MW00754742

The Commissioner
For Lost Causes

The Commissioner For Lost Causes

ARUN SHOURIE

PENGUIN
VIKING
An imprint of Penguin Random House

VIKING

USA | Canada | UK | Ireland | Australia
New Zealand | India | South Africa | China

Viking is part of the Penguin Random House group of companies
whose addresses can be found at global.penguinrandomhouse.com

Published by Penguin Random House India Pvt. Ltd
4th Floor, Capital Tower 1, MG Road,
Gurugram 122 002, Haryana, India

Published in Viking by Penguin Random House India 2022

10 9 8 7 6 5 4 3

The views and opinions expressed in this book are the author's own and the facts are as
reported by him which have been verified to the extent possible, and the publishers are
not in any way liable for the same.

ISBN 9780670096404

Typeset in Sabon by Manipal Technologies Limited, Manipal
Printed at Thomson Press India Ltd, New Delhi

www.penguin.co.in

For
Anita
Our very life

From
Adit and me

Contents

This book

'*Main tumhaarey* office *ke baahar ek* Board *lagaaungaa,* "The Commissioner for Lost Causes."'[1]

Ramnathji[2] had walked into my little cabin at the *Indian Express*. He was—and looked—mighty pleased. My colleagues and I had been documenting the condition of undertrials in our prisons. The series had been going on for months. Critics of the kind of work that the paper had begun to do—among them some of the seniors in the paper itself—were complaining, 'This is not journalism. This is pamphleteering. Our job is to give news, not run campaigns.' But Ramnathji was all for pursuing issues to the bitter end. And in this instance, he was especially pleased. He was a dogged litigant and so he keenly followed courts. He personally knew several of the great legal minds, and loved every little moment he could get with them. Even in cases that did not concern him or the paper in any way, he would seek out submissions by rival counsel, and relish taking them apart. He would pore over and dissect judgments. Moreover, he always looked to the courts as our ultimate dyke: '*Naheen, naheen. Abhee hathiyaar chhod deney ke*

---

[1] 'I am going to put a board outside your office, "The Commissioner for Lost Causes."'

[2] Ramnath Goenka, the redoubtable founder of the *Indian Express* group.

koi aavashyaktaa naheen,' he would say. *'Abhee* courts *hain.'*[3] He
was, therefore, especially pleased with the series. Together with
the work of a public-spirited lawyer, it had occasioned hearing
after hearing in the Supreme Court, which led to it giving a series
of far-reaching orders.

This particular pursuit was certainly not a 'lost cause', and,
what with his contacts in high legal circles, he knew it better than
most of us. The orders of the Supreme Court led to the release
of thousands of persons who had been rotting in jails for years
and years—not because they had been convicted of any crime but
because their cases had not come up. By one estimate, 40,000
prisoners had been released, 27,000 in Bihar alone.[4]

Yet, taken as a whole, the work my colleagues and I did
could certainly be seen as the pursuit of lost causes. We exposed
corruption. It is hundreds and hundreds of times larger today.
We nailed malfeasance. Standards have fallen so low that the
departures from the norm that used to shock everyone those
days are not even noticed today. We railed against the misuse
of an institution. Today, all institutions are instruments, and are
accepted as such. We nailed the lies of a Minister, of a Prime
Minister. Today, that the ruler has heaped yet another truckload of
falsehoods on our heads is just what we expect. We fought against
misrepresentation of one observation in one report by a rival
newspaper. Today, fake news is an entire genre. We bemoaned the
fall in the quality of persons in public life. Today, one is astonished
to come across quality in any institution of State.

So, 'lost causes'? Yes. But I am scarcely their only Commissioner.

As you go through writings of that time, dear reader, you
will find many precursors to what sends us screaming today.
The twists and turns of Judges, for instance. The lies and perfidy

---

[3] 'No, no. There is no reason to put down our weapons just yet. The courts are
there still.'

[4] So pleased was he that in an interview he gave at the time, he claimed that
the series had led to the release of 80,000 prisoners, that he planned to make
investigations a regular staple of the paper, so much so that it would carry
every day the result of some new investigation: *India Today,* 31 May 1979.

of rulers, for another. The attempts to throttle the media, for yet another.

But the fact that what is happening today was also happening then is no excuse. For one thing, scale and acceptance themselves matter. Murder has been going on forever. That does not explain away organized slaughter, it does not explain away either serial 'encounters', or sanctioned and sponsored lynchings. I, therefore, sincerely hope that incidents set out here will not fuel 'Whataboutery'. *Kam-bhakts*[5] tempted to put this volume to use that way would find it prudent to wait for the next one!

There are lessons from those years, of course. The first, that an individual, even a JP, cannot save us. Nor can even a Brahmaputra-scale movement. After all, we have had so many of these—in time: the Freedom Movement, JP's and the students' movement, the movement led by the All Assam Students' Union (AASU); and across our geography: from Chipko in the Himalayas to the exemplary reform movements of Kerala. Indeed, such occasional bursts can leave a residue of hopelessness. When the next great leader comes along, when the next movement gathers traction, people fall back in cynicism: 'Nothing came even of Gandhi, nothing came even of JP's movement. Why should this upsurge be different?' Only the proper functioning of institutions, day in and day out, their proper functioning without let, can pull us out of the ditch. That requires that the right sort be placed in them. And then that everyone in every institution lives up to high standards, that she and he live by lofty values. But even the best will slacken unless they are monitored, unless they are rewarded for standing up for what is right and severely punished when they transgress. And so anyone who does wrong, howsoever high or well connected he may be, must be dealt with swiftly and decisively. Everyone who does right, howsoever low on the rung he may be and howsoever isolated, must be shielded by all as if by a fortress. The 2000-year-old *The Book of Three Strategies* describes a country disintegrating in disorder, and thus ripening to be undermined, ripening for an outright assault:

---

5   The worshipper-pests.

When officials cluster in cliques, each promoting their friends, nominating crooks for appointments, suppressing and thwarting the good and intelligent, turning their backs on the public for the sake of their own private interests . . . When powerful clans gather crafty villains . . . [When] the country is in an uproar but the government ministers do not report it . . . The *Military Pronouncements* states, 'When the good are recognised as good but not promoted, the evil recognised as evil but are not dismissed, the wise are obscured while the corrupt are in office.' . . . The *Military Pronouncements* states, 'When deceitful ministers hold superior positions . . . [When] they rely on their awesomeness to grant personal favors, and act in a manner that offends the masses. [When] advancement and dismissal lack any basis, the evil are not dismissed, and men seek gain with any appearance possible. [When] they slander and vilify those of great Virtue, and make false accusations against the meritorious . . . [When] they gather and detain affairs of government so that commands and orders are not put into effect . . . When the ruler employs such wanton characters, he will certainly suffer disaster and calamity' . . .

A proximate description of those days? A precise description of these?

The lesson of those years is that values collapse, that institutions disintegrate with the rush of an avalanche: after all, episodes that figure here occurred just thirty–forty years ago. They show how one wrong by a ruler makes it that much easier for him to wreak the next one, just as one lie strengthens a habit, and thus makes it that much easier for him to utter the next one. Indeed, it makes the next perfidy necessary, just as that one lie makes a landslide of them unavoidable. The episodes show how malfeasance in one institution does not just facilitate, it makes inevitable, malfeasance in all.

So, the time to arrest decay, to check the ruler, is yesterday. Disintegration, too, has no hindlocks. The place to do so is anywhere and everywhere.

But it is never enough to set rulers and institutions right once or twice, howsoever completely and drastically this may be done. They have to be set right one by one, they have to be set right again and again, and we have to go on doing so forever. Therefore, reformers, their very lives, teach us, 'Begin, yes, but also persevere.'

Now for some *neti, neti.*

This book is not by any means a history of those times. It is just about the episodes it sets out.

Various persons appear in it. But it does not draw a well-rounded portrait even of the ones who appear frequently in it. We glimpse only those facets of their ways which the particular episode revealed.

The book is not an account even of my work. Episodes that led me to write books have been left out altogether: the evil that organized religions wreaked; their use in politics; the evil of caste; terrorism; national security; the debasement of discourse; economic reforms; and many others.

The book is an account of some of the work that my colleagues and I did at the *Indian Express*. The popes of the time frowned on much of it. Others cheered it on as the new journalism.

At places, I have reported conversations and remarks. 'How does he remember them?' some will ask. Some of them I had included in articles that I wrote at the time, and so there was no difficulty with regard to them. In several articles, I had included clues that would remind me of what was happening and being said at the time. Third, where I could check with either the person concerned, or, where the person himself had passed away, with someone close to him, I have done so. For instance, Giani Zail Singh was killed some years ago in a most unfortunate accident; and so I checked the instances and remarks with the one person who was closest to him, my friend Tarlochan Singh.[6]

But the answer that applies to most of the remarks that I have reported is different. Ramnathji, Gianiji, a Devi Lal, spoke in such colourful language that even if you tried, you wouldn't forget what they said on what occasion. I could, of course, have

---

6 Gianiji's Press Secretary when the former was the President of India. Later, member of the Rajya Sabha and Chairman of the Minorities Commission.

reported their remarks as indirect speech. I could have confined the text to English translations of what I remember them saying. But indirect speech, English translations just will not do. When Gianiji was cornering Rajiv Gandhi, and you asked him what his 'policy' in such situations was, would he say, 'Don't hit the man, frighten him,' or '*Maaro naeen, dhareeko*'? And which expression would give us a better glimpse of him?

Consider an example. When the Deputy Prime Minister of India rings you up and shouts at you for letting your colleagues go on writing about the deeds of his son, and not writing about that '*bhen****'—a colleague of his in the Cabinet—even though '*voh haathi saaraa baagh khaa gayaa hai*',[7] you are not liable to forget it. Especially when the very next day you reported the entire telephone call on the front page of the paper—including the '*bhen****'. And will 'sister-fucker' do? First, that Deputy Prime Minister would himself be puzzled by the expression. Second, 'sister-fucker' is an abuse, but for the Deputy Prime Minister, '*bhen****' was just a colloquialism! As it was for Ramnathji—he could abuse fluently in thirteen languages!

In a word, the expressions that I have typed are vivid in my mind. But, having pointed out the lapses in the memory of others, I would readily admit that I may be wrong in some particular. Therefore, the general impression that the remarks convey is of the circumstance, of the person, and not, even when they are within quotation marks, so much the specific word.

---

[7] 'That elephant has swallowed the whole garden.'

1

On the way to, and out of jobs

As first jobs go, the job at the World Bank in Washington was a very good one. Anita and I had just got married. We had all the time for each other. Washington was a very fine, green place to be in. As part of my work, I got to visit several countries.

But the charm soon wore off. All our relatives were in India. As for work, in those days, at the World Bank you were not assigned to work on your country, and all my interests were in and about India.

So, I kept looking for an opportunity which would enable us to return. At last, I got the Homi Bhabha Fellowship. Plus a consultancy at the Planning Commission—with a pay of Rs 500. The Planning Commission of those days was the hub of intense activity. Five Year Plans were still taken seriously. Chief Ministers would be coming and going. The operational head at the time was an elegant, colourful Minister, D.P. Dhar. A court politician, he was in Mrs Gandhi's circle of Kashmiris. Like everyone in that circle, and perhaps everyone of significance at the time, he liked to think of himself as being somewhat to the Left of everyone else. 'A master of dialectics,' Ashok Mitra, the erudite Secretary of the Commission at the time, warned me. 'Strong to the weak, weak to the strong.'

I was assigned to work with Dr B.S. Minhas—a scholar with an earthy common sense, as sparkling as he was pugnacious.

He had a natural adversary in another member, Sukhomoy Chakravarty—a snobbish intellectual, best known for writings that few understood and fewer read. Dhar was a charmer. He could set people at each other's throats as smoothly as he could bring them together. He fanned the natural differences between Minhas and Chakravarty.

Her circle persuaded Mrs Gandhi to take several 'progressive' economic decisions. Minhas thought poorly of these. In particular, he opposed the nationalization of the wholesale trade in wheat. Everything 'Left' was holy in those days. And everyone who opposed it was traduced and abused by the righteous, the *bhakts* of those days. Minhas was dubbed a 'Rightist'. But he turned out to be right: Mrs Gandhi soon had to reverse the nationalization of wholesale trade in wheat, for instance.

I wrote a few things for what used to be the zenith of our ambition in those days, the *Economic Weekly* (later renamed *Economic and Political Weekly*). The pieces had but to be published that I became a bit anxious. Would I lose the cubbyhole at the Commission? My mother's elder sister was visiting Delhi from Jalandhar. She was the jester and sage of our family, and the astrologer too. Few things were done, certainly no marriages were finalized, without seeking her approval. Teasing her, I said, '*Vadhey Behanji, meri patri dekhnaa zaraa.*' '*Kyon, kaakaa? Patri dekhan dee kee lodh ai?*'[1] I told her that I had written a few things against Mrs Gandhi. Would I lose my job at the Planning Commission? '*Lai, edhey layee patri dekhan dee kee zaroorat ai? Kaakaa, tu likh daa reh. Kisi nein padnaa ee naeen*'[2]—and she and my mother laughed and laughed.

As things turned out, not me, but Dr Minhas lost his job at the Commission. All sorts of indefensible assumptions had been made to pad up estimates of resources that would be available for the Fifth Plan. Minhas pinpointed the exaggerations. But

---

[1] 'Aunty, glance at my horoscope.' 'Why, my boy? Where is the need to look at the horoscope?'

[2] 'Goodness, what is the point of looking at the horoscope for this? My boy, you keep writing. No one is going to read any of it!'

Dhar and Chakravarty—the latter was one of the principal ones responsible for the wishful estimates—prevailed. Minhas wrote to Mrs Gandhi. To no effect.

One afternoon, the phone rang in my little office. *'Aa jaa. Aakhri vaari ethey dee chaa pee layiye'*[3]—it was Minhas on the line. *'Aakhari vaari'?* I rushed down to his room. He explained that Mrs Gandhi was not heeding his warnings about the wrong estimates in the Draft Fifth Plan document. So, he had sent in his resignation.

I was so sorry to see an honest, straightforward man have to go. That made me even more incensed at Sukhomoy.

After the gloomy tea, I too left for home. But by the evening, I felt that I must go and see Minhas.

I had imagined that he would be his fighting self. But to my surprise, I found him downcast. The reality of what he had done had begun to sink in, it seemed. He more than expected Mrs Gandhi to be taken aback by his resignation letter, to call him over, and talk him out of it. The afternoon had gone by, and there had been no reaction. By now, his feeling of being let down was tinged with bitterness.

I asked him whether he wanted to keep the matter quiet or to have the news published. He said he wanted to meet some totally reliable journalist, for he wanted people to know the reason why he had resigned. He said he wanted them to see through the fraud that was being committed on them in the name of the Fifth Five Year Plan, and to realize before it was too late the harm it would do to the country. Perhaps his expectation was that, once the news hit the headlines, there would be quite a reaction, and Mrs Gandhi would ask him to stay on. After some silence, he said yes again, and emphasized, but it must be done through someone totally trustworthy. And it must appear in a manner that Mrs Gandhi cannot ignore it.

The best person would be George Verghese at the *Hindustan Times*, I said. He readily agreed that Verghese would be best: he was well known, he was totally reliable, and he could determine how the item would be displayed as he was the Editor of the paper.

---

[3] 'Come along. Let us drink this place's tea for the last time.'

The next morning's *Hindustan Times* had the Minhas resignation as its lead story.

I was at Minhas's house early. I had thought that the display is what he would have wanted, that the text was factual, and by no means unsympathetic. But I found him even more downcast. He was still in his dressing gown. Where he might have felt last evening that the publication of the news would force Mrs Gandhi's hand, and she would ask him to withdraw his resignation, the story and its prominent display must have brought home the finality of what he had done. Far from being forced to call him, he now tended to think, Mrs Gandhi would be furious at what she would conclude was an effort to pressurize her.

I made it a routine to visit Minhas every day. And was very sad to see a fighter, a person whose grit and straightforwardness were widely admired, wilt. The reason was apparent: hope lingered. Minhas still expected that Mrs Gandhi would see the truth of what he had been pointing out. And so, the cut, when it came, cut very deep indeed.

A few days after his resignation, there was a full meeting of the Planning Commission. 'A full meeting' had long ceased to be a meeting about substance. It had become a ceremonial occasion: and as ceremony, its importance lay in the fact that it was one of the few occasions on which all Ministers who were nominal members, in particular the Prime Minister, attended a meeting of the Commission. At this meeting, Mrs Gandhi administered a totally unjustified rebuke, and she did so by using a cruel comparison: during the freedom struggle also, she said, apropos of nothing, there were a few who doubted our capacity for achieving great things.

It was the unkindest cut, and cut deep into Minhas's heart.

I learnt an important lesson. When one takes a step like this, remember the fate of Lot's wife: never look back.

I sought an appointment with D.P. Dhar, the Minister. Should I leave?

No, no, Dhar said. Do some work here. What did you do for your doctorate?

I told him that my thesis was a critique of our licensing system.

Just what we need, he said. Review the industrial licensing system, and tell us how it can be improved.

Of course, I did that review, repeating several of the points that I had made in my thesis. And I did odd jobs. But I was anxious to see if I could get a job somewhere in Government.

A stroke of luck

A position opened up. Dhar asked me to meet the Minister for Petroleum, D.K. Barooah. He was an important member of the Congress(I) from Assam. He was said to be, and fancied himself as a Leftist ideologue of the Party. In fact, his core usefulness was in making caste calculations for selecting candidates. In the coming years, he would rise to become President of the Party. And become justly notorious as a drum-beater. He is the one who coined the slogan, 'Indira is India, India is Indira.'

Barooah talked for just a while. And soon enough, asked whether I would join as Economic Adviser of the Ministry. I was delighted as Anita and I really wanted to stay on in India.

One day, out of the blue, I got a call from Barooah's office: the Minister was sorry, the post was no longer vacant.

I set about finding out what had happened. It seemed that Sukhomoy Chakravarty had got wind of the offer. He had told Barooah that I was a 'World Bank man', and that, at a time when Government was steering the country in a 'progressive direction', I would be just the wrong man, etc.

I was very upset: all our hopes for staying on in India had been shattered by a mere phone call.

I phoned Mahbub ul Haq at the World Bank in Washington, told him what had happened, and requested him to somehow get me the job again at the World Bank which I had told him I was quitting.

It was only much, much later that I read one of the Dalai Lama's sterling aphorisms:

Often
Not getting what you want
Is a
Splendid stroke of luck!

Back where I didn't want to be

In the World Bank at the time, everyone was dazzled by McNamara: all the talk was about how early he came to the office, how late he left; about his incredible focus and energy, his phenomenal ability to glance at 20x30 tables and pick the precise figure that revealed the problem, and which others had missed; about the impossible deadlines he set; about his determination to reorient the Bank from being a *bank* to being a development institution, from one that lent primarily for large infrastructure projects to one that lent for projects that directly helped the poor. What he had been doing in Vietnam never seemed to be on anyone's mind.

Mahbub[4] was very active as the head of the Policy Planning Department, one that provided inputs for the reorientation that McNamara wanted to engineer. Like others in the Department, I also must have been busy writing papers and preparing proposals. But I don't remember being happy or engaged.

The one set of events of those two years that stays in my mind lay outside the World Bank. Mahbub felt that economic discourse, even about our countries, was being set and steered by economists from the developed world, that economists from the Third World must have a more prominent say. Apart from being a lucid thinker and writer, he was a great networker. He organized the Third World Forum. And through his contacts in Pakistan, he made arrangements for its first meeting to be held in Karachi.

We flew in from the US. I couldn't sleep—in part because of jetlag, but even more so at the excitement of being in Pakistan.

Two in the morning, and I still had not fallen asleep. So, I rang room service. '*Ji* Horlicks *hai*?'[5] I asked. The person at the other

---

[4]   Mahbub ul Haq, a well-known Pakistani economist. He had been Chief Economist of Pakistan's Planning Commission, and twice the Finance Minister of the country. Later, he was the moving spirit and mind behind UNDP's annual World Development Report, and the Human Development Index—both of which led analysts to look at development in terms of what it did for the dispossessed.

[5]   'Do you have Horlicks?'

end said, '*Ji haan, main lehaanaa.*'[6] I scolded myself, now I have
to wait for the Horlicks to arrive. But in the shortest possible time,
a bearer brought a steaming glass of the drink. '*Tusee badi chheti
lai aa-e-o,*'[7] I said as I thanked him. '*Phone te ee pataa lag gaaya,
ki bandaa aapney ilaaqe daa ai,*'[8] the bearer responded.

The next day there was an inaugural session. Delegates were
grouped by continent. We were asked to prepare draft points
for a Declaration that would be released at the end of the
conference. When the hour that delegates had been given was
over, the Latin American Group had their draft for the entire
Declaration. Others had jotted points of varying length and detail.
But from South Asia, we had not been able to get a line written
as an argument had broken out the moment we had sat down: a
delegate from Pakistan objected to the presence of a delegate from
Bangladesh. The argument went on, with others joining in—along
'party lines', so to say—we couldn't do much about the business
of the conference. But Mahbub had already made up for us:
he had prepared the Karachi Declaration long before we had got
to Karachi.

From Karachi we were flown to Larkana where Zulfiqar
Ali Bhutto—who was Prime Minister at the time—had his
family house. I remember nothing of Bhutto at the reception,
except his fashionable, well-trimmed suit, and his pointed
spit-polished shoes.

From Larkana, we went to see Mohenjo Daro, a short drive
away. I had grown up looking upon it as the beginning of the
journey of our civilization. But here, it was the culmination of the
journey of Islam that began in Saudi Arabia, and at last reached
its climax in the founding of Pakistan.

Mahbub had asked where else I would like to go. I had said
Lahore. In Lahore, what would you like to do? he had asked.
Two things. I would like to see Faiz, even if it is from a distance
and for a moment. And, second, I would like to see the house

---

6 'Yes, sir, I will bring it over.'
7 'You have brought it so quickly.'
8 'From the phone itself I could make out that you are from our own region.'

my grandfather had built and where we were staying at the time of Partition.

An officer of the State Bank of Pakistan had been deputed to show me around Lahore. Of all things, I had forgotten to ask my parents for the address of that house. I remembered only that it was in an area called Qila Gujjar Singh. And me standing with my mother in a balcony—Nalini, my sister, is in her arms. We are looking down at a wedding procession as it winds its way through the street below. In an effort to locate the house, the officer took me through the lanes of that area. But so many houses had balconies. We gave up the search. In the evening, he took me to what must have been a press club—'Faiz Sahib comes there in the evening sometimes.' He was there indeed, a cigarette in one hand and a glass in the other, quite the centre of a little crowd. At least one wish had been fulfilled.

I returned to Karachi to catch the flight to Delhi. The flight was to leave around 6 a.m. I had put the alarm for 2.30 a.m. I was awakened by knocking on the door. I looked at the watch: just 1.15 a.m. As I opened the door, a man from the hotel said, 'Sattar Sahab *ne eh bhejeyaa ai*.'[9] A small envelope with negatives, and a handwritten note: 'I am sorry we could not locate your family house. Here are photographs of houses in the colony that have a balcony. Your parents will be able to recognize the house.' Talk of thoughtfulness.

In Delhi the talk was all about how the students' movement was gathering pace. And of L.N. Mishra who had been killed.

I went to call on D.P. Dhar. I was ushered into a bedroom, and was absolutely shocked to see a broken man. Most uncharacteristically, he was unshaven. He was sitting on his bed, his legs hanging to the floor. He told me that he had been expecting to be designated Ambassador to Moscow. Moscow had sent its concurrence, but there had been no answer thus far from Mrs Gandhi's office. I was very sorry to see such an elegant man reduced in this way. As if the sight were a warning, a couplet ran

---

[9] 'Sattar Sahib has sent this.'

through my mind—'Had I not been licking her feet like the colour of *mehndi,* today I wouldn't be crushed like the *mehndi* plant.'

A blow

The second round in Washington was almost depressing as we wanted to be in India. But one thing happened which changed our lives.

Back in India, Mrs Gandhi had proclaimed the Emergency. We were even more determined to return to India. I gave notice to the World Bank of resigning my job, and leaving for India. But Adit was born, and we were told that he had suffered a brain injury. We were in a quandary: How would we find the medical facilities in India which would be required for looking after him? A kindly doctor cleared the way. As I have narrated what he advised us in *Does He Know a Mother's Heart?* I will just reproduce the relevant paragraphs:

Three months later [after Adit's birth] we were advised to take the child to the head of pediatric neurology at the Georgetown University Hospital. We were exhausted, felled. The doctor was a kind, elderly gentleman. 'I am going to use a word that you have heard—it is used a lot these days to raise money. The word is cerebral palsy. It only means that the baby's brain has suffered an injury . . .'

We were too stunned to ask what exactly this was going to mean for our Adit's future. I told the doctor, 'We had planned to return to India. But if you feel that, for the sake of the child, we should stay on in Washington, of course we will. I will take back my resignation from the World Bank.'

'I have not been to your country, young man,' that kind doctor said. 'If you are here, all that we will be able to do will be to tell you how your son is faring against the milestones. But as observant parents you will notice that yourselves . . .'

'I have not been to your country, as I said,' he continued. 'But from what I have heard, you have strong, well-knit families there. That is what this child will need as he grows up—a net of love and security. So, if I were you, I would stick to your decision, return to your country, and bring him up in the embrace of your family.'

Among the wisest bits of advice we ever received.[10]

In those final, desperate months in Washington, I wrote to organizations and individuals in India, but, try as I might, I could not find a job. One day, as I sat in the World Bank office unable to focus on the work at hand, a visitor from India turned up. He had come with a message from Dr J.P. Naik, one of the foremost educationists of the country and at the time the Member-Secretary of the Indian Council of Social Science Research. I had met Dr Naik during our two years in Delhi, but only briefly. The message, in effect, was, 'Your work is here, especially now. Send me any proposal. I will find a way to have it approved.'

True to his word, he got me a Senior Fellowship of the Council.

I begin writing

Back in Delhi at last. My parents had a house with two bedrooms, and one sort of bedroom-cum-storeroom. My father moved into that solitary room on the first floor. Anita, Adit and I moved into his room.

Among the persons I met in those initial months were Raj and Romesh Thapar. They ran *Seminar,* one of the three small magazines which were continuing to publish independent stuff— the other two were A.D. Gorwala's *Opinion*, and Rajmohan Gandhi's *Himmat*. Raj and Romesh became our close friends, in many ways our buoys as far as public affairs were concerned. One of the pieces that I wrote for *Seminar,* 'Symptoms of Fascism', had two consequences—one for the Thapars and one for me.

The magazine used to be composed and printed at the press of *The Statesman*. As my piece was long, most of the issue was to consist of that piece. When the persons in charge of *The Statesman* in Delhi saw the piece, and because the pre-censorship

---

[10] *Does He Know a Mother's Heart?*, HarperCollins, Noida, 2011, p. 7.

order had been served on the magazine, they told Raj and Romesh that they could not compose or print the issue; they would have to send it to the Censor for clearance. Raj and Romesh were furious. They called me to their house in the evening and told me what had happened. What should be done?

The next morning I took Gandhiji's counsel to them in their office. Gandhiji had written that when authorities step in and an editor or writer cannot publish what he thinks should be published, he must not compromise and dilute what was going to be published. Were he to do so, he would be giving the signal that things are more or less normal when, in fact, the situation has completely changed. He must stop publication altogether so that readers realize what has happened.

Raj and Romesh, who had fought censors earlier,[11] were elated. *That* is what we are going to do, they exclaimed. Through a letter, they informed readers of what had happened, and how they were suspending publication of *Seminar* in accordance with what Gandhiji had counselled should be done in such a circumstance.

I was, of course, as furious as them, but, by that time, another avenue had opened up. Among the persons I had met were Krishna Kant and his wife, Suman. He was a Member of Parliament, and one of the famous trio that had stood up to Mrs Gandhi—Chandra Shekhar and Mohan Dharia were the other two.[12] Krishna Kant used to run an underground cyclostyled news-sheet for persons who had been detained. I had started

---

[11] One of the first cases dealing with freedom of speech concerned the magazine they used to run, *Crossroads*. The Supreme Court held that in the Constitution as it then stood, no restrictions had been placed on free speech. As a result, by the First Amendment, Article 19(2) was incorporated: it allowed the State to impose 'reasonable restrictions' on free speech on grounds specified in the new Article.

[12] Chandra Shekhar and Dharia were in jail at the time. Krishna Kant rose to become Vice President of the country. Chandra Shekhar became the President of the Janata Party, and later Prime Minister, for four months. Dharia became a Minister in the Janata Cabinet, and later, Deputy Chairman of the Planning Commission.

leaving pieces at their flat. I took 'Symptoms of Fascism' to them. It was cyclostyled, and sent on to the jails.[13]

I acquire a treasure

Several things happened during this period. One of these led to my getting what has since been one of our prized treasures. A person I had got to know as a result of writing for that cyclostyled news-sheet came to our home late one evening. He gave me a thermal copy of the diary that JP had been maintaining during his detention. He said that a few copies had been made and were being handed to a few persons for safekeeping. Some days later, a cautious friend and his wife had come for dinner. I showed him the bound copy. He recoiled, horrified. It was as if I had opened a box of snakes. He told me to 'get rid of it at once'. That copy of JP's diary has been one of our most prized possessions.

'You don't know who this is?'

A week or so later, I had gone to see Radhakrishna, the Secretary of the Gandhi Peace Foundation. He had just come out of jail. I was anxious to find out what was happening in the jails. What were the conditions inside? Who was where? How was their morale?

We were talking, and a dhoti-clad elderly man walked in. 'Hello Fatty, Hello Fatty,' he said to Radhakrishna cheerfully, and sat down. I glanced at him, said a perfunctory 'Namaskar, Sir,' and resumed talking to Radhakrishna.

After a few moments, Radhakrishna asked the gentleman, 'You don't know who this is?' gesturing towards me. 'No,' the gentleman said, 'must be some friend of yours up to your mischief.'

---

[13] The publication of *Seminar* remained suspended from August 1976 to January 1977. As everyone who had known them would have expected of Raj and Romesh, when *Seminar* commenced publication again, the first issue carried—along with an article by Ashish Nandy and a communication from Ashok Mitra—'Symptoms of Fascism' exactly as it was to have been carried in the issue that could not be printed.

Radhakrishna turned to me and asked, 'You don't know who this old man is?' I apologized, 'I am sorry, I don't.'

'Ramnathji, just yesterday you were asking me who "Arun Shourie" is who is writing these articles. This is that boy. And Arun, *just now* you were saying that you want to meet the Mr Goenka who is putting up such a splendid fight against Mrs Gandhi. Well, *this* is your Mr Goenka.'

I immediately rose from the chair, and held his hand.

The banter with Radhakrishna over, Ramnathji took me in his car to the *Express* building. I began visiting him often. He was always full of fight and stories—of what was happening, of the 1930s and '40s, of how he had been the first to shut his paper in response to Gandhiji's call, of the errands he had run for the Sardar and Panditji.[14]

From South Bloc to AIIMS

Apart from Raj and Romesh Thapar, who had become friends, and who were dead opposed to what Mrs Gandhi had done— they had known her well but had distanced themselves—I would visit one person from time to time, and give him my reactions to what was happening, and that was Mr R.N. Kao. He was one of the most elegant men I got to meet over the years, and while he said little, in those few words he said what he thought— often pointing out where he thought I was wrong and where right. In doing so, he was both straightforward and obviously felt secure—not the sort, like so many in Government, looking over their shoulder. I had got to meet him by an accident.

---

[14] Among the latter was hiring Feroze Gandhi as Manager of the *Indian Express*. Ramnathji said that Panditji had called him one day, and told him that Feroze and Mrs Indira Gandhi were staying apart too long; worse, that, away in Allahabad, Feroze was indulging himself in ways that would bring a bad name to all of them. Panditji wanted Feroze to be brought to Delhi. For this, he had to be given some job. The only job Feroze had held was as Manager of the *National Herald*. Panditji could, Ramnathji reported him to have said, ask Ghanshyam Das (G.D. Birla) to take Feroze as Manager at *Hindustan Times*. But that would raise a stink. So, could RNG help?

7. 9. 75

The Attorney General makes it out that Parliament is supreme & can do what it wishes with the Constitution; it can any part of the Constitution any way it likes. ~~They that~~ This is a horrendous picture of our ~~democratic~~ democracy. No wonder Gandhiji called parliamentary democracy a dictatorship of the majority. What genius had he to go to the root of things! If this view is or right then the Constitution has to be drastically changed. The Supreme Court must clearly & categorically lay down what ~~~~ constitutes the "basic structure" of our democracy, which parliament cannot alter. Alternatively, the Supreme Court must clearly decide that the concept of a basic structure is a fiction & that there is no such thing at all. After the Constitutional Bench of the Supreme Court might as well be abolished for all time.

Let us turn to politics. For M.P.s, no matter of which party, the words "Parliament is supreme" must sound grand. ~~It means they are supreme or at~~ ~~least It implies further that they themselves are~~ ~~supreme or at least, partake of that supremacy.~~ But politically what does the supremacy of Parliament means. It means something sordid, some thing revolting to a Democrat. Parliament virtually means the Cabinet (it is as true of Great Britain as of India) and the Cabinet ~~means the party working~~ the leader, the P.M. In a spineless party like the Congress, the leader is a virtual dictator. In India the Cabinet means Mrs. Gandhi. So, when the sonorous words are pronounced "Parliament is supreme", what

JP was among the first to be picked up when the Emergency was proclaimed. Frail and in poor health—ultimately his kidneys gave way—he wrote occasionally while in detention: stray notes, a fable, drafts of letters. Facsimiles of these pages were given to a few persons for hiding and safe keeping. They have been one of my treasures since.

is being declared is that Mrs. Gandhi is supreme in another vast party, like the Conservative Party or the Labour Party, while the P.M. for the term may be much more than a mere "first among equals", as Wilson is. But there is internal life & vigour & vitality within these parties & leaders have been replaced. So their performance counts for more than party manifesto. The role of public opinion, shifts the marginal among the non-committed voters, who decide of them play decisive roles, the international situation, the price of bread, butter & meat the employment position — all these & several other factors play their role. Most important, the existence of two parties, capable of replacing each other depending upon the above-mentioned & other factors, also radically affects the "dictator" position of the P.M. in the main. In India how different is everything? So let not any one be beguiled by the concept of the supremacy of parliament. The concept just does not fit into the picture. Here there must be clearly laid down checks & balances. No organ of the State should be supreme. All this has to be very clearly worked out by competent persons sharing these views.

जीवन निष्फलताओं से भरा है,
सफलताएं जब कभी आईं निकट,
दूर हेता है उन्हें निज मार्ग से ।
तो क्या वह सफलता थी ?
नहीं ।

सफलता और निष्फलता की
परिभाषाएं भिन्न हैं मेरी ।
इतिहास से पूछो कि तबों पूर्व
बन नहीं सकता प्रधानमंत्री क्या ?
किंतु मुक्त क्या जो शोषक के लिए
~~~~~~~~~~~~~~~~~~~~~~~~~~~~~~~

पथ आगे के, सेवा के, निर्माण के
पथ संघर्ष के, सम्पूर्ण क्रांति के ।
किसे कहता निष्फलता
थी शोषक की वे मंज़िलें,
मंज़िलें तो अनगिनत हैं,
गंतव्य अभी अति दूर है ।
रुकना नहीं मुझको कहीं
अवरुद्ध जितना मार्ग हो ।
निज कामना कुछ है नहीं
सब है समर्पित देश के ।

substitute them with another caucus of usurpers. This unfortunate country would then be set on the slow path of misery, autocracy & degradation as so many other countries of Afro-Asia. Heaven save India from this fate!

2.10.'75

बापू, आंध्र के गांवों में अद्भुत पूलिर नगल।
महात्मागांधी की जय। महात्मा गांधी अमर हों।
आज बापू का १०६वां जन्मदिन है। बापू को
गये आज २२½ वर्ष हुए। इस अनार्थ में इनका
नाम तो बहुत लिया गया, लेकिन उनका काम
बहुत थोड़ा हुआ। पिछले कुछ वर्षों से देश
के निर्माण भी अनुभव करने लगे हैं कि बापू को
बताया हुआ, को भारत ने बहुत बड़ी गलती
भी। परन्तु जवाहरलाल जी के जमाने में इन्हीं निर्माणों
ने, आ इनके जैसे ही निर्माणों ने, गांधीजी के भारत
को दरिद्रानुस भारत और जवाहरलाल जी ने
"आउटलुक" (outlook) के प्रशंसक बने
रहे। यशिलाम साबने हैं अभिमति गांधी, जिन्होंने
मिथ्याचार को सदाचार का बाजार करने में
बड़ी सफलता पाई है। बीच बीच में यह दशा
कहती रही है कि गांधीजी के ही मार्ग पर चल
चल रही हैं। शायद आज में जनोत्थान के
उपलभ्य में कुछ इस क्षण के बद्द ... नवर करें।

His younger brother, S.N. Kao, was at the World Bank at the time I was. We had got to know each other well. Kao Sahib used to visit Washington once in a rare while. I met him at his brother's apartment.

On one of his visits, he asked me if I could send him reports of the World Bank on Pakistan, Sri Lanka and other neighbours of India. But they are all available with the Indian Executive Director, I said, and he must be sending copies to the Finance Ministry. 'It will take less time for them to reach me from Washington than from across the road,' Kao Sahib said in return—his office was in South Bloc, across the road from the Finance Ministry. I concluded that he was just throwing a bait to see if I would bite, assessing whether I looked upon RAW (Research and Analysis Wing) as something evil. Though much was made of the World Bank's reports, there was nothing very confidential about them: they were based largely on material which anyone working on a country would be able to acquire; and they were prepared by run-of-the-mill staffers like me. In any case, I have always thought that intelligence services are imperative for a country like ours, and that they should get all the reliable information that they need, as well as sound, independent assessment from outside the organizations. So, I told Kao Sahib that if he was having the slightest difficulty in getting the reports, I would be happy to send them, but also that if anyone asked me, I would tell them that, yes, I was sending them to him.

Kao Sahib told me that one 'Devshankar' would be in touch with me from the Embassy. Weeks passed. There were new reports, but no 'Devshankar'. I thought that Kao Sahib would think that I had not lived up to my promise. I rang up the Embassy and asked for 'Devshankar'. Without a pause, the operator said, 'There is no "Devshankar" here. There is a Bharadwaj who goes about calling himself "Devshankar".' So much for covers!

Now that I was back in India, and felt strongly that the country had been pushed in a perilous direction, I would visit Kao Sahib in his immaculate office. A visitor had to wait a while in an anteroom: the coolth of the air-conditioned room was a welcome respite from the oppressive heat outside, as was the ice-cold Coca-Cola that was brought in by a liveried peon. His own room and desk would always have the latest books on international affairs. His presence was never intimidatory. I never felt the slightest apprehension in stating my views, severely critical though they were of what was happening. He would listen, and say a sentence or two.

Adit began to have convulsions. The 'myoclonic jerks', as they were called, would occur ten or twelve times a day. Even a sudden, loudish sound would trigger them. We took him to AIIMS (All India Institute of Medical Sciences). The neurologist couple who examined him told us that he must be admitted in the hospital. They said that we would not be able to get a room unless we could get some high-up Kashmiri to put in a word with the Director. Mr P.N. Haksar got us a room. What a relief that was. The three of us—Adit, Anita and I—stayed there for several days. The room was a boon for us, but one in which cockroaches were everywhere. Even a little inattention, and we would see them climb on to, and into Adit's cot.

Our room was one room away from the end of a corridor. The corner room always had a policeman sitting outside it, complete with a rifle chained to his belt. Every evening, at 5 p.m. sharp, the man inside would be taken to the patch outside the Eye Centre—his waist tied to the belt of the policeman. He would walk for an hour, energetically, rapidly, straight as a ramrod. Two/three days into our stay, I befriended the policemen, and they began allowing me to meet the person in the room. That became a long-lasting acquaintance, for the person was Mr Bhairon Singh Shekhawat—he rose to become the Chief Minister of Rajasthan and eventually Vice President, and, thus, ex officio, the Chairman of the Rajya Sabha at a time when I was a Member of the House. I began discussing matters with him, and bringing him books: including, I remember it well, Marx's *The Eighteenth Brumaire of Louis Bonaparte*. Bhairon Singhji was a most engaging man. Isolated, with a policeman outside the door, he would somehow have news from all over the country, and would share the latest snippets from different jails.

'March iktees tak'[15]

One day—I remember the incident as if it were happening in front of my eyes at this moment—I found Ramnathji downcast. I asked what the reason was. He kept looking away. '*Waisey, apni patni sey mujhey kuch lenaa-denaa to thaa naheen. Voh to saaraa din poojaa mein he lagi rehtee thi. Par phir bhi, patni ke zewar bechney par dil toot jaataa hai.*'[16]

I asked what had happened. He said that he had kept some jewellery in Nepal. To keep the paper going somehow, he had had to sell much of it. He had not known that doing so would upset him this much.

'Ramnathji *aap kab tak yon ladtey rahengey?*'[17] I asked.

'March *iktees* 1977 *tak,*' he said. '*Agar tab tak aisey he chaltaa rahaa, to main Devi*[18] *ko kehlvaa doongaa, "Devi, aap jeet gayee ho.* Paper *aap kaa hai. Jo chaaho karo.*"'[19]

What is going to happen by that date? I inquired.

'*Baba*[20]*nein kahaa hai ki us din tak merey saarey* problem *hal ho jaayengey.*'[21]

'Ramnathji, problem *hal to kayi tareh sey ho jaatein hain.*'[22]

'*Haan, haan. Mainey bhi Baba se kahaa, "Baba, kaheen mujhey gaadi par to naheen chadhaa rahe ho?" Baba nein kahaa, "Naheen nahhen. Voh ghalatee karegi. Sab theek ho jaayegaa.*"'[23]

---

[15] 'Till 31 March'

[16] 'In a way, I had little in common with my wife. She used to spend her entire day in prayer. Even so, having to sell the jewellery of one's wife does break the heart.'

[17] 'Ramnathji, till when will you continue fighting like this?'

[18] He used to refer to Mrs Indira Gandhi as 'Devi'.

[19] 'Till 31 March 1977. If things continue like this beyond that date, I will tell the Devi, "Devi, you have won. The paper is yours. Do with it what you will."'

[20] Satya Sai Baba of Puttaparti.

[21] 'Baba has said that by that day all my problems will get solved.'

[22] 'Ramnathji, all problems can get solved in many ways.'

[23] 'Yes, yes. I also asked Baba, "Baba, are you putting me on the train by then?" He said, "No, no. She will make a mistake. Everything will come out all right."'

And sure enough, on 18 January 1977, Mrs Gandhi announced that elections would be held in March.

JP's sixth sense

JP would have to come to Delhi, everyone knew, he would have to react. His health had broken down during imprisonment, in particular his kidneys. I was sent to Patna to prepare JP's reaction to the announcement.

From the airport, I was taken to the Gandhi Sangrahalaya, bordering the vast Gandhi Maidan. The room was cold and damp, and even in that cold it was infested with mosquitoes. 'Why is it that keeping things shabby is always taken to be a mark of authenticity?' I cursed. The complete opposite of how Gandhiji kept his surroundings. What with the mosquitoes, and the sheer excitement of being on such an errand, I did not sleep at all.

Early next morning—a somewhat foggy, cold winter morning—a gentleman came in a rickshaw and we rode to the part of town where JP's house was situated, Kadam Kuan. There were concentric circles of policemen at the house. I was patted up and down. After the police had satisfied themselves, I was taken to the first floor of the house.

JP was very frail by then. In spite of the cold, he was sitting on a *chabutra* outside his bedroom on the first floor, wrapped in a dressing gown, chewing what I later learnt was *lavang*. After I had paid my respects, he turned the conversation to what should be done in view of Mrs Gandhi's announcement. Those days, I used to smell villainous designs behind every move. I said that she must have devised some devious ways to capture the elections, and so we should boycott the elections. JP put that aside gently, as was his nature. '*Aap kehtey hain to usmey kuchh to hogaa he,*'[24] he began with the softness and extreme politeness which, I was to see in the coming months, was characteristic of him.

Par voh aagey ki baat hai. Abhi to teen maheenein hain. Inkaa istemaal karnaa chaahiye. Is samay logon mein dar hai. Dar

---

[24] 'You are saying this, so there must be something in it.'

public meetings *se toot-taa hai—jab har koi dekhtaa hai ki voh akelaa naheen hai to uskaa dar jaataa hai. Aur jab havaa chalti hai to voh* municipal limits *par naheen rukti. Is liye, is samay* boycott *ityaadi ki baat naheen karni chaahiye. Is samay, saari shakti badi-badi* public meetings organize *karney mein lagaani chaahiye.*[25]

We discussed what he might say in a statement. He explained what he had in mind, and said that I could bring a draft statement the next day.

As I was leaving to return to the Sangrahalaya, I was told that 'X' would come to fetch me at 8 the next morning. I should have the statement ready. 8 . . . 8.15 . . . 8.30 . . . and the person had still not turned up. Fearing that I would be blamed for being late, I got into a rickshaw and reached Kadam Kuan.

I was searched and patted again. But as the policemen had seen me the previous day, the searching was perfunctory. Though the statement was innocuous, I had kept the draft inside my shirt at the back. They did not discover it.

When I arrived upstairs, to my surprise, I saw that preparations were on for JP to leave for Delhi. I mentioned to the person who seemed to be handling things that I had brought the draft that I had been asked to prepare, and requested that they should have it typed as JP may not be able to read my handwriting.

'*Typing to kewal Satchitanandaji kartey hain aur voh Dilli ke liye train se ravaanaa ho gaye hain,*'[26] the gentleman said.

'*To kisi aur ko bulaa lein.*'[27]

'*Aur to koi hai naheen.*'[28]

---

[25] 'But that is something in the future. As yet we have three months. These should be put to work. Fear is what prevails today. Fear is broken by public meetings—when each person sees that he is not alone, that is when his fear breaks. And when the wind blows, it does not stop at municipal limits. Therefore, at this time there should be no talk of boycott, etc. At the moment, all our strength should be deployed in organizing large public meetings.'

[26] 'Only Satchitanandji does the typing, and he has left for Delhi by train.'

[27] 'In that case, please call someone else.'

[28] 'But there is no one else.'

Here we were at the headquarters of the fight against fascism and we could not find a typist.

There was no alternative but to send my handwritten text to Delhi and for someone to type it there.

I asked for an envelope, put the draft in it, and wrote 'Radhakrishna' on it. I was giving it to JP's faithful attendant with the request that he place it at the top of JP's meagre clothes so that the moment the suitcase was opened at the Gandhi Peace Foundation, it would be found, and Radhakrishna would have it typed.

'*Yeh aapne kis kaa naam likhaa hai?*'[29] the person directing the preparations asked.

'Radhakrishna *kaa*,' I said, '*kyonki Dilli mein JP unheen ke saath to reh rahen hain.*'[30]

'*Naheen, naheen. Yahaan Radhakrishna ko koi naheen pehchantaa. Aap Satchitanandji ka naam likhiye.*'[31]

I did as I was told, and took the rickshaw to the house-cum-office of K.P. Krupakaran, the long-standing correspondent of the *Indian Express* in Patna.

I don't know what happened to that draft. The statement was never issued. Before leaving his house, and in Delhi, JP spoke extempore.

Days later, JP was again in Delhi to address a public meeting, the first of its kind since Mrs Gandhi's announcement. I was asked to come to Radhakrishna's house at the Gandhi Peace Foundation: 'We will discuss points that JP might make in his speech.' There was a discussion of sorts. Everyone was urging his pet themes—some of them better suited to a manifesto than to what was certain to be a speech of momentous importance. Though he listened politely, JP was withdrawn. He knew what he was going to say. Soon, to my immense relief, Radhakrishna said that we must let JP rest before he heads to the public meeting.

---

[29] 'Whose name have you written?'

[30] 'Radhakrishna's,' I said, 'because in Delhi, JP will be staying with him.'

[31] 'No, no. No one here recognizes Radhakrishna. You write the name of Satchitanandji.'

I went over to the *Express* building nearby. We had planned
to drive down in Ramnathji's car to the Ram Lila Ground. But the
road was as if the Brahmaputra was in spate: there was a flood
of people walking—fast and animated. There was no way anyone
could drive through that flood. Ramnathji and I decided to walk.
A few recognized Ramnathji, and raised slogans in his honour.

The ground was packed, festive. Everyone was delighted—to
be present, and to see that he was not alone. JP was carried up
the stairs in a chair. The Government had tried various devices
to keep people away from the rally. From screening a popular
film on television at the time the rally was scheduled to putting
out that agents would be photographing all who went there.
Nothing worked.

In his feeble voice, JP began, '*Sab doctron ne kahaa ki mat
jayiye. Par aise maukey par to aadmi jaan ki baazi laga detaa
hai . . .*'[32] The crowd was delirious. The fear was blown to
the winds.

The days that followed were hectic ones. Manifesto. Statements.
Talking points. All these were hammered out at Krishna Kant's
house, at the Jantar Mantar building of the newly formed Janata
Party, at sundry offices.

In the final days of the election campaign, I was sent again to
Patna to draft an appeal from JP to the voters. The months had
tired him more visibly. He was lying in his bedroom, chained to his
tormentor, the dialysis machine.[33] How he dreaded it. Siddharaj
Dhadda, the Sarvodaya leader, was with him. We discussed the
broad themes. I was to bring the draft the next day.

The following day, I took the draft—two parts that were to
be issued on successive days—and read it out first to Siddharaj
Dhadda. He suggested an addition. We then went up to the
verandah where JP was seated. I still remember reading the draft
to him, and his moist and kind eyes as he listened. He changed

---

[32] 'All the doctors told me not to come. But at such a moment, a person wagers
his life.'

[33] JP had to undergo dialysis regularly till the end.

<u>FREE INDIA FROM THE DICTATORS</u>

<u>J.P.'s Final Appeal - I</u>

[In the name of all those who struggled for our country's freedom, I appeal to each one of you: FREE INDIA, DEFEAT THE DICTATORS.

[This is the last chance. If you falter, 19 months of tyranny shall become 19 years of terror.

[Our goal is progress with justice.

[Freedom is the first requisite for this. We have seen during the past 19 months how, when freedom is crushed, the poor, the workers are bludgeoned to slave for enriching a small coterie at the top.

[We want our officials & our elected representatives to be accountable to our people. To

[Freedom alone can ensure that they are. How can you end corruption if you cannot even talk about it? How can we have accountability if power is exercised by shadowy back-room operators who do not even hold office? How will the rulers be accountable if the judiciary is robbed of all effectiveness?

[The terrors of the black 19 months —

4

enthusiasm for the cause of freedom.

[I congratulate you.

[You have made an excellent beginning. Now you must persevere.

[• Cast every single vote to the Janata party

[• Defeat every single candidate of the ruling clique

[• Make India a free, progressive Gandhian country.

Jayaprakash Narayan

one word: 'if the judiciary is crushed' was to read 'if the judiciary is robbed of all effectiveness'.

'*Bahut sundar likhaa hai*,' he said. '*Par koi chaapegaa bhee?*'[34]

I requested him to autograph my handwritten text, handing him a ballpoint pen with red ink. He did. The pages have since been a family treasure for us.

I took the rickshaw to Krupakaran's house. And he sent it by teleprinter to the *Express* office in Delhi for copies to be made and distributed. Within an hour or two, I got a call. 'But there is nothing about employment . . . There has to be something about tribals and SC/STs . . . What about forests? . . . Women?' The usual committee—Verghese, Surendra Mohan, my friend Lakshmi Jain, etc.—was wanting the usual dhobi list. I resisted: this is an appeal; it is a call to arms, not a Five Year Plan draft. I didn't get anywhere.

In exasperation, I talked to Ramnathji and Lakshmi. I pleaded with them to talk the committee out of the nonsense they wanted to shove into the appeal. After a moment of my talking to him, Ramnathji asked, 'Has JP seen it?' I told him JP had not just seen it, he had made the change he wanted; he had, in fact, said, '*Bahut sundar likhaa hai*.'[35]

'*Us samay wahaan koi aur thaa?*'[36] Ramnathji asked. I told him that Siddharaj Dhadda had been present throughout.

'*Voh* change *jo tum keh rahey ho, kyaa JP nein apney haath me kiyaa hai?*'[37]

I said, '*Ji naheen. Par unhon ney* statement approve *kee hai. Unhon nein us par* sign *bhee kiyaa hai*'[38]—that last bit—about mixing the signature at the end with approval—a white lie.

'*To phir mushkil kyaa hai? Mujh par chhodo. In clerkon ko main sambhaal loongaa.* Statement *vaisey ki vaisey he chhapegi.*'[39]

---

[34] 'You have written beautifully,' he said. 'But will anyone publish it?'

[35] 'You have written beautifully.'

[36] 'At that time was someone else there?'

[37] 'Did JP make that change in his own hand?'

[38] 'No, sir. But he approved the statement. He has signed it.'

[39] 'Then what is the problem? I will take care of these clerks. The statement will be published as it is.'

The statement was published far and wide on 14 and 15 March 1977. Such had been the disappointments into which the Janata rulers had plunged all of us that when I reproduced it in a book published in 1980, I had to note, 'I reproduce it as it reflected JP's aspirations, his wishes on the eve of the 1977 election. It now reads like a parody. Such has been the legacy of those who rode to power on his name.'

Since then, I have seen so many statements, so many in which I had a hand, become parodies—what was written at the time of the Assam elections that brought the Assam Gana Parishad to power, what was written as NTR fought back for the Chief Ministership, what was written as V.P. Singh was vaulted up the hurdles . . . Here it is—after over forty years, a parody all the more:

~

Free India from the Dictators
JP's Final Appeal to the Electorate

In the name of all those who struggled for our country's freedom, I appeal to each one of you: FREE INDIA, DEFEAT THE DICTATORS.

This is the last chance. If you falter, 19 months of tyranny shall become 19 years of terror.

Our goal is progress with justice.

Freedom is the first requisite for this. We have seen during the past 19 months how, when freedom is crushed, the poor, the workers are bludgeoned to slave for enriching a small coterie at the top.

We want our officials and our elected representatives to be accountable to our people.

Freedom alone can ensure that they are so. How can you end corruption if you cannot even talk about it? How can we have accountability if power is exercised by shadowy backroom operators who do not even hold office? How will the rulers be accountable if the judiciary is robbed of all effectiveness?

The terrors of the black 19 months—herding hundreds and thousands into jails, the tortures inflicted on them, the untold sufferings of their families, mutilating 'laws' so that a citizen does not even have the right to life, illicit as well as illegal extortions, firings, destroying homes of the poor—these are not chance happenings. They are what dictatorship is about.

None of these atrocities could have happened in a free society. If you could have talked about them, if you could have met and organised to resist them, if the press could have written about them, an aroused and informed public opinion would have held back the hand of the oppressors.

Contrast the black 19 months with the relative freedom of the last two months. The very rulers who were asserting that the people do not want elections, who were saying that the people do not have even the right to life, those very rulers are today compelled to offer apologies. Just two months of freedom—and limited freedom at that—has forced them to once again take account of the people.

Do you want the unaccountability, the brutality of the 19 months to return? Do you want your 30,000 brothers and sisters who have still not been released to continue in prison indefinitely? Do you want the set-up to continue in which each of you can be arrested without explanation, in which you can be held indefinitely without trial, in which the rulers are free to do what they will with you—even to the extent of denying you food and shooting you?

And my brothers and sisters in the minority communities must remember that fundamental rights, as a free and open society, are even more important for them than for the majority. In addition to restoring fundamental rights and the rule of law, the Janata Party will establish a Civil Rights Commission to specifically protect the interests of minorities. Similarly, nothing will benefit the poor in general and the minorities in particular as much as the Janata Party's pledge to make the right to work a fundamental right.

Many efforts have been made to hoodwink you and to distract you. Destabilisers whose party is breaking up have talked of stability. They have tried to inflame communal passions, to frighten minorities, even to capitalise on Bapu's murder. They have tried to scare you with stories of violence, of external and internal threats. They have issued sham apologies. They have tried to pass the blame for their dastardly deeds to officials, even to us who were in jails. They have tried to bribe you with last minute concessions. With nothing but a record of corruption and stagnation, they have tried to mislead you with lies about the Janata Party's programme.

Do not let any of this mislead you. Be like Arjuna, and like him do not let your eye wander from the central issue: freedom or slavery, democracy or dynastic dictatorship.

Remember that the ruling Party still swears by the black laws and amendments that it used as the basis of its dictatorship. It will use them ruthlessly should it get another chance. Its leaders have clearly said that there is no room for difference of opinion in India, that they are the country, that far from being unhappy the hundreds and thousands who were jailed should be grateful that they were not shot to death this time round.

The Janata Party, by contrast, is pledged to a free and open society. It is pledged to repealing the black laws and amendments. The very process by which it will be acquiring power—that is, through the current struggle for freedom, through your support for the cause of freedom—will guarantee that it will fulfil its pledge.

Remember that each seat counts, and that for each seat each and every vote counts. Translate your enthusiasm into votes and vigilance for the Janata Party.

I will be happy only when every single candidate of the ruling clique which has heaped so much suffering on our country is defeated.

II

The India of my dreams is a community in which every individual, every resource is dedicated to serving the weak—a community dedicated to *Antyodaya*, to the well-being of the least and weakest.

It is a community in which individuals are valued for their humanity—a community in which the right of every individual to act according to his conscience is recognised and respected by all.

It is a community in which different views contend peacefully, in which disagreements are settled in a civilised manner.

It is a community in which fellowmen persuade each other, not bludgeon each other.

It is a community in which all have work—work which affords them a decent living and which fulfils them. It is a community in which each individual has enough to develop his creative potential to the maximum, in which everyone who toils with his hand has a share in owning and a say in managing the factory or farm in which he toils. It is a community in which all have equal opportunities—a community in which strong, the majorities themselves recognise the handicaps of the weak, of the minorities, and go out of their way to assure them preferential facilities so that their historical handicaps are removed.

It is a community in which every resource is bent to meeting the needs of the masses—to providing them enough to eat, to ensuring cloth, housing, drinking water for them.

The India of my dreams is a community in which every citizen participates in the affairs of the community, in which every citizen understands and participates in matters that transcend his immediate, personal interests, it is a community in which citizens—specially the weak—are organised and awakened to implement reforms and to keep an eye over their rulers.

It is a community in which officials and elected representatives are the servants of the people, a community in which the latter have the right and the opportunity to bring them to book if they go astray.

In short, my vision is of a free, progressive and Gandhian India.

The Janata Party is pledged to this vision.

The ruling clique is opposed to it in every particular.

It is this vision which is the basis of the Janata Party's manifesto. Many of the practical steps that are needed for realising the vision are spelled out in it. As you know, every successful candidate of the Party will take an oath at Gandhiji's Samadhi to work together with his colleagues, to work for the fulfilment of the Party's pledges and in his personal conduct to abide by Gandhian ideals.

Once the elections are over, I will myself launch a crusade to set up People's Committees at every level for ensuring that the pledges are honoured.

But the first step is to ensure that the Janata Party wins decisively at the polls.

All of you have shown remarkable resilience. In just two months you have dispelled the fear that had gripped our country. In every corner of the country you have shown the greatest possible enthusiasm for the cause of freedom.

I congratulate you.

You have made an excellent beginning. Now you must persevere.

o Cast every single vote for the Janata Party.
o Defeat every single candidate of the ruling clique.
o Make India a free, progressive, Gandhian country.

~

When I went to call on JP in Patna again, I took along the original drawing that Abu Abraham had done on the day the election results had come out. In the cartoon, JP is sitting on a *chaarpaai*. A farmer is seated on the ground, a hookah in hand. The farmer asks, 'Has my Revolution been Total enough?' I requested JP to answer the question, and autograph the drawing.

And I made a great mistake for which I have scolded myself since that day. I had a ballpoint pen with red ink, and a felt-tip pen with red ink. I thought that the ink of the felt-tip pen would stand out even more. So, I handed JP the felt-tip pen.

'*Kyaa likhein?*'[40]

The only truthful thing that could be written was, 'It was a good beginning.' JP wrote that, signed the drawing, and handed the pen and drawing back to me.

That cartoon became another family treasure. But with the years, and even though we have protected the drawing from direct sunlight, the ink from that felt-tip pen has faded. You can just about make out the pale shadow of JP's handwriting. What a blunder.

Jawaan ladkaa

One result of these events had been that I had got to know Ramnathji. In 1978, we were staying in the *Express* guest house in Bangalore. Ramnathji came for a few days. He was an ardent walker. I would walk with him under the beautiful, sprawling trees of the guest house.

'*To aajkal tum kyaa kar rahey ho?*'[41] he asked.

'*Sir, main kitaab likh rahaa hoon. Koi* job *he naheen miltaa.*'[42]

'*Tumhey koi naukri naheen mil rahee. Mujhey koi jawaan ladkaa naheen mil rahaa. Koi tumhaari kitaab naheen padhega. Tum meraa* paper join *karo. Main* Mulgaokar *ko kehtaa hoon ki tumhaarey liye koi achhaa saa* designation *dhoond le.*'[43]

That became my letter of appointment!

We had an eventful three years together. I was dismissed—but that is a different story, one we will come to in a while, for much happened before that happened.

---

[40] 'What should one write?'
[41] 'So, what are you doing these days?'
[42] 'Sir, I am writing a book. Just can't find a job.'
[43] 'You can't find a job. I can't find a young man. No one will read your book. Join my paper. I will ask Mulgaokar to find some good designation for you.'

2

'If someone hammers
a nail into our heads . . .'

'Once I told Rajaji,'[1] Ramnathji told me one day, '"Rajaji, you are a very great man. I am a nobody. But we have one thing in common: If someone hammers a nail into our heads, it will come out as a corkscrew!"'

An accurate description of his complexities.

Ramnathji was a great fighter, and a very resourceful one. Cornered, he would look for a toehold, and from that tiny perch, launch his fight back. One of the excitements of working with him was that he was a bundle of convolutions. You could never infer what he would do in one situation from what he had done in that situation last time.

Every few days, Ramnathji would interrupt what he was saying and enunciate yet another *gurumantra* asking me to keep it in mind. These ranged from tiny ones to ones that could be of considerable consequence.

---

[1] C. Rajagopalachari, one of the principal leaders of the Freedom Movement. The first Indian Governor General. Later, Home Minister, and much else. Founder of Swatantra Party. The sharpest of minds, a deep scholar.

A *tiny one*

'*Tum* business *ke kaabil to ho naheen,*' he said once as we were walking in the guest house grounds in Bangalore.

> *Par kabhi awsar miley,* business *kaa hi naheen, auron ke saath mil kar kaam karney kaa, to hameshaa chhotey aadmi ke saath rishtaa karnaa. Jab voh mushkil mein hoga aur apnaa udhaar lautaa naheen sakegaa, voh tum sey praarthanaa karegaa ki tum usey ek varsh ki aur mohlat de do. Jab tum de do gey to voh saari umar naheen bhoolegaa. Uskey baad voh tumhaaraa ghulaam ban jaayegaa. Par agar Birla tumhey ek saal paisey naheen lautaa sakegaa to voh na denaa apnaa haq samjhegaa.*[2]

Two substantial ones

One day, we heard that RNG had shouted at V.C. Shukla, the then Minister of Information and Broadcasting, and rumoured to be one of the executors of the Emergency regime. Ramnathji had stormed out of his office, and sworn at the top of his voice for all in the corridors to hear that he would bring all of them down—he had, of course, known Ravi Shankar Shukla, the father of V.C. and S.C. Shukla.[3]

---

[2] 'You don't have it in you to do business. But if an opportunity arises, not for business but for working with others, always bond with the little person. When he is in trouble and he cannot defray his debt, he will beseech you to give him another year. When you give him that extra year, he will remember it all his life. He will become your slave. But if a Birla cannot return what he owes you, he will look upon it as his right that you should cancel his debt.'

[3] Ramnathji narrated a much more colourful version to Vir Sanghvi. Recalling the hours he spent listening to Ramnathji, Vir wrote about this incident:

> He reveled in stories about his exploits during those days [of the Emergency], though to be honest, some seemed so outrageous that I had to frequently suppress the unworthy thought that perhaps he was saucing them up a little bit.
>
> There was the favourite anecdote about going to see VC Shukla, the Emergency regime's information minister, shortly after the government seemed to have tamed the *Express*. (Goenka had stepped down as chairman and S.

'*Yeh he to meri museebat hai aaj kal*,'[4] he was to tell me later—twice actually: once when Mrs Gandhi returned to power; and later when he and the paper were being harassed during Rajiv's time. '*Mahatma aur Sardar aur Pandit ke* time *se koi* leader *naheen huaa jis ko main unkey pehaley naam se pukaar kar unsey baat naheen kar saktaa thaa. Sri Arvind aur Maharshi*[5] *ke time se koi bhagwan purush naheen hua jis se mainey mazaak naa kiyaa ho. Aur aaj meraa paalaa in kuttey-billion se padaa hai. Aaj in kutte-billion se bhidnaa pad raaha hai.*'[6]

Ramnathji learnt that Mrs Gandhi had decided to take over the paper. He requested Iyengar[7] to come over to Delhi. Iyengar was a well-known lawyer, and Ramnathji knew that he had direct access to Mrs Gandhi. He asked Iyengar to convey two requests on his behalf to Mrs Gandhi. The first was that she could do what she wanted to him, but that she should please not let any harm come to BD or Saroj in any way. If Government does harm them, 'I will be helpless.' Iyengar was to tell Mrs Gandhi that he—RNG— had left letters her mother[8] had written to Prabhavati[9] with a London solicitor. They described her agony at the indifference

---

Mulgaokar was no longer editor.) Shukla's father had been a friend of his and Ramnathji was confident that he could make him see reason.

In fact, he recalled, Shukla was arrogant, rude, pompous and offensive. Finally, Goenka could take it no longer. He stood up and said gravely: 'My only regret about our meeting is that I have had to revise my opinion of your mother.'

Shukla looked bewildered.

'You see,' he continued, 'your father was my friend. He was a great man. But you are clearly not the son of that great man. So, regrettably, the only conclusion I must come to is that I had misjudged your mother.'

As Shukla gaped at him incredulously, Goenka stalked out . . .

4 'This is my trouble these days.'
5 Sri Aurobindo and Ramana Maharshi.
6 'Since the time of the Mahatma, the Sardar and Pandit, there has not been a leader to whom I could not talk, addressing them by their first name. Since the time of Sri Aurobindo and the Maharshi, there has not been a godman with whom I did not crack jokes. And today, my lot is thrown with cats and dogs. Today I have to grapple with these cats and dogs.'
7 I don't remember Ramnathji mentioning his initials, and have not been able to narrow the search to one Iyengar.
8 Kamala Nehru, the wife of Pandit Nehru.
9 The wife of Jayaprakash Narayan.

of Panditji towards her, and the ill treatment she had received from his sisters. 'I had given instructions that if something is done to BD and Saroj,' Ramnathji said he told Iyengar to tell Mrs Gandhi, 'these should be released; that if there is a direction from me to the contrary then the Solicitor must know that it has been obtained under duress, and should release the letters immediately.' The second request concerned her plan to take over the paper. Ramnathji wanted Iyengar to tell her, 'I have served your father. I have done things for him.[10] Now I am old and dying. For my self-respect, let me appoint the Board. Just send me the names; I will appoint whoever you name. But for the sake of my self-respect, let me appoint them.'

V.C. Shukla sent the list. Going over it, RNG said he saw that two of the persons were ones on whom he could rely—one of them, he said, was actually someone who he had helped out of a difficulty. So, he had a toehold. The others were 'fools', Ramnathji said—headed by K.K. Birla whose father, G.D. Birla, Ramnathji had known for decades, and for whom he had the highest regard—and upstarts, 'kal ke chokrey'—like Kamal Nath. Ramnathji appointed all of them as the new Board.

Ramnathji fell seriously ill. He had a vision in the ICU, he said. He saw Lord Vithal in front of him. So, the moment he could get up, he drove to Pandharpur to give thanks at the shrine of the Lord.

The Board met a few times.

Ramnathji said he heard that a meeting was scheduled at which the Board would remove Mulgaokar from the editorship of the paper, and instead install Mohammed Shamim, the movie critic of the *Times of India* as Editor. The meeting was to be held at the Penthouse in Bombay. Ramnathji said he told Ranganathan to receive each member as he arrived, to garland him, to have a young girl perform *aarti* around each of 'the *maadarchods*'.[11]

---

[10] As I have noted earlier, on Ramnathji's telling, these included appointing her husband, Feroze Gandhi, as General Manager of the *Indian Express* in Delhi at Panditji's request.
[11] 'motherfuckers'

The group gathered. K.K. Birla was in the chair. Ramnathji said he—RNG—sat slumped in his chair.

They started discussing something. Ramnathji raised his head, looked at Kamal Nath and asked, '*To kaisi bhijwaa rahey ho aaj kal?*'[12]

Nobody could understand what he meant. Ramnathji repeated his question, '*To kaisi bhijwaa rahey ho aaj kal?*'

Kamal Nath asked, '*Babuji, mujh se pooch rahey ho?*'[13]

'*To aur kis se? Aur bhee koi bhijwaa rahaa hai kyaa? Sunaa hai musaltee bhijwaa rahey ho. Ek pahaadan bhee.*'[14]

Everyone was properly shocked.

'*Aap kaa dimaag kharaab ho gayaa hai kyaa? Kisey bhijwaa rahaa hoon?*'[15]

'*Arey, Sanjay ko. Aur kisey?*'[16]

He really *is* out of his mind, everyone was convinced. To talk in such terms, and of all persons about Sanjay Gandhi—even to be hearing such nonsense about Sanjay these days . . .

Now that I have your full attention, Ramnathji told me he told them, listen to me carefully. You have met to dismiss my Editor and appoint that Musalmaan, that film correspondent of *Times of India* as Editor. You do that and I will dismiss you.

K.K. Birla addressed him, and said in Marwari-Hindi, 'You seem to have forgotten that the paper is not yours any longer. We are the Board. Government has appointed us. You are not well, that is why you are talking like this, and thinking like this. You should go and rest. We will finish the agenda and leave.'

You don't know anything, Ramnathji said he said. You were born with *shrikhand* in your mouth. Ask your father before you say such things. You have no authority. You dismiss my Editor, I will dismiss you. That is all I had to tell you. Now all of you can leave.

---

[12] 'So, what kind are you providing these days?'

[13] 'Babuji, are you asking me?'

[14] 'Who else? Is someone else also providing? I have heard you are sending a Muslim girl. A hill girl also.'

[15] 'Have you lost your mind? To whom am I providing these?'

[16] 'To Sanjay, of course. Who else?'

Convinced that he was out of his mind, but that there was no point in discussing anything with him when he was in such a condition, they left.

Ramnathji dismissed the Board.

The fools did not know that the appointing authority has the power to dismiss, he explained. *This* is what I had kept from everyone—starting with the Devi. That is why I had told Iyengar to have her put anyone she wants on the list but let me appoint the Board . . .

'*Ab suno: mein tumhe do gurumantra sikhaataa hoon,*' he said, concluding his tale. '*Par pehley ek baat hameshaa yaad rakhnaa: mainey tumhey* appoint *kiyaa hai. Is liye main tumhey kabhi bhi* dismiss *kar saktaa hoon. Ab gurumantra suno. Pehlaa: hameshaa das kadam aagey ki socho. Doosra: agar doosra samajhtaa hai ki tum usey behan ki gaali dogey, to usey maa ki gaali nikaalo. Tabhee voh tumhaari baat achhi tareh suney gaa.*'[17]

Had things happened this way? Who knows? With RNG one never knew. Before typing this, I contacted Kamal Nath—through Anant Goenka, Ramnathji's great-grandson. The two of us talked for long, with Anant listening. Even though I asked him more than once, Kamal would neither confirm nor deny Ramnathji's account. The sum total of his responses was that [i] there had been several meetings of the Board, he could not recall everything that happened in each meeting; [ii] he had met Ramnathji many times; [iii] he could not remember if such exchanges had occurred at a meeting of the Board or some other time; [iv] when Ramnathji was ill, Kamal had helped get a bed for him in a Calcutta hospital; [v] Ramnathji had asked him to help get Kuldip Nayar released; Kamal had persuaded Sanjay Gandhi to agree to this: 'He won't be able to write anything in any case. We have censorship in place'; [vi] Ramnathji had asked Kamal Nath, '*Tum mujhey*

---

[17] 'Now listen. I will teach you a *gurumantra*. But first, always remember: I have appointed you, and so I can dismiss you any time. Now listen to the *gurumantra*. First: always think ten steps ahead. Second, when someone expects you to abuse him as a "sister-fucker", abuse him as a "motherfucker". Only then will he pay attention to what you have to say.'

maarney lagey ho kyaa?[18] Kamal had assured him of two things: that he would fight him but not when he is ill, and that he would not let the Board go beyond a point. He said he had ensured this.

Kamal said that Ramnathji did not have the power to dismiss the Board. 'We had been appointed by the Government. It had issued a notification. No one had the power to dismiss us.'

But the fact is that Ramnathji had dismissed them.

But *had he*? I asked Shobhna Bhartia, the daughter of K.K. Birla.[19] She said, 'No, the directors were not dismissed. They gave up the office on their own.' She said that her father had taken up the assignment at Mrs Gandhi's behest. But he felt very uneasy as the months passed. The reason, she said, was that he and Bhagwandas, Ramnathji's son, were very close friends. 'Whenever Father had to visit Madras, he used to stay with Bhagwandas. All trips to Tirupati used to be arranged by Bhagwandas. So, Father was increasingly uneasy being the Chairman of the Board. After a while, he and other members just gave up the assignment.'

Could these persons—who must have been regarded by Mrs Gandhi as loyal, reliable, obedient, and who had been assigned a duty by her—have walked out of it on their own?

So, could Ramnathji have removed them? If so, how had he done so? I asked my friend, the distinguished lawyer and authority on the Constitution, Arvind Datar. Under what provision of Company Law, as it stood in 1977, could Ramnathji have removed the directors?

He said,

Section 408 of the Companies Act, 1956, until 1988, empowered the Central Government to appoint directors to effectively safeguard the 'interests of the company, its shareholders or the public interest'. These directors could hold office for up to three years at a time. Section 408 also gave powers to the Central Government to appoint directors on a reference made by not less than 100 members of the company or members holding not

---

[18] 'Have you come to kill me?'
[19] She is the Chairperson of the *Hindustan Times* group.

less than one-tenth of the total voting power. It is very likely that the Central Government appointed the directors suo motu.

As for removal or dismissal, directors appointed by the Central Government could not be removed by the shareholders of the company or by its directors.

It is quite possible that these directors may have been appointed during the Emergency for three years and would have ceased to hold office thereafter. Under the Companies Act, 1956, neither RNG nor the Board of Directors nor shareholders of the Express Newspapers Ltd. had powers to 'dismiss' any director.

But what if Government had fallen for Ramnathji's trick and had not appointed them? What if it had agreed, and left it to Ramnathji to appoint as directors the persons it had listed?

If the Central Government had not appointed the directors under section 408 as applicable at the relevant time, then any appointment made by RNG would have been of 'additional directors' under section 260. The Board of Directors are entitled to appoint additional directors subject to the maximum number prescribed in the Articles of Association.

If RNG had appointed certain individuals as additional directors, then they would hold office only up to the date of the next Annual General Meeting (AGM)—for this, see the proviso to section 260. At such a meeting, the additional director has to offer himself for appointment.

It is possible that RNG would have appointed certain individuals as additional directors (as 'suggested' by Mrs Indira Gandhi) and the Emergency may have been lifted by the next AGM. The simplest thing would have been not to propose their names at all and they would have had to automatically demit office.

What had actually happened was closer to Arvind Datar's surmise than either to what Ramnathji had recounted to me or to what Kamal Nath and Shobhana remembered. The government had tried first to force RNG to sell the *Express* wholesale to its nominees; then to agree to a Board of its nominees with total control over editorial content; then to six directors being appointed by it—to outnumber the five of the family; then to editorial content to be regulated on a day to day basis by the Chairman of the Board—K.K. Birla; then to a three-man committee to determine and enforce editorial policy, including 'the right to dismiss, appoint, transfer and give day to day instructions to the editors' . . . Government pressed each alternative with explicit threats—that unless RNG agreed to the proposal, he, his son and daughter-in-law would be arrested under the notorious and draconian Maintenance of Internal Security Act, that income tax demands would be pressed.

RNG engaged the government in protracted exchanges. One day advancing points of law—that for the Board or its Chairman to interfere with editorial content would be contrary to law and to the proclamations of the ministers themselves. The next, agreeing that the majority of the Board shall consist of government's people but how these must be appointed 'with my consent'. The third, tying ministers and intermediaries up in knots over financial complexities that must be settled before such moves could be contemplated—the true valuation of the Group, the relationship of the holding company to other Group companies, liability of loans the Group had taken, the fate of personal guarantees that he and his son had given for these . . . The fourth, invoking practical considerations—how running a complex business required a 'homogenous Board'. The fifth, feigning helplessness: 'Apart from my personal and emotional reaction in coming to this decision [to part with the paper], I have been persuaded by the fact that I am now 72 years old and my power to resist the demands of the Ruling Party especially at present is almost negligible. I would like to die in peace if possible and would also like to see that the members of my family are not visited with the repercussions of my actions real or imaginary . . .' All this was part of his strategy, he was to tell the Shah Commission later: 'My idea was to prolong the fight so that the end did not come as inevitably sooner as it looked at several points in time.'

Eventually, government had agreed to his appointing the six persons it had chosen. He appointed them as Additional Directors towards the end of 1975. In the twists and turns of those days, RNG had filed a Contempt Petition in the Madras High Court.

Replying to this, VC Shukla had stated, *inter alia*, that he had not been party to the reconstitution of the *Express* Board. 'I took advantage of the said denial,' RNG recorded in the statement prepared for the Shah Commission, 'and on 19.10.76 I sent a message to Mr. K.K. Birla, inter *alia*, stating that according to facts, the Board was constituted on the suggestion of Mr. Birla and no shareholder had proposed Mr. Birla's name nor was any notice received by the company from individual directors proposing themselves as directors at the ensuing Annual General Meeting stipulated to be held on 29 October 1976. Under the circumstances, Mr Birla could not be elected as a director of the holding company . . . Consequent upon the said decision to do away with the government nominees at the Annual General Meeting of the respective companies, the government nominees were neither proposed nor elected by the shareholders. Other government directors who were appointed to fill the casual vacancies resigned from the Board . . .'[20]

Mut'ah marriages

RNG had worked closely with Kamaraj and others to twice block Morarji Desai from becoming Prime Minister—in 1964 when Pandit Nehru died and again in 1966 when Lal Bahadur Shastri died. But in 1967, he reproached Morarji—'a man of your eminence in public life on whom the country depends such a great deal for getting out of the rut'—for having made up with Kamaraj. He blamed Kamaraj for having 'contrived' to thwart Morarji twice from becoming PM. He professed 'hatred' for Kamaraj. He wrote that Kamaraj 'has become a menace to the Congress Party'. He placed the blame for all the setbacks the Congress had suffered on Kamaraj . . .[21]

---

20 For the exchanges and statement to the Shah Commission, see *The Goenka Letters, Agony and Ecstasy in the Indian Express*, TJS George [ed.], Pinnacle Books, Chennai, 2018, pp. 191–237.

21 For the letter, see *The Goenka Letters*, op. cit., pp. 160–163. Morarji cut him short: '. . . You may have hatred for Kamaraj for your own reasons but I have no hatred for him. If you have such implacable hatred for Kamaraj, I do not

A few days after Verghese was appointed editor of the *Indian Express*, RNG said to me, '*Sach mein paadri hai—subeh saadhey aath bajey aataa hai, raat ko saadhey aath bajey jaataa hai. Aur paisey bhi naheen maangtaa.*'[22] Six months later, he said, '*Kyaa yeh paadri meri Shivji kee baraat chalaaegaa?*'[23] I said, 'Ramnathji, you will say the same sort thing about me one day! Today you say, I am your "racehorse". Tomorrow you will say, "This race horse will wreck my *tonga!*"'[24]

Few had put up the fight against the Emergency that Ramnathji had, certainly no one who had the kind of assets he had. Did that mean that he would be wedded to the Janata Government? Quite the contrary. If I ever met an adherent of Shiite *Mut'ah* marriages—temporary marriages—it was Ramnathji! He was possessive about the Government, sure, about the Janata Party, sure. But that did not mean that he would shut his eyes to, much less shield from public view, its infirmities. Quite the contrary. Precisely because he was possessive about the Government and Party, he would be the first to come down on them if they faltered. As bickering intensified within the Party and Government, Ramnathji tried at first to dampen rival ambitions—always through others, like Radhakrishna, the Sarvodaya leaders, even JP. That didn't work. Mulgaokar wrote an editorial—'Time to go'. This was taken as the death knell of the Government—'If even RNG has turned . . .' it was said.

But an editorial or two were just the announcement. Ramnathji was active in other ways too. And not always to keep rivals together. One day Radhakrishna and I were sitting with him in his office. All of us were lamenting the way the Morarji Government

---

understand why you should have chartered a plane for him in January 1966 as you yourself told me . . . I do not, however, wish to interfere in this matter [a point about which he, Morarji, had spoken to RNG's son] nor do I want to argue about it. When you have made up your mind, I know, your passions and prejudices leave no place for reason or argument.' (Ibid, pp. 163–165)

22 'He is a real priest. Comes to office at 8.30 in the morning. Leaves at 8.30 at night. And doesn't want even money.'
23 'Will this priest run my Shivji's marriage party?'
24 Somehow, this remark got attributed to him later on.

was floundering. '*Auraton kee tareh roney-dhoney se kyaa banegaa?*'[25] Ramnathji burst out suddenly. '*Chalo, chalo,*[26] Fatty, let us do some mischief.' He said we should go and see an astrologer. The three of us got into his small car. The astrologer does not like Morarji, Ramnathji explained in the car, as Morarji has no time either for astrology or the astrologer. As a result, he is close to Charan Singh, or so it is said. We reached the astrologer's house in Delhi's Green Park. The talk was of this and that, about how long the then-current crisis in the Government would last, about how long the Government would last, about who would become PM if Morarji fell . . . Ramnathji praised Charan Singh's honesty, his simplicity, his devotion to the cause of farmers. And then slipped in a few words making fun of Raj Narain. 'If only people could see that he is not that close to Chaudhry Sahib . . .'

Back in the car, I asked Ramnathji why he had gone out of his way to deride Raj Narain. He is an irrelevant joker, I said.

'*Arey, tum kuch jaantey naheen. Darbaariyon mein hameshaa kheenchaa-taani rehti hai. Raj Narain aur yeh jyotshi Charan Singh ke sipah-salaar hain. Shaam se pehley voh jaakar Charan Singh ko kahegaa ki main uskaa prashansak hoon, bus ek chhotie si baat hai ki yadi Raj Narain itnaa kareeb naa dikhtaa . . .*'[27]

'*Tum kahaavat naheen jaantey?* "*Shaahukaar ko kaho 'Jaag'. Chor ko kaho 'Laag'. Kuttey ko kaho 'Bhaunk'. Aur khud tamashaa dekho!*"'[28]

Two editors

Kuldip Nayar had been arrested during the Emergency. Ramnathji made sure that his family was looked after. As Kamal Nath recalled

---

25 'What will come of wailing like women?'
26 'Come, come,'
27 'You don't know anything. Courtiers are always at drawn daggers. Both Raj Narain and this astrologer are Charan Singh's lieutenants. Before the evening is out, he will tell Charan Singh that I am among his admirers, just that there is one small thing—if only Raj Narain did not seem that close . . .'
28 'Don't you know the saying? "Tell the merchant, 'Awake'. Tell the thief, 'Steal.' Tell the dog, 'Bark'. And watch the fun."'

later, Ramnathji requested even him to have Kuldip released. Later, Kuldip and Ajit Bhattacharjea had resigned. Instead of appointing one of them Editor, Ramnathji had picked Nihal Singh—he had worked under Kuldip Nayar in *The Statesman*. As usual, the *Express* was in battle with the Government, and, as a consequence, was besieged by notices, inquiries and the rest. We needed legal advice. Ramnathji sent me to Bombay to seek the advice of Mr H.M. Seervai and Mr Nani Palkhivala.

After a day there, I returned to Delhi late at night.

It wasn't yet 7 a.m. the next morning. I was reading the papers with my father and drinking coffee. Ramnathji was at our doorstep, having driven himself all the way from the *Express* building.

'*To unhoney kyaa kahaa?*'[29] he asked as soon as had greeted my father and sat down.

I recounted the legal advice they had given, and then said that both of them mentioned the resignations of Kuldip and Ajit, and asked me in almost identical words, 'But why does the old man do these things? Wasn't there a better way to handle the two editors? They are senior people. They have been with the paper for long.'

'*Arey chhodo,*' Ramnathji said. '*Paarsiyon ki baaton mein mat aayo. Yeh hameshaa hakoomat ke saath he hotey hain. Ghar mein jab jawaan ladkaa bhi martaa hai to gyaarvein din ke baad usey koi naheen poochtaa. Aur yeh to do editor he gaye hain.*'[30]

My father said to Ramnathji, '*Jab se aap ke paas gayaa hai, issey ek buri aadat pad gayi hai—yeh* coffee *peeney lagaa hai aur voh bhi itnee* strong. *Aap iskee* coffee *band karvaa do.*'[31]

Ramnathji answered, '*Shourie Sahib, voh aap kaa tareekaa hai, meraa naheen. Aap kisi kaa aib dekhtey ho to sochtey ho, "Main is se yeh aib kaisey chhudwaaoon?" Main ultaa sochtaa*

---

[29] 'So, what did they say?'

[30] 'Oh, leave it. Don't get taken in by Parsis. They are always with the rulers. Even when a young lad dies in the family, no one remembers him after the eleventh day. And here, only two editors have gone.'

[31] 'Since he has gone to you, he has acquired a bad habit—he has started drinking coffee, and that too such strong coffee. Get him to stop coffee.'

hoon: "Main iskey is aib kaa prayog kaisey karoon?" Aap kaa ladkaa merey liye nikamma hai: issey naa to ladkee chahiye, naa ladkaa. Beer naa whisky. Club-wlab yeh jaataa naheen. To issey main kaabu mein rakhoon gaa kaisey? Bus, issey coffee chhaahiye. Isliye is aib ki poonch to main pakad kar rakhun gaa. Issey jitni coffee chhaahiye, utnee doongaa! Aapney chhudwaani ho to aap chhudwaiyen![32]

Haath ponchnaa[33]

I was working in my cabin. *'Idhar aayo. Ek dam idhar aayo,'*[34] it was Ramnathji on the phone. As I entered the room, he started shouting, *'Yeh tumhaaraa paper hai kyaa? Mainey tumhey kitni baar kahaa hai ki . . . ko Balia mein* stringer appoint *kar do . . . Kyon naheen kiyaa? . . . Tumhaaree jeb se paisa lagtaa hai kyaa? . . .'*[35] He went on shouting. Chandra Shekhar[36] was sitting with him. Chandra Shekhar tried to be conciliatory: *'Naheen, naheen, chhottie si baat hai, aur Arun to meraa mitr hai he.'*[37] Ramnathji turned on him: *'Isee tareh to aap log meraa akhbaar barbaad kartey ho.* Discipline *ki baat hai. Chhottie ho yaa badi. Agar meri kahi hui chhottie baat bhi naheen chalegi to badi kahaan chalegi, to phir akhbaar kaisey chalegaa? . . .'*[38]

---

[32] 'Shourie Sahib, that is your way, not mine. When you notice someone's bad habit, you think, "How should I make him shed this bad habit?" When I see someone's bad habit, I ask, "How can I put this to use?" Your son is no use to me! He wants neither girls nor boys. Neither beer nor whisky. He doesn't frequent clubs-wlubs. Then how will I keep reins on him? All he wants is coffee! So, I am going to hold on to this bad habit of his. Howsoever much coffee he wants, I will ply him with that! You want to have him give it up, you do that.'

[33] To wipe one's hands.

[34] 'Come here. At once,'

[35] 'Is this your paper? How many times have I told you to appoint . . . as our stringer in Balia . . . Why have you not done so? . . . Is the money coming out of your pocket?'

[36] At the time, President of the Janata Party, later Prime Minister for four months.

[37] 'No, no. It is a small thing. And Arun is my friend in any case.'

[38] 'This is how you people ruin my paper. It is a matter of discipline. If even a small thing I say has to be done is not done, then why will something big I want done get done? And then how will the paper run? . . .'

Chandra Shekhar had asked him to appoint someone as a stringer in Balia, his home town. Ramnathji had never said anything about appointing anyone in that place.

Soon enough, Chandra Shekhar got up to leave. I also got up to see him off till the entrance to the building.

As I came back, RNG said, '*Aao idhar baitho. Agar tumney iskey behanchod ko stringer-shringer lagaayaa to main tumhey nikaal doonga.*'[39]

I wasn't nonplussed as you might imagine—this was his way. '*Dekho, main tumhey gurumantra sikhaataa hoon,*' RNG continued. '*Jab mujhey mushkil padeygi to main tumhaari kameez par haath ponchungaa—ki Arun meraa kahaa naheen maantaa. Jab tumhey kuchh naa karnaa ho, tum merey kurtey par haath ponch lenaa—ki Ramnath yeh karney naheen de rahaa. Chalo apnee coffee piyo . . .*'[40]

This *gurumantra* was deployed often. Ram Jethmalani was, of course, one of the foremost lawyers of the country. In addition, he would take up public issues fearlessly. He had stood by the Sikhs through the darkest days in Punjab. He had argued against the execution of Mrs Gandhi's killers. And he was a very close friend of Ramnathji, of the paper, of all of us: he had defended the *Express* time and again. Because of a combination of factors—his incompetence; his inability to manage the Congress seniors—Rajiv Gandhi had begun to flounder. Bofors had stuck. One day, reporters asked him for an answer to a point that Ram had raised. 'I don't answer dogs that bark,' Rajiv had said. A suicidal response. Ram said, 'Yes, I am a watchdog. I bark when I see a thief.' He vowed to ask ten questions a day. We began printing these. The series became a huge success, and Ram gained even greater prominence. He began feeling that he was better suited to be Prime Minister than others. For this, he had to become the focus of public attention as an alternative. And the *Indian*

---

[39] 'Come here, sit. If you appoint this fellow's sister-fucker as a stringer-wringer, I will throw you out.'

[40] 'Look here, I will teach you a *gurumantra*. When I am in some difficulty, I will wipe my hands on your shirt—that Arun does not do what I tell him to do. When you don't want to do something, you wipe your hands on my kurta— that Ramnath is not letting you do it. OK, now have your coffee.'

Express, a paper and institution that he had defended, was to be the platform.

I had come on a visit to the Bombay edition, and was downstairs discussing matters with colleagues. Ramnathji called: '*Oopar aayo. Tumharaa dost* Ram *aayaa huaa hai.*'[41] Ram Jethmalani and Gurumurthy were with him in the Penthouse. As I entered, Ramnathji beckoned: '*Idhar aao . . . Dekho, aaj kal desh khatrey mein hai. Ek nipund aur mazboot aadmi chhaahiye. Ram hi voh aadmi hai. Hamaaraa kartavya hai ki* Ram public *ke aagey aaye, ek bhaavi PM ke roop mein. Is liye,* topic *dhoondo jis se* Ram *ki* publicity *hovey. Aur* Ram *ki har ek* statement front page *par aani chaahiye . . .*'[42]

The moment Ram left, Ramnathji exclaimed, '*Agar ek baar bhi tumney merey akhbaar kaa is sar-phirey ki* publicity *ke liye prayog kiyaa, to main tumhey is pacheesween manzil se neechey phaink doongaa.* Merit *par,* merit *par—har cheez* merit *par tolnee hai . . .*'[43]

I am fortunate that Ram was so shrewd and so large-hearted that he was not the kind to ever believe that I had aborted his plan to become PM by denying him the out-of-the-ordinary publicity which was his due . . .

A *fundamentalist Hindu?*

Ramnathji was this curious mixture of one who was always looking ahead, of one who could conceive the most complex moves to outfox his adversary and one who held archaic, superstitious beliefs. Roop Kanwar was a young, eighteen-year-

---

[41] 'Come upstairs. Your friend Ram is here.'
[42] 'Now, look. The country is in difficulties these days. We need a skilful and strong person. Ram is that person. It is our duty to ensure that Ram comes before the people, as a prospective Prime Minister. Find issues through which Ram gets publicity. And every statement of Ram must appear on the front page.'
[43] 'If you use my paper even once for giving publicity to this headstrong fellow, I will throw you down from this twenty-fifth floor. On merit, on merit—everything must be weighed on merit.'

old woman in Rajasthan. She had been married just eight or so months. Her husband died—this was in September 1987. Suddenly, the state was agog with news that she had committed 'sati'. My friend, Swami Agnivesh, received information that she had been drugged and burnt alive so that others could gobble up the assets that belonged to her husband. To cover up the murder, they proclaimed that she had immolated herself at the pyre of her husband. Thousands were said to have attended the cremation. Swami Agnivesh led a march to the cremation site. In the paper, we covered his march, and speeches along the route. I went to Jaipur and, joining Agnivesh, addressed a public meeting at a traffic circle. I wrote an editorial commending his march: 'Dayanand's work.'

One day, Ramnathji rang up, '*Tumhaari* coffee *thandi ho rahi hai.*'[44] When I sat down, he asked me to read a letter that he had received from his close friend, Jaidayal Dalmia. Written in tiny Devanagari letters, it was many pages long. Dalmia had written that such a great thing had happened, that his heart was longing to visit the site, that the two of them should plan a trip together. I was aghast as I read the letter. Seeing my reaction as I turned the pages, Ramnathji said, '*Is ghatnaa par doosraa pehlu bhi hai,*'[45] and that Jaidayalji was his close friend. I continued supporting Agnivesh's march. Ramnathji never mentioned the subject again.

'*Naa milee ke sadhu*'[46]

From this, or from the fact that Ramnathji was an early supporter of the Gita Press, could one infer his attitude towards Hinduism in general, to the Rashtriya Swayamsevak Sangh (RSS) in particular as the aspiring standard-bearer of Hinduism? One day I got a message that Bhaurao Deoras wanted me to go over and meet him at Jhandewalan complex of the RSS.

---

[44] 'Your coffee is getting cold.'
[45] 'There is another side also to this incident.'
[46] 'Monks because they didn't get one.'

When I returned, I went to see RNG. I told him how impressed I was by Bhauraoji: such austere living, a sharp mind, clear thinking . . . 'Arey chhodo,' Ramnathji cut me short:

> Yeh sab naa milee ke sadhu hain—chokree naheen milee to sadhu baney phirtey hain. Sattaa milegee, tab dekhnaa—kaisey us ke peechey bhaagengey, kyaa uskaa prayog karengey, ke kaheen voh panjey sey nikal naa jaaye uskey liye kyaa kyaa karengey . . . 'Austerity'! Meri baat yaad rakhnaa. Tum yaad naa bhi rakhogee to yeh log tumhey meraa kahaa huaa yaad dilaayenge. Satta mili to tumhein pataa lagegaa ki yeh kitney sadhu hain.[47]

I got to see the contrast between the reality and the facade early on.

Why not a Trust?

Ramnathji's relations with his relatives were fraught, the underlying tensions just about covered by banalities and innuendo. The most telling of this state was the effect that his presence had on his son Bhagwan Das. B.D. Goenka was a very friendly person, but high-strung to the point of being a little fidgety, always as if he had to be somewhere else, with other things to attend to. Sometimes, he would be in Delhi and we would have begun eating. Ramnathji had just to walk in, and poor BD, who had been talking jovially till that split second, would gulp down the morsel he had in his mouth, and hurry off—as if he was late for some urgent appointment.

BD was a friendly sort; as I said, his visits were a welcome diversion, but as for his influence in regard to the paper, we never noticed it. Saroj, his wife, on the other hand, was an altogether different entity—an ominous shadow, darkening things all the way

---

[47] 'Oh, forget it. All these fellows are monks because they didn't get one—they didn't land the girl, and so they are going about as monks. Let them get power once, and then see how they will be chasing it, what all they will milk it for, what they will not do lest it slip out of their clutches . . . "Austerity"! Remember what I am telling you. Even if you forget it, they will remind you of it. Once they get power, then you will learn how much of the monk is in them.'

from Madras. I never understood Ramnathji's attitude towards her. Suspicious, certainly. But there was more—apprehension. So concerned was he that she should not be inconvenienced, that she should not take anything as amiss, it was as if he was actually afraid of her. Her father was Sriyans Prasad Jain, the patriarch of the *Times of India* group. A connoisseur of Urdu poetry, a benign influence over the Bhartiya Jnanpith, he hardly spoke. But the way they had acquired the Bennett Coleman group spoke of much shrewdness. Ramnathji was wary of him, as he was of the Jain family. But all this was carefully hidden under banter. Once I was sitting with Ramnathji in his office. Sriyansji entered. Even before he had sat down, Ramnathji, pointing to the wall, said to me for Sriyans Prasad to hear, 'Voh dekho.'[48] I couldn't see anything special. 'Udhar dekho, phir se dekho.'[49] All I could see was a *chipakali*.[50] Ramnathji said, 'Dekhaa naa? Yeh'—pointing to Sriyans Prasad—'yeh voh hain. Moohn band. Machhar aaye, moohan ek kshand ke liye khulaa, machhar andar, moohn band.'[51] Sriyans was unfazed. In turn he recited a couplet, 'Aur inkey baarey mein sun leejiye:[52]

> *Zindagi mein aisey mukaam bhi aatey hain ki rehzan ko ameer-e-kaarvaan kehanaa hi padtaa hai . . .*[53]

smiled, and settled down in the chair.

The most telling incident occurred one evening. I had come over to Bombay from Delhi, and was staying in the Penthouse with Ramnathji. I was accompanying him as he walked in the open space around the rooms. The Air India building rose between us and the sea. Ramnathji was ageing. Many persons, Mulgaokar in particular, had been urging him to form a Trust so that the paper could continue to function as a strong and independent institution

---

[48] 'Look at that.'
[49] 'Look there, look again.'
[50] Common lizard.
[51] 'Saw it? He is that. Mouth shut. A mosquito flies near. Mouth open for a second, the mosquito in, mouth shut.'
[52] 'And listen to something about him:'
[53] 'Such occasions also arise in life that one has to proclaim the brigand as the chieftain of the caravan . . .'

after him. Ramnathji would always put off the matter—often by agreeing to have some eminent lawyer like Mr Nani Palkhivala, draft a Trust deed for his consideration. I felt he would never agree to formalizing any institutional arrangement to look after the paper after him. In his eyes, *he* was the paper. If the paper survived after him, he was *not* the paper. As we walked, I said that, if not a Trust, he should formalize who in his family would take over the paper after him. He stopped. Looked at me. '*Kyaa kahaa?* Family? *Voh dekho*'—he pointed to . . . and said . . .[54]

I just typed what he pointed to and what he said. But have deleted it. It is better left unsaid.

His singular possession

There was an important emotion behind what he had said. The paper was his and his alone. He was the paper. All of us got glimpses of this often—and, as we shall see, it was one of the things that persons who wanted me out of the paper played upon later. But that was in the future. I got to see the possessiveness many a time much earlier.

Mrs Gandhi had returned to power. Her Government had again unleashed steps to rein Ramnathji in. The Delhi administration had taken steps to take over, if not demolish, an extension to the Delhi building that Ramnathji had begun constructing. Ramnathji said that on behalf of the paper I should go to Kanchi and seek blessings of the Paramacharya.

I was delighted as I had read about the Paramacharya in Paul Brunton's *Search in Secret India,* and how he had pointed Brunton in the direction of Ramana Maharshi.

From Madras, Cho, Gurumurthy and I motored to Kanchi. On reaching the *math*, we learnt that the Paramacharya had gone to a nearby temple to consecrate a new idol.

We walked to it. Hundreds of devotees were seated, their faces towards a far-off wall. The Paramacharya was sitting with

---

[54] 'What did you say? Family? Look at that.' His grandsons, who eventually inherited the paper, were still in their early twenties and were not at that time in the minds of us employees at the paper.

his back leaning against the wall, a white scarf tied somewhat haphazardly around his head—we were to learn later that the scarf had been wrapped around his head to honour him when he had arrived. We had but to enter the enclosure and many started shouting, 'Cho, Cho, Cho'. One of the priests came and took us to the front row of devotees.

The Paramacharya was quite old by this time. His eyesight as well as his hearing were impaired. After a while, one of the attendants shouted in his ear that Cho, Gurumurthy and another person had come. The Paramacharya looked towards us, and regaled the devotees with an account of what had happened when Cho had come to visit him on a previous occasion—'Cho, Cho, Cho', people had begun shouting, and had forgotten all about him, the Paramacharya exclaimed!

He then asked who the third person was. When he was told that I was so-and-so from the *Indian Express* in Delhi, he told the attendant to bring me closer. The three of us moved closer. Gurumurthy told me to ask the Paramacharya for something I really wanted. I said that I would be grateful if he could give something for Adit.

The Paramacharya said something. An attendant brought an apple from a tray of fruit that was lying at a distance. The Paramacharya took the apple, and kept rubbing it on all sides. After a while, he asked the attendant to give it to me with the instruction that I feed it to Adit.

As there were so many devotees pressing to get close to the Paramacharya, the three of us got up, walked away and sat at the back.

There was quite a din. Mantras and the nadaswarams resounded in the enclosure. Devotees were talking and chanting. All eyes were fixed on the Paramacharya. Look at him, I said to Cho and Gurumurthy. Here is the Pope of Hinduism, sitting on the ground, in the simplest dhoti, a flat piece of wood supporting his back . . . What a wonderful contrast to the gold and glitter that surround the Pope in Rome.

We were talking thus but our eyes, like those of everyone else, were fixed on the Paramacharya. After a while, we saw, from the distance, him say something to an attendant, and gesturing first towards his head and then some way in the distance. The attendant slowly took off the cloth that had been wrapped around his head. Holding the cloth with much reverence, the attendant walked to the side of the crowd, and then seemed to be coming towards the rear. To our astonishment, he came to us. All eyes were now on us. He raised the cloth, chanted a mantra, and wrapped it around my head. The whole hall erupted in sounds and exclamations and hands striking the cheeks.

I returned to Delhi, the silken cloth a treasure. The next day I took the cloth to the office. I went to Ramnathji and recounted our visit.

Ramnathji had been listening with great interest and satisfaction to the description of the visit and all that had transpired. When I came to the final part, I showed him the cloth. He sat up, looked at it, and asked with some abruptness, '*Swami nein yeh tumhaarey sar par pehanaayaa?*' '*Naheen, naheen,*' I said, '"*Pehnaayaa*" *naheen, "pehanvaayaa"*.'[55] I again explained what had happened. He immediately handed the cloth back to me as if there was some contaminant in it, and changed the subject.

In a flash I realized what had happened. While to me the cloth was something that had been gifted to someone from the *Express,* in Ramnathji's mind the only one from the *Express* to whom such a sacred gift should have been given was him.

Gathering cyclostyled sheets on the floor

He was austere in his habits, and worked as hard as anyone else at the paper. Unlike most other owners of enterprises, he was ready to do every kind of work. As I mentioned, the Government had initiated steps to take over a portion of the *Express* building in Delhi. We were readying a petition for the Supreme Court. The draft had been settled by Fali Nariman. Typists were busy typing out the text. As pages would be typed and corrected, stencils

---

[55] 'Did Swami put this on your head?' 'No, no,' I said. 'He didn't, he made someone put it on me.'

would be cut, and the pages cyclostyled. It was well past midnight. We were still in the office. I went over to see how Ramnathji was amidst all the tension. As many persons were working there at the time, I opened the door to his office to find out where he was. And what do I find? Ramnathji was sitting on the floor helping gather the cyclostyled pages together. Who would grudge working late into the night? Who *could* grudge doing any sort of work to protect the paper after he saw a person of his age on the floor gathering sheets?

'I have never felt so small'

Ramnathji was most considerate towards Adit, Anita and me: he went out of his way to enable us to go to Ayurvedic centres in Kottakal and Coimbatore for Adit's treatment. But he could also be heartless in driving a bargain. He had decided to start an edition in Cochin. Gurumurthy had accompanied him to look for land. They were taken to a plot that belonged to a distinguished, by then retired educationist. The gentleman was quite infirm, and visibly besieged by problems, including the grave illness of a close relative. In distress, unable to meet the expenses that he had to defray, in particular the expenses required for his ailing relative, he had been compelled to put the only plot they owned up for sale. He asked for a sum that was certainly not too high, indeed well within the price of plots in that locality. Ramnathji named a figure half that amount. The poor man kept entreating him to agree to a higher amount. He kept narrating the compulsions that were weighing upon him. Gurumurthy tried to reason with Ramnathji. He wouldn't budge. Narrating the incident to me later, Gurumurthy said, 'I have never felt so small in my life. A poor man, a teacher, someone in such distress, and RNG would just not budge.'

There was no end to such incidents. Some endearing. And some shocking. Gurumurthy once said, 'We love Ramnathji for traits which, if we had them, we would hate ourselves for.'

3

Starting at the paper

There were several things about the paper that were crying out to be changed, and as my new colleagues and I attempted to change them, Ramnathji was the one person who supported us.

Much greater importance was attached to editorial comments than to reporting facts. Few read editorials, but, cooped up in their own tiny echo chambers, editors thought the world about their pronouncements. It was a hangover of British journalism, 'The *Times* thundered . . .' In part, therefore, the importance that was attached to editorials and edit page articles was a reflection of the small world which editors inhabited: a world in which they read each other. In part, it was a reflection of the class system implicit in journalism of those days: editorials and edit page articles were written by editors, news reports by those who had not become editors, the lowly reporters. Moreover, the edit page articles were contributed by a minuscule band—the tiny circle of an editor. There was also plain vanity. Pointing to two of them as examples, Ramnathji warned me, '*Ab tum paper mein likhney lagey ho. Yaad rakhnaa, paperon mein jo likhtey hain voh samajhney lagtey hain ki duniya unkey articalon sey ghoomti hai.*'[1]

---

[1] 'Now you have started writing in papers. Always remember, ones who begin writing in papers start thinking that the world goes round because of their articles.'

56

The paper must accord more importance to facts than to opinions, I felt. The paper must give far, far more importance to reporters. And to photographers. And most of all to cartoons and cartoonists: a single cartoon punctures rulers more surely than a dozen essays ever could. The opinions, too, must flow, as incidentals, from facts. And we must get a far wider circle of persons to write on the edit page. Why not build up the page opposite the edit page as a place for longer stories, and longer opinion pieces?

Reporters must not just be reporting news. What they write must *be* news. The paper should give them opportunities to ferret out facts. It must give them facilities to go out of large cities. It must give them and their work prominence; it must give them space. Bylines must be given to young reporters and photographers as readily as to editors. For a byline to be given or not given must not be determined by the number of years that the person has spent in 'the profession', but by the worth of the story.

There must be no limit to the length of the stories. The reporter must be allowed, he must, in fact, be encouraged to get all the details to the reader.

On the other side, I would urge the reporters to read documents. When you must, yes, hunt out the documents that they have hidden away. But don't forget to read printed documents. Often, what the printed document says, even oftener what it does *not* say, is enough to reveal what is really happening. Documents apart, visit places. Look for yourselves. Report the facts, write *your* conclusions; don't tell the reader, 'X says, Y says', and make-believe that you have done a 'balanced story'. The point is not what 'X' or 'Y' says; the point is what do *you* say?

While many seniors in 'the profession' prided themselves on their 'sources', I would urge our reporters to be very wary of 'sources'. You think you are cultivating him, I would say. Actually, *he* is using you. And be sure to maintain a distance from them. Otherwise, you will not be able to write freely about them: *lehaaz* will come in the way . . .

Many of the young reporters took to all this like ducks who have been let out of baskets to water. Some, no doubt, were inconvenienced: I learnt of one 'financial reporter' who used to take corporate press releases, just put his name under the heading and send it to the news desk with the byline, 'By our special correspondent.'

All this was anathema to the 'seniors'. Shekhar Gupta had been a young correspondent in Chandigarh. An aunt of mine developed cancer. I had to take her to the PGI (Postgraduate Institute of Medical Education and Research) there. Whoever I needed to meet, Shekhar knew him. Whichever department in the hospital I needed to take my aunt to, Shekhar would be there. His energy seemed as boundless as his contacts were numerous. A while later, a vacancy opened up in Shillong for covering the Northeast. I urged that we send Shekhar: 'He will be everywhere. He will bring the Northeast to the attention of the entire country.' But the editors in Delhi—living in their tiny echo chambers in which they heard the reverberations of only their own pronouncements—had not heard of him. But they gave in. When stories filed by Shekhar from the Northeast appeared again and again on the front pages with his byline, a senior editor, visibly upset, remarked, 'It took us ten years before we could have a byline. And you are giving these freshers bylines on the front page.'

Then there were their fabled 'sources' in high places. What the reporters were filing was based on no 'sources' at all. Their dispatches were based on what they had seen in the streets, in the district towns and the countryside, in jails.

Most of all, the space that was taken by, was set apart for the stories and the kind of stories that began getting done—these irritated the 'seniors' no end. I felt that an exposure must not be a flash in the pan. Rulers are deaf. And so we must continue to pursue the story, for months if necessary. By then, either the rulers would have been compelled to do something about the matter—we would then have given heart to hundreds that, yes, things can still be changed. Or, even though conclusive facts would have been brought to light, rulers would have done nothing—in which case, we would have shown readers how far the rot in the system had gone, so that, even though the rulers had no answer to the facts that we had brought out, they could get away by doing nothing:

we would have made an unanswerable case for large-scale reform. Like much else, this approach to our work became a source of constant grievance: 'Is this a newspaper or a campaign sheet?'

For all these reasons, persons who had invested years in 'the profession', who were accustomed to a particular way of doing things, and even more so to their own prominence, and who now suddenly heard young reporters and the reporters' stories being talked about rather than their 'scoops'—which were most often nothing more than what somebody had told them 'in the strictest confidence'—they would find fault with almost everything that was being done. Only Ramnathji stood by what we were doing. Apart from his intense interest in public affairs, and therefore in the facts that were being brought to light, he saw consequences flow, he saw his paper being talked about because of what the reporters were doing, he saw the paper's circulation rise. And so, he deflected the contrarians: '*Nayaa zamaanaa hai, nayee cheezein karni hongi. Abhee jo chaahtaa hai, isey karney do . . .*'[2]

We were fortunate in the Editor we had at the time, S. Mulgaokar. He was a reclusive figure, and seemingly disapproving of everything. But he had a hawk's eye for the unexpected fact, and for what was missing in a story. None of the others could match his turn of phrase. Everyone was apprehensive of him as one could easily fall even lower in his reckoning, and there would be no way to climb back. He was one for whom Ramnathji had very high regard. Reappointing him as the Editor of the paper had been the first thing that Ramnathji had done when he had dismissed the Indira Gandhi Board during the Emergency. Ramnathji would counsel me to remain on the right side of Mulgaokar. That was difficult—not because of things all of us wanted to do in the paper—Mulgaokar said little about them— but because of his silently disapproving, condescending, superior manner. I would go to his flat in Jor Bagh to discuss something. He would not lift his eyes from some British paper he was reading, or from the crossword in it. The much neglected and crestfallen

---

2 'It is a new world. We will have to do new things. For the time being, let him do what he wants . . .'

Mrs Mulgaokar would come in, ask me to sit down and inquire if I would like some tea. Ramnathji would say: '*Tum us-sey ladtey kyon ho? Mujhey dekho. Mulgaokar meraa mulaazim hai. Par jab main uskey ghar pahunchtaa hoon, pehley main Mulgaokar ko salaam kartaa hoon. Phir main uskey kuttey ko salaam kartaa hoon—"Kuttaaji, meraa salaam." Poocho kyon? Kyonki mujhey Mulgaokar se kaam karvaanaa hai, aur kutta Mulgaokar ko pyaaraa hai . . .*' '*Us sey lado naheen. Us sey seekho*—internal injury *kaisey kee jaati hai. Upar se ghaav dikhey naa, aur andar nasein phat jaaen.*'[3]

Very difficult for us, Punjabis! I said.

The paper had outstanding, daring reporters and photographers. Like every organization, it also had its share of backbiters and *Naradmunis*. I adopted a simple remedy, and was surprised by how well it worked. I heard that a reporter was going around spreading malicious lies, telling a senior Editor that I had said this and that. I was incensed, as it was, and has remained my practice not to say anything about anyone to others which I have not said to the person face to face. When the reporter was in my cabin, I asked him whether he had been telling colleagues that I had said such and thus, and especially about a senior Editor. He flatly denied having done so, and maintained, instead, that it was the Editor who had been saying this and that about me. 'We'll ask the Editor,' I said. He almost shot up from his chair, and said, 'No, no, there is no need. It is nothing, it is a small matter.' I picked up the phone and dialled the Editor. 'X is sitting with me. I was told he has been carrying tales to you that I was saying this and that about you. He says that he never did so, that on the contrary, you are the one who is saying such and thus about me . . .' The reporter was in a sweat. That sort of malignant gossip stopped. At least, it no longer reached my ears. But I had bought myself a slanderer for life.

---

[3] 'Why do you quarrel with him? Look at me. Mulgaokar is my employee. But when I reach his house, first I salute Mulgaokar. Then I salute his dog—"Mr Dog, my salutations." Ask me why. Because I have to get Mulgaokar to do some work, and the dog is dear to him . . .' 'Don't quarrel with him. Learn from him—how to inflict an internal injury. No wound on the surface, and inside the veins have burst.'

4

Unearth the facts,
and just don't let go

K.F. Rustomji was a distinguished police officer. He had been the first Director General of the Border Security Force, and had, among other things, played a key role in organizing the *Mukti Bahini*. At the time I got to know him well, he was a member of the National Police Commission. As part of his work at the Commission, he used to visit several places and institutions. He used to write 'Tour Notes' describing what he had learnt during these visits. He would circulate the 'Notes' among members of the Commission, and to some persons outside. I was lucky enough to receive these cyclostyled sheets.

In early January 1979, he sent a note about of his visits to two jails. They revealed a shocking picture: in particular, of prisoners who had been rotting in jails for years, not because they had been convicted of any crime, but because they were waiting for their trials to proceed. We carried these notes in two parts in the *Indian Express* on 8 and 9 January 1979.

A public-spirited lawyer, Mrs Kapila Hingorani, filed a writ in the Supreme Court about the undertrials. She annexed the 'Note' of Rustomji that we had printed. The matter landed before Justice P.N. Bhagwati. He waived all technicalities aside—that Mrs Hingorani was not filing the writ on behalf of any of the undertrials, that she was not directly affected, etc.—and took up the matter immediately.

I drew up a list of items, and requested our state correspondents to visit central jails in fifteen cities and collect information about them. The series continued throughout 1979, much to the annoyance of some traditional journalists and editors. 'Why is he going on and on about this?' they said. 'Aren't there other issues, after all?' they demanded.

'This is not journalism,' they pronounced. 'He is a pamphleteer,' they pronounced. But what was bad about being a pamphleteer? 'He is not a journalist,' they pronounced. What was so great about being a journalist? I was and am nobody, but like others, I could look up to the example of the greatest Indians: Would Agarkar and the Lokmanya's writings in *Kesari*, would Gandhiji's writings in *Young India* and *Harijan*, not have been dismissed on the same charge? I always had before my mind's eye the example of Gandhiji in Champaran. As was his invariable practice, Gandhiji placed his demand at the minimum—that the British set up a committee to examine the condition of Indigo cultivators. This posed a dilemma for the rulers. If they set up the committee, the mighty British Empire would have bent to a 'half naked fakir'. Who knows what he will come up with next? And the people would draw the correct lesson—that, yes, the mighty Empire *can* be bent. If they did not set up the committee, Gandhiji would have proven his point even better—when this Government will not so much as set up a little committee to help you, how can you continue to look upon it as your *mai baap*? In the same way, if truthful, detailed, relentless, uncontroverted work compelled rulers to initiate reforms, not only would a specific wrong be righted, so many would gain heart—yes, we too can change things. If, in spite of a mountain of facts having been brought out, the rulers did nothing, we would have made an even more important point—that the system had decayed so much that, unless the nature of persons we had as rulers was changed, we could not turn our country around.

In this instance, the series, packed as it was with facts, had visible effect. Often, we would time fresh exposures with the dates on which the hearings were coming up in the Supreme Court, and we would share raw data with Mrs Hingorani.

Along with fellow Judges, Justice P.N. Bhagwati gave far-reaching orders. As a result, a large number of prisoners were released back to freedom. The very journalists and editors who had been berating us now appropriated the results as examples of what a free press can and should do.[1]

Rustomji

K.F. Rustomji's account of undertrials, though it was confined to two jails, bore witness to inhumanity in our society as a whole.

Prisoner after prisoner was wasting away as an undertrial for five years, ten years, thirteen years; a prisoner who in all the years he had spent as an undertrial had lost his mind and could not remember why he was arrested; another who had been languishing for six years because his file had been lost and now no one could figure out why he had been hauled in; a child who had been born inside the prison because the mother's case had not come up in court, and who had never seen the outside of the wretched jail; prisoner after prisoner who was spending years upon years in jail as an undertrial, when the maximum sentence for the crime he was supposed to have committed was just three to six months; prisoner after prisoner who was desperate to confess to any crime the police specified, but who could not do even this much as the case had never come up in court . . .

---

[1] The following is based on articles I wrote between February and November 1979, and on the stellar judgments of Justice P.N. Bhagwati and his fellow Judges. In particular, *Hussainara Khatoon & Ors (I) v Home Secretary, State of Bihar*, (1980) 1 SCC 81; *Hussainara Khatoon & Ors (II) v Home Secretary, State of Bihar*, (1980) 1 SCC 91; *Hussainara Khatoon & Ors (III) v Home Secretary, State of Bihar*, (1980) 1 SCC 93; *Hussainara Khatoon & Ors (IV) v Home Secretary, State of Bihar*, (1980) 1 SCC 98; *Hussainara Khatoon & Ors (V) v Home Secretary, State of Bihar*, (1980) 1 SCC 108; *Kadra Pahadiya & Ors v State of Bihar*, (1981) 3 SCC 671; *Kadra Pahadiya & Ors v State of Bihar*, (1981) 2 SCC 104; *Munna & Ors v State of Uttar Pradesh & Ors*, (1982) 1 SCC 545; *Munna & Ors v State of Uttar Pradesh & Ors*, (1989) Supp (2) 1 SCC 154. Except for the last one, all of these judgments were authored by Justice Bhagwati.

Surveys

Visits by our correspondents brought more horrors to light. They established that the problem was by no means confined to two jails, that, in fact, it was a general one.

We found that at the time, about 85,000 men, women and children were rotting as undertrials in our jails—'about 85,000', for no one knew their exact number. The situation was particularly bad in the Northeast, and also where *everything* seemed to be, and it has continued to be 'particularly bad', i.e., in UP and Bihar. In Assam, Meghalaya and Tripura, about two-thirds of the detenus were undertrials. In UP and Bihar, the figure was 80 per cent— eight out of every ten persons who were in the jails in Bihar and UP were there, not because they had been judged to have committed some crime, but because their cases had not come up in court.

The problem was atrocious across the country. In the Secunderabad Central Jail, 80 per cent of the detenus turned out to be undertrials; in Surat—the constituency of our Gandhian Prime Minister at the time—78 per cent were undertrials; in Ahmedabad, 72 per cent; in Lucknow, as well as Shillong, 82 per cent; in Patna and Srinagar, around two-thirds; in Bangalore, 55 per cent; in Calcutta's Alipore jail, 50 per cent; and so on. The only jails that fared qualitatively better were Trivandrum and Bhopal (38 per cent), Indore (16 per cent) and Nahan in Himachal Pradesh (10 per cent).

Even a few months in one of our jails is filled with enough misery to last a lifetime. But here, it was not a few months, but years and years. Sixty per cent of the undertrials in Patna Central Jail had been rotting there for over six months; around 40 per cent had been there for more than a year; around one-sixth for a year and a half; fifty-seven prisoners had been awaiting trial for two to three years, seventeen for three to four years, eight for four to five years, thirty-two for five to eleven years.

In Srinagar, 53 per cent of the undertrials had been in prison for more than six months; about one-third for more than a year. In most other jails, the proportions were smaller. But, even in their case, anywhere from one-tenth to one-third of the undertrials had already been in jail for over six months.

Nor were these prisoners dreaded dacoits or murderers—the category 'terrorist', so common today, was unknown at that time. In almost all cases, 70 to 75 per cent of undertrials were ones who had been charged, not with murder or attempt to murder nor with dacoity, but with sundry, small offences. The jails in Srinagar, Nahan, Lucknow, Ambala and Calcutta turned out to be exceptions. In Srinagar, 80 per cent of undertrials were there on charges of murder or attempt to murder; in Ambala and Nahan, 45 per cent; in Alipore, a quarter had been charged with dacoity; in Lucknow, two-thirds had been charged with murder, attempt to murder or dacoity. Of course, the veracity of the charges was an altogether different dimension. At that time, 'dacoity' had become a handy charge for rounding up many political opponents in states like Bengal and Andhra, just as possession of *ek tamanchaa, chaar kartoos* had become the standard charge for picking up all sorts in UP.

The typical case was not Srinagar but Madras. Only 3 per cent of the undertrials in Madras Central Jail were charged with murder, attempt to murder, or dacoity. Sixty-one per cent were there for, of all things, prohibition offences! All rich men, all Government officials, all politicians in Tamil Nadu, seemed to have become teetotallers—not one of them seemed to be violating the prohibition laws. Only the derelicts. The derelicts drank; the politicians and policemen only helped transport the stuff from Pondicherry.

Mindless variation

Our survey revealed that variation between states and over time was mindless and entirely fortuitous.

Thus, for instance, things had improved a great deal in West Bengal. And the improvement seemed to be the work of a new IG (Inspector General) of Prisons. He had abolished the practice of putting fetters on prisoners; he had outlawed lathicharge inside the prison unless an officer was present; he had used an old circular of the central Government to free 400 Bangladeshis who had been rotting since 1971. (In neighbouring Patna, Abdul Rahman, a Pakistani, had been rotting for nine years. If he was a spy, why was he mixing with other prisoners? If he was not, why was someone not sending him back to Pakistan?)

In Maharashtra, the authorities were experimenting successfully with two open colonies, where convicts could live with their families; they had also set up an open-air prison for convicts. Gujarat, too, had set up two open jails, one at Ahmedabad and another at Amreli. But in Shillong, prisoners were still stuffed into a hellhole that had been constructed over a century earlier.

In Gujarat, the administration was experimenting with providing new amenities to prisoners. At the Sabarmati Central Jail in Ahmedabad, even a TV had been installed, a novelty at the time, and programmes from a small experimental radio station were being aired for the prisoners. But in Shillong, our correspondent reported, the jail was 'an ill-equipped, unhealthy, overcrowded, dilapidated, badly managed' institution, in which most prisoners had to spend all their time indoors as the prison did not have much open space, a prison in which, our correspondent reported, 'sanitation just does not exist'. In Rajasthan and Bengal, generous remissions had reduced the sentences of convicts by years; in Bihar, remissions had been few and niggardly. In one state, a model prison had been constructed. In Patna, the overcrowded Central Jail did not have even water to flush lavatories so that the excreta used to pile up, not just for days but for months and months . . .

The improvements that have occurred since would be as dissimilar. The ranking of the states would certainly have changed— what with some states having substituted false encounters for the tedium of taking and housing prisoners.

What they pray for

At the turn of the nineteenth century, in UP, for every 100 convicts in jail, there was just about one-half of an undertrial. Even in 1967, for every 100 convicts in jail, there were fifty undertrials. In October 1978, for every 100 convicts, there were 460 undertrials.

This reversal in ratios reflected how the judicial drains had clogged up over the years. It also reflected erratic factors, the 'acts of God', which determined the fate of anyone who happened to get thrown into jail on some charge.

Remissions illustrated the position. Though over thirty years had passed since the country had gained Independence, Governments dispensed remissions in the feudal manner. Mahavir Jayanti? OK, five months of every convict's sentence cut. Guru Gobind Singh's martyrdom? OK, three months cut . . .

Those days, in Haryana, prisoners used to pray for the visit of Chaudhry Devi Lal: he dispensed remissions to mark his visits. But there was a special effect of the remissions. Remissions worsened the ratio of undertrials to convicts. In 1972, when we were celebrating the silver jubilee of our Independence, generous remissions were announced. In UP, 8000 convicts were released. But naturally not the undertrials. After all, you couldn't remit the sentence of someone who had not even been sentenced.

Other 'acts of God' also affected the lives of undertrials.

'Political prisoners' or, a nomenclature that surprised me, 'satyagrahis', for one. The undertrials in Patna reported this to be one of their periodic plagues. These prisoners would insist on special treatment, special accommodation, special facilities, the moment they landed in jail. The warders, too, were a bit nervous about them. They are birds of passage, the jailers reasoned; they will soon be out again, they may shout and complain about the jail staff when they are out; and, in any case, who knows, one of them may be a minister tomorrow. The result? In the Patna Central Jail, whenever satyagrahis came, the long-term undertrials and convicts used to be thrown out of their dormitories into the open yard.

Sickness was another visitation. Medical facilities were and remain appalling in all our jails; they could not but be more so in Patna. Prisoners used to be taken to the prisoners' ward in the general hospital in Patna for treatment. By the time our survey was done, the jail authorities were doing all they could to avoid having to take a prisoner to the hospital. And that because policemen were loath to do guard duty in the general ward of the hospital.

Why the '*general* ward', and not the '*prisoners*' ward'? The prisoners' ward had been abolished some months earlier when house surgeons of the hospital solved their accommodation problem by forcibly occupying what used to be the prisoners' ward.

Deep and intense tragedy

Behind these anecdotes and figures, lay deep and intense tragedy.

In Patna Central Jail, Ghanshyam Mahto had rotted for seven years awaiting trial on the charge of obstructing public servants in the performance of their duties and preventing the arrest of a wanted man. Had he been convicted, his maximum sentence would have been three years. Charitra Majhi and Bundhi Majhi had rotted for eight years and six years, respectively, on the charge of having stolen railway property. Maximum sentence, if convicted? Three years. Bholu Mahto had rotted for eleven years on the charge of kidnapping and wrongfully confining a person. Maximum sentence, if convicted? Seven years. His record was lost. After looking for it for eighteen months, the jail authorities had moved the Patna High Court to 'cause the record to be traced'.

The tragedies were not confined to Bihar. In Indore Central Jail lay Mulya Ratna. He had been there since September 1977. Too poor to obtain bail, not having heard of legal aid, he had gone mad. In the same jail, Annu Anwar Khan had been languishing since October 1976. He had been arrested when about 100 persons died after drinking illicit liquor. His role in the episode was undetermined. The big guns of the trade were free and still prospering. He was consigned to wait for his trial. Meanwhile, many of his relatives, including his wife, father, mother, father-in-law and an uncle had died.

There was no end to such cases. Reading the accounts of our reporters, I was reminded again and again of two remarks of V.S. Naipaul. In *An Area of Darkness*, he had talked of our 'art of non-seeing'. How could any of this have survived so long and become so pervasive were it not for this ability, this acquired, well-honed skill *not* to see what is staring us in the face? And in a collection of essays that had been recently published, Naipaul had said that when one comes across and is revolted by a particularly wretched level of life in India, one can be certain that there is always a level lower than that. One had but to be outraged at women and children being kept in jails for years on the pretext that they were needed for giving evidence, and the judgments spoke of women who, if they were to be released, had nowhere to go.[2] We are appalled at poor men rotting in jails for years, only to learn that lunatics and those of unsound mind are also being kept in ordinary jails for years.[3]

At home, my father, a distinguished and innovative civil servant—as a young man, he had sat as a magistrate, he had helped rehabilitate lakhs and lakhs of refugees, he had managed districts—was astonished by the reports from the *Express* reporters. How could things have come to such a pass? Aren't jailers aware of the law? Haven't they read the Jail Manual? Aren't magistrates ensuring that these prisoners are brought before them every fortnight? How are they sending the poor prisoners back to jail again and again? Haven't they read the CrPC (Code of Criminal Procedure)? Aren't officers visiting the jails as their job requires them to do? Don't they talk to the prisoners? Aren't they going through the records that every jail keeps?

His puzzlement and questions led me to look at provisions of the CrPC. They led me to look at the Jail Manual. But first I had to look for it.

---

[2] 'Mrs. Higorani has pointed out to us that there is some difficulty in regard to women and children who have been released on personal bond pursuant to the order made by us inasmuch as there is no one to take care of them and they do not know where to go,' the Judges noted, and directed the jail authorities to immediately contact the state's Social Welfare Department so that necessary arrangements could be made for them. *Hussainara III*, para. 4.

[3] Confronted with this fact, the Judges held that the Government must explain why they were in ordinary jails, and what the state government proposed to do about them. *Hussainara V*, para. 2.

A rare book

After quite a search, and with the help of colleagues in Chandigarh, I was at last able to locate a copy of the *Manual for the Superintendence and Management of Jails in the Punjab*. This manual, I learnt, applied to jails in many of our northern states. Moreover, it had been the model for jail manuals in other states.

Even at that time, it was a rare book. Only 300 copies of it had been printed four years earlier, in 1975. Each copy cost Rs 260.30. You can imagine how much help it must have been to our undertrials, who had neither the money nor the relatives to even stand surety for them.

The manual was 562 pages long. It set out detailed instructions for all manner of things—including the *seers* and *chhatanks* of *bhusa*, gram, oilcake, salt, green grass and weeds, separately, that must be given to a working bullock, to a stud bull in the dairy, to a dry she-buffalo, to a dry cow, to a buffalo in milk, to a cow in milk, to a calf less than six months old, to a calf between six months and one year, to a calf between one and two years, to a calf more than two years, each separately, and so on and on.

While it listed minute details on such things, it did not spell out the rights of prisoners at any one place. The relevant entries—cast in obfuscatory legalese—were scattered in small print over 562 pages. Page after page on the qualifications of each jail official, on his pay, allowances, entitlement to leave, to the produce of the jail garden, to the mango and lime orchards in the jail compound, and not a single compact section on the rights of prisoners.

The Rs 260 bound volume of the Manual boldly proclaimed on its cover '*Corrected up to August 1975.*'

No wonder, then, that clauses 5.52 and 5.53 of the manual specified that no visits to the jail should take place on, among other days, 'the King's Birthday, Good Friday and Christmas day'; that according to note 11 to clause 11.445, all warrants must be in Urdu; that according to clause 1.477.5, European prisoners must be searched only by European warders; that according to clause 39.996, European prisoners must be assured one-third more ground space and one-half more air space than Indian prisoners in the cells; that clauses 39.920 to 39.927 guaranteed a much better diet to European prisoners than to Indian prisoners.

'Corrected up to August 1975.' No wonder, then, that clause 5.48.2 specified the number of times District Magistrates must visit Lahore and Multan jails; that clause 6.267 specified the jails in which warders may be posted in the Lahore, Multan and Rawalpindi circles; that to meet emergencies in our Punjab, clause 10.424 specified that fetters and bell-chains for 2000 prisoners should be stocked in Lahore and Montgomery central jails; that clause 11.476.2 specified that two months before the release of a prisoner, his documents should be sent to the SP (Superintendent of Police), Crimes Branch, CID (Criminal Investigation Department), Lahore; that clause 16.548.12 specified the manner in which orders for staying executions in Lahore Central Jail must be given 'when the Punjab Government is in Lahore'; that clause 18.601.2.d decreed that 'Baluchis shall not, while confined in the Dera Ghazi Khan jail, have their hair cut or removed in any way'; that clause 20.631 set out the rules for remission that shall apply to 'the whole of British India, inclusive of British Baluchistan and the Santhal Parganas'. No wonder then that clause 25.764.3 specified that the cost of travel beyond Sialkot and Murree of prisoners who have been extradited from Kashmir at the request of the British Government must be borne by the said British Government.

'Corrected up to August 1975.' No wonder, then, that clauses 29.828 and 30.841 and 30.842 specified that 'all female convicts who are Indians' must be transferred immediately to the Lahore female jail, and that all juvenile male convicts must be similarly transferred forthwith to the Lahore Borstal Institution.

And so on and on for 562 pages.

The text made plain that our laws and regulations are beyond the comprehension of our people. The 562-page jail manual is certainly not meant for the average prisoner—no more than our land reform laws are meant for our sharecroppers.

Second, it is easy enough to spot what needs to be done (and suggestions to this effect had been made again and again), yet, for all the familiar reasons, our society never gets around to doing the familiar things. Is the jail manual obsolete? 'Solution': update it. It does not enumerate the rights of prisoners? 'Solution': enumerate them in a five-page leaflet and give it to each prisoner upon his admission to the jail. Are the prisoners so illiterate that they will not be able to read the leaflet? 'Solution': permit a social worker to lecture prisoners once a week about their rights. All these were and remain obvious enough. And yet we had never got around to implementing them. If, once in a while, we do take a step or two in a burst of commitment and enthusiasm, we are not quite able to sustain the effort.

Third, and the persistence of such entries thirty years after Independence in the Punjab Jail Manual 'Corrected up to August 1975' bore testimony to the fact that even the lawmakers did not read the laws and manuals they passed so solemnly.

Fourth, and this is where Rustomji's account and the facts that our correspondents excavated came in, the state functionaries did not, and do not care a hoot for the laws that are passed or the regulations that are laid down. Today, do they care for Article 21 of the Constitution—'No person shall be deprived of his life or personal liberty except according to procedure established by law'—or for how many 'encounters' the current Chief Minister wants them to stage?

Anguish

The facts that the *Express* published, and which Mrs Hingorani channelled to the Supreme Court, certainly shook up the Judges.

'A shocking state of affairs,' they wrote in *Hussainara I* '. . . An alarmingly large number of men, women, children including, are behind prison bars for years awaiting trial in courts of law. The offences with which some of them are charged are trivial. Which, even if proved, would not warrant punishment for more than a few months, perhaps for a year or two, and yet these unfortunate forgotten specimens of humanity are in jail, deprived of their freedom, for periods ranging from three to ten years without even as much as their trial having commenced.' 'It is a crying shame on the judicial system,' they continued, 'which permits incarceration of men and women for such long periods of time without trial . . . Many of these unfortunate men and women must not even be remembering when they entered jail and for what offence. They have over the years ceased to be human beings: they are mere ticket numbers . . .'[4]

'Most distressing . . . It is a travesty of justice . . . bail procedure is beyond their meagre means and trials don't commence, and, even if they do, they never conclude . . .'[5]

It turned out that there were several women who were in jail though they had not even been accused of having committed any crime, to say nothing of their having committed it. They were in jail because they were required to furnish evidence in regard to some crime that someone else had committed, or for their own protection! 'Very distressing reading,' the Judges recorded. 'It appears from this counter-affidavit[6] that there are quite a few women prisoners who are in jail without even being accused of any offence, merely because they happen to be victims of an offence or they are required for the purpose of giving evidence or they are in "protective custody"'. . . 'We are not aware of any provision of law,' the learned Judges wrote, 'under which a woman can be kept in jail by way of "protective custody" or merely because she is required for the purpose of giving evidence . . . It is the duty of Government to protect women and children who are homeless or destitute and it is surprising that the Government of Bihar should have come forward with the explanation that they were constrained to keep women in "protective custody" in jail because a welfare home maintained by the state was shut down . . . We direct that the victims be released and taken forthwith to welfare homes or rescue homes and should be kept there and properly looked after.'[7]

So astonished were the Judges by the details about some of the prisoners that they incorporated them in their judgments.

---

[4] *Hussainara I*, para. 1.
[5] Ibid., para. 2.
[6] Filed on behalf of the Government of Bihar.
[7] *Hussainara III*, para. 2.

Bhola Mahto: he had been in jail from 23 November 1968 until 16 February 1979 when he was released on his personal bond. Why was he suddenly released? Because of the directions that the Court gave on 5 February 1979. He had been committed to Sessions Court on 13 September 1972, but his Sessions trial had not yet commenced, the Judges noted in 1979. 'It is amazing . . .' they wrote. Similarly, *Ram Sagar Mistry:* he had been admitted in jail on 28 March 1971; he had been committed to Court of Sessions on 28 June 1972, but the trial has not commenced . . . six years after commitment, eight years after being jailed, they noted.[8] *Lambodar Gorain:* he has been languishing in Ranchi Jail since 18 June 1970 for an offence under Section 25 of the Arms Act; he has been in prison for eight and a half years; the maximum sentence for the crime if he were to be convicted would be two years.[9] Similarly, *Budhu Mahli:* he has been in Ranchi Jail since 21 November 1972 for offences under the Arms Act and Section 395 of the IPC (Indian Penal Code). Maximum punishment for the IPC Section: ten years, under Section 25 of the Arms Act, much less. Yet he has already been an undertrial prisoner for six years. The judgments also mentioned several others who had already spent more than half the maximum term for which they could have been sentenced. At the next hearing, the state government should provide each of them a lawyer to seek bail, the Judges ordered.[10]

'Shocking state of affairs so far as administration of law and order is concerned . . .' they observed.[11] 'The legal system has lost its credibility for the weaker sections of the community,' they declared.[12]

After recording how several prisoners had been rotting in jails for periods longer than the maximum sentence that could have been imposed if they had been convicted, the Judges noted,

---

[8] *Hussainara III,* para. 3.
[9] *Hussainara III,* para. 6.
[10] *Hussainara IV,* para. 8.
[11] *Hussainara III,* para. 1.
[12] *Hussainara III,* para. 9. 'It is, therefore, necessary,' they added, 'that we should inject equal justice into legality and that can only be done by dynamic and activist scheme of legal services.'

This discloses a shocking state of affairs and betrays complete lack of concern for human values. It exposes the callousness of our legal and judicial system which can remain unmoved by such enormous misery and suffering resulting from totally unjustified deprivation of personal liberty. It is indeed difficult for us to understand how the state government could possibly remain oblivious to the continued incarceration of these undertrial prisoners for years without even their trial having commenced . . . We fail to see how the continued detention of these undertrial prisoners mentioned in the list of Mrs Hingorani can be justified when we find that they have already been in jail for a period longer than what they would have been sentenced to suffer, if convicted. They have in fact some jail term to their credit . . .[13]

Hence, the Judges ordered, the state must release them forthwith.

The Constitution is there, the laws are there, the regulations and manuals are there, the judgments are there, and yet . . .

What heightened both the anguish of the Judges as well as their astonishment was exactly what had struck my father—after all, had the government, had jailers and magistrates the slightest acquaintance with, the slightest respect for law, for rules and regulations, none of this could have happened.

Bail was the rule, not jail. Section 167(2)(a) of the Criminal Procedure Code by itself entitled these poor detenus to bail.

'It is a matter of great regret,' the Judges recorded,

that such a large number of cases should be pending investigation for a period of more than six months and the number of such cases in relation to minor offences should be over several thousand. It is difficult to understand . . . It is no doubt true that reasons have been attempted to be given by B Srinivasan[14] in the statement annexed to his affidavit, but we are not at all satisfied about the validity of these reasons, particularly insofar

---

[13] *Hussainara IV*, para. 5.
[14] An official of the Bihar government.

as investigation in relation to minor offences is concerned . . . we would be failing in our duty if we do not express our sense of amazement and horror at the leisurely and almost lethargic manner in which investigation into offences seems to be carried on in the state of Bihar.[15]

How can such a situation persist in light of the provision in the CrPC? Section 167(5) specifies that, if in a case which is triable by a magistrate as a summons case, the investigation has not been concluded within a period of six months from the date on which the accused was arrested, the magistrate must make an order stopping further investigation into the offence, unless the investigating officer satisfies the magistrate that for special reasons, and in the interest of justice, the continuation of the investigation beyond six months is necessary. Had the investigating officers been doing so? Had the magistrates been giving extension after extension year after year for the investigation to continue?

Court regulations required, jail regulations required that the authorities produce prisoners in court every fortnight. If the prisoners were not being produced in court, who was responsible for this gross dereliction of duty? If they had been produced as mandated, how did the magistrates just keep sending the poor prisoners back to jails for years on end? 'It is difficult to believe,' the Judges observed, 'that on each of the countless occasions on which these undertrial prisoners were produced before the magistrates and the magistrates made orders of remand, they must have applied their mind to the necessity of remanding those undertrial prisoners to custody.' They were entitled to bail under proviso (a) of subsection (2) of Section 167. How has this clear provision been disregarded for years and years, and the poor detenus sent back to jail again and again? the Judges wondered.[16]

When the time for which the prisoners had been rotting in jails exceeded the maximum sentence for which they could have been imprisoned, if they had been convicted, by what provision of

---

[15] *Hussainara V,* para. 4.
[16] *Hussainara V,* para. 3.

law could their continued detention be defended? Their continued incarceration is manifestly illegal, the Judges declared.

Did the authorities not see that this gross discrimination against these poor people was a blatant violation of Article 14?

Had the governments, magistrates, the police officers not heard that the Supreme Court itself had held that speedy trial is, as is 'a dynamic and progressive programme of legal assistance', an essential ingredient of the right to life and liberty? That these flow directly from Article 21 of the Constitution? The Article provided that no one could be deprived of his life or liberty except in accordance with procedure established by law, and that procedure could not be any arbitrary procedure—it had to be 'reasonable, just and fair'.[17] Far from the procedure being 'reasonable, just and fair', in these thousands of cases, no procedure had been followed at all.

Had the governments, the jailers and magistrates not heard of Article 39A of the Constitution that directs the state to provide free legal aid 'to ensure that opportunities for securing justice are not denied to any citizen by reason of economic or other disabilities'? Had such aid been provided to these poor souls? If such assistance is not provided to the accused when he cannot afford legal help, the trial itself may be vitiated as contravening Article 21, the Judges held.

'The figures of pending cases . . . are staggering,' the Judges wrote, 'and it is distressing to find quite a few of these cases have been pending for more than five years, sometimes extending beyond even to seven or nine or ten years . . .' What are the norms for disposal that have been specified for magistrates and Sessions Judges? the Supreme Court Judges inquired. Are these being complied with? The state should provide for supplying additional facilities that the courts need, and for additional courts.[18]

---

[17] The Supreme Court, in particular Justice P.N. Bhagwati, had held this in *Maneka Gandhi v Union of India*, (1978) 1 SCC 248.

[18] *Hussainara V*, para. 9.

Directions

Shocked by the facts, and as the state of Bihar had not even filed an appearance in spite of notice having been sent two weeks earlier, Justices P.N. Bhagwati, R.S. Pathak and A.D. Koshal directed that all undertrials named in the *Express* report must be released forthwith on their personal bond. In response to another writ by Mrs Hingorani, the Court ordered the release of seventy prisoners who had already served longer terms than the maximum sentence that could have been handed to them for the crimes of which they were accused. As the hearings progressed, the Court gave a series of far-reaching directions to governments so that they adhered to the law:

o   Where Sessions trial has not commenced for seven years—this shocking number of years was in reference to two specific cases—the Sessions Judge must submit an explanation as to why the trial has not yet commenced.

o   Government must file a proper affidavit stating whether undertrials were periodically produced before magistrates in compliance with the proviso to Section 167(2). The High Court should inquire how magistrates continued granting extensions of the detention for two to ten years.

o   The state must furnish details of prisoners who have been kept in prison for periods longer than they would have had to serve if they had been convicted of the crimes of which they had been accused and awarded the maximum sentence. These details are to be provided separately for those charged with minor offences and those charged with major offences. Those who have served more than the maximum sentence that could have been meted out to them must be released forthwith as their detention is clearly illegal and violates their fundamental rights guaranteed by Article 21.

o   The state must release prisoners against whom no charge sheet has been filed within the period of limitation specified in Section 468, CrPC as they cannot be proceeded against at all, and their detention is unlawful and in violation of their fundamental right under Article 21.[19]

o As Section 167(5) of CrPC provides that where investigation has been going on for more than six months without satisfying the magistrate that its continuance is justified and in the interests of justice, the undertrial prisoners are to be released, unless magistrates' orders are obtained within one month.

o Women who are being held in 'protective custody' or because they are required to give evidence or because they have been victims of an offence must be released forthwith: keeping them in prison is a 'blatant violation of their personal liberty guaranteed by Article 21'. The state must make arrangements for them in welfare homes.

o Lawyers must be provided at state expense for all undertrials who have been accused of bailable offences.

o Governments must make provisions for speeding up and improving investigations.

o As speedy trial is a necessary ingredient of 'reasonable, just and fair' procedure, governments must make provisions for increasing the number of courts as well as providing them the facilities they require for the proper discharge of their duties.

o They must ensure that provisions of law regarding periodic appearance of undertrials before magistrates are adhered to.

o The bail system is heavily biased against the poor: it is riddled with complex requirements, and is beyond the meagre means of the poor. Under it, 'either they are fleeced by the police and revenue officials or by touts and professional sureties and sometimes they have even to incur debts for securing their release or, being unable to obtain release, they have to remain in jail until such time as the court is able to take up their cases for trial . . .'

---

[19] The relevant provision specifies the period of limitation as six months if the offence is punishable with fine only; one year if it is punishable by imprisonment not exceeding one year; and three years if the offence is punishable between one and three years.

o   Nor are the ends of justice met by mechanically pegging the amount of bail to the nature of the offence for which the person has been charged. The system must be simplified, and made less property-centric. Magistrates and Judges must consider roots of the accused in his community, family ties, job security, membership of stable organizations, his reputation and monetary condition, his prior criminal record, including any record of prior release on recognizance or bail, the identity of responsible members of the community who would vouch for his reliability, the nature of the offence charged and the apparent probability of conviction, and the likely sentence insofar as these factors are relevant to the risk of non-appearance . . .

o   And so on.

Others take up the issue, Judges do not let go of it

Others took up the issue in the ensuing months, and to the great credit of the Judges, they did not let go. Among the significant writs that were filed was one by Vasudha Dhagmawar, a researcher in law and a social scientist. She came across four tribal boys who had been in jail for ten to eleven years. They would have been 'naked goat-herds,' the Judges noted, nine to eleven years of age, when they were picked up; they were eighteen to twenty-two by now. Their cases had not come up for trial for eight years.

The four had been picked up and brought to jail in November and December 1972. Their cases were not committed to Court of Sessions until 2 July 1974. 'It is difficult to understand why their committal to the Court of Sessions should have been delayed for such a long period as 20 months after their arrest . . .' the Judges noted from the record. But that had been just the beginning. After committal, it took three years for trial to begin. 'This discloses a shocking state of affairs,' they wrote. 'There is something wrong with the entire system. How can any civilised society tolerate a legal and judicial system which keeps a person in jail for three years without even commencing his trial?' 'But the atrocity does not end here: more is yet to come,' the Judges continued.

Though the trial of the petitioners commenced in August 30, 1977, it was merely a symbolic commencement, for it never proceeded further and it has not yet made any progress. The petitioners appeared in the Sessions Court on August 30, 1977 but thereafter, Dr Vasudha Dhagmawar says, they have not yet been in court again. Three more years have passed but they are still rotting in jail, not knowing what is happening to their case . . . It is a crying shame on our adjudicatory system which keeps men in jail for years on end without a trial . . .

The Judges recalled the directions that had been given in the *Hussainara* cases, and were constrained to note:

We had occasion in *Hussainara Khatoon's* case to criticise this shocking state of affairs and we hoped that after the anguish expressed and severe strictures passed by us, the justice system in the state of Bihar would improve and no one shall be allowed to be confined to jail for more than a reasonable period of time, which we think cannot and should not exceed one year in a Sessions trial, but we find that the situation has remained unchanged and these four petitioners, who entered the jail as young lads of 12 or 13 and have been languishing in jail for over eight years for a crime which perhaps ultimately they may be found not to have committed. It is obvious that after so many years of incarceration awaiting trial, either their spirit must be totally broken or they must be seething with anger and resentment against the society. We fail to understand how our justice system has become so dehumanised that lawyers and judges do not feel a sense of revolt at caging people in jail for years without a trial. It is difficult to comprehend how the Sessions Judge could have forgotten that he had called the petitioners to the court for commencement of the trial and thereafter done nothing in the matter . . .

The Judges directed that the trial of the four lads commence immediately, that it be held day-to-day without interruption. In accordance with what they had held in the earlier cases, they directed the state to provide legal help to the four at state expense.

But there was more. It turned out that the young boys had been kept in leg irons; that work was being taken from them outside and inside the jail. They were shackled with leg irons so that they would not run away when outside the jail, it was said. That justification could not stand scrutiny, for it turned out that the leg irons were not removed when they were back inside the jail. The Judges were angered. This is a 'flagrant violation' of prison regulations and contrary to the ILO (International Labour Organization) Conventions against forced labour, they wrote.

> It represents one more instance of the utter callousness and indifference of our legal and judicial system to the undertrial prisoners languishing in the jails. It seems that once a person accused of an offence is lodged in the jail, everyone forgets about him and no one bothers to care what is happening to him. He becomes a mere ticket number—a forgotten specimen of humanity—cut off and alienated from the society, an unfortunate victim of a heartless legal and judicial system which consigns him to long unending years of oblivion in jail.

The Judges ordered that the leg irons be removed immediately and the authorities desist from taking any work from them so long as they are undertrial prisoners.[20]

By the time the case came up before the Supreme Court again, the four had been acquitted after a trial. The Judges expressed satisfaction that at last the wheels of justice had moved, and they thanked Dr Dhagmawar for having brought the matter to them. But, as for the general situation, things seemed to be more or less where they were. The Judges recorded that the statements which had been placed before them by the High Court and by the state of Bihar disclosed an 'alarming state of affairs'. They recalled the strong observations they had been constrained to make in the *Hussainara* case, and noted:

---

[20] *Kadra Pahadiya v State of Bihar*, 1981 (3) SCC 671, paras 1 to 3.

But despite the observations made by us it does not seem that any improvement has taken place. The position continues to be very distressing and there are a large number of prisoners still languishing in jails without their trial having commenced. The figures furnished by the State of Bihar are sufficient to shock the conscience of any Judge or for that matter even of any citizen of this country . . . this most unsatisfactory state of affairs . . . incomprehensible to our mind . . . They have been in jail for such a long period even before commitment and we shudder to think how much more they would remain in jail after commitment before trial is commenced and brought to an end . . .

Indeed, in a large number of cases, the Judges noted, even the dates on which the prisoners were brought into the jails have not been given so that 'it is not possible for the Court to find out as to how long they have been in jail before their cases were committed to the Court of Sessions'. Shocked and dismayed, the Judges ordered that such long-pending cases be taken up at the earliest, that the trials proceed day-to-day, that the cases be disposed of 'in any event not later than six months from today'. Where cases have been pending since before 31 December 1976, magistrates are to proceed immediately, and conclude them 'within three months from today'. In view of this state of affairs, the government and the High Court should examine the norms of disposal that have been specified for magistrates, and higher category of Judges, and assess how these are being observed . . . The state should make provisions necessary for additional courts, and for ensuring better facilities for them to discharge their functions . . .[21]

The petitioner cannot be traced

Madhu Mehta was the head of Hindustani Andolan. He visited the Kanpur Central Jail incognito, and, to his horror, discovered that children were being kept in the jail—for doing menial tasks and for sexual exploitation by adult convicts. Apart from everything

---

[21] On the foregoing, *Kadra Pahadiya v State of Bihar*, (1983) 2 SCC 104.

else, if we were to confine ourselves just to formal laws, keeping the children in jail with adult prisoners was a clear violation of UP's own Children Act and the rules that had been framed under it.[22]

We published a report in the *Indian Express* of Madhu Mehta's account on 2 December 1981—remember that date for a moment. A writ was filed in the Supreme Court. In the meantime, another person moved the Allahabad High Court. The latter Court ordered the senior-most Sessions Judge of Kanpur to visit the jail, and report. The Supreme Court recalled the findings of the Sessions Judge:[23]

o   There were eighty-four undertrials in the jail
o   There were seven juvenile undertrials below the age of sixteen
o   Recall that the *Express* report had been published on 2 December 1981. 'Curiously' [the Supreme Court's word], the record of the jail showed that all but one of the seven happened to have been released between 7 and 16 December 1981, that is just days before the Allahabad High Court could pass its order on 18 December 1981. Hence, the Sessions Judge could not interview any of them.
o   'The Sessions Judge also reported that there appeared to be general ignorance in the Kanpur Central Jail about the provisions of the UP Children Act, 1951,' the Supreme Court noted, 'and observed, "All the child accused mentioned in Annexure B should have been produced before the Juvenile Judge after their arrest. Where there was doubt whether the detenu was above the age of 16 or below it, he should have

---

[22] In its judgment, the Supreme Court summarized the relevant provisions of the UP Children Act. Rules 15 and 16 of the Act specify that where a child is not released on bail, he shall be detained in a 'place of safety'—i.e., 'any observation home or any orphanage, hospital, or any other suitable place or institution the occupier or manager of which is temporarily willing to receive the child; or where such observation home, orphanage, hospital or other suitable place or institution is not available, in the case of a male child only, a police station in which arrangements are available or can be made for the safe keeping of a child separately from adult offenders.'

[23] The following is based on *Munna v State of Uttar Pradesh*, (1982) 1 SCC 545. The Bench consisted of Justices P.N. Bhagwati and R.S. Pathak.

been sent for medical report (*sic* examination) in connection with his age and on being found to be a child, should have been dealt with in accordance with the Children Act."' None of this had happened.

The Supreme Court directed the Secretary of UP's Board of Legal Aid and Advice 'to immediately contact these six children after finding out their addresses from the court proceedings or from jail records and take their statements with a view to ascertaining what was the treatment meted out to them in the Kanpur Central Jail and whether any of them was maltreated or sexually exploited'. And it directed the state to report 'by proper affidavit' what were the circumstances in which these six were released. It also directed the state to ensure that children were sent to a Children's Home: 'No words we can use would be strong enough to convey our feelings in this respect,' the Judges said. 'A nation which is not concerned about the welfare of its children cannot look forward to a bright future.'

The petition came up again. Munna could not be found.

Six years passed before the case came up yet again in the Supreme Court. Again, the petitioner, Munna was not present, and could not be traced. Helpless, the Judges reiterated the Court's order of 1982—that magistrates must be extremely careful to see that no person apparently under sixteen is sent to jail, that he is detained in a Children's Home or some other place of safety—and decided that nothing more needs to be done, and thus there was no point in keeping the case on record any further.[24]

Outcomes

Around 40,000 undertrials were estimated to have been released as a result of the Supreme Court's judgments, and our series beginning with K.F. Rustomji's initial account. Twenty-seven thousand of these were from Bihar jails. That showed what power

---

[24] *Munna v State of UP*, 1989 Supp. (2) SCC 154. The Bench now consisted of Justices G.L. Oza and K. Jagannatha Shetty.

the courts have. That, even our traducers now said, showed what the press can and should do.

Among the factors that brought about such a result was the fact that we did not just publish an essay bemoaning the condition of undertrials. Our accounts gave details; they named names. Moreover, we did not look upon one exposure as enough. We persisted for an entire year. Nor did we stop at printing the accounts. We actively collaborated with Mrs Hingorani to bring the facts to the attention of the Judges.

Even so, without the Judges, the accounts would have remained just that—accounts.

There was the most fortunate of coincidences: the cases came up before Judges, or the Judges were able to wrest the cases, who were genuinely committed to reforming the system, in particular to human rights—Judges like Justices P.N. Bhagwati, D.A. Desai, A.P. Sen, O. Chinnappa Reddy, Balakrishna Eradi. They waived all formalities; they treated letters as writs, they took notice of the facts from non-official sources. And they persisted: a single judgment, howsoever full of admonishment and anguish, would have remained one judgment. Because they scheduled hearing after hearing, because they took up different facets of the injustice in successive hearings and pronounced judgments on each, governments could not get away with homilies and promises.

The times, too, were propitious. The abysmal record of the Supreme Court during the Emergency was still in everyone's mind, in particular of the Judges. They were keen to make up for the dereliction of those years.

But these were coincidences. A public-spirited advocate, an activist and creative Judge, propitious times, a new type of journalism. Reformers can take advantage of, they *should* take advantage of coincidences, but lasting reform requires more than coincidences. At the time, I felt and emphasized that without institutionalizing some changes, the system would revert to what it had been. If only the Court had made it mandatory for state governments to conduct a census of prisoners periodically—say, every two years—and publish the results. If only it had made it mandatory for governments to allow social workers to visit jails, and report what they observed. If only, in addition to mandating free legal aid, the Court had made it possible for social workers to regularly lecture prisoners about their rights . . . And so I urged such steps.

One in particular. The judgments showed again and again that laws—the Criminal Procedure Code here, the Children Act there—were being flouted, that regulations that were to govern jails, that were to govern what magistrates and Sessions Judges did, were being routinely, in fact, shamelessly disregarded. Even during the hearings, governments and officials—including law officers—were ignoring and evading directions of the Court. When Justice Bhagwati first took up the matter, he caused notice to be issued to the Bihar government—and scheduled the next hearing for two weeks thence. Come the next hearing, and no one turned up for Bihar. The Judges merely noted with manifest regret that 'Bihar has not put in appearance despite notice'. The Court asked the Bihar government to state whether the undertrials were being produced before magistrates as required by Section 167(2) of the CrPC. The government furnished an affidavit, saying that the undertrials were being produced 'as and when required by the courts'. The Judges merely noted that this averment is 'wholly unsatisfactory', that it does not constitute compliance with their direction. The Court asked for a list of undertrials—the undertrials to be classified into two categories: those accused of minor offences and those accused of major offences. At the next hearing a month later, the Judges merely recorded, again with manifest anguish and exasperation, 'this direction has not yet been carried out'. The Judges asked the government to state through a counter-affidavit the reasons on account of which 'there has been such enormous delay in bringing undertrial prisoners to trial'. Only to note that the counter-affidavit has not been filed. The Judges asked for dates on which the undertrials were admitted to jail. Only to note that, in 'a large number of cases', the date of admission was not provided, as a result of which it is 'not possible for the Court to find out as to how long they have been in jail before their cases were committed to the Court of Sessions'. The Court directed that if, in a case triable by a magistrate, the investigation had not been concluded within six months, and the investigating officer did not satisfy the magistrate as required by 167(5), that continuation of investigation is necessary, and in the interest of justice, the undertrial prisoner must be released. Only to have to note that the government has not filed a compliance report. The Court directed the state to provide a lawyer at state expense to every accused charged with bailable offences. Eventually, the state government informed the Court that instructions had been issued to district magistrates to do so. The Court had to demand that the government inform it through an affidavit, not that instructions have been issued, but how many undertrials have actually been provided lawyers at state expense. 'We are repeating the direction about providing lawyer at state expense,' the Court was constrained to remark, 'because we find that barring a few, many of the state governments do not seem to be alive to their constitutional responsibility in the matter of provision of free legal services in the field of administration of criminal justice.' And so on.

The Court noted patent violations of the laws. It noted shameless disregard of regulations by the police, the jailers, the administration, in a word, the entire apparatus of State. It recorded the incomprehensible disregard by the magistrates and Sessions Judges of norms which have been laid out to govern disposal of cases by them. It noted the disregard of its own directions.

But not one person was punished—no police officer had his pay cut, no jailer was suspended, no magistrate lost his promotion. And, of course, no minister or civil servant suffered the slightest embarrassment.

Instead, in judgment after judgment, the Judges said, 'We hope and trust.' It almost became a School of Jurisprudence—the 'Hope and Trust School'.

Over the years, governments learnt that, while Judges will record their anguish, while they may wax eloquent, officials and ministers would not suffer a whit.

Soon enough, expressing 'hope and trust' became an embarrassment for the Judges themselves. Doing so only reminded everyone that the Judges were helpless.

It was, therefore, not long before courts became a part of governments. Lions well under the throne . . .

5

Moral responsibility

'*Par Shourie Sahib, main* resign *kyon karoon?*[1] I have already accepted moral responsibility.'

We had been publishing Arun Sinha's devastating reports on the blindings in Bhagalpur. Parliament had been in uproar. The Central Government and Mrs Gandhi had been deeply embarrassed. There was every indication that the Supreme Court would come down heavily on the barbaric deeds.

The evidence Arun Sinha had excavated was irrefutable, and it was overwhelming—both in weight and, even more so, in the emotional upheaval it caused in whoever went through it. On the other side, the Bihar Government's responses had been contradictory, they had been heartless, they had swung from covering up the cruelty to trying ever so hard to explain away the diabolic role of its police. The Chief Minister, Jagannath Mishra, had been summoned to Delhi. Our senior correspondent in Patna, P.K. Krupakaran, rang me up to say that Mishra was coming to Delhi, and would like to meet me.

As I entered the Bihar Government guest house where Mishra was staying, I found Mishra sitting amidst a small hillock of newspapers piled on four–five tables. He argued that the whole

---

[1] 'But Shourie Sahib, why should I resign?'

affair had been the doing of the people of Bhagalpur, not of the police; that the persons who had been blinded were criminals of the worst kind, and this is why common people had taken revenge on them. As evidence, he pointed to reports in Bihar newspapers. He said that he would send a set of the papers to me to study. And he asked me to see the popular upsurge that had erupted in Bhagalpur against his decision to suspend fifteen policemen. Even if one or two policemen had taken the law into their own hands, he said, clearly what they had done was the will of the people; it was 'socially sanctioned'—this was a phrase he had used in Chandigarh also.

I had, of course, read about demonstrations in Bhagalpur in support of the policemen. Arun's reports had but to hit the headlines, and the policemen's association, the bar association, the Chamber of Commerce, the truck owners' association, college teachers, students and even so-called 'journalists' had taken out processions and passed resolutions in support of the police. 'Police-janata bhai bhai,' they had shouted. They had said they would not allow the Government to transfer the SP. They had said that what had been done was the only way to curb crime.

Had they been 'encouraged' by the police to stage this show of popular sanction? Or was it the familiar dynamic at work? The police and administration do little to curb crime. The people get exasperated. They support any and every action taken ostensibly to curb criminals . . . Either way, the 'social sanction' that Mishra was speaking about cast a dark reflection on what Bihar had become under his Government.

Feigning innocence, I asked, 'Mishraji, *voh ek* aspect *hai. Par yahaan logon ke man mein doosraa* point *bhi hai. Aapki police nein aankhein phodi hon yaa logon nein, jo hua voh to* barbaric *thaa hi.* Either way, *aap ki sarkar* law and order *par kaaboo naheen rakh payee. Is liye, yahaan to sab keh rahein hain ki aapko* resign *kar denaa chaahiye. Aap ki ismein kyaa raaye hai?*'[2]

---

[2] 'Mishraji, that is one aspect. But people here have another point also. Whether your police shattered the eyes or the people did, what happened was barbaric. Either way, your Government was not able to keep a grip on law

That is when he educated me to owning moral responsibility as a substitute for resigning! He had said as much in the state Assembly.

A *fearless and conscientious officer, a brave and intrepid reporter*

In early November 1980, Arun Sinha learnt that the police and people had taken to blinding persons in Bhagalpur district. The victims were lodged in Bhagalpur's Central Jail. He began making inquiries with the police and the headquarters of IG (Prisons) in Patna, but they claimed 'supreme ignorance', Arun recalls. So, he went to Bhagalpur to find out the truth. I reproduce what he told me about what ensued:

> When I met the superintendent of the Bhagalpur Central Jail, Bacchu Lal Das, his response was initially very cautious. He would not answer my questions about blinded undertrials in his jail until he had ascertained through some interrogation of his own who I really was, whether I really worked for the *Indian Express* and what kind of reports I had filed earlier. His intention was but to make sure that he was not talking to an informer of the police! Once he was confident he wasn't, he opened up and opened up warmly, as though he had been waiting to pour out his heart.

Though forty years have passed, Arun remembers Das with great regard. He told me:

> I will always remember B.L. Das with great respect, because that day when he poured out his heart, I could see that he was an officer with a conscience, a rare breed in the government. He spoke with great indignation and pain about how policemen at various police stations of the district had pierced the eyes of

---

and order. That is why everyone here is saying that you should resign. What is your view?'

criminal suspects and poured acid into them to make them blind
in a savage campaign to make the district 'crime free'.

'Das was not only conscientious but also fearless,' Arun recalls.
'This showed in the way he fought the might of the entire
establishment for years against the state government's decision to
suspend him as soon as reports of blindings came out'—something
to which we will return in a moment. 'That day he showed me
the documents that clearly suggested the police were directly or
indirectly responsible for the barbarous acts. He called some
blinded prisoners to his chamber to speak to me.'

But there were officers of the other kind too, Arun recalls:
'When I met local Bhagalpur police officers, they blamed "mobs"
of villagers for perpetrating the barbarity on the victims,' Arun
tells me. 'Their defence was that the victims were brought to
police stations already blinded, and the policemen had no role in
blinding them.' However, Sinha noticed that a common thread ran
through their answers to his questions; namely, that 'there was no
need to shed any tears of sympathy for those "murderers, robbers
and rapists" who had been given by the people the punishment
they deserved'.

He returned to Patna and wrote a report which was carried on
the front page of the *Indian Express*. He was urged to investigate
the matter to the last possible detail. He went back to Bhagalpur
and did intensive interviews with the families of the victims, some
victims who were on bail, police and administration officials,
lawyers and doctors, and common people. His report, with a
photograph of a victim, appeared in the paper on 22 November
1980 under the headline: 'Eyes punctured twice to ensure
blindness'. This report and the next, even more detailed one—
which we carried in the issue of 28 November—triggered major
consequences to which we will return. But before that, a word
about what Arun had to face:

I wrote a series of reports in the *Indian Express* on the subject.
The documents and facts for them did not come to me in
one basket. I had to get pieces of information from all kinds

of sources—jail officials, police officers, officers in the civil administration, lawyers, human rights activists in Bhagalpur town and in the villages and small towns of the district where the incidents took place as well as sources in the departments of police and prisons in state headquarters.

There were risks to my life as many policemen were suspended and the public had come out on the streets in support of them, saying they had done the right thing. I had to go around Bhagalpur with a disguised identity.

Gangajal

It turned out—and this is alluded to in Supreme Court judgments on the events—that the campaign to blind suspects by piercing their eyes and pouring *'gangajal'* into their hollowed eye sockets had commenced in July 1980. The *'gangajal'* was nothing short of corrosive acid. The victims would be caught, and taken to a police station. There, policemen would tie them up, thrash them to the floor and sit on them, with some holding their legs and arms. Their eyes would be pierced with a *takwa*, the long, thick needle which used to be used to stitch gunny sacks. A 'Doctor Sahib' would come, and inject or pour acid into the pierced eyes—to make sure that no eyesight survived.

In a particularly poignant incident that Arun reported, seven or so of the blinded persons were lying, huddled in a room. The 'Doctor Sahib' was ushered in. In a voice dripping with solicitude, he inquired how they felt, and whether they could see anything. Hearts of the victims leapt in hope: maybe, the doctor has begun feeling sorry for what he did, maybe he will help us. Two of the victims said that they could indeed see something. The doctor wished them well, and left the room. One at a time, the two were taken out of the room, and guided to another room. There, to the horror and screams of the victims, the bandages were taken off, their eyes were pierced again and acid was poured into their eyes a second time.

Further inquiries by Arun Sinha revealed that 'at least one' Minister of the Jagannath Mishra Government had been aware of the campaign for at least four months, and had cautioned against it. Bhagalpur officials had pleaded in return that blinding was 'the only way out' for restoring law and order in the district. They had 'commended' subordinate officers for taking 'effective steps' to curb crime. The Inspector General of Police, Bihar, had sent a 'letter of appreciation' to the Bhagalpur SP. The SP was given a wristwatch. Subordinates were given cash rewards. The IG (Prisons) had been more cautious: he was reported to have told the policemen that 'killing the criminals in "encounters" was far better and safer than damaging their eyes, because in doing so [blinding them], you are leaving evidence. Some day it might land you in trouble.' 'He was understood to have told the officials that if any "trouble" arose in future, there were several ways for the Police to wash their hands off the matter'—an ambiguous statement that. Was it a warning to the policemen that, should such an occasion arise, the police would absolve themselves, and they would be on their own? Or was it an assurance, that they need not worry, for the police knew how to 'wash their hands off the matter'?

And sure enough, when the blinded eyes made it into the public gaze, the blindings were blamed, both by the Chief Minister and the DIG (Deputy Inspector General), (Eastern Range)—the latter's office was in Bhagalpur—on 'that anonymous entity, the "public" or "the mob"', Sinha reported. This in face of the fact that almost all the victims had directly blamed the police for having blinded them at or just outside the police stations. This in spite of the fact that the mode of blinding them had been identical. And if mobs are the ones who had blinded the victims, Arun Sinha was to inquire:

o   Where did the people procure acid?
o   Were all the people of Bhagalpur moving about with acid and needles all the time?
o   Did the public know when and where criminals would be caught, so they were ready with the needles and acid on the spot?
o   Do ordinary people have courage to overpower criminals?

o Usually criminals carry arms; how could unarmed people overpower them?
o Why didn't the criminals use their arms when cornered by people?
o If the public blinded the victims, why were they not blinded at the scene of crime? Why were the places of their blinding far from the places of crime they were accused of committing?
o If the criminals were blinded by the public, why didn't the police arrest those who had done it? Why didn't they see it as a violation of the rule of law? Did they gather information about the perpetrators from the victims? Did they try to get any witnesses? Did they try to reconstruct the scenes?

What the government did was to suspend Das, the Jail Superintendent. The grounds? That he had failed to make correct entries in the Jail Register about the condition of the victims when they arrived at the jail, that he had not scrutinized and signed the entries in the jail register, that he had failed to make proper arrangements for treatment of the victims, and that he had not recorded any 'special order' regarding medical treatment given to or to be given to the victims as required by Rule XYZ of the Bihar Jail Manual![3] These were concocted afterthoughts. His real crime was that he had enabled Arun to have access to the victims: the suspension order said that he did not 'make a report' about the blindings to the authorities, and, instead, 'supplied to newspapers his own version of the blindings'. And there was the future to ensure: this was manifestly a way to put pressure on him not to furnish any evidence to the Supreme Court should he be asked to do so.

Fact after fact that Arun unearthed, established that senior police officials, doctors and others knew about the *'gangajal'* blindings long before they became public knowledge:

o In July 1980, Gajendra Narain, DIG (Eastern Range), (whose office, as we just noted, was at Bhagalpur), requested M.K.

---

[3] Rule 474 (1), to be precise.

Jha, DIG (CID), (whose office was at the police HQ in Patna), to send an experienced CID inspector to Bhagalpur to make inquiries and suggest ways of controlling crime in the district, which was on the rise. The CID inspector toured the district for a week and submitted a report to Gajendra Narain informing him of the blindings that policemen had inflicted on suspects in a planned manner. The inspector urged Narain to stop the campaign as it was proving counter-productive. The inspector also reported the blindings to DIG (CID) M.K. Jha on his return to Patna. Jha visited Bhagalpur thrice between July and November 1980.

o   Far from acting on the report of the inspector, the higher police officials began pressurizing him to change his report. After touring the district for a week, the inspector had submitted a detailed report; in that, he had stated that the operation was 'barbaric' and 'planned'; that far from curbing crime, it had enraged criminals who were launching a campaign of their own; he had urged that the *gangajal* campaign be stopped at once. The DIG who had deputed him, sources told Arun Sinha, was 'exasperated' at the report; he said the fellow was 'of no use' and should be immediately recalled to headquarters. And that his travelling allowance should be withheld. It was.

o   In July 1980, eleven blinded undertrials lodged in the Bhagalpur Central Jail sent a petition to the Home department, along with a forwarding letter from the Jail Superintendent, appealing for justice. The petition received no response from the department. Quite the contrary: when the diabolic deeds broke into public view, police blamed the Superintendent of the Bhagalpur jail, Das, for having drafted the petitions.

o   In early September 1980, the Inspector General of Prisons, after his inspection of Banka sub-jail of Bhagalpur, where he met three blinded undertrials, sent a letter to the Home Department urging an inquiry into the blindings. His letter, too, received no response from the department.

o   DIG (Central Range) and SP of Bhagalpur held regular crime review meetings with *thana* officials. It was, and remains hard to believe that the series of blindings never came up at the reviews during the nine months the barbarity had been going on. If it did, the senior officials were complicit. If it didn't, they were derelict.

o   As for doctors, leaving aside the role of the 'Doctor Sahib', it turned out that several of the victims had been taken to the Bhagalpur Medical College Hospital. The doctors there did not give the victims any medical treatment. They did not give any advice to the jail authorities or doctor about what line of treatment should be pursued. They turned down the request of the Bhagalpur Central Jail officials that they appoint an eye specialist for the jail.

Governance

On 29 November, the UNI (United News Agency) reported that eighty-seven may have been blinded. Arun Sinha reported that after examining eight of ten blinded persons in Bhagalpur jail, the jail doctor had sent a report to the Supreme Court stating that at least eight of the ten had been blinded 'deliberately', 'by injury due to punctured wound caused by a sharp and pointed weapon, and burns caused by a corrosive substance'—he could not examine the remaining two as they had been 'released on bail and cannot be contacted'. He also noted that 'the manner of carrying out the operation was almost identical'.

Various arms of Government announced that they had taken action. 'A Union Home Ministry source said today,' the *Indian Express* reported on 29 November, 'as soon as we saw the report, we asked the State Government to send a report.' The state government, in turn, 'sent a preliminary report saying it had appointed an inquiry committee to go into it'. On inquiry, it was found that none of the legislators who were said to have been appointed to the committee had heard anything about a committee having been formed from the Government. That just about summed up the reaction of the rulers to such devilry.

'Physically sick'

Back in Delhi, the reports caused a commotion. Ministers, even a literate and level-headed minister like Vasant Sathe, and others, said that we were 'demoralizing' the police, that Opposition parties were 'politicizing the issue'. But others—among them the venerable Acharya Kripalani—addressed public meetings condemning the entire operation. Motions were tabled in Parliament for a full discussion. At first, the Government tried to shove the motions off, by saying that these happenings, unfortunate though they were, were the provenance of the state government, that law and order was a state subject, and that the proper place to discuss them was the state Assembly. But this deflection could not hold for long. Both Houses of Parliament took up the matter.

Mrs Indira Gandhi spoke briefly. She just wanted to express 'my own very deep agony', she said. 'When my attention was drawn [to the incidents], I could not believe that such a thing could happen. I was physically sick and even now cannot talk about it.'

And that was that.

That expression, 'physically sick', was picked up by many in her Party. In short order, it almost became an accusation—that, apart from demoralizing the police, we had made her, a sensitive lady, 'physically sick'. But making rulers 'physically sick' was the objective. That such things should be happening and they should not even feel sick?

All sorts of other assurances were given. The Central Government announced that it had instructed the Bihar government to approach the Patna High Court to take action against the District Judge who had refused legal aid to the blinded persons. It announced that it had instructed the Bihar Government to oppose bail to the fifteen police officers who had been suspended. It announced that an ex gratia relief of Rs 15,000 would be given to each of thirty-one victims so that they could live off the interest. The Government was keen to assist the families of the victims also, the Home Minister, Giani Zail Singh, told Parliament, but a decision on this would and could be taken only after the criminal cases against the victims were disposed of. He appealed to members 'not to blow up this incident much more' as doing so would harm India's image abroad . . . We shall soon see what happened to the assurances.

There were difficulties within the paper also. 'This amounts to sensationalizing a tragedy,' an editor declaimed in blunt Punjabi.

'The way the paper is going about this business, it is as if such a thing has happened for the first time, as if it has been discovered for the first time. Who does not know about police brutalities? Who does not know that areas like Bhagalpur are torn by gang wars, by caste wars, by dacoities, by violence of all kinds? But we are going about this as if we are the ones who have made this great, new discovery. What was the need for putting that damned photograph on the front page? I couldn't eat my breakfast.'

A small price that—the breakfast—for giving the people the jolt they need.

Small mercies

In any case, 1 January 1981 dawned. Those in Government were busy wishing Mrs Gandhi a Happy New Year. But the cussed Federation of the Blind organized a procession. About a hundred totally blind men assembled at Jantar Mantar and began trudging towards the Prime Minister's house. Their ambition was quite modest: they just wanted that two or three of them be allowed to present a memorandum to the PM urging that the agreement that the Labour Ministry had reached with them months earlier be implemented. When they were still three-quarters of a mile from Mrs Gandhi's house, a contingent of 400 policemen stopped them. The poor, helpless blind men were kept waiting for an hour. As they tried to resume their journey, the police roughed them up, pushed and thrashed many to the ground. Many fell into the drain nearby. They were packed into two buses and taken away.

Talk of being 'physically sick'.

But we must be thankful for small mercies: the last time they had trudged to do the same thing—on 16 March 1980—they had been lathicharged by the police, and many of them had suffered injuries.

The Supreme Court

The Supreme Court took cognizance of the blindings in two streams of cases. The first was a set of petitions filed by the victims. The second was a petition filed by a public-spirited advocate, Mrs Kapila Hingorani. She had received the initial information from Ram Kumar Mishra, a conscientious advocate in Bihar. We used to send her whatever Arun Sinha gathered— not just his reports but also photographs, file notings and other evidence that he gathered. In all, the Supreme Court passed seven orders on the blindings.[4]

To get the shortest thing out of the way first, lawyers appearing for Das had filed his plea against the suspension as 'an incidental proceeding' to the petitions that had been filed by the victims.

This was the liberal phase of the Supreme Court: it was making up for its lapses during the Emergency. It used to treat even letters as writ petitions. But it dismissed Das's petition: ordinarily, an order of suspension cannot be challenged in an incidental proceeding, it ruled; and on the ground that the appellant had not proven that he had been suspended to prevent him from filing an affidavit in the Supreme Court. It said that Das would be at liberty to file a petition in 'properly constituted proceedings'.

---

[4] An order dated 10 October 1980 and two judgments were delivered by Benches headed by the then Chief Justice, Y.V. Chandrachud:

1. *Anil Yadav & Ors (I) v State of Bihar & Ors*, (1981) 1 SCC 622. This followed the order of 10 October 1980.
2. *Anil Yadav & Ors (I) v State of Bihar & Ors*, (1982) SCR (3) 533.
   In these, the Court directed the Registrar of the Supreme Court to visit Bhagalpur, examine documents, interview the victims as well as officials of the jail and the police.
   Five judgments were delivered by Benches headed by Justice P.N. Bhagwati:

1. *Khatri & Or. (I) v State of Bihar & Ors*, (1981) 1 SCC 623.
2. *Khatri & Ors (II) v State of Bihar & Ors*, (1981) 1 SCC 627.
3. *Khatri & Ors (III) v State of Bihar & Ors*, (1981) 1 SCC 635.
4. *Khatri & Ors (IV) v State of Bihar & Ors*, (1981) 2 SCC 493.
5. *Khatri & Ors (V) v State of Bihar & Ors*, (1983) 2 SCC 266.

These directed relief of various kinds to the victims and expressed the Court's 'hope and trust' that such atrocities would not take place in the future, that decisions of the Court would be followed, and that the guilty shall be brought to book at the earliest.

But to proceed: the Court did note, 'Whether these barbarous acts were committed by members of the public after the prisoners were caught or by the police after they were arrested, is not a matter directly in issue before us. The greater probability is that these acts may have been committed mostly by the police.'[5]

The judgment gave a glimpse of what Das was up against, and, even more so, of the condition of governance, in particular of the judicial system:

The petitioner Bachho Lal Das, who has filed these Misc. Petitions, had assumed charge as the Superintendent of the Bhagalpur Central Jail on April 19, 1979. On October 26, 1979 a prisoner by the name of Arjun Goswami was sent to the Bhagalpur Central Jail. On November 20, 1979 he addressed an application to the Chief Judicial Magistrate, Bhagalpur, asking that an inquiry be held into the torture inflicted upon him, especially the blinding of his eyes. That application was forwarded by the petitioner to the Chief Judicial Magistrate. Later, eleven prisoners made similar complaints which were forwarded by the petitioner to the learned Sessions Judge, Bhagalpur, on July 30, 1980. The complaints made by these prisoners unquestionably demanded the most prompt and careful attention. But, instead of directing a full and proper inquiry into the allegations made by the undertrial prisoners, the learned Sessions Judge, on August 5, 1980, sent a cold and indifferent reply to the petitioner's covering letter, saying that 'there is no provision in the Cr. P.C. to provide a lawyer to any person for prosecuting a criminal case as a complaint' and that the petitions of the prisoners were forwarded to the Chief Judicial Magistrate, Bhagalpur, 'for needful in accordance with law.' On October 9, 1980, ten blinded prisoners filed a Habeas Corpus petition in this Court (Criminal Writ Petition No. 5352 of 1980) asking that: (1) they should be produced in the Court, (2) they should be examined by a Medical Board, (3) they

---

5   For this and the following: *Anil Yadav & Ors v State of Bihar & Anr* on 23 March 1982, 1982 SCR (3) 533.

should be paid compensation for the damage done to their eyes and that (4) the police officers guilty of committing atrocities upon them should be suitably punished.

And that is how the Supreme Court had taken up the matter. The Court had the victims examined at AIIMS in Delhi: the examination confirmed the worst. The Judges observed:

> The report of the doctor will shock the conscience of mankind. There has been the most flagrant violation of the safeguards provided by Articles 19 and 21 of the Constitution. There is nothing that the Court can do to restore the physical damage, which seems irreparable. But the offenders must at all events be brought to book, at least in the hope that such brutal atrocities will not be committed again.

The state of affairs and the Supreme Court

We were new at all this, and were quite cheered by the fact that the Supreme Court was taking note of an issue that had been raised in the paper. The Court's findings nailed what we had been saying about the state of governance and, in particular, about the police and the judicial system over which the Court itself was presiding. The Court's anguish was manifest. As was the fact that it believed the victims when they said that policemen had blinded them. The arguments in court were also bringing out what I had been stressing for long: that the casuistry of lawyers and the tendency of courts to allow themselves to be led astray by legalisms will be the end of justice in the country.

As I said, we were quite happy at the time at the attention that the highest Court was paying to the issue.

We are wiser now.

But first, two or three things from the Court's judgments.

The first thing that strikes one is the state of affairs that the proceedings revealed. Recall that these blindings had taken place from at least July to November 1980. Well before this period, in March 1979 in fact, in the well-known case *Hussainara*

Khatoon that we have encountered earlier, the Supreme Court had laid down that securing legal assistance is a fundamental right, that it is an indispensable ingredient of the right to justice and fair procedure guaranteed by Article 21 of the Constitution. It turned out that no legal representation was provided to any one of the victims—not when they were initially produced before a Magistrate, nor in subsequent proceedings. To no one in no proceeding. And invariably, the Magistrates and others had said that they had not provided legal assistance because none of the victims had asked for it. Bereft of the assistance of any lawyer, 'save a few who were released on bail, the rest of them continued to languish in jail'. 'It is difficult to understand how this state of affairs could be permitted to continue despite the decision of this Court in Hussainara Khatoon's case,' the Court said. It did not order any penalty for those who had so blatantly disregarded its clear verdict and directions.

And its helplessness was not confined to this case. The Court observed:

> It is unfortunate that though this Court declared the right to legal aid as a Fundamental Right of an accused person by a process of judicial construction of Article 21, most of the States in the country have not taken note of this decision and provided free legal services to a person accused of an offence. We regret this disregard of the decision of the highest court in the land by many of the States despite the constitutional declaration in Article 141 that the law declared by this Court shall be binding through-out the territory of India.

But should we feel sorry for this helplessness? Had the Court not made itself helpless by not punishing any official who disregarded the law it had laid down? Helplessness? Or self-inflicted helplessness?

'It is also regrettable that no inspection of the Central Jail, Bhagalpur, was carried out by the District & Sessions Judge at any time during the year 1980,' the Supreme Court said. And what did it do? Did it punish those who had been derelict? Instead: 'We would request the High Court to look into these matters closely and ensure that such remissness on the part of the judicial officers does not occur in the future.'

Next, '. . . in a few cases the accused persons do not appear to have been produced before the Judicial Magistrates within 24 hours of their arrest as required by Article 22 of the Constitution.' Did it punish those whose responsibility it was to produce the accused before the Judicial Magistrates?

> We do not wish to express any definite opinion in regard to this irregularity which *prima facie* appears to have occurred in a few cases, but we would strongly urge upon the State and its police authorities to see that this constitutional and legal requirement to produce an arrested person before a Judicial Magistrate within 24 hours of the arrest must be scrupulously observed.

And then, ' . . . the accused persons were not produced before the Judicial Magistrates subsequent to their first production and they continued to remain in jail without any remand orders being passed by the Judicial Magistrates.' 'This was plainly contrary to law,' the Court pronounced. So, what did it do now that this plain illegality was before it? 'It is difficult to understand how the State continued to detain these accused persons in jail without any remand orders.'

It placed its trust in hope:

> We hope and trust that the State Government will inquire as to why this irregularity was allowed to be perpetrated and will see to it that in future no such violations of the law are permitted to be committed by the administrators of the law. The provision inhibiting detention without remand is a very healthy provision which enables the Magistrates to keep check over the police investigation and it is necessary that the Magistrates should try to enforce this requirement and where it is found to be disobeyed, come down heavily upon the police.

But here was a chance for the Court itself to 'come down heavily upon the police'. What kept it from doing so?

The record also showed that when the victims were eventually produced before them, the judicial officers did not so much as inquire how they had received the grievous injuries to their eyes, injuries so horrible that they made even those who looked at photographs of the gouged-out and burnt spaces 'physically sick'. So, what did the Court do?

'We also cannot help expressing our unhappiness at the lack of concern shown by the judicial magistrates . . .' it declared, and moved on.

The beleaguered Superintendent of the jail forwarded petitions of the victims. And what happened?

> The District & Sessions Judge by his letter dated 5th August, 1980, addressed to the Superintendent of the Bhagalpur Central Jail stated that there was no provision in the Code of Criminal Procedure under which legal assistance could be provided to the blinded prisoners who had made a petition to him and that he had forwarded their petitions to the Chief Judicial Magistrate for necessary action. The Chief Judicial Magistrate also expressed his inability to do anything in the matter.

But the record revealed another, fatal thing:

> It appears that the Superintendent of the Bhagalpur Central Jail also sent the petitions of these blinded prisoners to the Inspector General of Prisons, Patna on 30th July, 1980 with a request that this matter should be brought to the notice of the State Government. The Inspector General of Prisons, forwarded these petitions to the Home Department. The Inspector General of Prisons was also informed by three blinded prisoners on 9th September 1980 when he visited the Banka Jail that they had been blinded by the police and the Inspector General of Prisons observed in his inspection note that it would be necessary to place the matter before the Government so that the police atrocities may be stopped.

'The facts disclose a very disturbing state of affairs,' the Supreme Court observed. And that was that.

In any case,

> . . . one thing is certain that within a few days after 30th July
> 80 the Home department did come to know from the Inspector
> General of Prisons that according to the blinded prisoners who
> had sent their petitions, they had been blinded by the Police,
> and from the inspection note of the Inspector General of Police
> it would seem reasonable to assume that he must have brought
> the matter to the notice of the Government.

The Court could have paused right there and nailed the authorities
that had scotched the whole affair. It asked the very Government
that had taken no notice of the matter to now take notice:

> We should like the State Government to inform us clearly and
> precisely as to what steps they took after July 30, 1980 to bring
> the guilty to book because we should like to satisfy ourselves
> whether the blindings that took place in October 1980 could
> have been prevented by the State Government taking appropriate
> steps on receipt of information in regard to the complaint of the
> blinded prisoners from the Inspector General of Prisons.

Did it get the clear and precise information it asked for? Did
it then 'bring the guilty to book'? Did it then 'satisfy ourselves
whether the blindings that took place in October 1980 could
have been prevented by the State Government taking appropriate
steps on receipt of information in regard to the complaint of the
blinded prisoners from the Inspector General of Prisons'? Whether
the information came, whether the Court was able to satisfy itself
one way or the other, we do not know. But one thing is certain: it
did nothing as a consequence.

What the Court had said

Now, recall two observations from the Supreme Court's rulings in
Anil Yadav's case. First, 'The greater probability is that these acts
may have been committed mostly by the police.' Second, 'There

is nothing that the Court can do to restore the physical damage, which seems irreparable. But the offenders must at all events be brought to book, at least in the hope that such brutal atrocities will not be committed again.' Recall the horror that the facts sparked in the Court. Recall who, in its view—expressed in the *Khatri* judgments—was manifestly responsible:

> The police are supposed to enforce the law and not to break it, but here it seems that they have behaved in a most lawless manner and defied not only the constitutional safeguards but also perpetrated what may aptly be described as a crime against the very essence of humanity. It is a barbaric act for which there is no parallel in civilised society and deserves the strongest condemnation from all sections of community. It is difficult to believe how any person, much less an enforcer of law, can be so ruthless and inhuman as to deprive fellow human beings of their eyesight. It shows to what depths of depravity the administration of law can sink in the state of Bihar . . .

At one stage, two of the victims were present in the Court: 'We are shocked to see the plight of these two unfortunate persons who have been the vicitms of the barbaric cruelty of the police. They are standing before us with their eyes corroded and destroyed and tissues around the eyes burnt and scarred.'

Stern action

In the weeks that followed Arun's exposures, what with the outcry in Parliament, what with the observations made in the initial hearings of the Supreme Court, the Bihar Government just had to show that it was taking stern action.

First, it organized an 'identification parade' of the police officers and asked the totally blind victims to identify which police officer had blinded them.

Next, it suspended fifteen police officers. Three months had not passed, and it 'revoked the suspension' in each case. A few of the senior officers were just transferred: the officer who had been SP, Bhagalpur City, was made SP, Ranchi; another officer who had also been SP in Bhagalpur was made SP of Muzaffarpur. Not just that, the Government shifted key figures to even more important assignments. The DIG (CID)—of course, 'by way of normal process'—was made head of Bihar Military Police; the DIG (Bhagalpur) was made DIG (Vigilance).

The Supreme Court heard the matter from December 1980 to 1983; it delivered seven judgments. The text of the judgments leaves no doubt that the Court's disclaimer in, say, *Khatri V,* about not prejudging guilt notwithstanding, the Court had accepted the fact that 'probably' the police officials had blinded the victims. But it never deigned to take notice of the large-heartedness that the state government had shown even by February 1981 to the policemen. As we have seen, the Supreme Court expressed great anguish. It used grandiloquent words to denounce the atrocities. It urged that those guilty of such heinous crime be brought to book at the earliest. So much 'sound and fury' signifying—what?

Soon, the Court had allowed itself to be led into the quagmire of weighty 'constitutional questions'. Can a police diary be examined in such proceedings? If not the case diary, can a report by a senior police officer be examined in such proceedings? In its order, had it stayed the investigations into the deeds of the victims or their trials?

As for the pensions, you will recall that the *Khatri* judgments, arising from the blindings, were the first instance in which the Supreme Court directed that compensation be paid by the state for violation of human rights. It had the state deposit Rs 30,000 for each victim so that each could receive Rs 500 every month as pension. Later this was raised to Rs 750 per month. On 11 February 2020, Ram Kumar Mishra, the advocate who had supplied the initial information to Mrs Hingorani, was compelled to write to the District Magistrate of Bhagalpur. Of the twenty-eight victims about whom he had records, he mentioned, eleven had died. Seventeen remained. But from November 2019, they had stopped receiving even the Rs 750 that had been decreed. When they would be taken to the State Bank of India branch to collect the amount, the victims would be asked to first produce 'life certificates'—namely, certificates to the effect that they are still alive. As you would expect, the Supreme Court had not noticed.

Was Jagannath Mishra the only one 'morally responsible'?

The discordance

I once asked my dear and distinguished friend, the late Ashok Desai,[6] for this discordance between the Court's anguish and its action. He told me that he had discussed this very point with Justice P.N. Bhagwati once. Justice Bhagwati had told him that he had focused on laying down general principles, rather than on the actual relief that would be given in an individual case. The reason for this was twofold, the Judge had explained. He did so, first, in cases in which he was finding it difficult to get a consensus on the actual amount and terms of the penalty or, in these cases, the compensation: he would agree to the lowest common denominator, and press others to subscribe to the general principles that he was laying down. Second, he felt that what the subsequent Benches would use as a guide was not the amount of punishment or compensation that he and his colleagues decreed in the specific case that they were handling; they would use as a benchmark the general principles that had been laid down.

Of course, the difficulty of securing a consensus could not have explained the discrepancy in the amount decreed and the principles in the *Khatri* judgments. Justice Bhagwati's companion Judges on the Bench in these judgments were Justices A.P. Sen, E. Venkataramiah, and others—as stern and upright and compassionate Judges as any. In any case, the discrepancy between the high principles that the Court laid down regarding responsibilities of the State and the meagre compensation that it actually directed the State to provide, is just one aspect of the matter. There is the other question: Why did the Court never

---

6 He is the one who got the initial judgment in the Bombay High Court against Antulay's claim that the Governor could not sanction his prosecution without the advice of the Council of Ministers—the latter being firmly in Antulay's own control. Later, Ashok became the Attorney General of India, and one of our most respected advocates.

really go back to verify whether even this meagre compensation was actually being paid? And what about bringing the guilty to book at the earliest?

So, the question that remains is: Does the actual record of the Court confirm the hopeful premise—that the principles that it was laying down were the ones that would set the precedent?

For an answer, do compare the salutary principles that the Supreme Court laid down about the responsibility of the state to compensate those whose human rights its personnel had violated with what it did in regard to those whose eyes were damaged by police and paramilitary forces in Kashmir. Do compare those principles with what it did regarding the persons who have been killed in 'encounters' by the UP Government during Yogi Adityanath's regime.

6

A precursor?

'I have little intelligence . . . I am a layman . . . How can I know anything about these legal matters?'—that was one of the characteristic responses, repeated again and again, of Jagannath Mishra, the Bihar Chief Minister, to our queries about provisions of the Bihar Press Bill.[1]

Three of us—K. Narendra of the *Daily Pratap*, K.R. Malkani of *Organiser*, and I—were in Patna on behalf of the Editors' Guild to ascertain facts about the Bill. Mishra had returned around 11 a.m. on Sunday 8 August 1982, from Delhi, having gone there to meet Mrs Indira Gandhi, the Prime Minister. 'He is very busy, many appointments,' the Director of Public Relations had told us, 'and he has to go on an official tour by train at 4 p.m.'

So, we were particular to be punctual, entering his office at 3 p.m. sharp. Mishra's attention was immediately taken up by the file in front of him. I have always found this to be a very remarkable coincidence: the moment you enter a Minister's office is the very moment that he finds he must dispose of a file!

In any event, Mishra, a rotund man with four huge rings on his right hand and two on his left, disposed of the file in ten seconds or less, and we were off with our questions.

---

[1] This section on the Bihar Press Bill is based on a series I wrote and published at the time.

But first the Bill. And even before that, its passing.

'Passed'

31 July 1982 was the last day of the Bihar Assembly's current session. Twenty-four notices had been listed for sending the Bill to Select Committees and for eliciting public opinion. Sixty amendments were also listed. The House assembled at 9 a.m. Even by the Bihar Assembly's standards, the chaos was unprecedented: 'uproar', 'howls', 'fisticuffs', 'mikes snatched', 'papers torn to pieces', 'free for all'—that is how the papers had described the 'deliberations'. The House had to be adjourned five times. When it met for the sixth time, the din, tumult, chaos were the worst. Almost everyone was in the well of the House, shouting, gesticulating, shoving. This continued for four to five minutes. Suddenly, the Speaker announced that the required three readings of the Bill had been completed, that the Bill had been passed by a voice vote, and that the House stood adjourned sine die.

None of the twenty-four notices had been dealt with. None of the amendments had been discussed or put to vote. Indeed, the Bill itself had not been put to vote. Mishra didn't get to say a word. And yet—in keeping with everything else about this episode—the Bihar government placed six-column advertisements in the newspapers, giving what it claimed was the text of 'the Chief Minister Jagannath Mishra's statement in the Bihar Vidhan Sabha on July 31'. The text, almost 4000 words long, would have taken Mishra at least forty minutes to read out in the Assembly.

And things did not end with the newspaper advertisements. Karpoori Thakur told me that the Assembly proceedings that were circulated showed that the statement had actually been made in the House.

Customary lies

The Bill had been preceded by the Bihar government's customary lies. One example will do.

On 25 February 1982, *Aryavarta*, one of the two leading Hindi dailies in Patna, led with a dispatch that said that the Bihar government had sent its officials to Tamil Nadu to study the new laws regarding the press that had been passed there.[2] The dispatch said that this was part of the government's plan to put further curbs on the press, and it raised the question whether the government would promulgate an Ordinance to give effect to these plans.

On 3 March, Mishra addressed a press conference. The dispatch was completely 'baseless', he said. First, he said, no officer had been sent to Tamil Nadu to study the new law promulgated there. Second, he said, the government had no plans to promulgate an Ordinance on the matter. Third, he said, in fact, the government had no proposal before it for putting new curbs on the press to prevent 'objectionable' writings.

On 6 March, both *Aryavarta* and *India Nation* printed the photocopy of the Home Commissioner's order dated 25 January 1982, asking designated officials to proceed to Tamil Nadu for studying the new law and for formulating similar legislation for Bihar. They also gave the names of officials who had gone to Madras in mid-February and had filed their report about the proposals.

As expected, the Patna High Court refused to take cognizance of these facts on the ground that what the legislature does was not the Court's business.

Steps leading to the Bill

The Bill had been preceded not just by lies, but by concrete and far-reaching steps. A month before the Bill was hustled through, the Bihar government had amended the Press Accreditation rules. Henceforth, it said, a journalist would be disaccredited and a newspaper or news agency would forfeit all 'facilities' if he or it

---

[2] In 1981, MGR's Government had amended the law to enhance punishments under Section 292-A of the Indian Penal Code, and to make offences under it cognizable and non-bailable.

'misused' the facilities or access or if it violated the Official Secrets Act, or if it published reports 'violative of journalistic ethics'.

And just three days before the Bill was passed, the government pushed through a far-reaching amendment to the Criminal Procedure Code. The vital Section 190 of the Code was amended, so that from then on, the vital powers to take cognizance of cases, to direct investigations, and to institute trials, would vest with executive magistrates. The Press Bill specifically provided that cases under it would be triable by 'any' magistrate. The two Bills taken together would thus ensure that cases against the press under the Press Bill would henceforth be processed, not by judicial magistrates who function under the High Court, but by executive magistrates, who were completely under the control and direction of Mishra's government itself.

Provisions

The Bill amended Section 292 of the Indian Penal Code. It added a new Section—292-A—that prohibited the publication, sale, even possession of any material that government considered 'scurrilous', 'grossly indecent' or 'intended for blackmail'.

The key words were left vague. Thus, 'scurrilous' was to encompass 'any matter which is likely to be injurious to morality or is calculated to injure any person'. *'Likely to be'*— in the eyes of the rulers. *'Calculated to injure any person'*— even a well-documented exposure of an officer's or minister's, corruption could certainly be construed to be 'calculated to injure' that person. Nominally, exceptions had been included. 'It is not scurrilous to express in good faith anything whatsoever' regarding the public conduct of a public official in the discharge of his public duties, or his character as it bears on his public conduct, an exception provided. It was also provided that comments made in good faith regarding 'any person touching any public question' would be exempt. But these defences could only be offered and argued during the trial. Moreover, by virtue, rather by the vice of the amendment to Section 190 of the Criminal Procedure Code that we noted above, the defences would have to be argued before magistrates who would be under the control and supervision of the government. And what was this about the conduct being 'public'? The contract that a minister diverted to undeserving contractors was undoubtedly a 'public question'. Assume that the contractors provided favours in kind to the minister—say, women. His conduct vis-à-vis them was not public. Would exposure about the liaison be protected by the liberal-sounding exception?

Next, Section 292-A of the Criminal Procedure Code was changed. Offences under the Bill were made cognizable and non-bailable: a policeman could take cognizance of a 'complaint' or some undisclosed 'source information', and detain a person for up to 180 days without a warrant and without even an FIR being registered.

Third, it was not just the writing and publication of matter that the government deemed objectionable which would henceforth be an offence. The distribution, selling and purchasing, the mere 'possession' of 'any printed or written document' containing such material would be an offence punishable with imprisonment of up to two years for the first offence, and for any subsequent offence, with imprisonment ranging from six months up to five years. This provision would effectively frighten off newsagents, retailers and hawkers and even readers from handling any publication that—ignorant or, at best, ill-informed of the law as they were bound to be—they were told the government was liable to find objectionable.

The clause dealing with the distribution, selling and purchasing, the mere 'possession' of 'any printed or written document' containing such material, would naturally apply to everything printed elsewhere as much as to things written or printed within Bihar. Assume a magazine published from, say, Bombay was sold in Bihar: its contents could therefore be held to be adversely affecting and having been calculated to injure the repute of public servants in Bihar.

How would a vendor or a reader know beforehand whether the publication he was holding contained material which the government held to be objectionable?

In a word, the 'chilling effect' would paralyse and be used against not just publishers, editors and journalists but just as much against workers in printing presses, vendors, readers—everyone.

The background

Just five years had passed since the Emergency had ended. Memories of what was done to the press during it were still fresh in people's minds. There was also the apprehension that the Bihar Bill was part of a clear strategy. Mrs Gandhi and her circle had learnt a lesson. This time round, they would not be the ones to assault the press directly: states would change the laws and lead the charge. And the way that several local leaders—say, MGR—had moved against sections of the press that were critical of them—MGR against publications leaning towards his rival Karunanidhi, for instance—showed that rulers in the states were not that committed to democratic norms, and that they were as much in need of concealment as any ruler at the Centre. Recall that this was 1982, and that Mrs Gandhi's Government had already begun to lose legitimacy—Punjab had begun to heat up, economic policy was getting nowhere.

As if to confirm all apprehensions, in her public statements about the Bihar Bill, Mrs Gandhi had been, at best, ambivalent. She had come down heavily against the 'irresponsible press'. She had told a meeting of her partymen in Lucknow that, while she herself had not read the Bill, persons with knowledge of law had told her that there was nothing in it that could be said to gag the press. No section of society—and that included the press—could be allowed to misuse the freedoms granted by the Constitution to harm others: just as the Constitution does not allow anyone to murder anyone else, so also no one could be allowed to assassinate anyone's character. As it touched on central laws, the Bill would eventually have to receive the assent of the President, and the President was bound to act on the 'aid and advice' of her Government. On more than one occasion, Mrs Gandhi refused to say that her Government would advise the President to withhold consent. Her subalterns—the new Information and Broadcasting

Minister, N.K.P. Salve, for instance—were more categorical. Apprehensions about and criticisms of the Bill were unjustified, they said. While the Government was open to dialogue, while some changes too could be made, the Bill would not be withdrawn, they said.

For all these reasons, Mishra's Press Bill was seen not just as bad in itself but as a precursor of things to come. And so it had triggered concern far beyond Bihar.

Evidence

As a consequence, the three of us were in Patna, seated in front of the Chief Minister who was 'a very busy man', who 'had to leave on tour by train at 4'.

Had the government collected examples of objectionable writing in the press which had impelled it to bring forth the Bill? we asked.

No, Mishra said, the government had no compilation to which he could refer us. It had drafted the Bill purely on its 'impression'.

When we pressed him to furnish us at least some examples of the kind of writing he had in mind, he furnished three. During the Biharsharif riots, he said, a news agency stringer had filed a report saying that a pond had been poisoned and 500 persons had died as a result. Second, he said, the majority of writings in the press in Bihar aimed at fomenting casteism and inflaming communal passions. Third, he said, some papers had been printing editorials that 'not a single acre' had been brought under irrigation in Bihar in the last thirty years, and that 'there has been no agricultural progress at all'.

Now the Bill dealt only with writing that was 'grossly indecent', 'scurrilous' in that it injures a person, or was 'intended for blackmail'. Therefore, presuming his account of these press reports to be correct, we asked him how would the new Bill help the government combat the sort of dispatches he was referring to.

He said that the poisoned pond dispatches would be covered under the provisions against 'scurrilous' writing, and ones dealing with writing 'intended for blackmail'! And that dispatches that fomented casteism and communalism would be covered by provisions against 'scurrilous' writing! He did not specify what provision would deal with the third example of objectionable writing he had mentioned.

We laughed at the construction he was putting on the words and advised him to change his legal officers. But there was a sinister side to all this creativity. As we have seen, every critical term in the Bill had been left vague—indeed, in the Hindi Version of the Bill, 'scurrilous' had been transcribed as *gandi*, i.e., 'unclean' or 'dirty'. And, the statements of the Chief Minister showed that the government intended to put an extremely creative and elastic construction on the words and provisions of the Bill.

'I have little intelligence,' he said every time we drew his attention to the exact words of the Bill—'grossly indecent', 'scurrilous', 'intended for blackmail' successively—'I am a layman . . . How can I know anything about these matters?' We reminded him that he was *Doctor* Jagannath Mishra, that he had a doctorate.

What he was saying was the standard response in Bihar, I told him. We had requested an appointment with the Chief Secretary; he wasn't available. We had requested an appointment with the Additional Chief Secretary, who, we were assured was the major-domo at the moment; he, too, was not available. We had requested an appointment with the Home Secretary; he told us, 'You better leave me out of this.' On Saturday 7 August, one minister had agreed to meet us. The meeting was set for 11 a.m. on Sunday. At 10.30 a.m. his personal assistant rushed over to our hotel to say that the minister would not be able to meet us as he had suddenly remembered that he had to be in Arrah that morning. At last, the Director of Public Relations had come over on behalf of the government, files and all, after talking over the telephone to the Chief Minister, who was then in Delhi. But every time we asked him a specific question, his answer was along the lines that the Chief Minister was now pursuing, 'I am such a small fry. How can I answer that?'

Mishra wasn't the kind who would dub himself 'a small fry'; so he was again and again on the, 'I have little intelligence' bit.

If the press had been fanning riots and inflaming casteism and communalism all these years, we asked, why had the Government not proceeded against it under the Indian Penal Code? After all, just a few years ago, Sections 153A and 153B had been specifically introduced into the Penal Code to prevent anyone from 'promoting enmity between different groups on grounds of religion, race, place of birth, residence, language, caste or community or any other ground whatsoever', and to prevent 'imputations and assertions prejudicial to national integration'. Offences such as these had been made punishable with up to three years imprisonment. Mishra looked away.

Mishra had asserted in the statement he was said to have made in the Assembly that 'a majority of writings in the newspapers are those which (i) tend to promote communal hatred and enmity; and (ii) infringe or offend decency or morality . . .' I asked him whether he stood by this statement.

He was most emphatic: Yes, the Bihar press does nothing but this.

If the press had, in fact, been promoting communal hatred and enmity, if it had, in fact, been offending decency and morality for so long and so consistently, why had his government not launched cases against the papers? Had it not been derelict in its duty?

He said that the existing laws were '*bakwaas*', and it was his government's experience that it took very long to prosecute anyone under them. He was in a good position to know, I said. By then, the Urban Cooperative Bank case, in which he was himself an accused, had been successfully stalled for eight years!

How many cases had his government filed? we asked.

Many, he said.

Had he a list?

No, he said, no such list had been compiled.

We had done our homework. We put it to him that, in fact, his government had filed only one case—a case of defamation against a newspaper. This case had been filed on 20 February 1982 against the *Indian Nation*. Since cognizance was taken of the case, the magistrate had to adjourn the case six times—on each occasion the reason was that the state, not the *Indian Nation*, had failed to produce any witnesses and sought more time.

He said he did not know the details of such instances.

Could he recall any other case?

No, he said, he could not.

He had said that the Press (Objectionable Matters) Act, 1951, had been found to be 'a poor weapon' to deal with objectionable writings.

Had his government filed any case under the Act? we asked.

Yes, several, he said.

We put it to him that, in fact, his government had not filed any case under the Act since it had come to power two years earlier.

He shifted ground swiftly. He was not talking of the experience of his government in filing cases under this Act, he said. He had actually been thinking of the cases that had been filed by the previous Janata governments also, cases, he said, that had been filed in the previous five—and not just two—years.

We then informed him that the Act he had been talking about, and under which he had been claiming several cases had been filed in the last two and then the last five years, had not been on the statute book for the past thirty years! The Act of 1951 had a term of only one year—in keeping with the prevailing convention that Acts of this kind were in those days given lives of only one year at a time. The Act was not renewed. And having enlightened him, we laughed. How had so many cases been filed in the last two or five years when the Act itself had not been in existence for thirty years?!

He was taken aback and did not respond. But the government's Director of Public Relations, who was also present, did. He said that the Chief Minister was not to blame. He had stated in the Assembly and was telling us just what the concerned department had written out for him.

Which was the 'concerned department'?

Home.

Who is the minister in charge of the Department?

Mishra himself!

We were laughing again.

Mishra was now intimidated enough to bare his smug self. The opinion of the press on the Bill, he said, did not matter. 'It is an interested party.'

'Aren't you also an interested party,' I asked, 'and shouldn't your opinion be ruled out of court for the same reason?'

'No, the people have put me on this chair,' he insisted. 'As long as I am here, it is my duty to do whatever I think is necessary.'

It was this smugness which we encountered again and again those days, it was this argument—the final refuge of every political scoundrel in this country, then and now—which always sent me up the wall. And it did this time, too. Here were these fellows pillaging the country, destroying institutions and everything else, and they were insisting that it is the poor people of India who had given them the right to do what they will.

We had raised our voices, and the meeting would have ended but for the tact of my colleagues.

Mishra relaxed and put forth his general approach: '*Hum to hamesha Indira Gandhi ke hi programme laagu karte hein.*' ('I always put only Indira Gandhi's programmes into effect.')

He had slipped again. So, the Bill was the Central Government's programme, was it? Was it true, then, as he had insinuated to his partymen in Patna, that he had obtained the Central Government's approval for the Bill from Vasant Sathe, the Minister for Information and Broadcasting in Delhi? Was it true, then, as he had also told his partymen, that he had, in fact, obtained the clearance of Mrs Gandhi herself when he had met her on the eve of her departure for the US?

He realized the costly blunder. 'No, no,' he rushed in to say. 'I was talking of the twenty-point programme.' And that, without so much as a blush.

He had recovered enough by now to put forth a new argument. The Janata government had passed the same Bill, he said, 'Venkataraman has said so in Parliament. How could he say so if it weren't true?'

Just the way others do, I said, reminding him of his own record in the Assembly in the recent past.

My colleagues laughed. Malkani tried to cajole Mishra to share the joke.

He didn't succeed.

'I believe in serving the people,' he said in conclusion, '*Bhagwan mein atoot vishwas rakh kar . . .*' ('With eternal faith in Bhagwan . . .')

That was too delicious. I was transcribing it in Hindi.

'No, no,' he said in a raised voice, 'You don't have my permission to write that.'

'Your *permission*?' I had raised my voice too. 'Who told you that I need your "permission" to write? You have been spoilt by these Bihar journalists who seek your permission to write. We have not come here for a chit-chat. If we had been told that we needed your "permission" to write, we wouldn't have wasted our time. What do you want me to scratch out? Do you want me to scratch out "Bhagwan"?'

'*Naheen, naheen,*' Mishra said, '*Bhagwan mein mera atoot vishwas hai, zaroor likhiye.*' ('Do write about my eternal faith in Bhagwan.')

Is that all? I asked.

'*Aur Indira Gandhi ke netriyeta mein bhi atoot vishwas.*' ('And also about my eternal faith in Indira Gandhi's leadership.')

We were laughing, but he was keen that I take his words down verbatim.

'*Bhagwan upar aur Indira Gandhi yahaan,*' he said—'God above and Indira Gandhi here'—'It is with this faith that I serve the people.'

There was one final lie.

It has been alleged, I said, that you hustled this Bill through. But surely that isn't true, is it? You and your Government must have deliberated over it for long, isn't it, drafting and redrafting it, assessing your experience with existing laws?

Yes, he said, they had had the measure under consideration for a long time.

How many months, we asked. Five to six months, he said. Recall Mishra's statement of 3 March, that the government did not have anything under consideration, and here he was himself telling us that he and his government had been considering the matter for five to six months!

It was a quarter to four. We reminded him about the train he had to catch and thanked him for sparing time till just fifteen minutes before the scheduled departure of his train.

We got into our car and reached the airport to await our flight back to Delhi.

And guess who should turn up at the airport, accompanied by two carloads of hangers-on?

Jagannath Mishra himself!

The cars sped up to the state plane. Four large suitcases were put into the plane. A few members of his family climbed into it. And then Mishra heaved himself upstairs, reached the door of the plane, turned about swiftly as his leader does, waved to the hangers-on, the very gesture he must have picked up in Delhi, and was off.

'Where to?' we inquired.

He has gone to perform puja at the Devgarh shrine, we were told.

So much for the official tour by train!

The singular purpose versus the evidence

Why had Mishra hustled the Bill through the legislature? What should be done about it?

Clearly, Mishra's Bill had just one purpose: to intimidate and frighten the press into silence. It had nothing to do with the objectives that had been proclaimed on its behalf by the Bihar government.

The kinds of writing that Mishra and others said they wanted to curb were not covered by the Bill at all. On the other hand, they *were already* covered by existing provisions of the IPC; like Sections 153A and 153B, which Mishra's government had never even attempted to use.

In the statement Mishra claimed he had made in the Bihar Assembly, he had made many factual claims:

In the very large number of newspapers we studied and the variety of topics in respect of which the study was carried out, there have been many instances where a report was twisted . . . Yellow journalism of one type or another is increasing in this state . . . We have also come across news items strongly suspected to be false, if not known to be false, that have been published to increase circulations . . . Instances . . . have come to our notice when financial concerns and other institutions have been subjected to false and malicious attack . . . A majority of writings in the newspapers are those which (i) tend to promote communal hatred and enmity and (ii) infringe or offend decency or morality and publish scurrilous or obscene matter defaming individuals . . .

He had made other such claims.

Then or later, the Bihar government was not able to produce any evidence worth the name to substantiate even one of these assertions. After what must have been an extensive search, the representative of the Bihar government was able to produce only two rags as evidence.

One was a 4 January 1981 issue of the eight-page weekly tabloid, *Splinter*, said to be published from Patna every Sunday. And the other was the 10 July 1981 issue of an even smaller six-page tabloid called *Magadh Dharti,* said to be published from Gaya. The dates told the tale: if they had been published at all, they had been published a year and a half and a year, respectively, before the Bill was hustled through the Assembly.

The first carried an account of how things had deteriorated to such an extent that strip-tease dancers had been entertaining audiences at a religious fair. The second had an account of a woman who was said to have been kept by a priest and had now been abandoned by him. The first carried three single-column photographs of naked strip-tease dancers, which were said to have been taken at the fair. The second carried one photograph of a man holding on to a woman's breast.

Was the government really horrified by such photographs and write-ups? we asked.

Oh, yes.

Why, then, had it not prosecuted the papers under the IPC?

No answer.

Indeed, one could buy pornographic books around Patna's principal maidan for public meetings, the Gandhi Maidan. Why had the government never acted to curb this trade?

No answer.

Even more: the very issues that we had been given carried advertisements from the government; one full-page advertisement in the six-page *Magadh Dharti,* and a half-page one in the eight-page *Splinter.* Why was the government patronizing publications, which, on its reckoning, were publishing filth?

No answer.

What was the circulation of these two publications?

About one hundred copies each.

What, only one hundred?

Well, actually one thousand . . .

Such was the 'evidence' on the basis of which Mishra and his Government had brought the Bill.

Real reasons

The real purpose was simply to frighten the press into silence. Mishra's government was impelled to silence the press for four reasons.

First, corruption and maladministration in Bihar had reached such enormous proportions that, even though the press was not very vigilant, even though it was shy of pursuing cases involving high-ups in government, with increasing frequency, while investigating other matters, it would stumble upon and thus print some material relating to corruption and inefficiency; the material was not easily refutable and was thus an inconvenience to the government. Arun Sinha's reports on the blindings in Bhagalpur and the ensuing discomfiture of the government in the Supreme Court were examples, and they had dealt a heavy blow.

Second, during the preceding two years, Mishra had felt compelled to lean more and more heavily on tantrics and the like. Correspondingly, the influence of these characters in his government had become more and more apparent. Newspapers and magazines had been documenting this liaison. These reports, what with all the sloganeering about socialism, secularism and the scientific temper, had been as embarrassing for Mrs Gandhi and the Central Government as for Mishra and his government.

Third, the large section of the press that Mishra's government had successfully 'managed' had fallen out with him over the past year. The government had thus not been able to 'balance' adverse and truthful reports about its corruption and maladministration. Something more had to be done.

Fourth, there were, at the time, four major mass movements in Bihar and about a hundred small groups of persons who were working for and among the poor in the state. Their activities and what the government was doing to crush them figured in the press and gave the lie to the government's professions.

It is for reasons such as these that the Bihar government had been propelled to frighten the press into silence.

The Bill raised several questions, as relevant now as then. If Bills were to be concocted on evidence of the kind we had encountered in this case, what would not pass muster? If existing laws were not going to be used to curb malpractices, and continuance of the malpractices was to provide the rationale for more stringent laws, where would the process of endowing the state with more and more arbitrary powers end? If Bills passed in the manner in which this one had been passed, were going to be law, where would parliamentary democracy end? Who was a danger to our institutions and our country—the ones who indulged in wanton misdeeds or those who reported these to the public? When a system shuts out the truth, does it protect itself or does it preclude reform and hence ensure its eventual collapse? The country apart, could such measures save even the rulers? Did the Shah of Iran not have total control over the press, radio, TV? And of what avail was it in the end?

Prescriptions

Newspapermen across the country were in ferment over the Bill. Our visit to Patna on behalf of the Editors' Guild was part of the reaction. In lectures, meetings with pressmen and my writings, I urged four steps—the sort of steps that I would urge on several occasions in the coming years.

First, arrangements should be made all over Bihar so that information about the harassment or arrest of anyone under the new law could be swiftly disseminated within and outside Bihar; and groups of lawyers should be organized in Patna, Ranchi and as many other places as possible, so that legal assistance could be proved without delay to anyone who was apprehended under the new legislation.

Second, the press should pay the Bihar government back in its own coin. All official functions should be boycotted. If handouts about ministers' speeches at such functions are distributed, only the truly newsworthy content in them should be reported, and that, too, briefly. The names of ministers should not be reported. Thus, if X, the minister for education, announced with the customary fanfare that he had decided to open twenty-four schools in Biharsharif, a report should merely state that 'it has been announced on behalf of the government that twenty-four schools will be opened in Biharsharif'. The press should not describe the function. It should not report the minister's name. Moreover, it must not carry photographs of ministers of the Bihar government.

Third, we must have the confidence that, try as it might, the Bihar government will just not be able to sustain prosecution under this Bill of any comment or exposure of the kind that have been really upsetting Mishra and Co. Explanations one and two of the Bill that exempt from the purview of 'scurrilous' writing anything written in good faith about the conduct of a public servant, including whatever is written about his character inasmuch as it affects the discharge of his public function, should be pressed to the hilt to defeat the design of the Mishra government.

Finally, the most effective remedy was to show the Bill to be a toothless scarecrow by continuing to write truthfully about the true state of affairs in Bihar. As it was likely that once the Bill becomes an Act, much of the press in Bihar would be successfully intimidated into silence, the press outside Bihar should redouble its coverage of Bihar. And, as representatives of these outside publications who are stationed in Bihar will be vulnerable, these publications should make it a practice to send correspondents located in other centres into Bihar to collect material and file reports. The best way to pay Mishra back, I argued, is to teach him that the Bill he passed to shut off coverage of his deeds has in fact redoubled it.

The storm

Neither the Central Government nor Mishra's government could have anticipated the storm they had whipped up.

Demonstrations. Public meetings. Lawyers, university students, all joined the protests. Pressmen in Bihar returned their accreditation cards. They stopped covering government functions. They stopped reporting proceedings of the Assembly. One day, their colleagues in Parliament desisted from reporting the Question Hour. Memoranda were sent to, and delegations went to, the President, Giani Zail Singh, urging him not to sign the Bill. Soon, Opposition parties joined the protests.

After a year of ignominy, Mishra withdrew the Bill.

The Centre's role

Years later, in interviews—especially the ones he gave when he was criticizing the Ordinance that the Vasundhara Raje government issued in 2017—Mishra acknowledged that he should never have introduced the Bill. We know why he was dead against what was appearing in the press, and why he had tried to intimidate and silence it. But in these interviews, Mishra also acknowledged the other prod.

He said that once, when he had come to Delhi, he had found Mrs Gandhi to be distraught. She was particularly upset about what the press had been writing regarding her differences with her daughter-in-law, Maneka Gandhi, Mishra said. Can you not pass a law of the kind Tamil Nadu has? she had asked him, Mishra told correspondents. She had suggested that he meet Vasant Sathe.

Mishra had called on Sathe, and Sathe had given him a detailed briefing about changes that were required in existing laws.

But this was exactly what had been rumoured all along. And had been studiously denied by Sathe, Salve and others.

Moral of the story—a line well known among journalists: never believe a rumour till it has been officially denied!

7

'Fourth chapter, ninth verse'

The Janata Government had disintegrated. Mrs Gandhi had returned. Sanjay was again everyone's nightmare. Mrs Gandhi, it was said, is afraid of him. Mrs Gandhi, it was said, has surrendered power to Sanjay. All the old fears had surfaced again—within the *Indian Express* as much as outside.

One morning—that of 21 June 1980[1]—I got a call from Kishore Lal, a former MP and a close associate of Chandra Shekhar. Kishore Lal said that I should come over to his house for lunch as Chandra Shekhar wanted to meet me.

I went. Chandra Shekhar did not turn up till it was time for us to disperse. He had been detained at a meeting. But Chandra Shekharji has some work for you, Kishore said, so come for dinner tomorrow at 8.30 p.m.

I went. Chandra Shekhar came around 9 p.m. We talked of the way things were, of where they were headed. I delivered, what a friend used to call, my 'usual gloom and doom prophecies'. We talked of what should be done to re-establish credibility with the rank and file of the Party—though the three of us had no doubt that the Party was disintegrating, though we knew that neither

---

[1] I am using words from what I wrote at the time, something to which I will return as we go along.

rank nor file was visible. We talked about the need to reach out to good men, irrespective of parties—though none of us could have named many 'good men' in the dozen or so parties that were pulling in different directions. We talked of the need to rebuild the Party from the ground up, to build it around work—how many times had we talked of this, recalling Gandhiji and his constructive programmes, and how many times since then have we talked of the same imperative.

An hour and a half passed. Chandra Shekhar's interest was only in a convention of youth that he was going to inaugurate in Bihar a month later—and this is the work for which I had been summoned. He wanted me and a few others to draw up a 'Charter for Youth', a programme that he would announce at the convention.

'*Chandra Shekhar ji, voh to main kar he doonga,*'[2] I said, as he and Kishore walked me to the car. '*Yeh to Kishore yaa aap mujhe phone par he keh detey. Itnee takleef karney ki kyaa zaroorat thi? Par aap* politicians *ko yeh sab kehnaa to divaar mein sar phodnaa hai. Naa aap kuch karenge aur naa is abhaagi* country *mein kuch hoga.*'[3]

'*Haan, hamaarey baarey mein to tum theek kehtey ho,*' he replied. '*Hamaare sye kuch hogaa naheen. Par jahaan tak desh kaa sawaal hai, voh Murli Manohar hai naa, tum usey jaantey ho naa? Uskaa jyotshi keh rahaa hai ki kal taees taareekh hai, aur subeh hogee naheen ki aisi ghatnaa hogee jiskaa ham anumaan hi naheen kar saktey.*'[4]

We shrugged it off. Every two months some damned astrologer is forecasting deliverance, I said, and nothing happens.

---

[2] 'That much of course I will do in any case, Chandra Shekharji.'

[3] 'You or Kishore could have told me this over the phone. Where was the need for taking so much trouble? But to say all this to you politicians is to break one's head against the wall. Neither will you do anything nor will anything happen in this accursed country.'

[4] 'Yes, what you say about us is right. We will not be able to do anything. But as far as the country is concerned, that Murli Manohar, you know him, don't you? His astrologer says that tomorrow is the 23rd, and the day shall not break and such a thing will happen that we cannot even imagine.'

It must have been just before 11 p.m. that I reached home. My mother opened the door to let me in. '*Chandra Shekhar ki kehndaa?*'[5] she asked.

'*Mama ohney ki kehnaa? O vi jyotshian de chakkraan vich ghum reha-ai.*'[6]

The next morning, as usual, I got into the car and began my drive to the *Express* building. As I was crossing over a culvert near the International Hostel, I saw a number of persons running along the *nullah* below. They were all running in one direction. Something must have happened, I thought, and continued driving.

I had just about settled into my cabin and the phone rang. It was an officer in the IB (Intelligence Bureau)—someone who used to give us useful tips. '*Tumeh pataa hai kyaa huaa hai, ki Sanjay mar gayaa hai?*'[7] And he told me how Sanjay's plane had crashed, and he as well as his co-pilot had died.

I got up at once, and headed for the small cubicle in which Ramnathji used to stay.

I opened the door. He was reading a paper. I said, 'Ramnathji, fourth chapter, ninth verse.'

He caught the allusion at once.[8]

'*Devi gayee?*'[9] he asked.

'*Naheen, Sanjay gayaa.*'[10]

And I described the call from the IB officer.

He lifted himself out of the low chair in which he used to sit, put his head on the ground, and said, '*Arun, Bhagwaan hai.*'[11]

I then told him what Chandra Shekhar had said the previous night at dinner.

'*To kar kyaa rahey ho, phone lagaao naa.*'[12]

---

5   'What does Chandra Shekhar say?'
6   'Mama, what is he going to say? He is also caught up with astrologers.'
7   'Do you know what has happened, Sanjay has died.'
8   '*Yadaa yadaa hi dharmasya glaanir bhavati Bharat . . .*' in the Gita.
9   'Has the Devi gone?'
10 'No, Sanjay has.'
11 'Arun, there is God.'
12 'Then what are you doing? Dial the number.'

I dialled Chandra Shekhar's number.

'*Sharmaji,*[13] *Netaji hain?*'[14]

Chandra Shekhar came on the line: '*Arun, ek shabd naheen. Milengey to baat karenge*'[15]—and he put down the phone.

After spending some time with Ramnathji and making a few calls, I returned to my cabin, and wrote all this down.

But a dispute erupted. Publishing the exchanges when the accident had just occurred, it was argued, would indicate foreknowledge, and foreknowledge would point to a conspiracy, and a conspiracy would prove sabotage . . .

So, the few words I had written were not published.

The year went by. The anniversary of Sanjay's death came round. I submitted the small article to Nihal Singh, the Editor of the *Express* at the time. He refused to publish it, as he would refuse to let me do many of the things that I suggested—we did not think much of each other.

I was incensed, and thought of getting back at him. I then did what Ramnathji used to call 'mischief'—'*To aaj kyaa* mischief *kiaa hai?*'[16] he would say.

I gave the article to Nandini Mehta who used to edit the Sunday magazine of the paper.[17] I requested her to use it as a single-column box item—I did not tell her that Nihal Singh had turned it down.

She did.

Now it was Nihal Singh's turn to be incensed.

'*Nihal aayaa thaa,*' Ramnathji said, '*aur keh rahaa thaa ki tumney badmaashi kee hai.*'[18]

'*To aapney usey kyaa kahaa?*'[19]

---

[13] H.N. Sharma, a teacher at the Delhi Arts College, close to Chandra Shekhar.

[14] 'Sharmaji, is Netaji there?'

[15] 'Not one word, Arun. We will talk when we meet.'

[16] 'So, what mischief have you done today?'

[17] 'The second coincidence,' *Sunday Standard Magazine,* 21 June 1981.

[18] 'Nihal had come, and was complaining that you have done something wicked.'

[19] 'So, what did you tell him?'

'Arey bhai, mainey kyaa kehnaa thaa? Meiney kahaa ki main jaantaa hoon ki jo tumney likhaa hai, vahee hua thaa. Aur jahaan tak article *kaa sawaal hai,* that is history. History *chaapnaa to hamaaraa kaam he hai.'*[20]

---

[20] 'Come on, what was I going to say? I told him that as far as what you have written is concerned, I know that that is what happened. And as far as the article is concerned, it is history. And printing history is our job, after all.' This must have been the sort of incident that lay behind one of Nihal Singh's several complaints about me. In his autobiography, Nihal Singh wrote,

> Shourie exploited his proximity to Goenka to terrorize the reporters and subeditors.

The reporters and subeditors? The first time I heard this charge. The sentences that follow perhaps indicate who really felt terrorized.

> As executive editor, he was the No. 2 man in the editorial hierarchy but often assumed the airs of a prima donna. His office being twice as large as the editor's room and far better furnished always puzzled me. Shourie believed that rules were made for others, and our clash began when he took umbrage over my cutting his extensive opinion piece to conform to the paper's style.

'The paper's style'? Most of us would have been hard-pressed to say what it was—save independence.

> On one occasion, I had to spike a piece he had written on Indira Gandhi, in language unbecoming of any civilized newspaper, just before it was to go to press.

Memory lapse! As the sentence that follows makes clear, the little piece he had spiked was not about Mrs Gandhi but about Sanjay's death.

> In an underhand move, he quietly sent it to the magazine section, printed in Bombay, without inviting censure from Goenka. [C.f., S. Nihal Singh, *Ink in My Veins, A Life in Journalism,* Hay House India, New Delhi, Kindle, Loc 3057.]

And what was uncivilized about the language of this little piece?

8

A daring reporter

Ashwini Sarin was a daring young reporter in our Delhi team. He would go into the field and document the facts—from the excesses of authorities during the Emergency in the name of family planning to irregularities in disposing of old defence vehicles. To substantiate conditions in which prisoners were being kept in Tihar jail, he had himself arrested for 'drunken behaviour', and got himself into the jail. While he was inside, he collected information about the conditions, of course, but, more important, about the free flow of drugs there. He wrote about this trade when he came out, to great acclaim from readers.

While covering elections in the Dholpur-Morena area, Ashwini had learnt that trade in women was widespread at the junction of Madhya Pradesh, Rajasthan and UP. From time to time, social workers used to draw attention to this evil practice, and officialdom used to deny it. Ashwini told me that he was prepared to go to the area, actually purchase a woman, and bring her to Delhi.

We kept the project from everyone—at home and in the office. Even Ramnathji was not taken into confidence. The rationalization was that we must not implicate them as accomplices in case the authorities proceeded against us for having violated the law. The lurking fear was that someone high up would veto the project—

most of all the then Editor, another Brown Sahib of Brown Sahibs, S. Nihal Singh.

Of course, we had no doubt that purchasing a woman was a serious matter—Ashwini would be committing an offence far graver than 'drunken behaviour', and he would be doing so with my prior knowledge. I wrote to five eminent persons—starting with the then Chief Justice of India, Justice Y.V. Chandrachud, and Justice P.N. Bhagwati. In addition, I wrote to Justice V.M. Tarkunde, former Judge of the Bombay High Court, one of the most respected lawyers of the country, and the head of the Civil Liberties movement at the time; to Achyut Patwardhan, the socialist leader and former associate of JP; and to Siddhraj Dhadda, the Sarvodaya leader. I explained what Ashwini was about to do, and the reason he was going to do it. The reason was plain and simple: instead of taking steps to eliminate an inhuman practice, the Madhya Pradesh Government was just covering it up with lies. We were going to expose the facts in a way that would render them undeniable. This would put pressure on the Government to at last take steps to educate the poor tribal people to stop visiting this terrible fate on their sisters and daughters.

Ashwini began visiting the area to get to know the lay of the land, to forge contacts, to win the confidence of the local people. For winning confidence, he made himself out to be several characters, including a Thakur from Punjab on the lookout for a girl. On returning from his visits, to ward off any curiosity about his visits, as well as inquiries from our hard-pressed accountants, Ashwini would file stories, but on absolutely unrelated matters. This subterfuge continued for almost eight to nine months; four to five of these were taken up by actual negotiations with touts, controllers of the trade and others. Ashwini went to the area ten times. No one else in the office knew what the eventual target was.

At immense risk to himself, Ashwini established direct contacts with persons who were in the business of buying and selling women. After intense and diligent work, he struck a deal at the Morena Circuit House, and purchased the lady, Kamla. She was delivered to him at the Delhi railway station. Ashwini's account began with sentences that were to be echoed for long:

Yesterday I bought a short-statured skinny woman belonging to a village near Shivpuri in Madhya Pradesh for 2,300 rupees. Even I find it hard to believe that I have returned to the capital this morning after buying the middle-aged woman for half the price one pays for a buffalo in the Punjab.

I visited the area ten times to win the confidence of the sellers but in the end it was as if I were just buying a pair of shoes. And that's what an elderly resident of Morena, the nearby district town notorious for dacoits, had told me would be the case: 'People here buy women more often than they buy pairs of shoes' . . .[1]

We hadn't planned the subsequent steps well enough. After a frantic and unsuccessful search for a place in which to keep Kamla safe—this included taking her to Ashwini's own house—Mrs Pramila Dandavate, well known for her social work and the wife of Mr Madhu Dandavate, agreed to keep Kamla at their house.

We thought it best that after Ashwini's initial story, Kamla should be met by and be interviewed by a lady. Coomi Kapoor, our Chief Reporter in Delhi at the time, went to meet her. During the conversation, Kamla often referred to herself in the third person. Apart from gleaning other things, Coomi came back with a distressing fact: from time to time, Kamla lapsed into incoherence; she did not seem to be in full possession of her faculties. Even making allowances for the effect of what she had been through during the preceding day—having been sold, being brought to a large, unknown city—Coomi judged her responses to be erratic. 'She has been used and abandoned again and again,' Coomi wrote. 'No wonder she is now on the edge of madness.'[2]

---

[1] Ashwini's first dispatch appeared in the *Indian Express* of 27 April 1981. The follow-up stories on which this account is based appeared in the paper on 27, 29, 30 April, and 2 May 1981.

[2] When I send Coomi a message to double-check a point, she adds a detail I had forgotten: 'Yes, you took her first to the Dandavate house where I interviewed her, and you very sweetly brought Ashwini and me lunch boxes from Nirula's. In those days, editors didn't take notice of humble reporters' requirements.' I must have done so only because the reporters in our team were not that humble!

At times, far from being distressed, Kamla expressed a measure of pride at the fact that the price for her had been pegged so high. Kamla's reactions also established another distressing fact. So widespread must the trade in women have been that, at times, Kamla thought her fate to be the normal one: Ashwini's wife told reporters that Kamla asked her how much Ashwini had paid for her, Uma; that as Ashwini had already paid for her, Kamla, why could the two of them not stay together with him. On meeting her, and listening to her rambling, sometimes contradictory, sometimes somewhat incoherent responses, Coomi concluded that Kamla was 'in urgent need of psychiatric care'.

The story created a sensation.

Ashwini was already known for his daring. Within the day he became a household word in every city where the *Express* was published. On the other side, governments flew into a rage. They had been shown up doing nothing about an abhorrent practice. The local police at Dholpur let it be known that they would be filing a case against Ashwini for trafficking in women. To forestall that, we filed a writ in the Supreme Court requesting the Court to give directions on steps governments must take to curb the trade, and about where Kamla should be housed.

To our great relief, an Arya Samaj institution that maintained a home for orphans and destitute women, the Arya Anaathalaya, agreed to provide her shelter. She was taken there. But, the moment the Dholpur police let it be known that they would be filing a case against Ashwini, a posse of Delhi policemen swooped down to the Arya Samaj shelter to take possession of Kamla—they will be needing her as a witness, they said, in the Dholpur police's case. Someone at the orphanage rang up the *Express* and informed that the police had descended on them to take Kamla away. Colleagues rushed to the orphanage. The policemen just wouldn't listen to the pleas of the women in the orphanage, nor to those of our colleagues. They moved her to a police station, saying that she will be taken to Nari Niketan, a government-run home—all this to keep their potential witness safe! Coomi rushed to the Chief Metropolitan Magistrate, and filed an application to restrain the police. He directed that Kamla should not be moved. Colleagues

rushed to the Chief Justice of the Supreme Court. We argued
that the police were liable to browbeat Kamla into saying
what they will—this was all the more important in view of the
declared intention of the Madhya Pradesh police that they were
going to file a case against Ashwini for trafficking in women.
Moreover, Kamla herself was in a disturbed state of mind.
Convinced about the urgency of the matter, the Chief Justice
requested Justice P.N. Bhagwati to hear the matter on an urgent
basis at his residence. Late in the evening, Justice Bhagwati
directed that Kamla be returned to the orphanage, and should
not be shifted 'till further orders'.

The dispatch filed that evening after all this rushing around
concluded: 'Kamla, removed from the Home around 5 p.m., came
back at 7.30 p.m., visibly dazed and upset: "Am I a monkey to be
pushed around like this? You have not been kind to Kamla," she
said. "Have you?"'

Not to be outdone, the Madhya Pradesh Government
approached the Subdivisional Magistrate's court in Morena, and
got him to issue a warrant for recovery of the woman. The police
party left for Delhi post-haste.

Ashwini received a call from T.R. Kakkar, the DCP (Deputy
Commissioner of Police), Central Delhi: get lost immediately.
The DCP was known to Ashwini. Kakkar told Ashwini that
the Madhya Pradesh police had come to arrest him, that he
had asked them to wait outside his office while he made the
necessary arrangements. In those—distant—days, formalities were
still observed. As we fell in the Central Delhi range, the MP
police party had come to the DCP, Central's office to report their
mission, and seek assistance. Ashwini vanished. We rushed to the
Court of Justice P.N. Bhagwati. He passed an order granting a
stay on Ashwini's arrest.

Ashwini, Coomi and I filed a writ in the Supreme Court.
Justice Bhagwati and Justice A. Vardarajan admitted the petition.
They directed that Kamla not be shifted; that AIIMS immediately
depute a psychiatrist to assess the kind of help that Kamla
needed; that governments should not initiate any action based
on the subject matter of the writ against anyone among the three

of us without prior permission of the Court. And they issued notice to the governments of Madhya Pradesh, UP, Rajasthan and the Centre to explain what steps were being taken to suppress trafficking in women.

The Madhya Pradesh government, which had done nothing to curb this cruel trade, now directed the Commissioner of the Morena Division to inquire into the matter and file a report within ten days. The 'ten days' were over by the middle of May. Had the Commissioner submitted his report? No answer. In any case, the Government wouldn't make the findings public. We had an outstanding correspondent in the state, N.K. Singh. He got hold of the report, and filed a story giving details of the Commissioner's findings.

There was a flourishing trade in women centred in Morena and the surrounding areas, the Commissioner's inquiries confirmed. Girls and women were brought from faraway places, bought and sold, and sent to centres like Delhi and Meerut. The trade was rampant among some tribes—in some, girls were especially trained for prostitution. The practice was so widespread that it was almost customary: 'Discussing the sociological aspect of the problem,' NK wrote, 'the report said that in a society where dacoity was considered an "honourable" profession, trafficking in women naturally failed to touch the sensitive cord.' A large number of persons were involved in the business, N.K. Singh reported the Commissioner to have stated. 'In fact,' NK reported, 'a social reformer of Bedia community, which specialises in prostitution and trafficking, furnished a list of 75 persons belonging to his own tribe who were in the trade.' 'The traffickers,' NK quoted the report to have recorded, 'are influential in local politics and enjoy patronage of political and social bigwigs.'[3]

What was the government going to do about the Commissioner's findings? 'The Government was studying the report for follow-up action,' sources told NK.[4] 'It is, however, learnt from reliable

---

[3] N.K. Singh's dispatch was carried by the paper on 9 August 1981.

[4] Either the subeditor on the news desk or the compositor in the press was prescient, it seems: in the printed version of the paper, 'follow-up action' appears as 'follow-up auction'.

sources that the authorities are reluctant to accept the report which they feel has become more of a sociological treatise than an administrative inquiry.' This in August 1981. The next month, explaining what the government was going to do about the report and the trade it had documented, the Chief Minister, Arjun Singh was telling NK that 'The Madhya Pradesh Government will conduct a sociological study of flesh trade in northern parts of the state. A reputed agency like the Indian Council of Social Sciences and Research may be commissioned for this purpose . . .'[5]

Ashwini's story, and his daredevilry, became a household word. The famous playwright, Vijay Tendulkar, wrote a play with Kamla's fate as its peg. In proceedings later, to which we will come in a moment, it was stated that in the ensuing months, the play was staged 150 times in thirty-two cities in seven languages. The play became the basis for a movie, *Kamla,* with Tendulkar writing the screenplay for it.

Ashwini's spectacular effort had a tragic end, in more ways than one.

Even as efforts to find Kamla a shelter were continuing, one day we learnt that the poor lady had 'disappeared'. How could that be? Kamla was not of sound mind, and so she could not have escaped on her own into a city that she knew nothing about. More important, entry to the orphanage was strictly controlled. The building had only one entrance—a high gate that was always closed. And the police had been posted outside the gate. How could she have got out or jumped out?

Efforts to trace her continued. In November that year, the Supreme Court directed the Police Commissioner of Delhi to make all efforts to locate her. She was never found.

The most likely explanation? Persons buying and selling women who would have been exposed had removed her somehow.

As I mentioned, Tendulkar's play was enacted far and wide. No one at the *Express* objected. That a film was being planned was published in newspapers, including the *Loksatta,* the Marathi paper of the *Express* Group, and *Screen,* the film magazine, of the

---

[5] N.K. Singh's dispatch in the *Indian Express,* 22 August 1981.

Express Group itself. Nobody in the paper objected. But when the film was about to be released, the Group filed a writ in the Bombay High Court with prayers that were quite out of character of the paper: that distribution of the film must be stopped, that all copies must be destroyed, that the producer be directed to pay a huge amount as damages. The grounds were that the paper's copyright had been infringed; that in the film the reporter had been pictured as an oppressive, domineering husband; and that the proprietor had been shown as succumbing to political pressure—in the film he gets rid of the reporter to appease a minister through whom he was hoping to get a ticket for a forthcoming election.

The Court allowed the film to be distributed subject to some scenes being cut.[6]

There is a comic aspect to the case also. I had been removed from the paper long ago, and had to be made a non-person. In the writ, as well as in the judgment, the normal—minor—work which I had done about coordinating the effort, of keeping the office off-track, of writing to those five persons, of standing by Ashwini, etc., was attributed to the 'Executive Director' of the Group—someone whom we hadn't heard of at the time![7]

Ashwini continued in the paper for a few years. Later I heard that he had left journalism all together, and taken to business.

I had lost touch with him. To make sure that my memory was not deceiving me on some details, I got his number from an old colleague. Almost forty years would have passed since I had spoken with him. We were hardly a few minutes into the conversation that Ashwini was overwhelmed with tears. He said he had become 'too emotional', that he couldn't talk at the moment, and would get back later. He put his wife, Uma, on the phone . . .

Talk of bonds forged in those years.

---

[6] For details, *Indian Express Newspapers (Bombay) Pvt. Ltd v Dr Jagmohan Mundhra*, 1984. SCC OnLine Bom 256: AIR 1985 Bom 229, decided on 12 October 1984.

[7] Ibid., para. 2.

As for his leaving journalism, well, he had been at the *Express* for twenty years. And while the point does not apply to him, there is the curse of success that all whose work brings them into the public eye should bear in mind. Often, spectacular success—especially if it has come early in life—comes to taunt one. It raises expectations, say, of readers or viewers: 'What will he come up with next?' But it is difficult to keep coming up with stories of equal significance. Pressure builds on the journalist or writer or actor, as the case may be. He strains to measure up to the high standard that his initial success had set. People begin to exclaim, 'He has lost his touch.' The journalist or actor moves around in the afterglow of his previous work. As that fades from people's memories, he forsakes the profession altogether, and takes to doing something entirely different—something in which his past work will not be held up to measure him.

9

'The people want him'

'*Chalo, chalo. Do chaaloo logon sey miltey hain*'—Ramnathji had walked into my little cabin. '*Unkey paas maal bahut hai. Par naa dil, naa saahas. Badey dhanee aur badey darpok. Yahaan aaney sey dartey hain. Hamein he unkey paas jaanaa padegaa. Chalo, chalo.*'[1]

We got into his little Fiat. He drove. He told me that Srichand—Hinduja—had contacted him, that he had something important to tell us, but he was afraid of coming to the *Express* building. '*Aisey logon sey kabhee rishtaa naheen karnaa par aison sey miltey rehnaa chaahiye.*'[2]

'*Yahee to meri mushkil hai,*' he continued. '*Tumhaaraa vaishayon se lenaa-denaa he naheen. Unko saarey shahar kaa pataa rehtaa hai—kaun kis kee beewee udaa kar le jaa rahaa hai, kaun kis mein chhuraa dhaunsney vaalaa hai.*'[3]

---

[1] 'Hurry up, get up. Let us go and meet two fast dealers. They have a lot of wealth, but no courage. Very rich and very fearful. They are afraid to come here. We will have to go to them. Come on, come on.'

[2] 'One should not forge relations with such persons but one should keep meeting them.'

[3] 'That is my problem. You don't have dealings with prostitutes. They know everything that is going on in the city—who is going to elope with whose wife, who is going to thrust a knife into whom.'

We reached the Oberoi Hotel. And went up to a suite. Srichand and Ashok Hinduja greeted us warmly. Ramnathji introduced me.

Srichand started by saying that what they wanted to tell us was most important, but that no one should know they had met us. You have known our family for long, he said, addressing Ramnathji. You know we don't want anything for ourselves. You know everything, you know how much we have done for others, how much we have given away in charity . . . You know how our father started a small clinic after Partition. Land was purchased. We made it a 100-bed hospital. We want to expand this, make it the best hospital in India, and a great centre for medical research. We are in touch with Harvard and the best institutions in Europe.

'*To phir mushkil kyaa hai?*'[4] Ramnathji asked.

Srichand looked around, bent a little closer to Ramnathji. '*Voh Sultan.* Hospital *ko, ek* hospital *ko* expand *karney ke liye voh paisey maang rahaa hai.*'[5]

'*Kitney?*'[6]

'*Paanch crore.*'[7]

Ramnathji said that Antulay must be doing so, but was somebody prepared to stand up and speak out? '*Tumhein bolney ko main naheen keh rahaa. Par koi aur hai maan kaa laal jo khadaa hone ko tayyaar hai?*'[8]

'*Aap to sab jaantey he hain—kaun kitney paani main hai.*'[9]

'*To matlab, kaam mujhey he karnaa hogaa. Lathi chalee to sehnee mujhey he padegi. Tum tamshaa dekhogey.*'[10]

'*Main apney saath apnaa sher laayaan hoon,*' Ramnathji continued, pointing to me. '*Isey main Bambai bhejtaa hoon. Agar*

---

[4] 'Then what is the difficulty?'
[5] 'That Sultan, he is asking for money to let us expand the hospital.'
[6] 'How much?'
[7] 'Five crore.'
[8] 'I am not asking you to speak up. But is there someone else who is prepared to stand up?
[9] 'You know everything—who is prepared to take a stand.'
[10] 'So, you mean, that I am the one who will have to do the work. When the blows rain, they will fall on me. And you will watch the fun.'

koi dhoond saktaa hai, to yeh dhoond legaa. Tumhaarey paas jo kuch masaalaa hai isey bhijwaa denaa. Aagey hum dekh leingey.[11]

'*Hamaarey paas to keval sacchh hai,*' Srichand said. '*Baakee aap ko he dhoondnaa hogaa. Par ek shart par—naa hamaaraa naa hospital kaa naam aanaa chaahiye.*'[12]

'*Dekhaa?*' Ramnathji said as we got back in the car. '*Mainey kyaa kahaa thaa—mahaa dhani aur mahaa darpok. Par yeh baat sahi hai ki Antulay aisey he kar rahaa hogaa. Saaraa Bambai jaantaa hai ki usney choongi khol rakhi hai.*'[13]

Ramnathji returned to Bombay. I joined him there, staying at his Penthouse.

I started meeting various persons. Civil servants wouldn't talk. Retired civil servants were more forthcoming, but they did not have concrete information. Businessmen would speak as if the walls of their own offices and homes would hear, so elliptically, in fact, that one really had to strain to establish any connection with the question at hand.

In any case, the general pattern became apparent in little time. Antulay had centralized all licences and clearances, allocations of scarce materials like cement, and was extracting money for giving them. This much was standard governance in those days. The novelty was that he asked businessmen to pay into Trusts that he had set up. One of these was named after Mrs Indira Gandhi herself. I learnt that he could not have used her name for his Trust without her consent. Clearly, for our work to have consequences, *this* was the Trust which had to be the focus of inquiries.

Among the persons I met was Govindrao Talwalkar, the editor of the *Maharashtra Times*. I had come to know him through Justice V.M. Tarkunde as Govind was an admirer of M.N. Roy.[14]

---

[11] 'I have brought a lion. I will send him to Bombay. If someone can find it out, he will. Send us what you have. We will see to the rest.'

[12] 'We only have the truth. As for the rest, you will have to find it out. But on one condition—neither the name of our hospital nor our name should come.'

[13] 'See? What did I tell you? Very wealthy and very cowardly. But this much is right, Antulay must be doing what they say. The whole of Bombay knows that he has set up an octroi post.'

[14] Justice Tarkunde had been the Secretary of M.N. Roy in the 1940s.

He loved books and wrote books. The walls of his apartment were full of them. I explained the project to him, and recounted what I had learnt till then. It was enough for a general story. But that was not my way, and a general story recounting what I had been told would never have the impact that a story based on, in fact, a story with overwhelming facts, would have. And while Antulay seems to have set up several Trusts, I said to Govindrao, we should focus on the one he had named after Indira Gandhi—that is the one that will shake these fellows up like nothing else will, the fact that he had made commerce of Indira Gandhi.

Govindrao told me that the Trust was known but that he had not asked any of his colleagues to find out about it, nor did he know anyone connected with the Trust. But there were two persons who hated Antulay. They had worked in the Trust that had been set up for helping people after the Koyna earthquake. They had been removed from it because they objected to decisions that Antulay was taking about the funds. If they knew whom I should meet, they would point me to him, Govindrao said. You can go and try to persuade them, but you must never let them down; you must not mention their names, he said. They have already been persecuted enough.

I went to meet them in a building diagonally across the Churchgate station.[15] They were most forthcoming. Yes, Antulay was a crook and a curse. He would rob and ruin the state. I mentioned that I was after information, specific information about the Trust named after Indira Gandhi.

But the office of that Trust is in this very building, they said, on this very floor, they said, and a clerk working in it had worked with them earlier. One of them got up and walked to the office of the Trust—just plywood partitions away. He came back saying we were in luck. Some government person had come from Delhi, and so information about donations, etc., had been compiled for him.

Could I come back in the afternoon?

---

[15] Their office was on the fifth floor of the Industrial Assurance Building across the *chowk* from the Churchgate railway station.

When I returned, they had sheets listing the names of companies, donations they had made to the Trust, dates on which the cheques had been deposited.

This was a gold mine. I would have to get the facts verified, but, at last, what a start!

Could they also share the tables with Govindrao, they asked, as they knew him?

Of course, I assured them. After all, he is the one who sent me to you.

I returned to Ramnathji's Penthouse, and began collating the information, rearranging the names by industry, and comparing the industry-wise names with what I had learnt about decisions that Antulay had been taking, with circulars that had been issued, etc.

I worked on Ramnathji's dining table through the day and night till about 4 in the morning. Two vital circulars were missing: the one relating to the construction and cement industries, and one relating to the sugar industry. The former turned out to be relatively easy to secure. After some search for possible sources, a young man, almost a lad, Rajan Raheja brought it, to the strenuous objections of his family members. But I couldn't get the circular related to the sugar manufacturers.

Ramnathji said, '*Us badmaash ke paas jaao,* Sharad Pawar *ke paas. Voh sab* sugar *millon kaa kartaa hai.*'[16]

Sharad Pawar was an important leader of the Opposition in Maharashtra in those days. I was able to get an appointment for the evening. The veranda and anteroom of his house were full of people. He received me, as he received everyone, as if we had known each other forever. I explained the project, what I had been able to get, and the one missing link that was holding up the story—the circular sent to the sugar mills and cooperative societies.

Is that all? he asked. You already know what has been taken from the cement and sugar mills, and the formula by which every

---

[16] 'Go to that rogue, Sharad Pawar. He is the master of all sugar mills.'

mill owner's contribution has been fixed. Why don't you write your story? Why do you need the actual circular?

I told him that that was not my way. I won't publish the story till I have the circular in my hand.

You won't publish the story? Does RNG know about this?

When I explained the position, he asked me where I was staying, told me to go back, start writing the story as if I had the circular, and that someone will come to the Penthouse that night with the circular.

Sure enough, late into the night, a young man arrived with the cyclostyled circular. It was Ajit Gulabchand, who later became Chairman of the Hindustan Construction Company.

It must have been around 3 a.m. by the time I completed the story. I did not know typing in those days: I would write in longhand, and the typist attached to Ramnathji would type. Ramnathji would come out of his bedroom from time to time to check whether I needed anything.

Our practice used to be to creed sensitive stories around 10.30 at night so that governments would not have time to get to learn about them and somehow stop them. But in this case, the article would take a third of the front page and the entire page inside, and a third of the latter was to consist of just names and numbers: names of the 'contributor' classified into industry groups, the name of the 'contributor's' bank, the cheque number, date on which the cheque was made out, the amount. These were pre-electronic years: we used to creed our stories over the teleprinters to all the editions; in each edition, the copy would have to be composed laboriously letter by letter, digit by digit by the compositors in the press—though no one could match the speed with which they picked and placed the lead mould, reversed, for each letter or digit in the ill-lit press halls; many of them were not really fluent in even the language. A mistake in any digit, and the critics would jump at it to discredit the whole story. So, I decided that there was no alternative but for us to creed the text and table as soon as the teleprinter lines opened.

All the work had been done, but there was still one hurdle: the Editor in Delhi, S. Nihal Singh. In his own view, a sahib who had to teach us the alphabet, he would feel compelled to tamper with what I had written, I feared. My greatest fear was that he would decree that there was no need for the table of numbers, names, etc. That would kill the story. My rule was that the first salvo must have so much evidence as to be a fatal blow—but that one must keep a third of the ammunition in reserve. The subject of the account would deny what we had published. One must be able to come back at him with another ton of bricks. Nihal Singh was the 150-word-editorial writing type. He would not see the reason for all those details.

In the morning, I went over to Ramnathji's bedroom, gave him what I had written, and the table of names and figures. Unlike his editors, he revelled in details. He went through the names and figures as a starving man would go at food. I explained my apprehension about the story, especially about the details being cut out, and I requested him to tell Nihal Singh not to tamper with the copy.

'Nihal, *mainey ek-ek shabd* clear *kiyaa hai*,' Ramnathji told him as soon as the phone was put through. '*Sab subs ko keh do ki ek shabd bhi idhar-udhar huaa to main unki jaan ley loongaa. Ek shabd bhi idhar-udhar huaa . . . Tum khud sab ko yeh meri taraf se keh do, khud.*'[17]

Two hours later, from the press downstairs, we had proofs of the story that would appear the next morning in Bombay and every other edition, beginning from page 1, 'Indira Gandhi as commerce.' I went over the proofs, and handed each galley to Ramnathji. He read the story again, visibly elated, and left for the mandir.

The next morning had but to break and visitors started coming to the Penthouse. A beaming Sharad Pawar was among them.

What the Sultan had been doing

It turned out that Antulay had set up seven Trusts: five of these were named after and centred on the village, the taluka, the

---

[17] 'Nihal, I have cleared every single word. Tell all the subs that if even one word is misplaced, I will kill them. If even one word is here or there . . . You personally tell everyone this on my behalf, personally.'

constituency, the district and the region from which Antulay came. The sixth was named after a businessman, one of his main 'counsellors and helpers'. The seventh was named after Mrs Gandhi, the *Indira Gandhi Pratibha Pratishthan*.

This Trust had been incorporated about ten months before I was writing. The objectives were declared to be to help creative artistes in literature—'which includes', the Trust deed stated, 'poets, authors, critics . . .'—and fine arts—'which includes singers, dancers . . . *tamasha* and *nautankimen* . . .'—domiciled in Maharashtra. Antulay had already garnered for it around Rs 5 crore—a big sum in those days. Alas! Not enough, as the phrase goes, to wet even a man's teeth now.[18]

To get businessmen and those who needed other favours to 'contribute' money to the Trusts, Antulay had taken over functions that different agencies of the Government used to execute. Cement distribution from the Civil Supplies Department; allotment of plots for housing societies from the Revenue Minister; how much one could build on a plot from the Urban Development Department; no objection certificates to build on land held in excess of the urban ceiling from the Revenue Department. And so on, all along the lucrative line.

Everything was systematized. Rs 40 per bag of cement to be donated to the *Indira Gandhi Pratibha Pratishthan*. A graded levy for sugar mills—those recovering 10 per cent, Rs 1.75 per tonne of sugar cane crushed; those recovering between 10 and 10.75 per cent, Rs 2.25 per tonne of sugar cane . . . for recovery rate higher than 11.5 per cent, Rs 2.5 per tonne. Similarly, each of the nineteen distilleries that produced liquor in Maharashtra was asked to contribute one paisa per litre. Rumour was set afloat that licences to sell liquor will be cancelled, and given to new parties— the proposal was set aside when the Maharashtra Country Liquor Association agreed to cough up the prescribed toll.

---

[18] A publication of the Maharashtra Government, *Inner Voice*, indicated that Antulay planned to collect Rs 55 crore. Other accounts put the target at Rs 125 crore.

Antulay decreed shortages. Allocation of industrial alcohol was slashed by 20 per cent. Units using it could get their quota restored if they paid into the Trust. And the 20 per cent that Antulay now had in his hands was assigned to firms that he chose—they happened to be producing whisky. The black market premium on the raw material was Rs 5 per litre. They could get it upon their contributing Re 1 a litre into the Trust.

Routine, across-the-board decisions were replaced by decisions 'on merits': for instance, on how much land you owned in excess of the urban ceiling, you would be allowed to build; and how much you could build on each square foot of land within or beyond the urban land ceiling was decided on a '(suit)case-by-(suit)case' basis.

The result was predictable. The list that I gave and the text showed that even mills that had been certified as being too sick to continue without Government loans, even firms that could not pay salaries to their staff, and, of course, firms whose affairs were under examination by the state's agencies, were coughing up 'donations'. To top it all, the firms producing sugar, for instance, could deduct their 'donations' from the amount that they owed to farmers growing sugar cane!

While it was made out that the Trust was a government trust, it was nothing of the sort. By virtue of clauses that I enumerated, Antulay was Chairman, and his associates—all trustworthy cronies—were members of the Board of Trustees in their private, not official capacity. Antulay's wife, Nargis, had been a trustee in five of the seven Trusts. Furthermore, absolute power was vested in the trustees—for instance, to amend, alter or abrogate all provisions of the Trust deed; to amalgamate the Trust and its properties into any other Trust or institution that had even one objective in common with those of the Trust, etc. And among Trustees, Antulay had overwhelming powers—to enlarge the number of Trustees from five to eleven, to use the majority to expel any member; he had the exclusive power to nominate anyone to fill in the vacancies and appoint additional members. The Board would be subject to the Chairman's control. The Trust deed provided that he would 'direct activities' of the Trust; that 'his decision in matters of dispute of any nature shall be final and binding' . . . The Government of Maharashtra, controlled by Antulay, had kindly donated Rs 2 crore into this Trust controlled entirely by Antulay.

The other Trusts that Antulay had set up followed the same pattern. Each of them was in the complete and personal control of Antulay and his chums. The deeds were innocuous. The *Konkan Unnati Mitra Mandal,* for instance, was said to have been set up to provide scholarships, employment information, temporary accommodation to visitors from Konkan to Bombay; to arrange social gatherings, cultural shows, sports events, meetings and exhibitions to maintain social contacts and increase cordial relations among residents of Konkan; to enable them to examine problems the region faced, to make effective representations to authorities in Bombay, etc. And, as one would expect, the Income Tax Commissioner had granted 100 per cent exemption from income tax for donations made to the Trust . . .

It turned out, and Antulay had to admit this later while answering a barrage of questions in the Legislative Council, that he had given 8000 sq. yds of land in Central Bombay to this *Konkan Unnati* Trust on a lease for ninety-nine years. In return, the Trust would pay Re 1 per year for the lease! He said that this land had been given to make a grand studio to screen Marathi films, as there were few facilities for screening Marathi films.

Everyone waits for her

The article appeared on the morning of 31 August. As soon as the Houses met, both the Lok Sabha and the Rajya Sabha were in turmoil. Opposition members had come armed with the *Express.* They had given notices to the presiding officers and insisted that the collections of Antulay be discussed before anything else. The presiding officers ruled that Antulay and his collections were a subject that concerned the state, that members should ask their partymen to take them up in the state Assembly—which was meeting at that very time.

It has always struck me how everyone becomes such a strict constitutionalist the moment he is cornered.

In the Assembly, members stormed the well of the House. They clambered on to the Speaker's podium, and would have come to blows but for the fact that they were pulled away from each other.

Shalinitai Patil, the Revenue Minister and Number 2 in Antulay's Cabinet, stated publicly that she had been forced to collect funds for the Trusts, that she had done so because she had been told that these were Government Trusts, that sugar factories had been compelled to 'donate' money even when they were in crisis.[19] She was dismissed. The Assembly's sitting on the next day, 1 September, was also marked by 'uproarious scenes and slogan shouting'. The Speaker refused to allow the discussion. Members then filed motions to discuss the sudden dismissal of Shalinitai Patil, the Number 2 in the Cabinet. The Speaker rejected these also, ruling that it was the prerogative of the Chief Minister to decide whether a Minister would serve in his Cabinet. The entire Opposition walked out. No business could be conducted for the day.

During the days that followed, Parliament, as well as the state Assembly, was dominated by Antulay's Trusts. Notices followed notices, each to be rejected by the presiding officers. And the rejections naturally led to chaos in the Houses, and thus to adjournments and walkouts. All sorts of procedural issues erupted. Should the Question Hour be suspended? Should the matter be taken up during the Zero Hour? Under which sort of motion could the matter be discussed? An Adjournment Motion? A Call Attention Motion? As a Special Mention? Should the Government make a statement, and the House discuss points arising out of it? How can the House discuss Antulay when he is not present to defend himself? But you had brought motions against Kanti Desai[20] and family members of Charan Singh . . . Pandit Nehru

---

[19] Shalinitai was married to Vasantdada Patil, a powerful politician of the state. At the time, he was a General Secretary of the Congress(I); later, he became the Chief Minister of the state.

[20] Son of Morarji Desai, the then Prime Minister.

had agreed to discuss the charges against Sardar Pratap Singh Kairon, the then Chief Minister of Punjab . . . Cement is an essential commodity, a large proportion of the allocations that states receive come from the Centre . . . All right, not Antulay, but the income tax exemptions given by the central Government to certain Trusts in Maharashtra . . .

In the end, it was decided that the Government would make a statement. R. Venkataraman, then Finance Minister, a gentleman, was chosen to lie and evade on behalf of Government. Antulay 'air-dashed' to Delhi with a team of officials to brief him.

Venkataraman told the two Houses that Mrs Gandhi had not agreed to let her name be associated with the Trust; that the moment she had learnt of this, she had directed that it be dropped; that she had not inaugurated the Trust; that there had been no link between donations and cement allocations; that the Trust was a 'non-Government body though it had been sponsored by the State Government'; that tax exemptions had been given to the Trusts, as to thousands of other Trusts doing charitable work. He did not explain how the Konkan Unnati Mitra Mandal Trust had been granted exemption under Section 35 CCA, when under this Section, exemption could be given only to bodies engaged in rural development; nor how Indira Gandhi Pratibha Pratishthan had been granted exemption under Section 80 G of the Income Tax Act, when under this Section, exemption could be granted only if the Trust was irrevocable . . .

Alongside the report of his speech, we published a facsimile of a Maharashtra Government publication—*Maharashtra Marches Ahead*, with a picture of Antulay on the cover—affirming,

To give recognition to and encourage the talented people in the fields of Literature and Fine Arts, *the Government of Maharashtra has set up a foundation called 'Indira Gandhi Pratibha Pratishthan (Maharashtra)'*. The Pratishthan will have a fund of Rs 5 crores at its disposal. Out of this, the State Government will contribute Rs 2 crores and the remaining Rs 3 crore will be collected by way of donations from the public . . .

I took a marker pen and circled these lines in black ink, and underlined the phrase about the Government having set up the 'Foundation'.

Naturally, that caused a commotion the next day.

In the Lok Sabha, Venkataraman had said, 'She did not agree to her name being put in. The Prime Minister did not inaugurate it.' In the Rajya Sabha, he had said, 'I have definite information that not only does she not approve of her name being associated with any of these things, but she did not . . . What she agreed to was that the Pratishthan should be established, and not that her name should be associated with it, and when she came to know about it, she asked them to withdraw her name . . . I want to place this on record that she did not. I repeat, she did not inaugurate this . . .'

But there had been an official function in the Raj Bhavan on 11 October 1980. The Directorate of Information of the Maharashtra Government had distributed a photograph of Mrs Gandhi signing the document, agreeing to be a *sahabhaagi*—a partner, a participant—in the Trust, and it being named after her. The caption of the photograph, as given by the Government department, was,

> Prime Minister Indira Gandhi affixing her signature on the document giving her consent to name the Maharashtra Government's trust for promoting talent in literature and fine arts as 'Indira Gandhi Pratibha Pratishthan' at Raj Bhavan, on Saturday. Watching keenly is Chief Minister A.R. Antulay.

Paper after paper had carried the photograph and the description in their issues of 12 October 1980. More important, the Maharashtra Government's official publication, *Lokrajya* had carried these in its issue of 15 October 1980. And this is how the event had been described in this government publication:

> The Prime Minister, Smt Indira Gandhi, affixed her signature on the document giving her consent to name the Maharashtra Government's Trust for promoting talents in literature and the

arts as 'Indira Gandhi Pratibha Pratishthan' at Raj Bhawan in Bombay on October 11, 1980.

Two assertions in the account flatly contradicted what Venkataraman had told Parliament: the Trust was a government trust, and Mrs Gandhi had given her consent to having it named after her.

Moreover, that very day, 11 October, Mrs Gandhi and Antulay had addressed a large gathering of Congress(I) legislators. Antulay had thanked Mrs Gandhi for granting permission to name the Trust after her. In his speech Antulay had said:

> He [i.e., Antulay] announced that Mrs Gandhi had given her consent for naming the proposed trust to promote talents in literature and fine arts after her. The 'Indira Gandhi Pratibha Pratishthan' would grow very fast, Mr Antulay said . . .[21]

Our Chief Reporter in Bombay, Manu Desai, had a hobby: he collected government publications and stored them. He sent me the issue of *Lokrajya*. I wrote an article, 'Petty little lies in Parliament'. Several members filed breach of privilege motions against both Venkataraman and me—if Venkataraman had been truthful, I had denigrated the House; if I was right, Venkataraman had lied to the House. The fate of these privilege motions is delicious in itself. I will return to it later.

To deflect matters, the Minister of State for Parliamentary Affairs distributed sheets among Congress MPs containing allegations against Atal Behari Vajpayee, Charan Singh, George Fernandes—that they had collected huge amounts. Congress members created a din, demanding that the Houses discuss these charges. In the Lok Sabha, Arif Mohammed Khan led the pack. He filed a motion to this effect, and insisted that the Speaker allow discussion on his motion.

Shalinitai wrote to Mrs Gandhi. She said that Antulay had used 'coercive methods' to secure funds for the Trusts. She said

---

[21] A host of newspapers had reported these remarks in similar, some in identical words. I reproduced several of them.

that Antulay was annoyed with her because while she had acceded to one of his requests for money—Rs 21.27 lakhs from the Sangli Sugar Cooperative factory—she had not obliged him in regard to two other demands—Rs 12.5 lakhs from the State Farming Corporation, and Rs 3 per litre in cash for sanctioning industrial alcohol for the Sangli Sugar Cooperative factory. In regard to the first 'donation', she made it a point to record that Antulay had insisted that the cheque be sent immediately when she was busy making arrangements for the funeral of the President of the Maharashtra Cooperative Sugar Federation. As for the Farming Corporation, Shalinitai said she had told Antulay that it was registered under the Companies Act, and so paying such an amount required approval from the Central Government. As for industrial alcohol, the Sangli factory would pay by cheque, she told Antulay, but the latter, she wrote, insisted that the amount be given in cash.

Eighteen Congress legislators in Maharashtra signed a memorandum repeating some of the charges against Antulay, and adding new ones—that he had been building a personality cult, that in the fourteen months in which he had been in power, he had been behaving in 'an arbitrary and high-handed manner', that he had been 'flirting with persons with shady background', nepotism, hobnobbing with Shiv Sena (which in turn had urged that he be made Deputy Prime Minister), spying on colleagues (the operation being supervised by a retired Chief Secretary). As a result, the image of the Government and party 'has dipped like never before', the legislators said. They 'earnestly beseeched' Mrs Gandhi to act 'before it is too late'.

But she wouldn't.

Every second day brought out more and more embarrassing facts.

Defences

With details of the Trust deeds having been exposed, the first defence—that these were, in some sense, government Trusts—could no longer be advanced. Antulay, at the Congress legislators' meeting, and his megaphones in the press, therefore, advanced the second dodge: the amounts that had been deposited were not extortions; they had been given voluntarily as donations. But why had companies that were so sick that they couldn't even pay wages, 'donated' money into the Trust accounts? In a typical case that I listed, the company's General Body had voted unanimously that as the company was totally bereft of resources to run even its day-to-day operations, their company must not pay any 'donation'. The controllers, nevertheless, paid into the Trust. And did the government controlled and headed by Antulay voluntarily pay Rs 2 crore into the Trust controlled and headed by Antulay?

The third line of defence was soon deployed. Antulay said that the monies were not going to benefit him in any way. They were all going for charity. That was a non-starter. First, would the charity—say, looking after, providing accommodation to, entertaining, arranging social get-togethers for, giving scholarships, etc., to residents of his region/district/constituency/village—not help Antulay in the next election? More important, there were a slew of judgments that the form in which the money or favour was received by a public servant, and the ultimate purpose for which it had been received, was irrelevant—if it had been received in return for something done or not done by the public servant, it was corruption. Two cases, one from neighbouring Gujarat and one from Maharashtra itself, drove the nail in—for they concerned officials at the bottom of the governmental ladder and because the amounts involved were minuscule. A *mamlatdar*—the equivalent of a tehsildar in the North—in Broach had taken Rs 20 for certifying two affidavits. His defence was that he had taken the money to meet the target for the Flag Day collections. The trial court, and subsequently a Division Bench of the Gujarat High Court, imposed a fine of Rs 200 and sentenced him to rigorous imprisonment for one year, holding that the Rs 20 had been taken in lieu of an official act, and, therefore, was an offence, even if it were proved that the money had been taken for the Flag Day or for some charitable purpose. In the second case, a *talathi* in Parbhani district, Maharashtra, was said to have taken Rs 100 for making some entries in the mutation register. His defence was that he had not taken the money for himself but to fulfil targets under the small savings and postal deposits schemes. In *M.S.R. Koshinsagar v State of Maharashtra,* the Bombay High Court held that even if he had taken the money to fulfil targets under these schemes, he had done for a consideration what it was his official duty to do. It sentenced him to one year's rigorous imprisonment. If lowly officials were to be sentenced to rigorous imprisonment, and that too for such puny amounts, was a Chief Minister, having collected crores, to go scot-free?

Every defence Antulay and his team thought of got knocked out by the next edition of the paper.

But those defences were only for public consumption. The real defence was directed at Mrs Gandhi, the exact defence that had been directed at her by every crook around her. 'This is not an attack on me. I am nobody. The real target is you. The aim is to weaken you.' Gangrene in her hands, I felt—and wrote. If she cuts them off, she is without hands. If she doesn't, the gangrene spreads through the body.

In the beginning, Mrs Gandhi stood by her man. At first obliquely: 'Our Party is committed to ensuring the highest standards in public life,' she said. Did that mean that, committed as her Party was to ensuring the highest standards, Antulay could have done no wrong? Or that he would go soon? And then, 'Corruption is a global phenomenon.' That hadn't worked in 1974/75, why would it work now? Rajiv Gandhi removed the ambiguity: what Antulay has done is not corruption at all 'in the strict sense of the word', he proclaimed. That was new: Antulay had not done even what so many leaders the globe over were doing. And a week later, 'The people want him,' Mrs Gandhi declared. So, he was to stay, not because Mrs Gandhi wanted him to do so, but because the people wanted him.

With each new dispatch, Antulay's defence became less and less tenable.

The focus now shifted to insulating Mrs Gandhi from the facts. She did not know, it was said. Antulay had used her name without her consent, it was said. The moment she had come to know that Antulay had used her name, she had directed him to remove it . . .

Poor Antulay himself had to swallow a shovelful of his own words. Addressing the press in Delhi on 6 September, he said that Mrs Gandhi had never given consent to her name being used for the Trust; that the document she was shown signing in the photograph was only a blessing from her for the Trust; that it was only he who had assumed that he would eventually be able to persuade her to allow them to use her name in the name of the Trust named after her . . .

Everyone waited for Mrs Gandhi to do something, either way. But Mrs Gandhi wouldn't act. And so tea leaves were scrutinized minutely. She had given 'an audience' to Shalinitai Patil—this meant she was furious with Antulay: 'Observers are of the view that considering she had met Mrs Gandhi at a relatively short notice, it can be safely assumed that the decision to dismiss Mrs Patil had not been cleared by the party high command and that Mr. Antulay had taken this decision on his own. This, the observers say, lowers Mr. Antulay even further with the high command' . . . But just days later, addressing the Congress(I) Parliamentary Party, Mrs Gandhi censured the statements of Shalinitai 'in strong words', and declared that 'indiscipline and dissidence will not be tolerated at any cost'. Pundits now saw Shalinitai's dismissal from ministership as 'a warning to dissidents in other states' . . . One day that Mrs Gandhi had 'snubbed' Antulay, and that as a result Antulay, 'who is generally very careful about his dress and appearance, looked haggard and restrained' . . . The next, that he came out after a thirty-five-minute meeting with Mrs Gandhi and looked 'cheerful'. Asked by the PTI (Press Trust of India) correspondent if this meant he was staying, he replied cheerfully, 'You can draw your own conclusions' . . . Ministers and MLAs from Maharashtra came to Delhi to urge leaders to stand by Antulay, said the newspapers, with some adding that it was not altogether clear whether they were also simultaneously campaigning for their 'own man' to be chosen as successor . . . Mrs Gandhi was to leave on a tour of four countries. Chief Ministers flocked to Delhi to see her off. A directive was issued asking them not to come to the airport. But Antulay was

there. Had he been singled out for the privilege of seeing her off? Or
had he defied the ban? What you thought about Antulay's future
depended on your answer to these weighty questions . . .

One day, 'sources' said Antulay would be removed, 'but not
just now'. Removing him just now would be seen as 'surrendering'
to the Opposition and 'a small section of the press,' and that Mrs
Gandhi 'will never do'. The next, that he will be replaced after the
Parliament session. One day, 'sources' told correspondents that his
departure was imminent. The next, that he could not be removed
just now as Mrs Gandhi was leaving on a four-nation, nine-day
foreign tour, and she would not want uncertainty to prevail in
an important state like Maharashtra while she was away. One
forenoon, that the Congress(I) Working Committee was about to
meet to take a decision. That afternoon, that the Committee could
not meet to settle this 'internal Party matter'.

And then, out of the blue, on 9 September, while answering
a debate on the collections in the Assembly, Antulay announced
that the very day the controversy had broken out, he had sent
his resignation letter to Mrs Gandhi with the request that she
forward it to the Governor whenever she thought appropriate.
This led many to jump to the conclusion that his departure was
imminent. 'A successor to Mr Antulay is expected to be decided
soon—within a week, high command sources said,' reported our
correspondent covering the Congress(I).

And that had an amusing consequence in our offices. Not
to be seen not leading us, Nihal Singh seized the moment. He
wrote a signed piece, 'Mr Antulay goes'—a box item on the top
of columns 1 and 2 on the front page. Even more important than
Antulay's 'impending departure' is 'that the public outcry against
a mushrooming scandal has forced him to go'. 'That Mr Antulay
and some others of his party have chosen to blame, at best in part,
the *Indian Express*, is beside the point. Our shoulders are broad
enough to withstand such attacks.' That caused some merriment:
'*Our shoulders*'? 'Arun,' Pandita exclaimed, '*ab to Antulay gayaa
hi gayaa*—Nihal *bhi beech kood padaa hai*.'[22]

---

[22] 'Arun, now Antulay is gone for sure—even Nihal has jumped in.' K.N.
Pandita was a senior subeditor at the paper, as acerbic as he was meticulous.

But days passed, weeks passed, and Antulay remained. Quite the contrary. On 16 October, a PTI dispatch reported that the Congress(I) High Command has decided not to shift Antulay, and instead has given him a free hand to reshuffle his Cabinet. With no decision being taken, pundits discovered 'reasons' that were holding up a decision. Mrs Gandhi has made up her mind that Antulay should go, but she has not decided who his successor should be. She has yet to decide whether the state should be put under President's Rule for a spell. She is yet to make up her mind about what should be done to the Trusts: Should they be taken over by the state or the central Government? After all, it would not be prudent to leave so much money in the hands of a disgruntled politician.

Opposition leaders started reading their own theses into the absence of a decision. Ramakrishna Hegde said that this only showed that Mrs Gandhi had been involved in Antulay's collections. Atal Behari Vajpayee surmised that Antulay had some document which showed Mrs Gandhi's complicity and might be blackmailing her . . .

A devastating judgment

Soon after the article was published, P.B. Samant and others filed writ petitions in the Bombay High Court. They submitted that the method by which cement had been distributed was contrary to the rule of law and probity in public life, that allocations had been made to builders and others as a quid pro quo for 'donations' they were required to make to the Trusts.

The Government fielded Ashoke Sen, as well as the Advocate General (AG) of Maharashtra and other lawyers. Ashok Desai argued for the petitioners—pro bono. Justice Lentin's judgment is an education to read[23]—it illustrates how an able Judge cuts

The schoolmaster in our paper, he had sharp words for everyone and everything. He was never satisfied with our copy. His names for me varied by the day: 'Sergeant Major' one day, 'Band Master' the next.

[23] The following is based on *P.B. Samant and Ors v State of Maharashtra and Ors*, Misc. Petition No. 1165 of 1981, decided on 12 January 1982.

through deceitful arguments, contrived affidavits and doctored records, and how he sifts through a heap of evidence and gets at the truth. Justice Lentin held that the allocations were arbitrary, that they were made on the explicit instructions of Antulay, that they were made in patent violation of procedures that the Government itself had decided must be followed, and that they were made in return for the 'donations' that the builders made to the Trusts. In the process, Justice Lentin also established how, to help the Chief Minister escape responsibility, a counsel as well-known and senior as Ashoke Sen fabricated arguments, how officers were sought to be made scapegoats, how some of them falsified records and put mendacious constructions on their own directions—to the extent of asserting that they had written such and thus because they had misunderstood the directives and minutes that they had themselves drafted.

Cement was a terribly scarce commodity in those days, and hence commanded a very high premium in the black market. One turned a neat profit merely by getting an allocation of cement. Allocations used to be of two types: for the regular quarterly supplies, and for ad hoc quantities allocated to the state. It turned out that successive meetings had been held by a High Level Committee to settle the processes by which cement would be allocated in the state, in particular the quantities that were to be allotted ad hoc. Minutes were prepared of the proceedings and decisions of the Committee. Eventually a circular was issued on 31 March 1981 embodying the decisions and prescribing the procedures that must be followed for seeking cement and for allocating it.

Minutes of the crucial meeting in which the procedure to be followed was finalized were kept from the Court by the government. When, at last, on the Court's direction they were produced, it was evident as daylight that they had been tampered with; 'corrections or alterations' had been superimposed on and

---

Coram: Justice B. Lentin. MANU/MH/0352/1982. Equivalent citation: 1982 (1) BomCR367. [A few of the spelling and transcription mistakes in MANUPATRA have been corrected.]

interpolated in the text. The matter proceeded in court for several days. The Secretary of the Department, who was in the best position to clarify the matter, offered no explanation for the alterations and additions. He had submitted three affidavits; he could have submitted a fourth one, Lentin noted. After three, a fourth would not have 'overburdened the record'. 'Instead,' Lentin noted, letting Sen off for the unsustainable construction he was pressing as if he had not been properly briefed, 'the onerous task was placed on the shoulders of Mr. Sen to advance an explanation which can be no better than an ipse dixit.'[24] 'These minutes—bristle as they do with additions, alterations and interpolations—are not exactly calculated to inspire any confidence,' Justice Lentin concluded.

As we noticed, the Department had issued the crucial circular on 31 March 1981, embodying the decisions that had been taken at the meeting of the High Level Committee about the norms and procedure to be followed for ad hoc allocations. The officers, led by the Secretary of the Department and Sen, now maintained that the entire circular—it had been issued in the name of the Government and the Governor—was based on a 'mistake', a 'misunderstanding', a 'misconception', a 'wrong interpretation' of what had been decided by the High Level Committee. But it had never been withdrawn!

Lentin noted,

This circular was not a private note to lie forgotten in the morass of Mantralaya files. It was widely circulated. It was made public. It was intended to be acted upon. Even a notice was placed outside the Food and Civil Supplies Department,[25] Mantralaya, that no applications would be received at Mantralaya. This notice remained displayed in any event till June 1981, if not later. No one has yet told me that this notice too was a 'mistake' or the result of 'misunderstanding'. This Government Circular was in fact acted upon . . .

---

[24] A statement based on neither evidence nor reason.

[25] This was the Department that had the formal responsibility for determining how cement would be allocated.

Justice Lentin pointed to an instance. An Association of manufacturers of RCC Grills had sent a request for allotment of cement; the Department had issued a letter to it, reiterating the decisions embodied in the circular, in particular that no requests would be entertained at the Mantralaya. 'Happily,' Lentin noted, 'it was not urged that this letter from Mantralaya itself was also written under "mistake" and "misunderstanding". When I put this query to Mr. Sen, he had the modesty to blush.'

'There is not the slightest doubt in my mind,' Lentin concluded, 'that the hypothesis of "mistake" and "misunderstanding" now advanced at the hearing stage is a myth and a cover-up operation indulged in by the State Government in a belated attempt to extricate itself from the Circular dated 31st March, 1981 . . .'

There had been an earlier meeting, it turned out. About this, the Secretary and the Minister 'have chosen to slur over the minutes', Lentin had to record. And that an effort was now being made to 'lay a red herring, cloud the issue and make a belated basis for mistake and misunderstanding for which there can be no possible foundation except to willy-nilly circumvent' the circular which 'had been issued in the name of the government and the Governor'.

At one crucial point, the AG had mentioned a critical fact that was in flat contradiction to what officials had been telling the Court. Though present when he spoke, they had not corrected him. They had submitted affidavits—'long, tortuous and repetitive affidavits', Justice Lentin noted. They could have submitted a clarification, giving a different version from what the AG had stated. They did nothing of the sort. To get over what the AG had said, the Secretary now asserted that at the time, the AG had spoken as he had because he, the AG, 'did not have full instructions', and that he, the AG, was not aware of an earlier meeting. Lentin was properly upset at this effort to blame the AG: 'The statement made by the learned Advocate General was in the highest traditions of the Bar which he leads. The criticism levelled against him was unwarranted. The attempt on the part of the State Government to mulct the learned Advocate General cannot but be deplored.'

Such efforts having floundered, the blame was shifted to the poor Undersecretary who had signed the circular. The Secretary said that the Undersecretary 'was under a misconception'. The helpless Undersecretary was made to submit an affidavit asserting that he now realized that it 'was not correct and in fact is misconceived'. This affidavit is 'the most pitiable affidavit of the lot', Lentin observed. It is 'supremely vague. It is vacuous in thought and abject in content and gives an uncomfortable feeling whether he too is being made a scapegoat.'

The officers and the Minister 'have chosen to observe a studied and discreet silence as to the point of time when realisation dawned on them that the Government circular dated 31st March, 1981 was begotten in mistake and conceived in misunderstanding'. 'It did not occur to them'—neither to the officers nor to the Minister—'to instruct their own Counsel the learned Advocate General that the Circular dated 31st March, 1981 was the result of mistake and misunderstanding. Mr. Sen cannot blithely dismiss all this as a comedy of errors. It is neither. It is an afterthought, with [the three officers] as willing or unwilling tools, suppression having failed to achieve its purpose.'

Sen argued that the procedures that had been decided by the High Level Committee of the state government could not have been meant for ad hoc allocations as the Central Government had stipulated that the regular quarterly allotments were to be picked up from the manufacturers and moved only by rail, and all ad hoc allotments must be lifted from manufacturers and transported only by road. Even a cursory examination of the movement of cement showed that this was a patently false assertion.

But Sen was not done. He had another argument: the procedures set out in the circular just could not have applied to ad hoc allotments as 'not less than 10%' of the cement moved by road was liable to be 'eaten away by rats and rodents'. Lentin ascribed this argument to Sen's 'piquant sense of humour'.

The circular, the notice that had been put up in the Mantralaya, the letters that had been sent to associations had all stated that no requests for cement would be entertained at the Mantralaya. And yet requests from those who contributed to the Trusts had reached the Chief Minister directly, and they had been acted upon. How? There was no explanation.

And they had orders in Antulay's own hand and over his own signatures. Asked about these, Sen argued that they were 'mere recommendations and not directives'. The Chief Minister received over a thousand representations a day, and met over a hundred persons, each of whom brought representations, Lentin was told, and he sent these to the concerned departments to be acted upon in accordance with prescribed norms and procedures.

The Secretary stated on oath that no quotas were allotted by the Chief Minister personally. That was typical of the pettifogging by which Sen and the government were trying to shield Antulay: of course, he would only direct, and the concerned underling would allot the cement; ergo, Antulay had not allotted any cement! Moreover, said Sen, while forwarding the representations for cement, the Chief Minister had merely written that the Department 'may' allot the cement, that it 'may' try to help, etc.

Lentin called for a random sample of representations for cement from builders who had made contributions to the Trusts. In instance after instance, Antulay had given unambiguous directions that builder 'X' be allocated 'Y' tonnes from supplier 'Z'. Lentin set the results out in the judgment and in an annexure, and noted that they 'unmistakably reflected orders and directives emanating from the 2nd respondent'—that is, Antulay; that:

> These endorsements made by the 2nd respondent unmistakably disclose the peremptory order for allotments. There is nothing in the tone and tenor of these endorsements to indicate an opinion or a recommendation. Even the particular quota from which the allotments must be made has been ordered by the 2nd respondent, leaving the department no choice or discretion in the matter. The explicitness of the tenor of the endorsements conveys the implicitness and exactitude with which they must be carried out.
>
> Despite the protestations of Mr. Chari [the Secretary of the Department] and Mr. Kamale [the Minister] and the 2nd respondent to the contrary, even this limited random survey

unmistakably reveals that allotments were ordered by the 2nd
respondent himself. Mr. Chari and Mr. Kamale have been less
than frank when on oath they say otherwise . . .

When Chari asserted that in some cases, the Chief Minister's
'recommendations' could not be and had not been accepted,
Lentin examined the record, and had to conclude that here was
another assertion without proof or reason, 'with not an iota of
documentary evidence produced before me to establish it'.

Ashoke Sen came up with yet another argument on Antulay's
behalf: 'Mr. Sen says the builders were given allocations so as to
enable them to complete their projects in hand so that the poor
and underprivileged for whom they were constructing, would
not suffer,' Lentin noted, and observed, 'not a single builder has
ventured forth to express this admirable sentiment on affidavit.'

Sen came forth with yet another reason why the builders made
the donations, and did so voluntarily: they made the donations for
their own benefit as they saved taxes by doing so. 'Mr. Sen says
that the tax exemptions enjoyed by the Trusts [were] a potent
factor for attracting donations by persons with surplus income
liable to taxation, with the result that it was in the interest of the
donors themselves to make generous donations to the Trusts,'
Lentin noted, and remarked, 'significantly enough not a single
builder has himself come forward with this explanation. The result
is genius in its very simplicity—the donors got the exemption, the
Trusts got the donations and the builders got the cement.'

Recall that the circular had stated that no representations
should be submitted to the Mantralaya, and yet they were being
received by Antulay directly, and orders on them were being
recorded. Looking at this pattern, Lentin observed,

What also is not without its own significance is the manner in
which the allotment applications found their way to the 2nd
respondent and the manner in which allotments were ordered
by him. Both appear to be cavalier. The applications do not
bear any inward number. They do not even appear to have been
processed. The endorsements themselves do not suggest any

guidelines having been followed or that any enquiries were even
made to ascertain the correctness of the contents of the builders'
applications, which appear to have been taken at face value.

'Arbitrariness and *mala fides* are writ large,' over the decisions,
Lentin observed, after examining more of the record.

For the reason was not far to seek. The random sample of files
revealed that just around the date of the allocation, the builder
in question had, in return, made 'donations' to the Trust. No
explanation was forthcoming for, to use Lentin's phrases, 'this
sudden outburst of generosity', 'this sudden munificence and
outburst of charity the very next day of the allotment . . .' 'The
enthusiasm of the builders, their associates, friends and relations
in making large donations, often in unusual figures, is heart-
warming and bespeaks a generous disposition in the noble cause
of cement,' Lentin concluded.

The effort to conceal the nexus between the 'donations' and
the allocations' was equally manifest, and told the tale. Often,
the payments were made separately in the name of individual
members of the family and in the name of sister concerns.
Unfortunately for Antulay and the Government, in instance after
instance, the 'donations' were made on the same date, and from
related bank accounts. And while, of those examined at random,
one 'donation' was as low as Rs 27 per bag and another was as
high as Rs 70 per bag—'presumably depending on the capacity
of the builder to donate', as Lentin noted—most hovered around
the rate of Rs 40 per bag. 'The rate need not be uniform,' Lentin
noted upon studying the figures, 'what you lose on the swings you
make up on the roundabouts.'

Setting out the allocations, the dates of the allocations, the
dates of the 'donations', in instance after instance, Justice Lentin
concluded that the proximity of the dates of allotments and
payments, of the quantities of cement allotted and the amount
'donated', 'reveal a set and consistent pattern between allotments
and donations', and lead to 'the irresistible inference' that one was
related to the other. In case after case, the record showed that 'the
nexus is established'.

The Judge awarded Rs 7500 towards costs, and directed the Maharashtra Government to pay the amount to Samant.

On 12 January, Justice Lentin delivered his judgment at 3.15 p.m. Maharashtra ministers and legislators who were in Bombay passed a unanimous resolution requesting Mrs Gandhi not to accept Antulay's resignation. And there was a little rapier in the resolution. 'It will be laying down a dangerous precedent,' the resolution declared, 'to accept the resignation of a highly placed person only because of the judgment of a high court, which is subject to appeal'—as clear an allusion as one could frame to the judgment by Justice Jagmohan Lal Sinha of the Allahabad High Court against Mrs Gandhi herself. The resolution said that the issues raised before the High Court 'were also raised by the Opposition at the time of the Nandurbar Lok Sabha and Balapur Assembly by-elections and the people have given their verdict that they are with the Chief Minister'.

But by now the damage to the image of the Party, and to her image, was so grave that even Mrs Gandhi could no longer shield one whom 'the people want'.

As we saw a moment ago, Justice Lentin delivered his judgment at 3.15 p.m.

At 4.20 p.m. Antulay offered to quit.

At 6.50 p.m., there was an announcement from Delhi that the Congress(I) High Command was asking Antulay to resign.

At 9 p.m., the Congress(I) spokesman said that Mrs Gandhi had permitted Antulay to resign.

In Bombay, Antulay said that he was expecting someone to come from Delhi carrying the resignation letter (addressed to the Governor) which he had given to Mrs Gandhi. As no one had come, he had written the letter afresh, and sent it to the Governor.

At 10 p.m., it was announced from the Raj Bhavan that the Governor had accepted Antulay's resignation.

But that was by no means the end of the matter. Cases before Judges other than Justice Lentin had been filed, and they acquired a life of their own. Even to this day, they show how a litigant and his lawyers, with unwitting help from courts, can waylay justice in a maze.

10

The popes are indignant

A BJP corporator, Ramdas Nayak, filed a petition with the Governor of Maharashtra requesting permission to file a complaint against Antulay under the Prevention of Corruption Act and under the Indian Penal Code for cheating, extortion, conspiracy and misuse of public office.

It was soon realized that this meant, in effect, that before filing a complaint against Antulay, Nayak and others should obtain sanction from the Governor, which, in effect, meant from the government, which, in effect, meant from Antulay himself. So, without waiting for sanction from the Governor, Nayak filed a complaint in court urging that Antulay be tried on thirty-three grounds. The question of sanction, and of whether charges should be framed, and, if so, how many and which ones went from the Trial Court to the High Court, and thence to the Supreme Court. And back to the High Court and then back again to the Supreme Court. At least five times. The focus shifted from facts to points of law. As a result, in these judgments Antulay was not the one who was found to have been at fault. The Supreme Court found that the Supreme Court had been at fault.

First Round:[1] While the petition he had filed with the Governor was pending, Nayak filed a private complaint against Antulay—who was still the Chief Minister—before the Court of the Chief Metropolitan Magistrate, Bombay. The Court held that Nayak's complaint was not maintainable as Antulay was a public servant, and no prior sanction from the government had been obtained for filing the complaint. A second writ petition was filed by P.B. Samant against Antulay, alleging abuse of power in several decisions, including decisions that had figured in Nayak's petition. This petition was allowed. Nayak filed an appeal in the High Court against his petition being disallowed.

The High Court rejected Nayak's appeal against the Metropolitan Magistrate's order. As a new government was in office, the state filed an appeal in the Supreme Court against the order of the High Court on Nayak's petition. But the Supreme Court also upheld the Metropolitan Magistrate's view and that of the High Court that, because Antulay was a public servant and prior sanction had not been obtained, the complaint had been rightly dismissed.

Second Round:[2] On the day the Supreme Court gave its order in Delhi, another thing happened in Bombay. The Governor in Maharashtra gave sanction to proceed against Antulay. Armed with it, Nayak filed a fresh complaint before the Court of the Special Judge, Bombay. The Special Judge issued process, as well as bailable warrants against Antulay. Antulay filed objections maintaining that the Special Judge did not have jurisdiction to hear and decide the case. The Special Judge dismissed the objections. Antulay filed a criminal revision petition in the High Court. The Maharashtra government issued a notification assigning the case formally to an Additional Special Judge. The High Court dismissed Antulay's criminal revision petition. The Additional Special Judge began hearing the case. Antulay argued that the charges were baseless, and, as he was no longer the Chief Minister, the sanction

---

[1] *State of Maharashtra v Ramdas Shrinivas Nayak, (1982) 2 SCC 463.*
[2] *R.S. Nayak v A.R. Antulay, (1984) 2 SCC 183.*

that had been accorded by the Governor was irrelevant. He was an MLA and, therefore, sanction was required from the Speaker. The Special Judge accepted Antulay's contention and discharged him. The matter came back to the Supreme Court again. A Constitution Bench of five Judges went into the issue of corruption in public life, the issue of prior sanction, and the meaning of 'public servant'. It held that an MLA is not a 'public servant', and hence the question of obtaining sanction does not arise, and, therefore, it set aside the Trial Court's order of discharge, and held that an accused must be a public servant at the time when cognizance is taken for the issue of sanction to be relevant, and that the sanctioning authority had to be the one which could have removed the public servant at the time when he was accused of abusing his office. On this reasoning, the Court restored the trial against Antulay. It noted that two and a half years had passed since the case had commenced, and it 'has not moved an inch further'. To ensure an expeditious disposal of the case, it directed that the matter be transferred to the High Court, and that 'the learned Judge [to whom the cases are assigned] may proceed to expeditiously dispose of the cases preferably by holding the trial from day to day'.

Third Round:[3] When the matter was taken up by the High Court for being tried, Antulay contended that, even though it was taking up the matter on the direction of the Supreme Court, a Judge of the High Court had no jurisdiction to try the matter, and the case could be tried only by a Special Judge appointed under the Criminal Law Amendment Act of 1952. His contention was rejected by the High Court. Antulay filed an appeal in the Supreme Court.

In another stream, the case was transferred from one Judge of the High Court to another Judge. The latter framed charges on twenty-one grounds, but declined to frame them on twenty-two other grounds which Nayak had listed. Nayak went to the Supreme Court against the decision. The Supreme Court held that

---

[3]   *A.R. Antulay v R.S. Nayak*, (1988) 2 SCC 602.

'the trial court had *prima facie* taken a wrong view and it was a fit case where the charges in respect of which the trial court had made a discharge should also have been framed'. Delivering a strong rebuke, the Supreme Court observed,

> The trial court extracted at great length both the oral evidence as also the contents of documents but there was not much of analysis to justify rejection of the material. It adopted two different standards in the matter of weighing the same evidence, when it agreed to frame 21 charges which were interlinked and interconnected with the rest of the prosecution story with reference to which the 22 draft charges had been given.

On behalf of Nayak, Ram Jethmalani urged that, as the Judge had already expressed himself in regard to the twenty-two charges, the case should be transferred to another Judge. The Supreme Court said that it had no doubt that the Judge had dealt with the matter as seemed just to him, but Nayak had reason to apprehend that he—the Judge—may be constrained by the initial view he had taken. And so, the case may be transferred to another Judge.[4]

The case was thus transferred to a third Judge in the High Court. He framed seventy-nine charges. Antulay approached the Supreme Court, questioning both the decision of the High Court Judge to frame seventy-nine charges, and the constitutionality of the section of the Criminal Procedure Code under which the matter had been assigned for trial to the High Court. The Supreme Court stayed proceedings in the High Court, proceedings which had been initiated at its own directions and which it had said should 'preferably' be held on a day-to-day basis. A Bench of seven Judges examined the extent of the Supreme Court's power to correct its own errors, given the competing principles of 'in the interests of justice' and the 'finality of order'. Judges differed from each other on some points, agreed on some. But overall, they held that the earlier direction of the Supreme Court's five Judges to transfer the matter to the High Court was not good law.

---

[4] *R.S. Nayak v A.R. Antulay, (1986) 2 SCC 716.*

They granted relief to Antulay. A distinguished and erudite Judge, Justice Venkatachalliah, agreed with his fellow Judges on their reasoning but felt that the earlier order transferring the case to the High Court should not be overturned as it would mean that all the evidence that had been recorded before the High Court—and this had taken a year—would have to be recorded all over again before the Special Judge. The majority still sent the case back to the Special Judge to be tried under the 1952 Act.

In a subsequent judgment to which we will come in a moment, the Supreme Court observed,

> The record does not disclose what happened after April 29, 1988. It is not clear whether, and if so when, did the Bombay High Court send the record of the case to Special Judge and if it did so, to which Special Judge. Be that as it may, the fact remains that no further progress was made in the case. It does not even appear that the case was taken up by any Special Judge appointed under the 1952 Act.

Could there be a more pathetic sigh of helplessness? But how can we be surprised? Such circumvention of explicit and urgent orders of the Supreme Court—recall it had urged day-to-day hearings—was a natural result of the Court not punishing anyone for dereliction, a natural result of the 'Hope and Trust' School of Jurisprudence that we have encountered in the cases of undertrials and Bhagalpur blindings.

In May 1989, Nayak approached the Supreme Court to have the Special Judge treat the evidence recorded before the High Court as evidence in the Court of the Special Judge and proceed with the case. Two years passed. The request was never taken up.

Although two years had passed since its 1988 order, the state government had not even appointed the Special Judge under the 1952 Act, to say nothing of his proceeding with the case. An advocate filed a petition requesting the Supreme Court to direct the state government to notify the appointment of a Special Judge for the purpose. A year passed, and nothing happened. Eventually, this petition was tagged on to another case, one involving the trial of another advocate in the murder of L.N. Mishra, a murder that had taken place in 1975—fifteen years earlier. When the matter was taken up, the Advocate General of Maharashtra said that there was no need to take it up as the state government would notify the appointment within two months. Accepting the assurance of the Advocate General, the Supreme Court decided that 'the relief sought in the petition no longer survives and the rule issued earlier stands discharged'.

Fourth Round:[5] It was now Antulay's turn to approach the Supreme Court under Article 32,[6] requesting it to quash all proceedings against him on the ground that his Right to a Speedy Trial had been violated. This time, the Supreme Court held that Antulay's plea did not stand in the face of his own conduct in raising objections, all of which save one were rejected by the courts. Hence, the Court held, ' . . . we are of the opinion that this is not a fit case for quashing the criminal proceedings. The proper direction to make is to direct expeditious trial on a day-to-day basis.' In a word, the Court was back to giving the direction it had given years earlier, and noted now that *that* direction had had no effect!

Fifth Round:[7] What Justice Venkatachalliah had warned would happen, happened. The Supreme Court now held that evidence

[5] *Abdul Rahman Antulay v R.S. Nayak, (1992) 1 SCC 225.*

[6] Article 32: *Remedies for enforcement of rights conferred by this Part:* (1) The right to move the Supreme Court by appropriate proceedings for the enforcement of the rights conferred by this Part is guaranteed. (2) The Supreme Court shall have power to issue directions or orders or writs, including writs in the nature of habeas corpus, mandamus, prohibition, quo warranto and certiorari, whichever may be appropriate, for the enforcement of any of the rights conferred by this Part. (3) Without prejudice to the powers conferred on the Supreme Court by clauses (1) and (2), Parliament may by law empower any other court to exercise within the local limits of its jurisdiction all or any of the powers exercisable by the Supreme Court under clause (2). (4) The right guaranteed by this article shall not be suspended except as otherwise provided for by this Constitution.

[7] *R.S. Nayak v A.R. Antulay, (1992) 1 SCC 279.*

recorded before the High Court—which had taken one year
to record, had run to over 1200 pages, and had involved the
examination and cross-examination of fifty-seven witnesses and
a large number of documents, 963 to be precise—was non est in
view of its 1988 judgment. The entire evidence would have to be
treated as not existing and would have to be led again before a
Special Judge.

What happened in the ensuing years, I leave as an exercise for
the reader to find out.

Mrs Gandhi's 'the people want him' defence also having failed,
Antulay had resigned. And though, later on, he was inducted in
the Central Council of Ministers in some marginal portfolios, in
effect, his public life never quite acquired the dazzle of those years.

In the years that followed, I ran into him on two/three
occasions. He was invariably polite, even affectionate. Once he
rang up. I wasn't home. Anita had picked up the phone and
explained that I had gone out. '*Mainey unhein khaaney par
bulaaney ke liye phone kiyaa thaa,*' Antulay said. '*To, Bhabi, aap
khaaney par ayengi?*'[8]

He died in 2014.

'*Are we idiots and nincompoops?*'

As I mentioned, with their demands for the Question Hour to be
suspended, for them to be allowed to mention Antulay's collections
in the Zero Hour, with their Calling Attention Motions, and their
Adjournment Motions being rejected, several Opposition members
filed breach of privilege notices against Venkataraman. Other
Opposition members filed notices against me. If I was right, he
had misled the House. If Venkataraman was right, I had tarnished
the image of a member of Parliament even as he was performing
his duty in Parliament. Furthermore, said P. Ramamurthi, the CPM
member, I had made members of Parliament out to be 'idiots and

---

[8] 'I had called to invite him for dinner. So, Bhabi, you will come for dinner,
    won't you?'

THE POPES ARE INDIGNANT

nincompoops' who just sat and listened to lies. So, I had brought the entire institution into disrepute.

Two gentlemen

Venkataraman was a soft-spoken, competent gentleman. He would go on to become a fair and gracious President who stuck by the rules, 'a copy-book President' he said of himself. All that could have been said of him in regard to his statements in Parliament was, 'He is just doing what he must have been told to do.' The Lok Sabha was presided over by a conventional, physically lofty politician—Balram Jakhar. The Rajya Sabha had a distinguished Vice President at the time: Justice Mohammad Hidayatullah. He had been the Chief Justice of the country. More than that, he was a fair and gracious gentleman, a man of wide learning. But, like Venkataraman, he too was in a fix. So he mixed courtly hair-splitting with loftiness, and let both of us off!

Jakhar dismissed all privilege motions post-haste on two grounds. He said that Venkataraman had not misled the House when he said that Mrs Gandhi had not given her consent to the Trust being named after her, and, second, when he told the House that she had not inaugurated the Trust. He had seen the original document which Mrs Gandhi had signed, he said. It mentioned the name of the Trust as 'Pratibha Pratishthan'—by affixing her signature, that is what Mrs Gandhi had agreed to be associated with, not some 'Indira Gandhi Pratibha Pratishthan'. And the Trust had been registered only on 11 November 1980. So, there was no question of her having inaugurated it during the function in the Raj Bhavan on 11 October 1980.

The grounds were specious as can be. I will deal with the 'Pratibha Pratishthan' versus 'Indira Gandhi Pratibha Pratishthan' in a moment—as it was common to Jakhar's ruling and to that of Vice President Hidayatullah. On the 11 October versus 18 November, the facts were glaring. There were the photograph and caption distributed by the Maharashtra Government which spoke to the contrary, and the effusive thanks that Antulay had showered on Mrs Gandhi for consenting to have the Trust named after her. Jakhar dismissed all these. That newspapers had given a wrong impression 'does not alter the basic fact that the document signed by the Prime Minister referred only to "Pratibha Pratishthan, Maharashtra"', Jakhar maintained. But what about what had been stated by the Maharashtra Government in its publications, and what the Chief Minister himself had said? I am not concerned with what the Maharashtra Government or the Chief Minister said outside the House, Jakhar ruled; I am only concerned with what the Minister—Venkataraman—has said in the House. That was odd, to put it mildly. What Venkataraman had said had to be weighed against contemporaneous evidence.

In addition, there were a host of other facts. Madhu Dandavate brought these to the notice of Jakhar and the House, and also the press. He showed that between the function on 11 October and the date of registration, 18 November, the Maharashtra Government had itself deposited the first instalment of Rs 10 lakh from the Rs 2 crore it had decided to donate to the Trust. Nine other 'donors' too had deposited their 'donations'. So, registered it may not have been, but the Trust was receiving monies, all right. Dandavate also produced a letter written by Sudarshan Arya, the Honorary Secretary, of the 'Indira Gandhi Pratibha Pratishthan' on 4 August 1981. It was typed on the letterhead of the 'Indira Gandhi Pratibha Pratishthan'. It asked the Secretary, Deccan Sugar Factories Association, Bombay, to obtain contributions for the Trust from the Association's members 'on the basis as has been done by the Cooperative Sugar Factories'. Dandavate said that he also had in his possession a number of receipts for the 'donations' that had been deposited but was not making them public as he did not want to cause difficulties for the 'donors'. We published the text of the letter that Dandavate released as he told the press that he was filing a fresh breach of privilege notice against Venkataraman. Later, Dandavate also pointed to a letter that had been sent out by Vasant Deshmukh, the Liaison Officer in the Chief Minister's Secretariat, on 27 October 1980 stating that Mrs Gandhi had been so kind as to permit association of her name with the Trust. To top it all, the bank account was in the name of 'Indira Gandhi Pratibha Pratishthan'. But Jakhar, having writ, would not budge.

While Jakhar was merely brazen, Justice Hidayatullah was both erudite and condescending.[9] Justice Hidayatullah noted that when Venkataraman was asked for his response to the privilege motions against him, Venkataraman had said—I am using the words of Justice Hidayatullah from his ruling:

> Now what happened in this case was that the Chief Minister said that he wanted to establish a Pratibha Pratishthan, which would do all sorts of services, being [bring?] an El Dorado into the world to help the poor people, serve the poor people, help everybody and so on. What she agreed to was that the pratishthan should be established, and not that her name should be associated with it and when she came to know about it, she asked them to withdraw her name. Therefore, there is no question of her having called them to associate her name with these things.
>
> He also said, as he put it later in his reply to me, 'I had also stated that the Prime Minister did not inaugurate the Trust.' These two facts were stated to be misleading.

'There is no document, letter or other,' Justice Hidayatullah ruled, 'in which this consent [of her name being used for the Trust] was given or asked for, except the document the Prime Minister is signing as shown in the photograph. The document mentioned the name of the Trust as "Pratibha Pratishthan, Maharashtra". There was no mention of the new name or that the old name would be changed.'

While such subterfuge might have been all right for a conventional politician like Jakhar, it was not befitting of such a learned and good man. The use of the name of a high dignitary such as the President or Prime Minister was governed by 'the Emblems and Names (Prevention of Improper Use) Act' of 1950.

---

[9] For the ruling of Justice Hidayatullah, see https://rajyasabha.nic.in/rsnew/privileges_digest/priv-40.pdf; or Rajya Sabha Debates, 11 September 1981.

Hidayatullah would have been well acquainted with it, given his long and distinguished judicial career. In any case, he could have easily looked it up: it is just a two-page Act, after all. This Act forbids the use of the name, among others, of a Prime Minister 'without the previous permission of the Central Government or of such officer of Government as may be authorised in this behalf by the Central Government'. As a result, a Prime Minister's name could not have been associated with an organization without the written consent of the person. In other words, the Trust set up as 'Pratibha Pratishthan' could become 'Indira Gandhi Pratibha Pratishthan' only *after* she gave her written consent. And things had happened in that exact sequence: the Trust was set up as 'Pratibha Pratishthan'; she signed the papers; and it was rechristened as 'Indira Gandhi Pratibha Pratishthan'. We had been told all this by none other than the Office of the Charities Commissioner, Bombay. Soon after Justice Hidayatullah gave his ruling, I spelled it out with some glee.

And there is a reason for this legal requirement, I wrote.

> What if Gundu Rao established his 'Indira Gandhi Natak Mandali,' and Bhajan Lal his 'Indira Gandhi Bhajan Mandali,' and someone else the 'Indira Gandhi Salon'? While formally registering the trust named after Mrs Gandhi the Charities Commissioner required by law a document showing that Mrs Gandhi had consented to her name being associated with the trust. That is why Mrs Gandhi signed the document—there being no other reason for her doing so—and that is why the document was filed with the Charities Commissioner—there being no other reason for Antulay and Co. doing so. This is what A.R. Antulay, bar-at-law, did on October 11, 1980. And in this entire episode that was the one thing that he did strictly as required by law.

The Trust just could not have been named after her till she signed the document, and it was so named after she signed it. 'Before advising me to be more careful on my facts, Mr Hidayatullah, should you not have been more careful on your law?' I ended with:

I am afraid, therefore, the question posed by Mr P Ramamurti, CPM, in the Rajya Sabha is the one that really does demand an answer, 'Are we,' he asked, referring to himself and his fellow members, 'in this House idiots to accept the charge that deliberate lies are told to Parliament?'[10]

Well?

Justice Hidayatullah disposed of the photograph by similar reasoning. 'There is a photograph, and a caption,' he observed: '*Pratibha Pratishthan, Maharashtra brobar Sahabhaagi houvas male atiyashe anand ahe (Sd. Indira Gandhi).*'

The dictionary meaning of the word '*Sahabhaagi*' is 'co-partner' or 'associated with', Justice Hidayatullah noted. So, Mrs Gandhi was simply saying that she was happy to associate herself with the good work that was going to be done by the Pratibha Pratishthan.

Justice Hidayatullah went further, and stepped deeper into the mire of facts. He ruled:

> There is only one letter from the Prime Minister's office, dated June 23, 1981 in reply to the letter of the Chief Minister, dated 7th May, 1981. That was long before this matter in Parliament. In that letter the Special Assistant to the Prime Minister said:
>
> '. . . The Prime Minister does not approve of her name being used by the Pratishthan. She desires that the name may be changed even at this stage.'

But there was a problem. 'It is asked by Shri Shourie what the Prime Minister was doing from 11th October, 1980 to 23rd June, 1981, when she asked that her name be dropped?' Justice Hidayatullah observed, and provided an ingenious explanation:

> If Government machinery moved [at] the speed of an express train, it would be possible, but we know that it does not. The

---

[10] P. Ramamurthi of the CPM was one of the MPs who had submitted privilege notices against me. He had said in his speech that in my article, I had made MPs out to be 'idiots and nincompoops', sitting and listening to lies.

criticism against the Trust had not built up till lately. It appears
that between the P.M. and the C.M. there was a communication
gap and one thought that the consent was given and the other
was clear that it was not.

So, no one was wrong, just the speed of governmental trains!

But then what about photographs and accounts of the function
at the Raj Bhavan in which Antulay was reported as having
thanked Mrs Gandhi for allowing the Trust to be named after her?
Justice Hidayatullah was again very gracious and understanding.
He ruled:

> I have read both the English and Marathi versions and I feel
> that Shri Antulay probably spoke in Marathi. If that were so
> the Prime Minister would not be fixed with knowledge with
> that move. Even if this was spoken in English, the purport could
> be missed.

And so in conclusion, Justice Hidayatullah ruled:

> I have not expressed any personal opinion, but have gone from
> 'Facts to Facts only'. These facts clearly prove that if anybody
> told a lie it was not the Finance Minister.

But then, who had erred?

> It is perhaps to be inferred that the Maharashtra Government
> went too far with so little from the Prime Minister. I accordingly
> withhold my consent to raise a question of privilege against the
> Finance Minister.

But that still left the privilege notices against me. Here, loftiness
came to the rescue:

> As regards Shri Arun Shourie, I do not think this is a proper
> case for action. Newspapers always look into things closely
> and critically. They must, however, ascertain their facts better.

Although the item is phrased in language which is not high-toned or polite, I am going to ignore it. Arun Shourie was doing a journalistic duty according to his lights. I have said before that the newspapers are the eyes and ears of the public and if every citizen has a right to criticize the actions of others, so also the newspapers whose profession is to turn the light of publicity on the irregularities of public actions. Perhaps the Maharashtra Government itself presented a wrong picture of the events and it is enough to show that Shri Shourie was wrong in his inferences. I must however say that Shri Shourie could have said the same thing in inoffensive language. He went too far because he accepted as true which was false and described as lies which were the real facts. I propose, therefore, to let this matter rest in his case. I withhold consent in his case also.

Forty years later, I remain a votary of such loftiness—in others!

Calumny

Antulay had many megaphones in the press—for among mountebanks, he was a likeable one, one who spread his 'hospitality' far and wide. And then there was the strongman aura, 'the Sultan of Bombay'—always a lure for businessmen, including businessmen with magazines, and intellectuals running papers.

Across and on top of a page, a Bombay-based society glossy magazine, printed a photograph of our little Adit laughing in my arms. In the text below, it declared that I had written against Antulay because, hold your breath, Antulay had attacked America for supplying arms to Pakistan, and I was in the pay of the CIA![11]

---

[11] The originator of this canard was not far to seek. Recall that, replying to a five-hour debate on the collections, Antulay had addressed the Assembly on 9 September. He had alluded to dark conspiracies behind what I had written. He had said that he was 'surprised to notice that the Opposition and Mr Goenka had suddenly started criticising his decisions and fund collections although they were started almost a year ago'. Our reporter covering the Assembly debate had added, 'The Chief Minister implied that there were

That wouldn't have hurt at all. After all, it was the sort of dung that was flung at everyone those days. Just a few years earlier, Mrs Gandhi herself had been proclaiming that JP's movement was being run by 'the foreign hand', and her drummers were proclaiming that JP himself was a CIA agent. What incensed me no end was what followed. The magazine told its readers that I had been using the *'pretext'* of our son's illness to 'regularly visit [my] foreign bosses abroad'. Since I had returned in 1976, I had been abroad only once. And that for a heartbreaking reason. As I have noted earlier, Adit had been having spells of myoclonic jerks—ten to twelve spells a day. For his treatment, he—and Anita and I—had been staying at AIIMS. He had been so heavily drugged by the neuro-physicians that he had become like a handkerchief, and yet the frightening jerks were continuing. The doctors advised us to take him to the Great Ormond Street Children's Hospital in London. That was the only time I had been abroad. And this poor child's illness had been converted into a *'pretext'*?

I filed a defamation case against the damned magazine. They were represented by a well-known—and no doubt a very expensive—lawyer, Pherose R. Vakil. During the hearings, his expertise and value were certainly evident in one sphere of law: getting adjournments for his client. Adjournment followed adjournment. As for the submissions of the magazine, they said that they had the highest regard and respect for Arun Shourie. That they did not believe the story to be true at all. They said that they had printed it to alert readers that if such things can be said even about Arun Shourie, then what cannot be said about anyone else. That was rubbish, of course. But by that time I had been removed from the *Express* and didn't have the money to keep journeying from Delhi to Bombay for each hearing. Most against my will, I had to settle for an apology being printed in the magazine.

CIA connections behind the campaign that was launched against him more vigorously after his address at the intelligentsia convention held recently in Bombay.' This was the address in which Antulay was said to have denounced America for supplying weapons to Pakistan.

But there were bigger guns round the corner. Girilal Jain, the Editor of the *Times of India,* devoted an entire page and the third of another page to 'the new journalism' and the 'new journalist'. He called us 'Galahads of the press'.[12] He must have thought it to be a devastating assault. To me it seemed an unnecessarily defensive and a nervously on-the-one-hand-but-on-the-other-hand one. And '*Galahad*'? Wasn't he one of the most illustrious knights of King Arthur's table, one of the three who achieved the Holy Grail? Giri must have thought his piece to be not just devastating, but devastatingly ironic!

As I was lecturing others, I should get used to being lectured to, Giri wrote. While 'old' journalists were as 'self-righteous and self-assured' as new ones like me, there was a difference, he wrote. The former had 'come up the ladder the hard way and have had something to do with the freedom movement'—'something to do with the freedom movement', you mean these very ones who had just risen from singing hosannas for the Emergency? The latter, 'brash young men', had 'shot into well-paid jobs and prominence literally overnight'. It is the 'prominence' which must have rankled, for no one could have thought that anyone working for Ramnathji was 'well paid'. He compared himself to 'an old Marwari who went to Calcutta with a pair of dhotis and a lota'— that was how Ramnathji used to describe himself. And us, with 'his son or grandson who has had enough exposure to the West to be able to borrow its lifestyle—the safari suit, Scotch whisky, night-long parties, visits to discotheques and dancing'. Inaccurate, to the dot! I hadn't had, and have still not acquired a safari suit, and was, in fact, traduced in those days for being an Arya Samaji ascetic, a moralizing teetotaller.

But, Giri continued, while in business, 'irresponsibility quickly leads to bankruptcy, someone else bears the cost of brashness in journalism. That someone else can be poor Mother India.' Paragraphs followed describing, actually, how easy it was for me to have gathered evidence against Antulay—he had condemned himself by his own words; in any case, he had got money by

---

12 *Times of India,* 11 October 1981.

cheques; in any case, he had set up Trusts which were open to scrutiny.

This exculpation of Antulay was instructive in itself because it was, and remains, typical of apologia. Here is how Giri put the defence:

> The muckrakers have been divided on the Antulay issue. Some of them have bravely risen to his defence, arguing that the whole system is corrupt and rotten to the core and that, if anything, Mr. Antulay has acted more honourably than many others in office inasmuch as he has collected the funds in question openly through cheques and put them into trusts whose activities and expenditure can be scrutinised. There is merit in this view, but only by the standards of the new public morality that has come to prevail in our country. Mr. Antulay may be an honourable man. But he has violated the elementary rules of decent and honest public life. As such, it is only proper that his actions should have been exposed to public scrutiny.

First, notice that the absolutions Giri was offering had been advanced almost to the word by that buffoonish supporter and advocate of Antulay—Kalpnath Rai, then General Secretary of the Congress(I). Speaking to the press in Hyderabad on 28 September, he had declaimed, 'Mr Antulay has done no wrong . . . no wrong . . . no wrong.' He had praised Antulay, saying that he has been extorting money 'openly and not secretly'. Moreover, 'It is all by way of cheques. Therefore, what is the secret about it?' He has stood by Mrs Gandhi, Kalpnath Rai reminded the pressmen, and 'is a trusted friend of Congress-I'. Kalpnath Rai had denounced the campaign being built against 'a competent and minority chief minister.' 'It is for the High Command to decide whether Mr Antulay should continue or step down,' he declared. But if he has done nothing wrong, why should he step down? the pressmen asked. 'Sometimes a man who enjoys the confidence of the people is also asked to step down in the national interest.'[13]

---

[13] *Indian Express,* 29 September 1980.

Echoing the official drummers was just one feature of what Giri Lal had written. The equally instructive aspect was the way he had deployed two well-practised devices of the apologist. First, always put the exculpation you want to advance in someone else's mouth: 'Some of them have bravely risen to his defence . . . There is merit in this view . . .'—and then cushion it with a few words that exculpate you—'but only by the standards of the new public morality that has come to prevail in our country.' Second, give currency to the apologia and immediately follow it up with censure: 'Mr. Antulay may be an honourable man. But he has violated . . .' Contrast this sort of on-the-one-hand-but-on-the-other, with the clarity with which Justice Lentin recapitulated the principle involved, and the principle is a simple one:

> . . . Once nexus is established, *mala fides* must be a natural sequitur, and it cannot militate from the principle involved to say that from several other builders donations were received but no allocation was made. And the principle involved is that there can be no *quid pro quo* in allotment of an essential commodity, however laudable the object of the charity donated to may be considered to be. It cannot be said in defence or mitigation that the donations were openly received by cheque and are accounted for by the Trusts or that they did not go into the pocket of the 2nd respondent [Antulay] himself. None of this would make any difference. It would even have made no difference had the 2nd respondent not been connected with these Trusts. That he is, makes it worse.[14]

The real crime of the brash new, always-on-an-ego-trip journalist—yours truly, that is—was that he did not realize that there is a difference between persecution and exposure, Giri declaimed, that many things had to be done for reasons of State, for the security of the country, which persons like me, steeped in partisanship,

---

[14] Justice B. Lentin, *P.B. Samant and Ors v State of Maharashtra and Ors*, Misc. Petition No. 1165 of 1981, decided on 12 January 1982, para. 40.

did not realize. What this had to do with Antulay's collections, I did not know; even he had not claimed that the collections in lieu of decisions were for defending the Motherland. Not being able to discern the connection we may have been, but we learnt of a new explanation for Nixon sending that team to break into the Watergate apartment, and how it explained some remittance during Mrs Gandhi's Prime Ministership into a foreign account. Far-fetched? Read what Giri wrote to damn me without directly damning me:

> This [the difference between persecution and exposure] is beginning to be recognised in the United States itself which has fathered 'new' journalism, like much else in our times. There the more discerning among the journalists have come to feel that perhaps President Nixon was unjustly pilloried and that there were security reasons which led him first to set up the special group which broke into the Democratic Party headquarters and then to try to hush up the Watergate affair. It has since been disclosed that he was worried lest a Soviet diplomat in contact with the CIA be exposed. It has turned out that the Soviet diplomat was deliberately misleading the U.S. administration. He has returned to Moscow. But that is a different issue. At that time, his reports were going directly to Mr. Nixon and Mr. Kissinger and Mr. Nixon regarded it important to protect this source.
>
> A certain payment by the government of India into a foreign bank account when Mrs. Gandhi was the Prime Minister fell into the reasons of the same category. This was apparently why the Janata government finally chose to drop this matter. But it was raised in order to malign Mrs. Gandhi.

But how would the 'new journalist' care? He is 'on an endless ego trip', 'he is highly self-righteous and aggressive—a Savonarola-like figure who does not mind setting fire to the city so that the "evil" in it is expurgated [sic]'. What the 'new journalist' is doing will lower the country's image abroad, and that will make it more difficult for the country to get the loans it desperately needs. 'Such considerations cannot bother the crusader clad in his armour of self-righteousness,' Giri pronounced. 'He must destroy the cities of Sodom and Gomorrah whatever the cost.'

Did this 'new journalist' not realize, Giri asked, that by attacking Antulay, he was weakening Mrs Gandhi, that by weakening Mrs Gandhi he was putting the country in danger of foreign invasion? Too far-fetched? This is how Giri put the argument:

> The haters of Mrs. Gandhi and the Nehru family will not mind a general or a colonel in power in New Delhi . . . Perhaps things have been allowed to drift too far. Perhaps Mrs. Gandhi has been too lackadaisical in bringing to book men and women who have allowed their greed to run away with not only their moral values but also their discretion. The way out, however, is not to destroy the one possible instrument for getting hold of the situation at home and of coping with the gathering storm on its borders.

And who is 'the one possible instrument'? Mrs Gandhi, of course.

> Ayub Khan ordered the infiltration into Kashmir in 1964 because he felt Lal Bahadur Shastri was weak and indecisive. Zia-ul-Haq is arming Pakistan with U.S. help. Can anyone guarantee that he will not try to seize Kashmir and humiliate India if there is loss of authority in New Delhi? And can he dare so long as Mrs Gandhi is around and is known to be in command of the affairs of this nation?

Presumably, it was this exact identification—of Mrs Gandhi, security of the Indian State, and the Indian State itself—which must have led Giri and his mentor, Shamlal, to have supported the Emergency as zealously as they did. The 'new journalists' did not seem to have these doubts about what my colleagues and I were doing. *India Today* carried a cover story about the article, and what I was doing:

Journalistic coup:
Arun Shourie exposes Maharashtra CM
A.R. Antulay's collection of funds

Almost overnight Arun Shourie, the executive editor of the Indian
Express, *became a national 'hero'. In a swift bloodless journalistic
coup, Shourie achieved the impossible—exposing Maharashtra's
blue-eyed boy, Chief Minister A.R. Antulay's collection of funds.
Behind the barbed-wire writings is a man with a cause, a solitary
chronicler holding up the mirror to degenerate political values. A
profile on the media's lone crusader and his work.*

It was the classic journalistic coup, swift, bold and utterly
bloodless. What nearly a million readers of the 10 English-
language editions of the *Indian Express* found on the front
page of their newspaper on the morning of August 31 was not
just another sensationalist story involving a chief minister and
his arm-twisting fund collection drive but the beginnings of a
national cause celebre that involved the highest authorities in
the land.

As the sordid Antulay saga unfolded over the next two
weeks, challenging the institution of Parliament and its presiding
officers, involving the prime minister and the finance minister,
and mobilising the Opposition and ruling parties in a series
of assaults, the focus never shifted from the originator of the
mammoth media exercise: the lone, crusading figure sitting
in his newspaper office, slowly but single-mindedly compiling
evidence, cultivating sources and collecting clues before
mounting the most savage scenario indicting public and political
life in modem Indian times.

What has since come to be known as India's Watergate—or
Antulay's Trustgate scandal—was the result of no random leak,
no subversive hint surreptitiously passed on, nor the sum total
of common tittle-tattle gleaned from a bunch of squealers; it was
a consciously studied and calculatedly pursued investigation of
organised corruption in high places, a meticulously-researched
exposure with supporting evidence that ran into 7,500 words
and 140 column-inches of blistering copy.

In one fell blow, one journalist had achieved the impossible: of not only putting together the pieces of a complex financial puzzle, but presenting them in the highly personalised charge of not a hack polemicist but a pulpit preacher . . .

Even more sensational than Shourie's exposure of Antulay was the sustained tone of his counter-attacks in the forum of his newspaper. When Finance Minister R. Venkataraman stood up in the Lok Sabha to categorically deny the allegations Shourie's expose contained—of the prime minister consenting to her name being used for Antulay's trust—Shourie retaliated by accusing Venkataraman of 'petty lies'.

When Rajya Sabha Chairman M. Hidayatullah, former chief justice, further ruled that Venkataraman was not only right but that both Shourie's facts and language were incorrect, Shourie bounced back with yet more incriminating evidence 'to be able to trap even a former chief justice.' As for Venkataraman, Shourie stepped up his condemnation with the proviso that 'the fact is not just that Venkataraman's statement was a lie but it could not but be a lie.'

As for Hidayatullah, in a massively documented letter answering the breach of privilege notices against him, Shourie not only ascertained why the finance minister had lied and evaded questions but also claimed that as a free citizen it was his constitutional right and duty under Article 51A 'to alert as many citizens as I can reach if a minister misleads MPs, and that by writing "Petty little lies in the Parliament" I acted as a friend of the House, as one who cherishes its functions and values its role, as one who is outraged that an attempt was made to mislead it.'

Shourie's arguments, adhering to parliamentary jargon, were obviously so cogent that the presiding officer preferred to disregard the breach of privilege rather than pursue it and cause further embarrassment to the Government.

It was the kind of head-on confrontation between press, and Parliament that had seldom been witnessed before, with the individual journalist baiting the might of ruling authority in public and equally blatantly denigrating Parliament to defend his beliefs.

Shourie emerged from the imbroglio, miraculously unscathed: he had not only rocked Parliament but for a moment numbed it to the point of paralysis: with both Houses rejecting breach of privilege motions against himself and Venkataraman, Shourie had won his victory . . .

And, if Shourie represents a new phenomenon in Indian journalism, the greatest irony lies in the fact that he is a non-journalist, someone who neither earned his spurs in a newspaper environment nor coveted the conventional clout of Indian editors whom he refers to as the *'Times of Indira'* phenomena with as much disdain as he talks of the profession as the 'Indian Journalists Service' . . .

Arun Shourie has the mentality of a flagrantly driven religious zealot among mildly self-opinionated priests. Among everyday cruisers he is a crusader extraordinary.

No wonder the popes were indignant.

11

A trader in Unions

Ramnathji was well known for paying much less than journalists got in other papers. The freedom he gave them was the real emolument. I remember sending him a clipping once from some British paper in which an employer who was going to pay substantially more than his rivals had remarked, 'If you pay peanuts, you will only get monkeys.' RNG sent the cutting back with a scribble in the margin, 'If I have monkeys, should I not pay them peanuts?' But in one instance, I. Mahadevan, a scholar of the first rank who had been in the IAS (Indian Administrative Service) and was at the time editor of *Dinamani,* the Tamil daily of the *Indian Express* group, Gurumurthy and I were able to persuade Ramnathji to go against his usual practice.

Every few years, a 'Wage Board' headed by a retired Judge used to be notified. It would specify emoluments that should be paid to workers and journalists in the press. Almost invariably, the Award would be challenged by proprietors. Ever so often, the Award, challenged or not, would just not be implemented. A Wage Board, headed by Justice Palekar, had submitted its report in August 1980. The government had announced its acceptance of the Board's recommendations for journalists in December that year, and for employees other than journalists a year later. This time round, the *Express* group was among the very first to announce that it would implement the Award. We were quite proud of this, given what was expected of Ramnathji.

I was in Delhi. Ranganathan, the Manager in Bombay, called. He told me that Datta Samant was going to bulldoze our workers into a strike. Samant was a dreaded figure in those days. Along with a few other 'Trade Union leaders'—I looked upon them as 'Traders in Unions'—he had brought Bombay's industry to its knees. He was also known for instigating his followers to violence. Ramnathji said that he would rush to Bombay and deal with Samant—not to settle terms of some compromise but to tell Samant that he would not budge a hair's breadth. 'If he comes in as union leader,' Ramnathji said, 'the issue will be who owns the paper, me or him. He will run the paper.' Gurumurthy and I talked Ramnathji out of rushing to Bombay to meet Samant. We felt that Samant should stew in uncertainty about Ramnathji's next moves, and Ramnathji should remain the court with which the final decision will lie. Ramnathji then decided that I should fly to Bombay instead.

I was told that I could meet Samant in Rajni Patel's office. Rajni Patel was equally famous. He had known Panditji, and was said to be close to Mrs Indira Gandhi—he had been made head of the Congress in Bombay. He was plugged into many circuits— from the courts, to the Communists. He had been the spirit behind setting up the Nehru Centre in Bombay. I was told that there was a sort of routine with Samant also. Samant would decree a strike. Rajni Patel would step in, mediate, and settle the dispute.

I went over to Rajni Patel's office. I remember it as being rather small for such a prominent man. Rajni Patel was seated behind his desk. Samant and I sat in front of him on the other side.

After the usual preliminaries, I asked Samant in Hindi, '*Par kyon? Aap hamaarey yahaan* strike *kyon karwaanaa chaahtey ho?*'[1]

'*Goenka ne Palekar Award laagoo naheen kiyaa,*'[2] he said.

---

[1] 'But why? Why do you want to stop our paper?'
[2] 'Goenka has not implemented the Palekar Award.'

'*Aapko bilkul ghalatfehmi hai*,'[3] I said. I told him that the *Express* group had, in fact, been the first to implement the Award. The arguments went to and fro. It soon became evident that Samant didn't care for the facts, nor for the workers. He had started on the assertion that the group had not agreed to honour the Palekar Award. The moment I had explained that this time round Ramnathji had announced that he *would* increase emoluments to scales prescribed in the Award, Samant said, '*To phir har ek ko 3,000 rupaye aur do.*'[4]

'*Teen hazaar kyon?*' I said. '*Paanch hazaar kyon naheen?*'[5] There has to be some basis for demands, I said. This way the paper would be driven to bankruptcy. I told him that persons working in the paper were proud of what the paper stood for and what it was doing, that they would not agree to drive it to bankruptcy.

Arguments continued. He then took my hand: '*Merey log tumhein voh he karenge jo unhon ne Godrej ko kiyaa hai*'—and he made a motion as if to stab me.[6] With my hand still in his but with the grip reversed, I said, '*Aur hum* Express *vaaley aap ki dhakhaa-baazzi ko aise haraaen gey ki aapke paanv saarey Bombay se ukhad jaaengey.*'[7]

Ramnathji had the capacity to risk everything at the very first throw, to play the last card first. So, Gurumurthy and I had little difficulty in persuading him to issue a notice of closure of the paper. A statement was issued and notices put up in and around the *Express* offices in Bombay that the offices and press would be locked and editions shut for three months, and after that, they would be permanently closed.

Samant was flummoxed by RNG's response. At that time, under the Industrial Disputes Act, an enterprise needed to take

---

3   'You are completely mistaken.'
4   'Then give another Rs 3000 to each.'
5   'Why three thousand? Why not five thousand?'
6   'My people will do to you exactly what they have done to Godrej.' N.B. Godrej, senior member of the Godrej family, had been stabbed in Poona and had died. Datta Samant was charged with murder, later acquitted.
7   'And we at the *Express* will defeat your strong-arm methods so completely that you will lose your foothold in Bombay.'

government permission to close down an establishment.[8] We announced that Samant and Antulay had come together, and it had become impossible to carry on newspaper publication in Bombay. We approached the High Court, saying that we would not apply to a government that was bent on destroying the paper. We contended that closing down a newspaper is its right to silence, and the right to remain silent is absolute. Only the right to freedom of expression is subject to limitations, not the right to silence. The great constitutional scholar, and the former Advocate General of Maharashtra, H.M. Seervai, settled the writ, and appeared for us, bringing to the Court his great authority, his scholarship and his absolutely uncompromising presence.

All this was new to Samant, and was altogether different from the kinds of responses to which he was accustomed.

The Bombay edition was closed down. Workers explained that they had no alternative but to stay away from work. They were being threatened. Persons from Samant's Kamgar Sangh were visiting them at their homes and telling them what would happen to their families should they even go near the *Express* building.

We had played the last card first, true, but now did not know how to proceed. Ramnathji suggested that I meet Dattopant Thengadi, the head of the trade union movement of the RSS. He had a formidable reputation, having built one of the largest trade unions in the country, the Bharatiya Mazdoor Sangh (BMS).

I met Dattopantji at Palam airport. Almost a silent presence, he exuded confidence. He spoke softly and little. I began explaining our problem in Bombay. He cut me short, and said he knew about it. I recounted the meeting in Rajni Patel's office, right up to Samant threatening me. '*Kuch naheen kar saktaa*,'[9] Dattopantji said.

---

[8] In October 1981, an Ordinance had been issued by the Maharashtra government making it mandatory for establishments employing 100 or more workers to seek government permission before closing operations. The Ordinance was based on a section of the Industrial Disputes Act which had been struck down by the Supreme Court as unconstitutional. This mistake of the government gave us a good opening.

[9] 'He cannot do anything.'

'*Par voh to tufaan hai,*' I said. '*Hum uskaa aur uskey aadmiyon kaa muqaabalaa kaisey karengey?*'[10]

'*Dhairya se, sehansheeltaa sey. Tufaan hai? Tufaan ko bahut der chaltey dekhaa hai? Jitnaa tez aataa hai utnee he jaldi jaataa hai. Us sey bhidney ke aavashyaktaa naheen hai. Usey aatey dekho, usey jaatey dekho. Dhairya rakho.*'[11]

He told me that he would depute two persons in Bombay to guide us, closed the subject, and switched to something I would have least expected. '*Tumhaare lekh dikhaatey hain ki tumney* Communism *par gehraa adhyayan kiyaa hai,*' he said. '*Apnaa samay vyarth mein mat ganvaao.* Communism *khatm ho chukaa hai. Kisee aaney vaaley vishay par soch-vichaar karo.*'[12]

Back in Bombay, Gurumurthy, Hiranmay Karlekar, the resident editor of our Bombay edition, and I started meeting Dr P.R. Kinnare and Vasantbhai Puriya, the two who had been assigned to guide us. Vasantbhai was a somewhat elderly, slightly frail person. Dr Kinnare was strongly built. He inspired trust as well as confidence.

Ranganathan rented two/three rooms in a nondescript hotel, some distance from the *Express* building. Dina Vakil—she and her little team used to prepare our Sunday supplement—and others began working from there. Karlekar, Gurumurthy and I attended to the strike, and kept doing what we could for the other editions of the paper.

Every second or third day, Karlekar would drive us in his small car to Vasantbhai's modest place. We would keep pleading for this, that and the other to be done. Dr Kinnare would give us news of what was happening among our workers, about the talk among them, about what they were feeling. We would ask impatiently about the steps that had been discussed earlier; we

---

[10] 'But he is a hurricane. How will we match him and his men?'

[11] 'With patience, with forbearance. He is a hurricane? Have you seen a hurricane last for long? The faster it comes, the sooner it goes. No need to confront it. See it coming, see it going. Have patience.'

[12] 'Your writings show that you have made a deep study of Communism. Don't waste your time. Communism has finished. Think about something that is to come.'

wanted to know when those would be taken. Both would counsel patience. So much so that we started suspecting that they, and the BMS behind them, did not have the strength that they were rumoured to have.

We used to receive information directly from some of our workers also. In particular, about the meetings that would be held. Two–three weeks into the strike, the tone seemed to change a bit. Workers started to wonder how long the closure would continue. Some began to wonder what they could expect: after all, the paper had agreed to give the higher scales that the Wage Board had prescribed. Goenka will never give a paisa more. What are we fighting for? . . .

We learnt that such doubts were being met by the rumour that actually, Ramnathji had met Samant, that he was meeting some of the workers, that an agreement would be signed soon, one that would bring them substantial gains.

That Samant's men had to resort to such fabrications to keep the spirits of the workers up was for us a sure sign that the workers' heart was not in the strike. We moved swiftly to disabuse them of such expectations as the fabrications might have aroused. There will be no negotiations at all, we put out. And RNG is just not in India to be meeting anyone. He has gone to Europe and is not going to be back for three–four months. Far from agreeing to give something more, he was furious at having been persuaded to agree to the Award . . . Newspaper owners were getting together to collectively challenge the Award in court.

Kinnare also told us that Samant was very rough with our workers. He would scarcely meet them. When he did, he wouldn't listen to them; he had no patience for their difficulties. He was rude and rough towards them, almost abusive. When they asked what he would get them, from whom, he silenced them. His men were menacing.

What was more, Samant's figures had started slipping! He had asked me to get RNG to give Rs 3,000 a month more to every worker. In his talk with the workers, that had come down to Rs 1,000. Then to 'I will get each of you Rs 300 more per month.'

On one rare occasion, he came to one of their meetings at the Churchgate maidan. We got a recording of his speech from the police. Among other things, he exhorted the workers to break my legs. Everything will be settled then, he told them.

Emboldened by news of the mood of the workers and their progressive disillusionment and eventual exasperation with Samant, at long last, through Dr Kinnare and some of our colleagues, we began contacting each journalist and worker separately in his house and quarter.

There were many ups and downs. And some shocks. One that we should have anticipated. RNG was not one to pursue just one line. With the closure dragging on, with nothing in sight, Samant had opened a line to Ramnathji through Ashok Padbidri, a member of the *Lok Satta* staff. We did not know any of this at all. When we learnt of it, we were stupefied and furious. Our whole strategy rested on convincing the workers that they could not gain a paisa by following Samant, that Ramnathji would concede nothing at all. 'We will throw you down from this floor,' we shouted at him. 'We are going back to our families,' we shouted. At first, Ramnathji denied all knowledge of the matter. Soon enough, he promised that he would not meet Samant, that he would shut this aperture.

Two and a half tense months went by. At last, we began feeling from the information that we were getting and from Dr Kinnare's assessment that we could start preparations for restarting the editions. This involved planning a series of steps at many levels. What is the minimum number we will need to print editions of *Indian Express* and *Lok Satta*? How will the workers be brought from their homes to the building? At what distance must they disembark? How will they be smuggled in? As it will not be possible for them to leave the building once they have come in, where will they sleep? What kind of bedding will do? How many toilets and showers could we muster for them on other floors? From where will the food be arranged? How will it be brought into the building? For how many days must we, for how many days *could* we plan? Will the police help shield our workers from Samant's men? How will the morale of the families be sustained, and how will security be ensured if the workers do not return home for some days?

We proceeded with one thing and the other. The date that we had set for recommencing the papers neared. Karlekar, who had been a stalwart throughout, suddenly said that his dog was ill in Delhi, and he had to fly back. With fury in his stomach, RNG offered to get Karlekar's dog to Bombay by air. But Karlekar insisted—the dog will not be able to stand the flight; in any case, he will not be able to adjust to a completely new environment suddenly. That became a joke among us: '*Ramnathji, Karlekar kaa kutta phir se bulaa rahaa hai.*' Years and years later—almost forty years later, to be precise—when I mentioned this to Gurumurthy, he burst out in peals of laughter.

We cleared the twenty-fourth floor of the building. We spread out bedding.

The date arrived. Late that evening, the operation was begun. We were able to bring eighty-odd workers and subeditors into the building. With this meagre staff, we brought out *Lok Satta* and *Indian Express*.

The print run was naturally small. The printed copies were sent out in trucks with RSS men sitting in the rear, just in case Samant's men tried to stop the trucks.

Though just about half the normal print run, the printed copies were an announcement that the 'strike' was over, that the terror of Samant had been broken.

Given the harrowing three months that Samant had been able to put us through, it was not enough to restart the paper. We had to ensure that such an episode would not be repeated. We had to drive the lesson home to the workers. Far from thinking that a Samant could get them something, they must learn to stand up to the threats of such men. Therefore, keen though we were to recommence the editions, we erected a condition.

We insisted that anyone who rejoins work will have to give an undertaking of good conduct. The few who had been carried away by Samant's militancy and reputation for browbeating everyone would regard such an undertaking a humiliation. They would not be able to bring themselves to sign the undertaking. The undertaking would act as a sieve. It would keep them away.

Datta Samant challenged the undertaking in court. The case was listed before Justice Sawant. Ramnathji saw in this an ill-omen. The petition is by 'Samant', he told Gurumurthy and Janakiraman as they were leaving for the Court, and the Judge is 'Sawant'. The order will go against us. And that is what happened. Justice Sawant ruled that workers could rejoin work without signing the undertaking.

Mr Seervai went to the Division Bench, mentioned the matter orally, and got the order stayed. The few Samant enthusiasts that there were also had to sign the undertaking.

It had been a very costly tussle. For three months, the largest editions of the Group had remained shut. But there is the other side also: forty years have gone by; there has been no 'strike' at the paper in Bombay. Later, the textile industry followed some of our techniques, and Samant's reign of terror in Bombay was shattered forever. But so was the textile industry of Bombay. It was ruined.

12

A Judge, and some drama

'RNG wants you to come to Bombay urgently'—it was Ranganathan, the General Manager of the paper in Bombay.

I took the evening flight. By the time I got to the Penthouse at Express Towers, Ramnathji was asleep.

Early next morning, he came into the bedroom in which I was staying. '*Kyaa huaa hai? Bhagwati mujhey kal sey phone par phone kiye jaa rahaa hai.*'[1]

What had happened was as follows.

A seven-Judge Bench of the Supreme Court, headed by Justice P.N. Bhagwati, had delivered a judgment on the Transfer of Judges case.[2] I felt that it had handed the key to the robber—the Executive. I called on Justice Bhagwati. He explained the reasoning which had led him to hand down the judgment he had delivered. Apart from spelling out what the consequences of his judgment would be, I pointed out that what he had held now was in flat contradiction to what he had said in a case he had decided earlier. He asked his assistant to bring the volume containing that

---

[1] 'What has happened? Why is Bhagwati ringing me up since yesterday?'

[2] *S.P. Gupta v President Of India And Ors.*, delivered on 30 December 1981, 1981 Supp (1) SCC 87. Author: Justice P.N. Bhagwati. Bench: J.J., A. Gupta, D.A. Desai, E. Venkataramiah, P.N. Bhagwati, R.S. Pathak, S.M. Fazal Ali, V. Tulzapurkar.

earlier judgment, and, when this was brought, he handed it to me. I quickly located the passages and handed the volume back to him with the relevant page open. He went over the passages carefully. After a moment, he said that there had been a mistake.

The next day, in open Court, he said that, unwittingly, in the Transfer of Judges judgment, there had been an omission: the typist had skipped some passages while typing. He read these out in open Court, and instructed the clerk to see that they were incorporated.

I felt this grafting made matters worse. And so I wrote a three-part article criticizing, in parts lampooning the judgment.

The first of the three parts had been carried by the paper. Ramnathji was in Bombay, and the Bombay edition was shut because of the strike. So, Ramnathji would not have seen the article that had appeared that morning in other editions, in particular the Delhi edition.

Now, Justice Bhagwati was well known to Ramnathji. He was naturally very upset, and his staff must have been ringing up Bombay for the Judge to talk to Ramnathji.

I told Ramnathji that the judgment was going to weaken the Judiciary enormously, and that therefore, even though I knew how close Bhagwati was to him, I had written a three-part article.

'*Voh chhap gayaa hai kyaa?*'[3]

I explained that the first part had been published the previous day. The second part would have appeared that morning. And the third part would be appearing the following day.

'*Laaye ho?*'[4]

I gave him the typed script of the complete article.

'*Tum apni* coffee *piyo. Main yeh padhtaa hoon. Bhagwati yahaan aa rahaa hai, abhi subhey ki* flight *sey.*'[5] A keen litigator, Ramnathji used to love reading judgments and their dissection.

---

[3]   'Has it appeared?'
[4]   'Have you brought it?'
[5]   'You have your coffee. I will read this. Bhagwati is coming here, just now, by the morning flight.'

After about an hour, he called me back to his room. '*Bhagwati meraa dost hai. Par jo tumney likhaa hai, bilkul theek likhaa hai. In* arguments *kaa koi jawaab naheen hai. Dekho, tumney apnaa kaam kar liyaa hai, ab mujhey meraa kaam karnaa hai.*'[6]

He called Ranganathan. Asked him to receive Justice Bhagwati with much ceremony, and to bring him up to the Penthouse. '*Oopar laaney sey pehley mujhey* phone *kar denaa.*'[7]

Ramnathji told me that when Justice Bhagwati came, I should go back into the bedroom. '*Darwaazaa thodaa saa khulaa rakh saktey ho, par hargiz moohn naheen dikhaanaa jab tak Judge chalaa naa jaaye.*'[8]

Justice Bhagwati had but to step out of the elevator that Ramnathji greeted him most effusively. His brilliance, his erudition, their friendship . . .

'*To kyaa khabar hai? Bombay kaisey aanaa huaa?*'[9]

Justice Bhagwati explained that I had written against his judgment.

Ramnathji erupted, '*Kahaan likhaa hai?* Times of India *mein? Main usey abhi* dismiss *kar doongaa. Merey yahaan hotey hue voh kisi aur akhbaar mein likh he naheen saktaa.* Contract *mein hai.*'[10]

Justice Bhagwati explained, no he has written in the *Indian Express.*

'*Kyaa, merey akhbaar mein merey mitr ke* against? *Kyaa likhaa hai? Naheen, naheen, kuch bhee likhaa ho, main usey jeetey jee maar doonga . . .*'[11]

---

[6] 'Bhagwati is my friend. But what you have written is exactly right. There is no answer to these arguments. Now look: you have done your job, now I have to do mine.'

[7] 'Ring me before you bring him up.'

[8] 'You can leave the door ajar a bit, but under no circumstances must you show your face till the Judge has gone.'

[9] 'So, what is the news? What brings you to Bombay?'

[10] 'Where has he written it? In the *Times of India*? I will dismiss him at once. Being here with me he cannot write in any other paper. It is in the contract.'

[11] 'What, in my paper against my own friend? What has he written? No, no, whatever he may have written, I will skin him alive . . .'

Bhagwati explained that I had written against him even though he had gone out of his way to spare time for me to discuss the judgment.

'Judge, *aap us haraamzadey se miley? Aap us sey swayam miley?*'[12]

Ramnathji was shouting by now. He could put on an act as few could.

So worked up he must have seemed to have become that Justice Bhagwati would have thought that he—RNG—would have a heart attack. He was the one who was now trying to pacify Ramnathji. No, no, it is just an article. The judgment will stand on its own.

'*Par iskaa karein kyaa? Mein to usey abhi dismiss kar doon. Par log kahein gey ki mainey aapkey liye kiyaa hai.*'[13]

No, no, don't dismiss him. I will get a thorough reply written to his articles. Please have that carried at the earliest.

'Reply *aayaa naheen ki mainey chaapaa. Aap nishchint rahiye. Iski main khabar lekar he chodoongaa.*' [14]

Justice Bhagwati left.

'*Kal kaa* article *chapney do. Jab iskaa uttar aayegaa, dekhengey,*'[15] Ramnathji said as he called me back and we resumed our banter.

What was the judgment? What had upset such a distinguished Judge.

I felt that, as it is apt to do whenever the going gets tough, in the new Transfer of Judges case,[16] on general principles the Supreme Court had waxed eloquent, but on specifics it had given the government enough to pummel the Judiciary into obedience. And had written accordingly.

---

[12] 'Judge, you mean you met that bastard? You mean you met him yourself?'
[13] 'But what should we do about this fellow? I would have dismissed him on the spot but people will say I have done it for you.'
[14] 'The reply has but to arrive, and I will publish it. Don't worry at all. I will not leave this fellow till I have driven him to his senses.'
[15] 'Let tomorrow's part be published. When his reply comes, we shall see.'
[16] *S.P. Gupta v President Of India And Ors., op. cit.*

A representative judgment

Ever since Mrs Gandhi had returned to power two years earlier, she and her minions had been engaged in a systematic campaign to vilify and intimidate the Judiciary. The law minister and others had been saying that they will shunt Judges around at least till the Chief Justices, as well as at least one-third of the Judges of each High Court, were from some other state—with the Executive picking and choosing to determine which Chief Justice shall go to which state and which Judge shall be part of the outside third of which High Court. They had dropped Additional Judges at will, given them humiliating short-term extensions after having kept them waiting till the last humiliating moment . . . Nor was all this new. In the Emergency also, we had the same propaganda, the same terminations of Additional Judges like Justices Lalit and Aggarwala, the same punitive transfers (disguised then as being necessary in the interest of national integration) of sixteen Judges who had given judgments that the government did not fancy.

Such were the proclaimed policies, such the record. And the facts were once again as clear as they could be. O.N. Vohra, an Additional Judge in the Delhi High Court, was being reverted to the local courts because he had indicted Sanjay Gandhi and Co. in the *Kissa Kursi Ka* case. S.N. Kumar, another Additional Judge in Delhi, was being thrown out as his wife, once a municipal councillor from Mrs Gandhi's party, was said to have developed links with the Opposition . . . In an insolent circular, the law minister had asked the Chief Ministers to obtain the consent of all existing Additional Judges and all who might be in line for judgeships for being appointed to posts outside the state. They were to give their consent and list their preferences, while being told that, although they were to furnish their consent and preferences, the government was not bound either to appoint them as Judges or to abide by their preferences.

Articles and conventions

Formally, the controversies involved the first clauses of three Articles of the Constitution.

Article 217(1) provides that in consultation with the Chief Justice of India, the Governor of a state (in effect, that is, the government of the state) and, in the case of a Judge of a High Court other than the Chief Justice, the Chief Justice of the High Court, the President (in effect, that is, the Central Government) shall appoint Judges of the High Court.

Article 222(1), an Article of bitter controversy during the Emergency, provides that in consultation with the Chief Justice of India, the President (that is, the Central Government) may transfer a Judge from one High Court to another.

Article 224(1), the Article around which the greatest bitterness was generated this time, provides that the President may appoint Additional Judges for periods not exceeding two years in a High Court to meet any temporary increase in the business of the Court or to clear the arrears pending in the Court.

Provisions like Article 224(1) regarding Additional Judges are only a little less important than those relating to permanent Judges. The sanctioned number of Additional Judges is around one-third the sanctioned number of permanent Judges. In the Delhi High Court, for instance, there were seven Additional and fourteen permanent Judges.

Next, as far as the letter of the Constitution goes, for appointing a Judge of a High Court, the Central Government must consult three entities—the government of the state where the High Court is located, the Chief Justice of India and the Chief Justice of the High Court; that for transferring a Judge, it must consult the Chief Justice of India (specifically, the Judge being transferred need not be consulted); that for appointing an Additional Judge, it need consult no one.

Over the years, a series of conventions had been assiduously built up to ensure that the power to appoint and transfer Judges did not become a weapon by which the Executive could browbeat the Judiciary.

First, once appointed, during his term, an Additional Judge was in all respects on par with a permanent Judge.

Second, in almost all instances, a person was first appointed as an Additional Judge for two years. When a vacancy occurred in the High Court for the post of a permanent Judge, the senior-most Additional Judge was almost invariably elevated to fill that post. If no vacancy was available when the two-year term of an Additional Judge came to an end, he was almost invariably reappointed for another term of two years. Thus, almost invariably every Judge was first appointed as an Additional Judge, and, just as invariably, every Additional Judge became a permanent Judge. No Additional Judge ever needed to fear that he may lose his job after two years because the government did not, for instance, like his judgments.

Third, if a Judge had to be transferred, he was transferred only with his consent. Therefore, no Judge needed to fear that he would be sent off to some godforsaken place at the government's whim.

Fourth, it was axiomatic that on appointments, as on transfers, the Chief Justice of India and of the High Court would be consulted truly and fully and not just for form's sake, and that it would be the duty of the Central Government to place all the relevant facts before the concerned Chief Justice while seeking his advice.

Fifth, the advice of the Chief Justice of India was looked upon as almost binding.

Finally, the suitability of a person to become a Judge was assessed only at the time of his initial appointment as an Additional Judge. If any doubts arose about the Judge, the Chief Justice of the court concerned would swiftly bring them to the former's attention and give him an opportunity to refute or confirm the facts.

These conventions were carefully developed on two premises: that an independent Judiciary was central to the system envisaged in our Constitution; and that these conventions were necessary to ensure the independence of the Judiciary.

The new dispensation

Much of this was dealt a disastrous blow by the new judgment. The net effect of what the Bench led by Justice Bhagwati laid down was as follows:

o   Normally, persons should be appointed as permanent Judges and not as Additional Judges.

o   A permanent Judge may be transferred where the Central Government wills without his consent; indeed, he may be transferred in the teeth of his strenuous objections.

o   The Additional Judge should be appointed for at least one year.

o   Upon the completion of his term, an Additional Judge has a right to be considered for appointment as a permanent Judge, but no more. In particular, when his term comes to an end, his or her suitability is to be assessed all over again, and there are to be no restrictions on the criteria that the Central Government may use to decide whether or not the person should be reappointed as an Additional Judge, be made a permanent Judge, or dropped.

o   In all these matters, while there must be full and effective consultation, the advice of the Chief Justice of India is to carry no greater weight than that of the Governor of a state or the Chief Justice of the High Court. In particular, his advice is not to be binding in any way.

There were many caveats and ifs and buts ('a transfer can only be ordered in the public interest,' etc.). And some of these were consequential: introducing 'public interest' into the matter made the decision justiciable. But the total effect was as unmistakable as it was brutal: every Additional Judge (and recall that the sanctioned number of Additional Judges was one-third the number of permanent Judges) was now a probationer, in that he would have to pass the Central Government's tests each time his term came to an end; and every permanent Judge could now be shunted around by the Central Government, so long as it clothed the transfer in the garb of public interest.

Moreover, the Chief Justice of India had been cut down to being just another adviser to the Executive. Nothing—no collegium, for instance—had been put in his place. This too would prove injurious. The Executive had already acquired the unquestioned right to appoint a Chief Justice of its choice. Citizens had been left to rely on chance. Some Prime Minister might come along who genuinely valued an independent Judiciary; he might appoint an independent man as Chief Justice; the term of this Chief Justice might extend beyond the term of that particular Prime Minister. Or the Executive might make a mistake and appoint a strong man as Chief Justice thinking he is pliable. Or a pliable man may (as pliable men seldom do and yet as people continue to hope they will) grow in office.

But by the new judgment, even chance had been defanged. For the Executive had been assured that should such mistakes occur, it could disregard the advice of the Chief Justice with impunity.

The key had been handed to the robber. True, because of the post-Emergency liberalism of the Supreme Court, citizens had freer access to the courts, but the one who was the largest litigant in the country, indeed the principal violator of laws—the Executive—had been given a near absolute right to determine who will hear citizens there. Because of what had been held, and even more because of its announcement effect, I felt that, unless events overturned it, as the years pass the disastrous effects of this judgment shall far exceed those of the habeas corpus judgment that the Supreme Court delivered during the Emergency. That judgment, terrible as it was, affected one issue, a matter of life and death though it was, for a specific and limited period. This new judgment affected the Judiciary itself, and thus all issues before it, and it did so for the indefinite future.

But even in this there was a redeeming feature: the Supreme Court had warned us that it shall not be a buffer between the people and the potential oppressor, that the people will have to rely on themselves.

How is it that these Judges fail us at precisely the critical time? How do they come to cut their own feet? How do they shut their eyes to what is staring them in the face? How do they rationalize what they do?

One judgment and why

There are several answers. I shall draw attention to one or two by taking up the judgment of one Judge, Justice P.N. Bhagwati, in this case.

There are several reasons for the choice. Justice Bhagwati presided over the seven-Judge Bench that considered the case. He was regarded as the most outstanding legal craftsman in the Supreme Court at the time. He had built up a sizeable constituency by some liberal initiatives. If one more Judge had expressed himself the way three—Justices Bhagwati, Fazal Ali and Desai—had done against the affidavit and conduct of Chief Justice Chandrachud, the latter would almost certainly have had to resign, and Justice Bhagwati would have been in line for the Chief Justiceship. Finally, a reason that was specially important for me, I had the opportunity to partially discuss his judgment with him. As we noticed above, when, during a conversation, I mentioned to him that, given the things he had said in his past judgments, I found his latest judgment to be incomprehensible, he was gracious enough to send me a specially prepared five-page summary of his 308-page judgment and to spare an hour and a half for a discussion. As we parted, he also said that, in the interests of the country, the judgment should be discussed extensively, although no motives should be attributed as many persons were doing, he said.

This was the third major case dealing with the Judiciary in which Justice Bhagwati had pronounced a judgment. This time around, he held that Judges should normally be appointed as permanent Judges; that no permanent Judge should be transferred without his consent; that Additional Judges should be appointed for terms of two years each, solely to meet a sudden increase in the Court's work or to clear arrears; that on the expiry of two years, the Additional Judge should have no more than a right to be considered for appointment as a permanent Judge; that the Central Government must reassess his suitability at the expiry of the two years; that all material about him which has come to light in those two years can be taken into account, and that there are no restrictions on the criteria by which the government may assess the man's suitability; that in assessing the suitability of an Additional Judge for further appointment, the Chief Justice of the concerned High Court must go by the reputation of the Judge, in particular, that while he should carefully sift the information he receives, inquiring into it is neither practical nor desirable; furthermore that, as the decision to drop an Additional Judge on the basis of information received is 'neither adjudication nor condemnation', there is no need to introduce notions of fair play and natural justice; there is no need, that is, to give the man a hearing before deciding to drop him; that, while in all these matters, there should be full and effective consultation, the opinion of the Chief Justice of India is not to bind anyone, that it is to carry no more weight than the opinions of others, that, in fact, as the Chief Justice of India is liable to suffer from prejudices and weaknesses, and as the Chief Justice of the concerned High Court is liable to have more intimate knowledge of his colleagues, the latter's opinion should ordinarily carry greater weight; by inference, therefore, the opinion of the Chief Justice of India should carry no greater weight than that of the Governor of a state.

There were elements in this judgment which could indeed help secure the independence of the Judiciary. But these had come to nought, partly for reasons over which Justice Bhagwati had no control, and partly because he hesitated to go far enough.

Thus, his stand that no Judge should be transferred without his consent had no practical effect because the other Judges had held otherwise—a factor beyond our Judge's control. His stand that Judges should be appointed directly as permanent Judges did not go far enough, for he had desisted from issuing a direction to the government—as Justice Venkataramiah had done—that it appoint the requisite number of permanent Judges. Similarly, having knocked the primacy of the Chief Justice for reasons and with consequences that we shall soon see, the Judge had not put anything like a collegium in its place. The result was to hand things over entirely to the Executive.

But being let down by others, not pursuing one's instincts far enough—these were not the gravest of problems. The real problems were the ones that become apparent when we seek answers to deeper questions.

How did the notions Justice Bhagwati had put forward in this judgment square with one another? How did they square with what the Judge had held in the past? How did the Judge treat facts in any particular instance? We should go through the answers at some length because the danger lay not just in this particular judgment but in the way even the best of our Judges used to go about, and the way they still go about, such matters of life and death.

Consistency

Yes, Justice Bhagwati declared, citizens have the right to raise issues of public importance before the courts even though they are not directly affected by them. Yes, Tarkunde and others have the right to request the Court to examine the cases of Justices O.N. Vohra, S.N. Kumar and Wad, three Additional Judges of the Delhi High Court who had been given humiliating short-term extensions at the last possible minute. Yes, in the case of O.N. Vohra, both legal and factual mala fides are clear—as information regarding him was kept from the Chief Justice of India by the law minister and the Chief Justice of Delhi, the mandatory consultation was not full and effective as it must be. Moreover, the letter of Prakash Narain, the Chief Justice of Delhi, to the law minister, which had been kept from the Chief Justice of India, clearly showed that Prakash Narain had examined Vohra's judgment in the *Kissa Kursi Ka* case before recommending that Vohra be dropped. True, all this and more is true, Justice Bhagwati conceded. But, in a surprising volte-face, the Judge decreed that as Vohra had not come before the Court, he, Justice Bhagwati, will not look into the case. Had the undertrials, the women of the Agra Protective Home, had Kamla, the woman purchased by the *Indian Express* reporter, come personally to the Court before Justice Bhagwati agreed to examine their cases? Indeed, isn't the entire point about the Court's declamations on public interest litigation in this case that issues would be examined, even if the direct victim is not before the Court? Having declared that Tarkunde had the right to raise the issue on behalf of O.N. Vohra, how did the Judge refuse to consider the case on the ground that Vohra was not personally before the Court?

Yes, Justice Bhagwati said now, as he had said often in the past, when the Executive exercises power mala fide and for collateral considerations, the Court shall most certainly review the matter. But the moment the question of examining whether in a particular case the Executive had indeed exercised its power mala fide came up, the Judge declared: We won't go into the facts. If a person is detained mala fide or out of mistaken identity or under detention orders that have not even been signed, the Court, Justice Bhagwati had declared in the habeas corpus case, will certainly set the matter right. But, he declared in the same case, the Executive is entitled to keep the grounds on which a person has been detained secret, both from the detenu and the Court. If an Additional Judge, who, as Justice Bhagwati held, has a right to be considered for the post of a permanent Judge, is dropped for irrelevant or mala fide reasons, the Court, he said, will certainly review the decision to drop him. But, just as he will not look into the case of Justice Vohra as he was not before the Court, in the case of Justice Kumar, where also, as we shall see, the facts were damaging as they could be, Justice Bhagwati, having brought the facts on record, suddenly decided not to look at them: we will only consider, he said, whether there was full and effective consultation and not the facts about the reasons on account of which he was dropped. If Judges will not examine the facts, how will they decide what they say they invariably will whenever the occasion arises, that is, whether the Executive has exercised its powers mala fide or for reasons that it should not have taken into account?

A Judge's social philosophy is of paramount importance, Justice Bhagwati said in his judgment, and should certainly be a criterion for selecting him or dropping him. (Justice Bhagwati's pages—and I shall give a sample in a moment—on what the proper role of a Judge is, could scarcely have been improved upon by any enthusiast of a 'committed judiciary'.) When reassessing an Additional Judge, all material, Justice Bhagwati said, that has surfaced in the two years—including, one must infer, evidence about the man's social philosophy—is relevant. But his judgments, says the Judge simultaneously, should not be examined (as the Chief Justice of Delhi had recorded he had done in the case of Justice Vohra that Justice Bhagwati refused to examine). What better evidence of a man's social philosophy, I can hear a law minister ask, than his judgments? An assessment of the man's social philosophy being of such paramount importance, how come I should not look at the best evidence I have of it?

Trusting one Chief and not another

The advice of the Chief Justice of India should not be binding, Justice Bhagwati ruled this time around; it should carry no greater weight than the advice of others as he may be prejudiced. Bhagwati quoted a few lines of Ambedkar the way the Chinese quote classics of the remote past, as a device, that is, of commenting on the present: 'I personally feel no doubt,' Bhagwati quoted Ambedkar as saying, 'that the Chief Justice is a very eminent person. But the Chief Justice is a man with all the failings, all the sentiments and all the prejudices which we as common people have . . .' Ergo: no primacy for the Chief Justice's advice. Primacy would mean veto, Justice Bhagwati said now; veto would mean giving one man, who is liable to be prejudiced, etc., power that no one man should have.

But when it came to assessing the suitability of Additional Judges for further appointment, Bhagwati counselled that the assessment of the Chief Justice of the High Court was liable to be best informed, that he, in turn, should go by his opinion of the man, in contrast, that is, to inquiring into the allegations he hears, that we must accept his subjective assessment even when, as in the case Justice Bhagwati had before him, the Chief Justice of the High Court in writing had said that what he had heard were 'chance remarks', even when he had stated not once but twice in writing that he had no machinery to investigate the allegations! Furthermore, Justice Bhagwati held, it was not necessary for the Chief Justice to give the condemned man a hearing before reaching a decision.

But isn't the Chief Justice of the High Court as liable to be prejudiced, à la Ambedkar, as the Chief Justice of India? Here was Bhagwati's answer:

It is possible that the Chief Justice of the High Court may go wrong in a given case and arrive at an erroneous opinion in regard to the suitability of an Additional Judge for appointment for a further term and that may result in injustice to the Additional Judge who may suffer by reason of such erroneous opinion *but that cannot be helped because ultimately some constitutional functionary has got to be entrusted with the task of assessing* the suitability of the person to be appointed an Additional Judge or a permanent Judge and no better person can be found for this purpose than the Chief Justice of the High Court. The Chief Justice of the High Court may err in his assessment as anyone else may, fallibility being the attribute of every human being. *But that is a risk which has necessarily to be taken* and it cannot be avoided howsoever perfect may be the mechanism which human ingenuity can evolve . . . *These errors are inevitable in every process of assessment* and the Constitution has sought to minimise them by entrusting the task of assessment to a high dignitary like the Chief Justice of the High Court who would be expected to act with a high sense of responsibility and, who by reason of training and experience, would be able to sift the grain from the chaff and arrive at a correct opinion on the material before him . . .

Notice but two features. First, no consideration of this kind led the Judge to repose similar trust in the Chief Justice of India. Second, notice how far he went to find a constitutional basis for his a priori decision, that as someone had to be trusted, it might as well be the Chief Justice of the High Court: '. . . the Constitution has sought to minimise them [the errors in assessing the suitability of persons for Additional Judgeship] by entrusting the task of assessment to a high dignitary like the Chief Justice of the High Court . . .' Where does the Constitution do this? The relevant Article 224, as we have seen, mentions the Chief Justice of the High Court no more than it mentions the Chief Justice of India.

Is and ought

We must read the Constitution as it is, Justice Bhagwati said in the opening pages of this judgment, not as it ought to be. By the time he came to the last part of the judgment, the one dealing with the power to transfer Judges, he was himself reading the Constitution not as it is but as he thought it ought to be. Article 222(1) says, 'The President may, after consultation with the Chief Justice of India, transfer a judge from one High Court to any other High Court . . .' But we must, Bhagwati held in this judgment as he had in *Union of India v Sankalchand H. Sheth* in 1977,[17] read the Article as saying '. . . The President may . . . transfer a judge *with his consent* from one High Court to any other High Court . . .' inserting the three words where they are not.

He did so by the following steps. An Article of the Constitution must be interpreted in a manner that harmonizes with the Basic Structure of the Constitution. Independence of the Judiciary is part of the Basic Structure. Hence, Article 222(1) must be interpreted so as to preserve the independence of the Judiciary. Now, a transfer always entails hardship and often a stigma. And so the Executive can always browbeat a Judge by threatening to transfer him. The requirement in Article 222(1), that the President consult the Chief Justice of India, is not a sufficient safeguard, recent history having shown that, as Bhagwati had put it in 1977, when 'the highest in the land'—remember, as this will be relevant before we reach the end of this account, that at that time 'the highest in the land' was Mrs Indira Gandhi—abused this weapon, the then Chief Justice could not or did not safeguard the interests of the Judges. Nor can we expect a Judge to seek legal redress when he is arbitrarily pushed around. Hence, the only way to safeguard the independence of the Judiciary, Bhagwati concluded, is to read the words 'with his consent' into Article 222(1) and ensure that no Judge is ever transferred without his agreeing to the proposal.

Wouldn't that mean that if a Judge had set himself up in business in a High Court, you will not be able to deal with him by transferring him to a High Court far from his touts as he would veto the proposal?

Here was the answer Bhagwati gave in the *Sankalchand Sheth* case and to which he adhered in the current judgment:

---

[17] *Union of India v Sankalchand Himmatlal Sheth*, (1977) 4 SCC 193.

Now, it is true that there might be some cases where the dictates of public interest might require transfer of a judge from one High Court to another, but such cases, by their very nature, would be few and far between and I do not think that it would be right, on account of a few such cases, to concede power in the Executive to transfer a High Court Judge without his consent which would impinge on the independence of the Judiciary. Here there is a competition between two categories of public interest, one is the public interest in seeing that a High Court Judge does not continue to remain at a place where he is polluting the pure fountain of justice and the other is the public interest in securing the independence of the High Court Judiciary from Executive control or interference. *The latter public interest clearly outweighs the former* and if the Court has to choose between the two, the latter must obviously be preferred to the former. The transfer of an undesirable Judge may secure public interest and his continued presence in the Court from where he is to be transferred may be an evil, *but it is necessary to put up with that evil in order to secure the larger good which flows from the independence of the Judiciary.* I cannot accept a construction which sacrifices the independence of the Judiciary in order that it should be possible to transfer a few undesirable Judges. The relative benefit to the public interest by transferring a few unworthy incumbents of the office of High Court judgeship is insignificant compared to the injury to the public interest of the people of India in the independent administration of justice. The public interest in the independence of the Judiciary must, therefore, clearly prevail and a construction which subserves this higher public interest must be accepted . . .

But, as Justice Tulzapurkar, in his judgment on this very case showed, was this not the very logic, indeed, were these not the very words, that constituted the reason why the Executive should not be given the power over Additional Judges that, as we saw, Bhagwati had given it? Did the words not constitute the reason, among others, why an Additional Judge should not be dropped as Bhagwati would have him dropped, on the basis of uninvestigated allegations? Was the argument of those like Shiv Shankar, who would drop an Additional Judge at will, not that if in the two years of service, an Additional Judge turned out to be undesirable, then it was much better that he be removed forthwith than that an undesirable Judge continue and pollute the Judiciary as a whole, precisely the argument Bhagwati had rejected in *Sheth's* case? And was the argument of the petitioners not the precise argument which Bhagwati had laid down in *Sheth's* case, namely, that difficult though it be, the right course for removing an undesirable Judge is to impeach him, rather than to give the Executive a handle by which it could at one go browbeat a third of the Judiciary into subservience?

We cannot expect transferred Judges, Bhagwati observed, to resign and adduce proof of mala fides; we cannot expect them to fight protracted legal battles. Only one of the sixteen who were transferred abruptly in the Emergency, he had pointed out in *Sheth's* case, had the inner strength to take the matter to court. The same Justice Bhagwati now declared that he will not examine the case of Justice O.N. Vohra, an aggrieved Judge who had been reverted from the Delhi High Court to the local courts, just because he had personally not approached the Court, even though the case had been brought before the Court by persons whose right to bring the case to the Court Bhagwati and all the other Judges had upheld most fervently, and even though the record, clearly and beyond doubt, established that Vohra's judgment in the *Kissa Kursi Ka* case was the reason for his reversal.

Looking with eyes shut . . .

A transfer, Justice Bhagwati had ruled, almost always inflicts great hardship; it often inflicts a stigma. But discontinuance of an Additional Judge in office because of allegations of corruption, he maintained, is not even condemnation! A Judge, he said, must always be told the reasons why he is being transferred, he must be given an opportunity to explain all his personal difficulties, and, even after that, the Judge concerned must have a veto over his transfer. But the Additional Judge, Bhagwati held, whose Judgeship is being discontinued, need not be given any opportunity to clarify the facts, indeed, he need not be told what the reasons or allegations were on account of which his services were being discontinued. If the transfer was challenged in court, our Judge held, the burden of proving that it had been done in the public interest, and that no collateral considerations had gone into the decision, lay with the government. But when the Additional Judge was dropped, when he was deprived of the job for which, even Bhagwati agrees, he had a right to be considered, he shall have no recourse to the courts because, according to our Judge, he was not being 'dropped', he just 'goes' as his term had come to an end! And there seemed to be an esoteric reason, too, and here was how Justice Bhagwati put it:

> It is not open to the Court to hold an inquiry and determine for itself the correctness of the opinion of any of the constitutional authorities required to be consulted by the President. The opinion given by any such constitutional authority may be mistaken or erroneous but the corrective for such mistake or error is to be found in the constitutional provision itself and it cannot be provided by judicial intervention. The Court cannot take evidence for the purpose of determining whether the facts on which the opinion of a constitutional authority required to be consulted is based are true or not or whether the opinion expressed by such constitutional authority is well founded or not. That is a function entrusted by the Constitution to the President, that is, the central government and it is for the central government to judge whether the opinion expressed by the constitutional authority such as the Chief Justice of the High Court is well founded or not and whether it should be accepted or rejected . . .

This from the same Judge who had, again and again, held that the courts will never hesitate to examine an Executive decision to see if it was mala fide or to determine whether it had been taken for collateral reasons. What was the reality: The hortatory pronouncements on what the courts will look into or the tightly shut eyes?

But inconsistencies between one part of the judgment and another, and the divorce between general principles that were laid down and how they were applied, were by far not the most surprising part of this judgment.

Flip flop, flip . . .

While inconsistencies between one part of the judgment and another, between general principles and their application, are merely surprising in such instances, the felicity with which Judges switch from one view to another as times change is startling. Justice Bhagwati's judgment in the present case afforded example after example of such felicity. I shall confine myself to just a few examples.

What is one to do with allegations or information of corruption about Judges? Here is what, Justice Bhagwati, together with Justice Krishna Iyer, said in August 1974 in *Shamsher Singh v State of Punjab*:

> The true intendment of judicial independence is fulfilled not by declining to investigate into delinquencies of judicial personnel nor by holding an open enquiry by a judge which is a poor substitute for collection of evidence *but by creating an apparatus for collecting intelligence and presenting evidence which is under the complete control of the High Court.* This is no new idea but had been mooted in the '50s at an All-India Law Ministers' Conference but at least, now after such a long lapse of time, this felt want may be remedied.

And now? Far from recommending an investigation machinery under the control of the High Court, our Judge declared that investigations are neither practical nor desirable.

Full and effective consultation, Justice Bhagwati and others had repeatedly held, meant, at the minimum, that each of the parties to the consultation—for instance, the Central Government, the Chief Justice of India and the Chief Justice of the High Court—must have all the facts that any one of them had. *Whose responsibility is it that all the facts come before, say, the Chief Justice of India?* Here are representative passages that set out the Supreme Court's view, as expressed just four years ago in *Sheth's* case:

> But there can be no purposeful consideration of a matter in the absence of facts and circumstances on the basis of which alone the nature of the problem involved can be appreciated and right decisions taken. It follows therefore that while consulting the Chief Justice of India, the President must make the relevant data available to him on the basis of which he can offer to the President the benefit of his considered opinion. If the facts necessary to arrive at a proper conclusion are not made available to the Chief Justice, he must ask for them because in casting on the President the obligation to consult the Chief Justice, the Constitution at the same time must be taken to have imposed a duty on the Chief Justice to express his opinion on nothing less than a full consideration of the matter on which he is entitled to be consulted. In the discharge of this constitutional obligation the Chief Justice would be within his rights, and indeed it is his duty whenever necessary, to elicit and ascertain further facts either directly from the judge concerned or from other reliable sources. Consultation within the meaning of Article 222 (1) therefore means full and effective, not formal or unproductive, consultation . . .
>
> Consultation implies taking counsel and seeking advice. To consult is to apply for guidance, direction or authentic information and to ask for advice of the person consulted. Necessarily, all the materials in the possession of one who consults must be unreservedly placed before the consultee. A reasonable opportunity for getting the information, taking other steps and getting prepared for tendering effective and meaningful advice must be given to the person consulted. The consultant, in turn, must take the matter seriously since the subject is of grave importance. Therefore, the President must communicate to the Chief Justice all the material he has and the course he proposes . . . Where a proposal of transfer of a judge is made, the Government must forward every possible material

to the Chief Justice so that he is in a position to give an
effective opinion.

And now? The question had come up in the case of Justice S.N.
Kumar. The correspondence between the Chief Justice of Delhi
and the law minister showed that they came to possess what they
regarded as vital facts which cast doubts on the integrity of Kumar,
and that both of them, deliberately and in consultation with each
other, withheld these from the Chief Justice of India. Did the
law minister not fail in his constitutional duty when he withheld
facts in his possession from the Chief Justice of India? While all
the facts must come before each of the parties, Justice Bhagwati
held, this time around, the Constitution does not prescribe any
sequence or procedure by which they must come before, say, the
Chief Justice of India. In particular, therefore, it is not part of the
Central Government's duty to ensure that the facts reach the Chief
Justice of India whose advice on the matter it is seeking. And so
the law minister did no wrong!

*Should the advice of the Chief Justice of India be binding,
save in the rarest of cases?* Here is what Justice Bhagwati joined
Justice Krishna Iyer in saying in *Shamsher Singh v State of Punjab*
in August 1974:

> In all conceivable cases, consultation with the highest dignitary
> of Indian justice will and should be accepted by the Government
> of India and the Court will have an opportunity to examine
> if any other extraneous circumstances have entered into the
> verdict of the Minister if he departs from the counsel given by
> the Chief Justice of India. *In practice the last word on such a
> sensitive subject must belong to the Chief Justice of India, the
> rejection of his advice being ordinarily regarded as prompted by
> oblique considerations vitiating the order.*

And now? Far from holding that the advice of the Chief Justice
should ordinarily be binding, Justice Bhagwati held, in effect, that
the gentleman's advice should carry no greater weight than that of
a Governor of a state! The Constitution places all consultants on

par, he declared; giving primacy to the advice of the Chief Justice would amount, as we noted above, to giving one man a veto, he said; as Ambedkar taught us, the man is liable to be prejudiced, etc., he says; and in any case, he concluded, the Constitution explicitly places the final power to appoint or transfer Judges in the Central Government and in no one else!

When, during our conversation, I reminded Justice Bhagwati of his earlier stand on the matter, he told me that some sentences had got left out from the typescript of his judgment. He was so kind as to later send me a copy of the official corrigendum to his judgment issued by the Supreme Court.

The position, thus, became as follows. While in *Shamsher Singh v State of Punjab*, in practice, the last word was to be with the Chief Justice of India and a decision of the government contrary to his advice was to 'ordinarily be regarded as prompted by oblique considerations vitiating the order'; while in Justice Bhagwati's present judgment as originally delivered, a decision of the government to go against the unanimous advice of *three* entities—the two Chief Justices and the Governor—'may become vulnerable to attack on the ground that it is mala fide or based on irrelevant grounds', after the corrigendum 'it may *prima facie* become similarly vulnerable to attack', if it is contrary to the unanimous advice of *two* entities—the Chief Justice of India and the Chief Justice of the High Court. And Justice Bhagwati was careful to reiterate that if the two do not agree, the government may pick the advice it fancies, and that even when all the consultants are unanimous, the government had the ultimate right to do what it wants.

Similarly, while in *Shamsher Singh v State of Punjab*, Justice Bhagwati felt that 'in practice the last word is such a sensitive subject must belong to the Chief Justice of India'; in his current judgment, as originally delivered, he felt that '. . . where a Judge is to be appointed the Chief Justice is required to be consulted but again it is not concurrence but only consultation, and the central government is not bound to act in accordance with the opinion of the Chief Justice of India'; with the corrigendum, the Judge came to feel that '. . . but again it is not concurrence but only consultation and the central government is not bound to act in accordance with the opinion of the Chief Justice of India though it is entitled to great weight as the opinion of the head of the Indian judiciary.'

These examples can be multiplied; three more should prove sufficient. The first concerns a concept—natural justice—on which Justice Bhagwati had expressed himself with great eloquence in the preceding years; the second concerns the likely misuse of power by the Executive and what one's attitude should be in the face of such possible abuse, a factor that will determine the Court's approach every time Executive actions are at issue; and the third concerns the manner in which one must interpret the Constitution, a matter that would naturally affect all decisions and not just the one at hand.

Natural justice

In 1976, when thousands were rotting in prisons and when nine High Courts had unanimously held that they were entitled to relief, Justice Bhagwati held that the Constitution, having been enacted in 1950, we must presume that all relevant aspects of the rule of law, including natural justice, had been incorporated in Article 21 (which says that 'No person shall be deprived of his life or personal liberty except according to procedure established by law') and that as the operation of Article 21 had been suspended by the proclamation of Emergency, the detenus could not secure any relief by appealing to any eternal or other principles of natural justice or the rule of law.

What does 'law' mean in the expression 'according to procedure established by law'? Merely that it has been enacted by the State, ruled Justice Bhagwati. Thus, he held:

> The only safeguard enacted by Article 21 therefore, is that a person cannot be deprived of his personal liberty except according to procedure prescribed by 'State made' law. If a law is made by the State prescribing the procedure for depriving a person of his personal liberty and deprivation is effected strictly

in accordance with such procedure, the terms of Article 21
would be satisfied and there would be no infringement of the
right guaranteed under that Article.

It is true, he held further, that the law must be valid law and
must not be repugnant to fundamental rights. But as fundamental
rights had been suspended, he held, the laws under which, and
the procedure by which, people were being detained could not be
challenged on this ground either. The next step was conclusive but
requires a bit of history.

In November 1974, just seven months before the Emergency,
in *Khudiram Das v State of West Bengal*, Justice Bhagwati held
that the grounds on which a person had been detained must
be communicated to him because, as he put it, 'If the grounds
are not communicated to him how can he make an effective
representation?' He held, citing several earlier cases, that not
just the grounds but all the basic facts and materials on which
the grounds were based must be communicated to the detenu.
Come the Emergency and the Judge decreed, in *A.D.M Jabalpur
v S.S. Shukla,* that far from the basic facts and materials, even the
grounds need not be communicated, either to the detenu or the
courts. He characterized MISA's[18] bar on communicating such
grounds as being 'a genuine rule of evidence'. From this conclusion
it followed that their paeans to liberty notwithstanding, the courts
would not entertain even the challenge that a person had been
detained in violation of the law and procedures as they had been
laid down, howsoever arbitrary the law and procedures were to
begin with.

The Emergency ended in 1977. In 1978 Maneka Gandhi
wanted her passport back, a passport that had been impounded
without her having been told the reasons and without her
having been given an opportunity to state her case. Holding that
fundamental rights had been part of our legacy since the times
of the *Brihadaranyaka Upanishad*, that freedom of speech and
expression is a vital fundamental right, that travelling to other

---

[18] The infamous Maintenance of Internal Security Act.

countries is an essential part of this right, Justice Bhagwati laid down the following propositions about natural justice and about giving each person a hearing before taking an action that might injure her or his interests:

o that natural justice is 'the great humanizing principle', that it is a 'majestic conception';
o that under it no one must be a judge in his own case, and no one must be condemned without being heard, that the latter is 'the cardinal rule';
o that the soul of natural justice is 'fair play in action';
o that the essence of 'fair play in action' is to give a person an opportunity to state her or his case before coming to a judgment about him;
o that the practical test of 'fair play in action' is that the person be shown the materials relevant to the decision and be given an opportunity to state her or his case;
o that you must hear the person, even when the statute does not specifically ask you to do so;
o that the rules of natural justice apply equally when an authority is performing a judicial, a quasi-judicial or an administrative function;
o that procedures established by law must not merely have been formulated under a law enacted by the State, they must conform to fundamental rights, and, in addition, they must be reasonable and fair.

And now? Justice Bhagwati laid down the following principles regarding the manner in which an Additional Judge's suitability was to be assessed:

o Even though the Chief Justice of India and the Chief Justice of the High Court must by law have identical material before them, the latter is in the best position to assess the man's suitability;
o In assessing the information he receives about the man, the Chief Justice of the High Court must make personal and

discreet inquiries but he must not investigate the facts, as such investigation is neither practical nor desirable;

o   As the High Court Chief Justice's final recommendation that the person should be discontinued or appointed permanent Judge will be based not on an examination of facts but merely on the opinion he has reached, what is involved is 'neither adjudication nor condemnation';

o   Hence, there is no reason to import notions of fair play and natural justice into the proceedings; there is no reason, that is, to either inform the Additional Judge about the allegations that have been received about him or to give him an opportunity to present facts and thereby refute the allegations.

Consider the second example.

What if power is abused?

Here is what Justice Bhagwati held at the height of the Emergency in *A.D.M. Jabalpur v S.S. Shukla*, when he was, in effect, hearing the cases of thousands and thousands who were actually (and not just potentially) in jail:

> It was strongly urged upon us that if we take the view that the Presidential Order bars the right of a person to move a court even when his detention is otherwise than in accordance with law, there would be no remedy against illegal detention. That would encourage the Executive to disregard the law and exercise arbitrary powers of arrest. The result would be—so ran the argument—that the citizen would be at the mercy of the Executive; every one would be living in a state of constant apprehension that he might at any time be arrested and detained; personal liberty would be at an end and our cherished values destroyed. Should we accept a construction with such fearful consequences, was the question posed before us. An impassioned appeal was made to us to save personal liberty against illegal encroachments by the Executive. We were exhorted to listen to the voice of judicial conscience *as if judicial conscience*

were a blithe spirit like Shelley's skylark free to sing and soar without any compulsions. I do not think I can allow myself to be deflected by such considerations from arriving at what I consider to be the correct construction of the constitutional provision. The apprehensions and fears voiced on behalf of the detenus may not altogether be ruled out. It is possible that when vast powers are vested in the Executive, the exercise of which is immune from judicial scrutiny, they may sometimes be abused and innocent persons may be consigned to temporary detention. But merely because power may sometimes be abused, it is no ground for denying the existence of the power. All power is likely to be abused. That is inseparable from the nature of human institutions. The wisdom of man has not yet been able to conceive of a government with power sufficient to answer its legitimate ends and at the same time incapable of mischief. In the last analysis, a great deal must depend on the wisdom and honesty, integrity and character of those who are in charge of administration and the existence of enlightened and alert public opinion . . . It is true that, if, in a situation of Emergency judicial scrutiny into legality of detention is held to be barred by a Presidential Order specifying Article 21 illegalities might conceivably be committed by the Executive in exercise of the power of detention and unlawful detentions might be made against which there would be no possibility of redress. The danger may not be dismissed as utterly imaginary, but even so, the fact remains that when there is a crisis-situation arising out of an Emergency, it is necessary to vest the government with extraordinary powers in order to enable it to overcome such crisis-situations and restore normal conditions . . . Now, when vast powers are conferred on the Executive and judicial scrutiny into the legality of exercise of such powers is excluded, it is not unlikely that illegalities might be committed by the Executive in its efforts to deal with the crisis-situation . . . *But howsoever unfortunate this situation might be, that cannot be helped.* The Constitution permits judicial scrutiny to be barred during times of Emergency, because it holds that when a crisis arises in the life of the nation, the rights of individuals must be postponed to considerations of State and national safety must override any other consideration. I may add that there is nothing very unusual in this situation . . . . But at the same time it must be remembered by the Executive that, because judicial scrutiny for the time being is excluded, its responsibility in the exercise of the power of detention is all the greater . . .

So, it is over to the good sense of the people and the sense of added responsibility of the Executive.

After the Emergency, in 1977, the Judge considered the possibility that one specific power—that of transferring Judges— could be abused by the Executive and concluded as follows:

It is often said by courts that the entrustment of power in the hands of high functionaries of State is itself a guarantee against its abuse, but we have seen in our times that *this power of transfer has been abused by the highest in the land* and the so-called safeguard of consultation with the Chief Justice of India has proved to be of no avail. And, as pointed out by the Judicial Committee of the Privy Council in *Don John Francis Douglas Livanage vs. The Queen:* 'What is done once, if it be allowed, may be done again.' *It is a terrifying thought, a frightful possibility, which cannot be allowed to recur if judicial construction can help avert it. Lord Acton said with a profound sense of history. 'Power corrupts and absolute power corrupts absolutely.'* The history of the development of supremacy of the rule of law has been a constant struggle between assertion of power on the one hand and efforts to curb and control it on the other. The interpretation which has found favour with me places a limitation on the vast power reposed in the Executive and this limitation is necessary—indeed it is fully justified by all recognised canons of construction—in order that the Superior Judiciary may be free from Executive influence or pressure. Of course, this view would render it almost impossible to transfer an undesirable Judge from one High Court to another, but for that, the remedy is not to read the power conferred on the Executive as a power exercisable without the consent of the Judge but to create an independent authority which is not controlled by the Executive and where power is exercised by a plurality of hands and to vest the power of transfer in such independent authority so that it may objectively and impartially examine each individual case of proposed transfer on merits and decide whether the transfer should be made or not and where such provision is made, the consent of the Judge may be specifically dispensed with . . .

As the Executive was liable to abuse power and as the requirement that the Chief Justice of India be consulted did not guarantee that the interests of the Judges would be protected, Bhagwati held that the words 'with his consent' must be read into the Article authorizing transfer of Judges. He, having held in 1976 that nothing could be done about the abuse of power as the Constitution allowed the Executive to do what it liked, now said that words should be read into the Constitution which were not there as power was liable to be misused.

But here again is the Judge in 1978 when Maneka Gandhi wanted her passport back:

It is true that when the order impounding a passport is made by the central government there is no appeal against it, but it must be remembered that in such a case the power is exercised by the *central government itself and it can safely be assumed that the central government will exercise the power in a reasonable and responsible manner.* When a power is vested in a high authority like the central government, *abuse of power cannot be lightly assumed.* And in any event, if there is abuse of power, the arms of the Court are long enough to reach it and strike it down.

This time around, in 1981, there was the old trust and hope in the good sense of the Executive, plus, as regards the Chief Justices of India and of the High Courts, a bit of both the earlier attitudes to the possible abuse of power. As the Chief Justice of India is liable to be prejudiced, his power (a power merely to recommend), Justice Bhagwati held, must be hedged in and his advice must be deprived of the primacy that it had in practice enjoyed. On the other hand, said the same Judge, the Chief Justice of the High Court must proceed on the subjective opinion he forms about a colleague on the basis of information he receives but which he most emphatically may not investigate. May the Chief Justice of the High Court not abuse this power? Yes, he may well do so, but that, the Judge maintained in the passage I have already cited, can't be helped. Someone has to be trusted and so, as it was the entire Executive in the habeas corpus case, it might as well be the High Court Chief Justice this time around.

Consider now the third example.

How to interpret the Constitution

In November 1974, speaking for a four-Judge Bench in *Khudiram Das v State of West Bengal,* Justice Bhagwati affirmed how it was the right and duty of the Court to reach out to protect the liberty of the citizen:

> Where the liberty of the subject is involved it is the bounden duty of the Court to satisfy itself that all the safeguards provided by the law have been scrupulously observed and the subject is not deprived of his personal liberty otherwise than in accordance with law . . . It is therefore not only the right of the Court, but also its duty as well, to examine what are the basic facts and materials which actually and in fact weighed with the detaining authority in reaching the requisite satisfaction. The judicial scrutiny cannot be foreclosed by a mere statement of the detaining authority that it has taken into account only certain basic facts and materials and though other basic facts and materials were before it, it has not allowed them to influence its satisfaction. The Court is entitled to examine the correctness of this statement and determine for itself whether there were any other basic facts or materials, apart from those admitted by it, which could have reasonably influenced the decision of the detaining authority and for that purpose, *the Court can certainly require the detaining authority to produce and make available*

to the Court the entire record of the case which was before it.
That is the least that the Court can do to ensure observance of
the requirements of law by the authority . . .

Having held six months before the Emergency that 'where the
liberty of the subject is involved it is the bounden duty of the
Court to satisfy itself that all the safeguards provided by the law
have been observed . . .', having held that it would look not just
at the formal and bare grounds but at the material on which they
were based, in 1976, in *A.D.M. Jabalpur v S.S. Shukla,* Justice
Bhagwati declared that even the bare grounds—to say nothing
of the underlying material—could be kept from the Courts! Here
is how he stated his general position on liberty as a guide to
interpreting the Constitution:

> Before I leave this question, I may point out that, in taking the
> view I have, I am not unaware of the prime importance of the
> rule of law which, since the dawn of political history, both in
> India of *Brihadaranyaka Upanishad* and Greece of Aristotle, has
> tamed the arbitrary exercise of power by the government and
> constitutes one of the basic tenets of constitutionalism . . . But
> at the same time it cannot be overlooked that, in the ultimate
> analysis, the protection of personal liberty and the supremacy of
> law which sustains it must be governed by the Constitution itself.
> The Constitution is the paramount and supreme law of the land
> and if it says that even if a person is detained otherwise than
> in accordance with the law, he shall not be entitled to enforce
> his right of personal liberty, whilst a Presidential proclamation
> under Article 359, clause (1), specifying Article 21 is in force,
> I have to give effect to it. Sitting as I do, as a Judge under the
> Constitution, I cannot ignore the plain and emphatic command
> of the Constitution for what I may consider to be necessary to
> meet the ends of justice . . . I have always leaned in favour of
> upholding personal liberty, for, I believe, it is one of the most
> cherished values of mankind . . . But I do not think it would
> be right for me to allow my love for personal liberty to cloud
> my vision or to persuade me to place on the relevant provision

of the Constitution a construction which its language cannot reasonably bear . . .

And here he is after the Emergency when Maneka wanted her passport: 'The attempt of the Court should be to expand the reach and ambit of the fundamental rights rather than attenuate their meaning and content by the process of judicial construction . . .'

Here is Justice Bhagwati as the activist in *Sheth's* case soon after the Emergency was lifted in 1977:

It has therefore been said that the words of a statute must be understood in the sense which the legislature has in view and their meaning must be found not so much in a strictly grammatical or etymological propriety of language, not in its popular use, as in the subject or the occasion on which they are used and the object to be attained . . . The context is of the greatest importance in the interpretation of the words used in a statute . . . *The literal construction should not obsess the Court,* because it has only *prima facie* preference, the real object of interpretation being to find out the true intent of the law-maker and that can be done only by reading the statute as an organic whole . . . It must be remembered that when the Court interprets a constitutional provision, it breathes life into the inert words used in the founding document. *The problem before the Constitutional Court is not a mere verbal problem* [sic]. 'Literalness', observed Frankfurter, J., 'may strangle meaning' and he went on to add in *Massachusetts S. & Insurance Co. vs. U.S.* that 'there is no surer way to misread a document than to read it literally' [sic]. *The Court cannot interpret a provision of the Constitution by making 'a fortress out of the dictionary'. The significance of a constitutional problem is vital, not formal;* it has to be gathered not simply by taking the words and a dictionary, but by considering the purpose and intendment of the framers as gathered from the context and the setting in which the words occur. The difficulty of gathering the true intent of the law-giver from the words used in the statute was expressed by Holmes, J., in striking and epigrammatic fashion when he said, 'Ideas are not often hard but the words are the devil,' and this difficulty is all the greater when the words to be interpreted occur in a constitutional provision, for, as pointed by Cardozo, J., 'the process of constitutional interpretation is in the ultimate analysis one of reading values into its clauses . . .'

And now here he was in the opening pages of the present case, the strict constructionist:

> It is very easy for the human mind to find justification for a conclusion which accords with the dictates of emotion. Reason is a ready enough advocate for the decision one, consciously or unconsciously, desires to reach . . . We have therefore to rid our mind of any preconceived notions or ideas and interpret the Constitution as it is and not as we think it ought to be. We can always find some reason for bending the language of the Constitution to our will if we want, but that would be rewriting the Constitution in the guise of interpretation. We must also remember that the Constitution as an organic instrument is intended to endure and its provisions must be interpreted having regard to the constitutional objectives and goals and not in the light of how a particular government may be acting at a given point of time. Judicial response to the problem of constitutional interpretation must not suffer from the fault of emotionalism or sentimentalism which is likely to cloud the vision when judges are confronted with issues of momentous importance . . .

But the situation this time was more complex than in either 1976 or 1977. Hence, having just propounded the strict constructionism of his habeas corpus judgment, simultaneously and in this very judgment, Justice Bhagwati also stated the following:

> It is necessary for every Judge to remember constantly and continually that our Constitution is not a non-aligned national charter. It is a document of social revolution which casts an obligation on every instrumentality including the Judiciary which is a separate but equal branch of the State, to transform

the *status quo ante* into a new human order in which justice social, economic and political, will inform all institutions of national life and there will be equality of status and opportunity for all. The Judiciary has therefore a socio-economic destination and a creative function. It has, to use the words of Glanville Austin, to become *an arm of the socio-economic revolution and perform an active role calculated to bring social justice within the reach of the common man.* It cannot remain content to act merely as an umpire but it must be functionally involved in the goal of socio-economic justice. The British concept of justicing, which, to quote Justice Krishna Iyer, is still 'hugged by the heirs of our colonial legal culture and shared by many on the Bench' is that 'the business of a Judge is to hold his tongue until the last possible moment and to try to be as wise as he is paid to look' . . . Now this approach to the judicial function may be all right for a stable and static society but not for a society pulsating with urges of gender justice, worker justice, minorities justice, dalit justice and equal justice between chronic unequals. When the contest is between those who are socially or economically unequal, the judicial process may prove disastrous from the point of view of social justice, if the judge adopts a merely passive or negative role and does not adopt a positive and creative approach. The Judiciary cannot remain a mere bystander or spectator but it must become an active participant in the judicial process ready to use law in the service of social justice through a pro-active goal oriented approach. But this cannot be achieved unless we have judicial cadres who share the fighting faith of the Constitution and who are imbued with the constitutional values . . . What is necessary is to have Judges who are prepared to fashion new tools, forge new methods, innovate new strategies and evolve a new jurisprudence, who are judicial statesmen with a social vision and a creative faculty and who have, above all, a deep sense of commitment to the Constitution with an activist approach and obligation for accountability, not to any party in power nor to the opposition nor to the classes which are vociferous but to the half-hungry millions of India who are continually denied their basic human rights. We need Judges who are alive to the socio-economic realities of Indian life, who are anxious to wipe every tear from every eye, who have faith in the constitutional values and who are ready to use law as an instrument for achieving the constitutional objectives . . .

This time around, therefore, the Judge had armed himself with both swords—the sword of strict constructionism as well as that of judicial hyper-activism. The result was predictable: what was 'strict constructionism yesterday, activist interpretation today', became 'strict constructionism on this page, activism on the next . . .'

No primacy for the Chief Justice's advice, as the Constitution puts all consultants on par. But the words 'with his consent' must be read into an Article where they do not exist. Conventions of three decades regarding Additional Judges must be whittled down as they resulted from the 'unfortunate' and 'peculiar' manner in which Article 224(1) came to be implemented. On the other hand, the conventions regarding locus standi are to be dramatically enlarged as the courts must be an agent of revolutionary change. The Constitution and the laws must be read as they are, not as they ought to be. But governmental claims regarding privilege must be scuttled as they rest on a law passed a hundred years ago . . .

Were the flips random, or the flops? Or was there a pattern to them all?

The pattern

Variable attachment to propositions of the kind we have seen— 'Yes' today, 'No' tomorrow; 'Yes' in this part of the judgment, 'No' in that part—is bad enough for the poor fellow who lands up in the Supreme Court, and in the present case, it was every Judge in every High Court who was before it. But the judgment showed that the matter was, in fact, worse: even if a person falls within the propositions that the Judges currently fancied, he may still fail to secure justice. For the manner in which four of the seven Judges had dealt with facts in this instance—quite apart from what they had said on the law and the Constitution—was, to use the only word that seemed to fit the bill, startling.

As an illustration of the Court's approach to facts, recall the case of Justice S.N. Kumar. Justice Kumar had been an Additional Judge of the Delhi High Court since 7 March 1979. After much tugging and pulling, he was dropped on 6 June 1981, the law minister having chosen, ostensibly, to believe the allegations of the Chief Justice of Delhi that Justice Kumar's integrity was doubtful. (There were many aspects of this case. I shall focus, and that too only briefly, on the two on which the Supreme Court focused.)

The following facts were clear from the record which came before the Supreme Court. (Even in reviewing the record, I shall focus on the question of integrity alone as the matter eventually turned on this):

o   On 2 February 1981, Prakash Narain, the Chief Justice of Delhi, wrote to the law minister saying that there had been 'serious complaints' against the Judge, that 'I have no investigating agency to conclusively find out whether the complaints are genuine or not. All the same the complaints have been persistent.' He added that 'some responsible members of the bar and some of my colleagues have also expressed doubts about Justice Kumar's integrity'. The letter mentioned no evidence or facts to buttress the charge of doubtful integrity.

o   The Chief Justice of the Delhi High Court never mentioned the allegations to Justice Kumar, and never, but never, asked him to explain the facts regarding any of the allegations he had received. In fact, he repeatedly told Justices Kumar, Wad and Vohra, as well as other Judges (and I personally verified this from them), that he had recommended that the three Judges, including Justice Kumar, be given further appointments. The Chief Justice of India asked the Chief Justice of Delhi to substantiate his surmise about Justice Kumar's integrity because what the latter had stated in his letter 'seems to me too vague to accept' as a basis for doubting Kumar's integrity.

o   The Chief Justice of India never received any details from the
     Chief Justice of Delhi or from the law minister.
o   The two Chief Justices had a meeting on 26 March 1981. No
     minutes were available of this meeting. The only written record
     was a subsequent letter from the Chief Justice of India to the
     law minister, which indicated that Prakash Narain, the Delhi
     Chief Justice, did not furnish any evidence to substantiate
     his surmise.
o   The Chief Justice of India asked Kumar to furnish him
     facts regarding the points (allegations of slow disposal of
     work, retaining part-heard cases, etc., that Prakash Narain
     had mentioned to him). He never asked for Kumar's
     explanation regarding any question relating to his integrity—
     strong evidence that he had received no evidence that
     required explaining.
o   The Chief Justice of India made independent inquiries and
     came to the following conclusion which he communicated to
     the law minister: 'I have made the most careful and extensive
     inquiries in regard to both of these matters and I am satisfied
     that there is no substance in any of them . . . Not one member
     of the Bar or of the Bench doubted the integrity of Justice
     Kumar. On the other hand, several of them stated that he is a
     man of unquestioned integrity.'

The law minister also asked Prakash Narain to furnish details to
substantiate his surmise. Prakash Narain wrote to him on 7 May
1981. Two facts about this letter were vital. First, by marking
this letter 'Secret (For Personal Attention Only)', and by a later
and specific clarification, he requested the law minister to keep
the letter secret from the Chief Justice of India. (The law minister
assured him that it would be kept secret and it was so kept.)
In the letter, Prakash Narain adduced two bits of 'evidence' to
substantiate his allegation, and recounted the steps he had taken
since he had heard the rumours.

    First, he said, in 'the first half of 1980' he heard 'chance
remarks' about Kumar's 'conduct in court as well as about his
integrity' when Kumar was sitting singly on the original side.

Second, he said that *in early May* 1980 (note the 'in early May' for this will be important in a moment) a colleague told him that he had information with him to the effect that if a substantial amount was paid to Justice Kumar, suits brought by a particular party against an insurance company would be decided in favour of that party. Third, he said that as 'a safe way to finish the rumours if the same were incorrect and thus safeguard the reputation of a Judge', he shifted Kumar to a Division Bench on the Appellate side so that Kumar would henceforth sit, not alone, but with another Judge. Even so, Prakash Narain said, 'Justice Kumar did not release the original suits regarding which allegations had been made from his board.' Fourth, Prakash Narain said that as these allegations persisted, he looked into the matter carefully and found that 'it was not only the three suits mentioned above but that there were other single-bench matters also which had been retained by Justice Kumar on his board despite being on the Division Bench'.

The 'evidence', which in any case was not supplied to the Chief Justice of India, was a concoction through and through.

The three specific cases that Prakash Narain mentioned related to marine insurance claims made by a company called Jain Shudh Vanaspati against the New India Assurance Company.

Jain Shudh Vanaspati, the company from which Kumar was said to receive money, was opposing the application of the insurance company that the latter be granted leave to defend. Prakash Narain said that in early May, a colleague told him that he had information that Kumar would decide the matter in favour of Jain Shudh for money. The fact is that the matter had been settled on 11 April, that is, at least *three weeks before* the alleged conversation in which his colleague is said to have told Prakash Narain that Kumar would (in future) settle the matter in favour of the company. Second, on 11 April, Kumar had issued an order not in favour of Jain Shudh but *against* it! Third, after this order was passed, the suits went back to another Judge—Justice D.R. Khanna—so that in May, when Prakash Narain had said he had heard his tale, *there was just no question of the cases being dealt with by Kumar*!

The solicitude for the reputation of Kumar and the interests of clients which ostensibly led Prakash Narain to shift Kumar to a Division Bench for the latter half of 1980 was also an ex post concoction. For the fact is that in the first half of 1980, Kumar had sat alone for only five weeks. For *three and a half months*, he had already been sitting on a Division Bench with Justice Sachar. So there was no question of shifting him to a Division Bench in the second half of 1980. He had already been on one for three and a half months!

The next fact was comic. Prakash Narain had said that as he came to doubt Kumar's integrity, he had made sure that Kumar would no longer sit alone. But, having shifted him to a Division Bench in view of his conviction that Kumar could not be trusted to sit alone, in January 1981 Prakash Narain himself again posted Kumar to the original side to sit alone!

Prakash Narain's aspersion that Kumar, after being shifted to the Division Bench, had 'retained' cases, that he did not release cases he had heard in part while he was on the original side, was also patently a fabrication. First, the records showed that Kumar never ordered that any case remain with him. That was a function of the Registry of the Court. And the Registry functioned mechanically in this matter: if a matter had been heard in part by a Judge, it was automatically reassigned to him. There were good reasons for this: if the case was shifted each time, all the arguments would have to be gone through all over again, a contestant, having divined in the course of hearing that the particular Judge seemed to be going against him, may have his case shifted to another Judge, etc. So well-settled was the practice that at least two Judges in the past had threatened contempt proceedings against the Registrar when the latter's office shifted cases they had heard in part to other Judges.

How did Justice Bhagwati deal with all these facts?

He didn't deal with them at all! Each one of the facts that blew Prakash Narain's letter of 7 May to bits was placed before all the Judges with the specific permission of Justice Bhagwati. Indeed, at his direction, Kumar's Supplementary Affidavit, in which the facts were set out, was sent by a special messenger to the residence of each of the seven Judges. This document formed part of the Court's record.

Having received the facts, having held repeatedly that the Supreme Court would never hesitate to examine facts if a decision had been taken mala fide or for collateral reasons, Bhagwati and his colleagues decided not to look at the facts at all. We won't assess whether Kumar was justly done in, we will only examine whether there was full and effective consultation, the Judges declared. Why did they not throw out the document then, the document that had been sent to each of the Judges at his residence at the presiding Judge's direction? So much for the justice that Kumar had gone to seek at their hands.

Consultation

And what of full and effective consultation? Now, it had been repeatedly held that for consultation to be full and effective, each participant must have all the facts the others have, that all must have the identical set of facts. Whether Prakash Narain or Kumar had been right, the relevant facts had clearly been held back from the Chief Justice of India. Such as they were, and we have seen what they were, the 'facts' were set out by the Chief Justice of Delhi in his letter of 7 May to the law minister alone, and this letter had been concealed by the two of them from the Chief Justice of India. This was manifest from the record. As facts which were crucial and which Chief Justice Chandrachud had specifically sought, which were in the possession of both the Chief Justice of Delhi and the law minister, had been concealed from the Chief Justice of India, it was clear as daylight that consultation had not been, as under law it must be, full and effective.

How had our Judge dealt with this hurdle? The two Chief Justices, he maintained, must have discussed the matter in their meeting of 26 March, because, in a subsequent letter, the Chief Justice of Delhi told the law minister that all the details had been explained to Chief Justice Chandrachud. There were no minutes of the meeting. The only record of the meeting was the letter that the Chief Justice of India wrote to the law minister which clearly suggested the opposite.

Moreover, if Prakash Narain had already narrated to Chief Justice Chandrachud all the details that he was later to set down in his 7 May letter to the law minister, why was he so particular that his letter be concealed from Chief Justice Chandrachud?

Justice Bhagwati's reasoning on this vital matter exceeded mere craftsmanship. It was inventive. I will mention just one reason he gave in the hope that it will persuade you to read his judgment—at least this part of it—for a real education. The Chief Justice of India, he said, gave the Chief Justice of Delhi the impression that he would not like the latter to put on record facts that might injure Kumar. And that is why, when in response to the law minister's request Prakash Narain decided to put the facts down on paper, he naturally wanted that the letter be kept from the Chief Justice of India.

Here is how Justice Bhagwati put the matter:

> There is an undercurrent of suggestion here that the Chief Justice of India did not approve of the idea of the Chief Justice of Delhi setting out in a letter the facts discussed by him with the Chief Justice of India and perhaps that is why the Chief Justice of Delhi stated that it was both embarrassing and painful for him to write that letter setting out the facts on which his opinion was based . . .

As if repetition would lend weight to conjecture, the Judge repeated the supposition seventeen pages later:

> . . . but the letter dated 28th March 1981, was written by him in the terms in which it was couched as per the desire of the Chief Justice of India and therefore it was embarrassing and painful for him to write the letter dated 7th May, 1981. This reason given by the Chief Justice of Delhi carries a veiled suggestion, though not expressly articulated but implicit in what he has stated, that the Chief Justice of India did not want him to place on record the details and concrete facts in regard

to the allegations against SN Kumar and that is why he wrote the letter dated 28th March, 1981 in the terms he did according to the desire of the Chief Justice of India. This was perhaps the reason why the Chief Justice of Delhi found it embarrassing as well as painful to write the letter dated 7th May 1981 setting out the 'details and concrete facts in regard to the allegations' against SN Kumar, such a course being presumably contrary to the suggestion of the Chief Justice of India. *We have, of course, no definite material before us on the basis of which we can conclude* that the Chief Justice of India must have asked the Chief Justice of Delhi not to place the detailed facts relating to the complaints and doubts against SN Kumar in writing, but it does appear that *some discussion must have taken place* between the Chief Justice of Delhi and the Chief Justice of India as a result of which the Chief Justice of Delhi bona fide carried a feeling that the Chief Justice of India might feel offended if the Chief Justice of Delhi were to put the detailed facts in regard to the allegations against SN Kumar on record, contrary to the view held by the Chief Justice of India. That is why the Chief Justice of Delhi was anxious that his letter dated 7th May, 1981, should not be brought to the attention of the Chief Justice of India. It was not because the Chief Justice of Delhi did not want the facts set out in the letter dated 7th May, 1981, to be disclosed to the Chief Justice of India that he requested the Law Minister not to place that letter before the Chief Justice of India, but because in view of the impression given or perhaps a suggestion made at the meeting by the Chief Justice of India, he apprehended that if he placed those facts on record contrary to the wish of the Chief Justice of India, the Chief Justice of India might feel offended and his relations with the Chief Justice of India might be spoilt . . .

There are many things to be said about this reasoning. Let me mention just one: in concluding that the Chief Justice of India influenced the Chief Justice of Delhi to concoct a document so that the facts he had himself sought were kept out of it, Justice Bhagwati had discovered an explanation that neither the Government of India nor the Chief Justice of Delhi ever put forward.

The end of the matter, too, was curious. Having concluded by such reasoning that there was full and effective consultation as the Chief Justice of Delhi must have mentioned all the relevant facts to the Chief Justice of India in their meeting of 26 March, Justice Bhagwati ordered that there was no ground for directing the government to re-examine Kumar's case and thus rejected Kumar's plea for relief. Having done that on page 270 of his judgment, on page 271 Justice Bhagwati suggested to the government that 'it would be a good thing if . . . the Union of India could see its way to place the letter of 7th May, 1981, addressed by the Chief Justice of Delhi to the Law Minister before the Chief Justice of India and elicit his opinion with reference to that letter and then consider whether SN Kumar should be reappointed as an Additional Judge in the Delhi High Court.'

If all the facts contained in the 7 May letter were in fact placed before the Chief Justice of India, as Bhagwati was saying they were, and there was full and effective consultation, as he was maintaining there was, why this little 'suggestion' at the end? Covering both sides?

A pattern

Flip-flop, therefore, was not the only pattern in the judgment. There was more, for neither the flips were random nor the flops.

The law minister had issued a circular asking Chief Ministers to obtain the consent of Additional Judges and others to being appointed Judges in other High Courts. Its tone was minatory and presumptuous. Even by its own words, it was part of an overall policy to shunt Judges around. It came in the wake of concerted attacks on the Judiciary, characterizing the Judges as obstacles to social progress, as being incapable of rendering justice. It came in the wake of statements that the government definitely intended to use the weapon of transfers as a device for bringing the Judges to heel. It came in the wake of the government's record of using the weapon to devilish purpose during the Emergency. But our Judge was considerate as can be: 'It would not be right,' he said, 'to read the circular letter with a suspicious eye as if it was designed to cow down the Additional Judges into submission by holding out an implied threat to them . . . '

The law minister was insolent in asking Chief Ministers to obtain consents from sitting and prospective Judges. Could there be a clearer signal than this that the Executive was determined to put and to show that it had put the Judges beneath it? Justice Bhagwati, who in *Sheth's* case, to cite just one passage, had spoken stirringly on the need to insulate the Judiciary from the Executive:

> And hovering over all these provisions like a brooding omnipresence is Article 50 which lays down, as a Directive Principle of State Policy, that the State shall take steps to separate the Judiciary from the Executive in the public services of the State. This provision occurring in a chapter which has been described by Granville Austin as 'the conscience of the Constitution' and which embodies the social philosophy of the Constitution and its basic underpinnings and values, plainly reveals, without any scope for doubt or debate, the intent of the Constitution-makers to immunise the Judiciary from any form of Executive control or interference . . .

now declared that while the law minister, in fact, asked the Chief Ministers to obtain their consent from sitting and prospective Judges, he *must have meant* that the Chief Ministers do so through the Chief Justices of the High Courts. This is how he put it:

> It is true that the Law Minister did not state in so many terms in the circular letter that the Chief Minister may make this enquiry through the Chief Justice of the High Court but that *was clearly implicit in the circular letter,* because a copy of the circular letter was also sent to the Chief Justice of each High Court with the endorsement 'for necessary action', and moreover *it must be presumed* that the necessary inquiry would be made by the Chief Minister only through the Chief Justice of the High Court. The Chief Minister would not be expected to contact

directly the Additional Judges or the persons recommended for initial appointment, for the purpose of ascertaining whether they are willing to be appointed as Judges in any other High Court. Since the Chief Justice of the High Court is the head of the judiciary in the State, the Chief Minister would invariably route his enquiry through the Chief Justice of the High Court and request the Chief Justice of the High Court to ascertain whether any of the Additional Judges or persons recommended for initial appointment are willing to be appointed to a High Court outside the State. This enquiry could have been made by the Law Minister by writing directly to the Chief Justice of each High Court but, instead of doing so, the Law Minister chose to address his enquiry to the Chief Minister of each state, *presumably because* he thought that it would be more appropriate for him to make this enquiry through the Chief Minister of the state rather than by direct communication with the Chief Justice of the High Court . . .

Justice Bhagwati's assessment was that the transfer circular had, in fact, nothing to do with transferring Judges from one High Court to another. It was only meant to ascertain whether Judges would agree to being appointed to another High Court, he said. Now, it so happens that in statements in the Lok Sabha, the law minister had clearly used the word 'transfer' and did so more than once. Here is how Justice Bhagwati dealt with this inconvenience:

It is undoubtedly true that in columns 271 and 274, the Law Minister used the expression 'transfer' or 'transferred' while referring to the circular letter, *but one cannot fasten upon a stray use of a loose expression for the purpose of determining what is the true effect of the circular letter.* The speech of the Law Minister has to be read as a whole and if it is so read, it is clear that what was contemplated by the circular letter was not a case of transfer but a case of an appointment under Article 217 vide column 273 . . . The expression 'transfer' or 'transferred' in columns 271 and 274 *was obviously used in a loose sense meaning physical locomotion.* It must be remembered that this expression happened to be used by the Law Minister in an extempore speech made on the floor of the House and not in a document or letter prepared after much care and deliberation. No undue reliance can therefore be placed on behalf of the petitioners on the use of the expression 'transfer' or 'transferred' in the speech of the Law Minister . . .

What can one say about such pulling and stretching of plain words?

Double standards

In terms of judgments of the Supreme Court itself, the law minister was duty-bound to place all relevant facts in a case such as that of S.N. Kumar before the Chief Justice of India. He had received information (such as it was) from the Chief Justice of Delhi and had come to a private deal with him that neither of them would pass the relevant document to the Chief Justice of India.

Once again, Justice Bhagwati was consideration itself. Putting aside earlier dicta of the Supreme Court to the effect that it is the duty of the Central Government to place all the facts before the Chief Justice of India, he now said that nothing had gone wrong, as 'it is not necessary that the full and identical facts . . . should be placed before the Chief Justice of Delhi and the Chief Justice of India by the central government itself or that they should be brought to the notice of the Chief Justice of Delhi and the Chief Justice of India in any particular order or by following any particular procedure'. So the law minister did no wrong.

Contrast all this with the way in which Justice Bhagwati handled material regarding the Chief Justice of India. Chief Justice Chandrachud's unequivocal counter-affidavit that all facts regarding the transfer of K.B.N. Singh, the Chief Justice of Patna, to Madras were brought to the notice of the Central Government, Justice Bhagwati characterizes in terms such as 'vague and indefinite', 'this statement, even if it be accepted as wholly correct . . .', 'this statement made in the affidavit is delightfully vague', and so on. When the Chief Justice of India stated that the facts had been discussed by him and the Central Government, both before and after the transfer was proposed, Bhagwati dismissed it as just a 'vague allegation'.

In Kumar's case, as we saw, although there were no minutes of the 26 March meeting between the two Chief Justices, and although the only written record, the 22 May letter of the Chief Justice of India to the law minister, showed that the facts had *not* been placed before him, Justice Bhagwati concluded that, minutes or no minutes, 'there is no doubt in our minds that the facts were discussed . . .' In K.B.N. Singh's case, although the Chief Justice had sworn in his counter-affidavit that all the facts were discussed, although thirteen documents released by the government on the orders of the Court revealed that the matter was discussed by the Chief Justice with the law minister as well as the Prime Minister, Justice Bhagwati concluded that, these averments and documents notwithstanding, as there were no minutes of the discussions, he could not but conclude that the facts had *not* been discussed!

A *thread of three strands*

The examples can be multiplied. But the few we have encountered are enough to reveal the thread of three strands that strung the flip-flops together.

First, Justice Bhagwati believed, as set out in the passages quoted above, that the Judiciary must not be an umpire but an agent of social change. Second, he believed, as he set out with such grandiloquence in his letter of 15 January 1980, to Mrs Gandhi to which we shall turn in a moment, that she and her government were the great hope of social progress in India. Writing a month and a half after the end of the Emergency in *Rajasthan & Others v the Union of India*, Justice Bhagwati had recorded how unequivocally the people had rejected Mrs Gandhi and her Party:

This is not a case where just an ordinary defeat has been suffered by the ruling party in a state at the elections to the Lok Sabha. There has been a total rout of candidates belonging to the ruling party. In some of the plaintiff-states, the ruling party has not been able to secure a single seat. Never in the history of this country has such a clear and unequivocal verdict been given by the people, never a more massive vote of no-confidence in the ruling party. When there is such crushing defeat suffered by the ruling party and the people have expressed themselves categorically against its policies, it is symptomatic of complete alienation between the government and the people . . .

Writing six months after the Emergency ended, in *Sheth's* case, Justice Bhagwati recalled how power—in that case the specific power to transfer Judges—had been abused by 'the highest in the land', how 'what had happened once, if allowed, may happen again', how this was 'a terrifying thought, a frightful possibility', and how, therefore, it must be guarded against. His new assessment about who could best be the prime agent of social change was contained in the letter he wrote to Mrs Gandhi on 15 January 1980, that is just a week after her electoral victory:

Dear Indiraji,

. . . Your resounding victory . . . your triumphant return . . . a most remarkable achievement . . . you have fortunately the greatest asset any politician can ever possess . . . voted to power with an amazing outburst, amounting almost to an avalanche, of affection and enthusiasm . . . I am sure that with your iron will and firm determination, uncanny insight and dynamic vision, great administrative capacity and vast experience, overwhelming love and affection of the people and above all a heart which is identified with the misery of the poor and the weak . . . Today the reddish glow of the rising sun is holding out the promise of a bright sunshine . . .[19]

---

[19] The letter is an important document in marking yet another high in genuflections. It also illustrates the ease with which skilled craftsmen dress up their flattery in high principles and lofty objectives: in this instance, judicial reform and social justice. For these reasons, and so that it is not lost in hard-to-get old issues of newspapers, I reproduce Justice Bhagwati's entire letter at the end of this chapter.

Third, since 1977 Justice Bhagwati had grown increasingly disenchanted with the leadership of the Supreme Court and was by now convinced, at the least, that Chief Justice Chandrachud was not providing the leadership that would enable the Judiciary to be the engine of change that he thought it should be. In December 1980, in the *Minerva Mills* case, he went out of his way to castigate the Chief Justice of India for the manner in which he had conducted that particular case, and it was on that unprecedented page in his judgment that Mrs Gandhi's new government relied when, after its return, it filed a petition urging a review of the decision. In his January 1980 letter to Mrs Gandhi, the Judge put the matter a bit more obliquely but clearly enough:

> I also wish to bring to your notice that the judicial system in our country is in a state of utter collapse . . . The Supreme Court is also reeling under the weight of arrears . . . The position is almost desperate and yet there does not seem to be any sense of urgency in the Court . . .

Everyone knew what and who the Judge had in mind. And now Justice Bhagwati had gone further to characterize the Chief Justice of India, his conduct, his averments, and therefore the need to hedge his role in ways that I have indicated earlier. He had gone so far as to say that, in his view, Justice Chandrachud influenced the Chief Justice of Delhi to concoct a document; he had gone so far as to imply that Chief Justice Chandrachud had leaked secrets; he had gone so far as to dig up a convenient passage from Ambedkar and misrepresent it to boot. Ambedkar said what he did while opposing an amendment of Mr Pocker Sahib, which would have given the Chief Justice a veto over appointments, etc. Ambedkar said that as the Chief Justice was but a man, he might suffer from prejudices like other men, and so a veto should not be given to him as it should not be given to any other individual. Bhagwati used the passage to argue that, far from having a veto, the advice of the Chief Justice of India should carry no greater weight than that of a Governor of a state.

No one can say that these three strands were the motives that had impelled Justice Bhagwati to hold what he had in his judgment. We must assume that he had gone exclusively by the law and by the facts as he saw them. But these three strands were what ran through the judgment, and the 300-odd pages it spanned could only be understood by keeping them in mind.

Last words

From the fact that this analysis has been devoted to Justice Bhagwati's judgment, we should not conclude that his judgment is the one that is exceptionally or even specially suitable for examination. None can surpass Justice Fazal Ali's judgment in that respect.

Having held in *Sheth's* case, that 'the power (to transfer Judges) under Article 222 however, is to be exercised exceptionally', that 'the transfer of judges under the Article was intended to be an unusual step . . .' Justice Fazal Ali now had the longest of paeans for a policy under which wholesale transfers would be the order of the day. Even though the relevant policy had not been formulated, Justice Fazal Ali gave it his enthusiastic benediction in advance. Indeed, he gave practical advice to the government: you do not have to amend the Constitution or pass an Act or even formulate a rule or a by-law or any other instruction to give effect to the policy you propose to enact, he told the government; just decree it by a Presidential Order. And once this Presidential Order is decreed, he told the government, all this claptrap about full and effective consultation before transferring a Judge will fall in place: once the policy is in effect, he said, consultation will be limited to the exceptions only. As for the well-known fact that the Chief Justice of India had opposed wholesale transfers disguised under the garb of some 'policy', here was Fazal Ali's advice:

> Although the CJI has at present shown his stiff opposition to the policy we hope and trust that when the matter is reassessed and a policy is finally formulated, the CJI would eschew his opposition in view of the various factors and circumstances

indicated above as also in due deference to the view of some of the Judges of this Court who have decided these cases, which, as pointed out by us, is not only in great public interest but also in national interest of the country. Moreover, the policy has been amply supported and sponsored not only by the government but also by a very large body of public men including jurists, politicians, lawyers, parliamentarians and others. If despite these circumstances the CJI does not change his view and sticks to his opposition of the policy, then we think this will be a fit and proper case where the President might overrule the CJI and enforce the policy. We however solemnly hope and trust that such an eventuality would not arise . . .

Having held in *Sheth's* case that it is the duty of the Central Government to place all the facts before the Chief Justice of India when it seeks to consult him, Fazal Ali now held that the law minister was right to withhold Prakash Narain's letter from the Chief Justice of India. '. . . the role of the Law Minister,' he observed in a representative passage, 'has been very fair and just from start to finish . . .' As for Prakash Narain's conduct in asking the law minister to conceal his letter from the Chief Justice of India, Justice Fazal Ali did not merely find it bona fide but held it up as an example of 'tact and wisdom', and said that when 'we put ourselves in the place of CJ, Delhi, we would have done the same in the circumstances'.

Far from faulting Prakash Narain, Fazal Ali faulted Kumar for approaching the Supreme Court for relief:

Indeed, if a really conscientious judge would have been in the position of petitioner Kumar he would have silently walked out of the show in the larger interests of the great and sacrosanct institution which he was serving instead of insisting on disclosure and thereby drawing himself into a serious controversy to vindicate his supposed right. I have already pointed out that it is not for the first time that the term of an Additional Judge has not been extended: in the past also judges have been dropped and one of the schedules given by the Solicitor General is full of such

instances. Such judges never raised any controversy regarding
their not being reappointed and got reconciled themselves [*sic*]
without any protest or objection perhaps in due deference to the
maintenance of the purity of the great institution of justice . . .

How did Justice Fazal Ali conclude that, although the 7 May
letter was withheld from Chief Justice Chandrachud, all the
relevant facts were brought before him? On page 215 of his
judgment, he said, 'After sending the letter he [Prakash Narain]
had a full discussion with the CJI on all the points . . .' On the
next page he says, '*the possibility* that he [Prakash Narain] may
have discussed all matters including the materials put in writing to
the Law Minister with the CJI *cannot be excluded* . . .' On page
202 he says, 'It is obvious that the CJ, Delhi, expressed his desire
that the full material which was supplied to the Law Minister
may not be sent to the CJI but that was perhaps because the CJ,
Delhi had oral discussions with the CJI in respect of all relevant
material . . .' A strong argument there! The man has mentioned all
the details orally and, therefore, requests that the written version
of the same details be concealed! Two pages later, Justice Fazal
Ali is more definite: 'As the data and material supplied to the Law
Minister in the letter dated 7.5.1981 had already been supplied to
the CJI or, at any rate, orally discussed with him . . .'

But these remarks are hardly surprising from a Judge who has
characterized the petitioner's plea that the independence of the
Judiciary was in danger as a mere 'egotistic slogan'.

So it isn't Justice Bhagwati's judgment alone that
merits attention.

The lessons from this sorry episode are so manifest that we
need not expend time on them. I shall leave the last words to
Justice Bhagwati. The two passages figured in his judgment in
Sheth's case and, though they set out the perils of craftsmanship
and of ambition in the context of transfers, they have
wider relevance:

It must be remembered that though, by and large, our judges
(and their number, I am sure, is quite large) are made of sterner

stuff and no threat of injury, however grave or serious, would deflect them from doing their duty 'without fear or favour,' some judges may, on account of threat of transfer, be induced, albeit not consciously or deliberately, to do that which pleases the Executive to avert such injury, and *if they are competent and skilled in judicial craftsmanship, it would not be difficult for them to find arguments to justify their action in falling in line with the wishes of the Executive, because reason is a ready-enough advocate for the decision one, consciously or unconsciously, desires to reach* . . .

And, Justice Bhagwati further observed, 'I think it was Mr. Justice Jackson who said that "Judges are more often bribed by their ambition and loyalty than by money."'

Amen! And now for the incredible letter that Justice Bhagwati wrote to Mrs Indira Gandhi a week after she returned to power, and Sanjay once again seemed the go-to man for everything:

~

'The reddish glow of the rising sun'

Dear Indira Ji,

May I offer you my heartiest congratulations on your resounding victory in the elections and your triumphant return as the Prime Minister of India. It is a most remarkable achievement of which you, your friends and well-wishers can be justly proud. It is a great honour to be the Prime Minister of a country like India, but it is equally a heavy responsibility, particularly since you have to build a new order out of the wreckage of the old. You have fortunately the greatest asset which any politician can ever possess, namely, the love and affection of the people.

Your party has been voted to power with an amazing outburst, amounting almost to an avalanche, of affection and enthusiasm and now the people are looking forward to an era where there will be for everyone freedom from want and destitution. You have become the symbol of the hopes and aspirations of the poor, hungry millions of India who had so far nothing to hope for and nothing to live for and who are now looking upto you for lifting them from dirt and squalor and freeing them from poverty and ignorance.

It is a very difficult task which lies ahead of you, but I am sure that with your iron will and firm determination, uncanny insight and dynamic vision, great administrative capacity and vast experience, overwhelming love and affection of the people and above all a heart which is identified with the misery of the poor and the weak, you will be able to steer the ship of the nation safely to its cherished goal and the glorious vision of the founding fathers of the Constitution will become a living reality.

We must always carry in our hearts and never forget the intolerable burden of the misery and suffering of our people, for then only we shall be able to place our people and our country above ourselves.

It is in this spirit of dedication and service that I have taken up the task of setting up a legal service programme with a view to serve the poor and the weak, the have-nots and the handicapped, so that the benefits of the legal process may reach them, they may have equal justice under law and social justice may be assured to them.

During your earlier period as Prime Minister, you were good enough to appoint a committee under my chairmanship for making recommendations for establishing a comprehensive and dynamic legal service programme in the country and I made my report to the successor Janata Government on 31st August 1977. But unfortunately the Janata Government did not take any steps at all for implementing the recommendations made in the report and did not even make the printed report available to the public. The result is that the legal service programme is languishing and barring the States of Maharashtra and Karnataka, where I am guiding and supervising the legal aid programme, nothing is being done in this field in other parts of the country. There are some radical proposals made by me in the reports and I have personally no doubt that if they are implemented, we can go a long way towards bringing about socio-economic revolution through law. I would earnestly appeal to you to take up the legal service programme as a priority item.

I also wish to bring to your notice that the judicial system in our country is in a state of utter collapse. The British system of administration of justice which we inherited from our erstwhile rulers has developed serious constraints and has proved inadequate to meet the needs of a changing society in the context of vast socio-economic developments taking place in the country. This is evident from the incapacity of the system to deal adequately with the large volume of litigation coming before it and to adjust its methods and procedures and to forge new tools for resolving the new kind of problems that are continually thrown up by a society which is constantly on the move. Arrears are also mounting up in the courts and the entire judicial machinery is almost coming to a grinding halt. The Supreme Court is also reeling under the weight of arrears. There are more than 16,000 final hearing cases pending in the Court while the total number of special leave petitions and miscellaneous matters pending in the Court is over 19,000.

The Supreme Court has, at present, civil appeals of 1968–69, labour appeals of 1971, tax appeals of 1972 and criminal appeals of 1972 still pending on its files. The position is almost desperate and yet there does not seem to be any sense of urgency in the Court.

I am of the view that unless steps are immediately taken to remedy this state of affairs, the Supreme Court will go down. It is, in my opinion, absolutely essential that we should have a fresh and uninhibited look at our judicial system and consider what structural and jurisdictional changes are necessary in order to make it an effective instrument for dispensing social justice which is the signature tune of our dynamic Constitution.

It is necessary to restructure our entire judicial system and for that a bold, dynamic and imaginative approach is imperative. I would sincerely request you to see that immediate steps are taken to bring about drastic and radical changes in the judicial system with a view to restructuring it so that it may ensure not only speedy and expeditious justice but also social justice to the people.

Today the reddish glow of the rising sun is holding out the promise of a bright sunshine. May that sunshine fill our hearts with joy and bring comfort and cheer to the poor, hall-naked, hungry millions of our countrymen. That is my only prayer to God on this occasion.

With kind regards,

Yours sincerely,

(P. N. Bhagwati)

13

The case of the missing file

Late one evening, I got a call from R.R. Morarka. A businessman, he was as astute as he was soft-spoken. At the time he was a Member of the Rajya Sabha, and of Parliament's Committee on Public Enterprises. He asked whether we could meet the following day. When we met, he told me about a contract to purchase petroleum products, about how the Committee had been trying to get the facts about the contract, and how it was being thwarted at every turn. After much to and fro, the Ministry had at last agreed to provide the facts. But then, suddenly, it had said that it could not do so as the relevant file was missing. Two things were clear: government was trying to hide something, and the file was not 'missing'; it was lying somewhere from where the Ministry could not retrieve it. That can only be one place, I said. He agreed, and added that the officials who had appeared before the Committee were visibly under pressure, none more so than the Secretary—he had been so evasive as to have been misleading.

But I knew the Secretary, Lavraj Kumar. In fact, I knew him well.[1]

---

[1] He was an Adviser at the Planning Commission when I was working there as a Consultant to Dr B.S. Minhas. Several of us would often gather in Lavraj's room—you would get the best coffee there. His wife, Dharma Kumar was a

So, I rang him up.

When we met at his house, I recounted what I had come to know from members of the Committee, and explained how, from the way he had evaded questions, they had concluded that he personally had something to hide. And how could a file just go missing? Assuming that it had got destroyed somehow, why could it not have been reconstructed?

Lavraj told me that at some stage, the file had been handed over to R.K. Dhawan in the Prime Minister's Office, that, after strenuous efforts, it had been retrieved, that, in fact, he had brought it home for me to see. Officials were absolutely in the clear, he explained. The then minister had given explicit directions about who should be given the contract and on what terms. The Chairman of the Indian Oil Corporation—the government firm through which the purchases were made—had been sent the directions in writing.

All this was delicious! Lavraj took me through the important notings in the file.

Having had a glimpse of what the file contained, I became all the more anxious to get it. Later, through two other officers, I got to study the file and take notes.

I had already been through the COPU (Committee on Public Undertakings) report, in particular the few paragraphs in it that dealt with this deal. I had talked at length to Morarka and two other members of the Committee. I had been through the minutes of the Committee's meetings that dealt with this deal. The file completed the picture. The details about the deal were interesting, of course. But even more telling was what had been happening to the file, for this pointed to the ones who were interested in covering up that affair.

I wrote a three-part article, and handed it to B.G. Verghese, the editor of the *Indian Express* at the time. He went through the article, and told me that the paper couldn't carry it. The reasons he gave were laughable—having stood up to the authorities to

---

well-known economist—a first-rate scholar, she was full of beans and barbs and information.

the point of being removed from the *Hindustan Times* during the Emergency, he just could not have believed them. He said that as the file had not been furnished to Parliament, for us to publish its contents would be a breach of Parliament's privileges, and the paper, and he as its editor, could be hauled up for the breach. Moreover, we could be hauled up for breaching the Official Secrets Act.

But when something is withheld from Parliament and we are supplying it, we are *assisting* Parliament, I said. How are we breaching its privileges? As for official secrets: in the eyes of government anything and everything that shows the rulers up is a State Secret. If we go by what you say about the contents of this file, we will be reduced to publishing nothing but government press handouts.

But Verghese just kept repeating the phrases: 'breach of Parliament's privileges . . . Official Secrets Act . . .'

I knew the real reason for his decision. Ramnathji was under immense pressure to not allow material to be published that would embarrass the government. And here was an article that pointed directly to Sanjay Gandhi and his friends.

I contacted Mr H.M. Seervai, the great authority on our Constitution, and explained Verghese's apprehension and my view. Mr Seervai was emphatic: of course, you would be assisting Parliament by publishing what has been withheld from it. As for the Official Secrets Act, well, you have to figure out what, after all, is the duty of the free press in such circumstances.[2]

---

2 In his autobiography, Verghese gives an equally laughable reason for withholding the article. He says that he asked me whether the COPU report had been published, and as neither I nor he was sure it had been, he had to turn down the article. And that when at last I could confirm that the report had been published, he at once allowed publication of the article. [B.G. Verghese, *First Draft, Witness to the Making of Modern India,* Tranquebar, Westland, Chennai, 2010, pp. 298–300.] That is laughable, as I said. We were talking in July 1982. The report had been tabled in both the Lok Sabha and the Rajya Sabha *two months earlier*—on 30 April 1982. [Committee on Public Undertakings (1981–82), (Seventh Lok Sabha), *Forty-Seventh Report on Oil Companies—Imports of Petroleum Crude and Products and Distribution of Gas, (Ministry of Petroleum, Chemicals and Fertilizers, Department of*

But Verghese would not budge. I sat down and wrote him a letter, with a copy to Ramnathji:

~

My dear George,

Since yesterday afternoon I have been a bit distressed. Two apprehensions have arisen in my mind and as I hope to work with you, I think it best to report these apprehensions to you as candidly as possible. I would not like to hold anything back in my mind.

You said that the three-part article I had submitted to you could not be used as it was liable to open us to the charge of violating the privileges of Parliament and of violating the Official Secrets Act. Over the last three years I have had occasion to study both these subjects in great detail. I can state with certainty that we would have an excellent defence, were someone to charge us on either of the two grounds.

As for the breach of privilege charge, our defence would be that a deliberate and successful attempt had been made to withhold vital material from a committee of Parliament and to influence the report of that committee. Therefore, as friends of Parliament, we were bringing the facts to the attention of Parliament both because we value the institution in itself and because under Article 51-A we are duty-bound to do so. There would be various other lines of defence also. On earlier occasions I have set out the principles involved in my letters to the Speaker and to Hidayatullah when breach of privilege motions were filed against me. The principles passed muster then and I am sure they will not fail us now.

Petroleum), Lok Sabha Secretariat, April 1982.] In fact, I had recounted the conclusions of the Committee's report in the article. And the reason he had no option later but to allow publication of the article, as we shall see in a moment, is that Ramnathji saw that blocking the article further would cause the paper to lose face even more.

I also do not think that a breach of privilege motion would enable the government to side-track the scandal by talking about Parliament's privileges rather than about the substantive issues involved in the Kuo oil deal. In fact, the moment a breach of privilege motion is filed, the initiative would be entirely in our hands and, their majorities notwithstanding, we could well-nigh orchestrate the debate.

Similarly, the whole tenor of the Official Secrets Act is to make it a crime to surreptitiously pass secrets to enemies of the country. Even with the most far-out interpretation of the Act, no one can successfully prosecute us under it for this article. On the contrary, were someone to initiate the prosecution, we would have precisely the opportunity we want to have the Act itself struck down.

My first apprehension therefore is that the two rules you seem to lay down in this case—namely, that we steer clear of the Official Secrets Act as well as of Parliament's notions of its privileges—will be too restrictive for the paper. Had these rules been in force in the last three years, I am certain, not one of the things that the paper is best known to have done could have been accomplished or even initiated.

These are the sorts of things that sustain the paper. Even from a commercial point of view, they are the best advertisement for the paper.

One does not everyday come across evidence of the kind I have gathered for this article. And there is no point in writing these things as if we are writing feasibility reports. As it is, people are not paying attention. We must present the material in a way which, while not having an iota of exaggeration, forces them to react. If we fail to do so, if we deliberately tone the facts down or suppress much of what we know—as I would have to do in this case if I followed your prescription—we are not doing our duty. We are letting slip an opportunity we have of making the people focus on an issue of public importance. This serves no one: not the country, not the paper, not Ramnathji, not us, no one.

My second apprehension is of greater concern to me. I hope that it is entirely misplaced but as it is in my mind, I will put it to you as candidly as possible.

After our discussion I went through the three parts of the article again to see what exactly would have to be cut out if we were to steer clear both of the Official Secrets Act and of the conventional notions of the privileges of Parliament. In substance about one half of the entire article would go— precisely those parts which document the unusual interest which the Prime Minister's House took in this case.

I can only pray that the knowledge that the Government has been making overtures to Ramnathji, that Ramnathji, as he always does on such occasions, has sent them the kind of signals that he always does to buy time and to explore possibilities, the knowledge that there has been an exchange of letters between Ramnathji and Mrs Gandhi—I can only pray that all this has not influenced you even in the slightest to conclude that the paper should go soft on Mrs Gandhi and company. For such an inference will, I am certain, spell disaster for the paper. In my mind this apprehension is reinforced by the fact that when Ramnathji rang me up yesterday afternoon from Bombay for some work about teleprinter lines and I casually mentioned to him that I had withdrawn the article, he, though he had not read the article and though he presumably did not know of our discussions, immediately mentioned the precise argument about our opening ourselves to breach of privilege motions, were we to allude to the proceedings of a Parliamentary Committee, etc. He again repeated the argument when he telephoned this morning till I had to tell him that as he had not seen the article how could he know whether I had reproduced proceedings of the Committee, etc. Hence my apprehension.

I have worked with Ramnathji closely for three years. Permit me to recount two or three rules of thumb, among many, by which he operates and one singular trait of his temperament. These form a background to the recent exchanges between him and the Government. A person not acquainted with these is liable to place greater store by exchanges of this kind than is warranted. First the rules of thumb:

o   Like every good guerrilla fighter Ramnathji, whenever necessary, concedes space to buy time.

o When he receives signals that could be interpreted either way, he sends back signals that can be interpreted either way.

o He believes that the time to reach out to a person is when the person is isolated and down-and-out—that is, when the other person is in need: recall the article he wrote just after Sanjay's death saying that everyone should rally round Mrs Gandhi.

Each of these rules of thumb today lead Ramnathji to go on with exchanges of the kind that he has been having with the Government. He feels at the moment that to ward off any difficulties from the State Bank we should buy time by opening some kind of a dialogue.

He also perceives that Mrs Gandhi is today isolated and is in need. And so on.

But the main factor is a trait of his which often misleads those who are working with him into carrying out the desires he expresses at a moment more literally than is good for him or for the paper. This trait is that when he is set on a course of action, he completely convinces himself that that particular course of action is not merely opportune but also completely and exclusively right, that in addition it is the only possible course in the circumstances—recall the enthusiasm with which he espoused the cause of Mahesh Yogi a year ago.

This trait is a great advantage in moments of crisis. It is the trait which enables him to engage in a fight without any reservations or doubts and therefore to throw everything into the fight. But it also leads him to over-react to dangers as well as to opportunities.

Having determined on a course of action, having convinced himself that that course is the inevitable as well as the exclusively right course, he puts forth arguments justifying it forcefully, skilfully and most insistently. He will, in fact, as he often says, produce 'the devil's own arguments' to justify the decision. (This morning over the phone he was on to one such argument: he said that in the Kuo oil deal 'X' had given me the documents only with the diabolical design of getting Ramnathji personally

into trouble—in fact, while 'X' had talked to me he had refused
to give the documents.)

Few who work for him are able to resist this combination,
his total conviction at that moment that what he is proposing
is right and the manner of his argumentation. Thereby they too
are led to overreact.

As these are just his traits, just his modes, I sincerely hope
that his conversations with you about the overtures from Mrs
Gandhi's side, about the exchange of letters with her on the
Maharashtra thermal plant, his almost child-like satisfaction at
having received a reply from Mrs Gandhi, I only hope that these
have not led you to decide that we must all soft-pedal the issues
at least for the moment if not for the indefinite future.

Having worked for three years with Ramnathji, I believe
that, given this marked trait in him, the best way for his
colleagues and subordinates to help him and the paper is to
counter his tendency to overreact rather than to go along and
actually and immediately translate into the paper his preferences
of the moment. I can give you instance after instance of cases
in which, if his wishes had been directly and immediately
translated into the paper, the paper would have suffered and
more than anyone else Ramnathji himself would have regretted
the translation of his wishes into the paper.

We may therefore help him draft his letters, get the necessary
information, etc. But we must keep that part of our work
completely separate from what we do and get done in the paper.
And at each moment when his rules of thumb and that trait I
mentioned are persuading him to push in one direction, we must
remind ourselves that the next week the same rules of thumb, the
same trait will be persuading him to push in another direction.
This isn't fickle-mindedness as much as it is an unusually strong
ability to persuade himself and others. Therefore, at a moment
don't go by his assessment of that moment.

The Express group has enormous problems. Many of these
would not be there to the same extent if the paper were not at
odds with the Government. But he is the one man who has the
skill and stamina to sail that close to the wind and still not let

the boat capsize. If going by his preferences of the moment, we draw in the sails, the paper would certainly have a quieter time but it would have lost its character, it would have lost the very reason for its existence.

I would therefore sincerely hope that you do not take the recent conversations, signals, exchanges, etc., seriously. Given Ramnathji's temperament, given what needs to be done in the country's interest today, our job is to continue to speak out in the public interest *whatever the compulsions of the paper.* Ramnathji's job is to keep the paper alive *in spite of us.* He has the skill and the stamina to do his part of the job. Please, *please* do not pay too much attention to his problems. If you do, the paper is done for and so is Ramnathji. Today he has but two treasures—his sense of purpose and his self-respect. If out of deference to him or because of his shouting, pounding, cajoling we compromise and this gets reflected in the paper—as it certainly will—we would have robbed him of the only treasure he has. And that is quite apart from the fact that we would have done something wrong.

Sense of purpose apart, please remember, not on this occasion necessarily, but in the years you work with Ramnathji, that he isn't just mischievous, he is fond of mischief! He will often set two of his friends or colleagues (or if he gets half a chance, husbands and wives!) on contrary courses. In part this is one of his standard methods of man-management: the moment their horns are locked, he is automatically the Supreme Court! But he will do so even when he does not need to do so; it is a habit, an amusement—'as flies to wanton boys . . .'

For all these reasons I request you once again to allow the article to be published. If you still feel that the article will expose the paper to an unacceptable degree of risk, please permit me to hand it to the publishers who are bringing out my book, 'Mrs Gandhi's Second Reign'. They would like to place it somewhere as 'an extract from Arun Shourie's forthcoming book . . . etc.' The facts narrated in the article would then have been brought to public attention; the paper would not have been exposed to risk.

As I have said a number of things about Ramnathji, some of which will enrage him and some of which will amuse him, I am sending him a copy of this letter.

18.6.1981   Arun

~

Why did I write the letter? Did I not know Ramnathji well enough to know that he would not tolerate it? Would I write it again today?

The answer to the first question is simple. I had urged the points to Verghese orally several times over a fortnight. But would putting the same points in writing have made him change his mind? Perhaps, I might have reasoned: for Verghese would find it difficult to answer the points in writing. But when my friend, Ashok Desai[3] read the letter and asked me what I hoped to attain by writing the letter, I said, 'It is a Subba Rao dissent!'[4] Asked what he sought to achieve through his dissents, Justice Subba Rao remarked, 'They are directed to the brooding sense of the future!' That would imply that I thought nothing would come of the letter, but that it was written for the future. Ashok laughed.

Did I not know Ramnathji well enough to know that the letter would lead him to throw me out? Most probably. But then, caught in a quandary, my instinct has been what Vinoba has prescribed: 'Rassaa kaat deney kee neeti.'[5] When in doubt, cut the ropes so that there is no way to retreat. Maybe I had concluded that, in any

---

[3] I had only recently got to know Ashok. He is the one who later took up cudgels against Antulay in the Bombay High Court. In the years that followed, he became a close friend, protector in courts, and guide: he introduced me to many a Buddhist teacher and scholar, and to their writings.

[4] Justice Subba Rao was as famous for the dissents he wrote as for his judgments.

[5] Two brothers have led their band over the walls right into the fort of the adversary. The battle is fierce. It is poised as if in a balance. It can go either way. Seeing this, one of the brothers runs on the rampart, severing the ropes by which they have climbed. The confederates now have no alternative but to fight to the finish.

case, I was no longer going to be allowed to do the sort of work that I thought ought to be done.

Would I write the letter again today? Almost certainly. Thirty years later what I said in public when I concluded that the BJP had changed irretrievably, and for the worse, was no different from writing that letter.

But to get back to the Kuo Oil matter.

Cutting stencils through the night

The next day—8 July—I had the text cut on stencils. I took the stencils to a shop near our house. Through the evening and night, they made seventy-five sets of the article. Early in the morning, starting from 3 a.m., I had these copies delivered to seventy-five Members of Parliament—starting with Mrs Gandhi herself, and including the Speaker of the Lok Sabha and the Chairman of the Rajya Sabha.

As soon as the Houses met, there was much *hungaamaa*. Members waved the cyclostyled sheets. They demanded the file. They demanded that the government answer their questions. They shouted that they would file privilege notices against the minister and officials for having concealed information from a committee of Parliament . . .

The *Express* was in a dilemma. It had to report the *hungaamaa,* but it could not report the reason for the *hungaamaa.*

Worse, on the 9th, several senior members were on their feet. Atal Behari Vajpayee told the House that the previous day he had filed a breach of privilege notice against Mrs Gandhi for withholding information from a committee of Parliament, and the Speaker had told him that he, the Speaker, would not allow it. Madhu Dandavate, the leader of the Janata Party in the Lok Sabha, said that he had filed a breach of privilege motion against Mrs Gandhi: she was again doing what she had done in the Maruti case, that is withholding information from Parliament, something for which she had been expelled from Parliament. George Fernandes and Harikesh Bahadur demanded what had happened to their notices against me and Lavraj Kumar. To somehow get the notices admitted so that the issue could be pursued, they said that in the article that I had circulated, I 'had cast aspersions on the Public Undertakings Committee and its chairman', and that Lavraj Kumar had withheld information from the Committee.

From the point of view of the paper, the matter was clearly getting out of hand. After all, would the paper report this *hungaamaa* about privilege notices and again not mention who the notices were against and what had occasioned them? So, its edition of the 10th carried a report about these notices: 'Privilege move against PM, Shourie.' It also devoted space to reporting what I had written in the 'note' that I had circulated to Members of Parliament.

What is more, that day it carried the entire article—all three parts of it—in one go!!

'*Yeh kambakht yeh baazi to ley gayaa hai*,' Ramnathji exclaimed. '*Abhee to iskaa* article *chhaapanaa he padaa—is samay aur koi chaaraa naheen hai. Par main isey nikaal kar he chhodoonga.*'[6] All this to our mutual friend Radhakrishna, the head of the Gandhi Peace Foundation, with no doubt that his fury and his warning would be conveyed to me. In fact, I have no doubt with the intention that it be conveyed—he often conveyed things in this way: as the phrase goes, 'I talk so that my neighbours may hear.'

That is how the article got published in the *Express's* editions from 10 July onwards.

Once the article had been published, I knew that Verghese would not be able to block follow-up articles. The series continued till 30 July.

Within two days, another controversy arose. The convention had always been that minutes of a committee's meetings were tabled in the two Houses, along with the report of the committee. But this time round, even though the minutes had been finalized and approved by the committee's Chairman the day the report

---

[6] 'This scoundrel has bagged this throw. At the moment there is no alternative—we will just have to publish his article. But I will not rest till I drive him out.'

was approved, the government and its agents in Parliament had ensured that the minutes would be held back and not be tabled. But in my article, I had incorporated material from the minutes! That the issue had become a matter of public controversy and concern, that a journalist has got the minutes and we have not— this, the MPs said, was totally unacceptable. The new controversy gave second wind to the contents of the article.

Forty years later, details of the deal itself are of little interest. They presaged much of what we were to get accustomed to in the ensuing years: a tender was floated for import of diesel and kerosene; conditions in the tender were repeatedly changed, and eventually disregarded; fourteen parties sought to get the order; thirteen were disqualified one way or another; a Hong Kong-based company with a paid-up capital of *fifty dollars* was given the contract valued at *200 million dollars*; against government's announced policy, the contract with this Hong Kong firm was routed through an Indian go-between—*Hindustan Monark;* this Indian 'representative' was the Hong Kong company's secret weapon—a friend of a friend of Sanjay Gandhi; the contract was given at a fixed price when prices of the products were falling and were expected to fall. Officials pointed out repeatedly that what was being rammed through was against national interest. Eventually, the minister, P.C. Sethi, gave explicit instructions. These were recorded and then conveyed in writing to the Chairman of the IOC (Indian Oil Company). The loss to the country was Rs 9 to 12 crores, not even a grain of rotted wheat by the standards which we now regard as normal. But those days, the amount was large enough to be talked about. P. Shiv Shankar, who had since been given charge of the Ministry, had to admit on the floor of Parliament that, yes, a mistake had been made, but, he said in defence, it had been 'a courageous mistake'.

True, by today's standards, the deal is forgettable. But two things are of enduring interest. The fate of the file. And, as in the Venkataraman episode, the contortions which even presiding officers of the two Houses of Parliament—including the sagacious and erudite Justice Hidayatullah—and, of course, the loyal press, had to, and did put themselves through.

And so, from the series of articles that I wrote then, these two aspects are worth a glance even at this distance in time. There is another reason for doing so. These portions illustrate a feature that was somewhat new in our journalism: detailed analysis of documents, whether these be files or rule books or judgments and rulings. Many, in particular editors in the *Express* itself, objected to the detailed and longish analyses of documents. 'This is a newspaper not an academic journal,' they said. 'You are writing pamphlets, not newspaper articles,' they said. But I felt that detailed analysis of the documents was as necessary as facts, and, in the case of the latter, we must overwhelm the reader with an avalanche of facts. Those who would oppose what the paper had printed must not be able to get away with some obfuscation; they must not be able to get away by citing some so-called authority or expert. In a word, they must be left with no recourse. And the reader must be left in no doubt.

One of the compliments I treasure, undeserved though it probably was, came from a young lady who later became prominent in our public life. 'You don't know what you did,' she said. 'You taught us to *look*. You taught us to *read*, and not just shoot our mouths off.'

Where had the file been? Why would disclosing either that or the content of the file open us to prosecution under the Official Secrets Act? Or pitch us against Parliament?[7]

I get the file

On 20 February 1982, Parliament's Committee on Public Enterprises was examining C.R. Das Gupta, Chairman of the Indian Oil Corporation. Why did you go in for such and thus a transaction, he was asked. 'The contract was signed at the instance of the Government,' he said. 'We got a directive asking us to accept the offer.' He felt the government should give a reply.

---

[7] The following is based on articles published by the *Indian Express* between 10 and 30 July 1982.

Had the IOC not been consulted? 'No,' he said, 'we were not.' And so, when on 24 March, they were examining the Secretary of the Ministry of Petroleum, Lavraj Kumar, the Committee asked him about the transaction. He would like to have two to three weeks to give full information on the matter, he said.

But the written question had been with the Ministry since long. Three weeks would mean the middle of April, and the Committee's term was expiring on 30 April, a fact the government knew well. Perhaps that was the intention, not of the Secretary but of someone somewhere in the government? Drag it out. There were about 200 public enterprises of the Central Government alone. The Committee was able to look into the affairs of about ten a year. In the normal course, therefore, an enterprise having been examined once may escape examination for the next twenty years. And so, someone must have reasoned, if we can drag things out for just another month, we can be almost certain that no one would ever get around to examining the transaction. Who will think of raking it up twenty years hence?

The Committee said that it could not give more than a week and asked that the note be handed over to it by 31 March. It scheduled a meeting on 1 April to consider it.

The Secretary promised to do his best. He would have to consult other departments too, he said.

So, 31 March it was to be.

On 30 March, records of the Ministry of Petroleum showed the Ministry representative wrote to the Parliamentary Committee as follows:

> Please refer to our conversation today regarding the supplementary note to be submitted to the Committee on Public Undertakings. As discussed, the note relating to . . . will be submitted by the 31st March 1982 so as to circulate to the Hon. Members by that evening. The remaining notes, which are under preparation, will be submitted by the 2nd April, 1982.

Notice that on 30 March, just a day before the due date, the Ministry had once again assured the Committee that it would submit its note on the transaction the next day. There was no hint that the Ministry faced any difficulty in complying with the request.

But the next day, 31 March, the Ministry suddenly did a turnabout. It now told the Parliamentary Committee that despite the efforts made by the Department of Petroleum thus far, it had not been possible to lay hands on the File No. P-20 . . . in order to submit a reply to the Committee by the due date and time.

A week earlier, the Secretary had been helpfulness itself. He would do all to supply the 'complete picture'. No hint of any missing files. A day earlier, the Ministry had again assured the Committee that it would furnish the agreed note. No hint of any missing files. And then suddenly . . .

What was File No. P-20? Where had it gone? Who was interested in suppressing it?

The first written note relating to the file was dated 6 December 1980. On that day, the Deputy Director, Commercial Audit (Petroleum) wrote to the Secretary, Ministry of Petroleum. He said:

> I am to state that we have been conducting scrutiny of the contract of import of crude and other products. During the course of discussion with Chairman's office, Indian Oil Corporation, we find that the scrutiny is not complete in the absence of the relevant case file of the Department of Petroleum. The purchases are made and the record is maintained in the Ministry also. In view of this . . . the party may kindly be granted necessary facility for conducting the audit.

As little had come of this, the Director, Commercial Audit, himself wrote another letter to the Ministry asking for the file, stressing how important it was for their investigations that they have the file and stressing also the need for them to have it urgently.

As far as the Deputy Director and Director were concerned, nothing happened. The Ministry, however, was aflutter. They kept telephoning the Special Assistant to Virendra Patil, who had been Minister of Petroleum at the time and was now Minister of

Shipping and Transport, asking him to ask the minister where in hell the file had gone, explaining how the Audit fellows were breathing down their necks and how they, the Auditors, were beginning to suspect a conspiracy to keep the file from them, and how this was leading them to suspect more than there probably was to the matter.

Silence was all they got. And so on 10 February 1981, the Joint Secretary in charge wrote an official letter to the Special Assistant to Virendra Patil:

> You may kindly recall my mentioning to you over the telephone on a few occasions to send back the file concerning import of diesel, etc. As the file is required for reference, I shall be grateful if you could kindly arrange to return the file.

Virendra Patil's hand had been forced. The matter had now been formally reduced to paper, always a danger signal in governmental affairs. And so his Special Assistant had no option but to disclose the unmentionable.

'Dear Narayanaswamy,' he wrote back to the Joint Secretary on 16 February 1981, 'Please refer to your letter No . . . dated 10th February 1981. I had checked up the position from Shri K. C. Chennaveerappa (Private Secretary to the Minister). He confirmed that the file was sent to PM's house.'

The Director, Department of Petroleum, had sent another letter on 24 February 1981, to Virendra Patil's office: 'Kindly refer to your reply of 16th February, 1981. You are requested to get back the file and return it to this Ministry as early as possible.'

The Ministry also contacted the PM's office directly.

Two weeks later, things were where they had been. On 7 March 1981, Narayanaswamy, the Joint Secretary, recorded a note: 'I am trying to get the file. I have spoken to Shri Ghare Khan in PM's office, who is looking after the work which Shri Bakshi was looking after.'

The PM's office deigned to reply on 24 August 1981, that is, a full six months after it had been contacted directly by the Ministry of Petroleum. The reply was innocence itself:

Please refer to your DO . . . We are not able to trace your
department file No. P-20. If you can indicate the date on which
the reference was made to PM's office, or to whom it was made,
it would be possible to find the file.

The very next day, that is on 25 August 1981, the Director in the
Department of Petroleum wrote to the Private Secretary to the
minister of shipping asking him to give the precise date:

Dear Shri Chennaveerappa,

Please refer to . . . I have contacted PM's office . . . they desire to
know the exact date on which this file was . . . I shall, therefore,
be grateful if you indicate the date and the reference number,
if any.

Reminder had followed reminder, each yielding as little as its
predecessor. At last, on 8 December 1981, Chennaveerappa sent
his reply:

At this distance of time I am unable to remember the date on
which I handed over the file, referred to in your letter, to the
Special Assistant to the Prime Minister. Since the file was handed
over in person, no acknowledgement in writing was taken.

Helpless, knowing that the Parliamentary Committee was seized of
the matter, knowing that the Committee was after the transaction
recorded in the file, the Director, Ministry of Petroleum, had
recorded another note on 8 March 1982:

In spite of our best efforts we have not been able to lay hands on
the original file. No acknowledgement was obtained in writing.
We have requested him to meet the concerned official in PM's
office. No reply has been received.

Even so, the Ministry officials had kept up their dogged pursuit
of the file. Three successive ministers of petroleum—P.C. Sethi,

Virendra Patil and Shiv Shankar—were requested again and again to help get the file. The PM's office was also contacted repeatedly. The officials were assured on each occasion that the file would certainly be with them before the day was out, within a day or two at the most. Before the hearing on 24 April, too, they were told, 'Just ask for a few days, you'll get the file.'

And this is why the Secretary had sought time. Officials told me they were confident that the assurances would be honoured. They were also trying to reconstruct the file by obtaining copies of notes available in the originating offices. On 30 March, when the letter was sent to the Committee reiterating the promise to send the note by the next day, the officials were again assured that the file would be with them by the evening. All these assurances were widely known among officers of the Ministry. They thought they would prepare the note overnight and thus meet the deadline.

Not knowing any of this, going merely by the fact that it had suddenly been told that the written note that had been promised would not be available, the Committee had been incensed. The Secretary was summoned to a meeting of the Committee on 2 April. Under questioning, he candidly narrated the sequence of the Ministry's efforts to trace the file.

Well, we now know that the file was handed over to the Special Assistant to the PM. Who had been the Special Assistant?

He didn't know who the Special Assistant was at that time, the Secretary said.

Now, this was a file marked 'Secret'. The Chennaveerappas of the world couldn't and wouldn't really shunt such files around at will. There was a very strict procedure that had to be followed about their movement—the movement had to be noted in writing, the file had to be sent in a sealed cover, etc. Under what circumstances, and at whose initiative had the file gone to the PM's house? How had no record been kept of its movement at all? Was the person who was holding on to the file banking on this fact—that the Ministry officials would have to go by the written record, that as the movement of this particular secret file had not been 'diarised', the Ministry representative, confining himself to the written record, would say that he did not know who in the PM's office had summoned and obtained the file?

But was it all that difficult to find out the name of the Special Assistant in the PM's office? After all, how many Special Assistants did the PM have at the time? the Committee asked.

He didn't know, said the Secretary. He would like to check.

That the absence of the file was helping someone was clear from the only answers that, in the absence of the file, the Secretary was able to give: 'I am reading out from the information given to me by the IOC [recall that the IOC had told the Committee to find out the facts from the government]. In the absence of the file, I have no other way . . . My disability to reply to this really is that we do not have the file . . . It is difficult to answer . . .'

But had the concerned minister (P.C. Sethi, as he had been the minister when the deal was struck) not been asked the reasons justifying the transaction? Yes, the Secretary had asked him, and this is the written reply he had received from P.C. Sethi:

> I have taken this decision after careful consideration and I have clearly recorded my reasons for accepting this in the relevant file . . . It will be difficult for me to recall the precise reasons at this distant date.

And so, the IOC, when asked, had said: 'We were directed to do as we did; if you want to know the reasons, ask the Ministry.' The Ministry had said: 'We'd have gladly told you everything but the relevant file is missing; let's ask the Minister.' And the minister said: 'O, I wrote everything down in the file. As I don't have the file and as so much time has elapsed, I can't recall what persuaded me to act the way I did.'

But the position was clearly untenable. Worse, it put officials of the Ministry on the mat when, in fact, they had done everything they could to prevent the minister from the course that he had insisted on taking.

Chennaveerappa, the Private Secretary to Virendra Patil, had owned up that he had himself delivered the file to the PM's Special Assistant. The Ministry had been able to extract this much from him in writing. Who would believe that it had not taken the next step and asked Chennaveerappa the name of the fellow?

The matter was taken up again. The Ministry officials pressed for the file. Meetings, exchanges, notes stressing the urgency of the matter . . .

Suddenly, on 5 April, the Secretary of the Committee on Public Enterprises got a phone call from the Ministry: the file has just been traced, a written note based on the file is on its way.

'But don't you see that Sethi gave his orders in writing? If he had been wheeling-dealing would he have taken the risk of putting things down in writing?'

Far from exculpating Sethi, the fact that he was compelled to reduce his silly little rationalizations to writing and then to explicitly order the Secretary to direct the IOC in writing to enter into the contract was a crucial clue. It indicated, as nothing else could, that the man had no option. In spite of three written notes from him, in spite of meetings in his room, officers, both of the IOC and of the Ministry, had refused to become parties to a deal that would defraud the country. Sethi was sandwiched between these obdurate officials and pressure from someone behind the curtain to conclude the deal which he could no longer withstand. His desperate hurry on the afternoon of 22 February told the tale. Having allowed Kuo Oil to alter the very basis of its tender (after the tenders had been opened and after he had himself and in writing ordered that no new counter-offers should be entertained), he had allowed them to alter the price they had specified in their contract; next, he had sent down a note; third, he had called a meeting and ordered that the offers must be taken to expire as of 10 p.m. that night, and that the IOC must be ordered to conclude the contract 'immediately' . . . The man had no option but to put things down in writing.

Who was turning the screws on him?

The clue lay in the journeys of file P-20 that we have glimpsed. The file, it turned out, had been in the PM's office since 22 April 1980. This exalted office had held on tenaciously to it for two full years. It was only on 5 April 1982, that it was delivered to the Ministry, and only then that the Ministry could send its note to the Committee on Public Undertakings. The note was woefully incomplete. Even so, the note at least was sent.

The Secretariat of the Parliamentary Committee itself

After this, strange things had started happening in the Secretariat of the Parliamentary Committee itself.

Members of the Committee were acutely aware that the Committee's term was to expire on 30 April, that if nothing was done by then, the facts would have been successfully suppressed for years. They kept asking the Secretariat to circulate the draft report. They were particularly anxious that facts about the Kuo Oil deal should be recounted in full.

On one pretext after another, the draft report was not circulated to them till their penultimate meeting. What with the delay in circulating the draft report, they could meet to consider the draft only on 26 April, that is just four days before their term was to expire.

They were astonished. There was absolutely no reference in the draft to the vital circumstantial clue about the effort to suppress the file and about its having been sequestered in the PM's house. Even more important, while the entire tenor of the discussion on this deal had been that it was a deliberate and successful attempt to enrich high-ups at the expense of the country, that it was a clear case of corruption, the Secretariat had sought to suggest that in the view of the Committee, the loss of 9.85 million dollars had resulted from an 'error of judgment'. Members were incensed.

They had met again on 28 April, insisting that the report refer to the journeys of the file and that the 'error of judgment' bit be taken out. Only the latter was done. Summoning the file would take time, they were told. And where is the time? The Committee would cease to exist in two days. If they left the entire question to the next Committee, it would mean consigning examining of the deal for a decade.

The matter had ended abruptly with Bansi Lal, the Chairman, saying that there must be some end to the discussion, that, in any case, he was leaving as he was not feeling well. With only two days to go, members had no option but to adopt the draft of the Secretariat minus the error of judgement part of the sentence. The abrupt end was reflected in the ultimate conclusion of the Committee: 'The Committee fail to understand why the normal procedure . . . was not followed in this regard. They await a further enquiry or an explanation in this regard.'

The manipulator had not been able to keep the facts totally out of the report. The 5 April note of the Ministry had provided the Committee with enough information to raise doubts about the deal. But in large measure, the manipulator had succeeded. He had almost succeeded in ensuring that things were swept under the carpet by being attributed to a mere 'error of judgment'; and he had definitely succeeded in ensuring that the final report merely contained an innocuous and incomplete narration of the facts of the deal.

Perils of relying on our independent press

The Kuo Oil deal was 'an error of judgement', Shiv Shankar, the petroleum minister, told Parliament. And the only grounds for solace he could find were two. First, that while an error of judgement, it was, as he put it in Parliament, a courageous one! Second, that 'errors of judgement of this nature could not be ruled out even during the regime between 1977–79'!

The relevant file was in the PM's office all the while, he admitted. And again, his grounds for solace were two. First, that it was 'genuinely misplaced', it having got lost amidst some old papers and files in R.K. Dhawan's office. Anyone who had been to Dhawan's office could testify that there just weren't any piles of old papers and files lying around. Second, Shiv Shankar was comforted by the thought that, though the file had been sent to the Prime Minister for 'policy guidance', she never got the file. It was, of course, reassuring that the Ministry which had so eagerly sought her policy guidance on 22 April 1980, never got around to asking what the advice was till 5 April 1982!

The Ministry began asking for the file itself in early 1981, Shiv Shankar acknowledged. There are all those notes about letters and phone calls and meetings that testified to its relentless, and, at times, frantic efforts to get it. But, Shiv Shankar said, it was not till early April 1982 that Dhawan 'was impressed about the urgency' of locating the file!

Moreover, Shiv Shankar said, many other independent observers had come to the same conclusion—namely, that signing the contract on a fixed-price basis would be advantageous for the country. As evidence, he cited reports that had appeared in newspapers, including the *Financial Express* and the *Indian Express*.

It was on 22 February 1980 that B.B. Vohra, the then Secretary in the Petroleum Ministry, was told to send a written directive to the Indian Oil Corporation asking the latter to award the contract to *Hindustan Monark*, the bicycle parts firm, and through it, to Kuo Oil.

Now it so transpired—and Shiv Shankar, unfortunately for himself, as we shall soon see, made much of this in Parliament—on 20 and 21 February, several newspapers—the *Financial Express, Indian Express, Hindustan Times, Economic Times*—carried a 'news' item about the impending oil deal.

It said that tenders had been invited for 5 lakh tonnes of diesel and 3 lakh tonnes of kerosene, and gave several reasons why the country must purchase the products not at variable prices but at a fixed price. The reasons it gave were as interesting as can be.

Under the escalation formula, the 'news' item said, prices would be pegged to prices reported in the *Platt's Oilgram*. But, said the item, 'Platt's is an organisation composed of some traders and some oil companies. Platt's readings can themselves be sometimes manipulated to give international price readings which do not reflect the actual price situation in the international market.' Furthermore, 'There is an apprehension that the traders will be able to manipulate the prices. It is learnt that some traders have formed themselves into a cartel and quoted prices based on an escalation formula which they can manipulate to secure higher prices after the contract is awarded at a lower price.'

Not just that. 'Strangely', said the 'news' item, 'the government is inclined to accept offers on an escalation basis which would make the liability of the government undetermined . . . The Indian Oil Corporation, for some unknown reason, is insisting that orders be placed on an escalation formula basis . . . whereas large purchases made by other major countries in the world are based on firm price so as to keep the liability predetermined . . .'

And here was how the 'news' item concluded: 'Currently international market for diesel and kerosene is at its lowest ebb and it should be the government's policy to purchase on firm price basis . . .'

Hence it is that Shiv Shankar was able to claim in Parliament that 'in the particular situation prevailing at that time some others also reached the same conclusion to prefer to purchase at fixed prices rather than at variable prices'. And he cited the 'news' item in the *Financial Express* and *Economic Times* as evidence.

But there is something that he didn't tell Parliament.

First, the 'news' item that appeared in each of the papers was identical! A plant, not a 'news' item.

Second, the arguments put forward in it were exactly, but exactly, the arguments that Kamal Nath, the MP from Chhindwara, was putting forth repeatedly in meetings at the Ministry of Petroleum.

Third, not just the arguments but the words—'undetermined liability', 'international market . . . is at its lowest ebb'—were the very ones that occurred in the notes that the hapless P.C. Sethi recorded on 19 and 21 February 1980, in the file that had at last turned up. The ghostwriter of the minister and of the newspapers was the same.

Fourth, the papers carried a telltale second item along with this one.

Time for some investigating at home. Therefore, when I learnt of these items, I began to inquire how the *Financial Express* and *Indian Express* had got the item.

'O,' said the special correspondent who had filed the story for the papers, 'I got a written note from the then editor Prem Shankar Jha to file it on the basis of a hand-out.' It transpired that Jha could not have given him the written note on 19 February 1980, as he did not join the *Financial Express* till 1 April 1980.

When I returned to the correspondent with this information, he said that, in that case, he could not remember how he filed that story. A cover-up at home.

So, I asked Prithvis Chakravarty, who was then the Chief of Bureau at the *Hindustan Times,* and was at the time of my writing the articles, the Chief of Bureau of the *Aaj Kal*. Here is Chakravarty's account of how the item saw its way into print.

Chakravarty's account

It was around noon on 19 February 1980, Chakravarty recalled, that K.K. Birla, the Chairman of *Hindustan Times*, telephoned him. You should meet Kamal Nathji, Birla told Chakravarty, he has very important news to give you. Why don't you come to my house at 3 p.m.? Kamal Nathji is coming. He is a high-high person.

Chakravarty went to K.K. Birla's house to be in time for the 3 p.m. meeting. Birla was there. Kamal Nath wasn't. Kamal Nathji is busy in a meeting, his emissaries—two men in their twenties— told Chakravarty.

They had important news which Kamal Nathji wanted published, they said. Without much ado, they gave Chakravarty two separate typed sheets. One proclaimed that the government had decided to shift the headquarters of Western Coalfields from Nagpur to Chhindwara district, Kamal Nath's constituency, and that this decision 'has been widely welcomed by both official and industry circles'. It spelled out the many boons that would accrue to the country from the shift. The second note was the handout about the impending kerosene and diesel deal.

Chakravarty returned to the office feeling that while the items were plants, they were good tips and he should have them checked out. He handed the diesel-kerosene handout to A.K. Sen, the *HT* correspondent who was looking after Petroleum and Chemicals then (he was the economic correspondent of Reuters in Delhi at the time I was writing my article), and the coal one to Tapan Dasgupta, another correspondent.

Sen, Chakravarty recalled, told him that someone was trying to have them do his job, that he didn't believe a word of the handout. Chakravarty told him that as the item had come via K.K. Birla himself, it would have to be checked out in any case.

From Chakravarty's telephone and in his presence, Sen telephoned C.R. Dasgupta, the then Chairman of IOC. Dasgupta laughed at what Sen told him about the advantages of buying diesel at a fixed price but refused to say anything more about the matter over the phone. At Sen's request, Dasgupta agreed to meet him the next day.

As nothing more could be done that evening, the item was held over for the next day.

Around 8 p.m., Chakravarty recalled, a secretary came rushing to his office. Birlaji is on the phone in Hiranmay Karlekar's room, come at once.

K.K. Birla was indeed on the phone. Is the item being published tonight or not?

Karlekar and then Chakravarty explained to him that the item was being checked and that the inquiries would be completed tomorrow.

But the item has been given by Kamal Nathji himself; he is a high-high person; it must be correct, they were told. In any case, why are you being so fussy? The *Express* has already decided to publish it.

There were some further exchanges about the merits of checking such items out. In the end, Birla asked point-blank: Just tell me, is the item being published or not?

His voice sounded like an ultimatum, Chakravarty recalled. Well, publish it then, Chakravarty said. After all, Chakravarty told himself, it is Birla's goat; he can slaughter it from the head or from the tail.

The problem now was that the handouts had been given to Sen, and Tapan Dasgupta and Sen had both left the office.

Chakravarty therefore telephoned Kamal Nath. He told him that they had decided to publish the items but that the copies were no longer available at the office.

Kamal Nath told him that he would have copies delivered immediately.

10 p.m. and still the copies had not arrived. Chakravarty telephoned Kamal Nath again. My men are on their way, the latter said; they will be there any minute.

And so they were. With the wet galley proofs of the two items from the *Indian Express* press!

I just changed the byline from 'By Our Special Correspondent' to 'By a Correspondent,' pinned the proofs on dry paper and sent them to the press, Chakravarty told me. That's all the original work I did.

And that is how the two items—one extolling the government's decision to shift the headquarters of Western Coalfields to Kamal Nath's constituency and the other providing his arguments for giving the diesel contract at a fixed price—appeared together in the *Hindustan Times* of 20 February 1980, as in other papers, and that was how valuable the 'independent' opinions were that Shiv Shankar had cited in Parliament to justify P.C. Sethi's orders!

How they bagged it

Kamal Nath was thus the crucial link. But he was not the originator of the contract. This is what had happened.

Hindustan Monark was a medium-sized outfit with an office in Delhi and two factories in Ghaziabad and Hyderabad. It manufactured equipment for making bicycle parts and engaged in some export-import business. It was owned by three brothers. The youngest of these was Harish Jain.

He was at Doon School with Sanjay Gandhi and Kamal Nath. Sanjay's stay there was brief, but Kamal Nath and Harish Jain ('Haru' to his friends) spent several years together. They had kept in touch ever since.

In early February 1980, Harish Jain heard that a huge contract was about to be concluded for diesel and kerosene. He mentioned this to Kamal Nath and proposed that they work together to bag it.

At that time, Kamal Nath was flush with victory. He was one of Sanjay's men and their word was law. Kamal Nath spoke to Sanjay. Sanjay telephoned P.C. Sethi.

After that, all that had to be done was to make sure that, to use Shiv Shankar's felicitous phrase, P.C. Sethi was 'impressed about the urgency' of the matter. Telephone calls, peremptory visits to

Sethi's office and airing the definitive arguments at meetings in the Ministry that Kamal Nath had no business to attend were enough. A little show of impatience on 21 February 1980 ensured that Sethi passed the orders on 22 February.

The country lost between Rs 9 crores and Rs 12.5 crores. Harish Jain disclosed that he received only $6000 (and that too by cheque) plus one paid holiday in Singapore. You can decide what happened to the rest.

Courageous indeed

It isn't just that *Hindustan Monark* had no experience in the oil business. It isn't just that they just did not have the resources to handle a deal worth $175 to 200 million, the largest oil contract handed over to a private party in India till then.

Who were Kuo Oil? Had officials from the Ministry or from the IOC, or P.C. Sethi, for that matter, made any inquiries about them? They were going to be given a contract to supply half a million tonnes of diesel worth $175 million. Shiv Shankar himself testified in Parliament that 'in the contracts of oil many suppliers fail to deliver against contracts'. Well, what had been done to verify whether Kuo Oil could indeed handle a deal of $175 million? What precautions had been taken to safeguard the country's interest in case Kuo Oil, like the other oil suppliers, as Shiv Shankar told Parliament, failed to deliver against the contract?

The Ministry told the Committee on Public Undertakings that, as directed by P.C. Sethi, the minister, on 21 and 22 February, the IOC obtained a 'Performance Guarantee' from Kuo Oil. The Committee recorded this in its report.

But were any inquiries made to ensure that Kuo Oil had the assets against which claims could be filed should they renege on the contract?

Things were being hustled through at such a pace that no inquiries could really be made, they said. Indeed, to the day I was writing, senior officers in neither the Ministry nor the IOC could tell one what the total assets or even the paid-up capital of

Kuo Oil were, the very assets and capital against which the much touted 'Performance Guarantee' would have had to be enforced.

I didn't know either. We therefore requested a source in Hong Kong to help us find out. Kuo Oil repeatedly refused an interview on the deal. And as it was not a public limited company, its balance sheet was not a public document. Hence, information on its assets wasn't easy to come by.

But the company was registered. And according to the records of the Registrar of Companies in Hong Kong, the paid-up capital of Kuo Oil was two hundred dollars. Two hundred Hong Kong dollars, that is, about fifty US dollars! A $175-million deal with a company having a paid-up capital of $50 plus assets that government didn't know anything about and the government expected to enforce the 'Performance Guarantee'!

No wonder Shiv Shankar said that Sethi's error of judgement was a courageous one!

14

Innovators and their innovations

The device of cyclostyling the article and sending it to Members of Parliament had left the paper no choice but to publish it. Once Parliament was seized of the matter, what else the paper published on the subject could not be ignored. No one charged the paper or me for having violated the Official Secrets Act. This is what I had tried to persuade Verghese would happen. I wasn't proved wrong on the second point either. No one charged that either the paper or I had fallen afoul of privileges of Parliament. That we had acted as friends of Parliament by bringing it information which had been kept from its Committee was readily acknowledged.

Breach of privilege notices were indeed filed—but against Bansi Lal, the Chairman of the Committee, as well as Lavraj Kumar, Secretary of the Ministry. Against the former for having blocked facts from being brought on record. Against the latter for being evasive as well as not ensuring that all relevant facts were furnished to the Committee.

But members who had filed the notices were handicapped by two facts. The practice had been that the minutes of meetings of a Parliamentary Committee were tabled along with the report of the Committee. But in this instance, the minutes had not been tabled. And neither the evasions by the Ministry officials nor the manner in which the Secretariat had kept crucial facts and observations out of the report, nor indeed the role of the Chairman in bringing proceedings to an abrupt end, could be nailed without the minutes.

Four rulings

After heated arguments about the minutes not having been tabled, at last, the minutes were tabled. But on every single matter that had a bearing on the privilege notices, the forty-seven pages of the minutes were silent. They were instructive on one point alone. It was now confirmed that the Secretariat of the Committee had in fact sought to attribute the enormous loss of Rs 9 crores to Rs 12.5 crores to a mere 'error of judgement'.

More arguments followed. These occasioned two rulings in the Rajya Sabha, one by the Deputy Chairman Shyamlal Yadav, and the other by the Chairman of the House, Justice Hidayatullah. The Speaker of the Lok Sabha, Balram Jakhar, gave two equally innovative rulings.

The net effect of these rulings was extremely helpful to the manipulators. Not one single fact brought on record about the Kuo Oil deal had been refuted or even contested by the government or by anyone else. And yet, for all their devices, Members of Parliament had not been able to have either House discuss any aspect of the deal. And this time around, this result had been ensured not so much by the Congress(I) MPs shouting the Opposition down—though there had been a good bit of that, too—as by the exertions of the presiding officers of the two Houses.

Yadav's innocence

Shyamlal Yadav, the Deputy Chairman of the Rajya Sabha, had been first off the mark. As I mentioned, while minutes of meetings of the Committee on Public Undertakings were almost always laid on the tables of the two Houses, along with the report to which they pertained, the minutes pertaining to the 47th Report of COPU—the one dealing with the Kuo Oil deal—had not been tabled even two and a half months after the report had been presented to the two Houses. Members were angry and sought the help of the Chair to get the minutes.

Yadav ruled that even though it was mandatory for such minutes and reports to be tabled, neither the Chair nor the Rajya Sabha Secretariat could help the members. They must, in effect, make private arrangements with the Chairman or Secretariats of such committees to secure the minutes. 'There is no point in your demand,' Yadav had pronounced one day. 'There is no convention or rule that the report and the minutes have to be tabled together,' he pronounced the next.

These pronouncements required little comment. Yadav had been quite candid, after all: he would not allow a discussion on the deal in the manner proposed by members, he said, 'as that will open a Pandora's box'. But one point couldn't escape notice: the ruling was just plain wrong. Rule 23 governing the procedures of the Committee on Public Undertakings specified as follows: 'The Minutes of the sittings of the Committee shall be laid on the table of the House along with the report to which they relate.'

Nor was this some secret rule known only to the select. It was listed on page eighty-two of the printed booklet, *Committee on Public Undertakings, An Introductory Guide,* published by the Lok Sabha Secretariat itself.

Hidayatullah's erudition

On 13 July—four days after Jakhar had announced in the Lok Sabha that privilege notices relating to the 47th Report were under his consideration—Hidayatullah told the Rajya Sabha that, while he had received a number of notices, he had not read them till then. Nor could he stay in the House to hear the members as he had an engagement.

The next day he rejected the ten motions he had received on two related grounds.

The privilege motions, Hidayatullah said, had been raised—as they had necessarily to be raised—under Rule 187 of the *Rules of*

Procedure and Conduct of Business of the Rajya Sabha.[1] 'Stated briefly,' Hidayatullah said, summarizing in a novel way the import of this rule, 'a question of breach of privilege has to be restricted only to a matter affecting the Committee of our House. Now, the Committee on Public Undertakings is a committee set up under Rule 312A of the *Rules of Procedure and Conduct of Business of the Lok Sabha.* It functions under the direction and control of the Speaker, Lok Sabha . . . [it] is essentially and primarily a committee of the Lok Sabha. Under Rule 187 which has been referred to earlier, a question of breach of privilege can arise only in respect of our Committee . . .'

This was indeed a novel interpretation of Rule 187—that under it, only those questions of breach of privilege could be raised which alleged that the privilege of a committee of the Rajya Sabha had been breached. The rule itself was certainly not as restrictive as the construction Hidayatullah had put on it. The rule permitted a member to 'raise a question involving a breach of privilege *either of a member, or of the Council or of a committee thereof*'.

And the gravamen of the motions of privilege that Hidayatullah was dismissing was not that the privileges of the Committee on Public Undertakings had been breached but that the privileges of the Rajya Sabha itself had been breached. And this had come about, members had urged, because crucial facts, having been suppressed from a document that had been presented to the House and on which they would have to rely for their work, their ability to perform their functions as MPs, had been impaired. That was precisely what breach of privilege was.

Now, one may or may not agree that facts had been suppressed, but to block the question at the threshold by the sort of reasoning Hidayatullah had adopted was indeed an innovation. Recall that one-third of the members of the Committee were from the Rajya Sabha; the reports and minutes of the Committee were formally

---

[1] For Justice Hidayatullah's ruling, Rajya Sabha, *Rulings and Observations from the Chair, 1952-2017*, Rajya Sabha Secretariat, December 2018, Item 688, pp. 384–90. Also, Rajya Sabha Debates, 26 July 1982, Cols. 159–70.

tabled in the Rajya Sabha; the Committee used to report on matters that were of vital concern to the Rajya Sabha; the veracity and reliability of its reports and minutes was crucial for the members of the Rajya Sabha to discharge their duties as MPs.

Several MPs had attempted to raise these questions. But Hidayatullah had another engagement, and so, on 14 July, as on the previous day, he had left the House, with the members trailing behind him, imploring him to stay for at least a few minutes.

Hidayatullah's ruling had consigned members of the Rajya Sabha to being second-class MPs in at least two ways.

First, if they complained that their privileges as members or the privileges of the Rajya Sabha itself had been breached, their complaints were henceforth liable to be interpreted, as they had been in the present case, as implying merely that the privileges of a specific committee had been breached, and that of a committee which was not of the Rajya Sabha.

Second, from now on, members of the Rajya Sabha—even those who were themselves members of, say, the Committee on Public Undertakings or the Public Accounts Committee (PAC)—would not be able to raise privilege questions about these committees. To assess how restrictive this ruling was liable to be, we have to remember that all the finance committees of Parliament— the Public Accounts Committee, the Estimates Committee, the Committee on Public Undertakings—as well as a committee such as that on the Welfare of Scheduled Castes and Tribes, had been formally set up under the *Rules of Procedure and Conduct of Business of the Lok Sabha*.

Apart from everything else, consigning members of the Rajya Sabha to being second-class MPs went against the specific understanding on which these committees had been set up. MPs like Dinesh Goswami and A.G. Kulkarni drew attention to past rulings and formulations that laid down that MPs of both Houses would have exactly the same rights and privileges in regard to these committees. Past Speakers of the Lok Sabha and Chairmen of the Rajya Sabha had given specific rulings to this effect. On behalf of successive governments, authoritative spokesmen, from

Pandit Jawaharlal Nehru to law ministers to industries ministers, had repeatedly given assurances to the same effect.

Here was a typical one (this one from Nityanand Kanungo, the then minister of industry) that figured in the records of the Rajya Sabha itself:

> Both the Speaker of the Lok Sabha and the Chairman of the Rajya Sabha in 1954 have made it abundantly clear that the membership of the Public Accounts Committee carries the same rights and duties to Members from either House. I would like to make it categorically clear that by using the same phraseology it is meant beyond doubt that the rights and duties of the Members in this Committee as proposed would be exactly the same with no restriction whatsoever.[2]

But now, by Hidayatullah's dispensation, while a member of the Lok Sabha who was a member of, say, the Committee on Public Undertakings could file a privilege motion relating to the report of that Committee, someone from the Rajya Sabha who was, like his colleague from the Lok Sabha, a member of the Committee, could not do so.

Furthermore, should a member of the Rajya Sabha receive irrefutable evidence that a report of one of the crucial Finance Committees of Parliament was a fabrication or that it was based on distorted and misleading evidence, he could henceforth do nothing about it. He must hawk the evidence around to some member of the Lok Sabha or the press.

Jakhar's first ruling

Hidayatullah refused to entertain the privilege motions, ruling that the matter was the concern of the Speaker of the Lok Sabha.

And what did the Speaker do?

The day after Hidayatullah rejected the motions, the Speaker delivered three rulings. Two of these deserve comment.

---

[2] *Rajya Sabha Debates,* Volume XLV, p. 1115.

First, Jakhar had rejected all motions of privilege filed against ministers and officials of the government. He said that these motions had been filed on the presumption that a file had been kept from the Committee, but upon careful reading of the report of the Committee, he noticed that the report did not state anywhere that any file had been kept from it.

That was precisely the point. The crucial file had been kept from the Committee, and the Chairman of the Committee, and the Secretariat had ensured that the report would not mention this. The fact would have also been clear from the minutes of the Committee's meetings but these had not been tabled. But Jakhar had shut his eyes.

To start off, Jakhar had narrowed the charge. The charge had not merely been that the government had kept a file from the Committee on Public Undertakings. The charge had been that it had suppressed a host of vital facts from the Committee, and that one of the devices by which this had been done was to withhold a file.

Next, in assessing the narrowed charge, namely, the charge that the government had kept a file from the Committee, Jakhar had adopted a very special rule of evidence. He did not find, he decreed, any complaint to this effect in the report of the Committee.

But that precisely was part—and a very important part—of the charge, namely, that the minutes of the Committee's meetings had been doctored, that crucial facts had been kept out of the draft report, that the draft had sought strenuously to whitewash the deal, and that the Committee had been hustled into signing a document that members knew was grossly incomplete.

Before Jakhar delivered his ruling, he had at least two letters on record through which two members of the Committee— R.R. Morarka and Harikesh Bahadur—had certified that to their personal knowledge, the minutes had been deliberately doctored to shield some transactions and certain individuals. Jakhar must also have known by then or could easily have ascertained that, in fact, the minutes (and the report he was relying on was based on these) were completely irregular. Rules 21 and 22, that had been put out and printed by his own Secretariat to govern the procedures of the Committee, prescribed that the minutes must be drafted after each sitting of the Committee, and that they must be circulated to the members of the Committee. This was never done.

Moreover, in a separate letter delivered three days before the ruling, Harikesh Bahadur had testified to much more: '. . . Soon thereafter', he had written to the Speaker,

> I requested our Chairman (Bansi Lal) that we should call the witnesses, Lavraj Kumar, etc., again as we wanted to examine this note and see the file. The Chairman said there was no time so we should leave this matter there. Later on at the time of considering the draft report when there was no reference to the missing file in the draft several members of the Committee objected to that and desired that the actual position as recorded before the Committee be submitted to Parliament. Then the Chairman said that, if the members were so particular, why did they not call for the file? At this stage one of the members reminded him that the request was made by Shri Harikesh Bahadur to the Chairman to get the file but the Chairman had not agreed. On this the Chairman said, in a huff, that you may call for the file now. Subsequent developments have already been brought on record. In the end the Committee had no option but to leave its investigation incomplete and recommend that the matter be enquired into further . . .

Such was the evidence on record with the Speaker. He chose to disregard it and go only by what appeared in the report.

But why had the members not recorded something about the matter in the report?

I have already explained how the circulation of the draft had been delayed, how when they met on 28 April, with just two days to go before their term expired, the members had to choose between dropping the entire section on the Kuo Oil deal altogether or letting at least a truncated one survive. The meeting had been brought to an abrupt halt by Bansi Lal first refusing to allow any reference to the missing file and then walking out saying that he was not feeling well.

Presuming that even though the matter had been brought to his notice at least five days before the session opened, presuming again that even though members had been agitating the matter before him from the very first day of the session, the Speaker knew nothing of what had transpired in the Committee, he had now been alerted to the facts about the file, and that too in writing by a member of the Committee itself. Thus alerted, he could have found out more. In any event, he could not be unaware of the formal rule which disabled members of a committee from bringing such facts on record in a report. The rule was none other than Direction 68(3) of the Speaker himself. The Direction prescribed that 'there shall be no minute of dissent to the report'.

Given the role of the Prime Minister's Office in the matter, given the fact that two-thirds of the twenty-two members of the Committee were from the ruling party, given the absolute prohibition against filing minutes of dissent, where was the scope for members to register the complaint that the Speaker said he could not find in the report?

Thus, apart from narrowing the charge, the rule of evidence that the Speaker had adopted for his first ruling was, to say the least, restrictive. And it was a manifestly self-reinforcing one: first a general direction is given which precludes complaints of this kind from being registered in the report, and then motions are dismissed on the ground that the report does not contain complaints of that kind.

Jakhar's second ruling

His second ruling would have consequences that extended far beyond the case in question. Several members had petitioned the Speaker that, in view of the facts that had been brought on record, they should be permitted to examine the verbatim records of the Committee. The Speaker refused his permission, citing one precedent and one ground.

He said that one of his predecessors, Sanjiva Reddy, had similarly refused permission on an earlier occasion. There were precedents to the contrary. For instance, when a similar request had been made in regard to the 50th and 55th Reports of the Public Accounts Committee, which dealt in part with the affairs of Amin Chand Pyare Lal, members had been permitted to examine the verbatim records. Nor had access been limited to Members of Parliament. For instance, in 1969 the Trombay Fertilizer Inquiry Commission had been allowed to examine the evidence given by the government as well as the Fertilizer Corporation of India to the Committee on Public Undertakings. The Committee's correspondence with the Comptroller and Auditor General, too, had been made available.

Attempts were made to bring such precedents to Jakhar's attention. His reply, repeated more than once, was laconic: 'I concur with Sanjiva Reddy.' And that was that.

An inventive reason

The reason he gave for his ruling was even more interesting. He had referred the request, he said, to the new Chairman of the Committee on Public Undertakings (Madhusudan Vairale, a former tourism minister from Maharashtra), and he concurred with Vairale's concurring with the view (expressed fourteen years earlier in another context) by a Chairman of another Financial Committee that 'the existing practice of keeping the proceedings as confidential and not making them available to any person other than members of the Committee, made for frank expression of views by the representatives of government'. Accordingly, he said, he was turning down the request of the members to examine the evidence received by the Committee.

Like everything else about the ruling, this reasoning was open to question on several counts.

First, witnesses who testified before Parliamentary Committees did not testify on the presumption that their evidence shall be treated as confidential. On the contrary, they were explicitly told that what they say shall be treated as public. Direction 58 of none other than the Speaker, Lok Sabha, bound the person who was presiding over the sitting of the Committee as follows:

> Where witnesses appear before a Committee to give evidence, the Chairman shall make it clear to the witnesses that their evidence shall be treated as public and is liable to be published, unless they specifically desire that all or any part of the evidence given by them is to be treated as confidential. It shall, however, be explained to the witnesses that even though they might desire their evidence to be treated as confidential such evidence is liable to be made available to the members of Parliament.

From where, then, did the presumption of confidentiality come? And just on a point of fact, in the present case, no one had so much as claimed that any assurance was given to any witness that any part of his evidence would be treated as confidential. Indeed, no witness even requested that any part of his evidence be treated as confidential. (Before giving his ruling on the 50th and 55th Reports of the Public Accounts Committee, the Speaker had ascertained whether any such assurance had been sought or given. Having found out the facts, he had announced in his ruling that, 'In view of the fact that the Chairman of the PAC stated in the House yesterday that he had not given any assurance to any witness that his evidence will be treated as secret, I am inclined to give permission to the members to make a specific request to see the documents and evidence. Such records will be available in the Committee Room of the PAC where they will be shown in the presence of an officer . . .') This time around, the Speaker had chosen not to make any inquiry of this kind. He just enunciated a blanket rule shutting out access in general.

Second, Rule 272 of the *Rules of Procedure and Conduct of Business in the Lok Sabha* prescribed an oath for the witnesses: 'I, A.B., swear in the name of God/solemnly affirm that the evidence which I shall give in this case shall be true, that I will conceal nothing, and that no part of my evidence shall be false.'

Was it to be presumed, from now on, that this oath was a conditional oath, namely, that a witness shall speak the truth and conceal nothing, provided the Committee shall keep what he says confidential?

Third, mere common sense instructs us that a witness was more liable to prevaricate when he is certain that what he says will never go beyond half a dozen members of a committee, than when he is certain that what he says will be made public.

Another innovation

Since 15 July, whenever any member had sought to raise issues related to the Kuo Oil deal, the Speaker had disallowed him on the ground that the Committee on Public Undertakings was still examining the matter.

Now, this, too, was an innovation. It had been repeatedly held in the past that a committee was seized of a matter till it submitted its report and only till then. This Committee having submitted its report on 30 April 1982, it must be deemed to have delivered itself of the matter.

No, said the Speaker. It had yet to submit an 'Action Taken' report. The House could discuss the matter only after the Committee submitted that follow-up report, he ruled.

The operational effect of this decree would shut all discussion for long. Under the rules, once it received the report, the government could take up to six months to file its statements about what action it proposed to take on suggestions of the Committee. Second, by convention, it need not furnish its responses to all the suggestions within the mandatory six months. Third, the reply may be laconic: for instance, the Committee had suggested that the Kuo Oil deal should be investigated further; the government could just say, 'Accepted; a departmental enquiry is in progress,' and that would be sufficient. Ever so often this sort of response is all governments gave. Fourth, the government could reject the suggestions and furnish its reasons for doing so. In any event, the government had six months for starters.

Once these replies were received, the Committee had to examine them. There was no limit on how long it may take over this examination.

Therefore, the customary lag between the filing of a report of a Parliamentary Committee and the filing of the report about the 'action taken' on the original report was one and a half to two *years*. That was just the customary lag. Longer delays occurred often enough. Thus, for instance, in the sixth Lok Sabha, the 'Action Taken' report on the 8th Report of the Public Accounts Committee was filed *four years and twenty-two days after* the original report. The 'Action Taken' report on the PAC's 35th Report was filed *five years and twelve days after* the original report!

Who won?

Thus, Hidayatullah consigned the matter to Jakhar. Jakhar consigned it to the Committee. And the Committee could keep it consigned for long. The net effect was to foreclose debate on an issue of public importance.

The rulers seemed to have won again.

But what is the ruler's strength is the system's weakness. If, when such issues were brought up, full discussion took place, the guilty were identified and brought to book, the rot would be stemmed. When presiding officers foreclose all possibilities of reform in this way, they foreclose prospects of salvaging the system. When one chokes a dam, the water will go over the embankments or break the dam itself . . .

Moreover, rulings of this kind, and they have become more and more frequent with each passing year, diminish the high office of the Speaker and the Chairman of the Rajya Sabha. Whatever the intricate processes of reasoning of these presiding officers, people see the pattern of the rulings, they see the net effect, and they notice that the pattern is the same from one session to the next, that the net effect is also always the same, namely to foreclose debate.

A timely book

People see all this and contrast it with what has been said about what presiding officers should be like:

The Speaker has to speak for the whole House. As Speaker he knows only one language—that of the House . . .

Every Speaker understands that his conduct and behavior are under close scrutiny and subject to constant criticism. But his hope is that the criticism will come in equal measure from both sides of the House . . . He cannot claim to be a repository of all wisdom and all constitutional niceties. He has to exercise the powers of his office more as a duty to the House and to the Members rather than as authority over them . . .

As the repository of the confidence of the various sections of the House, the Speaker has the solemn duty to be fair-minded, non-partisan and objective in the conduct of the debate and the proceedings of the House. In the exercise of his powers the Speaker must not only be impartial but must also be seen by the whole House and the country to be so . . .

In a parliamentary democracy the Speaker cannot act arbitrarily . . . In the Business Advisory Committee . . . a list of items for discussion is prepared. The Speaker may, in fact, add to rather than subtract from this list . . .

What the Speaker has to do is to ensure that no important issue is barred and no discussion is curbed . . .

The book in which these noble propositions had been set out?

The People, the Parliament and the Administration, Metropolitan, 1982, Delhi; Rs 150 a copy.

Foreword by?

M. Hidayatullah.

The author of the book?

Balram Jakhar himself!

It was all a misunderstanding

Hidayatullah's ruling deserves another word, for in it, he laid down two general principles that strain one's credibility even to this day.

He said that, first, even if a document presented to the Rajya Sabha on behalf of a committee, such as the Committee on Public

Undertakings, was manifestly a fraud and was known to be a fraud, neither he nor the Rajya Sabha could do anything about it, as to do what needs to be done would amount to meddling in the affairs of a committee of the Lok Sabha.

Second, he had ruled that 'there is really no place for members of the Council [i.e., the Rajya Sabha] on the Committee [on Public Undertakings] under the rules of the Houses'.

The first innovation

Now, the first proposition was startling enough by itself not to require any comment. Documents such as reports of Parliamentary Committees, of commissions of inquiry, etc., are presented to Members of Parliament to assist them in their functions. A ritual has been devised—that of someone specifically laying the documents on the table of the House—precisely to ensure that the documents are well-considered, accurate and authentic. And here was a presiding officer, and a former Chief Justice of India, pronouncing that even if a specific set of documents presented to the House was a complete fraud, he could not help the House; furthermore, that the person who had tabled the documents could not be questioned, to say nothing of his being hauled up, as he had merely performed 'a purely ministerial function', that therefore he 'cannot be personally held responsible for inaccuracies, if any' in the document in question; and, most startling of all, the House could not help itself either, that as far as this set of documents was concerned, it must, in effect, proceed with its business on the basis of documents it knows to be an out and out fraud.

The second innovation

The second innovation knocked the Rajya Sabha out of all the financial committees of Parliament. It had no representation on the Estimates Committee, in any case. Now, by Hidayatullah's benediction, it would not have any place on the other two financial committees—the Public Accounts Committee and the Committee on Public Undertakings.

This was quite an innovation, for the Rajya Sabha had provided one-third of the members of the Public Accounts Committee since it was set up in 1954, that was for almost twenty-eight years till the time Hidayatullah was giving his ruling, and one-third of the members of the Committee on Public Undertakings since it was set up in 1964, that is, for almost eighteen years before the ruling.

Hidayatullah felt compelled to knock the Rajya Sabha out of these committees for three reasons.

First, Hidayatullah noted, the committees were set up under *Rules of Procedure and Conduct of Business of the Lok Sabha*, the PAC under Rule 308 and COPU under Rule 312A. Therefore, he maintained, while they were known as *Parliamentary* Committees, they were actually committees of the Lok Sabha.

Second, he recalled that whenever the committee was constituted, the Lok Sabha invited the Rajya Sabha to—and the Rajya Sabha formally agreed to—'associate' with the committee. From this, Hidayatullah concluded that members of the committee who were from the Rajya Sabha were 'not even described as members but are associated with the committee', that is, they were not full members of the committee; at best, they were associate members.

Third, to add death to debility, Hidayatullah cited Rule 312B from the *Rule Book of the Lok Sabha* which, when dealing with the Committee on Public Undertakings, laid down, 'the committee shall consist of not more than fifteen members who shall be elected by the House [which Hidayatullah pointed out repeatedly meant only the Lok Sabha] every year from amongst its members . . .' From this, Hidayatullah concluded that there was really no place for the Rajya Sabha members to be on the Committee at all.

What about entry 13 in the *Official Handbook, Committee on Public Undertakings, An Introductory Guide*, published by the Lok Sabha Secretariat itself, which stated, 'The Public Undertakings Committee consists of 22 members, 15 elected by the Lok Sabha and seven elected by the Rajya Sabha . . .'?

'This is not an accurate statement,' Hidayatullah said.

This last bit was more devastating than might appear at first sight, for it struck beyond the Committee on Public Undertakings.

At my desk at the *Indian Express*. An editor of the paper was to write that he was always surprised why, though he was the editor, my room was larger than his. Talk of 'status anxiety'!

For a month and a half, employees were prevented by the Government from bringing out the Delhi edition of the *Express* on the plea that there was a 'strike' when there was none. We shuttled between police stations and offices and courts.

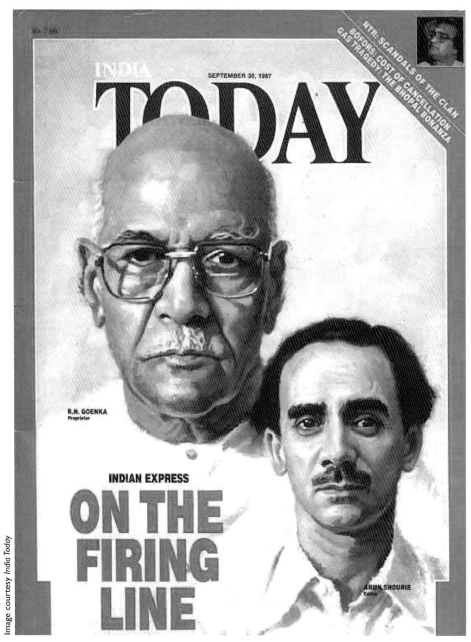

SEPTEMBER 30, 1987

INDIA TODAY

NTR: SCANDALS OF THE CLAN
BOFORS: COST OF CANCELLATION
GAS TRAGEDY: THE BHOPAL BONANZA

R.N. GOENKA
Proprietor

INDIAN EXPRESS

ON THE FIRING LINE

ARUN SHOURIE
Editor

Dismissed from the *Express*. 'Arun, *eh taan Guptaji dee sotee he niklee*,' my mother remarked, took my head in her hands and, as she always did, kissed me on my forehead. With that and her infectious laugh, in a flash she made me see that the job had been no more mine than that stick had been Guptaji's!

In the case of the Public Accounts Committee (which also had twenty-two members, seven of whom were from the Rajya Sabha) Rule 309 specified, 'The Committee shall consist of no more than 15 members who shall be elected by the House every year from amongst its members . . .' Indeed, why limit the self-abnegation to the financial committees? The Committee on the Welfare of Scheduled Castes and Scheduled Tribes, for instance, was also set up under a rule of the Lok Sabha alone—Rule 331A, to be precise. It had thirty members, ten of whom were from the Rajya Sabha. But Rule 331B, which on Hidayatullah's reading would constitute the final and exhaustive specification of its membership, said, 'The committee shall consist of not more than twenty members who shall be elected by the House every year from amongst its members . . .' The same reasoning therefore knocked the Rajya Sabha out of that committee too.

A *little history*

The decision that, whenever they sit together in a committee, members from both Houses shall have identical rights, privileges and duties, is as old as our Parliament. The question was explicitly raised and settled when the Public Accounts Committee was set up.

Some had argued that financial matters fell in the exclusive jurisdiction of the Lok Sabha, and so no one from the Rajya Sabha should be a member of the PAC. The matter was settled after Pandit Nehru and others clarified the position as follows: the Lok Sabha's exclusive jurisdiction on money matters is confined to the ultimate decision on the money bills; both Houses are equally concerned with other aspects of financial questions; in particular, the Rajya Sabha has an equal role to play in commenting on and tendering advice on financial matters; therefore, while the Estimates Committee would have members only from the Lok Sabha, the PAC would have members from both Houses.

Indeed, the specific point on which Hidayatullah had pronounced—that there is no place for Rajya Sabha members on such committees, that at best, they have the status of associate members—was raised and settled. An exchange from the debate on the matter that took place in the Rajya Sabha itself on 13 May 1954 was clear as can be:

> S.N. *Dwivedy*: May I know whether it is a committee of the Parliament or of the House of the People, and whether members who will be nominated from the Council would be full-fledged members or only associate members?

> S.N. *Sinha*: (Minister for Parliamentary Affairs): May I clarify this point, with your permission, Sir? So far as a clarification of this point is concerned, I would like to say that so far as the powers, function, or status of a member are concerned, there is absolutely no difference between the members of this House and that House . . . 'Associate' does not mean 'associate members'. There is a difference. If you ask them to associate with a thing it does not mean that they are associate members. I have made the position perfectly clear that so far as the powers, function or status is concerned, there is absolutely no difference between the members of this House and those of the other House.

And here is what Pandit Jawaharlal Nehru had observed on the same matter:

> Something has been said about associate members. Who are these associate members? If they come to the Committee, as the major function of the Committee is scrutinising, there is no question of two grades of members. They have the same grade and status . . . It should be the desire of the House to cultivate, to the fullest extent possible, cooperation and friendly relations with the other House: the conception of the Constitution is that of both Houses of Parliament shouldering the burden of Parliament.

And Dr Radhakrishnan, who then presided over the Rajya Sabha as Hidayatullah was doing at this time, before putting the matter to vote, summarized the position as follows:

Chairman: . . . So it is not a matter of any concession or sufferance. It is a matter of right in accordance with the motion of Parliament accepted by this House. It has also been made quite clear by the Minister for Parliamentary Affairs that we work in that Committee on terms of absolute equality with other Members . . . So we have a right to sit there now and our rights are absolutely the same as the rights of the other Members . . . I would advise the House to accept the motion and use their rights to the best advantage . . .

And yet Hidayatullah had read into being 'associated with' what was precisely and definitely read out of it twenty-eight years earlier.

Committee on Public Undertakings

As the number of and investment in our public-sector enterprises grew, Parliament decided that a separate Committee on Public Undertakings should be constituted so that their operations could be monitored closely. In regard to these enterprises, the functions of the Estimates Committee and the Public Accounts Committee were to be handed over to this new Committee. It is for this reason that COPU came to be set up under the Rules of the Lok Sabha: as the functions it was taking over had hitherto been exercised by two committees constituted under Rules of the Lok Sabha, the new committee too, it was felt, should be set up under the Rules of the Lok Sabha.

There was nothing more to the committee being constituted under Rules of the Lok Sabha than this.

The operational significance of a committee being set up under a Rule of one House rather than of the other is merely that the chairman of that committee comes from that House rather than the other, that it is serviced by the Secretariat of that House rather than that of the other, and that on operational matters, e.g., if there is a dispute within the committee, it is the presiding officer of that House rather than of the other who decides. In particular, the fact of the committee having been set up under the rules of one

House does not devalue the rights and privileges, just as it does not dilute the duties of its members who happen to come from the other House.

Thus, in the specific case of the Committee on Public Undertakings, while the Committee was being constituted under a rule of the Lok Sabha, this is what Nityanand Kanungo, the minister piloting the Bill through the Rajya Sabha, said about the rights and privileges of members from the two Houses:

> Both the Speaker of the Lok Sabha and the Chairman of the Rajya Sabha in 1954 have made it abundantly clear that the membership of the Public Accounts Committee carries the same rights and duties for members from either House. I would like to make it categorically clear that by using the same phraseology it is meant beyond doubt that the rights and duties of the members in this Committee as proposed would be exactly the same with no restriction whatsoever.

And one has only to read the speeches of member after member—K. Santhanam on, down—to see that this is the understanding on which the Rajya Sabha had agreed to join the Committee.

The matter having been well-settled so long ago, and it having been so clearly understood all these years, Hidayatullah had suddenly ruled otherwise.

A *distinction*

Hidayatullah had gone further. When his attention was drawn to these statements, assurances and understandings, he said that members could take them 'for what they are worth'. But that, in any case, if these assurances and understandings ensure anything at all, they only ensure that when they are functioning *in* a committee, members from the Rajya Sabha would have the same rights, etc., as members from the Lok Sabha. They do not ensure that outside the committee—specifically, when they are back in the Rajya Sabha—the Rajya Sabha members would have the same rights vis-à-vis that committee as members from the Lok Sabha.

This novel distinction was even more destructive than the original assertion that members from the Rajya Sabha were merely associated with the committee, that they were not members really.

First, members of the Rajya Sabha who sit on these committees do not sit in their individual capacity. They sit as nominees of and as representatives of the Rajya Sabha itself. The motion which the Rajya Sabha passes each time it sends persons to these committees, and which Hidayatullah himself cited, testifies to this:

> . . . the Rajya Sabha do agree to nominate seven members from the Rajya Sabha to associate with the Committee on Public Undertakings of the Lok Sabha . . .

The Rajya Sabha as a House agrees, not this member or that in his individual capacity, to send its nominees.

Therefore, when Hidayatullah struck down the status, rights and privileges of these nominees from full membership to associate membership, in fact, to an unwarranted membership, he struck at the status, rights and privileges of the Rajya Sabha itself.

But, even more important, by ruling that going by past assurances 'for what they are worth', even if the rights, etc., of these members *inside* a committee are the same as those of members from the Lok Sabha, *outside* the committee they are inferior, he whittled down the rights and privileges of every member of the Rajya Sabha. For outside the committee, a member of the committee is like any other member of the Rajya Sabha.

This distinction, too, was not fortuitous. The result—the rejection by Hidayatullah of all the privilege motions, almost all of them filed by persons who had not been members of COPU—would not have followed but for the distinction. The members were not saying that their privileges, as members of the Committee on Public Undertakings had been violated, nor that the privileges of that Committee had been violated, but that their privileges as members of the Rajya Sabha and the privileges of the House itself had been violated.

The wrong quotation

Even more incredible was Hidayatullah's ruling that as Rule 312B of the Lok Sabha does not provide for members from the Rajya Sabha, 'there is really no place for members of the Council on the Committee under the rules of the Houses'. As is well known, the Lok Sabha Rules provide only for what the Lok Sabha is to do. By convention, the Lok Sabha cannot, as part of its rules, direct what the Rajya Sabha should do. It cannot direct the Rajya Sabha, for instance, to provide seven members each for PAC and COPU, and ten members for the Committee on Scheduled Castes and Tribes. That is for the Rajya Sabha to do. Instead of directing his Secretariat to formulate the appropriate rule, Hidayatullah had ruled the members out of court.

The oddity will be obvious when we put the question the other way around. As the relevant rule of the Lok Sabha does not provide for any membership from the Rajya Sabha, how is it that for *twenty-eight years* in the case of PAC, and for *eighteen years* in the case of COPU, Rajya Sabha members had been sitting in these committees, presiding over their meetings, signing their reports? Had it all been just one big misunderstanding?

Conscious of the results of his findings, Hidayatullah said that the position was 'unfortunate' but that it could not be helped. He counselled the Rajya Sabha not to expend energy on mere sentiment, and instead to heed the advice A.K. Sen, the then law minister, gave in 1961.

'It will not be a good day,' Hidayatullah commended Sen for having said, 'when this House starts any conflict over these common matters of interest between itself and the other House.'

Someone had supplied him the wrong quotation. That was A.K. Sen's advice, not to the Rajya Sabha but to the Lok Sabha! And it was preceded by the words, 'to give one-third representation [on the Committee on Public Undertakings] to the Rajya Sabha would be a wise thing, because just as we are vehement here in asserting our rights, the other House will be equally vehement when this [the Bill on COPU] goes there.'

It was entirely in the fitness of things, therefore, that while Hidayatullah had insisted that he would not, as he said, 'sit in appeal over the Hon'ble Speaker', Opposition members resigned from the committees and forced the Speaker to sit in appeal over Hidayatullah and overturn his ruling swiftly.

It didn't deserve anything more than the two days it got.

15

'*Guptaji dee soti*'

I had been proven right as far as the Kuo Oil article was concerned. But the consequences were round the corner.

Ramnathji was under immense pressure. Mrs Gandhi's emissaries had made it clear to him that unless he reined in the paper, the might of the State would descend on him again. The attempt to seize the extension to the *Express* building in Delhi had already started. Financially, the paper was, as it always was, at the brink. Government advertisements were an important source of its meagre revenues. These could be stopped on any pretext; in fact, they could stop arriving without any pretext. One call, and the life-saving advances from the banks would stop. Newsprint had been held up at the Bombay and Madras ports earlier; it could be held up at a moment's notice again. In any case, there were enough cases in government departments to hobble Ramnathji and to cripple the paper.

Ramnathji was a great, and a very resourceful fighter. But from his long experience in battling odds, he had concluded that the occasional compromise, lying low till the opportunity to strike back arose, even a retreat, were stratagem. They were a part of fighting. '*Tum paristithee se lado gey kyaa?*'—'Will you fight circumstances?' he would ask me. '*Jab toofaan aataa hai, to jo pedh usey akad kar yon dekhtaa hai*'—he would turn, becoming rigid with his head and chin raised as if he were confronting a storm—'*usey toofaan ukhaad detaa hai. Jo chhotaa saa ghaas hotaa hai, voh jhuk jaataa hai. Toofaan gayaa, aur voh ghaas fauran phir yon-kaa-tyon khadaa ho jaataa hai*'[1]—he would open his curled hand.

The immense pressure was one element. But there were other factors too. Ramnathji used to tire of his editors and correspondents, as one might of a favourite dish or, as he would have put it, of a mistress! He was extremely possessive about the paper. It was his life. And so, the very success of the journalist—the success which he enabled, of which he felt proud—would kindle a sort of jealousy, almost a resentment. And there were enough persons to fan this jealousy. Once, Ramnathji himself told me—it was his way of telling me to let off a bit!—of a senior editor in the paper telling him, '*Aaj kal to log kehney lagein hain ki* Express *Ramnath kaa naheen, Shourie kaa akhbaar hai.*'[2]

For one reason or another, Ramnathji had opened a line to the government. Mrs Gandhi had asked Giani Zail Singh, then Home Minister, to handle the matter. Ramnathji used to visit Gianiji's house for the purpose. A person associated with the paper was close to Gianiji, and would tell me what was going on—how Ramnathji had met the Giani, and what had transpired. One day he told me that Ramnathji would be going to Gianiji's house at 4 p.m. To tease Ramnathji and to let him know that I knew what he was up to, I mentioned this to the editors of *India Today,* and requested them to post a photographer at a point from which he could photograph Ramnathji driving into the entrance—Ramnathji almost always drove his own car, and this was always a small Fiat in those days.

He was furious when this photograph was published.

I soon learnt that articles of the kind that I used to write and stories of the kind that I used to encourage would not be allowed, that, in fact, I was to be the goodwill gesture.

---

1 'Will you fight circumstances? When a storm comes, it uproots the tree that stands rigid, that confronts it. But the little grass, it bends. The storm passes, and it springs back to what it was.'

2 'These days, people have started saying, "The *Express* is not Goenka's, it is Shourie's paper."'

A *meeting, and another letter*

It is best to describe what I learnt and how by the letter that I sent Ramnathji and Verghese on 3 August 1982. Here it is.

August 3, 1982

My Dear Ramnathji and George,

In two meetings with Suman Dubey and again during a telephone conversation with him on Saturday, Kamal Nath told him to ensure that I met him. Accordingly I met him at Suman's place yesterday for three hours. Suman was present almost throughout the three hours and Manju, Suman's wife, was present for at least two of the three hours.

Kamal Nath, who seems to be fond of talking, was in a specially talkative mood. In fact, our meeting ended only because another guest arrived in the house and the two of us had to leave by another door.

Kamal Nath talked of many things and it will take very long to transcribe them. He mentioned a few things about the *Express* also, its past, its present and its future. One of these is of special concern to me and I am writing to you urgently so as to brief you about it.

Quite early on in the conversation Kamal Nath said that he had been receiving a lot of information from political circles, from journalists as well as from within the *Indian Express* about me. He said that he had a letter from some aunt of mine levelling allegations in connection with some property, and allegations against my father. (He had earlier told Suman that Congress(I) people had been telling him to release this letter.) I told him very firmly that allegations against me or my father were of no concern to me, that I did not much care for the opinions of 'journalists' either and that if he was thinking that he could hold out this letter as a threat to me, he might as well understand that I did not care a bit about this or any other letter that he might have, that in fact if such letters were released or published it would only give me an occasion to file a defamation case. This exchange occurred very early on in the evening. I told him that if he thought he could intimidate me with this sort of stuff, we couldn't proceed. His tone changed swiftly. He did not revert to the matter again. He then shifted to emphasising that we must all and I too must face realities.

He said that soon after the article dealing with the Kuo Oil Deal was written Ram Nathji conveyed both to him and to higher-ups in the Congress(I) that the article had been written, that he had made sure that it would not be published by the paper, and that there had been an exchange of communications by which he had told George that I must be removed from the *Indian Express*.

I asked Kamal Nath whether Ramnathji had personally spoken to him on the matter or whether he personally knew that Ramnathji had personally conveyed the assurance to Mrs Gandhi or someone. He was evasive. 'How does that matter?' he said, 'It is a fact.'

Why would Ramnathji go to this length? Suman asked him. Because, said Kamal Nath, Ramnathji wanted to make sure that they—Mrs Gandhi, Kamal Nath & Co.—knew that he had nothing to do with the article and that, in fact, he had done everything possible to prevent its publication, to the extent of directing that I be removed from the *Express* altogether.

He went on to say that the Congress(I) higher-ups had been specifically assured by Ramnathji that I would be removed but that 'I will do this in my own way.' He said that they had been assured that a situation would be created in which I would myself leave. (Kamal Nath had said this to Suman in the earlier meeting also.)

Suman asked him when this understanding had been arrived at. He said, 'It is older than you think; say, 1½ years ago.' He said that he had himself seen Ramnathji talking to Mrs Gandhi at a dinner and that he had personally met Ramnathji at Mrs Gandhi's house. He said that on the latter occasion he had accosted Ramnathji with the following words, '*Arey, Ramnathji, aap yahaan kaisey pahunch gaey?*' and Ramnathji had replied,

'*Kyaa tum he naatak kar saktey ho?* In any case, *merey liye*, the nation is more important than anything else . . .'[3]

Suman said that if such an understanding had been arrived at 1½ years ago, how could I have been allowed to publish the articles on Antulay? Kamal Nath shifted his ground somewhat, and said that articles on Antulay, PC Sethi etc. were all right as long as they did not touch the Prime Minister, Rajiv or Sonia. He said that nothing could be written against any one of these three in the paper as that was a part of the understanding.

He said further that before George was appointed, his name was sent for approval by Ramnathji with the observation that Ramnathji has to choose between George and me, and George would specifically ensure that I was 'fingered' and dealt with in such a manner that the situation would arise in which I would leave on my own, etc.

Suman asked him that, as Ramnathji was already 77 or 78, that as he had shown—for instance, during the Emergency—that he really stood for some principles, why would he compromise now? What would he hope to gain from such a deal?

Kamal Nath said that the answer was very simple and it was simply that 'he has lost his capacity to fight.' He said that everybody in the Government and people like him knew this, and that they also knew the inclinations and capacity of 'the Anil Agarwals and Pradip Ganeriwalas.'[4] He said that Ramnathji's only interest now was to safeguard the buildings, etc. He said that for this purpose, a Trust had been set up, of which I was one of the trustees! I quickly disabused him of this notion and also told him that the information about my being made a trustee did not harmonise with his entire thesis, namely, that Ramnathji had assured Mrs Gandhi & Co. that I would be removed from the *Express*!

He said that a specific assurance had now been given that no further exposures of the Kuo Oil type would be allowed to

---

[3] 'Ramnathji, how come you have reached here?' and Ramnathji had replied, 'Do you think you are the only one who can put on an act? In any case, *merey liye*, the nation is more important than anything else . . .'
[4] The husbands of two of Ramnathji's granddaughters.

appear in the paper, and that George would personally ensure that this assurance was adhered to. He challenged me to write another article exposing anything of a similar kind and get it published in the *Indian Express*. He said that I could write on the Quran or something like that and those articles might be published but nothing of the kind that had recently appeared.

He also recounted the favours he said he had done Ramnathji during the Emergency—of how he had ensured that while things would be pushed far enough to keep the *Express* in check, they would not be pushed so far as to finish it; of how he had got Ramnathji a hospital room in Calcutta; of how he used to visit him every day and how, holding his hand and with tears in his eyes, Ramnathji would tell him, '*Main mar rahaa hoon, abhi main tumhaarey se lad naheen saktaa,*'[5] and how he had assured Ramnathji that while he would fight him, he would do so only after Ramnathji had recovered; of how he had ensured that no Board meeting would be held while Ramnathji was ill in Calcutta; of how at Ramnathji's request, he had ensured that Express Towers was not put up for auction. Etc. And of how it was that as KK Birla and all had backed out after 1977, Ramnathji had told him—Kamal Nath—that he was withdrawing the *Express* case from the Shah Commission so as not to implicate him, i.e., Kamal Nath.

The whole tenor of his meandering presentation was as follows: (i) RN ji has lost the capacity to put up a fight; (ii) he has already assured Mrs Gandhi, Kamal Nath & Co. that no 'exposures' harmful to the Government would be published; (iii) he has already assured them that I will be removed by a situation being created in which I would myself leave; (iv) that Kamal Nath knew everything about the state of affairs in the paper; (v) that Ramnathji owed him many favours, and that (vi) therefore, I must accept the realities of the situation.

He did not put things as clearly as this. He doesn't seem to be the kind who does. He meanders and is carried away at each point. But this is the only way in which his remarks on this matter can be put together.

---

[5] 'I am dying, at this time I cannot fight you.'

On the presumption that his extended account of his proximity to Ramnathji, of the favours that he had done Ramnathji and of Ramnathji's assurances to the Congress(I) about my removal—on the presumption that all this was meant to cow me down, I told him emphatically that I did not attach as much importance to my work as a journalist as he and others seemed to imagine, and, therefore, the prospect of losing a job was not as daunting to me as he or others might think.

Towards the end of the conversation, he said that PC Sethi had been completely 'shattered' by these disclosures and that one of his problems was that he had to bolster the courage of people like Sethi who didn't know their own defence. He said that soon after the original article had been circulated, a meeting of a number of ministers had been held to decide how the matter should be handled. He said that another meeting had been held on Friday, July 30, which had been attended by four ministers. He reported that he had attended both the meetings.

At Friday's meeting, he said, one of the ministers asked, 'Can something not be done about this Arun Shourie?' and another minister had replied that he had activated something that morning which would work. 'Some people can be bought with a peg, others are bought by a bottle.'

Ramnathji, please don't react to this letter the way you did to the one I wrote to George by asserting that I am writing this for the gallery, etc. I would be derelict in my duty if I didn't report these exchanges to you and you would hold it against me. I have put all this in writing so as to be absolutely precise in reporting what transpired.

As on the last occasion much of the misunderstanding arose because a copy of my letter made its way to Saroj, I am specifically recording now that this letter is being sent only to Ramnathji, George and Gurumurthy. I am not sending a copy of this letter to anyone else.

Arun

~

Peace talks

Forewarned, I was not really surprised at Verghese blocking the Kuo Oil article—I *was* surprised at the laughable reasons that Verghese was advancing for doing so. That the article had been blocked, that I had sent the article to MPs, that, as a consequence, the paper had been compelled to publish the entire series became known in no time. Ramnathji was not one to hide his anger. By now, everyone in the paper knew of his fury at the fact that the paper had been driven into a corner and just had to publish the Kuo Oil articles. He had expressed his anger directly to Radhakrishna. Our friends—Lakshmi Jain, Radhakrishna and Rajni Kothari foremost among them—saw the rift between Verghese and me as something that would harm the work that needed to be done, now that Mrs Gandhi was back. They also knew Ramnathji well. They felt that he would fan the differences as that was his way—of managing his stable. Lakshmi told me that they wanted to discuss the matter with both of us, and so I should come to Rajni Kothari's place. George will be there, he said, and both of you have to iron things out.

The meeting lasted over an hour and a half.[6] But George Verghese and I ended up just restating our positions.

It was already around 11 a.m., well past the time we used to be in the office, so we got into our respective cars for the drive back. George did not tell me or anyone else at the meeting what Ramnathji told me much later.

'*Kayee baar pataa naheen kahaan sey aapati aa jaati hai,*' he said one evening: I was back in the *Express*, and Ramnathji was teaching me one of his *gurumantras*. '*Aur kayee baar naa jaaney kahaan sey kuchh insaan ko bachhaa letaa hai.*' '*Arey, tum bhee to phaansi sey ek din yon he bachhey the*'[7]—he added with a laugh.

---

6   Apart from L.C. Jain, Radhakrishna and Rajni Kothari, I remember that one other person was present. I think it was Ashish Nandy. While typing this portion, I rang up Ashish to make doubly sure. He told me that for a meeting of this sort, he would normally be present with Rajni, but that he does not recall being at this meeting.
7   'Many times one doesn't know from where some calamity bursts upon one. And many times one does not know what comes from where and saves us.'

What seems to have happened is this. From 9 to 30 July, I had had a free run of the paper—much to Ramnathji's chagrin. Once the issue had run its course, Ramnathji, still furious, had signed a letter dismissing me from the paper. He had given the letter to Verghese, and told him to hand it over to me once he—Ramnathji—had left for Bombay.

It turned out that Verghese was to hand me the termination letter the very day we were meeting at Rajni's place. But by the time we reached the office, the teleprinters carried the news that I had been given the Magsaysay Award! Not quite the day a person could be dismissed. That is how, in the nick of time, I had escaped the *phaansi*!

Gandhian themes

Coming as it did in a maelstrom of tension, the Award was, of course, a wonderful thing. It became all the more so because of the affectionate relationships that developed between the three of us from India who got three of the four awards that were given that year: Chandi Prasad Bhatt, Manibhai Desai and me. And because of Belen Abreu, an elderly lady who, unknown to me, had come scouting for that year's potential candidates. At the time, she was Secretary of the Magsaysay Foundation. She and a colleague used to tour countries assessing the work of persons—accounts and stories of whose work had reached the Foundation. She was a kind and perceptive lady. We remained in touch for several years. And once I heard her describe her job in a way that would make it the envy of us all. She and her colleague were at our home. An uncle of mine had dropped in to see my parents. After I had introduced him as one who had been a General in our Army, my uncle asked Belen, 'And what do you do?' 'O, I have the best job in the world,' she said with a laugh. 'I go around looking for good people and good work!'

The visit to Manila was all warmth and friendship. The function was a model by itself. The previous evening we were told that each recipient of the Award would be invited to give a response after the citation about him was read out. I wrote out

a little speech around Gandhian themes—in fact, at one point I
transposed for José Rizal, the national hero of the Filipino people,
lines that Gandhiji had written on the death of Tilak Maharaj.

Here is what I said at the function:

~

You have done me this great honor at a critical time. In several
of our societies rulers have become parasites. Indeed, parasites
have become rulers. Evil has come to be accepted as inevitable,
as natural, as a mere commonplace. Ideals have come to be
dismissed as idle dreams. Idealism has become a dirty word. In
these circumstances it is important to affirm three great truths.

First, it is important to show where all this will end,
to affirm that no good will come of this process. Already
in many of our societies the hopes people had when their
countries won independence have given way to despair. Already
the State apparatus has been brutalized to an alarming extent.
Semiliterate, vulgar, puffed-up bullies have converted the State
into private property. The people are becoming accustomed to
malfeasance, injustice, even to violence.

Second, it is important to affix responsibility for the process.
The responsibility is not primarily of the rulers—they are merely
pursuing their pleasure. The primary responsibility is ours. Their
evil is done with our hands.

No President, no Prime Minister tortures a citizen with his
own hands. Other citizens do the work for him.

Corruption is not the bribe the ruler takes, it is the bribe
you and I give.

We have an ancient saying in India: *yatha raja tatha praja,*
as the ruler so the ruled. Mahatma Gandhi used to say that this
is just a half-truth. The other half of the truth is *yatha praja
tatha raja,* as the ruled so the ruler. So, the state of affairs is what
it is because the ruled are what they are.

Hence, and this is the third point and it indicates the way
to the cure, the evil of the rulers will persist as long as we
partake of it, so long as we lend ourselves as instruments for its

execution, so long as we assist it by putting up with it, by doing nothing to end it. But, as we are its primary cause, it will cease the moment we withdraw the assistance we give it. The real tragedy of our times, therefore, is not that the rulers use their power for evil, but that the people do not use the power that is certainly theirs, to put an end to it.

Now, pointing all this out is not a popular task. The rulers naturally do not want to hear the truth. They are afraid of sunlight. But the people do not want to hear it either. For them also truth is an inconvenience; it demands of them at the very least that they stop assisting evil, that they change their conduct.

And yet there are at all times individuals who speak the truth to the bullies and to the people. At all times they are the special targets of the cruelty of the rulers, and all too often they are the targets of the derision and scorn of the people. But they hold on to the truth. The very efforts of the rulers to snuff out the man of truth proves his point. Eventually the man of truth bears testimony to how wretched the state of affairs has become by what is done to him; he bears testimony by his suffering. This is the ultimate service he does for his people.

In the end the cause of the truthful prevails. For one thing, as long as the man of truth suffers, as long, for instance, as he is in jail, and forever after he has been martyred, the people's attention remains on the lesson he was trying to teach them. If the great Rizal were still around, you and I would quarrel with this formulation of his or that, with this prescription of his or that. But, martyred, he today rules your hearts, his message is forever engraved in the minds of his people.

Day to day events also drive home what the prescient man of truth was warning the people to heed. You may kill a man for affirming there is corruption, for affirming there is torture. But the people learn of corruption from the bribe they have to give at every turn; they learn of illegal detention from the neighbor who disappears. Thus it is that even if the man of truth is killed, truth prevails.

These brave, tenacious men, these men who hold fast, throwing all rational calculus to the wind, constitute a fraternity in spirit. The fraternity cuts across national frontiers, it cuts across time. Few of us can claim to belong to it.

I take this great Award as being a command from you that persons like me should live up to the ideals of this fraternity, a command that we should aspire to it.

I accept the Award in this spirit, with the greatest humility and utmost gratitude. In return for this great honor I cannot promise you that I will make it to the fraternity, that I will succeed. But I give you my word that I will try.

~

But that reprieve turned out to be a brief one.

Dismissal

What 'my way' was that Ramnathji had in mind unfolded quite swiftly. Actually, there was little mystery to it. Anyone who had worked with him and seen him see editors out would have known the two prongs. First, and in this Kamal Nath was accurate, he would want a situation to be created in which I would myself decide to leave. Second, someone else had to be seen to have created that situation. I had myself seen these two prongs being deployed time and again: and I had often teased Ramnathji that he kept Mulgaokar around as the government keeps that hangman in Meerut—Mulgaokar was the one who would, in the end, tell the person who was being shown the door that 'the situation has become untenable', that the person should leave of his own accord.

As I was familiar with these two prongs, I was determined that I would not let either work. I had no illusion. I knew that when Ramnathji did not want me around, I could not keep my job. But even in that situation, there is one, and only one signal that I could give readers, I reasoned: that things are not normal, that the government has put such enormous pressure that even a fighter like Ramnathji has had to compromise. And so, I just would not resign, situation or no situation. And I would not let any middleman, any hatchet man, do Ramnathji's work for him. He had brought me into the paper. He would have to dismiss me by his own hand. That alone would give the signal that could still be given.

The Kuo Oil series over, Ramnathji called me to Bombay. I was told that he had various things to do in the forenoon, and that I should come up to the Penthouse around lunchtime. When I reached, Ramnathji greeted me effusively, 'Chalo, chalo, Oberoi mein khaanaa khaatey hain.'[8] I had no doubt what this meant, for he was not one who took persons out for meals in restaurants. The last meal before the hanging!

Ramnathji was sweet reasonableness. In passing, he even voiced appreciation for the work that reporters and I had been doing—'Kyaa tum jaantey ho ki mainey tumhaari ek baat kabhee kyon naheen maanee? Mainey tum ko kabhee koi paisey akhbaar ke advertisement ke liye kyon naheen diye? Kyonki jo tum log merey paper mein chaaptey ho, vahee paper kaa advertisement hai.'[9] In spite of an aside or two like this, and in spite of his overtly friendly demeanour, it was a strained meal. There was only one thing to talk about. He did not mention what was in his mind. I was determined not to be the one to initiate the subject. As a result, a perfunctory lunch with long silences, Ramnathji not even pecking at the soup that he had asked for, me eating as if the meal required close attention!

From Bombay I proceeded to Bangalore. The moment I reached the Express guest house on Brunton Road, I was handed a small envelope. It contained a letter from Saroj Goenka, the wife of Ramnathji's late son, B.D. Goenka. How could you have written such things about 'Father'? How can anyone who has written like this about 'Father' continue to stay in the paper?

The expectation obviously was that the moment I read Saroj's letter, I would shoot off a letter of resignation. But as this was

---

[8] 'Come, let us have lunch at the Oberoi.'
[9] 'Do you know why I never agreed to one of your suggestions? Why I never gave you a paisa for advertisement? Because what you fellows publish in my paper, that is the paper's advertisement.'

just an instance of the two prongs at work—a situation was being created in which I would leave on my own, and that situation was being created by someone other than Ramnathji—instead of going to the Bangalore office of the paper, I sat down and immediately wrote a letter explaining how what I had written was correct and why following a course contrary to what I had urged, suppressing articles, etc., would harm the paper. I had the answer sent by the paper's pouches to Saroj in Madras, and to Ramnathji in Bombay.

Ramnathji had to take the matter in his own hands. It was no longer enough that Saroj or someone else had the letter that I had written to Verghese. He had Dr J.K. Jain print the letter.[10] As the fact that the Kuo Oil articles had been held back became a matter of public comment, and as many inferred that this was an indication that Ramnathji was feeling compelled to soften the paper, and that, as part of this I would be thrown out, Shobha De asked him for an interview. In this interview, Ramnathji said all sorts of things about me. The least being that I had 'total lack of balance', etc. None of this could have hurt me. What outraged me was that he accused me of plagiarism! He said that I was being given credit and I was taking credit for stories done by others. As an example, he mentioned the articles on Antulay. He told Shobha that he and his 'sources' had put the entire story together, and I had taken the credit for it!!

Even in his tiny circle of elderly friends, among them Achyut Patwardhan and Radhakrishna, they told him that nobody would believe what he had said to Shobha. So, he sent a letter 'rebutting' the remarks that had been attributed to him. The interview was meant to be off the record, he said. But that remark would only confirm that what had been attributed to him was what he had said. So, he added that his remarks had been taken

---

[10] Dr J.K. Jain was close to all of us, and, to use one of Ramnathji's phrases, he was part of many of our 'mischiefs'. As I have mentioned earlier, he had taken over *Surya* magazine from Maneka Gandhi. How do I know that he gave the letter to Jain? Almost from Ramnathji himself, but only 'almost'! One day, after he had invited me back into the *Express,* we were laughing about things—'mischief'—that we had all done in the past. I asked him, '*To Doctor ko meri chitthie aap ne dee thi?' 'Aur kya? Tumney dee thi? Tum detey?'*—'So, did *you* give the Doctor my letter?' 'Who else? Did *you*? *Would* you?'

'out of context', that they had been distorted, that the story had 'omissions, inaccuracies, misjoinders, and overstatements'. Shobha was not one to be cowed. She confirmed that every word attributed to Ramnathji was accurately reported, that, in fact, he had said several other things but that these were so indecent that she had left them out.

I wrote to the magazine refuting what Ramnathji had said. As for the charge of plagiarism, and of my taking credit for his work on Antulay's doings, I wrote:

> Mr Goenka deserves great credit for the Antulay story as for everything else that has appeared in the *Indian Express*. It is only because of him that it has been possible for persons like me to publish stories like the Antulay one during the last four years . . . Hence it is that while I understand and well know the reasons that have led him to advertise his sudden discovery of my infirmities, I cannot understand the inner compulsions that have led him to lay claim to facts and files and sources— such petty things compared to what is his due and his real role . . .

By the time I returned from Bangalore, Ramnathji's interview was the talk among journalists, most of all in the *Express*. Verghese retained his studious composure, of always being busy with editorial work. At the morning editorial meeting, I asked him, in the presence of senior colleagues, what the paper intended to do about the *Celebrity* piece. I told him how the paper had stood up for its staff members when they had been attacked in the past. Verghese demurred. I will check with RNG, he said.

To me it was clear that Ramnathji was, of course, pursuing his goal of 'creating a situation' in which I would leave in a fit of outrage—hence that bit about plagiarism. But I felt there was more. That he should say all this in an interview, betrayed an anxiety: he was anxious that the high-ups notice that he was indeed squashing me, that he was doing everything to push me out.

Two days later, Verghese said that he had checked with Ramnathji, that Ramnathji had already sent a 'rebuttal' to the magazine, and that an 'understanding' had been reached.

'*An understanding?*' I asked—by now, I did not have to feign anger. An 'understanding' between whom? *Celebrity* and Ramnathji? Between him, that is Verghese, and Ramnathji? Between Ramnathji and me? And what 'understanding'? Tomorrow you will say that an 'understanding' had been reached between Ramnathji and me to such and thus an effect, and that I was violating it?

Verghese did not answer. He just got back to papers on his desk.

A few days later, Verghese delivered himself of the predictable phrase. 'The situation has become untenable,' he said, and that the 'parting should be amicable'. I told him again that Ramnathji had brought me into the paper, and that he is the one who will have to dismiss me—that I would not resign, nor would I go because some third party counselled me to do so, or even asked me to do so. Ramnathji has taught me, I told Verghese, that it is the 'appointing authority' which has the power to dismiss a person.

While all this was going on, a senior official in government told me that I would be dismissed definitely before 9 November. Why 9 November? I asked. That is the deadline that 'your Goenka' has been given. A case of his is coming up in the Court that day. If he has not removed you by then, government will go all out.

On 4 November, when I reached the office, a letter from Ramnathji was waiting. Ramnathji took exception to what I had written about him in the letter to Verghese, and which had found its way to *Surya*. He must have felt that there had to be more than personal hurt. What he chose to add was, uncharacteristically, a poor invention, even more far-fetched than what he had told Shobha De. He said that, actually, I had been inducted into the paper to work primarily on the management side, and that I had overstepped my assigned responsibilities by straying into editorial matters.

That was a poor invention, indeed. Not worthy of Ramnathji's vast experience in such matters, and his fertile mind.

Anyhow, I had been dismissed. I told the steno to pack my books and papers, and send them home.[11]

---

[11] For the older colleagues, my dismissal was 'inevitable' as well as 'well deserved'. And it must have been a relief. In his autobiography, Verghese refers to me as 'the polemicist turned pamphleteer . . . Though an outsider and never a journalist in the professional or traditional sense, Arun Shourie did certainly impact journalistic mores and styles in India but, not necessarily, always for the better. He was a stormy petrel, something of a maverick and ever so long-winded, particularly at a time when newsprint was in short supply.' Cf, B.G. Verghese, *First Draft, Witness to the Making of Modern India,* Tranquebar, Westland, Chennai, 2010, pp. 300, 303. The assessment of others had been different. Reporting the disagreements and my eventual dismissal, Dilip Bobb wrote in *India Today,*

> In the past four years, the turnover at the *Express* group has been phenomenal—13 editor-level employees have left in a steady procession including some of the brightest stars in the Indian journalistic firmament
>
> But the axing of Shourie will surely rank as the unkindest cut of all. Since January 1979, when he joined the *Express*, Shourie has taken the paper to new and unscaled heights, inspiring colleagues and the *Express* stable of reporters to some of the biggest scoops in the paper's history—work that has gained recognition not just in the Magsaysay Award but many others picked up on the way . . .
>
> Outsiders, too, are worried. 'Goenka has a nasty habit of playing his editors against each other but if he loses Shourie it will end the oppositional role that the *Express* has developed all these years. George (Verghese) is a good friend of mine but he is a bit of a boyscout. It will also add grist to the rumours that Goenka has made some kind of a deal with Mrs Gandhi to get rid of Shourie in return for something. Everybody knows he is financially very vulnerable,' says Romesh Thapar, editor of *Seminar* and one of the most respected journalists in the country . . .
>
> Above all, it could spell the end of a symbiotic relationship between the two that has restored the position of the media to its rightful place in the democratic scheme of things. Says Romesh Thapar: 'Shourie's leaving is not an internal matter at all. It affects all of us in the profession. Goenka and Arun are a two-man army and it would be tragic if both were to destroy each other in the bargain. The only winner, I fear, will be the ruling party.' [Dilip Bobb, *India Today,* 15 November 1982.]

By the time the next issue of the magazine came out, I had been dismissed:

> . . . Where does that leave the *Express* and Goenka? *Express* staffers are understandably concerned at what the future *sans* Shourie holds in store. For one, according to senior staffers, it has strengthened Saroj Goenka's efforts to assert herself in the organisation and added considerably to her accruing

'Guptaji dee soti'[12]

As I reached home, my mother opened the door.

'Tu ainee jaldee kidaayaan aa gayaa-n?'[13] she asked.

'Mama, unhaaney taan mainu dismiss *he kartaa.'*[14]

For the briefest moment she looked startled. She took my face in her hands, and, as she always did, kissed my forehead.

And then she burst out laughing: 'Arun, *eh taan Guptaji dee soti he niklee!'*[15]

'Guptaji dee soti' had a history.

In the early 1950s, I was in the boarding house at Modern School in Delhi. Swami Chinmayananda had just started visiting Delhi and giving lectures. The lectures used to be held in one of the grounds of the school, and we boarders used to be rounded up to fill in space.

Swamiji was a mesmerizing speaker. His lectures were full of dramatic pauses, of stories, of fun. 'Guptaji' was a character in several of his stories.

So, one day, the Ganges is in flood. Guptaji is out for his stroll along the bank of the river. As he is walking, the bank caves in. He falls into the river. The river is in spate. Guptaji does not know how to swim. He is flapping about, bobbing up and down,

---

influence. But it also means that there are unlikely to be any more Antulay exposes, no Kuo Oil deals and people like Jagannath Mishra can breathe a little easier.

That, in the ultimate analysis, can only reduce the *Express* to just another morning paper instead of the powerful oppositional role it had acquired. *Express* sources are convinced that the paper will harden its anti-government line for a month or so before tacking back to more tranquil waters.

Shourie himself has no intention of joining another newspaper or periodical and plans to complete two books that he has been working on. His absence from the journalistic scene will be felt universally but nowhere more so than at the *Express*.

It is, finally, a tragic interruption of a career that has been like no other in the field. The deliberate silencing of a man who is not just another journalist, but the most devastating chronicler of our times. [Dilip Bobb, *India Today,* 30 November 1982.]

[12] 'Guptaji's stick.'
[13] 'How have you come back so early?'
[14] 'Mama, they have dismissed me.'
[15] 'Arun, this has turned out to be Guptaji's stick!'

shouting for help. Suddenly he feels something in his hands. He has accidentally caught a stick that was being swept along. It is carved, and its handle is of silver. Now, Guptaji is doubly eager to survive: he has his life to save, and there is this precious stick. As he is thrashing about trying desperately to keep his head above water, the stick slips out of his hand. 'God,' he wails, 'I have lost my stick.'

In a flash, and with her infectious laugh, my mother had taught me that the job had been no more mine than that stick had been Guptaji's.

16

'Kitni naavon mein kitni baar . . .'[1]

The incandescence of the Freedom Movement still lit our lives. Yes, many things had soured. That leaders were far from the kind of persons who had led the country to Independence, that standards had begun to droop, that as a consequence, institutions were becoming instruments—all this was true, and all too visible. But in searching for what should be done, given this all-round enfeeblement, we hearkened back to the Freedom Movement—to Champaran, to Bardoli, to Kheda, to the agitation for repealing the Rowlatt Act . . . I almost continuously read Gandhiji's writings, Narhari Parekh's volumes about Sardar Patel, Tendulkar's volumes about Gandhiji, biographies of Tilak Maharaj, volumes by and about reformers like Swami Dayananda and Sri Narayan Guru.

One consequence of the afterglow of the Freedom Movement was that our generation looked with hope to people's movements. This in spite of the very circumstance that was leading us to gravitate to the next people's movement, namely, what had happened to the ideals of the movement for Independence. And in spite even of the most recent experience, namely, the landslide swiftness with which the hopes stirred by defeating Mrs Gandhi in the 1977 elections had evaporated. For every problem, we looked

---

[1] 'How many times, in how many boats . . .'—Ageya

for the institution we could stir into action, and, simultaneously, we looked for the kind of work, beyond awakening institutions, that would help. I was enamoured of movements like the Sasthra Sahithya Parishad in Kerala, and, as these gained strength, of movements like Chipko in the Himalayas.

Exemplary dedication, exemplary integrity

One of the windfalls from not having a job was that I had much more time to see these movements first-hand and to get to personally know the exemplary persons moving some of them. Another factor helped. Years earlier, I had been chosen to be the General Secretary of the People's Union for Civil Liberties. Some of the work we did was of consequence—like the evidence that was gathered, mainly by my friend K.G. Kannabiran, and the report that was prepared about the false encounters in Andhra. Over time, the tenor of the membership changed. At one of our national conventions, the more vocal members insisted on declaring that all private violence was a reaction to State violence, and hence, more than justified; it was called for. But our experience in Punjab was altogether different. I slowly drifted away from the organization.

Two of the many boons from this assignment were much more valuable for me than the work itself. I got to see a much wider range of good work being done across the country by people's groups. And to meet persons of exemplary dedication and character, persons I would not have met had I spent time just in my study. The bonds with some of them lasted for decades. Among them was my dear friend K.G. Kannabiran. A lawyer of the highest calibre, he devoted every waking moment to the victims of oppression—of oppression by society as well as the State. And Justice V.M. Tarkunde. A distinguished Judge, he had been chosen to be the President of the PUCL (People's Union for Civil Liberties), and so I got the opportunity to assist him in that work. It would take a volume to describe the character and work of these exemplary persons, and as this particular volume is already exceeding the bulk editors will permit, I must confine myself to just one instance to illustrate the kind of persons these were.

As a young man, Justice Tarkunde had been Secretary to M.N. Roy. He strove to keep the ideas and ideals of Radical Humanism alive. One of the things he did in this regard, in the midst of all his legal and public work, was to bring out a magazine—writing much of it himself. Another was to organize an annual lecture in memory of M.N. Roy. In 1984, he asked me to deliver the lecture. I chose to speak on the perfidious role of the Communist Party—with whom Roy had parted—and its 180-degree turn during the Quit India Movement of 1942.

I began to study the relevant files at the National Archives. Having waded through files on individual Communists and their Party, I thought that I should also learn more about the person in whose honour I was to speak, and so I started to look up files relating to M.N. Roy. There was a preliminary shock. I knew that Roy's approach was very different from Gandhiji's, but I hadn't known that he used to denounce Gandhiji and the movement he was leading in such extreme language. But there was more. One day, I chanced upon an Intelligence file that startled me. It contained information about the amount that used to be paid by the British government to Roy for anti-Gandhi propaganda. It consisted of two streams of Rs 12,000 per month, a very substantial amount in the 1940s. This was a shocking bit of information. It put in question all the work that I had done for the lecture till then. How could I speak about the treacherous role of the Communists in 1942 and not mention this fact about the person in whose memory I was speaking?

I telephoned Justice Tarkunde and said that I just *had* to speak to him. I planned to tell him that if he so desired, he should ask someone else to deliver the lecture. He said he had to argue a case at the Supreme Court that day, and asked where I would be around 4–4.30 in the afternoon, by which time he would be free of court work. I told him that I will be at the National Archives. He said he would come there.

I explained what I had found—Roy receiving Rs 24,000 a month from the British for anti-Gandhi propaganda—and the dilemma this posed for me. He said, 'But the allegation has always been of Rs 12,000.'

Yes, sir, but there were two streams going into two accounts— one in Simla and the other in Lahore.

I have never forgotten Justice Tarkunde's reaction. 'You have all the facts, Arun,' he said. 'You must reveal them.'

How this contrasted with the reaction of the Communists. Nothing that I had done till then had caused them to take offence. In fact, during a visit to Cochin, I had been taken to the office of their publications. Some leaders of the Party and quite a few journalists sympathetic to their cause were present. I was introduced to a senior member of the CPI(M), who was also a well-known editor, and was told that he had worked hard and long to translate a book of mine on the social consequences of the Vedantic world view. That was the first I had heard of the translation, and felt quite pleased. In any event, I was not anathema. Quite the contrary.

The lecture was delivered to a jam-packed University Hall in Bombay. Several Royists were present, including my friend, Govindrao Talwalkar. Many of them did not forgive me for mentioning the Rs 24,000. Talwalkar cut me off almost completely.

A few weeks later, Pritish Nandy decided to use portions of the script as the cover story of the *Illustrated Weekly* that he was editing then. The Communists descended on me. 'An old canard.' 'He has not established the authenticity of the documents he has relied on'—these included a report they used to submit to the British setting out the good work they had done to sabotage the Quit India Movement. Simultaneously, 'Old documents. Nothing new in them.' Pamphlets were printed in several languages denouncing me. A leading 'theoretician' of the Party sent a turgid reply dealing with I couldn't fathom what, but certainly not with any of the facts that I had set out. E.M.S. Namboodiripad, the General Secretary of the CPI(M), led the pack. He flew down to Bombay and addressed the press. An agent of the Right. Unnerved by the rise of secular and socialist forces. Of course, the standard question: *Why now?* And the standard answer: Shourie has rehashed and put out this old canard now because of the elections that are round the corner and the Rightist forces are dreading defeat.

No elections were round any corner. The lecture had been delivered on the date on which it was delivered every year—the birth anniversary of M.N. Roy . . .[2]

But I was on the great good fortune of getting to know and work with sterling persons like Justice Tarkunde and Kannabiran.

A shower of hope

The students' Nav Nirman movement had cornered Mrs Gandhi and her government. All that the students were demanding was that a corrupt Chief Minister and an inefficient one be replaced. But, as usual, the rulers took it as a personal affront. In Abu's cartoon, one Congressman told another, 'We refuse to end corruption and inefficiency under duress.'

The Emergency, too, had been ended by people's action—the 1977 election was a people's election. The Janata Party had just been formed. It had almost no cadre, and absolutely no resources. And yet what a resounding slap. Chandra Shekhar told me, 'Arun, hameshaa yaad rakhnaa. Jis samasyaa kaa hum samaadhaan naheen nikaal saktey, uskaa samadhaan janataa nikaaltee hai. Aur jab janataa chapat lagaatee hai, voh chapat naheen, jhaanpad lagaatee hai.'[3]

Students in Assam had launched a movement against illegal migrants from Bangladesh. It was the biggest people's movement since Independence. It lasted for six years. Over 850 students were killed by government forces. With each blow, the movement grew in strength. It was called off only after the Central and state governments signed an Accord with the students' representatives in August 1985.

---

[2] I have dealt with the episode in 'The Only Fatherland, Communists, Quit India, and the Soviet Union,' ASA, New Delhi, 1991, HarperCollins, 2004, Noida, India.

[3] 'Arun, always remember. People solve the problem that we can't. And when the people slap, they don't slap, they deal a blow.'

I wrote extensively on the problem and in support of the students. I felt that they were drawing attention to a life-and-death problem, a national problem.[4] I travelled to the state on occasion. I was astounded at the number who would turn up to the lectures in spite of the pall of fear that hung over the state.

And it was a thick pall, no doubt. Once, after a spate of killings, to tear through it, we took the aged Dada Dharmadhikari from Bombay to Gauhati for a prayer meeting. The meeting was to be held in the Judges Field near the High Court. No more than a score or two could be persuaded to turn up.

Three things in particular struck me.

First, in spite of the tightest possible bandobast, in spite of the lathicharges, arrests, firings, the movement continued.

Second, the wholehearted participation of women. Gandhiji always held this up as an index of the strength and genuineness of a movement, of the depth of feeling behind it.

Third, the fullest backing of the people. The students were in their teens. Even the leaders were just in their early and mid-twenties. The government had deployed its entire arsenal—of intelligence agencies, for instance; of security forces. But it could not locate the leaders. It just could not fathom who their advisers were. The reason was simple: the students were, to pluck a phrase of Mao, truly fish in water. Entire cities would turn up at their call. In a typical incident, students announced a programme of demonstrations. H.C. Sarin, a former Defence Secretary, and at the time Adviser to the Governor, placed the whole state under curfew. AASU—the All Assam Students' Union—which was leading the movement, issued a call to the people: 'Defy the curfew, come out on the streets.' There was a flood of people on the streets of Gauhati, of Nowgaon, of Dibrugarh, of Tezpur, and other towns. At the time, Assam and several other Northeastern states had a most sagacious civil servant, Mr L.P. Singh, as their Governor.

---

[4] For a sample, *A Secular Agenda, For Strengthening Our Country, for Welding It*, ASA, New Delhi, 1993, Rupa, Delhi, 2005, pp. 201–304. And *Where Will All This Take Us? Denial, Disunity, Disarray*, Express Group, Rupa, Delhi, 2008, pp. 82–84, 105–39.

When he received reports of how many were defying the curfew, he took a helicopter from Shillong and flew over the streets of Gauhati. The moment he saw the situation on the ground, he called off the curfew. Such was the force in the students' call.

One consequence of such deep and extensive support of the people was that the student leaders received ideas from all over the state. Clever ideas, sparkling ideas for each successive demonstration and campaign. At last, Mrs Gandhi had called the student leaders for a talk. How to unsettle Mrs Gandhi at the very start? How to put her on the defensive? An official of a nationalized bank brought an idea to my friend, Basanta Deka, a teacher, and in several ways one of the unknown guides of the movement.[5] The moment Mahanta, Bhrigu and others have been received by Mrs Gandhi and have been seated across her table, the bank official told Deka, they should suggest that everyone should stand in silence for a minute in memory of the students who had been killed. A simple idea. And this is exactly what was done. To tremendous effect. For Mrs Gandhi could not keep sitting while others stood in memory of the hundreds of students who had been killed—by her forces.

The enormous power of the students and the depth of feeling among the people were shown on the streets and in fields every other week. They were demonstrated again in 1983. The government decided to ram an election down Assamese throats. Students declared that elections must not be held till illegal migrants had been removed from the voters' lists. They had but to make the demand and the government could see only its *naak*. The students announced a boycott. The result? Violence broke out in several parts of the state. At 32.7 per cent of eligible voters, voter turnout was one half of what it had been in the 1978 elections—it varied from 3 to 4 per cent in six constituencies of Lakhimpur to 60 per cent in the districts adjoining Bangladesh like Cachar and Goalpara. The Dharmapur constituency had 69,308 registered voters; the Congress(I) candidate, Bhumidar Barman, won all of

---

[5] For his account of the movement and its sequel, Basanta Deka, *The Design, The Betrayal, The Assam Movement*, Orchid Publications, Guwahati, 2015.

267 votes; he was made a minister. Congress(I) won 52 per cent of the seats. It formed the government all right, but that government had no legitimacy, it could not govern at all, and had soon to be folded up.

Students continued to press ahead. Over the next two years, they began to feel that they would not be able to implement their programme on the ground till they acquired hold over the machinery of State. So the thought grew of forming a political party and contesting elections.

The Assam Accord was signed on the night of 14–15 August 1985. A grand Convention was organized at Golaghat in October 1985. I was called to inaugurate the Convention, a singular honour. Luminaries from several organizations—the Asom Sahitya Sabha among them—came. The Asom Gana Parishad (AGP) was formed.

Elections to the state Assembly and the Lok Sabha were held just two and a half months later—in December 1985. The AGP swept to power, winning sixty-seven of the 126 seats in the Assembly. It also won seven of the state's fourteen seats in the Lok Sabha.

Six months had not passed and the heartbreaking problems that I had witnessed so many times erupted here also. The government did last its full term of five years till 1990, but it couldn't govern after the first half. Leaders who had been the closest of comrades, Prafulla Mahanta and Bhrigu Phukan, became rivals. Bhrigu wanted to deal firmly with ULFA (United Liberation Front of Asom). Mahanta had kept a line open to them. As Home Minister, Bhrigu initiated steps to centralize records of the National Register of Citizens from the SPs in districts. Mahanta took away the 'political' portion of the Home portfolio from him. Bhrigu took steps to reform conditions in jails. Mahanta thought that this programme would add inordinately to Bhrigu's profile . . . As the two jostled, administration became paralysed.

Yet another organization that had taken birth from a people's movement, one that had come to embody the deep longing of a people to preserve their identity and land, was set on the road to marginalization and oblivion. In 1991, Bhrigu and other notable leaders left the AGP and formed the Nutan Asom Gana Parishad (NAGP). In 1992, the NAGP merged back into the AGP. In 2000, two other leaders formed the Trinamool Gana Parishad. In 2005, Mahanta was expelled from the Party on charges of corruption, illegal killings during his Chief Ministership, and anti-Party activities. In 2008, all the breakaway groups returned to Golaghat and reunited into the AGP. Three years later, another leader, Sarbananda Sonowal, broke away and joined the BJP. In 2016, the AGP joined a BJP creation, the North East Democratic Alliance (NEDA). In 2019, it first left, and, within two months, returned to the NEDA. Sonowal, a product of AASU, became Chief Minister of a BJP government. He was succeeded by Hemant Sarma, who had left the Congress and joined the BJP.

By now, the AGP is a marginal presence in Assam: it has just nine members in the 126-member Assembly.

Another upsurge of the people had gone the way of others.

'Brother, do something'

'Brother, do something. We need your help'—it was NTR calling from Hyderabad.

But first, two of the dramatis personae, and one obvious point of law.

N.T. Rama Rao was the Chief Minister of Andhra at the time. For the people of Andhra, he was a stand-in for deities, if not almost a deity himself. He had starred in 300-odd films, and in one of them he had played three contrasting roles. In an overwhelming number of those films he had portrayed deities— and had thereby acquired an almost mythic status in the hearts of the Telugu-speaking people. In other films, he had portrayed a sort of native Robin Hood or a beloved and compassionate elder. People looked up to him as a saviour who would help them in time of need.

The Governor was a disgraced Congress politician, Ram Lal. He had been Chief Minister of Himachal Pradesh, and had become a synonym for corruption and inefficiency. In one instance, his son and son-in-law had been caught red-handed smuggling felled trees out of Himachal. They had produced a permit, ostensibly allowing them to do so. The permit had turned out to be forged. They had been caught lying repeatedly to the investigating authorities. What they had been caught doing had turned out to be part of a pattern—felling precious trees and smuggling them out of the state had turned out to be what everyone in the state knew it was, a regular business. Indeed, a business that had, and could not have been continued, but for the collaboration and connivance of authorities right up and down the governmental ladder.

Subsequent developments in the case involving the son and son-in-law of the Chief Minister had established that officials of the police, of the Forest Department, of the Enforcement Directorate, of the Vigilance Department, right up to the high legal officers of the Himachal government had done everything they could to derail the case. In their files, they cautioned each other that the case was a 'sensitive' one. But in the courts— even in the High Court—they kept insisting that they did not know the name of the father and father-in-law of the accused! None of this could have happened without the knowledge of the Chief Minister. It certainly would not have happened—officers up and down the ladder would not have twisted their spines, and developed such acute amnesia—but for Ram Lal having been Chief Minister. The High Court had documented the forgeries, smuggling, etc., but held that the trial had been conducted in a manner so contrary to law that the case should be tried again. But the entire governmental machinery had been exposed for what it had become. There was no direct evidence against Ram Lal himself, and it was said that behind the developments lay a deep conspiracy led by the predecessor and would-be successor of Ram Lal. But the image of the Congress(I) had been tarnished so much that he had to be removed from his post.[6]

---

[6] Even after all these years, it is instructive to read the High Court judgment in the case—it shows how long the putrefaction has been fermenting from which our governance suffers today: *In the High Court of Himachal Pradesh, Criminal Revision No. 56 of 1982, Decided on 13.01.1983, Court on Its Own Motion v Mast Ram Tanta, Manupatra, MANU/HP/0034/1983.* A distinguished advocate brings me up to date. The High Court had held that

In true Congress style, he was removed from the Chief Ministership, but not from public life. Quite the contrary: he was immediately helicoptered to Hyderabad as Governor of Andhra.

An obvious but relevant point of law

Now the point of law—elementary but one on which events turned. Article 164 of the Constitution provides that ministers shall hold office at the 'pleasure' of the Governor. Now the 'pleasure', save in one instance to which we shall turn in a moment, is to be exercised in accordance with the Constitution and law, not on the whim and fancy of whoever happens to be Governor. Manifestly, the provision relates to ministers in their individual capacity. The clause that follows relates to the Council of Ministers as a collective body.

It provides, 'The Council of Ministers shall be collectively responsible to the Legislative Assembly of the State.' This has several implications. First, the discretion of the Governor is limited to the initial formation of a government after an election—if the result is ambiguous, he can decide to call whoever in his assessment can provide a stable government. After that, the tenure of the government depends on whether or not it commands the support of the majority of the Legislative Assembly. Furthermore, it has been held on several occasions that the proper place where rival claims of majority are to be tested is the floor of the Assembly, not in, say, the Raj Bhavan: to cite just one instance, this is what had been decided by the conference of Presiding Officers of State Legislatures in Calcutta in 1968; later, it was prescribed unambiguously by the Supreme Court in the well-known case

---

the trial was so vitiated and illegal that the case should be tried again. As a result, the case reverted to the trial court. All the accused were acquitted. In 1984 the state went in appeal and finally the matter reached the Supreme Court. In March 2020, the Supreme Court dismissed the case, observing that, thirty-six years having passed, there was nothing left to adjudicate. 'All ado about nothing except for poor Ram Lal, who lost his job!' adds my friend. And except that Andhra got a Governor, we may add, a Governor whose name is a figure of speech to this day.

involving the Chief Minister of Karnataka, S.R. Bommai, who was similarly dismissed and denied the opportunity to prove that he still commanded the support of the majority.[7]

But it had become customary for the Congress to [i] appoint and replace Chief Ministers from Delhi—in the case of Andhra, five years had seen five Chief Ministers, each selected in Delhi; [ii] settle its factional disputes in a state by imposing President's Rule; [iii] where non-Congress parties were in office, to engineer splits in that party, install as Chief Minister the one who had led the split. As he was dependent on the Congress for continuance in office, he could be relied upon by the Congress to act to its convenience. The most egregious of such cases, of course, was the installation of Charan Singh as Prime Minister.

Deep resentment

This had led to great resentment among people across states. In the 1978 state Assembly elections of Andhra, Congress(I) had got 205 of 294 seats. In the 1980 Lok Sabha elections, it had got forty-two out of forty-two seats. NTR founded Telugu Desam in 1982. In the Andhra Assembly elections of 1983, held just nine months after he founded the Telugu Desam, NTR ran on the slogan of *Telugu Vari Atma Gauravam*—Telugu People's Self-Respect. And swept the elections. The Congress got a mere sixty seats out of the total of 294. NTR's newly formed Telugu Desam Party won 205 of the 294 seats.

For Mrs Gandhi, this was both an affront and a danger. An affront because she was in the mind of her devotees, and possibly in her own mind, The Leader. A danger because [i] she had been thrown out once, in 1977, and such a defeat would further damage the image of invincibility on which her power—which, in effect, meant her ability to continue in office—depended; it did not depend on moral authority, for instance; [ii] NTR, a charismatic person, could be a rallying figure for the Opposition; and [iii] a

---

[7] *S.R. Bommai v Union of India*, [1994] 3 SCC, 1.

defeat in a substantial state like Andhra at anywhere near this scale in the next Lok Sabha elections would be debilitating.

In a move as ill-advised at the time as it turned out to be disastrous in the ensuing months, she repeated in Andhra what she had done at the Centre when she had installed Charan Singh as Prime Minister, and in state after state, most recently in Jammu and Kashmir just months earlier.

As I mentioned, NTR was a legend. Such a person, whom the people of the state had installed as Chief Minister, had just left for the US for open-heart surgery. Mrs Gandhi's clutch of henchmen conspired to break his party using as her front, NTR's finance minister, N. Bhaskara Rao—a former Congressman who had left the party and joined TDP, declaring that Andhra must be liberated from the corrupt and inefficient Congress! As you would expect, Mrs Gandhi claimed innocence, and denied— that too in Parliament—that she had any prior knowledge of the manoeuvre. A rubber stamp of a Governor, a timid Home Minister—Narasimha Rao—from Andhra no less, her ministers rushing to and from Hyderabad, all her intelligence agencies, and she was not in the know of anything that was being hatched.

This was, of course, Mrs Indira Gandhi's standard alibi. Here, for instance, is an item from the *Indian Express* of 24 July 1980:

> Prime Minister Indira Gandhi disowned any plan to topple the Sheikh Abdullah ministry in Jammu and Kashmir. Chief Minister Abdullah, who met Mrs Gandhi in Delhi on July 23, told journalists that she had told him that she was not aware of any conspiracy to oust his government and install the Congress-I in office. Nor did she ever support such policies. Since the PM had denied such a move, he had to believe her, Abdullah said. But the chief minister did not hide his feeling that someone in the Centre was supporting the state Cong-I elements who had been trying to create law and order problem and instability with a view to bringing down his ministry. Why could not the Central leadership and Mrs Gandhi discipline their party unit in the state, he asked.

Events swift as a gale

But to proceed with events in Andhra. NTR returned after his heart surgery on 14 August 1984. The very next day, Bhaskara Rao staked his claim to become the Chief Minister. And the day after that—on 16 August—the Governor proclaimed that NTR had lost the support of the majority in the Assembly, and directed him to resign. As NTR did not, the Governor dismissed him. NTR requested that he be given just *three* days, that the Assembly be convened and a trust vote taken. The Governor refused. Instead, he swore in Bhaskara Rao as Chief Minister, and gave him *thirty* days to prove his majority—enough to buy and sell loyalties.

To his disgrace, in Parliament, Narasimha Rao—at the time, as we noticed, the Home Minister—justified the actions of Ram Lal, saying that he had no option but to act as he did, and that, once in the assessment of the Governor, a Chief Minister had lost confidence of the Assembly, the Governor had the 'unfettered right' to dismiss him and his Ministry. Narasimha Rao went further: he twisted the provision in the Constitution that we have seen above—about the 'pleasure' of the Governor—to mean that this pleasure could be completely subjective. A scholar, a decent man, and such shameful display of fealty, I rued at the time.

NTR declared that he had the support of 168 MLAs. He repeatedly requested the Governor to convene a session of the Assembly so that the question of who had the support of the majority could be settled on the floor of the Assembly. As the Governor would not do so, NTR took his MLAs and twenty-two MLAs of non-Congress parties to the Raj Bhavan to demonstrate, by the physical presence of the MLAs, that he had the support that he claimed. The Governor refused to let them enter the Raj Bhavan. Instead, he got several of them, including NTR, arrested.

As soon as they were released, NTR took all 168 to Delhi—this time to demonstrate to the President, Giani Zail Singh, that he had the majority that he needed to continue as Chief Minister. The President met the delegation.

On the same day, in Hyderabad, the Governor, who had refused to meet NTR and his supporters, held a long meeting with

Bhaskara Rao and his associates—reports said that the meeting had lasted well past midnight. Bhaskara Rao paraded ninety persons before the Governor. He claimed that these were MLAs of the TDP. It turned out that among the 'MLAs' who were said to have accompanied Bhaskara Rao to the Raj Bhavan, thirty-seven were at the Rashtrapati Bhavan in Delhi at that very time! On returning to Hyderabad, these MLAs held a press conference and declared that their signatures had been forged, and that they had been in Delhi and not at the Raj Bhavan. Bhaskara Rao had not only forged their signatures, he had brought impersonators to the Governor. And the Governor had accepted them as MLAs!

This was too much even for the Congress(I) to defend. Ram Lal was removed as unceremoniously as he had been brought in. Shankar Dayal Sharma was brought in as Governor.

The question before NTR now was what to do with the MLAs. If they were taken back to Hyderabad and lodged there, they would be ready game for poachers. And yet they could not be kept in Delhi indefinitely: apart from other difficulties, the poachers here had an even larger arsenal than their agents in Hyderabad. So, NTR arranged to send the MLAs to Karnataka—at the time, a Janata government headed by Ramakrishna Hegde was in office there. Journalists were freely meeting them, but Mrs Gandhi declared that they were being detained as 'hostages'.

And, as usual, she said that the Opposition was 'exploiting' the developments in Andhra.

NTR began touring the state. The upsurge among the people for him was as tumultuous as their outrage at Bhaskara Rao and the Central Government was intense. The numbers that turned out for his public meetings were to be seen to be believed.

The Opposition had found a cause: to prevent the toppling of non-Congress(I) state governments. And in NTR, it had found a charismatic colleague. Protests at the happenings in Hyderabad spread beyond Andhra. Other Opposition parties joined the protests. Their leaders began addressing mass rallies. Many of them visited NTR in Hyderabad. A nationwide bandh was called. Its success became a symbol of people's anger at the kind of politics that Mrs Gandhi and her coterie were playing. Bandhs in the state were total. Violence and arson erupted in some places: at some places government offices, post offices, railway stations, as well as houses of some of the MLAs who were thought to have defected, were burnt. In Anantpur, thirteen agitators were killed— the total number who died in the state during the agitations exceeded twenty-five.

The *Eenadu* group, under the leadership of Ramoji Rao, took the lead in awakening readers to what was happening. Ramoji stood firm in the face of police high-handedness and attacks by hooligans on the offices of the paper. In him, I gained a friend.

It was around this time that NTR called me: 'Brother, do something. We need your help.'

A journey

The new Governor decided that the Assembly will meet on 11 September. Now the problem was of transporting the MLAs back to Hyderabad.

We formed a team of Observers. K.F. Rustomji, Ashis Nandy, civil rights activists like K.G. Kannabiran, and others joined the team. The apprehension was that on the way back from Karnataka, the MLAs would be diverted to some place and held. We could do little in the face of a police posse, but by being there, we could help focus media attention on what had happened.

The MLAs had been lodged in Nandi Hills. We joined their convoy. Late at night, perhaps around 1 a.m. or later, we reached a resting place near the border of Karnataka and Andhra. The plan was that NTR would join up with his MLAs sometime in the morning, and we would all proceed to Hyderabad.

We were awakened around 3.30 a.m. NTR had been on his *ratham* since the afternoon, had been addressing wayside meetings, and had arrived. We were told that he was saying his morning prayers, and wanted us all to start in an hour or an hour and a half. I was flabbergasted. Here was a man who had just had heart surgery, who had been travelling for ten–twelve hours, who had not slept at all, and who now wanted to start back for Hyderabad.

It took longer than that hour and a half to get the MLAs ready and set off.

The procession of NTR's *ratham,* our cars and the buses was something that I remember to this day.

The car in which I was sitting was sometimes in front of, sometimes immediately behind NTR's *ratham.* NTR was seated on top of the van. In spite of the early hour, people lined both sides of the roads. They would be chanting slogans, showering flowers. NTR would wave at them and sort of bless them.

But the most moving sight, the most memorable one for me, was something else. Among the thousands who lined the two sides of the road would be many, many women—with infants in their arms. They would make a circular movement with their hands in the direction of NTR—like gathering his aura—and swiftly rub their hand over the infant's head and face.

This is the man Mrs Gandhi is going to dislodge? I thought.

We reached the border of Karnataka and Andhra. The road was blocked by police jeeps and vans, and a few buses. We got down, as did some of the MLAs—among them Venkaiah Naidu and Jaipal Reddy. The police said that the cars and buses in which we had come would not be allowed to proceed, that everyone must board the buses which the police had brought, and we would be taken to Hyderabad.

Given all that had been happening, given the lengths to which the government in Delhi and Bhaskara Rao's goons had been going, like many in the convoy, I felt that the police would pack the MLAs into their buses, take them to some faraway place, and just not let them proceed to the Assembly building.

I was summoned to NTR's *ratham.* Venkaiah and Jaipal were already there. NTR asked us for our views about what should be done. Distrustful to the point of paranoia, I argued that this was a plot to whisk away the MLAs, and, therefore, no one should get into the police buses, instead everyone should sit in dharna on the road.

Venkaiah and, even more forcefully, Jaipal argued the opposite—that the main thing was to get to the Assembly— somehow, anyhow. And the first step to this was to get into Hyderabad.

NTR agreed with them.

After some argument, the police agreed to let all of us proceed in the vehicles in which we were travelling. But we were told that the Assembly area had been cordoned off.

NTR and his team decided that, in that case, we would all proceed to Ramakrishna Studios—his studio.

We reached the Studios. Venkaiah and Jaipal were proven right. The MLAs had entered Hyderabad, and, lodged in NTR's own studio, were secure.

The hours and days that followed were full of feverish activity. And gusts of rumours. One night, policemen forcibly entered the Studios, demanding that such and thus legislators be produced. Everyone kept asking them to show the search warrant. They had none.

Several leaders of other political parties had arrived, and were assuring the MLAs and NTR of their support. I remember the visit of Chandra Shekhar vividly. As he was talking to NTR, someone rushed in and said that large numbers of policemen had joined the ones who had been surrounding the Studio, and that plans were afoot to arrest the MLAs and take them away, that this operation was just about to begin—Mrs Gandhi had ordered it, the person said. Chandra Shekhar scoffed at the prospect. 'Vaisey to uskey paas atom bomb bhi hai. Voh atom bomb bhi phenk sakti hai . . . Arey chhodo, kuch naheen hogaa. Ab tak usko bhi reportein mil gayee hongee ki logon mein kitnaa gussa hai. Ab voh kuch naheen kareygee, aur kareygee to poori tareh asafal ho gee . . .'[8]

The Assembly did meet on 11 September. The MLAs travelled to the building, protected not by the police as much as by reporters, observers and the rest. The session was brought to order. But the Bhaskara Rao lot would just not let it proceed.

NTR sought an appointment with the Governor to apprise him of how the Assembly was being thwarted—and that was

---

[8] 'If you think about it, she has the atom bomb also. She can throw the atom bomb also. O, leave it, nothing will happen. By now she also would have received reports about how much anger there is among the people. Now she will not do anything, and if she does, she will be an utter failure.'

because it would take no time to establish who had the support of the majority and who did not.

A 'heart attack'

His misdeeds, more accurately the orders that he had been following, had brought such ignominy for the Central Government, and Mrs Gandhi in particular, that, as I mentioned, Ram Lal had been replaced. The new Governor, Shankar Dayal Sharma, was no flaming pillar of independence but he was a Congressman of the old mould—courteous, saying little, understanding much. He agreed to meet NTR.

The appointment that NTR had sought was duly given. That forenoon, NTR, his MLAs and some of us proceeded to the Raj Bhavan. The roads were bereft of all traffic save the vehicles in which we were travelling.

At the Raj Bhavan gates, only a few were allowed to go in. Luckily, I was among them.

The new Governor met NTR with due courtesy. We were ushered into a large room. The Governor seated himself at one end. NTR, the MLAs and persons like me were seated in an oval arrangement.

NTR's associates were stating the facts for the Governor, points that had been urged in public and to the press repeatedly. The Governor listened patiently. He did not nod a 'Yes, I know.' Nor did he move his head or raise his eyebrows to imply, 'No, I don't think that is so.' He just listened politely, without saying a word. But his demeanour was so benign that everyone would have got the impression that he was fully participating in the conversation, and, in fact, agreeing with the points that were being urged.

Suddenly, there was some disturbance, a little commotion. Someone raised his voice and said that a doctor be called. Everyone's eyes turned to NTR. It seemed that he was having a heart attack. His body had stiffened. His head and neck had arched back. He had stretched out on the chair. He was grasping his throat as if he was finding it difficult to breathe . . .

The meeting was wound up.

As we moved out, I got close to NTR, and asked, 'Sir, I do hope are you perfectly well?'

NTR winked, the slightest wink.

No wonder he had been, and has since been acclaimed to have been one of the greatest actors of Indian cinema ever!

Victory

The thirty-day deadline for Bhaskara Rao to prove that he had the support of the majority arrived. He could not prove that support. He was asked to resign. NTR was restored to the Chief Ministership on 16 September. Four days later, he proved on the floor of the Assembly that he had the support of the majority—171 MLAs voted in his favour. The Bhaskara Rao MLAs just evaporated.

There was a tumultuous function to mark the people's victory.

The people of Andhra did not forget what Mrs Gandhi and her coterie had done. While in the 1980 Lok Sabha elections, Congress(I) had won forty-two out of Andhra's forty-two seats, in the 1984 elections, in spite of the wave of sympathy because of the assassination of Mrs Gandhi, the figure came down to eleven. The TDP won twenty-seven of the forty-two—it became the principal Opposition Party in the Lok Sabha. The Congress(I)'s fate was no different in the Assembly elections: in the 1978 elections, it had won 205 of the total 294 seats. In the 1983 elections, its tally was down to sixty. In the 1985 elections, it got even less—a mere fifty seats against the TDP's 202.

But once again . . .

But once again, leaders failed the people. NTR won handsomely in 1985, and remained Chief Minister for five years. But his functioning became more and more wayward. His family members acquired more and more influence in affairs of government. Politics became more and more acrimonious—the acrimony against NTR often being fed from within his own Party. The Party lost to the

Congress in 1989. NTR returned as Chief Minister a third time in December 1994, but lost the Chief Ministership within nine months. His party split. And this time, it was a genuine split: one part, the larger part led by his son-in-law, Chandrababu Naidu; the smaller faction led by his recently wedded wife, Lakshmi Parvathi. NTR died within a year.

Kitni naavon mein kitni baar . . .

17

Ghalat shaadiyaan[1]

Out of a job, I returned to my unfailing friends, books. After what seemed a very long time, I got a call for which there was no reason, and which, for that reason, held promise. A person from the office of Ashok Jain, the head of the *Times of India* group, was on the line. The Chairman wants to see you . . . It was one of the few times I saw him. He was the complete opposite of Ramnathji. Public affairs were Ramnathji's passion. His paper was his singular concern. Ashok Jain also must have had some interest in public affairs. It is just that I never quite got a glimpse of it. And he too must have been interested in his paper—but as an instrument of business, it seemed to me. The only thing I remember of the few times that I met him was the desk in his office: an artfully hewn tree trunk. As for Ashok Jain himself, he was a bit vague, and a bit apprehensive, as if something might happen. He said little, but that little one had to take seriously, given his position. But these impressions were months in the future. For the moment, I was happy to be offered a job at the paper.

A few buildings away, Suman Dubey, my brother-in-law, took over as editor of the *Indian Express*.

---

[1] Wrong marriages.

Rameshji[2] was soft-spoken, always immaculately dressed in a white bush-shirt and white trousers, and famous for the annual flower show that he organized. I went to call on him in his office soon after I joined. '*Arey bhai, yeh to ghalat shaadiyaan ho rahee hain,*' he said as soon as I entered his cabin. '*Suman ko yahaan aanaa chaahiye thaa, aur tumhey* Express *mein waapas jaana chaahiye thaa. Yeh shaadiyaan chalengi naheen.*'[3]

With every passing week, I began to realize how right Rameshji had been. And therefore took to visiting him, and found him to be the one wise and straightforward man in the building. In just two/three sentences, he would spell out what a remark or incident meant. In even fewer words, he would educate me to what someone was about.

I should not have needed Rameshji to be forewarned. At the time, the paper was controlled by Shamlal and Girilal Jain. I should have needed no fresh evidence to know that they thought poorly of me. In 'Galahads of the press', which we have encountered earlier, Giri had roundly denounced not just some specific thing that I had written but everything about the work that my colleagues and I had done at the *Express*. And not just the work: he had detected so many flaws in my character, in my very nature.

Nor could I pretend to be among their admirers. Their pusillanimity during the Emergency had become a figure of speech—it was the butt of jokes among mutual acquaintances like Raj and Romesh Thapar. For nineteen months, the paper had peddled the thesis that JP had forced Mrs Gandhi into imposing the Emergency. That the country had needed the shock. That the shock had worked: the trains had begun running on time, officials were at their desks on time, the country was at last on the move. And the day Mrs Gandhi lost: 'We have passed through veritable hell.'

---

[2] Rameshji Chandra Jain, a distant relative of the owners of the paper. He seemed to oversee the administrative side of the paper.

[3] 'My friend, the wrong marriages are taking place. Suman should have come here, and you should have gone back to the *Express*. These marriages won't last.'

Shamlal always had the worried and absent look of an intellectual sans peer—he had a high reputation, built in part on esoteric pieces, including, in particular, reviews of books which few had heard about. He had been grooming Dilip Padgaonkar, the resident French intellectual, and manifestly thought me to be a lesser breed. He certainly did not look kindly upon an interloper who may have been brought in to derail his succession plan. Girilal fancied himself as the Grand Strategist, as the éminence grise of Mrs Gandhi's government. In his eyes, he was the one who had pivoted India's foreign policy, which included opening a channel between Mrs Gandhi and the Shah of Iran. Poor Anita had had a glimpse of how seriously Giri took himself. For a brief while, she had got a temporary job on the desk at the paper. I have not known a person who thinks as clearly as her, and she used to write so well. One day she took a brief 'middle' she had written for approval to Giri. He looked at it for a second or two, handed it back, saying, 'I don't do humour.' Girilal soon came to look upon me with even sharper wariness than might normally have been the case—I got the impression that while I was thankful for just having been given a job, he had concluded that I had been brought in to divide his authority, if not to take his position.

More than individuals, there was the culture of the paper. Smug as can be. And this smugness had rubbed on to the senior fellows there. When Dilip Padgaonkar became the editor of the paper, he declared that he had 'the second most important job in India'—the only more important job being the Prime Ministership of the country.

Moreover, while these editors thought so much of themselves and their weekly encyclicals, the focus in the running of the paper was on maximizing advertisement revenues, not on excavating facts or breaking stories.

And this was so evident in the transition that was on its way. Ashok Jain was receding farther into the background. His son, Samir, had been brought in. He made it a point to make me and everyone else realize that he thought poorly of editors and nothing of editorial content. Resident editors were soon rechristened 'Response Managers'—a euphemism for garnering advertising revenue. Soon enough, the paper launched 'Private Treaties'. A company would enter into a 'treaty' with the paper. Under this, the paper would give 'positive' coverage to the company. The company, in turn, would allot a specified sum of equity to the Bennet Coleman Group, and pledge to place advertisements above a specified minimum in the Group's papers. Next, correspondents were designated to look after the interests of each company in the paper. And both the company and the correspondent were told that the latter's advancement in the paper would be determined by how the former judged the contribution of the correspondent in advancing the company's interests. We heard that some of the younger ones among the editors, led by Padgaonkar, had been called to the Jain residence on Sardar Patel Marg to write addresses on some invitation cards, and they had gone. Every time I met him, Samir would fling another novel idea at me. Why should Laxman be given so much importance? He is just an employee. We should hire another cartoonist also. This about R.K. Laxman, a 'living national treasure', as the Japanese would consider him. Why should writers not pay us for publishing their articles? They are the ones who benefit by the publicity we give them. Why should the edit page not be shifted beyond the centrefold of the newspaper, why should it not be pushed to the back of the paper?

Each of these ideas seemed to have been self-consciously designed to shock. All of them had one thing in common: implemented, they would downgrade editorial content and editors.

Two incidents alarmed me, for they showed that these ideas were not a pose; they were beliefs. One day, a retired Army Officer came to see me at the office. He was manifestly in distress. He said that he had given his flat on rent to the *Times of India* several years earlier; that as he had retired from the Army, he, his aged and ailing mother, and his wife had no place to live other than the flat; that actually, the flat was lying empty. Could the paper not hand it back to him so that they could live in it? I went to Samir. I had barely finished making the plea that he shot it down. There can be no question of returning it, he said. But they are in need, I protested. And it isn't as if the paper is using it; the flat is lying empty. You don't understand. It is a question of business principles. When we used to play 'Monopoly' as children, we were taught how to cheat. When we get somebody's thing, we must learn to keep it. No, we will not return the flat.

Where had I come?

The second incident filled me with even more foreboding. Rajendra Mathur, a distinguished journalist, then the editor of the *Navbharat Times*, died. All of us went to Nigambodh Ghat. Samir was not there. Rameshji came and stood near me. Where is Samir, I asked him, I don't see him here. Rameshji told me that he had gone to the Jain house to bring Samir. But the latter said, '*Koi na koi editor to martaa hi rahegaa. To kyaa mujhe har-ek ke liye shamshaan ghaat jaanaa padegaa?*'[4]

'*Yeh akhbaar naheen, sarkar hai,*'[5] I concluded, and thought it best to leave the paper and return home to my faithful friends, books.

That was one of the best decisions I made in my life, at par with leaving the World Bank and returning to India. Sometime later, I met Samir on a flight to Bombay. Kashmir was in the grip of serious trouble. The paper's correspondent there was filing reports which were almost a verbatim reproduction of what the secessionists were saying. I pointed this out to Samir as we stood in the aisle, talking. '*Bhaiyaa yehee to aapmey aur ham mein antar hai. Aap abhee bhee hamaaraa akhbaar padhtey ho!*'[6] Whether he actually did not read the paper; whether the remark was meant to show his continuing disdain for editorial matter; or whether it was just a clever way to close the argument, I do not know. But it certainly achieved one thing: I could not pursue the topic.

Soon enough, I heard, Samir took to spending more and more time at Rishikesh and Haridwar for spiritual pursuits. His brother, Vineet, enlarged and institutionalized the new philosophy. We are not in the news business, he declared. We

---

4   'Some editor or the other will keep dying. Does it mean that I will have to go
     to the cremation grounds for each of them?'
5   'This is a Government, not a newspaper,'
6   'This is the difference between you and us. You still read our paper!'

are in the advertising business. News is what we use to fill the empty space between ads . . .

A *new appointment letter*

I had returned to my faithful friends, books.

Gurumurthy had kept in touch. One day he came over to our house and told me that Ramnathji wanted me to come and meet him in Bombay. I flew to Bombay. And called on Ramnathji in his Penthouse. He had visibly aged, but was still spirited. *'Jeevan mein ghalatiyaan ho jaati hain,'* he said. *'Merey se ghalati hui thi. Tum waapas aa jao. Mujhey pataa hai tum* paper *mein kyaa karogey. Main bhi chaahtaa hoon ki voh hi ho.'*[7]

That became my new appointment letter.

Within a few days of returning to Delhi, I remember being on a flight to Cochin along with Lakshmi Jain, Mark Tully and others. We were travelling for a conference there. Reading the paper in his hand, Lakshmi spoke to Mark Tully about some news item—'Have you seen this? . . .' Mark remarked, 'But the real news is in the *Express'*—and he showed Lakshmi the box item on the front page: that I was rejoining the paper! The three of us laughed.

---

[7] 'Sometimes in life we make mistakes. I made one. Come back. I know what you will do in the paper. That is also what I want done.'

18

The plots I didn't get, the judgment I did

'Arun Shourie is writing all this to protect his friend, Ramakrishna Hegde because Hegde has given him two plots in Indira Nagar.'

That was Subramanian Swamy.

I rang him up. 'Plots? I don't even know where this Indira Nagar is here.'

Not in Delhi, Swamy said. In Bangalore, near the airport.

But I have not been given any plot, I told him. In fact, I do not own any plot in Delhi or Bangalore or any other city.

'You mean Hegde has not given you any plot? In that case, you can issue a contradiction,' Swamy told me.

But *you* are the one who has said that Hegde has given me plots. Why should *I* have to issue a contradiction?

'I am going abroad,' Swamy said. 'I don't have the time. You can say that I have authorized you to issue the contradiction.'

What had happened was as follows.

Ramakrishna Hegde had acquired something of a reputation as a level-headed and proficient Chief Minister. He was being talked of as having Prime Ministerial potential. Naturally, the Congress party and others were eager to cut him down to size. Charges of corruption began flying around. The Centre declared that they would appoint a Commission of Inquiry to go into them.

They began pressurizing Justice R.S. Pathak, then Chief Justice, to spare Justice Kuldip Singh—he had just joined the Supreme Court—as the one-man Commission. Justice Pathak held his ground: first, we have a heavy backlog of cases in the Supreme Court, he told government; second, we have had a bad experience when sitting Judges take on Commission work: they get embroiled in public controversies; and, third, now that you have asked for a particular Judge, I will certainly not spare him in particular. Soon, Justice Pathak retired. And one of the first acts of the new Chief Justice, Justice E.S. Venkataramiah, was to make the services of Justice Kuldip Singh available for the Commission.[1]

G. Ramaswamy, the then Attorney General, assisted the Commission as its Counsel. Ram Jethmalani represented Hegde at the hearings.

One day, Ram had come over to see Ramnathji. We were quite upset with him. The paper had been carrying articles by Gurumurthy about the misdeeds of Reliance—articles in which Ramnathji was emotionally invested, and heavily so.[2] These had

---

[1]   Justice Pathak's mother and my grandmother used to look upon each other as sisters. After the passing away of his father, Mr G.S. Pathak, Justice Pathak used to look upon my father as an elder of their family also. He used to visit our house occasionally, and always touched my father's feet the moment he entered. He narrated the foregoing to my father and me on one of his visits. During that particular visit he also told us why he had to agree with the decision to hang Kehar Singh, a decision which we at the *Indian Express* had denounced in strong terms; and about the via media that the Court had to craft in the Union Carbide case.

[2]   In his autobiography, Kuldip Nayar, wrote,

> RNG, who wielded a lot of influence in the Janata government, began settling scores with individuals he did not like. One among them was Dhirubhai Ambani. He provided Arun Shourie, who had like a paratrooper, landed as executive editor of the *Indian Express,* with material relating to Ambani. Arun Shourie, who had come into the *Indian Express* through Nanaji Deshmukh, an RSS stalwart, used the material to make 'disclosures' against Ambani. (*Beyond the Lines, An Autobiography,* Lotus Roli, 2012)

Wrong on many counts! Gurumurthy wrote the articles on Ambani, not me. Gurumurthy did not get the material from RNG. He did a lot of legwork himself, and had a range of sources. I got to meet Nanaji Deshmukh long after

led to a case. Ram had been representing us. And suddenly, he had withdrawn from the case. We were as angry as we were flabbergasted. Ram was his candid self. He said that he had to withdraw from the case to save 'our common friend, Hegde'.

He told us what had happened. After a heated hearing of the Commission, GR—as G. Ramaswamy was known—had told him, 'Why are you straining so hard for your friend? Kuldip is an easy-going fellow. Let us go to his place and settle the matter over a drink.' Ram and GR had gone. According to Ram, Justice Kuldip Singh had said, 'I will agree to what GR says.' And GR had said that the report would go in Hegde's favour—but on one condition: Ram must withdraw from the Reliance case.

I joined the *Express,* and was no favourite of his. Similarly, later in the book, writing about the killings in Gujarat, Kuldip Nayar remarked, '. . . He [Atal Behari Vajpayee] lost his temper when he visited refugee camps and gave the chief minister [Narendra Modi] a piece of his mind in public hearing. His visit went down well, but later when he flew to Goa, he was brainwashed by Arun Shourie and Arun Jaitley who were sitting on either side of him . . .' Wrong on every count. I had accompanied Mr Vajpayee to Singapore and Cambodia immediately after his visit to the refugee camps. He was most distressed. I urged that he call Advaniji and tell him that Modi must resign before Atalji returned to India. Though extremely distressed, Atalji postponed doing so from day to day. The Party's National Executive was to meet in Goa soon after his return. Advaniji was to fly in his plane. Atalji decided that Jaswant Singh and I should be present. After discussions that I have described at other places, it was decided that Modi will announce his resignation at the meeting; Advaniji will inform him about this decision. As the meeting was going on, Modi got up and announced that he was resigning. By what I have described as a coup, Atalji was foiled: twenty–thirty persons started shouting that this could not be, that nothing wrong had happened, that Modi was not at fault in any way. I got up and explained the background to Modi's announcement, how what he had just said was the outcome of the decision that had been taken by Atalji and Advaniji in the plane. After a moment's stunned silence, the shouting resumed. The coup prevailed. Atalji was heartbroken but went along. He later explained to Shekhar Gupta that had he stuck to the decision, the Party would have split. I don't know how Kuldip imagined the 'brainwashing', not to speak of my doing anything with Arun Jaitley! It isn't that Kuldip Nayar was given to hearsay. It is that, in all probability, his disapproval of my having been brought into the paper as a 'paratrooper' had muffled his hearing.

In the event, Justice Kuldip Singh held Hegde to have been guilty of wrong-doing on several counts—giving undue favours to a builder, fraud and the rest. I telephoned Ram Jethmalani for his reactions. He was abroad, and at that moment, had not heard about the Commission's conclusions. I recounted for him the main conclusions of the report. 'What?' Ram exclaimed. 'But Kuldip has gone back on his word.'

The report is important, we felt; it is bound to be the subject of much debate, and also to have major political consequences. We thought we should obtain the assessment of some well-known Judge about its findings. Justice Y.V. Chandrachud's name came up. He had been Chief Justice, and was now living in retirement. Through our Bombay office, we got the report to him. He sent a scathing critique of the reasoning and conclusions of Justice Kuldip Singh.

The report was marred by 'contradictions and inconsistencies', Justice Chandrachud showed. The Commission had wholly disregarded well-established procedures, due process which was essential to ensure fairness, he showed. Its conclusions were 'unsustainable on facts and law', he showed; they were based on 'conjecture and suspicion', rather than on evidence. The evidence on record of the Commission's own proceedings was wholly ignored, he showed. Witnesses on whose statements the Commission relied 'heavily' were not called for cross-examination on specious grounds—first, that the request to cross-examine them had come late and was 'vague', and, when this could not be sustained, on the even more untenable ground that the Commission did not have the power to call them! Key findings were completely concocted, he showed: that a company was a 'front' for a builder who was hiding behind it when the builder had declared in bold type that he would be executing the project on a turnkey basis. Some of the central indictments were completely without basis, Justice Chandrachud showed: for instance, that amounts paid by customers had actually been provided by the builder himself. In other instances, he showed, that the conclusions were mere conjectures not supported by any evidence. In still other instances the conclusions were 'directly opposed to the evidence on record'.

At a crucial turn, in a move that Justice Chandrachud said was 'unparalleled', the Commission had taken shelter under a Section of the Evidence Act which had nothing to do with the point at hand, and dealt instead with a person's dying declaration! On the day the Commission was ready to submit its report, he showed, the Judge himself had observed, 'There is nothing on record to show that all these irregularities were ever brought to the notice of the Chief Minister by any one. There is nothing on record.' And the Commission's Counsel had stated, 'Therefore, if your Lordship asks today if I can give a report directly indicting the Chief Minister, my answer will be no.' But the very next day, Justice Chandrachud pointed out, notices were issued to Hegde and the builder as being under suspicion! We published Justice Chandrachud's devastating critique in full.[3]

Based on that opinion, I wrote an editorial: 'If shame had survived'. The editorial listed the points on which Justice Chandrachud had found the report wanting. And then it stated: 'If there had been any sense of honour or shame, a Judge would never have done any of this. If there were any residual sense of honour or shame, the Judge having done any of it and having been found doing it would have vacated his seat.' And as in the India of 1990, he is not liable to do so, such is the Judge before whom litigants would have to appear for securing justice.

The then Chief Justice, Justice Sabyasachi Mukherjee took offence, and initiated suo moto, contempt of court proceedings against me. Subramanian Swamy also filed a case against me for having committed contempt of court.

A sealed envelope

I prepared a lengthy draft affidavit. The editorial was about a Commission, and a Commission is not a Court. Even if the member of a Commission is a sitting Judge, observations about his work in the Commission, and about conclusions arrived at by the Commission, do not concern his work as a Judge or the

---

[3] *Indian Express,* 9 and 10 August 1990.

working of a Court. Second, while in India, even after decades of our having gained Independence, truth is still not a defence in contempt of court cases, I would really like to know whether in a country whose national motto is *Satyameva Jayate,* in which the Father of the Nation incessantly said 'Truth is God,' the highest Court of the land maintains that truth is not a defence. Third, what I had written was based on, and amply borne out, by the opinion that Justice Chandrachud had given, and which we had published in full. Fourth, as for the concluding two paragraphs in which I had advocated that the Judge resign and had lamented the fate of litigants if he did not do so, once again truth was my defence.

In support of the last point, I had drawn attention to what Justice Chandrachud had observed about the Commission having been oblivious of elementary principles of law and evidence, or having deliberately ignored them. And I had narrated what Ram Jethmalani had told us about having settled the matter over drinks. I summarized the latter in a general way in the main affidavit and described it in detail in a sort of annex, which I intended to submit in a sealed envelope.

Ram was a party to the proceedings, so to say. So, on behalf of the paper, we requested Mr Shanti Bhushan to represent me. Mr Shanti Bhushan went over the draft affidavit. When I met him, he asked me, 'Do you think Ram will state all this before me directly?' I said I would request him to do so.

One forenoon, I escorted Ram to meet Mr Shanti Bhushan in the largish room in the Supreme Court where advocates used to gather. Ram narrated the entire episode exactly as I had described it.

Now we can include it, Mr Shanti Bhushan said.

After I had made the changes he had suggested and taken the draft back to him, Mr Shanti Bhushan asked, 'Do you think we can get something in writing from Ram about the exchanges between Kuldip, GR and him?'

That would be embarrassing for me. After all, I could not ask Ram to swear an affidavit describing the evening. Therefore, I took the draft paragraphs relating to the exchanges to Ram. He said he was busy at the moment, but that he would look at them and send them back to me. My heart sank. But to my delight, he sent them back early the next day, with some corrections and improvements in his own hand.

I took these to Mr Shanti Bhushan. 'I am satisfied,' Mr Shanti Bhushan said. 'Now we can include them in your submission to the Court.'

The next year, the case came up before a Bench headed by the Chief Justice, Justice M.N. Venkatachalliah. He said that the Court did not entertain sealed envelopes. He asked the clerks to return it unopened, and said that, if necessary, we could submit a supplementary affidavit setting out the facts we thought relevant.

The case lay unattended for years. It eventually came up in 1998 before a three-Judge Bench. The Judges decided that as substantial questions of law were involved, the case should be referred to a Constitution Bench.

By the time it came up before the five-Judge Constitution Bench, twenty-four years had passed since the case was filed. After all these years, it will be too much to request Mr Shanti Bhushan to appear for me, I thought. And so I requested my friends, Ashok Desai and Arvind Datar, to argue on my behalf.

We were sitting in Court II waiting for our case to be called. Subramanian Swamy was sitting with two lawyers across the aisle. One of the advocates came up and asked whether I would mind if Swamy withdrew his complaint. I asked Ashok and Arvind—for they had spent time preparing our arguments. Ashok said that that would be the quickest way to resolve the matter and so, yes, it would be good if Swamy withdrew the complaint. 'But,' Ashok added, with the mischievous smile he so often had, as the advocate stepped back towards Swamy, 'let us wait to see what Swamy does. After all, it is a message from Swamy!' When the case was called, Swamy got up and, addressing the five Judges, said, 'I have placed the facts about the contemner and his conduct before the Court. It is now for Your Lordships to assess the facts,' and left the Court. That hardly amounted to withdrawing the case!

I was surprised and a bit upset—Swamy had sent his messenger just minutes earlier. Ashok was neither surprised nor angry. He was just amused. 'Now let us listen to Mohan,' he said.

Mohan Parasaran, the then Additional Solicitor General, representing the government, was the first to address the Court. He stressed several of the points that we had prepared. That was a good surprise, for our case was being made—and quite effectively—by the party that we thought would be opposing us. Ashok advanced the arguments that remained. He stressed the two points on which we had focused throughout—that a Commission was not a Court, and by now even the law recognized truth to be a defence.[4]

As for truth, apart from noting that by now the law itself formally recognized that truth could be advanced as a defence, the five Judges endorsed the view that had been taken in an earlier case by two Judges. They had held,

> In our view, if a speech or article, editorial, etc. contains something which appears to be contemptuous and this Court or the High Court is called upon to initiate proceedings under the Act and Articles 128 and 215 of the Constitution, the truth should ordinarily be allowed as a defence unless the Court finds that it is only a camouflage to escape the consequences of deliberate or malicious attempt to scandalize the court or is an interference with the administration of justice.[5]

---

[4]   The Commission to Study the Working of the Indian Constitution which had been headed by Justice M.N. Venkatachalliah had recommended that truth be recognized as a defence provided stating it was in the public interest. The government of Mr Vajpayee had introduced a Bill to this effect in 2003. That had been referred to a Select Committee of Parliament. But the Lok Sabha had been dissolved. With some changes, the Bill was reintroduced by the Manmohan Singh government, and became law in 2006. Section 13 of the Act now provided,

  (a) no court shall impose a sentence under this Act for a contempt of court unless it is satisfied that the contempt is of such a nature that it substantially interferes or tends to substantially interfere with the due course of justice;

  (b) the court may permit, in any proceeding for contempt of court, justification by truth as a valid defence if it is satisfied that it is in public interest and the request for invoking the said defence is bona fide.

[5]   *Indirect Tax Practitioners' Association v R.K. Jain*, (2010) 8 SCC (Civ) 306.

The Constitution Bench observed, 'We approve the view of the two-Judge Bench in *R.K. Jain*. Nothing further needs to be considered with regard to the second question [whether truth can be a defence] since the amendment in contempt law has effectively rendered this question redundant.' As part of the judgment, the Judges recalled with approval the words of the Privy Council in *Ambard*, words that are the shield of every commentator on courts, Judges and their judgments:

> ... The path of criticism is a public way: the wrong headed are permitted to err therein: provided that members of the public abstain from imputing improper motives to those taking part in the administration of justice, and are genuinely exercising a right of criticism, and not acting in malice or attempting to impair the administration of justice, they are immune. Justice is not a cloistered virtue: she must be allowed to suffer the scrutiny and respectful, even though outspoken, comments of ordinary men.[6]

Furthermore, the five Judges put to rest all doubts about the question whether a Commission of Inquiry could be considered as a Court in the context of the Contempt of Courts Act. We had advanced several reasons to affirm that a Commission was not a Court, and, therefore, even a sitting Judge, while he was serving as a member of a Commission, has to be considered as a member of the Commission and not a Judge functioning in a Court. We had argued, for instance, that:

o A Commission is a fact-finding body. Its function is not the 'administration of justice' as is that of a Court. It is to ascertain facts, not to adjudicate between the rights and claims of contending parties. A Commission does not pronounce judgments as a Court does. It is merely to gather materials on the basis of which an authority may act. The government or

---

[6] *Ambard v Attorney General for Trinidad and Tobago*, 1936 AC 322: (1936) All ER 704 (PC).

any other authority may or may not accept the conclusions that the Court has reached, nor need it act on its recommendations. Its report is not a 'definitive judgment' which binds everyone concerned. It is just a recommendatory document.

o   Unlike a Court, a Commission does not have the power to punish for its contempt. The Commissions of Inquiry Act of 1952 provides a specific procedure for a Commission to act against anyone who has committed an offence like bringing the Commission or its members into disrepute. And this procedure is very different from that which applies to the Supreme Court or a High Court, should either decide to proceed against someone for having committed contempt of it. The Commission has to complain in writing to a High Court to take cognizance of the alleged offence, and it has to set out the nature of the offence, as well as the facts relating to it. And no High Court may take cognizance of the offence if more than six months have passed since the offence is said to have been committed.

Building on a host of earlier decisions, the judgment accepted these submissions also, and held:

o   A Commission is not a Court, and its inquiries are not of a judicial character
o   Proceedings of the Commission are neither judicial nor quasi-judicial proceedings
o   A Commission's findings are not a 'definitive judgment'
o   Unlike a Court, a Commission does not have the power to enforce that its findings or pronouncement be acted upon
o   A Court must act in accordance with law. A Commission may do so on 'principles of administrative policy or convenience or what appears to be just and proper in the circumstances of a particular case'
o   A member of a Commission is not a Judge as he is not empowered to give a definitive judgment which, if not appealed against, would be definitive, or a judgment, if confirmed by some other authority, would be definitive

o   Though he may be a sitting Judge, when he functions as the
    Chairman or member of a Commission, he does not have the
    powers of a Judge

In a word, the judgment went entirely in our favour. The contempt
petition was discharged.[7]

The judgment had but to be delivered, and Swamy let it be
known that I had not been sent to jail because he had not pressed
the case.

One must be thankful for small mercies.

---

[7]   *Subramanian Swamy v Arun Shourie*, (2014) 12 SCC 344.

19

A conman takes us for a ride

Within a short time of my rejoining the *Express*, and entirely unexpectedly, we got into a fight with Rajiv and his government.

I had returned home from the office. The news editor called. There is an Agency item, he said. The Swedish Radio seems to have said in a broadcast that bribes have been paid to win the contract for supplying guns to India. I requested him to read it out. It was a brief item. So, I said that we should carry it as a single-column box item on page 1.

At that time, I did not think it would amount to much: the Radio had just stated this as a fact. They had not furnished any evidence. But later that day, and the next day, the reaction of the government was so severe that I concluded, 'There must be something in this.' From that day, we kept at the issue. Actually, the government and its spokesmen kept us on the issue. Their evasions and lies spoke for themselves. The more we asked, the more they lied. The easier it became to catch them out.

One result of our pursuing the government was that they pursued us even more comprehensively than they had been doing. Investigations. Notices. Cases. Raids. Holding up newsprint. A manufactured 'strike' to shut down the principal edition of the paper . . .

And as their assault became more determined, we became rash—welcoming help, even the prospect of help from all quarters. Among other things, we established a collaboration with *Expressen,* Sweden's spirited afternoon paper, in particular with its principal investigative journalist, Per Wendel.

The conman

'*Main andu bum laa rahaa hoon,*'[1] Chandraswami said one day over the telephone. He was calling from somewhere in Europe, he said, and was going to land in Madras. He said the government was after him, that he had explosive information, that he would share it with us—but first we had to keep him out of jail.

Colleagues in the Madras office of the paper, and Ram Jethmalani strained every nerve to make sure that the government did not get its hands on him.

Chandraswami got to Delhi. Gurumurthy and I would meet him from time to time. He kept us panting on a leash—never giving us the promised information but always keeping our hopes alive. That mustn't have been all that difficult: as I mentioned, we had become all too eager for information; we had become rash.

Once, when we went to meet him, Chandraswami told us that he would definitely give us killer information, but he couldn't do so there and then as there were too many people in the ashram at the moment. He was going to Kurukshetra in two–three days. We should meet him there, and he would definitely give us the information.

We trooped to Kurukshetra. After much rigmarole, and driving us mad with his diversions and evasions, Chandraswami gave us a sheet with two numbers. He said these were the numbers of the bank accounts of Rajiv and Sonia Gandhi in Switzerland.

We redoubled our efforts to keep Chandraswami from the clutches of government. Ministers and Chief Ministers bowing at his feet were a common sight. But I have never seen a man so full of fear as him.

---

[1] 'I am bringing an atom bomb.'

In the meantime, Ram Jethmalani heard from the Hindujas—he had known them for long. He told Ramnathji that the Hindujas had vital information, that they knew Martin Ardbo personally. But that to get it, he and one of us would have to travel to London.

Ram travelled to London—in the style to which he was accustomed. I went in the plebian way to which all of us at the *Express* were accustomed. 'They will send you a car,' Ramnathji told me. 'They will say they have booked your room in a hotel. If I hear that you have so much as put a step in their car, or if you stay in the hotel, I will throw you out.' In London I travelled by the Underground, and I stayed at the flat of a classmate of my mother-in-law.

Over lunch, Srichand said that he could easily put me in touch with Ardbo as he had known Ardbo personally for years. He put through a call, ostensibly to Ardbo, and said that I was someone well known to him, that I was coming to Stockholm, and Ardbo would do well to spare time for me.

For all I know, and knew then, Srichand was talking to his secretary in the next room.

Such expectations that I may have had about getting some facts about Bofors evaporated in a breath. Srichand took me aside. He said he had a very big 'project' in mind and wanted to know whether I would be interested to join him in it. He told me of how their father had started in Iran, of the vast and varied holdings they had acquired, and how they now wanted to play an important role in public life. The way to do so, he said, was to influence public opinion. Everyone felt that the way to do that was to set up newspapers. But the real way was by controlling news agencies—all newspapers used stories put out by the agencies. And so, he and his brothers were thinking of acquiring Reuters. The problem was finding someone trustworthy to head it . . . That was just a brazen bribe in the sky! I deflected it to Suman. I don't have the temperament, I told Srichand. But Suman would be ideal. He is quick. He is the best journalist of our generation. He is non-political . . .

I had one more call to make. Chandraswami had fixed a meeting with Adnan Khashoggi. I went up to his room—actually a suite of interlinked rooms—in the hotel. He greeted me with Arab effusiveness. 'Friend of my friend,' he exclaimed. After a few minutes, he got up, went to the adjacent room, had some words with the persons there; got up, went to yet another room . . . came back to where I was, resumed the conversation; got up as abruptly, walked to the adjacent room . . . This went on for a good half an hour. I got only promises, including the promise that he would speak to Ardbo. The others must have got their arms' deals.

On to Stockholm. I had no illusion that Srichand's call to 'Ardbo' needed to be followed up. But I had with me that sheet of paper with the two numbers that Chandraswami had given. I showed them to Per Wendel. 'Give me a minute,' Wendel said.

He made a few calls, and moments later, 'These are not account numbers in any Swiss bank,' he said. 'They are the telephone numbers of Ardbo—this one is his number in Karlskoga, and this one is his number here in Stockholm!'

We looked up some persons, decided what we should focus on. And it was back to Delhi.

But that was not the end of those numbers Chandraswami had given us. Once I narrated this incident of how we had been made fools of to a BBC correspondent who had come to discuss Bofors, Chandraswami and the rest. Some weeks later, V.P. Singh—by then he had left Rajiv's government, and had become a formidable challenge to Rajiv—said in a speech that he had details of the accounts in which the Bofors money had been deposited. He had the numbers of the bank accounts, he said. He would reveal them at the right time, he said. I went to see him, and asked him whether he really had the numbers. 'Of course,' he said. And showed me what would today be called a screen grab of the BBC programme. It was a picture of the piece of paper that Chandraswami had given us. I told him the history of the numbers, of what they actually were. He wasn't as deflated as I had been when Per Wendel broke the truth to me. But he did not make the claim again: the right time to reveal the account numbers never came.

I chance upon a letter

Even after these experiences, we kept up our contacts with Chandraswami. In retrospect, this seems unbelievable idiocy. Once, when I was going on about the information we needed and about Khashoggi's promise, Chandraswami exclaimed, '*Arey bhai,* information, information . . . Information *ki kyaa zaroorat hai? Main* Khashoggi *ko keh detaa hoon ki inkey naam ek account khol de aur usmein das million daalar daal de. Hum kahengey ki yeh* Bofors *walaa paisaa hai. Yeh lo, tumhaari* information *aa gayi*'[2]—and he giggled out loud.

What could be clearer proof that he did not have the 'explosive' information he had been promising us? That he could not get it?

Even so, we kept our contacts with him. Even so, we kept shielding him from the government. Demand and supply! We were too anxious for information. And he, a rogue he was, but a seductive rogue. And like the godmen I was to meet later, an artful one—he could keep one's hope alive.

Around 10.30 one night, Coomi Kapoor, the head of our reporters, called. 'They have arrived to arrest Chandraswami.' Where? 'At Dr Jain's Nursing Home.'

I rushed there. A posse of policemen were all over the entrance and in the parking space on the ground floor. Our friend, the pugnacious and fearless lawyer, Pran Nath Lekhi was keeping them at bay. He knew the law, of course. But he was much more: he was fearless. In addition, he could act furious and shout.

I was told that Chandraswami had learnt a while earlier that he would be arrested and had promptly got himself admitted into the Nursing Home. I went to the room where he was. I have never seen a man tremble as much. He was shivering,

---

[2] 'You keep saying, "Information, information." Where is the need for information. I will tell Khashoggi to open an account in their name and deposit ten million dollars in it. We will say this is Bofors' money. So, here it is—your information.'

pleading, hysterical, '*Bachao, bachao . . . Ram*[3] *kahaan hai? Usko bulaayo . . .*'[4] Here was the godman—with tantric powers, no less!

While I was trying to ascertain what exactly had been happening, in walked 'Mamaji', Chandraswami's Sancho Panza. His head was wrapped in a bandage—with red blotches. '*Sarvanaash ho gayaa, Maharaj, sarvanaash ho gayaa. Mercedez neechey khadi hai . . . Briefcase usmein reh gayaa hai . . . Agli seat par. Shaayad khulaa he reh gayaa.*'[5]

Apparently, Mamaji had been driven to the Nursing Home as if he had been in an accident and had sustained injuries. In the scramble to get past the policemen, he had forgotten to bring his briefcase with him.

But what is the problem? What is in the briefcase?

'*. . . Voh chitthee bhee hai . . .*'[6]

I was trying to make sense of what was happening, why this was such a catastrophe, and calm Chandraswami all at the same time, when who should walk in but my father. In his dressing gown.

It was around midnight. I had left around 10.30 p.m.—telling him and my mother as I ran out that I was rushing to the Jain Nursing Home. I had still not returned. He had got worried that I might have picked a fight with the police. He had got into his car, and driven over.

Here is a godsend, Swamiji, I said. Let someone take him to Mamaji's Mercedes. In the chaos downstairs, nobody will pay attention to him. He can take out the briefcase and take it to our home. I will deliver it to you tomorrow morning.

So scared were they that Chandraswami and Mamaji thought this to be sheer brilliance. In any case, it was the one way out.

I returned home around 1.30 a.m. My father had left the briefcase near my bed. Mamaji had been right—it was not locked. I opened it. There were just four–five sheets in it and a few

---

[3] Ram Jethmalani.

[4] 'Save me, save me . . . Where is Ram? Call him . . .'

[5] 'All is lost, Maharaj, all is lost. The Mercedes is standing downstairs . . . The briefcase has got left in it . . . On the front seat. Possibly open.'

[6] '. . . That letter is also there.'

envelopes. Among these was an envelope addressed to 'Shriman Rajiv Gandhi, Pradhan Mantriji'.

What is this? I took out the letter in it.

The letter was from Chandraswami to Rajiv.

. . . The country is in grave danger . . . Foreign powers are bent on overturning it . . . The first step in doing so will be to overturn your government . . . The *Express* is part of this conspiracy . . . I have explosive information that can overthrow the government . . . The *Express* people are after me to give it to them . . . I can give it to you, but only in a one-to-one meeting . . . For the sake of our country, please spare some time so that we can meet alone . . .

Five pages of treacherous bunk . . .

I was furious. Here we were saving this fellow from the government, and here he was denouncing us as accomplices of foreign powers to Rajiv Gandhi, and wanting to strike a bargain with us as offering.

I couldn't sleep, and got ready even before dawn.

Around 8 in the morning I drove over to Ram Jethmalani's flat. I recounted events of the previous evening, and handed him Chandraswami's letter.

He glanced through it. 'Aroon'—he always pronounced my name that way—'the bastard is cleverer than I thought.' Where I had broken into a fury, Ram seemed amused at, almost appreciative of Chandraswami's cleverness. 'This is a letter blackmailing the Prime Minister of India: that I have information so explosive that it can bring down your government. I can give it to you, but only if you agree to a one-to-one meeting.'

Later that day, I went to the Nursing Home and returned the briefcase to Chandraswami and Mamaji. And I told them about the letter. Mamaji was struck into embarrassed silence. Chandraswami let out a hyena-like, apologetic giggle. In less than the flash of an eyelid, he had made up a story: '*Arey bhaiyaa, voh to us badmaash nein*'—he mentioned a young lawyer, one of his errand boys—'*banaayee thi. Mainey to bheji bhee naheen.*'[7]

---

[7] 'That was made by that rogue. I did not even send it.'

I lost contact with him. Some years later, I chanced upon him on a flight. He was a sorry sight: his complexion had turned much darker, he had blotches on his cheeks and temples, his eyes furtive, he couldn't get up, much less stand without help. *'Milnaa zaroor chaahiye,'* he said as we parted, *'Main* phone *karoongaa.'*[8]

He did too. Rajiv had been assassinated by then. Narasimha Rao had become the Prime Minister. I went to his 'ashram' in the Qutab Institutional Area. *'To aap sarkaar chalaa rahein hai, kyaa?'*[9] I asked. *'Naheen, naheen, main kisi bhi sarkaari nirndaya mein hastakshep naheen kartaa,'* he said. *'Main to ministeron ko kehtaa hoon, "Aapney jo bhi nirndaya lenaa hai, leejiye. Bus ghoshnaa se ek din pehley mujhey bataa deejiye."'*[10]

That was one of the modes. He would tell each of the contenders that he was working for him. And take an advance, so to say. When he got to learn of the decision, he would return the advance to the unsuccessful fellows, and take an additional amount from the one who was going to get the contract the next day. He would tell him of the enormous difficulties in the way, of the pressure and tactics that his rivals were using, and of the intense work that he—Chandraswami—would have to do to swing the decision.

'To kyaa mainey unkey nirndaya mein hastakshep kiyaa? Jo honaa chaahiye thaa, vahee huaa. Beech mein hamaraa kaam ban jaaye to kyaa buraa hai? . . .'[11] He laughed.

As we were talking, a handsome lady came in, obviously a foreigner. She started stroking his feet. *'Yeh bahut achhee ladki hai. Jo bhee main kehta hoon kartee hai.'*[12] Accompanied by his smirk, the clearest declaration that she was available if I wanted her . . .

But I have run ahead of the story.

So much happened vis-à-vis the government.

---

8 'We must meet. I will ring up.'
9 'So, you are running the Government, are you?'
10 'No, no, I do not interfere in any governmental decision. I only tell the Ministers, "Whatever you want to decide, decide. Only that, one day before the announcement, let me know what the decision is."'
11 'So, did I interfere in their decision. Whatever should have been decided was decided. If on the way, our work also gets done, what is wrong about it? . . .'
12 'She is a very good girl. She does whatever I ask her to do.'

20

Rulers take to forgeries

Rajiv & Co. did the predictable thing. Instead of answering the facts that were coming out on Bofors, they began campaigns to make people believe that their critics were corrupt, that they had unclean hands, that they were acting on behalf of commercial rivals, that—and here we were back to Mrs Gandhi's 'foreign hand'—they were puppets of foreign powers who were out to destabilize India.

As part of this smear campaign, the rulers took to peddling forgeries. And this proved a boon. The forgeries were so inept that they recoiled on the fabricators the moment they were put out.

The CIA sets its plans down in writing!

The 1 August 1987 issue of *Blitz*—it was on the stands a few days before the date on its masthead—carried what it claimed was a facsimile of a letter from William Casey, the then Director of the CIA, to the head of a conservative think tank in the US, the Heritage Foundation. It was said to document how the CIA and this Foundation were coordinating their efforts to shake Rajiv Gandhi's government. When Parliament opened on 27 July, Congress(I) MPs were armed with reproductions of the 'letter' that had been printed by *Blitz*. They used these to paralyse both Houses. Is the CIA so foolish as to put its designs in writing? Is the letterhead of the kind that the CIA Director uses to convey proposals for coordinating steps against a foreign government? Doubts exploded the moment the 'letter' became a public issue. To counter these, *Blitz* printed 'the same document' a second time.

Nothing could have nailed the forgery, and shown up the clumsiness of the forgers, as their 'reproducing' the document. The two versions of the 'letter' had so many discrepancies that even a fool could detect them.

To begin with, the second version of 'the same document' had several additions. There was a stamp proclaiming 'Received'— much as would be the case in a government office in India. There was a new note said to be in the hand of the head of the Heritage Foundation. And while the original forgery had just had the seal of the CIA on the letterhead, the second version had the designation of Casey also—'The Director of the Central Intelligence Agency'. Cornered by the discrepancies, *Blitz* maintained that it had deliberately withheld these features so as to trap the Americans.

But the additions were just the beginning of the bumbling. Even a child could notice the discrepancies in the two versions. In the document as it was originally published, there was scarcely any vertical distance between 'Washington DC' beneath the seal and the name of the addressee and the date. In the second version, there was a distance of seven lines between 'Washington DC' and the name, and of four lines between 'Washington DC' and the date. In the original, the date is given in the same line as the name of the addressee. In the second version, it was three lines higher. Correspondingly, the diagonal distances between the seal, the name and the date were vastly different.

The forgery, having done its work of diverting Parliament for a day or two, was soon forgotten. Only to be overshadowed by new ones.

A series

As Rajiv and his associates boxed themselves into tighter and tighter boxes, they strove to divert public attention by more and more forgeries. To arrest my colleagues, S. Gurumurthy and A. Janakiraman, they produced a patently forged 'letter', ostensibly from the 'Vice President' of a private investigating agency, Fairfax, in which the latter acknowledged receiving $3,00,000 from Nusli Wadia of the total half a million dollars which Wadia had to pay. To get over disclosures about the Enforcement Directorate's report about the foreign accounts of a key member of Sanjay's and Rajiv's group, the original report was replaced by a forged report from which every incriminating fact had been removed. To puncture V.P. Singh's rising popularity, a 'hotel bill' and 'call records' were manufactured to allege that his associate, Arun Nehru, had stayed in New York and had been calling numbers in tax havens. To sow doubts in the minds of Opposition leaders, a 'letter' was produced, ostensibly from the head of Fairfax, in which he was telling V.P. Singh about the latter's request that Fairfax unearth foreign accounts of sixteen Opposition leaders. A member of V.P. Singh's staff was produced to assert that V.P. Singh had been regularly writing to a diplomat in the US Embassy in Delhi, affirming that his views coincided with those of the US, and seeking guidance about the next steps that he should take!

Every single forgery was as stupid as could be. The list of Opposition leaders whose accounts V.P. Singh was ostensibly after, for instance, included the poor Karpoori Thakur who had died much earlier! Yet, every single forgery became an instrument to divert Parliament from discussing facts about Bofors.

As these forgeries were being dished out, I forecast that, to put V.P. Singh at par with the Bofors beneficiaries, soon the government would allege that V.P. Singh also had a foreign account in which he had been receiving bribes and commissions, and will produce 'documents' to prove this. I forecast this on the basis of what Chandraswami had said could easily be done to establish Rajiv's guilt: '*Arey bhai,* information, information . . . Information *ki kyaa zaroorat hai? Main* Khashoggi *ko keh detaa hoon ki inkey naam ek account khol de aur usmein das million daalar daal de. Hum kahengey ki yeh* Bofors *walaa paisaa hai. Yeh lo, tumhaari* information *aa gayee.*'[1]

Within days, that is exactly what happened.

---

[1] See above, page 275.

Another botched attempt

A paper in, of all places, Istanbul, a paper that had hitherto displayed scant interest in Indian affairs, and was not known for investigating the doings of Indian politicians, published a story alleging that V.P. Singh had an illegal foreign bank account. No one noticed.

The story was repeated in the *Arab Times* of Kuwait. UNI (United News of India) picked up the story. 'The Kuwait based newspaper, *The Arab Times,* has alleged that former Finance Minister, Vishwanath Pratap Singh made six substantial deposits totalling $21 million in the First Trust Corporation Limited in St. Kitts,' the UNI dispatch reported. *'The newspaper says,'* the UNI dispatch continued, *'it has in its possession all the documents necessary to prove the authenticity of this story.* The account was opened in the name of Mr VP Singh's son Ajeya Singh who is a middle level employee in the Citibank in New York . . .' The UNI feeds landed on newspaper desks between 6.35 and 6.50 in the evening.

I was still in the office.

Soon a PTI dispatch also arrived datelined Bahrain. The opening sentence grabbed my attention. 'A Kuwait daily *quoting Indian political sources has alleged* . . .' That was very different: the UNI dispatch implied that the story was based on documents which the paper had in its possession. The PTI dispatch implied that the story was based on 'Indian political sources'. The difference between day and night. As I happened to be on the Board of the UNI at the time,[2] I alerted them to the omission. They *did* send out a new 'introduction' stating that the paper had said that its story was based on what it had been told by 'Indian political sources', but it was not sent out till midnight. As a result, most papers carried the original UNI copy.

But who had fed the concoction in the first place? The internal inquiry by the UNI established that the story had come from 'high government functionaries'.

---

[2] By virtue of being the editor of the *Express.*

By the next day, the 'documents' on which the story had supposedly been based began landing in offices of one newspaper after another. I got them from a senior journalist in one of the Delhi-based papers friendly to the government. We now had something for us to work on. We faxed the 'documents' to our correspondent in Washington DC, A. Balu.

What was in those days one of the main outlets for such concoctions—*The Telegraph* of the Ananda Bazar Patrika group—published them.

The story was that V.P. Singh had an illegal account in a bank in Basseterre, the capital of St Kitts, an island in the Caribbean. There was a number to the account. A person, one 'George Mclean', had been called on the phone. He would say nothing. So, he was asked, 'Can we read something into the fact that you are not denying the existence of the account?' He had said, 'Yes.' And that was said to establish that there *was* an account! What if he had been asked, 'Can we read something into the fact that you are not affirming the existence of the account?' and he had said, 'Yes'? But the ever so friendly paper had concluded not just that the account existed. It had concluded that the account belonged to V.P. Singh!

Ajeya Singh, the son of V.P. Singh, was said to have travelled to St Kitts and entered into an 'agreement' on 16 September 1986, about operating the account, etc. Balu found out that Indian and US citizens did not need to obtain a visa prior to their visit to St Kitts: it would be stamped on their passport at the time of landing there. Through V.P. Singh's family, we requested Ajeya Singh to fax us his passport from New York. He did, within the hour. He had never been to St Kitts. Balu followed up the matter with the authorities on the island—and got the same result.

We asked for three documents which had been signed by Ajeya long before this story about the 'account' broke, and which would be with governments—in India or the US. He sent them also. His signature bore absolutely no resemblance to the 'signature' on the 'agreement' that he was said to have entered with the bank.

On one thing the forgers had been meticulous: in choosing the date on which the 'agreement' had supposedly been signed—

16 September 1986. They had chosen the date on which there had been a meeting in the Caribbean of finance ministers of the Commonwealth. And as finance minister, V.P. Singh would have represented India. But it turned out that he had never made it to the finance ministers' meeting as he had been held up at the meeting of GATT (General Agreement on Tariffs and Trade) in Punta del Este, a resort in Uruguay. In the attempt to be meticulous, the forgers had been meticulously wrong.

There were other howlers. The account number had five digits. Accounts with the bank had six. The seal the bank used while opening accounts was completely different from the one that appeared on the 'documents'. The account was said to have been opened by Ajeya Singh in the name of his father, V.P. Singh. But for those wanting secret accounts, the bank did not require any name at all. It issued a bearer card—with no name. Whoever had the card and could mention the code could operate the account. And so on.

It wasn't difficult to nail the forgery. But with the help of friendly papers, of AIR and Doordarshan, and of the shouting brigade of MPs and others, like other forgeries, this one also did its work: it served to deflect attention from Bofors for a few days.

Saving grace

The sequence followed a pattern. The forgery was planted in one or two papers. It was broadcast by others. And even more aggressively by AIR and Doordarshan. But the one feature that was common to them all was the one that saved the intended targets: the forgeries were clumsy as can be. The supposed 'letter' from the 'Vice President' of Fairfax, on the basis of which Gurumurthy and Janakiraman were arrested, had been typed on a very Indian typewriter. The sentences and spellings had so many Indianisms that Jethmalani could tear into it in his sleep. The idiotic discrepancies in *Blitz*'s CIA letter. The numerous foolishnesses in the 'VP Singh's secret account' 'documents'.

The clumsiness of the forgers was their saving grace.

Roping in the Judges

Evangelists of governments take what governments put out very seriously. Governments realize much before them that fewer and fewer are believing what is being put out. They are forever on the lookout for others whose word may carry conviction. Often, Judges are, ex officio, the propagandists of choice.

And that is what happened. The forgeries would divert attention from Bofors for three/four days. But that was all. And so the government appointed a Commission of Inquiry. It was able to persuade the then Chief Justice to spare two sitting Judges, M.P. Thakkar, who had already 'done the needful' by his inquiry into the assassination of Mrs Gandhi, and S. Natarajan, for the job. The ostensible purpose of the Commission was to ascertain who had engaged, and who had financed the private investigating firm, Fairfax, to inquire into the accounts of Indians abroad, and whether, by engaging it to do so, national security had been jeopardized.

V.P. Singh swiftly killed the mystery about who had engaged Fairfax. He wrote to the Commission that as finance minister, he had approved the proposal of the Enforcement Directorate to engage it. And that he had informed the Prime Minister about it— this is what had led to the sudden decision to shift him out of the Finance Ministry to Defence. Moreover, it turned out that private investigators were routinely engaged to track down culprits with accounts abroad. But who paid it? That mystery, too, was swiftly nailed. The Enforcement Directorate had a fund for such purposes. Moreover, several informers and agencies worked on a finder's-fee basis: under the scheme then in force, the agency would have received a fifth of the amounts in the foreign accounts it detected. But why had the Enforcement Directorate been allowed to select Fairfax without reference to 'Government'? It turned out that the selection of agencies was an 'operational matter', to be decided by the Directorate on its own. But why had the Revenue Secretary sent the file to V.P. Singh when the latter had been shifted out of the Finance Ministry? Because the latter had asked for it, and the Secretary had done so after informing the minister of state in the Finance Ministry. Why were minutes of meetings with the Enforcement Director not kept? But discussions regarding clandestine accounts, etc. are just not reduced to writing. Why did the Director meet the head of Fairfax in a park and a hotel? Why did he not record the substance of the discussions with the latter in a file? Surely, you would hardly want your informer or investigator to come to your office, and let everyone know. Nor does anyone reduce discussions with investigators and informers to file.

Gurumurthy was one of the targets. Under the law governing Commissions of Inquiry, he had to be issued a notice to appear before the Commission. He flooded the Commission with offers to assist it once the Commission issued him a notice—his petitions covered 150 pages. But the Commission just wouldn't issue a notice. Reason? Once it issued him a notice, he would have the right to cross-examine witnesses.

Whenever such requests came up; whenever arguments or evidence was proceeding in a direction inconvenient to the design of the government; whenever the initial questions came up—what was the reason for engaging Fairfax? Whose foreign accounts was Fairfax asked to investigate?—Thakkar would intone: we will take up that matter at a later stage.

And one day, suddenly, the Judges decreed that there would be no later stages.

In the event, no one believed the Commission's report any more than they believed the forgeries. Everyone who had followed the hearings realized what the real problem with Fairfax had been. Government was alarmed at the persons whose doings Fairfax was going to investigate—Reliance, among others—and the rumour that it had stumbled on some trails of payments that it thought had to do with the purchase of howitzer guns from Bofors.

21

A Prime Minister unspools himself

Swedish police had received information that Bofors had been violating the law: shipments of arms to belligerent countries, bribes—both through pit-stop countries. Tipped off by a source in the police, on 16 April 1987, the news arm of Swedish Public Radio broadcast a report about these illegalities. Among other things, it mentioned that Bofors had made payments in India for bagging the howitzer contract. It said that three payments had been made by Bofors of 29.5 million Swedish Kroner in November 1986, and a fourth payment of 2.5 million Kroner was made in December 1986. But these were just the ones that had been made till then, the Radio reported: Bofors would end up paying 'a commission . . . of a couple of hundred million Kroner'.

The Swedish Radio broadcast its first dispatch on 16 April 1987. Indian readers learnt about it from a small Reuters item on the morning of 17 April. But of course the government had rushed its 'denial' out on the night of 16 April itself. 'Official sources,' the PTI dispatch reported, dubbed the Swedish Radio report 'entirely baseless and mischievous', and 'categorically denied that any bribe was paid to any Indian politician or defence officials in the Bofors deal'. These were standard phrases. Few would have believed them, and, as the original Reuters dispatch was just a short one, most would not have attached much importance to the dispatch itself.

But on the following day, 17 April, the government issued a formal denial, adding an assertion and an insinuation which were to be repeated ad nauseam over the next few months. The government declared:

> Government categorically deny the allegations contained in the news stories based on the reports broadcast by the Swedish radio and television in connection with an arms order placed on the Swedish firm Bofors. The news item is false, baseless and mischievous. During the negotiations the Government had made it clear that the company should not pay any money to any person in connection with the contract. Government's policy is not to permit any clandestine or irregular payments in contracts. Any breach of this policy by anyone will be most severely dealt with.

Standard government-speak thus far. And the implicit assertion, too, was true to form: as it is our policy that no clandestine payments must be made, none have been made. And then, the conspiracy theory:

> The report is one more link in the chain of denigration and destabilisation of our political system. Government and the people are determined to defeat this sinister design with all their might.

The Congress Working Committee met the next day, 18 April. Rajiv Gandhi presided. While rubber-stamping the 'categorical denial', the Working Committee made the smear even more strident. It declared:

> Not content with this, the security of India is being imperilled by uncalled for and unwanted reflection cast on the defence preparedness of our patriotic Defence Forces.

In fact, no one had cast any reflection on them nor had anyone raised any doubts about their preparedness:

An atmosphere of cynicism and despair is being fostered, undermining the confidence and determination of the nation. In short, a grand design of destabilisation is being implemented with meticulous attention to detail . . .

. . . A vicious campaign of falsehood, insinuation and innuendo, backed by baseless and malicious charges . . .

The direct threat posed by the supply of the most sophisticated weapons systems to Pakistan has been further aggravated by a massive campaign to undermine the morale of our Defence Forces by inspired and motivated stories regarding defence contracts . . . The consequence of the avalanche of disinformation let loose on an unsuspecting public will be to weaken our defence preparedness . . .

All manner of phoney issues are being generated . . .

The vehemence of the denials convinced me that there was definitely something wrong. That feeling was heightened when I learnt that on the very night of 16 April, intelligence agencies had pounced on a Swedish Radio correspondent who had come to Delhi. They had been hounding him since then. This, even though he had neither filed the dispatch nor had he been associated with inquiries which had led to it.[1] I was reminded of how Mrs

---

[1] The rapidity and force with which the government let fly the conspiracy theory calls into question a hypothesis that my friend Vir Sanghvi was to advance years later in his lucid reconstruction of the Bofors controversy. Vir wrote:

> If you examine Rajiv's responses [to the allegations surrounding the Bofors contract], he began as you would expect Mr. Clean to behave. He was outraged by the allegation . . . The Rajiv of early 1987 who banned the Hindujas, was completely different from the Rajiv of 1989 who had welcomed them back to the Prime Minister's House. My guess is that Rajiv genuinely believed that he had nothing to hide on Bofors. *Within a month or so,* he realised that he was wrong; that if the truth came out, he would be severely compromised. That is when his responses began to change, and that is when the Hindujas wormed their way back into his favour by offering to manage Martin Ardbo and to supervise the cover-up from Stockholm and London . . .
>
> What was it that Rajiv discovered that so compromised him? It is hard to say, but there are two obvious explanations. The first is that the Congress had

Gandhi's minions had reacted to our reports on the blindings in Bhagalpur—the very words were the same. I was to encounter the words and canard again—this time from Narendra Modi's government—when Prashant Bhushan, Yashwant Sinha and I nailed wrongdoing in regard to the purchase of Rafale aircraft.

With thirty-five years having passed, it is not necessary to recall the facts relating to the scandal. The main point to remember is that, within two years, the fact that there had been middlemen was established, the identity of several of them—Win Chadha, the Hindujas, Ottavio Quattrocchi and others—had been established, that Rs 64 crore had been channelled to them had been established, that the payments would have continued but for the scandal having broken out had been established. These and other facts have been summarized periodically.[2]

What comes to mind thirty-five years later?

---

taken the commission, but that Rajiv, never a details man, had been unaware of this when he had launched his outraged defence. The second is that it took him a month or two to realise that Quattrocchi was involved. Even if Quattrocchi had been operating in an individual capacity, any revelation that suggested an Italian connection would have severely compromised Rajiv. Sonia would have been the subject of the attack and it is unlikely that he would have been able to face that level of personal assault.

Hence, the turnaround from Mr. Outraged Clean to Mr. Cover-up . . .

—Vir Sanghvi, 'Bofors' Ghost', *Seminar,* Number 485, January 2000, pp. 32–36. Available at https://www.india-seminar.com/ 2000/485/485%20sanghvi.htm

But the fact is that the destabilization conspiracy theory was trotted out within a day of the broadcast.

[2] In particular, see the reports No. 2 of 1989 and No. 12 of 1990 of the Comptroller and Auditor General of India; Prashant Bhushan, *The Selling of a Nation,* Vision Books, New Delhi, 1990; Vir Sanghvi, 'Bofors' Ghost', *Seminar,* op. cit. In the following, I shall refer often to N. Ram, *Why Scams Are Here to Stay, Understanding Political Corruption in India,* Aleph Book Company, New Delhi, 2017; and the interview that Sten Lindstrom, the principal investigator in Sweden on the matter, gave to Chitra Subramaniam, *The Hoot,* 24 April 2012. Available at http://asu.thehoot.org/media-watch/ media-practice/the-bofors-story-25-years-after-5884

We lose out!

First and foremost, that, occasioning one of the great scoops of the time, Sten Lindstrom, the principal official of the Swedish National Investigation Agency who had led the investigation, gave the documents to Chitra Subramaniam and, through her, to N. Ram and his team at *The Hindu*, and not to us! Lindstrom gave them well over 350 documents.[3] *The Hindu* published the documents in three instalments: April and June 1988, and then in November 1988—the gap between June and November will come up again in a moment. Lindstrom's motives were of the highest order. His wife and he had imbibed the social-democratic ideals that we associate with Sweden and the Swedes. He learnt that Bofors had been giving bribes to get contracts, and had been selling arms to belligerent countries in violation of Swedish law. It had been selling arms by showing that they were being shipped to third countries, and making the payments through accounts in tax havens—facts that showed that the company and its senior executives knew they were breaking the law. Lindstrom was appalled by the extent of malfeasance: 'They claimed a tax-deduction for the money they had to pay as bribes,' he was to remark. The more information he received about the contract to supply howitzer guns to India, the more let down he felt:

> The $1.3 billion deal with India for the sale of 410 field howitzers, and a supply contract almost twice that amount, was the biggest arms deal ever in Sweden. Money marked for development projects was diverted to secure this contract at any cost. Rules were flouted, institutions were bypassed and honest Swedish officials and politicians were kept in the dark. Our former Prime Minister Olof Palme was talking peace, disarmament and sustainable development globally, while we were selling arms illegally, including to countries that were on our banned list. My office, the office of Hans Ekblom, the

---

[3]   In his account, Ram puts the figure at 'well over a hundred'. *The Hoot*, while introducing Lindstrom's interview with Chitra, put the figure at 'over 350'.

public prosecutor in Stockholm, our National Audit Bureau—
everything was ignored. So was the Swedish tax-payer.

Chitra asked him, 'How did the India angle in Bofors crop up?'
'It was an accident,' Lindstrom explained:

> We were conducting several search and seize operations in the
> premises of Bofors and their executives. I have some experience
> in this area, so I asked my team to take everything they could
> find. In the pile were one set of documents to Swiss banks with
> instructions that the name of the recipient should be blocked
> out. An accountant doing his job asked why anonymity was
> necessary since the payments were legal. Bofors was unable to
> explain and then we found more and more documents leading
> to India.

The difference one conscientious man, a single journalist who
perseveres, and an accident can make: a pebble moves and an
avalanche starts.

In particular, what stands out is the sterling role of Chitra. She
persevered for a year, and ultimately won Sten Lindstrom's trust.
Of course, as one would expect, recollections vary somewhat. Ram,
who led *The Hindu's* team, emphasizes that their investigation
was a team effort:

> *The Hindu's* investigation was not the work of any one
> star journalist but a collective enterprise, which I happened
> to lead and do much of the writing for; and for more than
> eighteen months from April 1988, when *The Hindu's* Geneva
> stringer, Chitra Subramaniam, struck gold in Stockholm, until
> October 1989, when we published the withheld secret papers
> of the Swedish National Audit Bureau's findings, *The Hindu*
> owned the investigation—thanks to the exclusive continuing
> relationship with the confidential source Chitra had formed and
> had persuaded to cooperate with us.[4]

---

4   N. Ram, op. cit., p. 90.

Ram records that the principal source was Sten Lindstrom. In addition, he lists several others whom he and the rest of *The Hindu* team interviewed.

Lindstrom underscored the role of an individual rather than a team, and much less an institution. He told Chitra,

> I knew what I was doing when I leaked the documents to you. I could not count on my government or Bofors or the government of India to get to the bottom of this. My only option was to leak the documents to someone we could trust.
>
> I believe I did the best I could. I watched you work for almost one year before I took my decision to leak the Bofors-India documents to you. You were one of many journalists from India and Sweden as well as many politicians from India who visited me during this period. I was lectured to and told how to do my job.

The crucial factor, he explained, was trust:

> People trust people. Trust is built over time. The one and only visit by your former editor N. Ram of *The Hindu* to my office in whose presence I handed over the documents is a detail. I would have leaked the documents to you even if you had worked for any other newspaper.
>
> *The Hindu's* role in all this was that of a medium of communication. I met them because you insisted. I was disappointed. They published the documents as and when they wanted without any respect for the risks other people were taking to get the facts out.

To drive home his point, he singled out one set of documents:

> The most explosive documents that involved the political payments were Ardbo's notes and diary. *The Hindu* published them several months after they had them. In the meantime there was a serious difficulty. I got a message that my name was circulating in Delhi's political circles as the whistleblower.

This caused a lot of stress and difficulty for me. You will recall the month you were not allowed to call me while we investigated who leaked my name as the whistle-blower in India. There were consequences for me and my family. The *Hindu* seemed unconcerned.[5]

You will recall that *The Hindu* printed the documents in three instalments. The first set was printed in April 1988, the second set in June. And then there was a long gap till November. Gurumurthy fills in the blank, and recalls how that long pause was eventually broken:

I distinctly remember that after *The Hindu* published the Hinduja papers and parts of Ardbo diary there was a long lull.

Then both of us decided to meet Ram. You came to Chennai and we went to him.

Then he brought down a huge pile of papers from his open shelf and said that he had not seen them. I asked his permission to see the papers.

As both of you were discussing the investigation he was doing and we were, I was quickly going through the papers.

There were hundreds and hundreds of sheets but one unmissable one set was the Ardbo diary.

---

[5] From *The Hindu,* Chitra moved to the *Express*. She got very angry with me once as some lines of her dispatch were missing from what appeared in the paper. She had sent the fax to my number at the office. I had taken it to the news editor with the instruction that it must be the lead on the top right of page 1. When Chitra told me the next day that some lines had been cut from her account, and felt that this had been done deliberately to shield Arun Nehru, I went back to the news editor. He told me that he had marked the fax as he had received it and then sent it down to the press. Together, we concluded that the fax machine must have sprinted over some lines. For us in Delhi, Arun Nehru was a marginal source, by no means a crucial one. And as a source, he was the kind who would be using the journalist with whom he was sharing any titbit. So, apart from being marginal, he was a source of whom we in the paper were wary. He was certainly not known well enough to any one of us, and certainly not to Ramnathji, for anyone to doctor copy to shield him. The explanation never satisfied Chitra.

The Hindu had already carried some parts of the Ardbo diary earlier—on 'Q', 'Nero', 'W'—on which I had written the commentary in our paper. So they knew about the Ardbo diary.

But that page which said meeting with 'Gandhi Trustee Lawyer' which I saw among the papers was too telling to be missed unless by accident.

At that time Ram was saying that there is nothing directly mentioning Rajiv's name except by inference.

When I heard that, I took out the 'Gandhi Trustee Lawyer' entry and showed it to both of you.

Then Ram said, 'Now we have found the clinching piece we always wanted.'

In fact, when I was looking at the papers, Ram even charged that I was stealing the papers. It made me angry. I reacted and then he apologised. In fact, Ram would never have allowed me to see the papers if you had not come.

In my view, after the initial rounds of publication, the papers were perhaps left lying just as a heap. That is how *The Hindu* had missed the most critical page in that pile.[6]

Guilt

The next thing that comes to mind is a personal loss that filled me with guilt for years. Quite apart from the fact that he has been one of the most outstanding journalists of our time, Suman Dubey is the most loved in our family. The best index: he is one of Adit's favourite uncles. Suman was the editor of the *Express* at the time. Something I did led him to leave the paper. I distinctly recall being called to Ramnathji's flat in Sundar Nagar one evening. Mulgaokar was there. The Bofors procession was hurtling along— the government lying, and us nailing the lies. Suman, scrupulous, conscientious, and better disposed towards Rajiv than us, felt that we were running ahead of the evidence. But then, out of the blue, another rock loosened, and came tumbling down.

---

6 Email, 26 April 2021, and exchanges over the phone.

Stories began to appear that there was a build-up of forces along the Pakistan border. V.P. Singh was suddenly shifted out of the Finance Ministry to Defence. The real reason, as we have seen, had nothing to do with build-ups, etc. It was the apprehension that Fairfax had stumbled on to something that had to do with Bofors, and dealings of some of Rajiv's friends. In the Defence Ministry, V.P. Singh was shown a message that had come from the Indian Ambassador in Bonn. It said that an Indian go-between had pocketed Rs 30 crore—a huge sum in those days—in exchange for the purchase of HDW submarines by India. V.P. Singh ordered an inquiry. He began to be denounced in one forum after another, in one meeting after another. The denunciations were all by Congressmen. It became impossible for him to continue in government. In effect, he was pushed to resign.

The three of us—Ramnathji, Mulgaokar and me—agreed that pushing V.P. Singh out like this confirmed the suspicion that something seriously wrong had been done. After some exchanges, it was decided that an editorial should appear the next day. I said that we must ask Suman. Ramnathji said that it was only after talking to him that they had called me to write it. Mulgaokar confirmed this with a nod. I asked, 'But then why is Suman not writing it?' They said that he had gone to some wedding. I wrote the editorial, 'To confirm suspicion'. After recounting the latest development, it urged the President to seek legal counsel on what could be done, and it urged the Opposition to take the issue to the people. In effect, it said that as Rajiv was neither going to alter course nor resign, other remedies should be explored.

The Desk would have sent the editorial to Suman. He felt that such an editorial could not be allowed to appear with him as editor. He sent in his resignation that evening. The editorial appeared on the front page the next morning.

Suman says that his differences with Ramnathji had been building up for some time. There had been that incident of the letter being drafted for Zail Singh to send to Rajiv Gandhi, he recalls—Mulgaokar's corrections were on the copy. They wanted Zail Singh to dismiss Rajiv—and you were there too, he tells me. The last straw was this editorial. 'In effect, it called for Rajiv's dismissal or resignation, and it was written without my knowledge let alone participation,' he recalls. 'I told them that such an editorial going with my name as editor was not acceptable, and I sent in my resignation the night before it appeared.' A great loss to the profession, and an even greater loss to us in the family.

Distortions

The next thing that still rankles after all these years is the familiar one: the complete distortion of what we were saying and doing. It was made out that we were depriving India of the best weapon, a gun that had been selected after rounds and rounds of tests by the Army. It was even hinted that we were doing so on the prompting of some rival—manufacturers of the Austrian gun, it was hinted at one stage. But we had repeatedly stressed—in my case, directly to officials in government,[7] among others—that we were not disputing the technical virtues of the Bofors gun. Nor had we the expertise to maintain in the least that guns of other suppliers—the French, the British or the Austrians—were better than the Bofors gun. Yes, there were, as there always are, differences of opinion among experts: on six occasions, the Army Headquarters had indicated its preference for the French Sofma gun; it had reversed its preference in February 1986, a month before the contract was signed with Bofors. All this was true, but we are not competent to sit in judgement on the final choice, I stressed; we are only on the payments that have been made by Bofors to procure the contract—as Yashwant Sinha, Prashant Bhushan and I were to do later in regard to the procurement of Rafale fighter aircraft, and the payments made to and by Dassault. But the distortion became a staple.

---

[7] Among them, Gopi Arora, then one of the principal aides of Rajiv Gandhi. I had known him for almost fifteen years as we had been together at the Planning Commission.

Another charge was added, and this has been routinely insinuated for years, the charge that what we did hindered defence purchases for long, that, in fact, it meant that the Indian Army could not get for decades the additional howitzer guns it needed. If our Army did not get the guns it needed, questions raised at the time were not the cause. The cause would lie with the government's handling of the controversy. There *is* a way to go about such matters. First and foremost, do not use defence purchases for any purpose other than equipping our forces—do not, to recall the rationalization that was given by some at the time, for instance, use them to collect money your party will need for the coming elections. Second, if something wrong has been done, and comes to, or is brought, to your attention, do everything possible to uncover the facts at the earliest, severely punish the guilty, and go ahead. It is because these simple things are not done that decisions remain stalled in the wake of such a scandal. Third, assuming that they are doing the right thing, why do officers not take decisions? The reason is not that some controversy erupted thirty years ago, but because ministers and Prime Ministers are not prepared to take responsibility, and to be shields for the officers in case there are baseless inquiries later. *This* is what needs to change—have ministers and senior civil servants in place who will stand up for their colleagues. The solution is not that if something wrong has been done, it should not be brought to light. The lie to the charge that the controversy stalled acquisition of guns in the decades that followed is given by the fact that, though Bofors had given the technology to manufacture the gun in India, the country did not avail of it for decades.

Discouraging advice

The next thing that comes to mind is the discouraging advice from so many, including the hostility of other papers to what we were doing. Like Rajiv, these papers and their editors were demanding that *we,* not the government, uncover evidence—presumably uncover such evidence that *they* would deem to be satisfactory! In the meanwhile, they were peddling the 'destabilization' thesis as enthusiastically as any other megaphone of the government.

You are going on and on about this, friends would say. But this is just a middle-class issue; it is only in your drawing rooms in Delhi that some of your friends get agitated about it. I had been inured to such comments by then—after all, they were a verbatim replay of what used to be said during the Emergency. Even so, the nagging was an unceasing annoyance. Among the things that settled it was an article by my friend, Jaswant Singh. Jaswant loved books. He was widely read, and he wrote very well. But everyone is writing the same commentaries on the same subjects sitting here in Delhi, I mentioned to him. Their pieces are just opinions they have formed or heard at their dinners. They are so alike. Fewer and fewer read them. Please tell us what is happening in your village. What are people there talking about? The 'national issues' that preoccupy us, do these register in the village? What do your relatives and friends there feel about them? In one of his articles, Jaswant Singh set out what they were saying about Bofors in his village. A village elder had said, as they sat on *chaarpaayees* smoking hookahs, '*Isney to topkhaaney se churaayaa hai*'—'He has stolen from the armoury.' A cardinal sin—remember that the areas from which Jaswant came sent large numbers of its young men to the armed forces. It wasn't just concern for the security of the country that the remark reflected. It wasn't just the possessive pride in the armed forces. It was that what had been done endangered the lives of their sons and brothers. That remark weighed more with me than the discouraging advice.

The charge that we were going on and on with an issue that reached no farther than our drawing rooms, and that I was exceeding the limits in pursuing it, reached a minor peak after the Swedish government released a truncated version of the report of their National Audit Bureau. In particular, the names of companies and persons to whom payments had been made were blanked out. I requested our readers to let the Swedish government know the depth of feeling on the issue in India by writing a letter to the Swedish Prime Minister, Ingvar Carlsson. Here is a sample, I wrote, improve and alter it as you think fit:

The Prime Minister of Sweden
c/o the Embassy of Sweden
New Delhi

Dear Sir,

Like millions the world over, I have looked up to Sweden for the institutions it has pioneered, for the values around which it has tried to organise its society and government.

I have, therefore, been distressed to read about the payments the Swedish company, Bofors, has made to Indians to secure the Howitzer contract from our government.

These payments are not commercial commissions. They are bribes.

Disclosures about these bribes have shaken the faith of our people in our government. They have paralysed institutions like our Parliament.

The names of at least some of the Indians who received these bribes are contained in the portions of the Audit Bureau's report which your government has withheld.

I believe that by doing so your government is shielding, however unwittingly, those who have made a barter of our country and our defence. Shielding them is contrary to the principles by which, I have been told, your people and government live. It puts in jeopardy not just the Bofors contract itself, that of course it does, but also the regard we have had for your society. It also puts the severest possible strain on Indo-Swedish relations.

I, therefore, request you to release the portions of the Audit Bureau's report that you have withheld, and to release them as you did the report itself, that is, openly to the world at large and not in any private communication to any individual.

Best regards,

'This is not journalism,' the editors lectured. So what if it isn't? 'You are using a paper to carry on a campaign.' But is the campaign for the right thing?

In response to the suggestion, 1,50,000 readers—a very big number in those pre-Internet days—sent us copies of their letters. We sent them in a truck to the Swedish Embassy. A good answer to the censors.

The torrent of abuse

The abuse was incessant, no doubt. The moment anyone questioned what had been done, the government and its hounds pounced on him. The Swedish Radio was said to be linked to the CIA. V.P. Singh suddenly became Jai Chand and Mir Jafar rolled into one. He was said to be linked to the same CIA, to be, in addition, 'a blackmailer . . . a coward . . . most corrupt . . . [with] property worth rupees 50 crore in Delhi', 'a gaddaar', 'a darpok', 'a bhagoraa', an occasional lunatic given to fits of lunacy—much of this was said in Parliament, much of it by ministers in Rajiv's Cabinet.

Arun Singh, at the time Minister of State for Defence, was among the staunchest and most loyal associates of Rajiv. As we shall soon see, he had been fielded several times to defend the contract in Parliament, and to advance the rationalizations. K. Sundarji was the Deputy Chief of the Army, soon to become its Chief. His expertise, and the fact that, ultimately, it was on his advice that the Bofors gun had been selected, had been paraded time and again to justify the contract.[8] As the controversy unfolded, the two came to feel that the government should hold out the threat that the contract would be cancelled unless Bofors disclosed the names of beneficiaries. Buffeted from all sides, Bofors offered to disclose the details. Bertil Bredin, a Vice President of Bofors and the person directly in charge of the matter, that is, its 'Project Coordinator, Field Artillery in India', came to Delhi and informed the Ministry of Defence that the company was ready to send a high-level delegation—consisting, among others, of the President

---

[8]   The CAG's report was to reveal later that in six rounds, the French gun, Sofma, had come first, that it was only after the relative importance assigned to different parameters was recalibrated that Bofors came out on top.

of Bofors, as well as their senior-most legal counsel—to disclose everything that the Indian government wanted to know. Arun Singh, the Minister of State for Defence, readily accepted the offer. Bredin therefore informed both his superiors in Karlskoga and the second senior-most official of the Swedish Embassy in Delhi, Rolf Gauffin,[9] that in response to their offer, Bofors had been asked to send the delegation. This was on 3 July 1987. Rajiv was in Moscow. He had but to return and, Arun Singh, happy at what he had been able to achieve, told him that Bofors had agreed to disclose the names, and was going to send a delegation consisting of its senior-most personnel to do so. As General Sundarji was to reveal later, Rajiv 'lit into' all those who had agreed to receive the Bofors offer. They were told to tell Bofors *not* to send any delegation. We learnt of this diktat and published it. Arun Singh resigned.[10] The guns were immediately trained on him.

Arun Singh suddenly became one who had been part of some unspecified shady deals and against whom 'fingers had been raised'! 'As a part of the new plan launched by Shri Rajiv Gandhi to refurbish his image and that of the party,' began the *Navbharat Times* account of his resignation, 'another minister and close friend of his, the Minister of State for Defence, Shri Arun Singh, has resigned from the central Council of Ministers.' 'The reason for Mr. Arun Singh's resignation could not be immediately known,' reported PTI, 'but according to reports in political circles the Prime Minister might replace those against whom accusing fingers were being raised. Some of them are close to him.' 'Having made up his mind to get rid of some of his associates against whom accusing fingers have been raised in the deals concerning defence equipment and civilian aircraft,' said the *Hindustan Times* apropos the resignations of Arun Singh and, believe it or not, Mufti Mohammad Sayeed, 'the Prime Minister is expected to call for some more resignations from the Council of Ministers, as also

---

[9] He was a close friend of Jaswant Singh, and an important source for us at the *Express*.

[10] In typing the foregoing, I have relied on what my colleagues and I learnt at the time. Arun Singh has continued to remain completely silent.

from the two Houses of Parliament'. The common words in such reports spoke to a common inspiration.

A full two years later, General Sundarji disclosed the advice he had given—that Bofors be asked to reveal the names of beneficiaries on pain of losing the contract, and how Rajiv had 'lit into' them.[11] The moment he did so, the shout went up that Sundarji was 'speaking out of frustration' as he had not been given the Ambassadorship that he had been hankering after. Stories appeared alleging that there had been a 'nexus' between Arun Singh and Sundarji for some unspecified purposes. Money? it was asked. Furthering each other's ambitions? Something else?[12]

Similarly, the moment it became known that the Comptroller and Auditor General had submitted a report listing how the evaluation procedures and other aspects of the contract had fallen short of the prescribed norms, he became 'that Charlie sitting as the C and AG' who'd better make sure that he continues to 'sit in his ivory tower and if he does come out, I do not know what will happen which I do not want to happen'. And was it some buffoon who used these words, and insinuated that threat? It was N.K.P. Salve, a minister many times over, at that time the Chairman of the Finance Commission, and Member of Parliament.

Of course, abuse was not the only weapon. As I have narrated elsewhere in the book, other steps were taken to muzzle us and stop the chase: the Delhi edition of the paper was shut down by proclaiming that there was a 'strike'. And then there was Rajiv's Defamation Bill.

Comprehensive failure of institutions

The abuse and the debasement of discourse would not have disabled us. The comprehensive failure of one institution after another to perform its duty ensured that little would come of

---

[11] The disclosures by General Sundarji led to another stream of falsehoods. I will return to these in a while.

[12] For instance, 'There Was a Sundarji-Arun Singh Nexus'. Available at https://www.outlookindia.com/magazine/story/quotthere-was-a-sundarji-arun-singh-nexusquot/203118

our efforts. Every institution functioned as the instrument of the rulers.

That there were three streams of payments was established beyond doubt. The most telling was the set that flew to AE Services, a company ostensibly registered in the UK. It had come in at the last moment. Payment to it was pegged to the contract being awarded to Bofors by a specific date—and it *was* awarded by that date. Given the labyrinthine ways our bureaucracy works, how could the person who was behind this front company be so sure about the date by which the contract would be signed to peg millions of dollars to that date? This was in 1986. By June–July 1993, it had become abundantly clear that the person behind this front company was Ottavio Quattrocchi, the long-time representative in Delhi of Snamprogetti, an Italian company, and one whose proximity to Rajiv and Sonia Gandhi was well known. The identity had but to become public that Quattrocchi was allowed to escape on 29 July 1993. Ostensibly, Interpol was approached. It issued a Red-corner notice. In December 2000, Quattrocchi was arrested in Malaysia. In December 2002, India requested that Quattrocchi be extradited. The Malaysian High Court turned down the request on the ground that India did not provide adequate grounds and evidence to substantiate its request. A year and a half passed. In March 2004, the Malaysian Supreme Court rejected India's appeal against the High Court order—the required papers had not been filed in time. In early 2007, Quattrocchi was arrested in Argentina. Three months later, the country's Federal Court rejected India's request that he be extradited. The CBI had not presented the Court order on the basis of which Quattrocchi had been arrested. The Indian government did not appeal this decision in time as the CBI, it was said, could not get the order translated from Spanish! In February 2007, the CBI withdrew all charges against Quattrocchi. The Red-corner notice was withdrawn. The CBI sought permission from our Supreme Court to withdraw the case against him on the ground that repeated attempts to get him extradited had failed. In 2011, the Special Court responsible for handling CBI cases in Delhi discharged Quattrocchi, and others from the case, saying that, while the payments in question were said to be only Rs 64 crore, attempts to prove their involvement and to get them extradited had already cost Rs 250 Cr. . . . Quattrocchi died of a heart attack in July 2013 . . . The same sort of sequence attended the cases that were filed against the others who had been chargesheeted. Each of them died before the cases filed against them could reach anywhere.

The whitewash committee

To make a show of doing something, a Joint Parliamentary Committee (JPC) was set up. Headed by a certified poodle, B. Shankarananda, it was a farce from beginning to end. Even so, it proved useful to us as we had a window into every sitting. My colleague, Surya Prakash, had two good sources in the Committee, one of them an invaluable one—the AIADMK MP, Aladi Aruna. Surya recalls the drill:

> The Committee used to hold its sittings in the Parliament Annexe. The Ministry of Defence had placed all documents pertaining to the deal on tables in the meeting room. I had two good sources in the committee. One of them was Aladi Aruna, MP, who I had known for a long time. We wanted the documents that had been put before the Committee. You suggested that I ask Aladi Aruna. Aruna agreed. We set up a standard drill for every day the committee met. The committee used to adjourn for lunch at 1 p.m. and re-assemble at 3 p.m. Aruna would take the MPs' mini-bus to his residence on Gurdwara Rakabganj Road. I would follow in my car at a safe distance. After he alighted and went in, I would park and walk in. Aruna would open his briefcase and pull out a sheaf of papers he had taken out that day. The office car would be waiting to take the papers to the Sundar Nagar flat[13] for photo-copying and return within an

---

[13] Ramnathji used to stay there.

hour. Aruna would take the papers with him and put them back before the others arrived.[14]

The fealty with which the Committee conducted itself was so shameful as to border on the unbelievable. An instance will suffice. On 6 April 1988, B. Shankarananda told members that a letter had been sent to Bofors on behalf of the Committee to depute two senior representatives to appear before the Committee. He said that there had been 'a positive response', but because of Easter holidays they were not able to come immediately. Members pointed to press reports that the two, Per Ove Morberg, the President of Bofors, and Lars Gothlin, the Chief Jurist of the parent company, Nobel, had already arrived in Delhi to depose before the Committee. Shankarananda said, 'I am officially unaware of their arrival,' adding, 'but they have agreed to appear before the Committee.' For three full days, the two were debriefed by officers from Rajiv's office and the Defence Ministry.

Shankarananda had another gem for the members. He said that on behalf of the Committee, Bofors had been told that they would like to meet Martin Ardbo but that nothing further could be done for the moment as Bofors had replied that Ardbo had left the company, and they did not know either his residential address or his telephone number. Ardbo had been visible as can be in Stockholm: he had been in the premises of Sweden's Parliament following proceedings of *their* Parliamentary Committee.

On 7 April, members were summoned at short notice. K. Parasaran, the Attorney General, 'will address the Committee', members were told. Just a while before the Committee was to meet, members heard—several of them from casual conversations with each other—that instead of Parasaran, the two Swedes would be meeting them. Suddenly, the meeting was preponed—to suit the convenience of 'our honoured guests', Shankarananda explained to the members. He then proceeded to give them a speech about how they must conduct themselves in front of 'our honoured guests'. You must not upset them, he told the members. You must

---

[14] Email, 30 June 2020.

not ask them questions that may give them the impression that we are cross-examining them. You must not ask them questions that may offend them. We must not create circumstances in which they refuse to give information. We are going to persuade them and put such questions that they will be pleased to come out with the true facts rather than withhold facts . . .

Aladi Aruna protested. They had not been given any time to prepare. We should hear Parasaran today and meet these two later. Shankarananda refused. Aladi Aruna persisted. Shankarananda said that he would put the matter to vote. As the majority were from the Congress, they voted to hear the two Swedes.

When the two appeared, the record of the meeting showed, Shankarananda took up most of the time asking inane questions, in particular, ones that would absolve Rajiv. The result was predictable. When a member asked them for the names of middlemen whom Bofors had paid, the two said that they had given these to the government and could not share with the Committee what they had told the government. It was a question of 'customer confidentiality'.

While Morberg and Gothlin were going on and on with their non-answers, S. Jagathrakshakan, leader of the AIADMK in the Lok Sabha, turned to Morberg and said that the company had told the Chairman that Bofors did not know even the address and telephone number of Ardbo. Does this not reflect 'the bad character of your company?' he asked. But we have said nothing of the kind, Morberg replied.

What? Members were taken aback. Aladi addressed Shankarananda, 'You said the opposite.'

'No, Aruna,' Shankarananda said firmly, 'we need not talk about this with Morberg. We can talk among ourselves.'[15]

From a distance, I had to get first-hand experience of the Committee. Rajiv Gandhi had been proclaiming repeatedly:

I have said so on the floor of this House that the minute we have any information, we will take the hardest possible action

---

[15] The preceding is from what I wrote at the time: *Indian Express,* 9 April 1988.

and you will see that action. It will not be hidden, it will not be concealed. It will be there for you to see, it will be there for the country to see. I would also like to reiterate that we are still waiting for the press to give us some information. The press has been saying for over two weeks now, and I forget on what date this whole thing started, it is almost two weeks now: it was around the 16th. The press has been saying, 'We have the information,' but they don't give us the information: even the newspaper today. I am quoting from the same newspaper that has raised the thing. A report just below says, 'The Swedish Radio may come out with some evidence.' I would request them to please come out with some evidence, not 'may come out with some evidence,' because then we can show you, show the Swedish Radio and show the nation and everyone that we mean business and we will chase it right down to the end and take action. We are awaiting information from the press and, well, from the Opposition. If you have it, you please give us, we will take action.[16]

He had repeated the assurance in the Lok Sabha the same day:

Let me just reiterate, we are waiting for information from the Swedish Government. The minute we get information, we will take action and we will show you that we have taken action. We will show the nation that we have taken action. Let me also reiterate once more that the press on numerous occasions have said that they have this information, they have that information. Now we could have gone over, I think I do not know for 10 days or two weeks of this 'We have this and we have that.' We have not got any information from the press except this sort of irresponsible reporting about who has done it. First they said politicians, then they said officers, now they are saying no officers, no politicians, it is somebody else. If the press has

---

[16] Rajiv Gandhi spoke in this refrain on several occasions. This extract is from the Rajya Sabha proceedings of 28 April 1987.

something, for heaven's sake, let them give it to us. We will take action and show you.[17]

Notice, first, that he was shifting the onus of providing evidence on to the Opposition and on to us in the press. There was not the slightest commitment that the government would chase the evidence. But at least there was the commitment that should such evidence be produced by others, the government would take action: ' . . . then we can show you, show the Swedish Radio and show the nation and everyone that we mean business and we will chase it right down to the end and take action.' I happened to be in Stockholm later. I received information about [i] the payments that Bofors had made—they totalled Rs 64 crore, and clearly would have gone on to a multiple of the amount but for the scandal having become public; [ii] the companies to which it had made the payments—Svenska, Moresco, AE Services; [iii] the code names which were used to disguise the payments—for Moresco 'Lotus', 'Tulip', 'Mont Blanc'; [iv] the addresses of the companies—in Panama, the UK, elsewhere; [v] the banks to which the monies had been sent; [vi] the dates on which the monies had been transferred; [vii] the numbers of the accounts into which the money had been transferred; [viii] names of the handler of each account in the respective bank. Each payment was listed separately. The paper carried the dispatch containing all these details on 2 February 1988.

I stressed that the payments were not made suddenly, impulsively. They were made because of written agreements that Bofors had entered into with the go-betweens. They were made in accordance with the schedule that had been written down in the agreements—the amount to be paid as the deal crossed milestone 'X', 'Y', etc. Lars Ringberg, the Swedish Prosecutor, had stated on record that the payments were not made for 'winding up' the agreements—which is what Rajiv and Bofors had begun saying after their lie that no payments had been made at all had crashed—but in accordance with the agreements. Swedish investigators had

---

[17] Lok Sabha proceedings, 28 April 1987.

noted that Bofors had not been able to point to a single, solitary service that any of the go-betweens had provided the company. Furthermore, I listed five authorities in Sweden, in addition to the courts and Bofors, which had the information, authorities from which the government or the JPC could secure it.

The JPC was in session. Aladi Aruna brought the article and the details to the attention of the Committee. Prashant Bhushan was to record the 'action' that the government and the Congress(I)-dominated and controlled Committee took:

> No notice was however taken of Shourie's information by the government or the JPC. The JPC was then in session and was examining Bhatnagar and other members of the negotiating committee on the technical and commercial negotiations with Bofors and Sofma. Aladi Aruna, the AIADMK member of the JPC, suggested the very next day on 3 February 1988, that the JPC should examine Shourie. Shankarananda rejected the suggestion saying that 'it would not be proper to give credibility to unfounded allegations,' and that 'press reports should not detract them from their tasks.' Regarding the proposal to approach Swedish agencies, Shankarananda said that 'unless the agencies were willing to extend cooperation in finding out the truth, there was no point in going there.' Shankarananda chose to forget that Ringberg had been crying himself hoarse that he wanted to cooperate with the Indian investigation but it was Shankarananda himself who had refused to cooperate with him on the ground that the JPC proceedings were confidential.[18]

In a word, every single institution—CBI, Enforcement Directorate and other agencies of government, courts, a committee of Parliament—which could have helped track down the payments and those to whom Bofors had paid, was perverted. The perverting shone through, and damaged Rajiv and his government no end. But there was one other factor which unravelled them completely.

---

[18] Prashant Bhushan, *The Selling of a Nation*, Vision Books, 1990, p. 60.

Rather, there was one other device by which Rajiv unravelled himself and his government completely.

And that is the one thing that stands out in my mind thirty-five years later—the lies.

The thing that undid him

First it was: there have been no middlemen, no payments have been made.

An uncle of mine, a distinguished officer in the Army, gave me two yearly diaries that Win Chadha used to distribute, and his visiting card. These explicitly mentioned that Chadha and his company, Anatronics, were the representative of Bofors in India. We printed these, and our reporters and photographer went to the office that had been mentioned.

This became the routine. Government would put out a lie. We would nail it. Government would just move on to the next lie . . .

You will recall that it was on 16 April 1987 that Swedish Radio broadcast that money had been paid to bag the howitzer gun contract from India. On 20 April, Rajiv told Parliament that he had personally specified to Olof Palme, who had, of course, died a year earlier, the conditions on which India would give the contract to the Swedish firm: that compared to the competitors, the gun must be the best technically, that it must cost the least, and 'I must get a firm answer from the Swedish Prime Minister that no middlemen were involved. I got confirmation [please note the word] back from Prime Minister Palme that there will be no middlemen or agents involved . . .' 'When a Prime Minister of the country assures us,' he continued, 'after having gone into great depth [note the words again] that there are no middlemen or agents [please note the words again] we have to accept his word.' He added: 'We have been assured by the Swedish Government that there is no agent who had been involved. We have got a telex from the Swedish Government saying that they had checked up [please note the words again] and on the basis of that they have said, "No".'

On 27 April, Rajiv met the Army Commanders. The official account of his speech to them said:

> The Prime Minister pointed out that the negotiations and purchase of 155 mm Swedish Howitzers were meticulously handled. He reiterated that he had made it clear to the Swedish Prime Minister, Mr. Olof Palme, that there should be no middlemen, the guns should be good and the prices reasonable. Sweden had confirmed that there was no middleman and no money was paid in Swiss Banks . . .

The minister for foreign trade in Sweden was asked about all this. 'The Government had made no inquiry,' the minister said, 'and the Government is not a police institution.' The Swedish Prime Minister was asked about the 'guarantee', he was asked about the results of 'inquiries'. 'I cannot guarantee,' he said, 'that Bofors has not used bribes in Switzerland, India or somewhere else in this affair.'

The Press Secretary of the Swedish Prime Minister was even more specific:

> The Indian Prime Minister had called the Swedish Prime Minister a few days ago and the Swedish Prime Minister made no such guarantees or assurance in that telephone call. It was a very short courtesy call. There were no questions asked about this matter. There have been no other direct contacts between the Prime Ministers on this matter.

Confronted with these statements in Parliament, Rajiv embellished the lie. 'When I said "Sweden had confirmed,"' he said, 'I hadn't meant the present Prime Minister but the previous one, Olof Palme'—who was, of course, long dead.

But how could Palme have confirmed 'there was no middleman and no money was paid in Swiss Banks', when these things had happened after his death? Rajiv was asked on 29 April.

'Now,' he reiterated, in the face of what the Swedes had explicitly said, 'this was confirmed to me by the Swedish

Government in part,' and then added a new source, 'and Bofors in part.'

Our policy is 'no middlemen', there were no middleman

The 'no middleman' assertion was itself a red herring. The absence of a middleman, for instance, was perfectly consistent with money being paid and received directly by politicians, their relatives or officials. And middlemen come in many guises: the real fixers don't go in for formal registration in any case; the 'middleman' may be not 'an agent' but 'a fixer', 'an intermediary', 'a representative', or none of these but, as Win Chadha as well as Bofors were to claim later, 'a consultant'. And the 'confirmation' by Bofors that it had not paid money to any official, etc., was perfectly consistent with it paying a subcontractor or 'consultant' and 'not caring' what the latter did with the money. This was obvious, and yet the 'Because-it-has-been-our-policy-therefore-it-is-a-fact' became the standard refutation on this deal, on HDW, and on so much else. The seemingly clinical speech of the then Minister of State for Defence, Arun Singh, in Parliament on 16 April was typical:

> I wish to categorically state before this House that the Department of Defence of the Government of India has not appointed any agent authorised to act on its behalf in respect of any defence contract.

That was just knocking a strawman down. The question was not at all about the Government of India having appointed and authorized an agent. Next came the 'our-intention-therefore-fact':

> On assuming office, the Prime Minister reiterated the existing instructions that the Department of Defence should not deal with any non-governmental agent of a foreign supplier in respect of any commercial negotiations. The Prime Minister also directed that foreign governments and suppliers should be told unequivocally about the decision. This policy directive has

been enforced rigorously by the Department of Defence with satisfactory results.

Rajiv was even more emphatic. 'On no occasion between 1980 and 1987,' he told the Rajya Sabha on 20 April 1987, 'has the Department of Defence ever dealt with any non-governmental agent, foreign or Indian, in any commercial negotiation.'

The existence or absence of an agent, we saw, was a red herring. But even on the point of fact, the assertions of Rajiv and Arun Singh were false. As I mentioned, for years, Win Chadha had been distributing his calling cards and diaries in which he described his firm as the representative of Bofors in India. Not just with him, the Defence Department had been routinely dealing with a host of agents of arms suppliers. Nor was this a secret. Just a while earlier, for instance, *India Today* had devoted its cover story to middlemen, 'The hidden persuaders', who were steering contracts and deals.[19] Among other facts, it had listed the names of several arms intermediaries, their companies, the foreign arms suppliers on behalf of whom they were lobbying, and the types of weapons for which they were striving. These firms, and the men behind them, were well-known figures in Delhi, with many a retired officer from the Defence Forces on their payrolls. They entertained freely and lavishly. They moved in and out of ministries freely and openly. Their operations were public knowledge.

Bofors itself was to express surprise over this claim of the government in an unguarded moment. Asked by a member of the Joint Parliamentary Committee on 18 September 1987 whether Win Chadha and his Anatronics General Corporation had been acting as agents of Bofors in years preceding their 'termination' in 1986, the company's Chief Jurist, exclaimed, 'I don't quite understand the question because up to the situation when your Prime Minister talked to our Prime Minister saying that no agents are to be allowed in this contract, it was completely legitimate to have Anatronics Corporation as an agent in India.'

---

[19] *India Today,* 15 September 1986.

But, 'On no occasion between 1980 and 1987', it was. As the weeks flew past, one thing after another revealed that, in this deal itself, various go-betweens had been shuttling between government and Bofors—Win Chadha, the Hindujas, Ottavio Quattrocchi behind the curtain of 'AE Services'. The final blow to this 'no middleman' chorus was delivered by the publication of the entry for 2 July 1987 in Ardbo's diary. In this he had recorded in Geneva: '. . . Myles Scott [the legal representative of AE Services in Geneva and one of its Directors], Bob [i.e., Bob Wilson, the frontman in AE Services] had talked with Gandhi Trust lawyer.' But that was in November 1989. Much was to come out before that.

'Everyone believes Olof Palme, therefore everyone must believe what we say he said to us'

K.C. Pant had replaced V.P. Singh as Defence Minister upon the latter having been sacked for ordering an inquiry into the purchase of HDW submarines. In a typical presentation, he told the Lok Sabha:

> Sir, many hon. Members have referred to what the Swedish Radio had said, what a single correspondent has said, and so on. And there has been a tendency to ignore what the Swedish Government has said. There has been a tendency to slur over the fact that a man of the stature of Olof Palme gave a solemn assurance. Can you slur over this fact? Is it reasonable or is it right to simply ignore them and put all your emphasis on one small aspect of this case? You balance the two. It is for you to balance and see whether it is right to put this one Radio in the balance against Olof Palme and the Swedish Government, not to speak of our own Government . . .
>
> Therefore Olof Palme's credibility in this House is, I hope, unquestioned on all sides, I take it. If anybody questions it, I would like to know now. This is the time to question it. Now. Therefore, once you do not question that, one of the problems is removed. Once you say you accept his assurances and when you

accept his assurances, one of the major problems of this debate
is removed . . .

Notice that Palme was depicted as having given 'a solemn assurance'.

On 21 April, in the Rajya Sabha, with uncustomary flourish and
to loud cheering from the Congress benches, Arun Singh produced
a letter the government had received from the Undersecretary of
Foreign Trade in Sweden as conclusive proof. Arun Singh told
the House, 'The company informed the Swedish government
representative in autumn 1985 that there would be no middleman
involved and that they would deal directly with the Indian Defence
Ministry,' the Swedish Undersecretary said, adding, 'this was
conveyed by Olof Palme in his personal conversation with Rajiv
Gandhi in January 1986.'

The letter represented Palme as having merely 'conveyed' what
Bofors had said, but it was presented as proof positive of Palme
having 'guaranteed' and given a 'personal', a 'solemn assurance'.

And Arun Singh did what was to become standard practice
from then on: he flaunted a certificate from Bofors as proof. The
government had been told by Bofors on 10 March 1986, he told
Parliament, that they did not employ an agent or representative in
India: this in spite of the fact that throughout the negotiations, Win
Chadha had been participating in the discussions, in preparing the
bids, etc., and the house journal of Bofors itself had published
photographs of him working along with the company's officials
on the contract and bids!

Replying to the discussion, Arun Singh zeroed in on what he
said was 'the first question', 'the fundamental question'—namely,
whether anything had been paid. The government, he said, had
categorically told both the Swedish government, as well as Bofors,
that nothing should be paid. If something had, nevertheless, been
paid, 'There must be something wrong with the payment,' and
that, 'we as Government, if we find that something has been paid
will definitely pursue each of these questions: What? To whom?
And why?'

And then he went on to add the crucial bit:

In our opinion, as a Government we have received a commitment both from the company and from the Swedish Government that nothing has been paid. In fact, it was a commitment that nothing was payable, because the commitment was received before the contract was signed. So we received a commitment that nothing was payable.

The 'commitment' that 'nothing is payable' had become the 'commitment that 'nothing *has* been paid'. And the '*In our opinion* we have received a commitment . . .' was soon forgotten.

The government is absolutely clear and determined about what it will do, should it discover that its conditions have been violated, Parliament was told. Rajiv told the Rajya Sabha, on 20 April 1987:

We have made it very clear that no middlemen or agents are to be involved. We have made it very clear that if we discover at a later stage, the severest action will be taken against those companies who violate this rule up to the extent of blacklisting them and not dealing with them in the future. We have made this clear at the negotiating level, we have made it clear government to government, in some cases, we have made it clear Head of Government to the Head of Government. We have not let this be at any point; our stand is very, very clear. We are only interested in one thing and that is to see that such middlemen and agents are cut out of this and the benefits from this, the benefits that flow from this cutting out of agents, flow directly to the Government and to nobody else. In our negotiations we have made it clear that the price must be reduced by the equivalent amount that these agents were to have been paid.

Please remember this bit, the last sentence, and contrast it with what actually happened when Arun Singh, by that time out of the government, said that this is exactly what should be done. Rajiv continued:

We have fought for lower prices and, perhaps, specially during these last two years, the way we have negotiated Defence contracts, we have never negotiated in our Defence contracts before. Perhaps, no other country in the world has taken such a tough stand. The reduction in prices that we have got are unimaginable.

Within months, evidence was to establish, not just in private to government but in the open to the people at large, that Bofors had violated the 'guarantee'. They themselves gave to government, on 16–17 September 1987, the names of the front companies into whose accounts in Switzerland they had paid huge sums. The government never returned to its minatory statements about disqualifying the company, not even to retrieving the money from the company.

'Winding up'

When it could no longer maintain that nothing had been paid, the government began saying that the payments were made to 'wind up' the agreements that Bofors had earlier entered into with the agents. In the paper, we published the agreement between Win Chadha and Bofors. That showed this new assertion to be just as false. The agreement was signed on 3 January 1986. On the government's assertions, it was cancelled before 23 March 1986, the date on which the contract with Bofors was signed. In fact, the agreement provided that it was valid in the first instance till 31 December 1990. That there had been no subsequent, retrospective cancellation became evident from the writ that Chadha filed in the Delhi High Court: his complaint, in essence, was that by freezing his account because of the clamour of his rivals and others, the government was preventing him from providing Bofors the services that he was obliged by this agreement to provide.

The agreement and the writ showed that Chadha had not been asked to 'wind up'. Second, even if he had been asked to do so, it was clear from the agreement that he could not have been paid the astronomical sums that had been disbursed by Bofors. The agreement contained no penalty clause for cancellation. In fact, the onus of living up to its provisions was all on Chadha, not on Bofors. The agreement obliged Bofors to pay Chadha Rs 2 lakh a month in lieu of the work he was to do. For the entire five-year period for which the agreement was valid, the total would come to Rs 1.2 crore. Which fool—to say nothing of one of the most experienced arms manufacturers in the world—would pay an amount between Rs 35 crore and Rs 64 crore for the privilege of not using services, which, if used, would have cost him only Rs 1.2 crore?

Worse, it was soon established that, while Bofors had acknowledged that it was told in October 1985 to eliminate middlemen, it had entered into an agreement in November 1985 with AE Services, specifically for help in bagging the contract. When Bofors produced a self-serving document later showing that this agreement had, in fact, been terminated in January 1986, it was quickly established to be an inept forgery. The termination document, said to have been signed in January 1986, it turned out, had anticipated the precise date in March 1986 by which the company would bag the contract! Later still, it was established that the payments to AE Services were being made in 1986, in accordance with an agreement subsisting at the time! The Prosecutor's Office in Sweden confirmed to me that not one shred of paper in the thousands they had examined, or in the ones that Bofors had submitted, showed any evidence that any one of the companies had provided any service at all to Bofors. The office also confirmed that, in spite of hours and hours of questioning, no one from Bofors was able to point out a single service that any of the so-called companies had provided in relation to the contract.

Excuses

Investigating agencies were sent to chase wild geese. The obvious thing—asking the Swiss about the payments that had been made into Swiss banks—was not done on transparent pretexts: that a Memorandum of Understanding needed to be signed, that the Criminal Procedure Code had to be amended. Eventually, a request was made in a form and on a ground that the Swiss were bound under their laws to turn down. The person at hand—

Win Chadha—was allowed to flee. He was then declared to be untraceable. But soon enough, it was established that he had not just been in regular touch with but had actually been visiting the Indian Consulate in New York.

The Public Prosecutor's lament, and the principal investigator's

The Swedes were blamed for not cooperating and disclosing information. In fact, Lars Ringberg, the Public Prosecutor, had had to close his inquiry precisely because the 'aggrieved party'—which he, in his formalistic way, had taken to be the Indian government—was not even responding to his requests to cooperate and exchange information. He publicly expressed his distress about this lack of even elementary cooperation. It was later to transpire that ministers of the Swedish government also had urged him not to pursue the matter. They were rapped for this by the Constitutional Committee of Sweden's Parliament. Sten Lindstrom, the principal investigator whom we encountered at the outset, had a similar lament. He told Chitra Subramaniam,

> After the LR [Letter Rogatory] was lodged in Switzerland, I was waiting for the official track with India and Switzerland to begin. It never did. Whenever the public prosecutor Ekblom and I heard of any Indian visits to Stockholm, we would speak to the media expressing our desire to meet them. Can you imagine a situation where no one from India met the real investigators of the gun deal? That was when we saw the extent to which everyone was compromised. Many politicians who had come to my office claiming they would move heaven and earth to get at the truth if they came to power, fell silent when they held very important positions directly linked to the deal.

Even while closing the inquiry, however, Ringberg established two vital facts. The payments, for which proof was on hand, were not Rs 35 crore to Rs 50 crore as had been discovered by the National Audit Bureau. They were Rs 64 crore. Next, Bofors was not able to indicate any service at all in recompense for which these payments had been made.

A *new reason*

Rajiv had a new reason for feigning unconcern. Whatever their purpose, he said in early November 1987, the payments had not, in any case, been made to Indians, and that if Bofors had chosen to pay some foreigners, it was really not at any business of ours. This is how he put his unconcern to the Independent Television Network of the UK:

> We believe that no Indian has been paid. In this we have been assured that no Indian has been paid. I am talking about the Bofors business. We have been assured that no Indian has been paid on this. We hope that we will be able to track down whoever has taken any money on this. But the feeling that I get is that we are not going to find any Indians. There may be others and . . .

He was interrupted and asked, 'Foreigners?' 'Perhaps,' he answered, and added, 'that is really not our business if somebody else has done it . . .' Toeing this line, the JPC declared towards the end of April 1988:

> There is no evidence to show that any middleman was involved in the process of the acquisition of the Bofors gun. There is also no evidence to substantiate the allegation of commissions or bribes having been paid to anyone. Therefore the question of payments to any Indian or Indian company, whether resident in India or not, does not arise, especially as no evidence to the contrary is forthcoming from any quarter.

Replying to the debate in the Lok Sabha on 5 May on the JPC report, K.C. Pant endorsed the contention of Bofors that it had had some consultancy agreements which it had terminated because of the government's insistence that there be no middleman.

'No evidence has so far emerged,' he said, 'to contradict the Bofors version.'

The Hindu published documents which left nothing of such assertions.

Rajiv finds 'confirmation'

The surge of public opinion forced the Swedish government— which Rajiv had been telling everyone had already inquired into the matter—to inquire into the matter. The latter asked its National Audit Bureau to look into it. Bofors promised to cooperate. And then reneged on the promise, saying they would not breach 'customer confidentiality'. Even so, the National Audit Bureau came to devastating conclusions.

The Bureau said that evidence on hand showed that Rs 35 crore to Rs 50 crore had been paid by Bofors to an agent; that, in addition to and apart from this, 'considerable sums' had been paid to this agent and to 'some others' as 'commissions'. It concluded in terms 'that an agreement exists between AB Bofors and . . . concerning settlement of commission subsequent to the FH 77 deal'—the names had been redacted from the version that was released.

The Bureau's report also established how totally untruthful the word of Bofors was. The Bureau listed the assertion of Bofors that no payment had been made in connection with the deal, and then pointed out that this assertion was falsified by the letter that Bofors itself had written to the Indian Ambassador on 25 April 1987. In that letter, the Audit Bureau said '. . . AB Bofors . . . has verified that payments had been made during the specified period and furthermore confirmed that they were related to the FH 77 deal but concerned payment to a Swiss company.'

At first, the Audit Bureau recorded, Bofors said it had no agent at all. Then, the Bureau recorded, it acknowledged that it had engaged Win Chadha's Anatronics General Corporation 'for administrative services'. (The phrase was of Bofors, not the Audit Bureau's. The government's propagandists—including friendly newspapers and their editors—made out that it was the Audit Bureau's conclusion!)

The Bureau said that Bofors informed it that the costs of this 'service' (the sceptical quotation marks were of the Bureau) 'amount to about SEK 100,000 per month'. The 'amount' that had to be paid had been referred to in the present continuous and not in the past tense. But that was the minor point. As we saw earlier, the explanation was belied by the amounts. At the time, a Swedish Kroner was equivalent to about two rupees. According to what Bofors told the Audit Bureau, therefore, Bofors had been paying Win Chadha around Rs 2 lakh a month. Now, if we assumed that Chadha was its agent from the beginning of 1977 to the end of 1985 (anything earlier or later would have gone against the dates Rajiv Gandhi had been giving), the total Bofors should have paid its agent was around Rs 2 crore and 16 lakh. But, as the Audit Bureau pointed out, in fact, Bofors had paid him and/or others something between Rs 35 crore and Rs 50 crore!

If the services, when availed of, were worth no more than Rs 2 lakh a month, which company would pay Rs 35 crore to Rs 50 crore so as not to use them in the future? And what were these services? Handling local telex messages, making hotel and airline reservations, etc., according to what the Minister of State for Defence told Parliament!

Unable to deny the evidence of payments, Bofors next asserted that the amounts represented 'the reimbursement of consultant services within the areas of marketing and counter-purchasing', and that these were made to a 'Swiss company'.

The Audit Bureau punctured this claim also. It said that, while there was indeed an agreement for 'counter-purchasing', on the admission of Bofors itself, 'no such counter-purchasing had taken place to date'.

There was a further, and much graver problem that this explanation of Bofors raised. Indeed, in its anxiety to explain away the payments, Bofors had let the fatal hint slip out. It had said, and the Indian government had been saying, that the two had negotiated directly, that there had been no third parties, no middlemen, etc. How come, then, that there was, in fact, an agreement—a separate and distinct one—for some undefined 'counter-purchasing' with someone else? Not just with 'someone else', but, on the statement of Bofors itself, with a 'Swiss company'. What was a 'Swiss company' doing in the midst of a direct, exclusive agreement between Bofors and the Indian government?

'We are vindicated'

The moment the report of the National Audit Bureau was released, Rajiv claimed that the findings of the National Audit Bureau bore out what he and his colleagues had been saying!

'We feel that to a great extent the Swedish Government's report has vindicated what we have said,' he told Aroon Purie and Prabhu Chawla of *India Today*. 'We had said that no middlemen were to be kept and it has been confirmed that there were no middlemen at the point of signing the contract.'

The tail was new: 'there were no middlemen *at the point of signing the contract*.' So that if there were some till just a moment before the contract was initialled, Rajiv Gandhi would still be technically correct.

Or was the fig leaf in the words 'to a great extent', so that whatever was shown to contradict what the government had been saying could be waved away as being of the lesser extent?

What about the payments which had now been documented? 'Now,' he said, 'unfortunately they have paid two per cent to three per cent in the winding up of an earlier middleman appointed in 1977.'

And an explanation struck him that had not struck Bofors itself. Aroon and Prabhu asked him, 'Do you think that a payment of Rs 50 crore means that it is not purely an agent's commission, that there were other payoffs?'

'Let me tell you,' he told them, 'what I feel has happened. Whoever signed the agent's contract in 1977, must have signed for some absurdly high figure, and that is why the winding up has cost two per cent.' Even Bofors had not claimed that high a level of absurdity.

If the agent had been dispensed with before the contract was signed—i.e., before March 1986—Rajiv Gandhi was asked in the interview, did he not find it strange that the payments were made six months later, i.e., in November and December 1986?

'I don't see that as a complication,' said Rajiv Gandhi, 'because a part of the payment for cancellation would come as part of their agent's contract'—whatever that meant.

Rajiv feigned injury: 'We did feel a little upset that they [the Swedish government] have gone and deleted half the things in the inquiry. Well, not half, but the critical things which could have helped us.'

Questioned in the hearings of their Constitutional Committee, the Swedish government revealed that the Indian government had been entirely satisfied with what they had received and had never asked for more! And recall the laments that we have come across earlier of both the Public Prosecutor and the principal investigator—about the absence of even elementary cooperation of the Indian authorities, indeed, of even minimal interest.

In his anxiety to claim credit for what could no longer be denied—the existence of the agent—Rajiv torpedoed what he and his colleagues had been saying till then. They had told Parliament just weeks earlier, 'On no occasion between 1980 and 1987 has the Department of Defence ever dealt with any non-governmental agent, foreign or Indian, in any commercial negotiation.' Now— 14 June 1987—he told the *Navbharat Times,* one of his stout propagandists at the time, 'In the report of the Swedish Government that has come, they have said that this large expenditure that was incurred took place in cancelling the middleman.'

The report had most emphatically not said this. 'This means that a middleman was there who was cancelled at our asking. When we go into the history of this, then it is found that [he was] possibly appointed in 77 . . .'

Rajiv finds 'confirmation'—yet again!

The Hindu published documents that knocked the bottom out of the 'no payments', 'no middlemen' chorus. Rajiv's reaction was as astonishing as it was typical. The documents, he told newsmen on 25 June 1988, 'corroborate the findings of the JPC'. And, 'They confirm that no politician is involved in the pay-off.' Furthermore, he said, there is nothing new in them. 'To the best of my knowledge,' he said, 'all the papers published in *The Hindu* were examined by the Chief Swedish Prosecutor, Mr. Lars Ringberg, who came to the conclusion that no bribe or commission was paid and only winding up charges were paid. We have no reason to disbelieve the findings of the Swedish Prosecutor who is an independent agency.'

But no one agreed that there was nothing new in the documents. Soon enough, therefore, Rajiv shifted ground. There are doubts about their authenticity, he and his colleagues now began saying. 'If I remember correctly,' he told Aveek Sarkar and Vir Sanghvi of *Sunday* in November 1988, 'these documents are said by the Swedish Bank to have some defects in them. There are some doubts about their authenticity.' It wasn't just that this was at variance with what he had said earlier; that there was nothing new in the documents as they were the ones Ringberg had examined. It wasn't just that neither the 'Swedish Bank' nor the Swedish Prosecutor had ever entertained any doubt about the documents—and this was immediately reconfirmed for the record by asking them again. It was that within days of their publication, Rajiv's fixer-sleuth, Mohan Katre, the then Director of the CBI, had confirmed their authenticity and, as was established by what he told N. Ram at that very time, he had informed Rajiv that the documents were authentic. Nonetheless, 'there are doubts about them' was to become one of the continuing refrains of Rajiv and his colleagues.

Somersault

But Rajiv went further. Speaking to reporters at the Bangalore airport on 10 November 1988, he asserted that all that the invoices, etc., showed was that commissions had been paid by Bofors. But that was of no consequence as, he said, the government had never maintained that commissions had not been paid!

This was just indefensible. So, the very next day the government denied he had said this. Only to have the Bangalore Reporters Guild issue a statement affirming that Rajiv had said exactly what had been attributed to him. Should anyone have any doubts, a tape recording is at hand, the Guild said. The government did not controvert the Reporters Guild.

Yet another invention

In any event, Rajiv by now had yet another explanation of the payments, yet another reason why Bofors could not be faulted for having made them. 'The question is to whom and for what [the amount was paid],' he told *Sunday* in November 1988. 'If it was paid for some genuine work done for Bofors, then we cannot question them.' Aveek Sarkar and Vir Sanghvi reminded Rajiv that Bofors had all along been forbidden from having any middlemen. 'So there could be no genuine work they were paid for,' they said. 'No, not genuine work in terms of middlemen,' said Rajiv. 'Genuine work gathering information about the French weapon, for example. That is industrial espionage,' said the Prime Minister of India. 'You can't grudge them for that.'

Apart from the question whether Bofors would have been right to use Indian public funds to pay persons conducting 'industrial espionage' for it, Ringberg's staff had already questioned officials of Bofors at great length on the point, and the latter had, as I mentioned above, been unable to point to a single service which the recipients of the money had performed for them.

The legal luminary

Rajiv was in the forefront of floating such inventions. His subordinates strove hard to do their bit for the cause. Shiv Shankar, who passed those days for a legal luminary of Rajiv's government, had an altogether novel explanation when the payments could no longer be denied. Speaking on the Joint Parliamentary Committee's report in the Rajya Sabha on 4–5 May 1988, he put forward a new, and absolutely original thesis:

> Nonetheless, the fact remains that 319 million Kroners has
> been paid—I am not saying that. Very rightly they have said
> and I agree with them that these companies seem to be hollow
> companies. Is it not a case? Are we not aware that in many
> companies in this country also, the directors themselves keep
> back the money? . . . This is a fact. These are all hollow
> companies; the money is transferred through them, if they want
> to divert some of the money for themselves or for whomsoever it
> may be . . . I agree that these three companies seem to be totally
> hollow companies. If they had paid money, I am sure, it must
> have been ploughed back to the directors which happens in this
> country day in and day out. This is what the directors have been
> doing . . .

And yet these were the very persons—the 'Directors', the President,
the Vice Presidents, the Chief Jurist—whose certificates of good
conduct Rajiv and his entourage had been flaunting. In any case,
this explanation was suicidal: for even the reluctant Swedes would
have to act if there was reason to believe that Swedish nationals
had siphoned off some of the money. In fact, that was exactly the
ground Ringberg's officers had been looking for to continue the
investigation. The invention was therefore allowed to sink swiftly.

The inventive explanations were accompanied by inventive
logic. P. Chidambaram told the Lok Sabha on 25 July 1989 that
Svenska was a front company of Win Chadha's; on this basis,
the government had sent a formal request to Switzerland for
assistance; the Swiss had rejected the request. 'In the absence
of any information or assistance from the Swiss authorities,' he
concluded, 'on the basis of other inquiries conducted so far by
the CBI into the Svenska account [the CBI had, in fact, indicated
that they had not been able to make headway in regard to the
account], a tentative conclusion has been arrived at that no Indian
or legal entity appears to be the beneficiary of the payments made
into the Svenska account.'

The next day, K.C. Pant had an even better reason on why
importance should not be attached to the devastating report of the
Comptroller and Auditor General of India. 'Look at the sheer size

of the reports,' he told Parliament. 'The JPC report runs into 240 pages with hundreds of other pages of information. It deals with all aspects. C and AG's report is an 18 pages report that does not deal with the entire matter.' QED.

The people were not convinced: in the elections, Rajiv's 410-odd MPs were reduced to 190. But even after the elections, the conduct on the issue remained just as telling. Every setback—for instance, the Geneva Court's order asking the government to revise the Letter Rogatory—was greeted as a triumph. Every advance—for instance, the mistake of the same court by which the names of two of the beneficiaries who had objected to disclosure of documents by the banks, that is S.P. Hinduja and Jubilee Investments, became known—with dismay.

And all pretence was shed in procuring the notorious order from Justice M.K. Chawla of the Delhi High Court and then using it to stop the case in the Geneva Court.

Only orally?

Even in July and August 1987, the government blew to bits its cover-up about the cancellation of the visit of the Bofors delegation. In a chat with T.C.A. Srinivasa Raghavan of *Indian Express* on 20 July 1987, Rajiv Gandhi inadvertently acknowledged that yes, Bofors had indeed offered to send the delegation, and that the government had asked them not to do so. 'Nothing would have been gained from it,' he explained, 'as they had not been prepared to give any details.' A few days later, he added a new detail. Bofors is not prepared to give any details; it is not prepared to give anything in writing, he told newsmen in Madras on 2 August 1987. 'Bofors is not prepared to reveal anything and there is no use talking to people who just don't want to talk,' he declared.

On 12 August 1987, Shivraj Patil, the replacement for Arun Singh, stuck to this line in the Rajya Sabha on the cancellation of the visit. 'Now we had asked for certain information,' he told the House,

and the information we had asked for is about the commissions paid [by now the expression had changed—'commissions', not 'winding up charges'] which has been mentioned in the Audit Report. We wanted to know who is the recipient of the commissions. That is the information we wanted. When we found that the information was not coming to us in writing but they wanted to convey that information orally, we thought it is not wise to have it at that point of time. At that point of time we were thinking of constituting this committee [the Joint Parliamentary Committee].

It was an idiotic stance, and brought to sharp attention the fact that Rajiv himself had relied on this alibi ten days earlier in Madras. What was wrong with receiving information which was given orally? Did the government not routinely act on oral information in regard to economic and other crimes, in regard to intelligence about terrorism and so much else? Rajiv, however, did not catch the point. Emerging out of an investiture ceremony at the Rashtrapati Bhavan, he told reporters, 'Bofors was willing to tell us something orally but not in writing in view of what they call the secrecy clause. What is the use of telling us something orally? It is no use to us.'

You mean the company was willing to violate 'the secrecy clause' orally but not in writing?

It was then that the absurdity struck the government. Shivraj Patil was packed off to the Rajya Sabha to make another 'suo moto' statement 'clarifying' what he had told the House two days earlier, though that was just what the Prime Minister had said in Madras ten days earlier, and what he, that is the Prime Minister, had just reiterated at the Rashtrapati Bhavan. 'Sir,' Shivraj Patil, told the House,

while speaking in this House on 12 August, on the motion for the constitution of the JPC, in response to the questions raised by some member I had endeavoured to clarify the circumstances relating to the visit of Mr Bredin, Vice President of Bofors on 3 July, 1987. Some misunderstanding seems to have been created in some quarters in regard to my aforesaid statement. The fact of the matter is that Mr. Bredin did not give a convincing indication that a delegation from Bofors would be prepared to give information required by us *in writing or verbally*. This is borne out by the totality of my observations on this point on 12 August, 1987 and this should set at rest all doubts.

It only confirmed the doubts! Three days later, the PMO, too, issued its own 'clarification'. Repudiating what had been said in the hearing of scores of reporters by Rajiv at the Rashtrapati Bhavan, the PMO said,

> The PM, clarifying certain aspects of the matter had stated that Bofors had not offered to give orally the information required by us. He added that there was no indication at any time that Bofors were prepared to give oral information about names of recipients and the amount paid to them. Any other information given orally or otherwise was of no use to the Government. In reply to a question whether the names of the recipients and account numbers had been deleted from the report of the Audit Bureau, he wondered why such a presumption should be made. He said that the report might also have contained information about banking and financial transactions which might have been deleted because of the Swedish law.

The latter, too, turned out not to be the case: as was evident from the context even at that time, the names and particulars of the recipient companies were the things that had been withheld.

And what happened just a month later? As we have seen, the President and Chief Jurist of Bofors did come to Delhi, ostensibly to testify before the JPC. For three days, they remained closeted not with this committee but with officials of the PMO and the Defence Ministry who were helping cover up the facts. In any event, they did give the names of the three front companies to the government at these meetings. How? We gave them orally, they told the JPC. But, as had so obviously been arranged, they insisted that, while they had given the names to government, they would not give them to the Committee of Parliament. The Committee got the names only later, by which time, as was established by N.

Ram and his colleagues subsequently, government and Bofors had, among other things, manufactured a decoy—'Moineau'—to hide the transactions that had taken place under the label, 'Moresco'.

'Customer confidentiality'

In public, even at this stage, the refrain was the familiar one. What can we do? the government asked. The Press and Radio are not giving us information. Bofors is not giving us information.

Why are you not giving the names? Bofors was asked repeatedly. Because of our centuries-old commitment to 'the principle of customer confidentiality'—that was the company's stock answer.

It was manifest nonsense, of course. The 'principle' could not be used, certainly not under Indian law, to hide criminal conduct. In any case, the 'customer' was the Government of India. And that 'customer' was on record any number of times asking for the names.

But with 410 MPs to shout down the Opposition, with so much of the press available to take up and run with these 'explanations', even such manifest nonsense was enough to block all inquiry.

'Global commissions'

First, as we have seen, the line was, 'Sweden has confirmed that there was no middleman, no payments to Swiss banks,' that they have confirmed this after an inquiry, that they have sent a telex to this effect. Then, when the payments could not be denied, they were said to be for 'administrative services', for 'practical assistance', for 'booking hotel rooms and airline tickets, for handling telexes', etc. Rs 35 crore to Rs 50 crore to Rs 64 crore for these services? As this was wholly implausible, Bofors, and the government, switched to saying that the payments were for 'counter-purchasing'. That too could not hold as no 'counter-purchases' had taken place. In mid-June 1987, therefore, Rajiv came up with yet another explanation. The payments which the

Swedish Audit Bureau had established, he now said, were 'in respect of the agent's global commissions and may not have had anything to do with the Bofors deal itself'. But the Bureau had disclosed that the payments were pegged at being a specific per cent of the value of this particular contract, he was told. He had an explanation for that too. Sweden's National Audit Bureau had arrived at the 3 per cent figure, he said, 'not because it had evidence about this, but as it corresponded to the payment that could not be explained by Bofors'. The new explanation, once again an explanation that Bofors in all the months that it had been besieged on this matter had not yet chanced upon, compounded the problems.

It was in flat contradiction of Rajiv Gandhi's earlier explanations, to begin with. Moreover, if the payments were 'global commissions', unrelated to the Indian contract, India was, in effect, paying someone for services that had nothing to do with India, services that the agents had rendered to a foreign company in some foreign country. If this was what Bofors was doing—i.e., paying agents working for contracts in one country out of the proceeds of contracts in another country, a practice that would certainly be good camouflage—had the government verified whether Bofors had rewarded those who helped it bag the contract in India out of the proceeds of some contract elsewhere? On the other hand, if the agent was indeed one who Bofors—itself a giant arms supplier—found useful for services on a 'global' scale, it certainly could not be mere Win Chadha. Who, then, was the agent who could operate on such a scale? Most important: the report of the National Audit Bureau had stated emphatically, and more than once, that the payments by Bofors were directly related to the howitzer deal. 'However,' the report had said, once again pinpointing contradictions in the Bofors account, 'in its letter to the Indian Ambassador of April 25, 1987, AB Bofors, as may be seen above, have certified that payments had been made during the specified period and furthermore confirmed that they were related to the FH 77 deal but concerned payment to a Swiss company.' The Audit Bureau had gone on to state, 'An agreement exists between Bofors and . . . concerning the settlement of commission subsequently to the FH 77 deal and that considerable amounts have been paid subsequently to, among others, AB Bofors previous agent in India.'

How did all this square with 'global commissions for services other than one relating to this deal', services rendered in some other country'? Yet, the invention was soon adopted by Bofors. Towards mid-August 1987, the government produced as conclusive proof a letter from Bofors saying that it had 'terminated international consultancy agreements signed long before the commencement of the Howitzer contract negotiations'. The payments, which had since been discovered, and which, of course, it had earlier sworn it had never made, it said were made for 'winding up these international consultancy agreements'. It emphasized that these termination costs were not paid to 'any Indian citizen or Indian company, consequently including any member of the Indian government and any other government official. The termination payments had nothing to do with the howitzer contract, it emphasized.

But this mixing of the 'winding-up charges' theory with the 'cancellation of international consultancies' theory caused problems of its own.

Why would they terminate the agreement they had with someone somewhere else in the world, with someone who had nothing to do with the howitzer deal, who wasn't even an Indian, when all that the Indian government had required of them was that they should not have any middleman in dealing with it, in regard to the howitzer deal?

How come the payments suddenly turned out to be for not using international consultancy services? Thus far, for instance, in the written explanations that Bofors had given to the Audit Bureau, Bofors had been maintaining that the payments were for the privilege of not using the famous 'administrative services' within India—the handling of telexes, the making of hotel reservations—and for the 'counter-purchases' by Sweden in India that did not materialize. There was not a word about these explanations in the latest letter, just as there had not been a word about 'international consultancy' in the earlier ones.

Another Chairman, another blow

Even as this new letter was turning out to be another boomerang, Lars Thunholm, the Chairman of Nobel Industries, the parent company of Bofors, complicated the matter. Interviewed by Swedish Radio, he disclosed that the 'winding-up' charges had been paid in the manner in which the agents had demanded they be paid. Why would agents demand sub rosa payments into secret accounts in Switzerland if the payments were being made in compliance with the Indian government's request to terminate agreements? The next answer he gave was worse for the Indian government's stand. Asked whether Indians were behind the front companies, Thunholm said, 'As far as I know it is both Indians and others.'

Time for us to step back and look at another stream of fabrications, a stream we noted in passing earlier.

22

Till yesterday, the oracle

General K. Sundarji had been the Chief of Army Staff (COAS) when the Bofors contract was signed. As the controversy mounted, the government invoked him and his authority. The Army Chief had recommended that the Bofors gun be bought, it said. It has what other guns do not—a 'shoot and scoot' capability—he had said. The Army Chief had affirmed, the government said, that cancelling the contract would expose the country to an unacceptable level of danger, and that, therefore, the threat of cancelling it should not be held out to Bofors. It was bound to go by the advice of the Chief of Army Staff, the government said.

This became its standard answer, inside and outside Parliament, to every argument: 'But the Chief of Army Staff himself had recommended . . .'

In August 1989, General Sundarji at last broke his silence. In a detailed interview with Raminder Singh of *India Today*,[1] he revealed among other things that:

o   He had advised the government both orally and in writing—and not once but on several occasions orally, and twice in writing—to get Bofors to disclose the names of the recipients,

---

[1]   *India Today*, 15 September 1989.

or they should be told that the contract would be cancelled unless they revealed the names;

o After assessing the consequences with due care, he had concluded that the risks inherent in holding out such a threat were acceptable;

o Bofors had agreed to disclose the names;

o The moment he came to know of this, Rajiv came down heavily on all who had sought to pressurize Bofors into disclosing the names;

o Suggestions were then made to Sundarji—much as they were to be made later to the Comptroller and Auditor General of India—to alter the advice he had tendered.

The government, which had to that day been touting General Sundarji's advice as the thing which had settled both matters— that of awarding the contract of Bofors in March 1986 and of not threatening cancellation after the scandal broke—pounced on the General. He was denounced by its propagandists. And the government issued elaborate 'refutations' of what the General had revealed.

The first thing that the government did by its 'refutations' was to confirm the central point which General Sundarji had made— namely, that twice in writing Sundarji had recommended that to get Bofors to reveal the names of the recipients, government should threaten to cancel the contract. And they also confirmed the point another key General, Hridaya Kaul, had made, one which gave a glimpse into the cut-throat competition that had preceded the final decision—namely, that a firm had offered to pay him Rs 2.5 crore, an amount that could be raised up to Rs 5 crore, if he would move its gun higher up on the evaluation. S. Bhatnagar, the then Defence Secretary, confirmed in his statement that General Kaul had told him that some intermediary had approached him with 'a high offer to help a particular company'. Bhatnagar's explanation for not doing anything about the matter was laughable but consistent with the sort of bunk the government was peddling—he said that he did not act as General Kaul did not submit to him a written report on the matter!

Government's case

Unable to deny that General Sundarji had advised that government use the threat of cancellation to secure the names, the government maintained that, in tendering this advice,

o   General Sundarji was merely expressing his personal opinion—the consequences which would have followed upon the cancellation of the contract, the government's statement said, were ones which he—i.e., General Sundarji personally as distinct from the government—was prepared to accept as a risk;

o   His two notes—the second one being 'in substance a verbatim copy of the first'—'did not contain any evaluation of the precise security implications, the attendant risks and the relative strengths and weaknesses of potential adversaries during this period, in relation to probable threat scenarios';

o   'National security is much larger than its military aspect,' the government said, and the Chief of Army Staff did not have the comprehensive information which the government had and on which it proceeded to set aside his advice;

o   The 'hasty cancellation' of the contract, and the consequent delay in the induction of the guns would have put the country at serious risk: 'it has to be borne in mind that in the first half of 1987,' the government said, 'there were serious tensions on our borders with Pakistan. Developments on our borders with China were also causing serious concern in the country';

o   In any case, 'there was no assurance whatever that such a risk, even if taken, would have yielded either a disclosure of the identities of the beneficiaries or a recovery of the amounts paid';

o   And after debunking the idea of holding out a threat of cancellation, the government maintained that the idea for cancelling the contract originated not with Sundarji but with Rajiv Gandhi himself! Immediately upon receiving the report of the National Audit Bureau of Sweden, 'that very day,' the government said, the Prime Minister 'not only directed that immediate action be taken to elicit the full facts, but also desired a complete evaluation of the implications of cancellation, including security implications, the financial impact, etc.'

Facts

First, General Sundarji was not conveying to the government just his personal view of the matter. It was not that he was in some sort of a personal capacity prepared to bear the risk to the country's security. He was conveying to government the considered assessment of the Army of which he was the Chief. He had consulted all the Army Commanders as well as all the senior officers at Army Headquarters.

Second, he had been asked to provide to the government, on behalf of the Army, 'the evaluation of the precise security implications, the attendant risks, the relative strengths and weaknesses of potential adversaries, probable threat scenarios . . .' The note was the occasion to restate the Army's views on these points. Detailed assessments of each of these matters were already with government. The question he was now to answer was: In the light of the relative strengths and weaknesses of potential adversaries, probable threat scenarios, etc., what does the Army think of the risks that would follow upon the cancellation of the contract? And to that he gave a specific, unambiguous answer: there will be risks of course, but they are acceptable.

A Chief who won't listen?

Through its statement, the government, howsoever inadvertently, confirmed that Sundarji said this in writing not in one note, but, as he stated to *India Today,* twice, on 12 June and 15 July 1987. Sundarji had stated that in the same period he conveyed this assessment to Arun Singh, S.K. Bhatnagar, etc., orally, and that it was suggested to him through the Defence Secretary that he reconsider the advice he had tendered. He was surprised to be told later that the PMO had not received the note which he had sent a month earlier, and that they were upset about this. He thereupon reiterated the Army's advice in a second note.

Now, look at how the government twisted the facts. It said that Sundarji's original note was just an expression of opinion and did not contain the details of threat scenarios, etc., which the government had asked for. 'These serious lacunae,' the government's statement maintained, 'were pointed out to the former COAS and the note returned for re-examination.'

Sundarji characterized the government's statements to be a lie. And the sequence, as attested to now by the government itself, fortified his characterization.

Recall that the original note was written on 12 June 1987. The second note was written on 15 July 1987, that is more than a month later. Is it plausible that the Chief of Army Staff, even after 'serious lacunae' in his note had been pointed out to him, in fact, even after he had a month to rectify these 'serious lacunae', would submit a second note which, to quote what the government said in its statement, was, in substance, a verbatim copy of the first?

Sundarji told my senior colleague, N.S. Jagannathan, that he would have been a fool or a knave if, the lacunae having been pointed out to him, and he having taken a month over the note again, resubmitted the old one.

Army's advice?

'National security,' the government said, 'is much larger than its military aspect. It is the Government which is answerable to the people. Therefore, the views of the COAS, though important, cannot alone determine national security decisions.'

How did this square with the statements that K.C. Pant and all had been making in Parliament till just a few weeks earlier? 'Madam, the point is the Chief of Army Staff is an expert and we have to rely on him,' Pant had said. 'I must tell my honourable friends that anybody who knows anything about the Army will understand that at the given moment you have to respect the opinion of whoever is the Chief . . .' 'In a matter like this the

Government necessarily relies on the Chief of Army Staff . . . It is the Chief's opinion which prevails and the Chief is supposed to give his reasons . . .' Each and every one of these statements was made in Parliament by the same K.C. Pant who had presided over the Defence Ministry's new statement: 'Therefore, the views of the Chief of Army Staff, though important, cannot alone determine . . .'

Moreover, if that was all there was to the opinion of the Army Chief, how come you invoked him so many times to justify the final award of the contract to Bofors? Remember that on *six* occasions, the evaluation had gone in favour of the French gun. In the end, the contract was given to Bofors, and the principal feature that was said to tilt the decision in its favour was the one Sundarji had specified—'shoot and scoot'. How come that, even though Sundarji, now on the government's own admission, had advised that we threaten to cancel the contract, the government, led as usual in such untruths by the Prime Minister, purveyed the impression again and again that the contract was not being cancelled because the Army did not want it cancelled—as Rajiv did while addressing the Maharashtra Congress(I) Committee meeting in Pune on 16 June 1987, that is within three days of Sundarji sending him the note?

At long last, Arun Singh, who had left his ministership amidst much controversy and had since remained silent, rose to speak. It was May 1988. He urged the government to ask Bofors to return Rs 64 crore. He urged that it blacklist the company. Congressmen, thinking that he had been put up to making these suggestions by the leader so that the latter could, with becoming grace, accept them, cheered him repeatedly. The Opposition was under the same impression. Gurumurthy was with Advaniji. The latter told him that Arun Singh would have advanced this idea on the prodding of Rajiv, that the government would accept it, and the Bofors issue would be forgotten in a month or two.

But the moment Rajiv heard what Arun Singh had urged, he put Dinesh Singh, his Cabinet minister, to pounce on him. Speaking on behalf of his leader and the government in the Rajya Sabha on 11 May 1988, the minister expressed the most touching faith in the authority and integrity of General Sundarji. As he put it:

> Now the question comes as to what is the point on which you must accept the finality of the advice that is given to you because the processing takes place by different committees and by different organisations. I would say that the person best qualified to assess all these reports and considerations that have been gone into would be Chief of the Army Staff, because he would be the person who would be able to assess the various reports and various opinions that may have come . . . I was somewhat pained that he [that is, Arun Singh] should have cast any doubt on the competence, if not anything else of the Chief of the Army Staff. I would say here we can have no better opinion than that of the COAS, General Sundarji, a distinguished soldier and an apt leader of the Indian Army whose concern for the defence of the country, the fighting fitness of the Forces and their welfare could not be less than of any of us here. Therefore we must accept the advice of the Chief of the Army Staff.

And this had become the theme song of the government, and its trumpeters in the press. From K.C. Pant down, everyone proclaimed that the 'experts', that is the Army, had advised against cancellation.

When the Army had advised the opposite, as the government statement was now acknowledging, how had these ministers sworn to the opposite?

Private intelligence?

And was it at all plausible that on these matters—i.e., the 'relative strengths and weaknesses of potential adversaries' during this period, and the probable 'threat scenarios'—the government had information other than what the Chief of Army Staff had? All intelligence information bearing on weapons of the Army, the howitzer guns in this case, and the tasks confronting it was, as it is today, made available to the Army Chief. In fact, along with other Chiefs, he receives the complete intelligence assessments of 'the relative strengths and weaknesses of potential adversaries', of 'probable threat scenarios', etc. That is but natural. After all, intelligence information is not meant for the private edification of a Prime Minister or a Defence Secretary. It is meant for those who are to direct the defence of the country, and foremost among these are the Service Chiefs. In addition, the Chief receives information from the Army's own intelligence set-up.

Moreover, if it had not been on the advice of the Army, on the advice of which other agency had the government come to the decision that threatening to cancel the contract would expose the country to an unacceptable level of risk?

Assume that there really was some information on the basis of which some agency came to an assessment of threat scenarios, etc., that was so contrary to the Army's assessment, the assessment on the basis of which the Chief of Army Staff had conveyed his advice. Why did the government keep this security assessment to itself? Did it never think of conveying the security assessment to the ones who were to ensure the country's security? After all, more than two years had passed between Arun Singh and Sundarji advancing that idea and Sundarji speaking out.

And for Rajiv and his government to invoke 'answerability to the people' as a reason was just as ludicrous as its concoctions. If only the government had considered itself answerable to the people . . .

There was no assurance?

In any case, 'there was no assurance whatever', the government maintained, that such a risk, even if taken, would have yielded either a disclosure of the identities of the beneficiaries or a recovery of the amounts paid.

No assurance? The Chief was suggesting a device for ascertaining the names. Was it the practice of the government to threaten culprits only when it had an assurance—in writing perhaps—that they would yield to the threat?

That apart, and the testimony of Sundarji that, confronted with the threat, Bofors would agree to disclose the names, apart too, the course that events took at the time itself belied the government's assertions. At the time, as we have seen in the foregoing, both Rajiv and Shivraj Patil had said things that conformed to Sundarji's version, and not to what the government was maintaining after Sundarji had spoken out.

The Minister of State for Defence had told the Rajya Sabha on 12 August 1987, that: 'The Bofors Vice President, Mr Bertil Bredin, had been willing to reveal the names of persons who received the commission orally but not in writing as the Government wanted it.'

On 14 August, after the conferment of the Bharat Ratna on Badshah Khan, Rajiv had said the same thing at Rashtrapati Bhavan. Here is how the PTI reported Rajiv's observations in a dispatch carried by the *Times of India* and therefore, from Rajiv's point of view, doubly reliable: 'Bofors were willing to tell us something orally but not in writing in view of what they call the secrecy clause. What is the use of telling us something orally? It is of no use to us.'

Equally telling were the circumstances in which Bofors was placed at that time. The company had run woefully short of orders. It was on the verge of laying off workers. This is why, as the Swedish government had testified again and again, as high an official of the Swedish government as the Prime Minister himself was compelled to take such an extraordinary interest in securing the Indian order. Was a company in such dire straits likely to disregard the threat of losing the order, which was quite literally its lifeline, just to protect some commission agents?

Cancellation of the visit

Sundarji recalled that, pressurized, officials of Bofors agreed to come over and furnish the details, that Rajiv 'lit into' those who had sought to pressurize Bofors. The visit was therefore cancelled. On the basis of what senior Swedish officials told me then, we had published information about the visit being cancelled within days of the event.

In its response to Sundarji's interview, the government gave a different reason for the cancellation of the visit. It said:

> The pros and cons of such a dialogue at a level higher than that of Mr Bredin were carefully considered. Keeping in view the fact that on 11th June '87 the establishment of a Joint Parliamentary Committee had already been proposed to the Presiding Officers of the two Houses of Parliament, it was decided that it would be appropriate to require Bofors to furnish through a written reply the entire information already asked for. Bofors were, therefore, addressed afresh on 16th July, and once again asked to furnish specific replies to the questions already put to them . . .

The dates first. Note that Bertil Bredin, its Vice President and 'Project Coordinator, Field Artillery for India', had arrived in Delhi in the last week of June. The government's statement itself said that it handed him a letter on 3 July. It was on this day that he informed them that he had received confirmation from Karlskoga, the headquarters of Bofors, that the President and Chief Jurist of Bofors had agreed to come over and disclose the names.

On 4 July, Rajiv returned from Moscow. The meeting Sundarji had recalled had taken place. And the next day Bredin was told to tell Bofors to cancel the visit. Thus,

o   Bofors were asked in end June to send their officials.
o   On 3 July they conveyed their willingness to come over and disclose the details.
o   They were told on 5 July to cancel the visit.

As calling them over was thought inappropriate in view of the decision to set up the JPC, and as this decision had been communicated to presiding officers on 11 June, how come they were being asked till 4 July to come over?

There was more. Recall that the JPC was not set up till the Lok Sabha and Rajya Sabha passed their motions on 6 and 12 August respectively. We know how the government suborned and prostituted the Parliamentary Committee after it was set up.

But we were to believe the government's new statement to the effect that a sense of propriety had prevented it from receiving information from the officials of Bofors from 11 June onward, as on that day, the decision to establish such a committee of Parliament was made known to the presiding officers of the two Houses!

And could the JPC explanation stand? The government would have us believe that, once the decision had been taken to set up a committee of Parliament, it thought it wrong to collect information behind the JPC's back.

The President and Chief Jurist of Bofors had come on 14 September 1987.

From that day till 18 September they were closeted, not with the ever so sacred JPC. They were closeted with officials of Rajiv Gandhi's entourage and those of the Defence Ministry. And when, after these confabulations, they met the Committee of Parliament, they refused to disclose the names of the beneficiaries to the Committee on the ground that they had already disclosed these to their 'customer', the Government of India! Who then could believe the 'As-the-decision-to-set-up-the-JPC-had-been-taken' explanation?

But there was comedy too. Provided as usual by Rajiv's cleverness. K.C. Pant and his team, though they had laboured so hard to put together an explanation for asking Bofors to cancel the visit, had forgotten that Rajiv had already provided an explanation for that cancellation. In November 1988, Aveek Sarkar and Vir Sanghvi of *Sunday* had asked Rajiv,

> But this was just one of the options that Arun Singh suggested. What he said was that the Government of India was one of the biggest buyers in the market-place. It was the Government of India that kept Bofors going. Surely, if you put a little pressure on them, you could get them to tell you who they gave the money to and not just give you the names of Swiss front companies. There was no suggestion that you ever did that.

And Rajiv had replied,

No. We did. With due respect, I think the information that Arun had, at the time he said that, was not complete. What happened was that a gentleman from Bofors had come here who was not a top-level official. And he had said that he does not have the authority to say more than what he has said. This was long before they came and deposed before the JPC and gave us everything that they gave. And there was some impression that he might say something if he was allowed to meet at a political level, which meant either Arun or me. And we had to take a decision whether he would or would not say something because if he did meet and did not say anything then it could be interpreted to mean that we told him to shut up. So the danger of that was very high. So we took a decision that we would not deal with that level. When we really wanted the information, we put the pressure at the top-level. The man went back. We started doing that. And that is when we forced the Swedish lawyer and Chairman or MD Ring . . .

Because Bofors offered to give the information orally, and not in writing?
    Because the decision had been taken to set up the JPC?
    Because Bofors officials wanted to meet 'Arun or me' personally?
    An alibi a day gives the crime away . . .

But it was his idea!

While devoting nine-tenths of its statement to arguing that not just cancelling the contract, even threatening to do so would have been ruinous for the country, the government tried to snatch credit for the Prime Minister for that very idea.

Recall that after insisting for months that there had been no middlemen, Rajiv had suddenly switched in June 1987 and claimed credit for having had the middlemen removed. Similarly, having claimed credit so long for not cancelling the contract and thereby safeguarding the country's security, even though by doing so he was having to 'take a beating', Rajiv was snatching credit for having been the first to come up with the idea of cancelling the contract.

As the government's statement put it:

> The Swedish National Audit Bureau Report received on 4th June, 1987 indicated that certain payments had been made by Bofors but did not disclose the identity of the recipients. On that very day, i.e., on 4th June '87 itself, PM not only directed that immediate action should be taken to elicit the full facts, but also desired a complete evaluation of the implications of cancellation, including security implications, the financial impact etc. It is thus clear that the idea of the possible cancellation of the contract emanated from the PM himself.

A picture thus of the PM surprised, awakened by a flash, incensed, if not shocked, at learning that payments have been made, ordering immediate action, coming up with stratagems to get at the names. Was this really his reaction to the Swedish National Audit Bureau's report? We have evidence from the day itself. The National Audit Bureau's report was released on 4 June 1987. That very day, Rajiv met the Opposition leaders. L.K. Advani pointed out it was suggested that the government cancel the contract, that at least it should threaten to cancel it so as to get all the names. And what was Rajiv's reaction? 'Sharply negative,' Advani said.

And we have confirmation that on that very day, the government had ruled out cancellation, confirmation from none other than the Defence Minister, K.C. Pant himself. For he too, in Parliament and on record, registered what the government said at that meeting.

Speaking in the Lok Sabha on 6 August 1987, K.C. Pant recited the by now familiar litany of reasons for not cancelling the contract, among these 'the conclusion of the experts'. It was not that he was conjuring up these reasons just for the occasion. He had listed them to the Opposition leaders earlier, he said. As he put it,

> Therefore, Sir, the question is whether the Government should have used the threat. As I said, if you had not pointedly asked me

again and again, 'Why did you not cancel the contract?,' perhaps
I would not have touched. I did take the Opposition leaders
into confidence when we met on 4th June: Prof. Dandavate
will remember. I also gave them figures. After all, they are as
patriotic as we are, though they are sitting on the other side of
the House. I told them everything including the reasons.

And later, through that statement over the drafting and issuing of
which he presided, K.C. Pant wanted everyone to believe that 'on
that very day, that is 4 June, Rajiv Gandhi initiated an exercise
to examine the consequences of cancelling the contract'. But he
was himself on record saying that on that very day—i.e., 4 June
1987—government had explained in detail to the Opposition
leaders why the contract could not/should not/would not
be cancelled.

And why cancel?

As we have seen, Rajiv had time and again come up with
explanations for what Bofors had paid. The payments were made
to 'wind up' the middlemen. They were 'absurdly high', true, but
that was because whoever in Bofors signed the agreement to wind
up agreed to an absurdly high figure. Maybe they were 'global
consultancy fees' that had nothing to do with India. They could
be legitimate payments for 'industrial espionage' . . . As nothing
wrong had been done, why should the contract be cancelled?

Indeed, we would rather be martyrs, Rajiv and his minions said.
Should we sacrifice the security of our country and put our Services
in danger just to shield our reputations from your allegations?
Speaking in the Rajya Sabha on behalf of the government, the
then Minister of State for Defence, Shivraj Patil, listed the horrors
that would follow cancellation. He echoed Rajiv:

> What will happen if this contract is cancelled? Let us understand
> it. The countries in the neighbourhood have the weapons of this
> nature in their armoury and if something happens unfortunately,
> would you like our forces to become more vulnerable simply

because you are alleging something against the Government? Simply because you are maligning me, should I sacrifice the interest of the security and sovereignty and the territory of my country? . . . For nine years we have waited for these guns and having entered into a contract, if we cancel it, we would be required to wait for a pretty long time again. Would you ask us to wait for a pretty long time and make our forces vulnerable? . . . And why do you want us to cancel the contract when the news is coming from outside? Why don't you try to understand it? . . . We cannot do that. We will not do that. We will not stake the security of our country simply because somebody is making some allegations against us . . . If you cancel the contract, are you going to be reimbursed? Are you going to make good the loss? Are you going to get anything out of it? [interruptions] Simply by cancelling the contract you will not be able to do that. Where is your justification for cancelling the contract? [interruptions] . . . What can be done in this matter will be carefully considered by all the responsible persons and that will be done which is in the best interests of the country, best interests of the Forces and in the best interests of our finance. Let there be proof of anything having happened and we will take action, proper action, against anybody in the country and, if it is necessary, we shall have to take proper action outside. But don't ask to cancel the contract simply because you want it.

But Sundarji had not advised that the contract be cancelled. He had advised that the threat that it will be cancelled be held out, and had said that, given the precarious condition in which Bofors was at the time, faced with the threat, the company was likely to reveal the names.

Rajiv had earlier spoken to the same effect as Pant. It had become his theme song—'The country's security over my martyrdom'—with a new twist. As he put it to Aveek Sarkar and Vir Sanghvi in November 1988:

Then there was the penalty, the money that we would have paid. And I forget there was one more part on the financial side. The evaluation was it would be hundreds of crores, perhaps closer to a thousand, that we would lose on a cancellation.

So obviously, trying to get 66 (crores) back and this is what I said at the meeting where this was raised . . . I said what have we've got, we've got Rajiv Gandhi's credibility on the one side which is, you know, that he is a great guy and cancelled the contract and in doing that, he has compromised the security of the nation. He has made the nation pay, I don't know, 800-1,000 crores extra. I said: Look, it is better that I take a beating rather than the nation take a beating.

In the following two and a half years, Rajiv spoke on the matter scores of times. Never, not even once, did he express the slightest disapproval of the payments by Bofors. But K.C. Pant and the statement that the government issued in the wake of Sundarji's revelations made out that so incensed was he at discovering from the Audit Bureau's report that Bofors had paid someone, that 'that very day' he ordered this, that and the other, including an examination of the consequences of cancelling the contract.

The last refuge

The Official Secrets Act was, as it has remained since, the last refuge of every scoundrel. 'It is unfortunate,' the government declared, 'that the former COAS has knowingly committed the impropriety of disclosing the contents of a "Top Secret" document especially when it contains an assessment of matters relating to national security . . .'

What had Sundarji disclosed? That he had written two notes which had said that the risks entailed in holding out a threat of cancelling the contract were acceptable. How was security jeopardized by that disclosure? Far from exposing to the enemy's view chinks in our armour, the statement would inform the enemy that, even without the 155 howitzers, we could stand up to him. Moreover, by the time Sundarji spoke out in public the guns had arrived and had been deployed by the Army. How did disclosing that two and a half years earlier he had suggested that they threaten to cancel the contract endanger the security of the country? Of course, disclosing official secrets never comes to the mind of rulers when the disclosure helps fortify their lies. It had been all right for them to have disclosed the results of field trials to assorted members of Parliament? It had been all right to disclose the delivery schedule of the weapon to them? To disclose all the technical specifications of the weapon to them?

It was perfectly right for this very Sundarji to have disclosed at the asking of the very government what he had come to know about the equipment Pakistan had acquired—the much vaunted radar—and to even disclose when we had come to know of it, thereby almost certainly endangering some vital source of intelligence.

Two questions

That Bofors had already paid Rs 64 crore hurt the government, no doubt. But it was this string of lies that destroyed Rajiv's credibility altogether. That is why the two questions I had asked at the time in regard to the lies seem just as relevant after all these years:

o   Would Rajiv Gandhi have done so much, and persisted so long in it, had you or I taken the money?

o   On the other hand, how could he not have done all this, and persisted as long as he could in doing it, if the money had been taken by someone or some organization indistinguishable in the public mind from himself, or one indispensable to him?

23

A boomerang

We had been pursuing Bofors—after having looked down upon, or at the least, neglected the matter for long, *The Hindu* had hit the jackpot: it had received telltale documents from the Swedish investigator. We had nailed the Fairfax forgery. We had established Ajitabh Bachchan's violation of FERA (Foreign Exchange Regulation Act). We had established that Reliance had violated several laws as they stood at the time, and it could not have done so but for the government's complicity. We had been publishing material about the misdeeds of other friends of Rajiv, like Satish Sharma.

The government had retaliated by slapping us with notices alleging violations of various regulations and laws; by holding up newsprint; by instituting cases; by raiding the residence of Ramnathji and our offices. They had physically stopped the publication of our principal edition, the one in Delhi.

None of this had deterred us, none of it had even slowed us down.

Most of the press was, as is always the case, singing hosannas of the rulers—Rajiv Gandhi and his circle. With his overwhelming majority in Parliament, and the Opposition's inability to get together, Rajiv had little more than condescension for it. 'There is no Opposition,' he said. 'There is just one newspaper.'

We were that paper.

One day, 28 August 1988, with just two days left for the session to end, the Question Hour of the Lok Sabha had but to conclude, and a Bill was thrust upon the House—'The Defamation Bill, 1988.'[1] Members were told that there would be no Zero Hour, that they had half an hour to table amendments, that the Bill would be taken up as soon as the House met after the lunch break. The Bill had just been sprung on them: it had not been so much as mentioned at any meeting of the Business Advisory Committee. It was evident that the government was determined to ram the Bill through the House that very day. The Opposition was up in arms. *Hulla* ensued. The government agreed to continue the discussion till the next day.

And rammed through the Bill was the next day. The government let it be known that it would take the Bill to the Rajya Sabha forthwith.

The government was asked repeatedly, in Parliament and out, what had happened which made defamation such an urgent matter. It offered no explanation. The government was asked what was about to happen which made it necessary to stop that event from happening immediately through a new law. It offered no explanation. During the debate, the government was asked to provide illustrations of the kind of publications that it thought were so indefensible and which, in its view, could not be dealt with by existing laws that a new law was required to curb them. It was not able to provide any illustrations. During the debate, Somnath Chatterjee, the CPI(M) member asked the minister piloting the Bill, P. Chidambaram, to provide just one illustration, just one. The government was not able to provide even one illustration. The demand was repeated outside Parliament. The government was not able to provide any illustration.

Asking for an illustration was just a way of putting the matter. There was no doubt about what sort of work the government wanted to throttle. Nor was there any doubt that the government

---

[1] The following is based on articles and news reports published in the *Indian Express* between 29 August and 24 September 1988.

could not cite that kind of work as an illustration of the kind of writing that just had to be stopped!

We realized that the Bill had to be stopped. Indeed, that it had to be killed 'in broad daylight', so to say—to be killed so conspicuously that future governments must not think of ramming through such legislation. But we also realized that the *Express* could not do so by itself. There would have to be a campaign involving the entire press. The campaign must be such that even the pro-government papers would feel compelled to join it.

And Ramnathji spelt out the sine qua non for organizing such a campaign. '*Andolan karnaa padegaa,*' Ramnathji said. '*Toofaan khadaa karnaa padegaa.*'[2] Of course, that was exactly what we thought had to be done. But he hadn't finished. '*Aandolan to hamein he karnaa padegaa; toofaan to hum sab ko hi uthaanaa padegaa. Par hamey aagey naheen aanaa hai. Har ek press-waaley ko lagey ki aandolan voh he chalaa rahaa hai. Tum sab peechey rehnaa. Main bhee peechey he rahoongaa.* Irani[3] *ko aagey karo—usey leaderee kaa bahut shauk hai, apni* photo *khinchwaaney kaa bahut shauk hai. Usey* leader *banaayogey, voh bahut phoolegaa. To jo chaahengey, voh karegaa, aur auron se karvaaega.*'[4]

'Objects and Reasons'

The government said that the Bill was intended to merely codify, consolidate and amend the law on defamation. The amendments, it said in the Statement of Objects and Reasons, were necessary to give effect to the recommendations of the 42nd Report of the

---

[2] 'A movement will have to be launched. A storm will have to be launched.'

[3] C.R. Irani, the *kartaa-dhartaa* of *The Statesman* at the time.

[4] 'The movement will have to be waged by us; the storm will have to be triggered by us. But we must not be in front. Every pressman must feel that he is the one who is directing the movement. You stay in the background. I also will remain in the background. Put Irani in the forefront—he is very fond of being a leader, he is very fond of getting his photograph taken. You make him the leader, he will swell like anything. And then we can steer him to do anything.'

Law Commission, and the recommendations of the Second Press Commission. That was, of course, a complete misrepresentation: the Law Commission and the Press Commission had, in fact, urged that the law be liberalized. In any case, that assertion did not explain the urgency with which the Bill was being rammed through. The 42nd Report of the Law Commission had been submitted a decade earlier. The Report of the Second Press Commission had been submitted four years earlier.

The falsehood implicit in invoking these commissions, and the utter inability of the government to state what kind of writing made the Bill so urgently necessary, made our task easier. The reading public as well as organizations of professionals—lawyers, trade unionists, and others—realized what the government was up to. As leading lawyers—H.M. Seervai, Ram Jethmalani, A.G. Noorani—set out the dangers inherent in the provisions, such doubts as might have remained about the goal of government evaporated.

Provisions

True to form, the Bill began in an innocuous manner. The Bill's Chapter II was the first substantive one. Its definition of defamation was no different from what existed in the Indian Penal Code of the time, essentially Macaulay's Code. It retained each of the ten exceptions of the Code. All that was missing were the masterly illustrations that Macaulay had penned to show what was and what was not defamatory.

Alterations began in this innocuous-looking chapter itself, in particular in clause 5 of the Bill. The first alteration could be said to be crafted to help the press. The Code as it stood provided a blanket punishment for defamatory statements or representations. The Bill graded these: for the first offence, the defamer could be sentenced to imprisonment which may extend up to two years or may be asked to pay a fine of Rs 2000, or both. For the second and subsequent defamatory statements, the person could be sentenced to imprisonment which could extend up to five years, and a fine which may be up to Rs 5000, or both.

The Bill provided that the publication would have to publish the judgment of the Court in the matter in the manner prescribed by the Court.

Clause 6 contained an omission that could go unnoticed at first reading. Here is the version in the IPC:

> 501: Whoever prints or engraves any matter, knowing or having good reason to believe that such matter is defamatory of any person, shall be punished with simple imprisonment for a term which may extend to two years, or with fine, or with both.

And this is what the Bill provided:

> 6: Whoever prints or engraves any matter, knowing or having good reason to believe that such matter is defamatory of any person, shall, in the case of the first offence, be punishable with imprisonment for a term which may extend to two years, or with fine which may extend to two thousand rupees, or with both, and in the case of a second or subsequent offence, with imprisonment which may extend to five years, or with fine which may extend to five thousand rupees, or with both.

The imprisonment up to '*five* years' would have caught the eye. But there was another change which was equally chilling: a word was missing—the one that in the IPC qualified 'imprisonment'. The IPC specified that the imprisonment would be 'simple'. The Bill omitted 'simple'. The Court could, therefore, sentence the writer and publisher to either simple or rigorous imprisonment of up to two years or up to five years as the case may be. That was certainly an ominous change, and would certainly have what the courts like to call a 'chilling effect' over what is written or published.

The next clause did what Mishra's Bihar Press Bill had attempted to do. It enlarged the net to ensure that even if some journalist was foolish enough to write or some publisher was foolish enough to print what could be regarded as defamatory, they wouldn't get far—as no one would dare to store, transport, sell or distribute the publication. The clause of the Bill provided:

> 7: Whoever sells or offers for sale any printed or engraved substance containing defamatory matter, knowing that it contains such matter, shall be punishable with imprisonment which may extend to two years or with fine which may extend to two thousand rupees, or with both.

How would the hawker know that the bundle he was distributing had defamatory matter? Would he take the risk of being able to prove that he did not know that the matter was defamatory? Or standing up to the well-heeled lawyers of the complainant or the well-connected ones of the government when they sought to prove that, indeed, he knew that the publication contained matter which was defamatory, and was yet distributing it?

The next clause brought into central law the undefined terms that Mishra had introduced:

> 8: Where any matter which is grossly indecent or scurrilous or is intended for blackmail is published [*sic*] . . .

'Grossly indecent' seemed to suggest that the clause was intended to curb pornographic writing or publications. The real mischief was in the next two categories: in material that could be alleged to be 'scurrilous' and in material that could be said to be 'intended for blackmail.'[5]

---

[5] The government tried to make out that an amendment piloted by the Janata government in 1978 was the basis for these words. Actually, as I pointed out at the time, the words were taken from *The Prevention of Publication of Objectionable Matter Ordinance, 1975,* which had been issued by the government to shield Mrs Indira Gandhi and her colleagues during the Emergency. The Ordinance had prescribed that papers and presses could be seized and shut down for publishing 'Objectionable Matter'. The latter was defined to include all statements 'which (i) are defamatory of the President of India, the Vice President of India, the Prime Minister or any other member of the Council of Ministers of the Union, the Speaker of the House of the

The dictionary meaning of 'scurrilous', all of us pointed out, was, 'Making or spreading scandalous claims about someone with the intention of damaging their reputation'—a very wide net indeed. The word in the Hindi version of the Bill was even more elastic: *bhadda*. And any politician could allege that what had been printed was 'intended for blackmail'. The journalist would contest this—he would argue that he had merely reported what he had found and had no intention to extort anything in return. But that would have to be done during the trial.

Of course, the 'explanations' contained some relief. The journalist was afforded the opportunity to establish that what he had reported was true and for the public good: these were said to be 'question[s] of fact', that is, he would have to establish both that what he had written was true and that it was in the interest of the public that those facts be brought to light. Second, the 'explanations' to the clause said that what had been written would not be defamatory if it had been written in 'good faith' and was about the conduct of a public servant in the discharge of his public functions, or about the conduct of any person touching any public question, or about their character, in as much as they appeared from their public function or their conduct in relation to the public question respectively. It was also provided that in deciding whether a person has committed an offence under clause 8, his 'general character', the 'nature of his business'; the 'general character and dominant effect of the matter'; and any evidence that the writer or publisher may offer to establish that the matter was not grossly indecent, scurrilous or intended for blackmail would be considered.

These provisions could be said to be in line with defences that had existed under the law as it had stood for a century. But, first, and especially in light of provisions relating to onus to which we shall turn, each segment would have to be established by the writer or publisher, and, second, in India, as had been said so often, the process is the punishment—getting the fellow

---

People or the Governor of a state; (ii) are grossly indecent, or are scurrilous or obscene or intended for blackmail.'

embroiled in a court case is punishment that by itself can cripple the fellow. If the journalist or publisher could establish that he had published the matter 'innocently', not realizing that it was defamatory, or after taking 'all reasonable care', he could seek to avoid punishment by 'an offer to make amends'. He could offer to publish a correction and apology 'in the same manner and with the same prominence as the matter alleged to be defamatory was published'. 'Fair comment' too was exempted.

It was widely expected at the time that foreign contracts—Bofors, HDW submarines—that were under discussion in India would figure in legislatures or courts or media of other countries—UK, Sweden, Switzerland, Germany. And that if the press merely reported what had transpired in those fora, or the rulings and judgments that had been given in those countries, it could be sued for defamation.

The next clause seemed to provide assurance that this would *not* be the case.

Clause 11 provided that it would *not* be defamation to publish 'a fair and accurate report of any proceedings in public of' a foreign legislature, the judgment of a foreign court, of an international organization of which India was a member, of an international court, etc.

This was very important for us. Especially because this clause opened with the words, '*Notwithstanding anything contained in this Act,* the publication of any of the following statements shall not constitute defamation . . .'

But three provisions at once set this relief to nought.

The last subclause of clause 11 provided:

(f) any notice or any other matter issued for the information of the public by or on behalf of government or a local authority shall not be defamation.

In a word, the CBI, the Doordarshan, any and every government department could state anything, they could cast any aspersion on anyone—'unaccounted money and jewellery amounting to 100 crore found in searches', 'drugs found' . . .—broadcast it over national networks, and that would *not* be defamation.

Second, the onus was shifted on to the accused. Clause 12 provided that if the writer or publisher sought to suggest that what he had written or published fell under one of Macaulay's ten exceptions (listed in clause 4 of this Act) or under the exceptions listed in clause 11, 'the onus of proving such claim shall be on him and the prosecution shall have the right to lead evidence in rebuttal'.

Opposition leaders pointed out, and so did we in the press, that in the initial stages of a controversy, all the facts are not known, and conclusive proof may not be available. Facts tumble out as the issue is joined. Often the truth of what was stated at first is established more by the evasions and lies of rulers and their friends than by one conclusive document. More important, in the case of, say, governmental contracts or decisions bent to favour a friend of the rulers, conclusive proof would be contained in official files—files to which government will not allow access. Such being the case, shifting the onus on to the accused was to ensure his punishment even before trying him.

The real problem lay in the next clause, clause 13. It wiped out each and every one of the exceptions that had been listed in clauses 4 and 11. Recall that clauses 4 and 11 were part of Chapter II of the Bill. Clause 11 of this chapter had started by affirming, 'Notwithstanding anything contained in this Act . . .'

Clause 11 done, Chapter III of the Bill commenced. It opened with clause 13. This clause read: '13. *Notwithstanding anything contained in Chapter II of this Act . . .*'

Didn't the words wipe out the ten exceptions? Didn't they wipe out the assurance that to accurately report what had been said in or decided by a foreign legislature or court would not constitute defamation? Clause 13 continued:

> . . . whoever by words, either spoken or intended to be read or by sign or visible representations, makes or publishes any imputation falsely alleging that any person has committed an offence, or has done or omitted to do any act which amounts to an offence, under any law for the time being in force, shall . . .

Clause 11 had stated, 'Notwithstanding anything contained in this Act . . .' That would imply that 'fair and accurate' reporting of what happened in foreign legislatures or courts would not constitute defamation. Clause 13 stated, 'Notwithstanding anything contained in Chapter II . . .' making an imputation which was false, that X had done what was contrary to law or had not done what the law required of him, would be defamation. Assume a prosecutor in Switzerland stated in a Swiss Court that, 'Yes, this account belongs to Y.' Y in India asserts the statement is false. The protection available under clause 11 would evaporate.

Imprisonment not less than one month and up to one year for the first offence would follow; not less than three months and up to two years for any subsequent offence . . .

The matter would go to or be taken up by a Sessions Court—i.e., one layer of courts would be skipped.

The Sessions Court would, if it thinks fit, try the case in 'a summary way', and 'in camera'.

The trial would proceed on a day-to-day basis.

It would be concluded within three months.

Day-to-day trial. To be concluded within three months . . . such swiftness was not mandated for even the far more heinous crimes like rape, murder, terrorist attacks.

The allegation would not constitute defamation if it was true and if making it was for the public good, the Bill stated. But also that the onus of proving that it was true and for the public good would lie on the accused, and the prosecution shall have the right to lead evidence in rebuttal.

Nor was that the end. Clause 18 provided that the Court shall *not* dispense with the personal appearance of the writer, editor, publisher if they 'refused within a reasonable time, to publish *any* reply of the person against whom any imputation relatable to such offence was made . . .'[6] Notice: the Court shall *not* dispense with personal appearance; second, 'publish *any* reply of the person . . .'

In a word, you could tie up writers, editors, publishers by having cases instituted in different parts of the country. And you

---

[6] Clauses 13 to 15, and clause 18 of the Bill.

could send *any* 'reply': whether true or not, whether short or long.

To make doubly sure, clause 20 provided:

20: The provisions of this Act or any order made thereunder shall have effect notwithstanding anything inconsistent therewith contained in any other enactment or any instrument having effect by virtue of any other enactment.

Things to do

At the *Express*, as I mentioned, we invited leading lawyers to analyse provisions of the Bill. Along with others at the paper, I wrote a good deal, analysing the clauses and pointing out the dangers inherent in them. But analysing and broadcasting the dangers was only one component of what had to be done, I argued in articles, at meetings, through lectures. The government was trying to choke our throats, the real answer would be to:

o   Redouble our efforts to expose its misdeeds.

o   Expose the duplicity of the government, evident even in this Bill: by saying it had brought the Bill to punish and thereby stop defamation, and at the same time exempting everything said by or on its behalf, the government was protecting the worst defamers—its agencies and instruments. Therefore, we should ask ministers and their minions why, given that damaging a person's reputation was so horrible, should this exemption not be dropped. In any case, we should remember that the relevant clause is in Chapter II of the Bill. And so, it is knocked out by the words with which clause 13 opens: 'Notwithstanding anything contained in Chapter II of this Act . . .' So, use this to the hilt: file cases against ministers and officials in different parts of the country the moment AIR or Doordarshan or CBI issues a false statement that lowers your reputation. Demand that they attend the hearings personally, day-to-day . . .

o Demand also that AIR and Doordarshan, and agencies like the CBI, broadcast your reply 'in the same manner and with the same prominence' with which they defamed you.

o Note every statement that Rajiv Gandhi makes which is defamatory under this Bill—that Ram Jethmalani is 'a barking dog', that V.P. Singh is 'Mir Jafar', that Opposition leaders are 'anti-national', that sections of the press are in league with foreign forces to destabilize the country. And set up legal cells all over the country to file defamation cases against him personally when the Bill becomes law. Under the law that he would have himself rammed through, he will not be able to escape attending court personally.

o Stop printing the names and photographs of ministers and the Prime Minister. If one of them makes an important announcement, carry that announcement so that readers are not deprived of information which they should have, but do not publish the name of the minister who has made that announcement. Instead, just say, 'At a press conference, the minister for industries announced . . .' Never publish his photograph. Even this mild exclusion from the papers will tell on them: so accustomed are they to seeing themselves in our papers that *unkaa khaanaa hazm naheen hogaa*.[7]

o As soon as the minister turns up for a press conference, ask him to state his view about the Bill. If he says he is for it, or if he gives a *gol-mol*[8] answer, just walk out.

o I strenuously urged a lesson we had learnt during our fight with Datta Samant. As I have explained in an earlier chapter, the *Express* staff quickly saw that they were just being used by him. They wanted to get back to work. He would get them to stay away from work through fear, of course, but also by telling them that his men were in touch with Ramnathji, that Goenka would agree to the new demands very soon, that it was just a matter of a few days, and so they should keep up the pressure. We made sure they realized that there was no

---

[7] They won't be able to digest their food.
[8] Roundabout

question of anyone meeting Datta Samant or his men, that there would be no 'negotiations'. To reinforce the point, we put out the rumour that Ramnathji had left for Switzerland and the UK, and would not be back for three months. With this in mind, as the campaign against the Bill gathers steam, I said in meetings of editors and journalists, the government will invite you for a dialogue. Declare at every available opportunity, 'There is no question of a dialogue. There is nothing to discuss. Just withdraw the Bill.' They will put out a lie that, in fact, some editors and journalists have begun meeting them and the 'dialogue' has begun. When they say so, we must demand that they release the names of the editors and journalists who have met them. If all they have been able to corral are some nominal journalists, the names will puncture their claim that a dialogue has commenced. If some genuine journalists have met them, those journalists will be shamed. So, 'Names please.'

o Defamation, like most other crimes, falls in the Concurrent List. Hence, we should persuade the non-Congress states to pass laws liberalizing the IPC provisions regarding defamation. And send these laws to the President for assent. He will then have two sets of laws—this Defamation Law rammed through by the Centre, and the liberal laws passed by some states. If, abiding by the 'advice' of the Central Government, he does not assent to the state laws but assents to the central law, he would be exposing the Central Government. If he assents to the state laws, by virtue of a provision in the Constitution,[9] the law passed by the state shall prevail in the state and not the central law. Of course, Rajiv Gandhi would persevere, and, under the same provision, pass a law that overrides the law passed by the state. But that would put him in conflict with the state. And, more important, it would expose the nature of his government all the more.

o The day the Bill becomes an Act, the papers can pledge, and print the pledge, that they will disregard it and continue to work to hold the government to account.

---

[9] Article 254(2).

o That day, and on a fixed day every week after that, they can all print one common statement or story which is true, dignified, in the public interest but actionable under the provisions of the Act. They can store up the results of their investigations between now and the day the Bill becomes an Act, and then with unremitting regularity print the results of their investigations.

o From the day that the Bill becomes an Act, papers should refuse to publish every statement put out by or on behalf of government that contains the slightest tendency to tarnish the image of anyone in anyone's eyes; and naturally, in deciding whether the handout is defamatory, it is the judgement of the paper, and not of the government department, which shall prevail.

o And so on.

The campaign

Journalists rose as one man. Dharnas, processions, articles and editorials in their papers. Walkouts at press conference after press conference. Blank editorial space encased in a black border. Refusal to accept awards from the hands of ministers. Journalists began wearing black badges. The highlights were a procession from India Gate to the Boat Club—Ramnathji, Irani, editors of all leading newspapers and magazines, everyone was there. And then a nationwide shutdown of all publications.

Rajiv Gandhi helped as he swung between seeking a way out and sticking to the last. I have an open mind, he would say one day. Let the press come and convince me. And then that he was convinced that the Bill was necessary, that the government was moving in the right direction, that those opposing the Bill had not read it, he would say, all there is, is *haahaakaar* . . . One day his minions were all determination. The next that the Bill is not being introduced in the Rajya Sabha as planned, that is on the next working day. Then that it is not going to be introduced pending a comprehensive dialogue with all sections, in any case, not in this session . . . Every twist added fuel to the journalists' engines.

Gandhiji

Members of other professions joined: lawyers, trade unions. And the Opposition parties. N.T. Rama Rao announced that Andhra would disregard the Bill should it become an Act. Fissures developed in the ranks of the Congress itself. Kamlapati Tripathi, former Chief Minister of UP and a senior leader, declared that the government should withdraw the Bill. The authors began to distance themselves: Chidambaram was visible much less; Siddhartha Ray, then Governor of Punjab, had a statement put out by his Secretariat that he had not contributed to drafting the Bill.

It really became a national stir. The cause was not just to get one Bill withdrawn. It was not just the freedom of the press. It wasn't even just the right of the reader to know facts about his rulers. The cause now was to ensure that rulers listen to the people. It was time to remind people of what Gandhiji had written in regard to the Rowlatt Bills.

The Bills are bad in law, he had said. But worse, they are an insult to the whole nation, he had said, as they are being 'steamrollered by means of the official majority of the government and in the teeth of the unanimous opposition from the non-official members'. After the speech of the official representative reaffirming the government's faith in the Bills, 'It is necessary,' he told the private secretary to the Viceroy in a telegram, 'to demonstrate to government that even a government [of] the most autocratic [kind] finally owes its power to the will of the governed.' 'The Bills require to be resisted not only because they are in themselves bad,' he told the thousands who had gathered to hear him in Madras, 'but also because government, which is responsible for their introduction, has seen fit to practically ignore public opinion and some of its members have made it a boast that they can so ignore that opinion . . .' 'It is common cause throughout the length and breadth of India,' he told the audience in Tuticorin, 'that that legislation, if it remains on the Statute-book, will disgrace the whole nation. We have asked our rulers not to continue that legislation. But they have absolutely disregarded the petition. They have therefore inflicted a double wrong on the whole nation. We have seen that all our meetings, all our resolutions and all the speeches of our councillors have proved to be of practically no avail . . .' And, therefore, he said in a written message, 'To my mind the first thing needful is to secure a frank and full recognition of the principle that public opinion properly expressed shall be respected by the government.'

The outcome

With every passing day, it became clearer and clearer that the parable L.K. Advani used to repeat would come true for Rajiv Gandhi.

A criminal was caught and brought to the presence of the ruler. But the ruler was in a magnanimous mood that day. 'I will give you a choice,' he announced to the criminal. 'You can either choose to eat a hundred onions or to be flogged a hundred times.'

'God, a hundred lashes of the whip will be too much,' the criminal thought. '*Jahaanpanhaa,* I will eat the hundred onions.'

He had barely eaten ten and his mouth was ablaze, his eyes dripping with tears. 'The whip won't be as awful,' he moaned.

He pleaded that he be exempted from eating the remaining ninety onions, and that he would rather suffer the hundred lashes.

The King, in his magnanimity, accepted the plea.

The criminal had suffered but ten lashes, and he screamed, 'Please, please stop this flogging, I will eat the ninety remaining onions.'

And so it went: onions . . . lashes . . . onions . . . lashes . . .

By the end, the poor fellow had eaten the hundred onions and also suffered a hundred lashes.

On 22 September, just three and a half weeks after he had rammed the Bill through the Lok Sabha, Rajiv's government announced that the Bill was being dropped altogether.

The high ground

The decision had been taken after receiving the report of an inter-ministerial committee, it said. It tried to take the high ground. The Bill had been designed to strike a balance between freedom of speech and the reputation of individuals, it said. However, it had aroused 'misgivings and misapprehensions'. 'The press and sections of the public have expressed their concern,' it said, and:

> We are alive to these concerns. We draw inspiration from Mahatma Gandhi, Jawaharlal Nehru and Indira Gandhi, who always responded to democratic expression of opinion. We, therefore, offered an unconditional dialogue on the subject. Some organisations and individuals have responded to the offer.

Really? Which organizations? Which individuals? The government wouldn't disclose. My friend, Sanjay Suri, one of our best reporters at the time, found out.

The dialogue

'The dialogue finally took place,' Sanjay reported. 'Two weeks the chosen ministers had waited for someone to talk to them on the Defamation Bill. Then on Wednesday the committee held three meetings.' The first was with a 'delegation' led by Mr Harbhajan Singh, editor of *Film Mirror* and *Indian Observer*, a gentleman who could be seen in the forenoon any day drifting from one restaurant in Connaught Place to another. 'He is a senior member of the press—"decades" old, he says,' Sanjay reported. 'He was charged under the Obscenities Act during a film festival. "If the films could show everything,"' Sanjay reported him as asking, '"why not my magazine?" But the cases came to nothing.' 'Nor did the cases of defamation against him filed by V. Shantaram and J. Om Prakash, for example. Hema Malini and Sridevi had sent him defamation notices. "But they never pursued the cases," he says. Now that he is a member of the Press Council, he says, he has become "very responsible". No more ads for sexual aids.' 'The latest issue of *Film Mirror*,' Sanjay reported, 'says on the cover, "Rape a must for a film." What follows would make every woman furious and college boys blush.' 'The Government has done a lot for him,' Sanjay informed our readers. He was recently given the National Integration Award. He is a member of the Newsprint Advisory Committee, Central Press Accreditation Committee, the Telephones Advisory Committee, and a member of the Governing Body of Kamala Nehru College'—a college for women. 'Mr Harbhajan Singh mentions several "illustrious journalists" who had accompanied him.' Sanjay listed the names of the illustrious ones: one each from *International Understanding, World Fair Guide, Prata Kamal, Sandhya Prakash* and *Tarun Duniya*. If you hadn't heard of the publications, you wouldn't be the only one who hadn't.

There was another meeting the same night, Sanjay reported, with Ahmed Mustafa Siddiqui 'Rahi' 'who brings out a weekly called *Nai Duniya* from Delhi, another publication called *Urdu Digest,* and several other *"risalas"*'—magazines. 'He heads the All India Urdu Journalists Congress,' Sanjay informed our readers. 'Mr Sidiqqui says his organization has 42 members, including some from Hyderabad and Lucknow. Many are from the family.' 'There is hardly a journalist from major Urdu publications who is a part of this Congress. Most members of this Congress are owners of small *"risalas"* not known for stands against the Government.'

'The third meeting surprised journalists the least,' Sanjay wrote. 'It was with Mr Vishwa Bandhu Gupta, a ruling party MP, who responded to the call of the Prime Minister. He heads the All India Newspaper Editors Conference.'

'On the Government Committee that talked to them were Mr Narasimha Rao, Mr HKL Bhagat, Mr KC Pant, Mr Shiv Shankar, Mr Gopi Arora and Mr Suman Dubey.'

'The Bill was dropped a day after this long-awaited dialogue with the "press". "The Bill was dropped so fast only because of us." Mr Harbhajan Singh says.'[10]

---

[10] For the foregoing, Sanjay Suri, 'The "Speakers" at the "Dialogue"', *Indian Express*, 23 September 1988.

Suddenly, for a national debate, for the spirit of understanding and cooperation, for national consensus

The government statement continued, 'We feel, however, that there should be a wider and fuller national debate. In order to facilitate such a debate, and in keeping with our heritage and traditions, we have decided not to make the Defamation Bill into law.'

Gandhiji, Pandit Nehru . . . Mrs Gandhi who had locked up free speech . . . Heritage and traditions . . . That some organizations and individuals have responded . . . The absurdity of it all.

But it had not given up, the government felt compelled to affirm: 'The issue of defamation remains.'

Till yesterday, Rajiv was saying, 'Critics of the Bill have not read it, all there has been is *haahaakaar.*' Till yesterday, he was saying, 'I am totally convinced the Bill is needed. We are heading in the right direction. The press should come and convince me.' Today his Government was reduced to hoping:

> It is our earnest hope that concerned citizens, jurists and the media will participate in the national debate on the issue of defamation. In course of time, Government may, if necessary, create a suitable forum to carry forward the dialogue in a spirit of understanding and co-operation. A solution based on a national consensus will strengthen the institutions of our Republic.

Senator Aitken's formula: when asked what advice he would give President Kennedy in regard to Vietnam, he said, 'Cry "Victory", and run.'

A victory we needed

The press had, and we had got a victory we very much needed. And all of us were elated. A good beginning it certainly was. But it was just a beginning. Like these rulers, future rulers also having a brute majority in legislatures, could just as easily dress up their oppression by such 'laws'. After all, the apparatus of oppression, in this case of silencing inconvenient voices, remained in place. That is why, while this was a good beginning, it was just a beginning.

24

A paper is closed

V.P. Singh, as we have seen, had been shunted out of the Finance Ministry to the Ministry of Defence. Murmurs had started about the purchase of HDW submarines from Germany. At the *Indian Express*, we had been nailing the lies and somersaults of the government on Bofors. V.P. Singh, then Defence Minister, wrote on file that the submarine matter should be investigated. Congressmen made it impossible for him to continue in government. He resigned, declaring that he was doing so to fight corruption. The government retaliated by putting out some documents that it—and its loyal pressmen—proclaimed established that V.P. Singh's son, Ajeya Singh, had an account at a bank in St Kitts, a tax haven in the Caribbean. It took us just a little effort to establish that the documents were out-and-out forgeries—I have always found this to be a great reassurance: the inefficiency of the system saves us. The government tried to change the issue. The issue is not whether the documents are forgeries. The issue is who has paid for the investigation in St Kitts that unearthed the facts that the *Indian Express* has relied on. And it appointed a Commission of two Supreme Court Judges to find out who paid for the inquiries that led us to establish the forgeries.

We persisted.

The government hit back with a vengeance. A year earlier, through a contrived 'election', a person who had nothing to do with the *Indian Express* group had been helped to become the leader of the Union in our Delhi edition. He now filed a complaint alleging malpractices. This complaint became the basis for officials from various agencies to raid our offices as well as the apartment in Delhi where Ramnathji used to stay. In forty-five days preceding the event with which I shall deal, ten prosecutions were launched against the *Express*, and it was suddenly served about twenty-five show-cause notices. Equipment worth Rs 4 crore—a very substantial sum in those days—was held up for seven weeks in Bombay in spite of every query having been answered, every requirement having been met. As the group was not picking up equipment—because it could not—it was asked to pay whopping amounts as demurrage! The group had to turn to the banks, but the banks—all in the control of government— began to drag their feet.

We persisted.

Kuldip Nayar was the first to bring us news of what was being planned. He told us that two days before the ongoing session of Parliament concluded, when he was talking to four or five MPs of the Congress(I) in the Central Hall, they told him, 'Let the session end and the *Express* will be stopped by a strike.' T.M. Nagarajan—the outsider who had been 'elected' as the President of our Delhi Union—would be the instrument.

The plan unfolded. The rulers turned to hired *gundas*. With their help and the tacit inaction of the police, the paper's principal edition—the one in Delhi—was physically closed down. It was made out that there was a strike.

We shift to an apartment

At the time, there were about 670 employees in the paper's Delhi office. As Delhi was in many ways the head office of the group, these 670 included managerial staff—staff that looked after accounts and other things of all editions. Once the trouble started, about a hundred left town. We began operating from the guest house in Sundar Nagar where Ramnathji used to stay. We opened an attendance register. Every employee who reported for work would sign it, affirming, 'I am not on strike. I am hereby reporting for work today.' Of the 570-odd who were in Delhi, around 350 signed regularly. Several told us that they would work—and they did—but were afraid to sign lest they were roughed up. One day, 500 signed.

It isn't just that the employees signed and did their work. The overwhelming proportion of them trooped to police stations, to the offices of the Labour Commissioner, to the ministries, proclaiming by word, in writing, by their very presence, that they were *not* on strike, that they were eager to resume work. To no avail.

The building was cordoned off by the police. The *gundas* were allowed to station themselves at the entrance, and we were kept by the police from approaching it on the ground that, were we to approach it, violence might erupt. Eventually we did go back. But the police and the *gundas* then blockaded us in. Food was not allowed in. Water was cut off.

Here is what happened on that fateful day, 28 October 1987— about a fortnight after the 'strike' had supposedly commenced.[1]

A day as fateful as frightening

About 370 of us resumed work in the *Express* building on Wednesday 28 October. But two things had happened on the evenings of the previous two days, events that saved us, literally.

The 'strike' that stopped the publication of *Indian Express, Financial Express* and *Jansatta* from 14 October had been a

---

[1] The following is based on articles I wrote between 1 November 1987 and 1 December 1987. I have deleted some portions that drew general lessons from the events. In one instance, where I had written 'one of the senior-most ministers in the Central Cabinet', I have supplied the name: Arjun Singh. In another instance, I have named the editor of the *Times of India*—Giri Lal Jain, who was the subject of an exchange with that paper's general manager, and the editor—Dileep Padgaonkar—who held forth on there being no right to reply under Indian press laws.

contrived strike all along. The executive of the Union had met me, and I had sought the opinion of several journalists. All had stressed two things: (a) The only real issue was the bonus that the management would pay; (b) There would be no strike, no occasion or issue for a strike, if the management were to pay something akin to what it had paid the previous year, that is 12.33 per cent.

On the basis of information that I had started receiving about who were controlling the Union and who in turn was manipulating them, I told Ramnathji and all concerned that the publication of the papers would be stopped, whatever bonus the management paid. The raids of 1 September, far from deterring the *Express* group, had rebounded on the government. The latter was determined to stop the publication of the paper before the next session of Parliament commenced.

The fifteen per cent

In the event, the management decided to pay not just what had been paid the previous year, but more—that is, it decided to pay a bonus of 15 per cent as against the 12.33 per cent which everyone who had talked to me had said would be adequate.

As the Delhi unit was expected to register a loss, and because of the information that those in control of the Union would be disrupting work in any case, the 15 per cent was split in two parts. The workers were to be paid the statutory 8.33 per cent as bonus, and 6.67 per cent as a goodwill allowance for the maintenance of industrial peace. The former was to be disbursed on 15 October, the latter on 15 November. 15 November was chosen as the Parliament session was expected to commence sometime in the first week of November.

The decision was communicated to the Union. It was announced on the noticeboard, and circulated to the workers.

Even so, the controllers of the Union executive insisted that the strike would commence on 14 October. The entire amount must be paid in one lump sum and immediately, they said. In spite of clear evidence of their design to stop the publication of the paper, issue or no issue, bonus or no bonus, the management agreed even to this insistence. The entire amount would be paid in one go on 15 October.

This was announced on the evening of 13 October. The journalists of all the three papers met—the editors were naturally not present. They discussed the situation. They decided— unanimously—that the 15 per cent decision settled the matter, and that therefore, should the strike be called, they would not join it. They informed the Union executive of their decision to desist from the strike and to continue working.

Late in the evening, the Union executive and management agreed on a draft agreement. The text was typed and brought in for all to sign. And just as that was about to be done, two bullies started shouting, disrupted the meeting and forced the rest of the executive to walk out.

The press manager read out the draft to the workers in his department. To prevent all concerned from resuming the meeting, half a dozen started shouting slogans, hurling abuse; they were joined by a dozen more, all now *gheraoed*[2] the general manager and the press manager successively.

No one knew what to do. The 'leaders' announced that the strike would commence the next day.

At 4.30 a.m. on 14 October the executive members telephoned S. Gurumurthy, Ramnathji's adviser in all matters financial. What had happened yesterday was a mistake, an unfortunate one, they said. They would like to sign the agreement that had been arrived at. Could they come over?

They came at 6 a.m. There was a slight shift, but only a slight one. They would sign the agreement, they said, but in view of the stand they had taken the previous night, they would like to have the general body ratify the agreement first so that no one could accuse them of a somersault. The general body would meet at 10 a.m., they said. It was just a formality, they said.

---

2 'Encircled'.

Strike yes, vote no

When workers and journalists gathered at 10 a.m., they were told that the meeting would be at noon. At noon the leaders insisted that the strike had already commenced. They specifically refused to put the strike decision to vote. When a journalist asked what was wrong with the draft that had been agreed to the previous evening, he was shouted down. No vote was allowed. Slogans took over.

The journalists reported for work the next day. As did persons from all the other departments.

The pattern was repeated day after day.

We felt that with more than 300 reporting for work day after day, with many more coming over to say that but for their fear of being beaten up they would return to work, we just could not let outsiders keep us from working at our place of work.

We took the matter to Court. The Court ordered that no employee or outsider is to obstruct workers, journalists or any other member of staff of the papers who wanted to work. It directed that no one trying to obstruct them would be allowed to picket or demonstrate within 50 yards of the entrance to the building.

It was therefore decided to re-enter the premises on Monday 26 October. Because of information that we received that day—to which I shall turn in a moment—the attempt to resume work from our building was postponed to 28 October.

Two incidents

Workers—especially those working in the press—and other staff had been beaten and threatened. In each of these incidents, men who were not employees of the *Express* group played the dominant, most aggressive part. On 26 October, two things happened within hours of each other which made us sit up.

A group of thirty to forty men went to two colonies and terrorized employees in the circulation and advertisement departments who had been working throughout. Only four or five of the posse were employees of the *Express* group. In both colonies, the intimidation, pushing around and abuse went on for over an hour. One of the *Express* staffers who lived in the colony and who had walked over to the colony—the intimidators apparently did not realize that he too had been working and filing his dispatches—struck up a conversation with one of them and asked an intimidator where the latter was from. 'We are from Sylvania Laxman (the bulb company), and Ajay Maken (a Congress[I] official) has sent us.'

Late that night, Prabhash Joshi, the editor of *Jansatta*, received a personal and urgent message from Arjun Singh, one of the senior-most ministers in the Central Cabinet; the two had known each other for years. Arjun Singh knew that we would not be able to enter the building that day, the 26, as we had planned, that we would just have to defer the attempt by two/three days. 'And day after tomorrow, you people will be thrashed at the entrance to your building,' the message said. 'Toughs are being sent from one of our unions. They expect your group to be 100 to 150 and those opposed to you to be about the same number. A melee will ensue at the stairs leading into the building. The toughs have been asked to make Arun Shourie, Prabhash Joshi and Gurumurthy their special targets, to thrash you three to pulp. In the melee, the police will order a lathi charge and make arrests from both sides. And it will be put out that the management-instigated attempt to break the strike has been foiled by the workers. Please be very careful, specially the three of you.' Arjun Singh gave the name of the person who had been engaged to supply the toughs to thrash us.

Several students had been meeting us ever since the papers had stopped appearing. We had discussed proposals for others and me to speak at the Delhi University and the JNU.

We put the new information about the toughs to them as it had just come and was much in our minds. They said that they would come and form a human wall between those who were going in and those who would try to obstruct them.

We gratefully accepted this offer. We also decided to request MPs and others to come and witness our procession. They were to look out for three things, in particular: (i) Does the police enforce the decree of the Court that no employee of the *Express* is to picket, demonstrate, obstruct, etc., within 50 yards of the entrance? (This had been a sore point with us as the police had consistently failed to enforce the decree. It was also a crucial point, for if the obstructers were kept 50 yards away, they would not be able to belabour those who were entering); (ii) How many would try to obstruct employees who were entering the building? (iii) Who indulged in violence?

A defection

Two of the students worked all night and the next morning and located the man—Yashpal Singh Yadav—who, Arjun Singh had told us, had been assigned the job of supplying toughs to belabour us. He was a prominent figure in a unit in the city and was well known for such work.

His mentor and friend was contacted.

Three absolutely fortuitous quirks helped. Yashpal turned out in his own way to be an idealist, a reader of *Jansatta,* our Hindi paper in Delhi. He knew of the work that we had been doing, and since the events in March, he had felt greatly drawn to V.P. Singh, as the man who was standing up and being made to suffer for the right things. He wanted to 'sacrifice his life' for V.P. Singh, he said.

It also transpired that he had had some arguments with Nagarajan, the outsider who was leading the *Express* 'strike' over the money that was evidently coming in to finance the 'strike'.

He said that he had asked Nagarajan where the money was coming from for the video and TV which had been installed outside the premises, for the free food at two nearby hotels, for the cars that were suddenly at the disposal of the Union leaders.

'Why are you worried?' he said he was asked. 'You say how much you want and you will get it. There is no shortage of money.' At last, he was told that the money was being given out by Kedar Nath Singh (one of the new General Secretaries of the Congress[I]), that there would be no shortage as 'the sarkar' was with them, that the meetings to plan everything take place at Gulmohar Park.

He set out the details of what had been planned for the next morning. They corresponded to the dot with what Arjun Singh had conveyed. Yashpal's description was, of course, more graphic: 'Four to five heads will be broken . . . Even if four to five are shot dead, there is to be no entry . . .'

All this came out in a long session he had with Gurumurthy. Gurumurthy led him through the work that the group had been doing and what was being done to the group. He told Yashpal that at that very moment, I was with V.P. Singh, as the latter had sent for me . . .

'I will just now go and tell them that I won't bring my men,' Yashpal told Gurumurthy.

'No, no—*don't*,' Gurumurthy told him. 'That will give them time to make other arrangements. When they have settled themselves at the entrance in the morning, that is the time to go and tell Nagarajan that what he is doing is wrong and therefore you are not supplying him the men.'

The entry

I was astonished at the turnout the next day. Over 350 turned up at the *Express* guest house to board the vehicles.

Reporters from various publications, from news agencies, photographers, a video crew turned up at the *Express* building. Around 8.30 a.m., one of India's best journalists who was at the entrance phoned me at the guest house. She told me that there were just about fifteen *Express* employees to oppose the entry. They were a dispirited lot.

'Why has nobody come from your side?' she asked Nagarajan. 'You say the overwhelming majority are with you. Why aren't they here?'

'They come in shifts . . .'

One man was dispatched to the *Times of India* to fetch workers from their press. About thirty came.

The mood of those resuming work was festive as we set out in twenty vehicles from Sundar Nagar, with police escort and all.

The students were waiting. As were MPs and leaders—Satyanarayan Reddy from the Telugu Desam, Sharad Yadav from the Lok Dal, Jaswant Singh and Madan Lal Khurana from the BJP, Kishore Chandra Deo from the Congress(S). Kuldip Nayar, too, had been invited and was there. My friend Cho Ramaswamy had flown all the way from Madras. He was not only there; he was at the head of the procession with me.

The entry was swift and peaceful. We had been saved by several things.

True to his word, Yashpal had not brought his men. At 9.15 a.m., he informed an astonished Nagarajan that he wouldn't be doing so. Second, it wasn't that there were 100 to 150 on each side. Our number was now nearly 370-odd, fifteen to twenty having joined us at the site; the protesters were just about fifty-odd; and only twenty to twenty-five of them were employees of the *Express* group.

The police had formed a good cordon.

And, true to their word, too, as we neared the entrance, the students—about twenty of them—rushed past us and formed the wall they had promised they would. I was almost swept in.

The entry was swift and peaceful, I said. But not entirely, I learnt half an hour later as I sat in my office talking to pressmen.

A senior police official tried to split our procession in two. Sharad Yadav and Madan Lal Khurana prevailed on him not to do so.

The procession proceeded. The police officer saw that employees in the last four vans were still disembarking. As they came over, the police officer asked an inspector to stop them. 'No,' the inspector told them, 'you are not to go from the front.' Instead he took them all round the building and brought them back into the group of twenty to twenty-five *Express* employees and the thirty-odd who had come over from the *Times of India*.

Here they were set upon mercilessly by outsiders and the *Times of India* men. S.K. Hazra, the head of our process department, was thrashed and dragged away. (He had to receive eight stitches later.) Another employee's leg was badly injured. A third fell back as he was struck. His scalp ruptured, and soon his clothes were red with blood.

No one did anything to protect these helpless men.

It was soon after this melee that a large stone hurled at one of these belaboured men struck the police inspector who had brought them into the waiting posse.

And it was then that the police swung into action. They set upon the *Times of India* workers, and chased them all the way into the *Times* building, which is a good way off from where all this was happening.

Many of the *Express* employees who had been beaten in this melee straggled in, some having taken shelter for a while in adjacent buildings.

Inside, work soon commenced.

But soon, a group of about ten were running past the rear of the building. They hurled stones and bricks and broke window after window. Two windows of my office, too, were broken—the shattered glass all over the room. The police looked on from one end of the lane.

'What has happened?' I asked. 'They are *Times of India* employees,' a colleague said. 'The *Times* has gone on strike in protest against the police action.'

'But what were they doing here in the first place?' I shouted in rage.

Soon the group of twenty to twenty-five protesters outside was joined by several more—first from the *Times*, then from *Patriot,* and finally from the *Hindustan Times*. A full-fledged meeting was on. Gurumurthy, Prabhash and I were the butt of the lies, the rage, the abuse, a precursor of the barrage to come.

The footage

Fortunately, the entire sequence of the entry was filmed by two crews of cameramen. The video film was seen in its entirety by several groups of journalists and others. It showed the twenty-five or so opposing the entry—barely half of them were from the *Express*. The slogan-shouting was being led by the General Secretary of the Union of another newspaper. Then one could see a group of outsiders march up and join them, most of them from *Times of India*. Even with this transfusion, the group was no more than forty or so. A very large group of us were seen entering peacefully. There was absolutely no incident of violence. The police could be seen preventing the persons in the last four vehicles from proceeding straight to the entry and, instead, taking them round the building and bringing them bang into the posse of outsiders. The outsiders and striking workers set upon them. The belaboured staff members could be seen trying to run into the building.

They could be seen as they were pushed back by the police and thrown over the entrance platform of the building, back into the hands of outsiders and the striking workers who beat them. They ran, and then, remarkably, though beaten and bedraggled, they marched peacefully into the building. It was after this that the police got into a lathi-wielding contest with striking workers and outsiders, and then lathicharged them. By that time, the 350-odd *Express* employees and the students were inside the building, and there was no way by which they could reach, to say nothing of hitting those who were outside.

The film nailed the lies that were being pasted on us. And it showed the outside instigation and participation as little else could.

A lot of money had certainly been in evidence. Since the day the strike commenced, the Union leaders had several vehicles—complete with drivers—to ferry them around. 'Strikers' and others helping them were able to obtain free food at two nearby hotels. Thousands of posters had come up all over Delhi supporting the 'strike', and condemning the *Express* management and me. One of the 'leaders' had suddenly acquired funds to travel to different centres by air to instigate workers there. At the site, there had been not just the usual tent etc.; there had been a video and TV with films. Food, too, was being served in the tent free of charge. In fact, in the three days preceding our entry, several of even the Union's executive had been asking the 'leaders', 'As the balance in the Union account was only Rs 2000 when the strike began, where is all this money coming from?'

The siege

Inside, work was on. By 2 p.m., a new problem surfaced. Even then, I did not realize the magnitude it would acquire by the night. Food that was being carried for the staff at work was set upon, seized and overturned into the dust. Not once but thrice.

By the evening, three vans carrying the food were smashed. On three separate occasions, four students who tried subsequently to bring food were severely beaten up. Only a little bit got in.

The snatching and beating took place within yards of the building, within sight of the police. The police—present in great strength—did absolutely nothing.

Late at night—around 10.30 p.m.—when no food had still been allowed in, three police officials told me that it was not part of their responsibility to see that the food that came to the building for us actually reached us inside.

Eventually, they said that if food could be taken to the Daryaganj police station—just a short distance away—they would escort it to the building. It was so taken. A lawyer and a lady waited with it for a long, long while.

'No, we cannot take it. The whole building is on fire,' the police said, 'where is the question of taking food inside?'

There was no fire. But an engineer from the Delhi Electricity Supply Undertaking appeared, insisting that all power must be switched off as there was a fire in the building. It took a lot of persuasion to keep him from executing the instructions.

Soon the police allowed fifteen-odd outsiders with lathis to storm the foyer of the building. These outsiders started beating those who were in the foyer.

There was panic. By this time, only about half a dozen of the students were still in the building. They took the blows, snatched and hurled away the lathis, and kicked the assaulters out. I shall always remember with gratitude, a young, well-built Sardar, R.P. Singh, who took the heaviest blows, and who also fought back the hardest.

A man in civilian dress came to ascertain facts. He met me also. He said he was an inspector with the CID. As he reached the foyer, he was dragged by the 'strikers', and beaten up savagely. The police did nothing for two or three minutes, till his shouts registered with them. 'I am from CID,' 'I am from CID.' The police then lathicharged those who were beating him.

Throughout the day, I kept telephoning official after official—from the highest in the civil and police hierarchy on down. The calls brought no relief.

They only incensed me further. 'Who did you expect? Snow White?' asked Gopi Arora, then the senior-most official in Rajiv Gandhi's office—we knew each other well: he had been special assistant to D.P. Dhar, the minister for planning, when I was working in the Planning Commission as a consultant. One official was full of platitudes which would have seemed polite invectives in an ordinary situation, but seemed outrageous then. Another advised me that the proper thing to do would be to file a written complaint with the police. A third gave a list of others I should ring up.

A fourth said that he had already issued the general instruction that all problems should be attended to. I told him the specific ones that had *not* been attended to at all—no escort for the staff to return home (this had been promised), no protection for the food that was being brought . . . But to give any directions in regard to such specific things, the official said, would amount to his giving operational directions to the local government which, as Secretary of the Union of India, he could not do.

It was like trying to raise the dead. I have not yet witnessed a greater contrast than the one I did that day between the dedication and idealism of the students on the one hand, and the pusillanimity of officials on the other.

By the end, the water supply to the building had also been cut off.

The paper

The staff continued to work. Well before the deadline for the city editions, the pages for both *Jansatta* and *Indian Express* were all ready.

I inquired from the police officials about the time at which the escort that had been promised for the vans that were to deliver the paper would be available. The escort had been promised, and a list of the centres to which the vans were to go, the times at which they would leave had been supplied in writing to the police. And this had been done at their request.

No, there will be no escort, the officials now said. Yes, we anticipate your vans will be damaged and men hurt. But there will be no escort. We have received no orders to provide any.

But why don't you ring up and ascertain? I asked. We don't seek orders, they said. When we receive them, we carry them out. And they walked out.

So, we started the printing. The machines were stopped after 5000 copies each of *Indian Express* and *Jansatta* were printed. We did this to establish that there was more than enough staff to produce the papers, that the papers were produced, that the print run was restricted to 5000 copies each because of the turnabout by the police.

The staff left the building in batches. The production staff, the editors and other senior personnel left at 2.30 a.m.

There were ten or so sleeping under the strikers' tent.

I reached home around 3 a.m. Anita and our Adit would be sleeping upstairs, I knew. If I went up, I might awaken them. So, I lay down in a room on the ground floor. It is then that I realized the condition in which I was; I was trembling from shoulders to calves.

A lesson from Gandhiji

We met the next morning. What is the position? we asked ourselves. That we want to work, that we are at work but that the place at which the equipment, etc., which we need for printing the paper are out of our reach because the police will not enforce the law or the court order.

As we could not go back to the *Express* building, we again started working from the Sundar Nagar guest house. We approached the Court again: the police are not implementing your order; they are not keeping outsiders and the fifteen to twenty *Express* employees, who insist they are on strike, 50 yards from the entrance of the building, we told the Court.

On 29 October, that is the day after we entered, the Court gave a second ruling in which it said:

> As held in the authorities of Andhra Pradesh and Calcutta High Court, law is clear that rights arising out of orders of the courts can be enforced with the help of the police. This is so because between the parties an order, judgement or decree of the court has status of law. It is the statutory duty of the police to enforce law. The police is supposed to be the servant of the law only. Whenever there is a violation of law between the parties to the decree, therefore, any flagrant violation of that decree calls for positive steps on the part of the law-enforcing agency.
>
> If police authorities fail to discharge this duty they will not merely earn reproach of having failed in their statutory duty but also this omission on their part will tend to lower the authority of the court which passed the decree. This clearly amounts to criminal contempt as defined U/S 2(C) (I) of the Contempt of Court Act.

We sent a copy of this new ruling also to the police. Not even an acknowledgement. We sent a reminder. Not even an acknowledgement.

And why did not, and do not the police care? Because while the courts have the power to punish for contempt, the police are confident that they will not exercise that power. And, in this day and age, who cares for more strictures and lectures, be they of a magistrate or a Judge?

I was reminded once again of the truth that Gandhiji used to speak about: in the end, every institution of the state, the law, the officials with their elaborate titles, are but the convenience of the powerful. And in the India of today, the 'powerful' are those who are in office at the moment. And why are they 'powerful'? Because officials and institutions are only too eager to act as their instruments.

Soon we learnt that Gulabrao Joshi, a 'labour leader' of the Congress(I) had been deputed to bring the Bombay edition of the *Express* to a halt by similar means. He had been quick to act. He lost no time to send a representation to Rajiv Gandhi, asserting that the *Indian Express* should not be allowed to function.

Another attempt

Over 600 of the 670 workers had begun reporting for work. One Tuesday, the workers met near the Sundar Nagar flat from which we used to operate. The General Secretary of the Union addressed them. They decided to hold a general body meeting at the steps of the *Express* building the following day. The decision was a brave one as individuals had continued to be thrashed day after day.

On Wednesday, they started gathering at around 10 a.m. near the building. As the individuals arrived—they had decided not to approach in a procession—many were set upon. Acid bulbs were thrown at some. Soda water bottles—their virtue being that they explode on impact—were hurled at others. Some were thrashed.

All this went on within yards of the police. They did nothing at all.

In fact, they did the opposite of what the law and the decrees of the Court required. They allowed twenty-odd employees and thirty or forty toughs from outside, equipped with lathis and all, to position themselves across the entrance.

And they formed a cordon across the approach road to make sure that none of the employees who wanted to resume work could get near the entrance.

'This correspondent,' wrote the special correspondent of the *India Post* in Thursday's issue of the paper,

> witnessed a curious exchange between the ACP (the Assistant Commissioner of Police) Daryaganj, Mr. Virender Singh, and Mr. Nagarajan (the 'leader' of the 'Strike'). Mr. Singh assured Mr. Nagarajan that no *Express* employee would enter the building since his men were posted even at the rear entrance. But at the same time, he urged Mr. Nagarajan not to use violence

and involve the police in it. 'Don't make the police clash with
the workers. If there must be a clash, let the workers fight it out
among themselves,' he said.

Complicity? Collusion? The advice of an officer charged with the
duty to enforce the law?

And he was true to his word.

In spite of the violence, 410 employees reached the venue. And
stayed on for hours. They couldn't reach the steps. And so they
held their meeting in the open space next to the building.

No one from the management was at the meeting. None of
the editors of the three papers was there. The staff had said that
they wanted this to be a purely employees' affair. And so it was.

At the meeting, they removed T.M. Nagarajan from the
presidentship of the Union. They formed a new team to negotiate
matters with the management. They formally called off the 'strike'.
They decided to resume work immediately.

The police, which had done nothing, but nothing till
then, now swung into action. Those in charge called in the
mounted police and the riot police. And all of them together
formed a barricade across the approach. No, you cannot go to
the building.

'But why not?' C.P. Raghavan, the resident editor of *Financial
Express*, demanded. 'Why are you doing this? By what authority
are you stopping us?'

'Orders from above,' said the senior-most police officer there.

Two hundred of the employees were then herded into trucks
and taken to the nearby police station. And kept there for
four hours.

Not one person who had indulged in violence was so much
as questioned.

The avalanche of calumny

By the evening of that day itself, the barrage of disinformation
had started: BJP–RSS–Arun Shourie have beaten up the striking
workers, and the police, too, for good measure, have joined them

in doing so. Doordarshan and AIR were the first to put out the lie—a difference from what things would be today: a posse of 'private' channels would be the megaphones of choice. The first part of the lie obscured every fact—issues settled before the strike, 370 v twenty-five, who hit, who was hit . . . The second part absolved the government and the Congress(I).

In fact, from the *Express* workers' side, not one person had hit anyone. As for the police, they had hit out only twice. Once when an inspector was hit accidentally, and that by the *Times of India* employees; and the second time when the CID inspector was set upon. But, who cares? The bigger the lie . . . the more often it is repeated . . .

In the next few days, the patriotic press, the very ones that had trumpeted the government's line that we were destabilizing the country, took the lie to a crescendo.

When there was a slight lull in the barrage of the *Times of India*, I showed to the general manager, Baljit Kapur, Ramesh Jain, a senior person in the management and a member of the Jain family who we have encountered earlier, and one of its editors, Dileep Padgaonkar, the video film which had recorded the events of 28 October, events which no one had misrepresented and distorted more than the *Times of India*. The executives were quick to see that, contrary to the impression which had been created by the *Times of India*, the overwhelming number of *Express* workers had resumed duty that day. They saw for themselves that there were just a handful opposing the entry, and that, in fact, a large proportion of these were from the *Times of India* itself. They recognized the man who was leading them in shouting—he was not from the *Indian Express* but from *Times of India*. (They asked me who the other person was who was leading the shouting. He too was not associated in any way with *Indian Express*. He was a worker who had been suspended from *Punjab Kesari* for violence.) They saw another bunch from the *Times of India* join that small group. They saw how some of the workers resuming duty were diverted to the back lane deliberately by the police. They saw that there was not the slightest violence by anyone or on behalf of anyone resuming duty.

Padgaonkar, the editor, also saw all this. He heard the comments of the senior executives of the *Times of India* itself. Now that both the premises on which the calumnies had rested— the premise that the overwhelming proportion of workers were for the strike, and that we had tried to break through with a handful, aided and abetted by outsiders; and the premise that these outsiders had belaboured the striking workers—had been seen to be so totally without foundation, what amends would the *Times of India* make? I asked repeatedly.

I was told that nothing could be done as far as the comments of the editor and the editorials on the subject were concerned, 'The editor's comments, as you know,' Baljit Kapur, the manager, always suavely dressed, said, 'are independent of the facts. His comments are on an entirely different level.'

As for my writing an article in their paper setting out the facts to nail the lies that they had been publishing, Padgaonkar, recently returned from Paris, said with a show of indifference bordering on superciliousness, 'There is no right of reply under Indian press laws.' I could, of course, write a letter to the editor, he said, and they would consider publishing it. As for the perverse coverage in the news columns, he said he would examine the coverage and get back to me. I am not sure whether he examined it. In any case, he did not get back to me.

I was very upset at, but not at all surprised by this supercilious attitude, just as I had not been surprised by the abuse. And there was a lesson in that abuse. Given what Indian society is, we just cannot contribute anything worthwhile to public discourse in India or to public issues, till we steel ourselves against slander, indeed against all sense of personal wrong.

The cardinal lesson was, and remains: the only protection that those who value free speech have is that they must work in the public weal as much as they can when they can, so that when they are silenced, their silence speaks. And so that when they are silenced, the reader feels that *he* has been silenced.

In any event, our routine resumed. We would meet every morning at the Sundar Nagar guest house. Employees would gather, sign the register. The editorial meeting. Stories to be pursued. Dictating edits. All this for the other editions of the paper as the Delhi edition remained shut.

We made repeated attempts to enter the building—singly and in groups. The result was always the same.

When employees attempted to enter the building individually, they were set upon. The police looked away. When they attempted to approach it in a group, the police physically prevented them from doing so.

'There will be violence at the building,' police officials deputed to the spot would say. 'You see, there are *gundas* there.' 'But why are you allowing the *gundas* to occupy and block the stairs?' I asked them on more than one occasion. 'Sir, what can we do? You must talk to the high-ups,' they counselled.

The high-ups were polite, even full of mock concern. 'We will look into the matter at once,' they told us, and they told the MPs; after exchange upon exchange, they counselled us to go the Labour Commissioner's office. 'It is a labour matter,' they said.

Not one or two but several hundred employees went to that office on several occasions. The agreement had been registered there. 'We already know the facts,' the officials at that office said. 'There is no need to convince us as we are already convinced. It is purely a police problem. All that has to be done is for the police to ensure protection.'

On returning to the police, we would find them solicitous—for themselves. 'It is really beyond us. You know what is going on, why don't you get the courts to order us to provide the protection?' But the courts have already issued two orders. You fellows are not putting even those into effect, we would point out.

'That is right,' the police officials agreed, only to add, 'but you see while the court said, "X and Y should be done," it did not say, "The police should do X and Y." Why not get the courts to say that?'

'And how long do you think it will take us to get that case through?' They were ever so understanding: 'Yes, it could be months, if not longer.'

'But is it the position that the police will not implement a law because the court does not say "this law is to be implemented" to the police?' we would ask.

'You are right, of course. There is no answer. And you know there is no problem either. Except that at our level we can do nothing. Please take it up at the high level.'

This routine continued till the end of November. It was only on 1 December that we could enter the building and begin printing the Delhi edition of the paper.

The staff, the students, all of us together had rolled back the might of the government. All of us echoed the chant of the students: '*Dam hai kitnaa daman mein terye, Dekh liyaa hai, dekhengey*'. Ravi Shankar caught the moment. Rajiv Gandhi is sitting in his veranda, having his morning tea. From his cycle, the newsboy hurls a rolled-up *Indian Express* into the veranda. Rajiv is startled out of his wits.

Rules of thumb

Here are rules of thumb that summarize some of the lessons we learnt from such experiences:

1. Our task is to educate people. For this, we may deploy facts and figures, good writing, humour, whatever. But these are just means. Our task is not to merely entertain people, to provide them diversions. It is to persuade, to cajole, to shame, to compel them to take up public issues, to act in the public weal.

2. We must be open to all, for information may come from anyone—low or high. We must weigh the evidence, not get taken in by who is providing us the information, opinion or that lead.

3. Of course, if someone is hiding some document, etc., we must try our damnedest to get it—for there must be a reason why that person is trying to conceal that document. But in the excitement of looking for the secret document, we must not neglect to study the documents available in the public domain.

4. If what we are to write is based on, or is to refer to some documents, we must have studied every single document ourselves.

5. We must have all the documents in our possession, so that if at any turn during the period the controversy lasts, and we need to refer to the document, or show it to prove our point, we must be able to do so without any hitch.

6. We must forge bonds with, cooperate with persons in other professions. Rare will be the journalist who will be a master of every issue on which he may have to write. Bonds with experts in those fields will be invaluable. Moreover, to have consequences, what we write will often have to find an echo in other chambers—courts and legislatures, for instance. Comradeship with persons in those fora, who will take up the issue in their own sphere, will be indispensable. We have to make friends before we need them. Once we are caught up in the chase, we will just not have the time to forge these links.

7. The first blow must be devastating.

8. But we must keep a third of the ammunition in reserve. The subject of the writing is bound to deny what we have written. The moment he does so, we must be able to smother his credibility with successive salvos.

9. We must be crocodiles, not grasshoppers. We must keep up the pressure. Churchill's formula for his troops: 'Continue to pester, nag and bite.' Pressed, rulers will make mistakes. They will evade, lie, raise some other issue, making it that much easier for people to see that what we are saying is true. Soon enough, they will pounce on us; thereby they will prove our point.

10. Gandhiji's formula: Persist with the issue till one of two things happens. Either persons occupying positions that give them, ex officio, the right, so to say, to pronounce on the evidence—a Prime Minister in the case of ministers, the courts, the reader—accept that the subject is guilty, or, in spite of overwhelming evidence, these referees refuse to accept that the subject has done wrong. In the former case, we would have proven that one individual, that a paper, can indeed bring even a high official to book—this will give heart to many that, yes, they too can bring oppressors to book. In the latter case also, we would have rendered a service: we would have shown

people at large how far the rot has gone, and taught them that they have to shed the illusion that they can get justice through existing institutions.

11. We must not equivocate, we must not hem and haw. Our task is not to 'present both sides of the picture'. Our task is to examine the evidence, and state what we think is right. We can leave it to others to weigh the evidence and come to different conclusions and urge these to the readers.

12. Even though we are pursuing an issue, what we do will touch people's lives, some of them innocent, some of them having little to do with the issue. In the heat of the chase, and especially when we follow the preceding rule, it is entirely possible that some innocent persons will get hurt. We would have done our best to verify the information, and yet may end up advancing the wrong conclusion. The moment we realize this, we must acknowledge the mistake openly, at once. And not just by writing about it. We must reach out to the person who has been hurt and apologize to him. Also, in future, we must be extremely wary of the source who misled us. In fact, the best would be to expose the person who gave us the wrong information—affirming that we accept full responsibility for what we wrote, but that we are revealing the name of the source so that others may not be similarly misused by him. From each such mistake we must learn to be more careful about the collateral hurt that our writing may cause.

13. In regard to issues as distinct from persons, when new evidence comes forth or we come to realize that there was some aspect that we had not examined, and we now see that what we said was in error, again we must acknowledge the error openly. And state as unequivocally what we think is right in light of the new evidence or on reconsideration of the evidence we had examined originally.

14. Readers may well turn around and say, 'Why should we believe you now? Maybe you are wrong this time too.' The answer must be, 'Indeed, do not accept what I say. Examine the evidence yourself. Think for yourself.'

15. Journalism, and writing in general, is one of the professions in which it is easy to get by without doing much—it resembles government service in this. Gather for coffee. Gossip with colleagues. Go to a press conference. Type 500 words about what the fellow said. Gather for coffee. Gossip with colleagues. The assignment is done. But so is the day. Never to return. We must beware of this trap of ease.

16. When, by chance, we happen to be a witness to something of consequence, when we get entangled with rulers, with some institution, we must carefully store what we write, of course. In addition, in spite of the extreme pressure that we will be working under at that time, we should write down the incidentals around that story. These notes will help us as little else reimagine and depict the episode, the ruler, the times themselves.

17. We must read incessantly. Read widely. Two things in particular. First, we have to master the laws, regulations, manuals of procedure that bear on the subject we are writing about. If we are writing about purchase of defence equipment, for instance, we must know the regulations and procedures that have been prescribed better than the fellows in government. Second, the laws that will be used to stifle our work: defamation, contempt of court, privileges of legislatures, sedition. We have to master these laws. We must keep up with the latest judgments about them. We must not leave the matter to lawyers. Few will work as hard on our case as we can, and as we need to.

18. We must invoke the laws, and seek protection from the institutions when harassed by the powerful—often just to show up the laws and institutions. But we must always remember that, in the end, these are not what will protect us. The laws will have been framed, and when necessary, altered by the powerful. The institutions to which we will have to run will have been manned by persons whom the powerful have assessed to be reliable. In the end, the reader alone will be our shield. And so, our work must be such that, when the powerful silence us, the reader must feel that *his* tongue has been yanked out.

19. Of course, we need sources. But while we think we are 'cultivating' him, we must beware lest he is 'cultivating' us to use us.

20. So that *lihaaz* does not come in the way, we must not get too close to anyone about whom we may have to write one day. That will include persons in public life, persons in authority—a government official, a Judge—and businessmen.

21. As well as the people—for just as often, we will have to speak truth to the people.

22. We must want little. Be satisfied with enough—'enough' being what we have at the moment.

23. In particular, we must not want anything that potential subjects of our writing can give us or withhold from us—an asset, a position, an honour. We must have no price, and everyone must know that we have no price.

24. We must always bear in mind that the Empire *will* strike back. So, we must be squeaky clean.

25. And if it strikes in any case, we must be prepared for the consequences of what we have been writing. 'Commitment' to a cause does not mean shouting a slogan and running away. It means commitment to the consequences of what one is saying and doing.

26. We must—each of us personally—stand our ground, of course: no one is going to listen to our lectures on the importance of free speech when they see that we ourselves have muted our voice. But there is also a related task: we must be fortresses around those who are standing up for the truth, and for the right to get it to the people.

27. In striking back, the rulers will use all the instruments of State, of course. But the instruments will include not just the agencies that formally count as agencies of the State. Among the instruments they will deploy are persons and institutions outside the formal apparatus of the State, persons—journalists, owners of papers, advertisers—they have suborned. We must expose these toadies mercilessly. They are not just a hindrance to our work. They are polluting, and thereby corroding the credibility of the entire profession. They are undermining

the freedom that is the basis of other freedoms—the freedom of speech.

28. Just as we must be alert to and expose quislings, we must be alert to the stratagems that rulers deploy. Cornered, they will raise some other issue, and get their agents in the media to make *that* the issue of the day. They will use each blunder of theirs, and the crisis that ensues as a result, to make people forget the previous blunder and the harm *that* blunder had inflicted. We have to awaken readers to these techniques of 'headline management'. We have to keep the reader's eyes on the great issues. The moment rulers deploy a device to distract, we should bring it to the notice of the reader—that is a part of, an important part of our work.

29. We must stay clear of one of the most frequently used excuses for mediocrity, of dumbing down—that the reader 'wants this only', that he is not interested in anything more detailed. We must not underestimate the average reader. The reader is hungry for facts, for details, for reason. Our job is to present facts and details to him, to present them in ways that will capture his attention. In any case, if the reader still does not heed facts and details, so much the worse for him—he will pay for his superciliousness, society will pay for not paying heed.

30. One way to avoid this curse of mediocrity is not to pitch our writing to the average reader. We should aim much, much higher. Our treatment of a subject must pass muster with the expert in that field, with the authority on that subject. Not the average reader, but *they* must regard our treatment as worthy.

31. We have to have a thick skin. When criticized, we should examine the criticism: to the extent that it is valid, we should alter our conduct or view. When the criticism is contrary to facts, especially when it is just abuse, we should learn to disregard it: to be able to do so with equanimity, it will serve us well to have a *kadhchi* full of contempt for calumners.

32. When motives are pasted on us and what we have written, a good answer is, 'Believe the worst about me—that I am a cheat, an ungrateful blackguard, in every way a wretch— but what about the facts?'

33. We must not compromise on any of these. We must not dilute what we have to get to the reader. If the editor or proprietor gets in the way, we must find some way around them.

34. As the Empire *will* move to push us out, as owners and editors may well give in, we must keep abreast of new ways that are emerging to get our message across: if not a regular publication, a blog; if not print, TV; if not a regular channel, YouTube; if not YouTube, books; if not books . . .

35. The point is not to compromise, not to dilute what we have to say. Beware of the rationalization: 'It is better to get at least *something* across than nothing.' As Gandhiji would remind us, if we compromise, if we dilute what we know must get across, we mislead the people into believing that things are more or less normal. If we are completely silenced, Gandhiji taught, we would have delivered the most important signal we can give in times of suppression: we will have awakened readers to how far things have gone.

36. If the reader, too, does not listen, well, he does not listen. He, indeed, the society at large, will pay for not having paid heed to our warning, for not having taken our advice to heart. We must not dilute it to make it more palatable for him.

37. We must learn not to worry, 'But I will lose this platform. How will I get my views across?' If we are being prevented from conveying truth to our readers, we don't have the platform in any case.

38. We mustn't worry about losing our job either. There is life after dismissal! It is prudent to have two/three professions going. If we are blocked in one, we can leap on to the next one.

39. But one thing above all. The expression Gandhiji used, 'My life is my message,' should be in our mind always. It has a dual meaning. One, he changed his view as situations changed, as he saw the result of the course he had recommended, as he reflected further on a question. Therefore, to glean his core, we should look not so much at what he said at some point in time. Rather, we should look at the principles—the search for truth, for instance, through the vicissitudes of life—to

which he held on. The expression has another aspect also, one that may not have been in his mind, but will be of use to us. He acquired the enormous influence that he did, not because of what he spoke or wrote, but by the life he led. That is what we must remember above all. In the end, what will determine whether people will heed us is not the circulation of the paper in which we write, or the 'hits on YouTube'. It is the authenticity of our life, the degree to which our life corresponds to our words. And this will be on view every day.

25

'Puerile, politically motivated, slanderous, utter depravity, sick mind, always out to destabilize India, manipulative journalism'[1]

For the past few weeks, some members of the Opposition have behaved like marionettes of manipulative journalism.

—Rajiv Gandhi, Prime Minister

All that I can say is what has appeared in the Press can be defined as puerile writing, highly mischievous, a politically motivated slanderous campaign to defame certain persons in the Government . . .

—Buta Singh, Home Minister

---

[1] The following is based on what I wrote in the *Indian Express* on 14, 17, 19, 29, 31 March, and 2, 5, 18, 19 April 1989. And on exchanges and debates that took place in the Lok Sabha and the Rajya Sabha on 14, 15, 17, 27, 28, 29, 30, 31 March, and 3, 10, 11 April 1989.

... a section of the media as well as certain political, leaders have continued to indulge in speculation, insinuation and innuendo. In the last ten days—days in which both Houses were often disrupted, members were suspended, Government was blundering its way from cover to cover—*they have attributed motives to the Government and tried to bring into ridicule the institutions of the State and those holding responsible positions in Government. When the reports are laid before Parliament, and when they are read by reasonable men and women, the truth will be known and the utter depravity of the campaign launched by [a] certain section will stand exposed ...*

—Buta Singh, Home Minister

... Only a sick mind of a newspaper editor can do this ...

—N.C. Chaturvedi, Congress(I) MP

I know at least one editor and one advocate for whom any stick is good enough to beat the Government and who will go to any length even to join hands with if necessary, and encourage anti-national and disruptive forces to put the Government in difficulty. They will not mind putting national interests into jeopardy in order to serve their narrow perverted interests ...

—Bipin Pal Das, Congress(I) MP

To demand [the] resignation of the Prime Minister is what if not an attempt to destabilize? Whenever we have passed or introduced any legislation to curb terrorism, or issued Ordinances, opposing these Bills or Ordinances is what if not an attempt to destabilize this country? To doubt the quality of Bofors gun and make it public and known to the world that we do not have a proper gun to defend our country, what is this if this is not an attempt to destabilize our country? Marching to the Swedish Embassy and handing over a memorandum to a Clerk in the Embassy [as I have mentioned earlier, a truck-load of over a lakh and fifty thousand letters had been addressed by readers to the Swedish Prime Minister] *when we have got Parliament, Supreme Court and other institutions, what is this if not an attempt to destabilize our country? They have, therefore, played this game of destabilization all through . . .*

—Shantaram Naik, Congress(I) MP

. . . this entire, this most vicious drama . . . I am respectfully submitting that this drama has been enacted on the basis of a particular news item which had appeared in the Indian Express *yesterday. I am respectfully submitting that this news item was under the name of one particular individual, the author. I am submitting, the character of this individual have [sic] been so malicious, petty, mean and untruthful that every writing which flows from the pen of this individual deserves to be rejected with the contempt he deserves. Here is the man, when he was kicked out of the* Indian Express *by Mr. R.N. Goenka, he started writing most abusive articles against his mentor and master, he started biting the very hand that had fed him and now he goes back to the* Indian Express *. . .*

—Madan Bhatia, Congress(I) MP
The Deputy Chairman: '*What are you speaking on?*
We are dealing with the Budget now. I cannot
allow a statement for no reason. There should be
something before the House . . .'

. . . This morning when I was reading the newspapers, I found that a particular newspaper, the Indian Express *. . . My personal friend Mr Shourie . . . He is my personal friend . . . I am not ashamed of it. I don't ditch people. Mr Shourie is an intellectual and I know him as that since he was in the World Bank. I find that many matters are being brought which have made the Parliament a laughing stock . . .*

Earlier, MPs used to unearth facts, they were leading exposures—like Feroze Gandhi. Now we are being led by newspaper people. Find out who leaked the report . . .

*I want to know how this matter which is called top secret
goes out. How is it published in the newspaper . . . I want to
know whether the Government will take stringent measures and
stern action against the culprits and against those who printed
this . . . But who has done it? And Mr Shourie with impunity
goes on publishing day [in] and day out any matter whatsoever
making Parliament a laughing stock . . .*

*. . . I do not want the Government to be impervious
to such acts of the newspapermen. They must be dealt
with sternly . . .*

—A.G. Kulkarni, Indian National Congress, MP

What had happened?

As you will recall, Mrs Indira Gandhi had been assassinated on
31 October 1984. One of the assassins, Beant Singh, had been
killed on the spot. The other, Satwant Singh, had been injured and
captured. R.K. Dhawan, Mrs Gandhi's powerful special assistant
for years, said that he had been walking a foot and a half or two
feet behind her. Fortunately for him, while she was sprayed from
two directions by bullets from semi-automatic weapons, he had
not been hurt—a fact that was to figure substantially in what we
are about to consider.

The assassination was followed by widespread killing of
innocent Sikhs in Delhi and elsewhere. At a public meeting, Rajiv
Gandhi, who had succeeded Mrs Gandhi as Prime Minister, said,
'When a giant tree falls, the earth is bound to shake.'

On 15 November, a Special Investigation Team (SIT) was
constituted to investigate the assassination.

Five days later, a Commission of Inquiry was set up to examine
the 'larger conspiracy' behind the assassination. In consultation
with the Chief Justice, a sitting Judge of the Supreme Court, M.P.
Thakkar, was appointed as the Commission. The Commission had
five terms of reference:

(1) Sequence of events leading to and facts relating to
the assassination

(2) Lapses, if any, on the part of individuals on security duty and others responsible for the security of the Prime Minister
(3) Deficiencies, if any, in the security system and its processes
(4) Deficiencies, if any, in the procedures and matters relating to provision of medical attention after the crime and whether there was any lapse or dereliction in that respect
(5) Whether any persons or agencies were responsible for conceiving, preparing and planning the assassination and whether there was any conspiracy

Arrangements were made for the SIT and the Commission to work closely together.

Thakkar presented what he termed as an 'Interim Report' on 19 November 1985. This was not 'interim', in the sense that its text or conclusions were tentative and liable to be revised as new material reached the Commission. It was 'interim' in that it dealt with only the first three terms of reference.

Thakkar submitted a 'Final Report' on 27 February 1986. He devoted scarcely eight pages to the possible role of any foreign agencies in the conspiracy to kill Mrs Gandhi. And in these also, Thakkar was as convoluted as can be. On page 138, he wrote:

> *Involvement of foreign agency to create a situation of instability*: A great deal of material has been gathered by the investigating agency, which tends to show that a foreign agency has, in fact, played such a role *inter alia* by inspiring, encouraging, assisting and training the terrorists. A full and detailed report carefully and assiduously prepared by the said agency is included in Part I(A).

Two pages later, Thakkar observed:

> Regarding involvement of foreign agency so far no adequate and satisfactory material showing that some foreign agency was involved in the conspiracy to assassinate the late Prime Minister has been placed before the Commission.[2]

---

[2] My dear and distinguished friend, Jaswant Singh, drew the attention of the Rajya Sabha to this contrast, while arguing why the SIT report and other

In contrast to the eight pages of such contortions about the possible role of foreign agencies, Thakkar devoted more than 120 pages to the role of individuals. He found fault with twenty-two individuals. His strongest strictures were reserved for R.K. Dhawan. According to Thakkar, Dhawan had been responsible for reversing the earlier decision not to place Sikh personnel in the inner circle after Blue Star; he had shifted the time of the interview Mrs Gandhi was to give on the morning of the 31st to a time by which Satwant and Beant would have had sufficient time to acquire complete mastery over the path Mrs Gandhi was to traverse to go for the interview; Dhawan had resorted to several untruths and evasions while replying to a range of questions—from whether he had known Beant Singh to a crucial entry in the master diary listing Mrs Gandhi's appointments.

Even as he said about Dhawan, 'the motive which operated on his mind has not become sufficiently evident from the material which has come to light so far', Thakkar used strong language to point what he termed 'the needle of suspicion' towards Dhawan:

> The Commission on its part has in the course of its exploratory exercise gathered certain material and on the basis thereof formed the opinion that there are reasonable grounds to suspect the involvement of Shri RK Dhawan, the then Special Assistant to the late PM, in the crime.
>
> . . . There is no escape from the conclusion that there are weighty reasons to suspect the complicity or involvement of Shri Dhawan in the crime . . .

Accordingly, Thakkar suggested that the SIT be asked to investigate the role of Dhawan.

In his 'Final Report', Thakkar wrote that some of the matters to which he had drawn attention needed to be investigated by the SIT, and therefore, both so that the criminal investigation is not hampered and so that no individual is unfairly harmed, the

---

materials that had been listed by Thakkar as being part of his Report should be made available to members. Rajya Sabha Debates, 3 April 1989, Columns 31–32.

government may consider not making the report public. This was in February 1986.

The government went a step further. It decided that the 'Interim' and 'Final' Reports dealt with what, in effect, was the same event, and so both should be kept secret. The Commissions of Inquiry Act required all reports of Commissions of Inquiry to be placed on the Table of the Lok Sabha. And so, on 14 May 1986, government issued an Ordinance to amend the Act. On 20 August 1986, the Act was formally amended, and now, by law, the government could keep the Thakkar Commission's Reports secret. A tiny detail which led to an amusing result: the Resolution to amend the Act was piloted by the then law minister, Ashoke Kumar Sen whom we have already encountered in the Antulay affair.

By early 1987, the decision to keep the Report secret from everybody became one of the causes for tension between President Giani Zail Singh and Rajiv Gandhi. Gianiji sought a copy of the Report. He specifically asked the Home Minister, Buta Singh for it. Buta Singh promised to send it. But didn't. The President's Secretary wrote to the Home Secretary, reminding him of the Home Minister's commitment. Nothing happened. As the months went by, Gianiji began feeling that information that he needed for discharging his role as President was being deliberately withheld from him—something I allude to elsewhere. That the Thakkar Report had been withheld from him became a prominent example in his mind.

The SIT examined Dhawan's role for four years. In January 1989, it concluded that Dhawan was completely innocent, that he had no role whatsoever in the assassination of Mrs Gandhi. It located some others who had indeed had a hand in the conspiracy to kill Mrs Gandhi. The government moved to proceed against them. The SIT's report was kept secret.

I get the report

Having become, in effect, the 'gatekeeper' of Mrs Gandhi, in that he came to control access of both persons and information to her,

Dhawan had stirred many jealousies. Several persons would have wanted to cut him out. Moreover, he had grown close to Sanjay Gandhi. After Rajiv took over as Prime Minister, Dhawan was removed from his post. But after 1986, Rajiv became entangled in political and other difficulties—the Bofors controversy among them. He brought Dhawan back as Additional Secretary in the PMO.

In the paper, we had heard that Thakkar had pointed a finger at Dhawan, and so had been on the lookout for the Report. This was all the more so as I knew first-hand that the fact that the Report had been withheld even from Giani Zail Singh, the then President, had rankled in his mind. N.S. Jagannathan was the editor of the *Financial Express*. He was sagacious, widely read, one of the best in our field, and my good counsel. Two officers known to him brought Thakkar's two volumes and asked him to hand them over to me. I found the Reports to be banal. The only news point, so to say, was the fact that the Judge had gone so far to point 'the needle of suspicion' towards Dhawan.

Given the fact that the Report had been withheld from the public, from Parliament, from the President, we realized that publishing it would require extra precautions. By then, we knew that what we were publishing was being carefully monitored. It was easy for government agencies to do so as the material had to be sent to our editions over teleprinter lines. On two or three occasions, the electricity to the building had been turned off as the paper was about to go to press. We had looked upon these as rehearsals for the day when the government would want to prevent some particularly embarrassing material from being published. Accordingly, after I had written the article, I had it composed by a trusted supervisor, rather than sending it down in the basement to be set by one of the usual typesetters in the press. It was proofread by a senior colleague. The bromides were sent by different courier services to our editions. Resident editors and news editors were told not to open the envelopes till they heard from the news editor in Delhi.

On 14 March 1989, more than three years having passed since Thakkar had presented his Reports, all editions carried the article.

It set out what Thakkar had said, and why. Mohan Katre, then
Director of the CBI and a key fixer of the Prime Minister, was to
say later that this was the first occasion on which the government
had not known what was appearing in the *Express* the next day.

'Cannot be discussed . . . in any circumstances'

Parliament was in a furore. The Opposition wanted the Thakkar
Commission's Report to be given to Members of Parliament.
The government could have finished the matter in a moment by
furnishing the Report. Instead, it dug in its heels. We won't do
the right thing under duress! The Home Minister, Buta Singh,
reminded members of the amendment that Parliament had passed:

> The provisions of sub-section (4) shall not apply if the appropriate
> Government is satisfied . . . that in the interest of sovereignty
> and integrity of India, the security of the State, friendly relations
> with the foreign States or in public interest, it is not expedient
> to lay before the House of the People or, as the case may be, the
> legislative Assembly of a State the Report, or any part thereof,
> of the Commission on the inquiry made by the Commission
> under sub-section 1 and issues a notification to that effect in the
> official gazette.

Buta Singh was emphatic, categorical:

> There is a decision of the House through resolution or through
> an amendment of the Act that this Report shall not be placed on
> the Table of the House and shall not be discussed in this House.
> We stick to that decision. We do not want to revise this decision.
> Therefore, this House cannot discuss or even raise questions on
> this. This is the sovereign decision of this House.

The House erupted in disorderly scenes. As things settled a bit,
Buta Singh said that the amendment had been piloted by Ashoke
Sen. But now Sen had joined the rest of the Opposition in urging
that Thakkar's Report be given to Parliament. Sen got up to

answer. He was not allowed to do so. At last, he was able to speak. He said:

> Sir, may I proceed? When this House was asked to vote upon this Bill they were not told that there were strictures of this character against a person and to shield that, this matter was being brought. If we were told, it would have been a different thing. Nobody was told. Even the Law Minister did not know of this. It was not placed before the Council of Ministers even. Therefore, the House voted without knowing the cause of shielding . . . [Interruptions] This was a trick played on the House. [Interruptions]

Buta Singh and others jumped on him. You were the one who piloted the amendment. You and V.P. Singh attended the Cabinet meeting in which the amendment was approved . . . Sen would not relent. 'The people of the country have been telling us that Mr Ashoke Sen is a man of integrity,' Buta Singh said. 'Today he has proved that this thing is not there.' 'Either he was not sincere when he brought the amendment or he is not sincere now . . . There is something called collective responsibility . . . I am sure that V.P. Singh has not taken that stand as yet because the Government has the collective responsibility to this august House . . .' And he continued,

> All that I can say is what has appeared in the Press can be defined as puerile writing, highly mischievous, politically motivated slanderous campaign to defame certain persons in the Government. Beyond that I am not prepared to say anything and this cannot be discussed in the House under any circumstances.

Even shriller uproar. V.P. Singh got up:

> My name was taken by the hon. Home Minister and he has talked of collective responsibility. I was in the Cabinet. I was also a member of the CCPA[3]; Shri Buta Singh was also there. May

---

[3]   Cabinet Committee on Political Affairs.

I say of collective responsibility? The Prime Minister did not show the Report to any member . . . [Interruptions] How does the question of collective responsibility come? [Interruptions]

It was now Buta Singh's turn to be the strict constitutionalist. 'Shri Ashoke Sen and Shri VP Singh are divulging certain things [which happened or did not happen] according to them,' he said.

What has happened in the Cabinet and the CCPA is not a property of this House, that cannot be discussed here. Both of them are breaking the constitutional obligations; they are breaching the privilege which they enjoyed as Ministers. They are not worthy to be called even members of Parliament, of this House . . . I request you to kindly expunge this from the proceedings of this House . . . [Interruptions].

With every syllable, Buta Singh was convincing members that the government had much to hide.

Outside Parliament, pressmen were told that the Report just could not and would not be released as doing so will prejudice the investigation into the conspiracy to kill Mrs Gandhi.

Members demanded that the Report be tabled. They filed Calling Attention motions. On the 16th, Shankar Dayal Sharma, then Vice President, ruled them out. He said:

I can tell you, I have given the matter the full attention that it deserved, and after receiving your intention to give notice I have ascertained the Government's viewpoint in detail. After fullest consideration of all aspects of the matter, I am entirely convinced that this matter for calling attention should not be admitted. That is my considered decision.

'The full responsibility is mine,' he continued as members protested. 'Posterity will judge me,' he said as members shouted against his decision. 'Nobody has the right to question my ruling,' he declared.

This was on 16 March.

I pressed the advantage, and on the 17th morning published another article. This one showed that what the government had been peddling to the Courts in the criminal case was different from what Thakkar had concluded; and that Thakkar's conclusions as well as the evidence that he had collected—both documentary and oral—had been deliberately kept from the courts. This led to even greater turmoil.

Somersault

By now, things were getting out of hand for the government. All sorts of allegations were being hurled at the government; all sorts of suspicions were being stoked. Neither House was able to transact business. That day, the government concluded that it just could not stick to the stand that it had taken—that the Report will not be placed before Parliament, that Parliament cannot discuss the issue at all.

So, it took the high road.

Rajiv Gandhi himself spoke later in the day, the 17th. He said that the Report had been held back only so that the criminal investigation would not be prejudiced. And because this was what Justice Thakkar himself had urged. He took a swipe at us, and implied that what I had published was distorted: 'A version of what is alleged to be stated in a portion of the Report . . .'

Casting three-layered doubts in one go: 'a version', 'alleged to be stated', 'a portion of'. '. . . has reached the Press. This is fuelling willful distortion, malicious innuendo and irresponsible character assassination.'

This time, three aspersions in one go: 'willful distortion', 'malicious innuendo', 'irresponsible character assassination'.

> To put a stop to this, it is important that the full text of the Report be made public. I have enquired about the current stage of the criminal investigations. I have been informed that the investigations are now complete and necessary follow up action will be taken soon. Therefore, the release of the Report would no longer prejudice the course of the criminal investigations.

And so:

> I seek your permission, Mr. Speaker, Sir, to inform the House
> that when the House reassembles on Monday, the 27th March,
> after the forthcoming recess, steps will be taken immediately
> to lay the Report of the Thakkar Commission on the Table of
> the House.

Even in this, government was being crafty, actually ham-handed.
There were ten days between this about-turn and the promised
27th. There could be no difficulty in getting the Report printed.
Rajiv could have said, 'We will lay the Report on the Table of the
House on the 27th.' But no: 'When the House reassembles . . .
steps will be taken immediately to lay the Report . . .'

'A laughing stock'

Come the 27th, and the government said that the Report *has* been
laid on the Table of the House. But members kept shouting that
they had neither received copies nor could they get them—not
from the Secretariat of the Rajya Sabha or the Lok Sabha, not
from the library, not from the sales counter . . . One copy has
been delivered to my chamber, the Deputy Chairman of the Rajya
Sabha announced; you can come to my chamber and read it. More
shouting . . . Later: a few copies have been received in the Rajya
Sabha Secretariat. They will be sent to the library . . .

28 March: Members kept shouting. At the very beginning of his
Report, Thakkar says that his Report is in four volumes. What
you have placed in the library are only two volumes . . . This
point led to heated exchanges over several of the succeeding
days. What is a 'Report'? What is a 'Complete Report'? Are
annexures a part of the 'Report'? Are affidavits that were
filed, evidence that was collected, replies that were given in
response to questioning, are testimonies, are proceedings part
of the 'Report'? Thakkar has listed these as part of his 'Report',
Opposition members pointed out. Government maintained that,

what the Judge had said notwithstanding, these could not be shared with members. These constitute the raw material on the basis of which he had arrived at certain conclusions. The conclusions are set out in the two volumes, the 'Interim' and 'Final' Reports. And these alone will be shared. But how can we assess whether the conclusions are sound without seeing the material that Thakkar took notice of and the material he ignored? the Opposition asked. Thakkar has used such strong and unequivocal words to describe Dhawan's role, Atal Behari Vajpayee pointed out. You have reinstated him to a high post. At least share the SIT report on the basis of which you say you have exonerated him . . .

29 March: Copies had still not reached members. As the shouting went on, fifty copies arrived. But these were only of the 'Final' Report and not of the 'Interim' Report.

It turned out that while the Prime Minister had announced on the 17th that copies will be made available, printing had started only after the 27th.

With the government stonewalling the MPs, on 29 March I published further details, damning details from the Reports— including extracts from the oral and written depositions and records of meetings of senior officers who had been responsible for Mrs Gandhi's security.

That day, both A.G. Kulkarni and L.K. Advani told the Rajya Sabha that Parliament is being reduced to a laughing stock. The House has been taken for granted, it has been taken for a ride, L.K. Advani charged. Thakkar himself says that his Report consists of four volumes. He lists what is in each volume. Yet the government has said that the complete Report consists of only two volumes . . . At first, the government maintained vigorously that under no circumstances would the Report be placed on the Table of the House because it would endanger the security of the country, that it would be against public interest, Advani reminded the House, adding that the entire ruling party had defended the government's stand 'with all the vigour and vehemence at its command'.

Now the whole Parliament is being reduced to a laughing stock. Day after day, you are bungling. You are committing one blunder after another. What do you want? Do you want these two volumes to be published in a special supplement of the *Indian Express* for Members of Parliament to read?

A.G. Kulkarni was cutting.

> . . . I find that many matters are being brought which have made the Parliament a laughing stock . . . I want to know how this matter which is called top secret goes out. How is it published in the newspaper . . . I want to know whether the Government will take stringent measures and stern action against the culprits and against those who printed this . . . But who has done it? And Mr Shourie with impunity goes on publishing day in and day out any matter whatsoever making Parliament a laughing stock . . .

Of course, Kulkarni, a mischievous and deceptively genial man, meant something else—that the government was being made a laughing stock. In demanding stern action against me he was pointing to the impotence of the rulers.[4]

30 March: copies were still 'on their way . . . they will be made available as soon as they are available.'

With members still waiting even for those two volumes, on the 31 March, and in even greater detail on 2 April, I published Dhawan's notes, his written and oral statements, as well as his evasions which had led Thakkar to turn the 'needle of suspicion' towards him.

Copies of the Report reached members in the coming days. Atal Behari Vajpayee nailed the point: on reading the Report, he said, 'I find that there is nothing in the volumes which required that they be kept secret. Yes, Thakkar had said that the second

---

[4] During the Antulay episode, he had composed the doggerel: *Idhar bhi lay Udhar bhi lay, Abdul Rahman Antulay* . . .

volume may not be made public at that juncture. But he had not said that it must be kept secret indefinitely . . .'

Conspiracies

When eventually Parliament got around to discussing the content of Thakkar's two volumes, ministers as well as Congress(I) members strained to outdo each other in advancing conspiracy theories.

As their rhetoric flew higher and higher, two sets of conspiracies got intertwined—the conspiracy to assassinate Mrs Gandhi, and the conspiracy to divulge the Thakkar Commission Report.

One thing members were certain about—that, Thakkar notwithstanding, R.K. Dhawan had absolutely no role in the assassination. Member after member, starting with Buta Singh, swore to Dhawan's loyalty and devotion to Mrs Gandhi. They said that Thakkar had written his Report 'under pressure'. Saifuddin Soz was first off the mark:

> . . . I feel that Justice Thakkar had been working under great pressure. He has not been able to come to the right conclusions. From the very beginning under which [sic] the Thakkar Commission had been working under pressure that is writ large in the Report . . . I feel that there are negative elements in these recommendations. Why? Because the Commission has been obsessed from the very beginning with Mr Dhawan.
>
> . . . I feel Justice Thakkar has been working under great pressure, or may be he was motivated . . .
>
> . . . Here I feel that the Commission was under some terrible pressure that Dhawan has to be out . . .
>
> . . . Sir, I can go on quoting so many paragraphs from his Report to prove the Commission's obsession with Mr. Dhawan. But the point is, why did the Commission do it? Well, there was a reason. Some people were interested in sending Mr. Dhawan out because they had to settle a score. I want to say that the political [politics?] of manipulation is responsible for this.

And then, obliquely, as was and remains his wont, Soz hinted at who had applied the pressure:

> It has already been pointed out by Shri Buta Singh in this House and by our knowledgeable and able colleague Shri Chidambaram in the Rajya Sabha that Shri Arun Nehru had access to this Report because he was the Internal Security Minister at that time. Therefore, I feel that there is a fit case against Shri Arun Nehru and his close associate Mr. Fotedar for a breach of privilege. But the Prime Minister has given an assurance yesterday[5] and so I might withdraw it. But I feel that this is a fit case for breach of privilege against Shri Arun Nehru and also Shri Fotedar. They were very close to each other when they were in the Government together and the Commission had worked under pressure from them. My conscience also tells me so.
>
>   . . . At their hatching a conspiracy at such a critical time and doctoring the Thakkar Commission to write something, I recollect an Urdu couplet. Iqbal had said this thing:
>   Khuda bandey terey seedhaa dil bandey kahaan jaayen
>   Ki darweshi bhi aayari hai aur Sultani bhi aayari[6]

Naresh Chandra Chaturvedi echoed the charge. He told the Lok Sabha that what Thakkar had written about Dhawan was 'highly objectionable'. He testified to Dhawan's devotion to Mrs Gandhi:

> I am among those people who know Dhawan since long. I know from my own experience that there was no other person at that time who worked as the personal assistant of Shrimati Gandhi and who was so honest, so active, so fair and so dedicated to his boss and so strong in his moral character. One thing I know

---

[5] In his speech, Rajiv Gandhi had said that government would find out who had leaked the Report, and no one, however high, who was responsible would be spared.
[6] O man of God, where should your simple-hearted go/Monkhood is fraud as is kingship

very well [is] that there has been no change in his devotion to
Indiraji when she was in power and when she was out of power.

And so,

> I agree with Prof. Soz when he says that Justice Thakkar
> worked under some pressure to have been so explicit about
> pin-pointing his suspicions against a particular person and if a
> Judge acts under pressure, it is not a very welcome sign and the
> Government should be more vigilant about such matters.

The second point, about which several MPs were certain, was that
Mrs Gandhi's assassination was not the doing of just two security
personnel. Her assassination was part of a pattern—CIA . . .
the attempts to kill Nasser and Castro, the killing of Patrice
Lumumba, of Allende, of Mujibur Rahman, of Anwar Sadat, of
Olaf Palme, of 'our mother' Indira Gandhi . . .

The great powers could not stand her as she was the leader
of the largest democracy in the world, they said, as she was 'the
strongest pillar of democracy', as she was pursuing an independent
foreign policy—in particular, because of the Indo-Soviet Treaty.
They wanted India to sign a military pact with the US. They
wanted her dead because of India's role in the 'Third World
Movement', because of its role in 'the cause of world peace',
because of its refusal to sign the Non-proliferation Treaty, because
of its role in Disarmament and against Nuclear Weapons . . .
Because she is the one who had liberated India from dependence
on US grains by ensuring the Green Revolution . . .

That last ground from the ever-alert Home Minister, Buta
Singh. Of course, he was as alert to international dimensions:

> I remember the day, when after the Non Aligned Movement
> had gained strength under her leadership, she went to United
> Nations and held there a conference of non-aligned countries,
> the big power blocks were stunned at the emergence of her
> phenomenal image as the leader of the Third World and they
> focused their attention as how to destroy it. The entire Western

press joined hands with the big powers. Attempts were made to disturb her meetings but she had the real [sic] and in the question of leadership in her mind and body received in inheritance from Pandit Jawaharlal Nehru. So she went ahead with her task undauntedly and gave an image to India of which even the big powers are scared . . .

Others were equally well informed.

Priya Ranjan Dasmunshi: . . . The 'nasty Camp David Agreement which encouraged the Israelis to continue their occupation'. It was welcomed publicly by Morarji Desai. Moshe Dayan came to Delhi incognito 'to understand quietly the whole operation of destabilization' . . . They followed twin tactics: destabilize India and attack 'the most popular leader of the third world movement'. . . Brand the leader as corrupt. And undermine the constitutional framework: appeal to armed forces to rebel . . . This had happened in the case of L.N. Mishra and later Chimanbhai Patel . . . Then they instigated the Khalistani movement . . . The *Express* was brought in, and even me:

> Mr. Chairman, Sir, I want to draw your attention to the campaign that started. On the one hand, there was an attempt to destabilize the country by terrorists and on the other, under the popular banner of ending corruption, a particular newspaper carried a campaign and invited the army to rebel against the Government. That was before 1977. If you see, it is the same newspaper, the same so-called journalists, one or two, who are even carrying the so-called battle today. I am shocked to inform you and it is below the dignity of the Members of Parliament, whether this side or that side, to assemble together to draw up their strategy in Parliament and in that meeting to invite a journalist to address them and give them counsel. Yesterday it so happened that in Vithalbhai Patel House Mr. Arun Shourie was asked to give his advice as to how to play the game further and how to go in the future. Mr. Chairman, Sir, this campaign started with the Bofors Deal. They tried to use or misuse the highest office of the country, the President of India. They failed as they undermined

the importance of the democratic institution. Then finally they came to this character assassination with regard to the Thakkar Commission Report, its findings and its observations . . .

V.N. Gadgil: In the assassination of Indiraji, the day was carefully chosen, the place was carefully chosen, the time was carefully chosen, the assassins were carefully chosen . . . This careful choosing and planning gives me the idea that there is some mastermind working. I see a pattern: Allende in Chile, Sheikh Mujib in Bangladesh, Sadat in Egypt and Indira Gandhi in India . . . You see the pattern. All of them took certain independent positions to the dislike of certain outside powers. All of them were killed by their own security guards. You see the pattern . . . Reads an extract from a book about Harold Wilson's tenure as the British Prime Minister. Gadgil reads on: how the CIA, businessmen, newspaper owners conspired to publish material that would harm Wilson and the Labour government and have them replaced by a coalition led by Mountbatten, and asks,

> Is it not the same pattern? The Commission has said that the timing of the assassination was important. I say that the timing of the character assassination was also important. What is the timing? When Parliament is in session. What is the place? Parliament of the country. What is the day? The day on which something appears in Swedish newspapers about Bofors, the same day something appears about Thakkar Report. And who is the character assassin? A newspaper which has an obsession about Rajiv Gandhi. So, in the character assassination also, the time is carefully chosen, the place is carefully chosen, the assassin is also carefully chosen . . .

The straightforward explanation that the assassins had been outraged by the events in Punjab, especially Blue Star, and had on their own, or incited by mentors, killed Mrs Gandhi was obviously too simple for the conspiracy theorists. It hardly found mention during the debates in Parliament on the Thakkar Report. Two did make the connection. The plan all along has been to kill

Mrs Gandhi, they maintained, create havoc in its wake, and break India—by creating Khalistan to begin with.

Why now?

Why has the Report been leaked *now*? the theorists demanded. Why has it been published *now*? they demanded. Why all this shouting about it *now*? they demanded. After all, its findings had found their way to *India Today*, to *The Statesman* in 1986 itself, they said, and been printed then. There had been no furore.

And they had their answers.

To get at the innocent Dhawan who had been reinstated, said many. To embarrass and harm the PM, said one or two—after all, he is the one who had reinstated Dhawan. To sow doubts in Rajiv's mind about those close to him—Buta Singh, Fotedar, Sheila Dikshit and others, said one—by causing him to wonder who among them had leaked such an embarrassing Report. Because elections are round the corner, said others.

The official explanation was more conspiratorial. And there were two strands to it.

The first was that the Report had been published to deflect attention from the larger conspiracy. And the second was it had been published at that particular time to derail the criminal case that was about to be launched.

P. Chidambaram[7] was the point man. He recalled events that had preceded the assassination, and then told the Lok Sabha:

> . . . It is in this background that one must ask again and again the question why was the Thakkar Report selectively leaked at the time when it was leaked and in the manner in which it was leaked. Unless we answer this question and unless each one asks this question and answers this question and unless each leader of the Opposition gives us an honest answer to this question, this

---

[7] At the time, the minister of state in the Ministry of Personnel, Public Grievances and Pensions; and minister of state in the Ministry of Home Affairs.

debate will never really end. The answer to this question and I
am convinced in my mind that the answer to this question is that
the purpose of the selective leak of a very selected portion of the
Final Report of the Thakkar Commission was nothing but to
deflect the attention and concern of the people of India from the
real conspirators in the larger conspiracy. The idea was to point
the needle of suspicion against some person so that the people
of India will not focus on the grave danger that threatens the
unity and integrity of this country, so that the largest conspiracy
will be clouded by a mist of suspicion and a miasma of rumour
and gossip . . .

Rajiv Gandhi spoke for almost an hour. Emotion, declaration
of eternal resolve, insinuation, conjecture, damn-by-association,
answers embedded in questions—all rolled into one. On the
Report finding its way to us at the *Express,* this is what he had
to say:

For the past few weeks, some members of the Opposition have
behaved like marionettes of manipulative journalism . . .

Sir, allegations about the contents of the Thakkar Report
reached the press three years ago. But no repercussion was heard
in this House or elsewhere. Why did this not happen Sir? Was
it because the journalists concerned did not instruct the stalking
horses of the Opposition on what to do? Or is there a deeper
significance to the timing of this latest brouhaha?

The Thakkar Report pointed to a larger conspiracy over and
above the crime on the spot. Those in the know of the leaked
contents also knew that criminal investigations were drawing
to a close. They knew that non-disclosure of the Report was to
preclude prejudicing the investigations into conspiracy and the
prosecution of the conspirators. Why then the leak now? What
was the intention of the accessories of the crime of leaking the
nation's secrets at this time and in this manner? Why did they
not disclose their hand earlier? Why now?

Sir, the noise was raised because we were on the point of
filing charges against the conspirators. The Thakkar Report

led to a line of investigation which exposed the conspiracy. So the friends of the conspirators acted to forestall the conspiracy being revealed. They knew the net was drawing to a close. They knew after Atinder Pal Singh was picked up late last year that the Investigation Team was close on their heels. They knew that it was only loose ends that had to be tied up. They knew that only chargesheets were to be filed. They knew once the case was in the Courts, the Thakkar Report would inevitably have been made public.

So, they chose a diversionary tactic on the eve of filing of the chargesheets. They thought up this exercise of reviving what was an old thing. The friends of the conspirators could, if they had wished, have leaked the portions of the Report relating to the conspiracy because if we believe what they say—they say they have the full Report—why then only a selective leakage pointing in one direction? Why not a complete leakage? Why were they trying to protect the conspirators? Was it not a ruse to divert the attention of the nation? If it was not, why was the leak a selective leak? And if not, why now and not earlier?

We do not have definitive answers to these questions. What we do have is a stackful of needles quivering on the magnetic field of suspicion that point to the conspirators, that point to their political peers, that point to their friends, that point to their accomplices.

The political conspiracy was with a criminal purpose and treacherous intent. Criminal because its means were assassination and anarchy. Treacherous because, it was aimed at wrecking our independence, our unity, our integrity, our very existence . . .

Rajiv got quite carried away by his conspiracy theory. On his reckoning, not just the killing of Mrs Gandhi, even the killings of innocent Sikhs in the aftermath of the assassination, killings in which his own partymen had been in the forefront, killings which he had said had been but the natural reaction of an outraged people—'Jab ek badaa pedh girtaa hai to dharti thodi hiltee hai'[8]—even that was part of that same 'larger conspiracy':

---

[8] 'When a giant tree falls, the earth does shake a little.'

The conspiracy relied on detonating the explosive mixture of religion and politics . . . Lahore Declaration of the Muslim League . . . Anandpur Sahib Resolution of the Akali Dal . . .

Sir, chargesheets have been filed against the conspirators. The objective of the conspiracy was clearly a 'Khalistan'. The means to be employed was the assassination of the Prime Minister to create chaos, confusion and anarchy.

From the start of terrorism in Punjab, the purpose of the killing has been to fire a communal reaction. For the maximum reaction, they chose to kill the Prime Minister. To the conspirators, it did not matter that thousands might be killed, thousands of innocent Sikhs, thousands of innocent Hindus, thousands of other communities, nor that their aim could only be achieved by drowning the country in rivers of blood. The conspirators' intent was to promote communal fratricide. The conspirators' intent was to climb to their objective on mounting corpses of innocent men, women and children. Through a holocaust, they wanted the country to break so that on one of its pieces they could establish their fascist fundamentalist rule. It was in this atmosphere that Indiraji was gunned down in cold blood. It was in this atmosphere that an orgy of violence was unleashed against our Sikh brethren in Delhi, Kanpur and elsewhere.

And then, of course, the salve to distance the party and government from the killings—which, of course, were the diabolic work of conspirators out to destroy the country, not of his partymen:

Sir, the terrible bloodbath of November 1984 was a carnage which will rest forever on the conscience of all decent Indians. It happened in the cusp of a traumatic transition. That is not an extenuating circumstance. We cannot forgive ourselves. It should never have happened. But let me say in all humility, Sir, we have prevented any recurrence of mass killings of Sikhs in the capital or elsewhere. Repeatedly agents provocateurs have sought to provoke horrors to fulfill their nefarious purposes. Repeatedly we have thwarted them. I am pledged to a life of

honour for every Sikh in India. I would not be my mother's son
if I were not . . .

Loud thumping and cheering.

For a moment, let us go along with these theorists and assume
that the Report came to us at the *Express* so as to bury the larger
conspiracy. It came to us so as to deflect attention from the
conspirators who were going to be chargesheeted.

The next question our conspiracy theorists naturally had to
address was, 'Who channelled it to us?' Who were, to use the
words of Rajiv, 'the accessories of the crime', 'the friends of the
conspirators'? Who had steered the Report to us to bury the larger
conspiracy, to 'protect the conspirators'?

Who?

Rajiv was circumspect. He resorted to indirection, and held out
a threat:

> Someone has betrayed the will of Parliament. Someone has
> breached the trust reposed in him. Someone has violated his oath
> of secrecy. Someone has been a traitor to his word. The leak has
> not come from us. We will institute inquiries to determine the
> source of the leak.

That last bit was greeted with loud applause.

Rajiv had given enough indications: 'Someone has breached
the trust reposed in him. Someone has violated his oath of secrecy.
Someone has been a traitor to his word.' He was clearly pointing
to one person—whom he had trusted, who had sworn the oath of
secrecy, who had betrayed his word.

By now, Arun Nehru had left the Congress(I), along with
V.P. Singh and a few others. So, it was open season. Where
Rajiv had been indirect, others removed all doubts. Buta Singh
said that the Thakkar Report had been lying with, or had
been kept by, one person for months. This is how he described
the person:

Sir, the less said about the former Minister of State for Internal Security, the better it is. He ruined the party the moment he joined it. His attitude was totally undignified towards the senior partymen who had struggled for the freedom of the country and for the Congress party and the Sewa Dal. He had no regard even for the Chief Ministers of a State. He did not call even the names properly and treated them as if they were his servants. Today he is talking about independence, self-respect and integrity.

Sir, his style of functioning was totally intolerable, I am sorry I cannot use those words. I know it very well how he created hatred between the two individuals. He did it by creating a unique thing like the Internal Security. The Minister of Home Affairs was seldom consulted in this regard. He never showed the concerned file to his seniors. I cannot describe in words how he misused his position. Report of Thakkar Commission is a glaring example. He did not let any body know about the reports of security agencies and he was so clever in manipulation that he did not let any paper move without his approval.

I think the nation owes a great deal to Shri Rajiv Gandhi who expelled such a person from the party and provided the much needed relief. His close associates know what type of communal feelings he has and how he incited the communal feelings among the people.

Buta Singh went on in this refrain, citing his personal experience:

. . . She [Mrs Gandhi] had never viewed the country from the caste, community or language point of view. Even today, I remember it very well that after Blue Star Operation she had assigned me a responsibility most benevolently and had directed me to make up the loss caused to the Akal Takht Sahib during the Operation at the earliest with a sense of decorum and in accordance with all the sacred Sikh traditions. Accordingly I went there and managed things . . . When we were yet managing things according to the orders of Shrimati Indira Gandhi, I do not remember the exact date, but perhaps it was 17th or 19th June and it was the incident of about 15-20 days after the Blue

Star that when everything had been settled and the only thing left was to deploy the soldiers who were hitherto inside the Temple, at the roof top of the *Parikrama* or at the main gate, to restart the '*kar sewa*', that I reached Amritsar according to her orders and some gentleman about whom I have already mentioned, issued a statement against me to torpedo the matter. They never wanted the peace to usher in the Punjab. It was Shri Arun Nehru and his friend Shri Arun Singh who had made a statement the next day. Mr. Dhillon Saheb was with me. We had gone there together. They disturbed the entire programme by issuing a statement, which again relegated us in the background. Just after that, terrorists gave a slogan that they would not allow it to be repaired. Even if repairs are carried out, the entire structure would be dismantled by them. I can say it with a stress that if the decisions of Shrimati Gandhi had not been violated, today the position in Punjab would have been quite different. Conditions in Punjab would have improved very soon. For all this I hold him responsible who had changed our decision. I have mentioned this here so that people of the country may realise it as to who are responsible for the present bloodshed in Punjab. Major share to it has been contributed by Shri Arun Nehru. These elements do not want a cordial atmosphere to prevail in the country . . .

No one conducting an 'Identification Parade' in a police lock-up could have pointed more clearly to the one who had 'betrayed trust', to the one who had 'violated the oath of secrecy', to the treacherous traitor.

Others joined the chorus. Bipin Pal Das put two and two together for the House:

. . . Shri Buta Singhji said that the same part of the Report was leaked in some journals in 1986. At that time, the Report was in the possession of the then Minister of Internal Security whose name is Mr. Arun Nehru. Everybody knows. Why should you want his name? Everybody knows it. It is, therefore, clear who might have leaked that Report at that time. It is natural to conclude that the same source must have done it this time also. At that time, it was obviously done to harm Mr. Dhawan whose case was still under investigation. But, this time it was done specifically with the sole objective of harming Prime Minister Shri Rajiv Gandhi because the Prime Minister has reinstated Shri Dhawan in his Secretariat ...

The 'elite magazine'

So, Arun Nehru was my source? One minister was sure he wasn't. Kalpnath Rai, then minister of state in the department of power, gave an interview to *Surya* magazine.[9] In this, he said that the Report had been leaked by M.L. Fotedar. At the time, the latter was not a former minister, like Arun Nehru, but a sitting full-fledged Cabinet minister—for steel and mines. Several members— P. Upendra, Dipen Ghosh, Satya Pal Malik, Renuka Chowdhury— picked up on this interview during exchanges in the Rajya Sabha. One day, Renuka Chowdhury filed a notice for a Special Mention. She told the House that Kalpnath Rai, a minister of state, had told *Surya* that Makhan Lal Fotedar, minister of steel and mines, had leaked the Thakkar Commission Report. Kalpnath Rai got up to assert his right to offer the House a 'personal explanation':

> Sir, with reference to the Special Mention made in this House, as a personal explanation, I would like to say that when from a certain elite magazine questions were asked, I only said that Arun Nehru and his gang were responsible for the omissions and commissions. I categorically deny taking any other name.

But Renuka Chowdhury had come armed: 'Sir, this pains me because I have said it with a true spirit. I have his voice on tape . . .' [Interruptions]

Aladi Aruna shot up. This must be referred to the Privileges Committee, he said, because a minister is making a charge against

---

[9] The interview appeared in the April 1989 issue of *Surya*. Kalpnath Rai's remarks appeared in *Sunday* also.

another minister, adding, 'Now she has another record to prove her charge.' Take the tape from her, members said, and verify it. And see if Kalpnath has spoken the truth or whether he has misled the House. The Deputy Chairman refused to do so. Kalpnath Rai again denied taking any names in the interview. 'Do you deny the tape also?' members challenged him. Yes, I deny the tape also . . .

I ask an astute man

Had I published the articles to cloud the 'larger conspiracy'? Had I done so to shield the ones who were about to be chargesheeted?

The fact is that two officers known to my senior colleague, one of the most sagacious journalists I had known, N.S. Jagannathan, had channelled Thakkar's Report to me. I had written the article as soon as I had finished reading the Report. It had been set, and the bromides made that very day. They had been dispatched to our editions in sealed covers. Within a day and a half, we knew that they had reached every edition. The article appeared in the paper the very next morning.

Had the officers been on Thakkar's staff, and thus had direct access to the Report?

Was Arun Nehru behind them?

Was Fotedar?

And were the great powers behind Arun Nehru? Were they behind Fotedar? So that my articles were at third remove prompted by the great powers!

Many, many years later, I asked an astute and knowledgeable person, one fully in the know of things. Did he think, did anyone high up think, that the publication of the Report was the result of a conspiracy? Did anyone up there think that I was part of a conspiracy to 'deflect attention from the larger conspiracy'? Did anyone think that I had published extracts from the Report to shield those who were about to be chargesheeted?

No one in his right mind thought so, he said. The fact is simple. The longer a report—*any* report—is kept secret, the more liable it is to get out, he said. Look at the most secret of all reports—the Pentagon Papers, he pointed out. They got out, didn't they?

26

'Maaro naeen, dhareeko'[1]

One of the boons of working at the *Express* was that all of us got to meet all sorts of people, and, one way or another, get involved in situations which otherwise we would only have heard about.

Among the most astute and the most diverting of persons I got to meet was Giani Zail Singh. I first met him soon after he had become Home Minister in Mrs Gandhi's Cabinet. Subsequently, I met him after he had become President.

An associate told me that Gianiji wanted to meet me, and would I join him for dinner at the associate's flat? Of course, I will, I said.[2]

I arrived early. Gianiji came—immaculately dressed as he always was in an achkan, a rose in the buttonhole, and churidar pyjama.

'*Gianiji, ki haal hai?*'[3] the host asked in tones of close friendliness.

'*Nighey ain,*' Gianiji replied. '*Bibi*[4] *ne keyaa ai ki main Amteshwar*[5] *te file banaawaan.*'[6]

---

[1] 'Don't hit, frighten'
[2] I would have typed the associate's name. But he says that he is certain it was not at his flat that I met Gianiji, just as I am certain that it was.
[3] 'Gianiji, how are you?'
[4] Mrs Indira Gandhi.
[5] Mrs Amteshwar Anand, Maneka's mother.
[6] 'Cosy. Bibi has asked me to prepare a file on Amteshwar.'

'*Gianiji pher taan tusi paunch he gaye o: koi kaye ki merey kudum te file banaayo—es to zayaadaa ki* proof *chaidaa ki os daa thodey te pooraa itbaar hai. Hun taa thaunoon* Beant Singh[7] *ne vee leader man litaa hai.*'[8]

'*Rehan de,*' Gianiji dismissed the cajolery. '*Aidaayaan leader mani de ne? Leader udaan mani de nein jidaan main Bibi nu man daa ain. Bibi kaye ki Asaamiayan de sir udhaa deyo, main sir udaa devaan gaa.*'[9]

'Sir, *ag lag jayu,*'[10] I said, breaking into the exchange.

'*Shourieji thaunoo ainaa cheezaan daa tajurbaa naeen,*' Gianiji turned to me with a smile. '*Main thaunoon Faridkot daa haadsaa dasdaan. Ansee Faridkot de Raja de khilaaf* movement *chalaayee. Mainu* police *ne giraftaar kar litaaa. Merey kes phad ke mainun galiaan vichon ghaseetyaa gaya. Kothdi-ch sutt dittaa. Aur chaudvein din jadon mainoon kacheri pesh keetaa gayaa, meraa bhraah vi meri fateh bolan nayeen aayaa.*'[11]

'Sir,' I ventured, '*magar Assam taan Faridkot naheen.*'[12]

'*Shourieji, magar Hindustani taa Hindustaani hai,*'[13] he said, laughing.

And that is what he did. Leaders of AASU had been called to Delhi for talks. The talks done, they headed back for Assam.

---

[7]   Chief Minister of Punjab, and a rival of Giani Zail Singh in state politics. Their rivalry cost the people of Punjab dearly.

[8]   'Then you have certainly arrived: what can be greater proof of complete trust than that someone were to ask you to prepare a file on her in-laws. Now even Beant Singh has accepted you as leader.'

[9]   'O, leave it. Is that how one acknowledges a leader? One acknowledges a leader the way I acknowledge Bibi. If she tells me to blow up the heads of the Assamese [student leaders], I will blow up their heads.'

[10]   'But sir, there will be a conflagration.'

[11]   'You don't have experience of these matters. Let me tell you what happened in Faridkot. We launched a movement against the Raja. I was arrested by the police. I was dragged through the streets by my hair. I was thrown into a cell. And on the fourteenth day when I was produced in court, not even my brother came to hail me.'

[12]   'But sir, Assam is not Faridkot.'

[13]   'But, Shourieji, an Indian is an Indian!'

The plane had but to land at the Guwahati airport, and they were arrested.[14]

Assam did not go up in flames as I had expected it to.

The conversation moved to Rajiv Gandhi. '*Bandey dee neeyat buri naheen. Par suljaheyaa hoyaa nayeen hai,*'[15] Gianiji said.

Look at the way he makes promises, Gianiji said in Punjabi. Look at the way he '*garuntiaan barsaandaa*'.[16] The one at the top should not be making promises. He should not be giving guarantees. What will happen depends on so many things. How can a man, howsoever big, control the winds? So, don't hold out guarantees yourself. If things turn out well, the credit will come to you in any case. If they don't, people should remember someone else!

And then he recalled an incident to illustrate how much Rajiv had yet to learn.

Main thanoon ik kissa das daan. Os veyley main Punjab daa Mukh Mantri si, aur Rajiv, kyonki o Bibi daa munda si, Congress daa General Secretary si. Mainu itlaa aayee ki o Simley jaa rehaa hai, aur jaan layee o Chandigarh hawai addey te utrey gaa. Main parbandh kitaa ki Chandigarhon main odhey naal odhi gaddi vich hi chalaan. Simley vich, saareaan de samney, aur baad vich gaddi vich driver *de samney, Rajiv nein Ram Lal di aisi fassiyat kiti ki puccho hi naan. Main sundaa reyaa.*[17]

'*Jadon asi gaddi vich vaapas Chandigarh aa rahe si, main Rajiv noon kayaa,* "*Rajiviji, gustaakhi maaf, magar aapko sab ke saamney Ram Lal ko is tareh daantanaa naheen thaa.*"'[18]

---

[14] January 1983.

[15] 'His intentions are not bad. But he isn't seasoned.'

[16] 'He rains guarantees.'

[17] 'I will tell you an instance. I was the Chief Minister of Punjab. Rajiv was the General Secretary of the Congress. I got information that he is travelling to Simla, and that he will get down at the Chandigarh airport. I arranged that I will travel with him in his car. In Simla, in front of everyone, and afterwards in front of the car's driver, Rajiv berated Ram Lal. I kept listening quietly.'

[18] 'When we were returning in the car to Chandigarh, I said to Rajiv, "Rajivji, pardon my impertinence, but you should not have scolded Ram Lal like that in front of everyone."'

'*Rajiv ne keyaa, "Magar us ke baarey mein itnein* charges *hain. Voh hamaari sarkar ki hi naheen, hamari Party ki bhi* reputation *khatm kar degaa.*"'[19]

'*Aap jo kehtein hain, bilkul theek hai,*' Gianiji said he told Rajiv.

Par aapko us ki beyizzati sab ke saamne naheen karni chaahiye thee. Aap Dilli wapas pahunchtey, us ke dushmanon ko batlaatey ki aap us se kitney naa khush ho. Voh saarey Himachal mein dhindhoraa peet-tey ki Ram Lal to gayaa, ki aap Ram Lal se nihaayat naakhush hain. Ram Lal aapke paas bhaagtaa hua aataa. Aap us se poochety, 'Kyon, kyaa baat hai? Itney pareshaan kyon lag rahey ho?' Voh apni safaai deney mein lag jaataa. Aap usey kehtey, 'Par aap yeh sab keh kyon rahey ho?' Voh batlaataa ki falaaney ne saarey Himachal mein afwaah udaai hai ki aap mujh se bahut naaraaz hain . . . 'Naheen, bilkul naheen,' aap kehtey. 'Mainey to us sey kuch kahaa hi naheen.' Un dono mein ladai badhti. Aap Supreme Court ban jaatey. Ab aap ne befaayadaa apney barkhilaf ek dushman khadaa kar lia hai . . .[20]

'*Naheen sunyaa, naa,* Rajiv *ney?*' he paused, and asked, '*Nateejaa? Apnee sarkaar de* Foreign Secretary *noo bharee* Press Conference *vich ee barkhaast kar dittaa. Faayadaa keedaa hoyaa? Nak kehdi katti gayee?*'[21]

---

[19] 'Rajiv said, "But there are so many charges against him. He will bring down the reputation not just of our Government but also of our Party."'

[20] 'What you are saying is completely correct. But you should not have demeaned him in front of everyone. You could have returned to Delhi, and told his rivals how dissatisfied you are with him. They would have gone around shouting how angry with him you are. He would have come running to you. You could have said, "Come, what is the matter? Why are you looking so worried?" He would have told you that so and so has spread the rumour all over Himachal that you are angry with him. And you could have said, "No, no, I have not told him anything." The tussle between the two of them would have sharpened. You would have become the Supreme Court. Now you have acquired an adversary for no reason.'

[21] 'He didn't listen, did he? Rajiv didn't listen. Result? He dismissed the Foreign Secretary of his own Government in a crowded Press Conference. Who gained? Whose nose got cut?'

I was taken in by his charm even more than by the shrewd advice he had given to Rajiv. I had earlier written in harsh words about his role and that of Sanjay Gandhi in promoting Bhindranwale; in the paper we had reported the terrible price that Punjab and the country were paying for his desire to put down Beant Singh, the then Chief Minister of Punjab; I had spoken harshly against his toadying to Sanjay Gandhi—'Sanjayji is my *rehnuma*,'[22] he had said; and even more to Mrs Gandhi—'I will sweep the floor if she asks me to do so,' he had declared. I had written and spoken in strong words about all these occurrences. But not once during that evening, as I listened to his tales, did those words and deeds cross my mind.

~

Mrs Gandhi had been assassinated. Two years into Rajiv's Prime Ministership, the *Express* had got into a tussle with him and his government. Gianiji had begun feeling that Rajiv and his circle were out to cut him out of everything. Even though the Constitution prescribes that the President be consulted and be kept informed about important matters,[23] consultations, he felt, had shrivelled to nothing. Members took up this grouse of his in Parliament. Rajiv Gandhi stoutly denied the charge—in Parliament and outside. Consultation aside, Gianiji felt that he was being shut out even from information. Gianiji had been

---

[22] 'Sanjayji is my guide.'
[23] Article 78, which prescribes:

> 78. Duties of Prime Minister as respects the furnishing of information to the President, etc.—It shall be the duty of the Prime Minister—
>
> (a) to communicate to the President all decisions of the Council of Ministers relating to the administration of the affairs of the Union and proposals for legislation;
> (b) to furnish such information relating to the administration of the affairs of the Union and proposals for legislation as the President may call for; and
> (c) if the President so requires, to submit for the consideration of the Council of Ministers any matter on which a decision has been taken by a Minister but which has not been considered by the Council.

naturally enraged by the killings of Sikhs right in Delhi after Mrs Gandhi's assassination, and even more so by the fact that in spite of his personally calling Narasimha Rao, then Home Minister, the government machinery had not stirred into action. By 1986, relations between Gianiji and Rajiv had become frosty. He had sought Ranganath Mishra's reports on the killings of Sikhs in the wake of Mrs Gandhi's assassination. Gianiji had sought Thakkar's Report on the assassination itself. This had been withheld from him. The excuse that was given was that the Commissions of Inquiry Act had been amended, that he had given his assent to the amendment. As a result, the Report was not going to be shared even with Parliament. Gianiji saw this for the excuse it was. After all, he was the President. He had been Home Minister, and that too in Mrs Gandhi's Cabinet. He had enjoyed her confidence. More than anything, he was a Sikh.

He asked Buta Singh to meet him in this regard. Buta Singh promised to send the Report. But it did not come. On instructions of the President, the Secretary, S. Vardan, wrote to the Home Secretary asking for the Report. Nothing happened.

When the Bofors controversy flared up, Gianiji asked the Secretary to write to government asking for files on the Bofors contract. The files may be sent for the President to examine them, the letter said. In an unprecedented move, the letter was placed before Cabinet, and the Cabinet dutifully rejected the request from the President.

Gianiji also started showing his annoyance. He raised objections to the Mizoram Accord the government signed with Laldenga. He nailed the government for the different yardsticks it deployed in approving or turning down appointments of Judges. He started meeting persons who Rajiv regarded as hostile to him. He would hold up routine things. Annoyance came to strain in an unexpected way. He took strong exception to an entire chunk having been cut out from his broadcast to the country.

Towards end 1986–early 1987, government got an amendment to the postal law through Parliament.[24] By virtue of this change,

---

[24] The Bill was to further amend the Indian Post Office Act of 1898.

virtually any officer designated by government was given the authority to intercept postal articles—letters, parcels, newspapers, anything and everything. Opposition parties as well as civil rights organizations took this up as a cause—as a grave invasion of civil rights and a potential instrument of harassment. Gianiji held up his assent to the legislation. Through his office, he told government of four ways in which the amendment could be misused. He let it be known that unless these loopholes were plugged, he would not give his assent, that, instead, he would send the Bill back to Parliament with a message. His message would have to be read out in Parliament, and it would become an occasion for the Opposition to mount a full-scale attack on the government. There was, in addition, an infirmity, drawing attention to which would embarrass everyone—the presiding officers, the government benches as well as members of the Opposition. As my colleague, Surya Prakash, pointed out at the time, the Postal Bill had been passed with just twenty of 555 members present. That is, it had been passed without the quorum—of fifty-five members—that was mandatory. Pushed to a wall, the President was certainly not going to hold back from pressing the advantage that this flagrant infirmity gave him vis-à-vis the Bill.[25]

At this stage, I got to see a file of the Home Ministry on this very Bill. From the file, I learnt that the Ministry had proposed almost identical changes in the postal law. And at the time, the Minister for Home had been none other than Gianiji himself. During Gianiji's tenure as Home Minister, there had been three occasions on which the Ministry could have taken back its proposal. But it had doggedly stuck to it. I printed an article giving the new amendment and what the Home Ministry had proposed, and showing that the two were virtually identical. I concluded that Gianiji was a somewhat late convert to civil rights, that he was among the most astute politicians, but that in this case, he

[25] A. Surya Prakash, 'Do 20 MPs Make a House?', *Indian Express*, 23 February 1987. That passing Bills in this way had become customary by then would not make the infirmity less bothersome. It would only make the embarrassment greater.

had picked a fight in which he could not prevail. He could send the Bill back to Parliament, yes. But, given the overwhelming majority that Rajiv commanded, it would be back at his desk in no time, and Gianiji would have no option but to sign the Bill into law. The article was carried very prominently—beginning as a large box item on the top of the front page.[26] I followed this up with a harshly worded piece in which I, of course, said that Rajiv had lost by alienating the President as the latter's mature counsel, his great charm and skill in managing persons were things from which an immature person like Rajiv had a lot to learn. But I also said that the President had been politicking, that he and two of his officers were the fount of stories about the many ways in which Rajiv had been doing him down, that he had taken a stand now against the Postal Bill, not out of conviction but for expedience. I even included two examples from an earlier conversation to illustrate how much Rajiv could have benefited if, instead of offending Gianiji, he had set out to learn from him.[27]

Any other politician would have been mighty upset. Instead, Gianiji called Anita and me over for tea at Rashtrapati Bhavan.

He was gracious. He talked frankly as if to a friend he had known for long. He expressed appreciation for the fight we were putting up against Rajiv Gandhi. He must have spared close to an hour for us. Not once did he say anything about my articles. Just once, he said obliquely while we were talking of governance in general, 'Home Ministry *taan a-thaa samundar hai. Keno pataa hundaa kee kithey kee-kee ho rehaa hai?*'[28] That was all: so many things would have been happening in the Home Ministry at any given moment that it wasn't reasonable for me to have thought that he would have known of some proposal on some old Bill.

---

[26] 'The President vs the Home Minister', *Indian Express*, 19 February 1987. My own views lay between those of the contending camps: 'What to Do about the Postal Bill', *Indian Express*, 25 February 1987. My dear friend, and our shield, Ram Jethmalani took me to task for not taking a stronger stance against the Bill: *Indian Express*, 3 March 1987.

[27] 'Is the President above Politics?', *Indian Express*, 10 March 1987.

[28] 'Home Ministry is an endless sea. Who knows what is going on where?'

'*Shourieji, gustaakhi maaf,*' he said with a teasing glance at Anita. '*Vaisey, tusi bandey kisi kam de naeen. Naa kuddi chaheedi hai, naa paisaa. Naa thaunu sharaab daa shauk hai.*'[29]

I interrupted him, and said, '*Vaisey, Ramnathji nein vee eheeyo shikaayat merey* father *noon keetee see*!'[30]

Gianiji smiled, and resumed,

Main thanoon ik gal das daan. Jadon main Home Minister *si, taan IB daa* Director *hairaan hovey ki mainun Akalian di androoni khabar os to pehlaan kidaan paunch jaandi hai. Gal e si, ki asaan chaar auarataan Akalian di* Working Committee *de aaley-dwaaley laayeeaan. Onaa ne wi onaahaan daa paryog kitaa, sanoon vi kudiyaan to khabar mildee rayee, tey saadaa vee kum hundaa rehaa . . . Tuseen aidaan de logaan naal milo gey hi naeen taan thaunoon pataa kidaan chalugaa ki shehr vich kee ho rehaa hai? Aur thaunoon koi shauk hi nayeen hoyegaa, taan tusi kis de kum aayogey?*[31]

He laughed, and pulled me to himself.

Before he had us leave, Gianiji asked, '*Seth poorey paise-vaisey dindaa hai ki naeen? Naa, meraa matlab hai ki koi zaroorat hovey—ghar dee, kisi hor cheez dee—taan dasnaa.*'[32]

I said, '*Naeen, naeen, Gianiji, baut shukriyaa, par koi zaroorat naeen. Aseen dono apney* parents *de ghar rehndey hain. Koi zaroorat naeen.*'[33]

---

[29] 'Pardon my saying so, but Shourie Sahib, in a way you are of no use. You don't lust after girls nor after money. And nor are you fond of liquor.'

[30] 'Ramnathji made the same complaint to my father!'

[31] 'I will tell you something. When I was Home Minister, the Director of IB would be surprised that I got to know the inner doings of the Akalis even before he did. The thing was that we posted four women around their Working Committee. They also used them, we also kept getting information from the girls, and our work also got done. When you will not remain in touch with such persons, how will you get to know what is happening in the city? And if you have no fancy, to whom will you be of use?'

[32] 'Does the Seth give you enough? No, I mean if you are short of anything—a house, something else—let me know.'

[33] 'No, no, Gianiji, many thanks, but we are not in need of anything. We stay with our parents in their home. We don't need anything.'

Next day, Tarlochan Singh came over to find out how the meeting had gone. I told him how charming and interesting Gianiji was, but that, sitting in the Rashtrapati Bhavan, to suggest what some would construe as a bribe to a journalist, was not befitting really.

'*Tusi Gianiji di policy samjhey hi naee,*' Tarlochan said.

*Onhaan dee policy hai, bilee di pith tey hath phero. Aur dekho.
Agar o apni pith chuk ke khushee ch aakd dee hai, agar o apni
poonch chak ke mod di hai, taan agey chalo, naeen taa gal rehan
deyo . . . Tusi samjhey naeen. Jo unhaan ney keyaa, thaunoo kuch
den layee naeen. Eh dekhan layee ki tusi bandey kis tareh de o.*[34]

~

Tensions between Rajiv Gandhi and Gianiji continued to mount.

Time and again, Gianiji felt slighted, and, that too, by a chit of a boy.

V.P. Singh and Co. left Rajiv's government and the Congress(I). Various manoeuvres were set afoot. Arun Nehru, V.C. Shukla and Yashpal Kapoor were the principal actors, with V.C. Shukla doing most of the running to and from the President. The three began meeting Gianiji—one at a time. And plans began to be made to oust Rajiv. The threesome readied Ashoke Sen, the many-times law minister, to be the alternative. He would be a weightless figurehead, they must have felt. They would be able to control him. At one stage, R. Venkataraman, the former finance minister, agreed. In one of their meetings, Gianiji mentioned this to V.C. Shukla. This time, Shukla hemmed and hawed—'*Dekhtey hain*',[35] he told Gianiji. And promptly went and told Rajiv that

---

[34] 'You haven't understood Gianiji's policy. His policy is, stroke the cat's back. If she arches her back and stiffens in pleasure, if she curls her tail, proceed. Else, leave the thing. What he said was not so as to give you something. It was to gauge what kind of a person you are.' Gianiji held on to the Postal Bill, and did not give his assent. Rajiv Gandhi's government fell. The Bill was eventually withdrawn by the V.P. Singh government.
[35] 'Let us see.'

Venkataraman had agreed to become the replacement when Rajiv was ousted. Rajiv met Venkataraman and offered him the presidentship. As a result, even though election for the post was months away, the Congress(I) announced that R. Venkataraman would be the candidate.

Gianiji's confidant, Tarlochan Singh, met me around this time. He hinted at the fact that such manoeuvres were afoot, and asked what I thought would happen if Rajiv was removed from office. I said that doing so would be terrible—that Rajiv was losing ground rapidly, that he will lose the next election, and that *that* would be the way to get rid of him, that any other way would be resurrecting the dead . . .

One evening, I was called by Ramnathji to come over to his Sundar Nagar flat, '*ek dam*'.[36] Mulgaokar was with him. RNG told me that the moves to replace Rajiv had reached the critical point, and that he had sent Rajmata[37] to the President to tell him that he—RNG—and the paper would support him fully if he dismissed Rajiv and put someone else in his place. He added that she was carrying the letter that Zail Singh was to write to Rajiv dismissing him—Mulgaokar has himself improved it, he said.

But that will be terrible, I argued, and went over the arguments I had given Tarlochan. In any case, it is just not going to work. Rajiv has almost 410 out of 520—eight out of ten—members of the Lok Sabha. How many MPs can these fellows pull to their side? We will be re-enacting the Charan Singh episode all over again. Like him, the new government will never be able to face the House. And the move would have revived Rajiv's stock . . .

This went on for ten to fifteen minutes. Mulgaokar sat silently.

'*To phir jaao, jaldi jaao. Zail Singh ko kaho ki ghalati hui. Voh chiththi par kuch naa karey. Hum sab milkar aagey sochengey. Chalo, chalo, jaldi karo. Driver hai?*'[38]

---

[36] 'at once'

[37] Vijaya Raje Scindia of Gwalior.

[38] 'Then go, go quickly. Tell Zail Singh that there has been a mistake. He should not do anything on the letter. We shall meet and deliberate. Go, go, hurry. Have you got a driver?'

'*Nahin ji. Main khud* car *chalaa kar aayaa hoon.*'[39]

'*Meri gaadi mein jao.*'[40]

From the large courtyard in front of the Rashtrapati Bhavan, I rushed in, almost breathless, towards the room where the President used to receive visitors. Gianiji had come out of it and was standing in the Military Secretary's room—facing the room in which he used to receive visitors. S. Vardan, Secretary to the President, was there. Tarlochan was there. I had clearly entered at a very inopportune moment—you could have sliced the tension in the air.

'*Chalo, uppar chaliye,*'[41] Gianiji said.

We took the lift to the first floor.

We sat down at a sort of dining table. He held my hand. He said that he had decided to dismiss Rajiv Gandhi. '*Terey Seth nein apnee razaamandi bhej tee hai. Rajmata aayi see.*'[42] The problem, he said, was that first Vardan, and then even Tarlochan, was refusing to draft the letter that had to be sent to Rajiv.

I told Gianiji of the arguments at Sundar Nagar, and how the message that the Rajmata had brought was a mistake, that no one, certainly not the *Express*, could support a move to dismiss the Prime Minister.

'*Aur koi PM banan noo tayaar vee nahee hoyegaa,*'[43] I added.

There you are wrong, Gianiji said. '*Shukla teyiyaar hai. Arun Nehru teyiyaar hai. Teraa yaar Venkataraman teyiyaar hai. Umeedwaaraan daa ghaataa naeen.*'[44]

'*Tunsee kisi noo chuneyaa hai?*'[45]

---

[39] 'No, sir. I have driven myself.'

[40] 'Go in my car.'

[41] 'Come, let us go upstairs.'

[42] 'Your Seth has sent his concurrence. Rajmata had come.'

[43] 'And no one will agree to become PM.'

[44] 'Shukla is ready. Arun Nehru is ready. Your friend Venkataraman is ready. There is no shortage of aspirants.'

[45] 'Whom have you chosen?'

'*Haan. Meri gal Vasantdada naal ho gayee hai. O manjheyaa hoyaa bandaa hai. Main* television *vageraa daa vi bandoobast kar litaa hai.*'[46]

'*Sir, e taan coup hoyegaa. Kadi chal hi naeen sakdaa. Kal o panj lakh bandaa baar le aawey. Rashtrapati Bhavan noo gher laye. Ki karogey? Saareaan no chittar pehngey . . .*'[47]

'*Too vee naeen mandaa?*'[48] he asked.

'*Phitey moon terey,*'[49] he said, got up, and hugged me.

By the time I reached Sundar Nagar, Vardan had called Mulgaokar, and narrated what had passed. 'The moment has passed,' he had told Mulgaokar.

The next day, Tarlochan came to our house. I told him what had happened, how the whole thing had been a lunatic plan . . .

'*Tuseen Gianiji dee* policy *samjhey hi naeen,*' he said. '*Onaan dee* policy *hai, "Maro naa. Dhareeko." Bandey noo maarnaa naeen. Onhoon dhakka deyo, kapdey phaad deyo, dhakel ke bhunjey laa deyo, daraa ke chhad deyo.*'[50]

The same day Advaniji rang up Tarlochan. Tarlochan told him that Rajmata had come, and the message she had brought. Advaniji said that Tarlochan should fix an appointment for Advaniji to meet the President urgently. Advaniji explained to the President that the Rajmata must have come on her own, that she had certainly not come on behalf of the BJP, that the BJP could not be part of any such manipulations.

Later, Tarlochan was to tell me that the 'policy' had worked to the dot. Rajiv heard about what had 'almost happened'. He got really rattled—exactly as Gianiji had planned. He realized that

---

[46] 'Yes. I have talked to Vasantdada [Patil]. He is a seasoned man. I have made arrangements of TV, etc.'

[47] 'Sir, this will be a coup. It will never work. What if he brings five lakh and surrounds Rashtrapati Bhavan? What will you do? Everyone will be thrashed with chappals . . .'

[48] 'You also don't agree?'

[49] 'Shame on you.'

[50] 'You haven't understood Gianiji's policy. His policy is, "Don't hit, frighten." Don't kill a man. Push him, shred his clothes, having thrown him to the ground, having frightened him, let him go.'

the President was prepared to go to *any* length, that there was no option but to make up with him.

All talk of impeaching the President stopped. Ministers and officials who had been staying away, even when the President asked them to come for discussions, suddenly started trooping to the Rashtrapati Bhavan.

Gianiji, sharp as he was, saw that his method—'*Dhareeko*'— had worked.

Rajiv invited Gianiji over for a dinner. He apologized for the misunderstandings.

Gianiji told Rajiv that, in that case, the first thing that Rajiv must do is to remove the minister, K.K. Tewary, who had spoken against him, who had said that the Rashtrapati had become a sanctuary for Khalistanis. Rajiv said that the minister would resign forthwith. Gianiji turned that down firmly: '*Istifaa naheen,* dismiss.'[51]

The minister, K.K. Tewary, was dropped.

Gianiji's term came to an end. He was a much loved person by then. On the last day of his term, we printed an illustration by Ravi Shankar. The left half had the Rashtrapati Bhavan. The right showed India with its heart. The legend on the left said, 'He lived here.' The one on the right said, 'He lives here.'

That day, Rashtrapati Bhavan had been opened to the public. People had thronged to wish Gianiji the best. Ravi Shankar and I made our way through the crowd. We had had the original drawing framed, and taken it with us. We presented it to Gianiji.

He was moved. '*Adaa kasoor teraa hai,*' he said laughing. '*Toon yaad karengaa.*'[52]

And whenever I called on him later, he would tell whoever was standing nearby, '*Adaa kasoor edaah hai,*' laugh, and would pull me to himself.

---

[51] 'No, not resignation. Dismiss.'
[52] 'Half the fault is yours.' 'You will repent.'

27

I manufacture an affidavit

'But are you sure it is not petrol?' My friend, Cho Ramaswamy was on the phone from Madras. Cho said he had received a call from Chandra Shekhar—for whom, and for whose judgement, he had high regard. Chandra Shekhar had told him to tell me that the *Indian Express* was doing quite the wrong thing in supporting and projecting V.P. Singh. V.P. Singh is a coward, Chandra Shekhar had told Cho; he is a rank opportunist, he believes in nothing, he is not fit to, and will not be able to run the country. Tell your friend not to rely on him, not to support him, Chandra Shekhar had told Cho.

'Cho,' I said, 'there is a proverb, "When your house is on fire, you can't wait for Ganges water. You have to make do with municipal water!"'

'But are you sure it is not petrol?' Cho retorted.

It wouldn't be long before I saw how right Chandra Shekhar and Cho had been. But first, an understanding, a sabotage, and the sequel.

An understanding, and a sabotage

In the *Express*, we were besieged by Rajiv and his government. Raids, inquiries, minatory notices, cases, the Delhi edition forcibly shut down . . . V.P. Singh had taken up the Bofors issue, and had left—or been pushed out of—Rajiv's government. By that step, he had caught the public's imagination. We were reporting his public meetings, his statements. Chandra Shekhar, on the other hand, remained dead against V.P. Singh becoming leader of the Janata Dal and hence the Prime Minister. Chandra Shekhar let it be known that even if he had just five MPs with him, he would himself contest, and seek to become the leader of the Parliamentary Party. Ram Jethmalani, another friend of ours, began a fast outside Chandra Shekhar's house. He was shooed away by the latter's men.

Biju Patnaik, Devi Lal and Arun Nehru visited Chandra Shekhar at his farmhouse in Bhondsi, a village in Haryana. They said that the leadership issue had been resolved. V.P. Singh would *not* be made leader of the Parliamentary Party; they told Chandra Shekhar, that, instead, Devi Lal would become the leader. Chandra Shekhar took them at their word, and agreed to the proposal.

This understanding was then conveyed to all and sundry— that the leader's election is to take place the following day, and that Devi Lal is to be elected unanimously.

The next day, V.P. Singh proposed Devi Lal's name. Instead of accepting the position, Devi Lal declined, and in his own place proposed that V.P. Singh become the leader and hence the Prime Minister. Outfoxed, a grenade of pent-up fury, Chandra Shekhar left the meeting.

A *man of the soil*

Even though no one in his right mind could have supported Devi Lal as Prime Minister, I used to quite like him as a person. He had gone to jail during the struggle for freedom. He always spoke up for the farmers. He was forthright, always saying what was in his mind. His manner of speaking, and especially his similes were graphic and earthy.

An *imaginer of conspiracies*

But there was another side to him. He would spot conspiracies where none existed. He would often let attachment to his sons sway his position on issues of great moment. And he had this habit of using his *Brahmaastra,* his ultimate weapon—resignation or the threat of resignation—every other week: once in 1978, when he was Chief Minister of Haryana, he led his entire Cabinet to resign, only to get himself and his Cabinet sworn back in later the same day! Such jolts used to rock governments and parties.

It wasn't long before I fell afoul of him. There was a by-election in Meham, a constituency in Haryana. Devi Lal's son, Chauthala was contesting it. His supporters indulged in a lot of violence and intimidation. Our reporters filed accounts of the fraudulent way in which Chauthala had won. I wrote an editorial or two arguing that the result should be annulled. 'Throw him out,' our editorial of 1 March counselled.

Phone calls

That night, after 10 p.m., the phone rang. I picked it up immediately for fear of letting the ring wake Adit up.

'*Arey, tujhey pataa naheen hai tujhey aisey naheen likhnaa chaahiye?*'—it was Devi Lal on the phone. '*Tu jaantaa naheen, apney faaydey ke liye yeh poonjipati kuch bhi kar saktey hain? Tooney pichhlee baar se sabak naheen seekhaa?*'[1]—a reminder and a threat: that I had been dismissed last time, and could be again.[2]

Nothing had happened in Meham, he said. A few reporters had cooked up stories to sell their papers.

But there are photographs, I said. Had the photographers also cooked up their photographs?

'*Sab ek he to hain.*'[3]

---

[1] 'Don't you know you shouldn't be writing like this? Don't you know, for their own benefit, these richies can do anything? Haven't you learnt a lesson from the last time?'

[2] The following is based on what I remember vividly and also on what I wrote for the paper at the time: the article—'*Deputy PM Sahib Baat Karenge*'—was carried in the *Indian Express* on 29 March 1990.

[3] 'They are all one.'

'*Tujhey pataa naheen, yeh Deputy Prime Ministry main jootey par rakhtaa hoon? Mujhey Deputy Prime Ministry chaahiye?*'[4]

It is all a conspiracy of you pressmen, he said. What more could I have done? he asked. I said count all the votes again in those booths . . . I ordered a judicial inquiry.

'*Main to aur bhi badaa khel khelney jaa rahaan hoon,*'[5] he said, and put the phone down.

The next morning I narrated the call and what Devi Lal had said, and the threat he had held out to my colleagues. Some felt that we should publish the text of the exchanges forthwith. Others said that doing so would be premature, that we should ignore the call and continue our work on Meham.

We continued our work on Meham.

Devi Lal phoned Ramnathji in Bombay. Ramnathji was unwell, and so he was curt. His nurse and secretary handed him the phone, whispering, 'Devi Lal.' Before Devi Lal could say anything, Ramnathji told him, '*Agar paper mein kuch chhapaa hai aur us ke baarey mein aap chaahtey ho ki main kuch karoon, to uttar hai, "Naheen." Agar kisee aur cheez ke baarey mein hukum hai to uttar hai, "Haan,"*'[6] and with that, he handed the phone back to his nurse and secretary.

The secretary told me that Devi Lal proceeded to bombard her with fulsome abuse of me and, she said, a colleague.

On 16 March, Devi Lal, as was his wont, resigned from the V.P. Singh government, throwing the coalition—just three months old, and fragile as it was—into turmoil. One Ram Pujan Patel had been abusing him, he declared, and now he has been made the head of the Janata Dal in UP. Ajit Singh—the son of Charan Singh, another leader who spoke in the name of farmers, and had been propped up as Prime Minister by Mrs Gandhi and her party for a few ignominious months—has gone to Meham and declared

---

[4] 'Don't you know, I keep this Deputy Prime Ministership on the tip of my shoe? Do I need this Deputy Prime Ministership?'

[5] 'I am about to launch an even bigger game.'

[6] 'If you want me to do something about something that has appeared in the paper, the answer is "No." If you want me to do something about something else, the answer is "Yes."'

that disciplinary action should be taken against Chauthala . . . Who are these fellows, *'Inkee aukaat kyaa hai?'*[7] They are afraid of me because they know that I do not need them, they need me. I represent the rural areas, and 107 seats of the 141 we have won have been won in the rural areas.

As the head of Janata Dal's Parliamentary Board, Devi Lal removed Ajit Singh as its Secretary General. Everyone becomes a constitutionalist at such moments: 'As per the Party's constitution, Devi Lal has no power to remove a Secretary General,' many said. Devi Lal couldn't care a buffalo's *pathee*. Where is the party? he hectored everyone, including our Bureau correspondents. Where is the constitution? he demanded. Committees of the party in Delhi cannot decide whether Chauthala should remain Chief Minister or not. It is for the MLAs to decide. And they have unanimously elected him as the Chief Minister.

Devi Lal resigned on these high principles. And then agreed to take back the resignation—because of the international situation, he said! Punjab was again on the boil. International conspiracies in Kashmir. Should I let the country go to ruin? In any case, he had resigned to give the party a shock, to strengthen it. He had resigned from the government, not from the party, he reminded everyone.

That night—of 16 March—Gurumurthy and I went to see him on a sort of pacification-cum-reconciliation mission, and also because we were as anxious as anyone that the Janata Dal government survive. Devi Lal was fuming. *'Voh behanchod . . .'*[8] about the editor of our Hindi paper and about Arun Nehru. *'Voh haathi saaraa bagheechaa khaa gaaya hai. Tum sab uskey baarey mein nuktaa tak naheen likhtey, aur merey chhorey ke baarey mein panney par panna bharey jaa rahey ho . . . Yeh saaraa kuch Arun Nehru likhwaa rahaa hai . . .'*[9]

---

[7] 'What is their standing?'
[8] 'That sister-fucker . . .'
[9] 'That elephant has swallowed the whole garden. You fellows are not writing a word about him, and you are filling page after page about my son . . . Arun Nehru is the one who is getting all this done . . .'

'*In logon ki aukaat kyaa hai? Log dekhney mujhey aatey hain . . . Mainey behanchodon ko kameti mein daalaa, aur maalik ban gaye hain . . .*'[10] He went on to shout about everyone—from that Ram Pujan Patel to Ramakrishna Hegde to NTR. But the choicest abuse was hurled at our Hindi editor and Arun Nehru.

We were conciliatory, we cajoled him. We let him blow off steam. I assured him that the reporter who had written the Meham accounts for the *Indian Express* was not the sort who would be meeting Arun Nehru, that in any case, she had already resigned and joined another paper.

He wasn't one to be assuaged. All five Janata Dal Chief Ministers are my men, he declared, letting us know what he could do to the Janata Dal and to V.P. Singh and his government.

Nor were we to be assuaged. On 19 March, I wrote an editorial, 'The next two steps', commenting on his withdrawing his resignation. In it, I urged that as its next steps, Janata Dal should once again field Chauthala from Meham, and, this time, make him lose his deposit. That day his office called *five* times.

A senior officer told us that Devi Lal accosted him immediately after the proceedings in Parliament. He asked the officer to ensure that Ramnathji was talked to, and our mouth shut. '*Main baniyaa to hu naheen. Main to aadmi bhijwaa ke pitwaa doongaa.*'[11]

The officer did not trouble Ramnathji. He narrated the thunder to me. Others came and reported Devi Lal's abuse. The *behanchods,* it seemed, were now reserved for me. '*Shourie ne mujhey vishwaas dilaayaa thaa ki jo voh azaariye* [editorials] *likh rahaa thaa, usey nikaal diyaa gayaa hai, par vaisey he azaariye chhap rahein hain . . .*'[12]

He had mixed things up. I couldn't have dismissed the writer of the editorials, and I could not have told Devil Lal that I had dismissed him, as I had been writing the editorials myself.

---

[10] 'What do these people matter? It is me whom the people come to see . . . I have put these sister-fuckers into the Committee, and they are strutting around as if they own it . . .'

[11] 'A *baniya,* I am not. I will send men and get them beaten up.'

[12] 'Shourie had promised me that the man who has been writing those editorials will be removed, and yet the same kind of editorials are appearing . . .'

In public, he would make a distinction: he had nothing against pressmen, he would say. It is a conspiracy of the capitalists—Goenka, Ambani, Birla, Jain.

That Sunday, our edition carried two articles—one on the Meham episode, and one on his fulminations. Monday's editorial, 'A tantrum a week', dealt with the dismissal of Ajit Singh. Tuesday's editorial began with references to Devi Lal.

His man Friday was on the phone early. When I shouted back at him, he suddenly retraced his steps. No, no, this is a campaign that the *Hindustan Times* people are waging, he said. I was talking about them.

But around 9 p.m., the familiar call, 'Deputy PM sahib *baat karenge.*'[13]

'*Arey teraa akhbaar to waisey he chal rahaa hai,*'[14] Devi Lal said.

'*Ji haan,*' I said, '*aur waisey he chalegaa.*'[15]

'*Kyon?*'[16]

These are issues of public importance, and you have taken to abusing us morning and evening, I said.

'*Gaali naa doon to aur tujhey kyaa karoon?*'[17]

'*Aap jo marzee kar leejiye.*'[18]

'*To achhaa,*'[19] and he put the phone down.

In my article I raised the questions that you would expect. How does such intimidation square with the Janata Dal's professions? Is he, and through him the government, not indulging in blackmail? How much time is the Deputy Prime Minister of the country spending on Kashmir and Punjab and how much on the depredations of his son? Should everyone in the Janata Dal be sitting back and just watching what the man is doing? . . .

---

13 'The Deputy Prime Minister will talk to you.'
14 'Look here, your paper is going on as before.'
15 'Yes, sir, and it will go on in the same way.'
16 'Why?'
17 'What else should I do to you if not abuse you?'
18 'Please do what you think fit.'
19 'All right, then.'

But as the Deputy Prime Minister was involved, as I would be reporting not just his fusillades aimed at me but also Ramnathji's conversation with him, as this would be the first time that an English daily would be printing *behanchod* on its front page, I thought I should talk the matter over with Ramnathji. He had come back to Delhi. Therefore, before handing the article to the press for composing, I had taken it to Ramnathji. His health had begun deteriorating, and, unfortunately, his mind was sometimes not as acute as it had always been. He had insisted on attending a public function that evening. I had taken the manuscript to the function, and explained its contents to him—the implied threats, the *behanchods*.

Ramnathji did not pay much attention to the details of what I had written, and the *behanchods* were of no consequence to him—he could himself abuse fluently in thirteen languages. He was on another point.

'*Kyaa, merey akhbaar ko dhamki de rahaa hai? Merey editor ko dhamki de rahaa hai?*' he had asked. '*Seedhaa karo, usey seedhaa karo. Yeh log apney aap ko samajhney kyaa lagein hain?*'[20]

Our photographer, R.K. Sharma had taken photographs of me talking with Ramnathji. That turned out to be fortunate for me.

For the paper had but to be distributed in the morning, and there was a furore in Ramnathji's immediate circle. Nusli Wadia, the industrialist who had invested heavily in the government and had acquired proprietorial airs about it, and Nanaji Deshmukh, the RSS leader, were the foremost in demanding that I be dismissed. Attacking the Deputy PM of our own government . . . '*behanchod*' on the front page of our paper . . .

Gurumurthy intervened. Arun says that he mentioned the article and its contents to RNG. We should at least check that out . . .

The moment passed.

---

[20] 'What? Is he threatening my paper? Is he threatening my editor? Straighten him out. Who do these fellows think they are?'

Devi Lal continued in his ways. V.P. Singh's government continued to totter more and more. Devi Lal made up with Chandra Shekhar. Various individuals and various factions set off all sorts of schemes to corner V.P. Singh and bring about a change in the government—oblivious of the fact that all of them would be in the dust were these manoeuvres to succeed. And then an unexpected explosion occurred.

Letters, affidavits and a notary public

July 1990.[21] Devi Lal shot off a letter to the Prime Minister. To counter the charges that were being made against his son, Chauthala, he set off charges of his own. The letter began with high-minded invocations of the need for 'morality and propriety'. It complained of colleagues who had gone to the press about 'the unanimous election of the leader by the Haryana Janata Dal Legislature Party'—the election of Chauthala as the leader, that is. Devi Lal said, 'I would like to bring to your notice that much more damaging acts, immorality and impropriety are being committed under our very nose by some of the same gentlemen who are raising the banner of revolt and declaring themselves to be the guardians of propriety and morality.' He then accused the then commerce minister, Arun Nehru, of having committed 'serious irregularities' in the purchase of phosphoric acid and DAP. He said that 'the [Commerce] Ministry decided to import phosphoric acid from Morocco through an Indian agency going under the name of Polisario which is associated with some very big industrial families of our country', and that 'very substantial commission' is 'being asked for and obtained running into several million dollars'. 'The amount has been pocketed by none other than one of our friends who has resigned from the Council of Ministers on the issue of the Haryana Legislature Party leadership,' Devi Lal continued.[22]

---

[21] The following is based on an article of mine which appeared in the *Indian Express* on 28 July 1990.

[22] Arun Nehru, Arif Mohammed and Satpal Malik had resigned in protest against the removal of Banarsidas Gupta as Chief Minister of Haryana and the reinstallation of Chauthala.

For all that we at the paper knew, commissions may have been asked for and received. But the letter did not make sense. The imports of phosphoric acid were canalized through MMTC. And we could not find any trace of any company called 'Polisario'—that was the name of a region in Western Sahara that was under dispute between Algeria and Morocco. Moreover, we found that the order for importing phosphoric acid was given to Morocco, not at the asking of the Ministry of Commerce but at the asking of the Department of Fertilizers. And Devi Lal himself was the minister in charge of the Department of Fertilizers. And so on.

Next, Devi Lal trained his plough at Arif Mohammed, then an associate of Arun Nehru. He charged that Arif had purchased huge tracts of land in 'a satellite city of Uttar Pradesh' for Rs 55 lakhs. And this amount he had received from a company against the purchase of power turbines. This too was swiftly shown to be a figment of imagination. Arif had purchased 2 acres of land near Ghaziabad—long before the V.P. Singh government was formed, and had declared them in the list of assets he had filed with the Prime Minister on joining the V.P. Singh government. And the contract for the turbines had been awarded by the *previous* government, well before the V.P. Singh government was formed.

Two days after releasing that letter to the press, Devi Lal declared that he had 'definite information from US and Morocco'. V.P. Singh kept asking him to share that information, to release it. Devi Lal wouldn't. Cornered, he took a different tack. He had not made any charges, he said. He had merely passed on to the Prime Minister the information he had received.

But he was not one to leave bad enough alone. He had to go to Bangalore for treatment at a nature-cure clinic. From there, he released a letter that he maintained had been written by V.P. Singh as Prime Minister, to the President of the country, asking the latter to dismiss Arun Nehru and Arif from the government. So, it wasn't as if Devi Lal was making any charges. V.P. Singh himself had come to the conclusion that these two had been involved in corrupt transactions and ought to be removed.

To make sure that no one would doubt the authenticity of the letter, Devi Lal had got the copy notarized by Ms M. Shantha, a Notary Public in Bangalore.

A *strange letter*

The letter was on V.P. Singh's letterhead. It listed the address as 28 Lodi Estate, and was dated 26 November 1987.

Everything about the letter struck me as strange.

The letterhead was suspiciously, in fact, exactly, like the one that had been used in the St Kitts forgery that we had nailed earlier.

And why on earth would a letter from the Prime Minister to the President have to be notarized, and that too by a Notary Public in Bangalore? If it was a copy that was being notarized, had the Notary Public compared it with the original as she was required to do by law? In any case, even if this was a genuine copy of a genuine letter, how had Devi Lal received the copy?

I was convinced that all this was a forgery, a forgery orchestrated at the command of none other than the Deputy Prime Minister of India. So, it must be nailed.

And there was one way to nail it.

I rang up my friend, E. Raghavan, then the resident editor of the *Indian Express* in Bangalore. We should locate Ms M. Shantha, and go about the business in three steps. First, we should take a simple, genuine document to her and have her notarize it. This would give us an idea of whether she was punctilious about the law—for instance, does she ask for the original documents on which a document is based? What other precautions does she take before notarizing the document? Next, we should take a more elaborate document that contains an obviously fabricated story. And finally, I told Raghavan, we should take a long and absolutely absurd 'affidavit' and request her to notarize it—an 'affidavit' that I have dictated, I told Raghavan, and am putting on the teleprinter. He must go to the teleprinter office and retrieve the 'affidavit' before anyone else has a chance to read it. After collecting it, Raghavan should take it to some senior lawyer and see if it needs to be modified in any way. Each of the three documents should be taken to Ms Shantha by a different reporter.

The first document was a simple caste certificate that was needed for admissions. Ms Shantha was swift, and most reasonable. She charged only Rs 5 for notarizing it.

In the second document, a fictitious person, S. Chandra Shekhar, declared himself to be the sole and absolute owner of the property situated at 112 JC Road, Bangalore, and recorded that he was selling it off. The property was actually the headquarters of the Canara Bank. Ms M. Shantha notarized that without any ado.

The third document was the long one—full of the most fantastical nonsense. In it, to begin with, the then Mayor of Bangalore, K.C. Vijayakumar, declared himself to be the sole and absolute owner of the building that housed the Bangalore Corporation. And he declared that he was selling it to Dinesh Goswami, the then minister of law in the Central Government. Their addresses and designations were given precisely and correctly.

Next, the Mayor declared himself to be the owner of the 'agricultural land' on which the Indian Institute of Management, Bangalore, stood. He then spoke of a death that was to take place a month later. And declared that, in view of the death, he was selling the 'agricultural land' to 'the legal heir of Devi Lal, i.e., Sri Om Prakash Chauthala who is the ex-Chief Minister of Haryana and the son of the Deputy Prime Minister of India Sri Devi Lal'. The Mayor swore in the 'affidavit' that he was selling the land 'due to high influences from the Centre'.

In the bargain, he also sold the Vidhana Soudha, the High Court and the Secretariat buildings to Chauthala. Each for a pittance.

Devi Lal entered the affidavit. He recorded that, committed as he was to morality and propriety, he was outraged at Chauthala buying government land and buildings in this way. Therefore, he declared, 'I, Devi Lal, the Deputy Prime Minister of India do hereby declare that I disown my son Sri Om Prakash Chauthala hereafter and we will not have any association with him whatsoever in any manner in future.'

Next, we made Ms M. Shantha make an appearance herself. She was made to declare that she knows that the law requires her to read a document before notarizing it; that she hereby certifies on oath that she has not read the document she is notarizing; that she realizes that, in doing so, she is violating the law, but she is doing so nonetheless. 'I, M. Shantha, notary, hereby certify that I have not read this affidavit and looked into any documents to ascertain the truthfulness of this affidavit sworn by the first person of the Bangalore City,' she was made to say in conclusion.

Ms Shantha notarized the document. Again, she was very modest in her charge.

But even the forgery was forged

The three documents showed that you could get anything notarized from the lady. But they revealed something more. That the notarization that had ostensibly been done of the Prime Minister's letter to the President was itself a forgery. For Ms Shantha had two rules she always followed. She always put a date on the document she notarized. And she always had an advocate identify the person who was swearing the affidavit, and sign the document himself, before she put her signature to it.

In the 'letter' that Devi Lal distributed, her name and seal appeared. But no date. And no supporting signature of an advocate.

And then, there was a telltale mistake in the letter itself. While the letter was dated 26 November 1987, and listed V.P. Singh's address as 28 Lodi Estate, New Delhi, our reporters found out that V.P. Singh had not moved into this accommodation till 23 March 1988!

The Deputy Prime Minister of India had not only been hurling charges against his colleagues and then failing to provide the proof he said he had; he had not only been saying, when confronted, that he had made no charges; he had been peddling a patently forged letter, ostensibly from the Prime Minister of the country to the President of India.

The sequel

There was an uproar—work of the *Indian Express* was, of course, a very tiny straw in the maelstrom.[23] The government's Political Affairs Committee met. Devi Lal's charges and letters were the subject of heated exchanges. Instead of furnishing the proof he had said he had, Devi Lal said that the letter—V.P. Singh's letter to the President—had come to him by post. He 'could not vouch for its authenticity'. Minister after minister came down on Devi Lal heavily: you have made serious charges against colleagues on the basis of a forged letter; now you must bear responsibility.

Three ministers resigned. Others threatened to do so. V.P. Singh sent his resignation to S.R. Bommai, the Party President . . . Everyone asked everyone else to be firm. V.P. Singh asked Bommai to be firm and settle the issue once and for all. All together asked V.P. Singh 'to remain firm and courageous', trying thereby to implant a backbone where there was none. As usual, R.K. Laxman captured the moment perfectly. The cavernous mouth of a cave, with 'Devi Lal' written outside. A shivering, midgety V.P. Singh with a backbone thrust into his achkan, sticking out from the top as well as the bottom, is standing at the mouth of the cave. Arun Nehru, Arif, Dandavate and others are looming over him, staring at him. Arun Nehru says, 'Now go in and show him that you have a backbone.' A stormy Cabinet meeting followed. Eventually, Devi Lal was removed from the government.

---

[23] For a glimpse, see the first-person account of I.K. Gujral, who would soon be Prime Minister himself, in his *Matters of Discretion,* Hay House India, New Delhi, 2011, pp. 285–92. Our work was a little straw, but it *was* a little straw! Writing about the stormy meetings and discussions, Gujral, who was at that moment on tour in Africa, observed, 'A little later, my son Naresh also telephoned me to say that the media reaction to the prime minister's line was "very harsh" and Arun Shourie's hard-hitting article in the *Indian Express* had caused immense damage to the image of the government and the party. I obtained, through the diplomatic bag, a copy of the *Indian Express,* which also reported that Chauthala had been nominated as one of the six general secretaries of the Janata Dal. He was thus wearing three hats simultaneously! (He was chief minister of Haryana, the state party chief and now a general secretary) . . .' Ibid., pp. 286–87.

Chandra Shekhar turns out to have been right

That was not proof that V.P. Singh had at last decided to 'stand firm and be courageous'. Quite the contrary, it proved how right Chandra Shekhar had been when he had warned that V.P. Singh was a coward, that he was an opportunist, that he believed in nothing.

Devi Lal threatened to bring 5 lakh farmers to Vijay Chowk on 9 August—the anniversary of the Quit India Resolution—occupy it, and not leave 'till justice is done', and 'the corrupt are brought to book'.

V.P. Singh panicked.

28

A beacon for me

'*Kahaan ho?*'[1]

　'Office *mein.*'[2]

　'*Kar kyaa rahe ho?*'[3]

　'*Kal ke liye* editorial dictate *kar rahaa hoon.*'[4]

　'*Yahaan* Vishwanath *paagal ho gayaa hai aur tum* editorial *likh rahey ho? Chhodo, chhodo. Merey daftar aayo. Abhee.*'[5]

That was Vinod Pandey, the Cabinet Secretary. He had been a friend of V.P. Singh for long. Though a civil servant, he was better known for his eccentricities, better still for his poetry, and even more for his astrology!

I wound up the editorial and went to his office in the Rashtrapati Bhavan complex.

'*Sab theek to hai naa?*'[6] I asked as I entered.

1　'Where are you?'
2　'In the office.'
3　'What are you doing?'
4　'Dictating the editorial for tomorrow.'
5　'Here Vishwanath has lost his head and you are writing editorials? Leave it. Come here. Just now.'
6　'Everything is all right, isn't it?'

'*Theek hai? Arey, tabaahee ho gayee hai. Yeh desh kaa satyaanaash kar degaa. Isey roknaa hai. Bilkul roknaa hai.*'[7]

But what has happened? What has the Prime Minister done?

Pandeyji, as he was universally known, explained. Devi Lal had declared that he would hold a massive rally. V.P. Singh had panicked. And to 'take the wind out of Devi Lal's sails', he had decided to announce implementation of the Mandal Report.

Mandal Report? What is this Report?

'What? You work in a newspaper and you don't know what the Mandal Report is? *Is desh mein rehtey ho yaa abhee* Washington *mein hee ho?*[8] It is the surest way to destroy the country.'

Pandeyji buzzed his PA. 'Get a copy of the Mandal Commission Report from the Labour Ministry at once.'

Through the afternoon, through the evening, through the night I read through the Report.

It had been submitted seven years earlier. And had been consigned to the government's almirahs.

No Prime Minister had thought of implementing it. But now, an opportunist, a panicked opportunist had resurrected it to save his chair. At the Cabinet meeting which was convened to ratify V.P. Singh's decision, Ramvilas Paswan said, 'Sir, *yeh jo aapney nirnday liya hai, hum iskaa pooraa samarthan kartey hain. Isko laagoo karney se ab hamey bees saal tak koi bhi satta se hattaa naheen sakegaa.*'[9] Arif said, '*Pradhan Mantri ji, bees saal to kya, isko lagoo karney ke baad agar aap bees haftey bhee satta mein reh gaye to meraa naam badal denaa.*'[10]

---

7 'Everything is all right? Calamity has come down. He will destroy the country. He has to be stopped. He has to be stopped completely.'

8 'Are you living in this country or are you still in Washington?'

9 'Sir, we totally support this decision that you have taken. Once this is implemented, no one can remove us from power for twenty years.'

10 'Mr Prime Minister, leave twenty years, if after implementing this if you can stay in office for even twenty weeks, you can change my name.' Arif told me that before the Cabinet meeting, three persons—Arun Nehru, Ajit Singh and Arif—had met and decided that they would strongly oppose the decision. At the meeting, Arun Nehru kept quiet and Ajit Singh did not open his mouth. Arif, on the other hand, spoke at length against the decision: people have not

V.P. Singh's government announced their intention to implement the Mandal Report in August 1990. It fell in November 1990! Arif retained his name!!

Done was done. A step that I considered would set the country back by decades had been taken.

Protests erupted in various places, especially in university campuses. A student at Delhi University poured petrol over himself and set himself on fire. There was commotion all round.

In the *Indian Express*, we covered the protests comprehensively. I wrote in detail about the Report and the decision.

Having grown up in boarding school and college, and, on top of that, being from Punjab, I had no awareness of caste. I remember being invited by Sharad Yadav for lunch. At one point, he said, as if he were admonishing me, '*Bhai, main aapkey lekh kab se padhtaa aa rahaa hoon. Par in mein mainey jaati ki mehak naheen paayee. Yeh kyon hai? Jaati hamaarey desh kee ek vaastaviktaa hai.*'[11]

As I began to read about caste, I became convinced that it was a curse on our society and religion. I also felt that it was being eroded by modernization. Books said that should an untouchable touch one, one would suffer pollution. Books said that if even the shadow of an untouchable fell on a Brahmin in the south, the latter would have to bathe God knows how many times. They listed elaborate rules about whose hands one could take water

---

given you a mandate to do anything of this kind; you are ruling with the help of BJP and the Left, have you talked to them . . .? Three persons attacked him fiercely—Ramvilas Paswan, Sharad Yadav, Nitish Kumar. 'You don't know anything about ground realities,' they maintained. Arif reminded them that he too had been fighting and winning elections since his college days, and, therefore, by their test, he also knew about realities on the ground. V.P. Singh said nothing, but, Arif recalls, he signalled to Madhu Dandavate to talk to Arif. Dandavate came over to Arif's seat, put his hand on Arif's shoulder and signalled to him that he should come out for a minute. Out of the room, Dandavate told Arif that 'X' number of OBC MPs from the BJP are set to revolt on this issue and support the V.P. Singh government, and 'Y' number of OBC MPs from the Congress are set to revolt and support the V.P. Singh government. So, don't worry on this score, etc.

[11] 'My friend, I have been reading your writings for long. But I have not found the odour of caste in them. How come? Caste is a reality of our country.'

from, whose hands one could take food from.[12] But in our school, in our college, we never thought of, nor did we know the caste of a fellow student, of our team-mate on the hockey field. We did not know the caste of the cooks who cooked our food in the school and college messes, of the bearers who brought it to the tables.

Even the person with the meanest intelligence would have seen that this diabolic institution was being eroded outside our schools and colleges also. After all, people were pushing each other to somehow get into the crowded bus. People were fighting for municipal water. Who was verifying the caste of the person squeezed against him in the packed bus? Who was verifying the caste of the person in the municipal water supply works? And what about workers in factories, in the new professions like journalism, sports? That did not mean that the inequities of centuries had been wiped out. Not by a long shot. But the erosion had begun. It was gathering pace as the economy modernized, as urbanization proceeded. And the way out had been shown by reformers like Sri Narayana Guru, Jyotirao Phule, Gandhiji, and so many others.

Electoral politics is what had given a second life to this evil. Unable to stand on any record of performance, parties had begun fanning caste resentments and sentiments. Socialists and the Communists, especially in north India, unable to extend their sway, had come up with a new thesis to rationalize their casteist sloganeering: 'In India caste is class,' they shouted. By that, their casteist strategies became progressive.

The evil design

I hated all this. And here was Mandal. Henceforth, seats would be reserved, not just for the Scheduled Castes and Scheduled Tribes; they would be extended to another lot of castes—'the

---

[12] A book listing all this which was widely read at the time was, Louis Dumont's, *Homo Hierarchicus: The Caste System and Its Implications*, Translated from the French by Mark Sainsbury. Weidenfeld and Nicolson, The Nature of Human Society Series; London, 1970.

economically and socially backward classes'. Seats on the basis of caste would be reserved in the administrative services also, and in public enterprises. And, persons who would be inducted to these posts on the basis of caste, would *by definition* be persons who were not qualified for the posts: if a person was qualified, he would enter the service in the general category. Only *if he was not qualified* would he be among the ones entering on the basis of reservations.

And the reservations would be not only at entry into a service or organization but in promotions also. The poison of casteism and groupism would enter government services also.[13]

The limit was ostensibly set at 49 per cent. But that would soon be breached. The Commission recommended, and these politicians argued, that if a sufficient number of candidates could not be found in a particular year to fill the number of seats that had been reserved, those seats would be 'carried over' to the next year. Assume that forty-nine seats out of 100 are reserved, but in a year only thirty candidates could be found who qualified on even the relaxed criteria. That would mean that in year two, not forty-nine seats but 49+19 would be reserved. In the third year, not forty-nine seats but 49+19+19 would be reserved. In one state, we found that the student who had come first in the examination for entry into medical colleges could not get in as all seats had been reserved as a result of the 'backlog'.

The consequences were obvious even then. As the standards had been lowered for reservationists, officials in state after state had vaulted over colleagues who had ranked much higher. The same, sad story was repeated in regard to students. In Kerala, the student who had ranked 413 in the common examination for entry into medical and engineering colleges was denied admission

---

[13] I got a sharp glimpse of this when I was in Atalji's Cabinet. The CEO of one of the enterprises under the Ministry had come to me complaining that engineer 'X' was thoroughly corrupt, that he was raking in commissions for equipment, for copper cables and the rest. But why don't you take action against him? I asked. 'But, Sir, he is from the reserved category. If I take action, he will say that I am casteist, that I am anti-SC/ST/OBC. He will file an official complaint against me and then *I* will be the one in trouble.'

while a student who had ranked 14,246 had got in. 'Some way to select doctors,' I felt. Our reporter asked a minister who was ever so vocal in favour of the Mandal recommendations, 'If you have to have an eye operation, will you go to a surgeon because of his caste or his proficiency?' 'Of course, I will go to the best surgeon,' he said. And I am sure he would have had a perfectly valid reason for that too, based though it would be on his caste: 'Just because I am from a backward caste, should I not get the best medical treatment?'

How would we compete with the rest of the world when half of our students, half of our civil servants—right to the top—half of the managers in public enterprises, would be selected on the basis of their birth and not on the basis of their merit?

V.P. Singh had a ready answer. What is 'merit'? he asked in Parliament. What is the merit of a system which keeps half of its people oppressed?

Ortega y Gasset's forecast was coming true. Merit had become a dirty word. Standards were dubbed as elitist, as a conspiracy of the upper castes to keep the lower castes down. Vulgarity was becoming a mark of 'authenticity', a right. Intimidation, the argument of choice. And assault, proof.

There were other anomalies in Mandal's report also. For one thing, his own listing of instances in which members of the Scheduled Castes and Tribes had been thrashed and killed showed that in so many of them the violence had been perpetrated by the castes immediately above them, the 'socially and economically weaker classes'—this word, 'classes' had become the code word for 'castes'—who were now the object of everyone's compassion. Among the Commission's members, only one had been from the Scheduled Castes. And he had appended a Note of Dissent.

The records showed, and the chief of the experts who had been tasked to help the Commission stated, that the questionnaires they had prepared as well as their views had been mutilated, that they had not been shown the data.

The way in which one caste after another had been able to get itself included in the reserved category told its own story. Reservations were being extended, not because someone suddenly realized that a caste was weak and had been left out. On the contrary, a caste had qualified for reservations when it had become strong enough and organized enough to wrest them from the politicians. These were not backward and weak castes. They were the dominant—they were the domineering castes.

And such juggernauts never stop, I felt and wrote. Increasingly powerful castes will wrest reservations: we will be plunged into 'a race for the bottom'. Even in the 1930s, castes used to vie with each other to be recognized as '*forward* castes'. A Census Commissioner had written how his office had become a 'College of Heralds'. Now, castes would fight to be acclaimed as 'backward'.[14]

With no conviction to anchor him, V.P. Singh and his small band swung from one position to the other. One day, 'Twenty seven per cent jobs will be reserved for OBCs.' Next, 'If the courts come in the way, I am sure with your help we will . . .' The next, 'No, I didn't mean that. I was just saying . . .' And the next, 'The recommendations of the Mandal Commission will be implemented without dilution . . .' And the next, '540 members [of the Lok Sabha] are not the country . . .' And the next, 'Prime Minister regrets the outburst of his minister.' And the next, 'Hit the streets and give a befitting reply.' And when the charge of casteism became shrill, news was put out that the Cabinet had met and decided that, in addition to the 22.5 per cent reservations for Scheduled Castes and Tribes, in addition to the 27 per cent reservations for 'Other Backward Classes', 5 to 10 per cent jobs will be reserved for the poor. That would take jobs that would be reserved to 55 to 60 per cent. Hadn't the courts laid down 50 per cent as the upper limit? But as he had said, 'If the courts come in

---

[14] Once I got into trouble with Atalji on this score. Elections to the Rajasthan Assembly were round the corner. Atalji had gone there to give a few campaign speeches. During these, he announced that Jats too would be given reservations. The following week, the announcement was put to the Cabinet for endorsement. I repeated my arguments—Jats were a dominant, a domineering caste, not a backward one, etc. Atalji interrupted me, '*Phir to mujhey yeh pad chhod denaa chhaahiye*'—'In that case, I should leave this position.' That was not what I was saying. But with the chorus that erupted, what I was saying was drowned out.

the way, I am sure with your help we will . . .' And if that didn't work, you would 'hit the streets and give a befitting reply'.

This was an opportunist in panic. And a government desperate for legitimacy—*some* legitimacy, *some*how, *any*how.

Of course, the poor and the disadvantaged must be helped. The help must be positive help: nutritious food at school; free places to stay and study; free textbooks; no tuition or other fees in school or college; guidance after school hours from the best teachers; help for them to continually raise their learning and professional skills even after they join professions. But standards must not be lowered. When the race starts, say for the civil services, all must be toeing the same starting line . . . *This* is the kind of help which will lift entire generations, and, at the same time, the country, I felt.

The individual, and not a group—say, a caste, or persons born in one state or other—must be the unit of selecting a beneficiary. And the individual must be selected on the basis of strictly secular criteria—income and assets of parents, for instance. Of course, such selection, as well as the help that will be rendered once the person had been selected, required first-rate implementation; it would require close monitoring. Decreeing reservations, by contrast, was the lazy politician's way of showing that he had done something dramatic for the poor and backward. In fact, these reservations would be gobbled up by the stronger and better-off sections among the 'socially and economically backward classes', I wrote. And as evidence, I pointed to what the Mandal Commission itself had written about who had cornered benefits and outlays under government schemes.

I wrote about these and other aspects of the decision, the Report of the Commission, the consequences that were sure to follow. My colleagues in the states unearthed fact after telling fact. The paper reported the agitations and the unrest among students. We were charged: 'High caste fellows', 'Instigating the students'— to agitate, to riot, to immolate themselves . . . But no one would answer the facts and arguments.[15]

---

[15] The principal articles that I wrote about the Mandal Commission appeared in the *Indian Express* between 21 and 28 August 1990. Politicians were not the

Pandeyji was on the phone again. The situation is getting out of hand, but don't give up, keep at it. Vishwanath has not yet come to his senses . . . I reminded him that some days earlier, when I had asked him how long this turmoil would last, he had said, '*Bas chaar haftey mein sab shaant ho jaayegaa,*'[16] and, in fact, things had got so much worse—in the country and for the government. 'When did I say this?' he asked. When I came to your office the other day, I reminded him. '*Arey "kahaan" naheen, "kab". Kis din mainey yeh kahaa thaa?*'[17] I had my desk calendar in front of me. I hastily turned the leaves, and told him the date on which I had last been to his office. '*To ismey aashcharya kee kyaa baat hai? Voh din merey liye bahut buraa thaa. Jo bhee mainey us din kahaa, voh to ghalat nikalnaa he thaa.*'[18]

Can't beat the astrologer in a Cabinet Secretary!

But another act was unfolding—in a distant city, unknown to me.

A teleprinter message

One evening, I had returned late from the office. I had just about entered our house and the phone rang.

'Sir, office *waapis aa jaayiye,*'[19] it was the subeditor looking after the Desk at the time.

'*Kuchh ho gayaa hai kyaa?*'[20]

---

only prisoners of populism. Later, I wrote a book, *Falling Over Backwards, An Essay against Reservations and against Judicial Populism*, ASA, Rupa, Delhi, 2006, HarperCollins, Noida, 2012. The book documented how Judges, too, had been carried away by populism dressed up as progressive-ism. And how, at every turn, after a moment of hesitation, they had fallen in line, and, in fact, legitimized the worst instincts of the politicians.

16 'Everything will quieten down in four weeks,'

17 'Not "where", "when". What was the date when I told you this?'

18 'Then where is the surprise in that? That day was a very bad one for me. Whatever I said that day just had to come out wrong.'

19 'Come back.'

20 'Has something happened?'

'Sir, *bas aap aa jaaiyey. Zaruree baat hai.* RNG *ke naam se aap ke naam ek* message *aayaa hai.*'[21]

A message from Ramnathji? At this hour? In any case, there was no alternative but to return to the office as the subeditor would not read out the message: he said it was a long one.

Before leaving home, I requested three colleagues to join me in the office, including N.S. Jagannathan, then editor of the *Financial Express.*

The teleprinter message was, to use the language of those days, ten takes long. The message said that the paper was being taken too far in the wrong direction; that he had told me about this; that, as the paper was continuing to proceed in the same direction, he had to conclude that irreconcilable differences had developed over editorial policy; and so, by this message, I was being removed as editor of the paper.

The four of us who had assembled agreed that Ramnathji could not have written or dictated the message. His health had broken down. He was bedridden. Those among us who had telephoned him from time to time knew that he was not coherent. It was evident to us that, in all probability, bedridden and cut off, Ramnathji was not even in the know of what had been unleashed by V.P. Singh, nor would he have any inkling of the reaction that the Mandal decision had triggered. Jagannathan suggested that the only thing to do was for me to go to Bombay and talk to Ramnathji, and find out what, if anything, was in his mind.

I got on to the first flight on which the office could get a seat. One thing I remembered to take along, and that was the cassette of *Newstrack* which had reported and filmed the protests and, in particular, the immolation.

On reaching the Penthouse in the Express Towers, I was literally shocked. Ramnathji was not even a shadow of himself. He was lying in bed, staring blankly at the ceiling. His tongue was lolling about. I stood in front of him. That did not register on him. Therefore, I spoke up, 'Ramnathji, *main Arun Dilli se aayaa*

---

[21] 'Sir, just come back. It is an important matter. There is a message for you in RNG's name.'

hoon.'[22] That too did not register. After ten minutes or so of such remarks, he surfaced into some degree of awareness. I mentioned that a long teleprinter message had reached us in Delhi last night, that it said I was dismissed.

Of course, Ramnathji could put on an act! But this time round, he clearly did not have any knowledge of the message or its contents.

I persuaded his nurse-secretary that, together, we shift him to the drawing-dining room in which the television set was lying. We brought him to a chair with considerable difficulty. I tried to explain to him about the Mandal decision, and what had followed. Feeling that the news was not getting through to him, I stepped towards the TV set and inserted the *Newstrack* cassette. The scenes had but to begin that two other persons who were present in the room started speaking in loud voices, 'No, no, stop this at once. We cannot upset RNG.'

That was that.

I had learnt what Jagannathan had said we had to ascertain. Ramnathji could not have sent the message. He was in a very bad way.

Clearly, others were acquiring control; actually, for all intents and purposes, they had already acquired control over the paper. There was neither any way for me to continue in the paper nor any point in continuing in it.

What a sad end

Even though thirty years have passed, I distinctly remember how I felt on the way to the Bombay airport. I wasn't angry at all about the job. I was just so sorry that Ramnathji had come to this pass.

I reached Delhi, and went home to Anita and my parents. I rang up my PA to pack up my books, etc., and have them sent home.

From then on, having been dismissed from a job became a badge of honour for me. When, while introducing me to

---

[22] 'Ramnathji, I am Arun, I have come from Delhi.'

audiences, the organizers would read out the awards, etc., that I had received, I would begin my speech by saying that they had forgotten the one thing that set me apart from the audience. There were three editors who had been removed from their jobs—George Verghese from the *Hindustan Times,* Pran Chopra from *The Statesman,* and me from the *Indian Express.* So, I am one of three, I used to say. But I was the only one who has been dismissed not once, but twice!

Many months passed. I got a call from Bombay. Ramnathji was in hospital, and he wanted me to come and see him 'one last time'. I went. A staff member from the *Express* met me at the airport: 'He is in Breach Kandy Hospital. It will be good if we go straight there.'

I can scarcely describe how very sorry I was to see Ramnathji. He was curled up in a bed, in a smallish room. The elegant Mrs Srinivasan[23] was the only person there. She spoke to him in a slightly raised voice, 'Look who has come to see you, RNG. You wanted Arun Shourie to come. Here he is.'

RNG's eyes focused a bit.

'He wants you to hold his hand,' Mrs Srinivasan said.

I took his hand in mine. A tear rolled from his eye.

A tiger had shrivelled into a little bird.

That was the last I saw of him.

I had no contact with the *Express* for many years, I did not even visit any *Express* building till many years later—by then, the group had split in two. The northern and western editions had fallen to Viveck. My dear friend, Shekhar Gupta, had taken over as its editor. Viveck had cast aside those who had tried to use him to take control of the paper. The paper had been brought back to what it had been under Ramnathji.

My beacon

Perhaps it was time to move on to other work. In any case, I could no longer have done what I thought needed to be done, given the state of affairs.

---

[23] Mother of Venu Srinivasan.

Many years ago, I had read what Gandhiji had written about the duty of an editor. As I mentioned, I had transposed an expression from it in Manila. Of course, it is absolutely presumptuous to think that any of it is written as a guide for nobodies like me. But I reproduce the passages that Gandhiji wrote a hundred years ago as it has always been my beacon, and, in the sort of circumstances that I have just listed, it has been my solace.

The occasion was the government's attempts to choke various newspapers, and their editors. Gandhiji wrote:

> . . . I believe that an editor who has anything worth saying and who commands a clientele cannot be easily hushed so long as his body is left free. He has delivered his finished message as soon as he is put under duress. The Lokamanya spoke more eloquently from the Mandalay fortress than through the columns of the printed Kesari. His influence was multiplied a thousand fold by his incarceration and his speech and his pen had acquired much greater power after he was discharged than before his imprisonment. By his death he is editing his paper without pen and speech through the sacred resolution of the people to realize his life's dream. He could not possibly have done more if he were today in the flesh preaching his *Mantra*. Critics like me would perhaps be still finding fault with this expression of his or that. Today all criticism is hushed and his *Mantra* alone rules millions of hearts which are determined to raise a permanent living memorial by the fulfilment of his *Mantra* in their lives.
>
> Therefore let us first break the idol of machinery and leaden type. The pen is our foundry and the hands of willing copyists our printing machine. Idolatry is permissible in Hinduism when it sub-serves an ideal. It becomes a sinful fetish when the idol itself becomes the ideal. Let us use the machine and the type whilst we can, to give unfettered expression to our thoughts. But let us not feel helpless when they are taken away from us by a 'paternal' Government watching and controlling every combination of types and every movement of the printing machine.
>
> But the handwritten newspaper is, I admit, a heroic remedy meant for heroic times. By being indifferent to the aid of the

printing room and the compositor's stick we ensure their free retention or restoration for all time.

We must do something more. We must apply civil disobedience for the restoration of that right before we think of what we call larger things. The restoration of free speech, free association and free press is almost whole Swaraj . . .[24]

Postscript: Those outside the family of Ramnathji who were wresting control of the paper thought that my friend, S. Gurumurthy, would be an even greater obstacle to their plans than me. And so, after I had been removed, they did not just push him out, they began circulating all sorts of allegations against him.

Post-postscript: The last time I saw Vinod Pandey, he was in a very sorry state. He had been made Governor of Bihar. Having learnt that I was in Patna for a lecture, he invited me for dinner, and insisted that I stay at the Raj Bhavan. He wasn't ready when I reached there. I was shown to the room in which I was to stay. It was damp, the air was fetid, the windows had probably not been opened in ages. The carpets were not just torn, they were so damp as to be termed wet—you could see the place from which water was leaking in through a wall. The heavy curtains were drawn so that all light was shut out. They had dust all over them. It did not take me seconds to decide that I must not stay there. At last, Pandeyji appeared. He was being supported by a liveried attendant, and had clearly taken a good deal to drink. He was wearing a white *bandgalaa* coat and white trousers, but they were both soiled. He talked on and on through the dinner. About the sorry state of Bihar, about the idiocies of its rulers, about the glories of the Patna University Library, how hardly anyone used it, how he had been able to obtain rare books, including ancient editions of Shakespeare's works . . . Dishes were brought by liveried attendants, but their cuffs and collars were enough to warn one against touching what they had brought . . .

---

[24] *Young India*, 12 January 1922. *Collected Works of Mahatma Gandhi*, Volume 25, pp. 427–28.

29

A new beginning, an ingenious device, an innocent question

'Arun Shourie *hain?*'[1]

　'Main bol rahaa hoon ji. Kahiye.'[2]

　'Main Thakre *bol rahaa hoon.'*[3]

　'Kyaa hukum hai, sir?'[4]

　'Main Kushabhau Thakre *bol rahaa hoon.'*[5]

　'Kahiye Thakre ji, *hukum kyaa hai?'*[6]

　'Arey bhayiyaa, main Kushabhau Thakre *BJP kaa adhyaksh bol rahaa hoon.'*[7]

　'Sir, kshamaa keejiye, mainey pehchaanaa naheen. Kahen, main kyaa kar saktaa hoon.'[8]

　'Party ke office *aa saktey ho?'*[9]

---

[1] 'Is Arun Shourie there?'
[2] 'I am speaking, sir. What can I do for you?'
[3] 'I am Thakre speaking.'
[4] 'What is your command, sir?'
[5] 'I am Kushabhau Thakre speaking.'
[6] 'Yes, Thakreji, what is it you want me to do?'
[7] 'Friend, I am Kushabhau Thakre, President of BJP speaking.'
[8] 'Please excuse me, I did not recognize you. What would you want me to do?'
[9] 'Can you come to the Party office?'

'*Jee haan, jab aap kahen.* Office *hai kahaan?*'[10]

'*Arey, tumhein* Party *kaa* office *naheen pataa! Das* Ashoka Road. *To phir aisey karo, abhee aa jaa-o.*'[11]

I reached the BJP office. Kushabhauji was in his dhoti and kurta.

'*Aaiye, aaiye.*'[12]

After some preliminary chit-chat, he said, '*Abhee in teen mahaarathiyon ki baithak hui hai*—Atalji, Advaniji *aur* Joshiji *ki. Unhon ne* Rajya Sabha *ke liye tumhaaraa naam bhee chunaa hai.* Party *kaa sadasya ban-ney mein koi kathinaayi to naheen?*'[13]

I said I was very grateful to the leaders for choosing me, and I would be happy to join the Party also.

'*Tum rehtey kahaan ho?* UP *kaa* address *chaaheeye hogaa.*'[14]

I explained that we stayed with my parents in West End, a colony in New Delhi. As for finding an address in UP, I would have to look for one.

'Party *kaa sadasya to main banwaa doongaa. Aap* UP *mein* address *dhoondiye. Turrant.*'[15]

I was to be elected to the Rajya Sabha from UP, and under the electoral law as it then stood, to qualify to stand from UP, one had to be at the least a resident of UP. This requirement used to lead to a number of 'anomalies': Dr Manmohan Singh had had to swear that he was a resident of Assam and stayed in the house of the Chief Minister there; Pranab Mukherjee had to swear that he was a resident of Gujarat. I had an obvious choice: Anita's family home was in Hazratgunj in Lucknow. But, the examples of distinguished persons notwithstanding, it did seem a stretch to say that I stayed in Lucknow. Fortunately, I had the family of a first

---

[10] 'Of course. Where exactly is the office?

[11] 'What? You don't know where the Party office is? Ten Ashoka Road. Then do one thing, come just now.'

[12] 'Come, come.'

[13] 'The three *mahaarathees* have met—Atalji, Advaniji and Joshiji. They have selected your name also for the Rajya Sabha. Will you have any difficulty in joining as a member of the Party?'

[14] 'Where do you stay? A UP address will be needed.'

[15] 'I will get you enrolled in the Party. You go and find a UP address. Without delay.'

cousin living just across the border, in Noida. My cousin had died young. My *bhabi* and their son readily agreed to allow me to say that I had a room in their house.[16]

With the address acquired, Kushabhau's people began the process of getting me enrolled in Noida's electoral rolls.

Armed with a slip from the Electoral Office, and with a nomination paper from the Party, in a few days I set off for Lucknow.

A doctor who lifted my spirits

I was a bit nervous, almost a little downcast. I was entering an entirely new venture—an election—one in which I would be entirely dependent on others. At the airport, I was met by a Sikh gentleman, Dr S.S. Dang. He had been assigned the task of being my Election Agent. In fact, he became my shepherd, so endearing was he, so full of good cheer and humour. Meeting him at once lifted my spirits. He was a gregarious, hearty gentleman, full of stories. From the very first greeting we talked in Punjabi. Few things break barriers as a common mother tongue.

There were still two/three days for the voting. Dr Dang took me to the Party's office—a monument to studied negligence. Rajnath Singh was the Chief Minister. Kalyan Singh was the leader of the state BJP. I wanted to meet them. Dr Dang said I would indeed—at a dinner on the night before the voting.

But at least I should be meeting the MLAs who are to vote for me.

'Why?' Dr Dang asked.

'Doctor Sahib, they will be voting for me. Maybe they have some questions about me. Shouldn't I clarify any doubts they may have?'

'*Kamaal hai, Shourie saab. Tusee RSS no naeen jaandey? Soochnaa aayi, sochnaa band. ML-eyaan nu milan dee kee*

---

[16] The law was changed later, and the residence requirement was dropped.

*zaroorat ai? Taintee bandeyaan nu soochnaa mil gayee ai ki vote
thaunoo denee ai. Bas, kam hogyaa.'*[17]

'Elect *hon layee taintee votaan chahidiyaan nein, aur taintee
nu kehtaa? Koi os din bimaar ho jaaye? Kisi de ghar koi bimaar
ho jaaye? Taan?'*[18] I asked.

'*Eh thaudi pehli election hai, esi layee tusee ainvi ghabraa
rae-o. Koi bimaar-shimaar naein hundaa. Taintee de taintee vote
den layee paunchan ge.'*[19]

I could hardly be less convinced. But I got nowhere. In any
case, the Party has fourteen surplus votes, I was told. If one of
your MLAs fails to turn up, one of these fourteen will be assigned
to you . . .

There was a dinner, all right, at the Chief Minister's house.
Much like dinners at our weddings. Apart from perfunctory
namaskaars, I did not get to interact with anyone. I could not even
find out who had been tasked to vote for me.

A fatal omission

Not familiar with the fact that this is the informal way political
affairs are conducted, I was quite nervous when the next morning
we reached the premises where the nomination papers had to be
filed. Someone had already filled the form for me. '*Yahaan* sign
keejiye.'[20] I did as I was told. After a while, we were ushered into
the room of the officer who was conducting the proceedings. We
were quite a crowd in that small room. Rajnath Singh was there,
as was Kalyan Singh. Dr Dang was with me.

---

[17] 'Strange. Shourie sahib, you don't know the RSS? Message comes, thinking
stops. Where is the need to meet the MLAs? Thirty-three have been informed
that they have to vote for you. The work is done.'

[18] 'Thirty-three votes are needed to get elected, and just thirty-three have been
assigned? What if someone falls ill that day? What if someone in someone's
family falls ill? Then?'

[19] 'This is your first election, that is why you are nervous. Nobody is going to
fall ill. Thirty-three of the thirty-three will reach for casting their vote.'

[20] 'Sign here.'

I was handed the form—'Rajnathji *ko dikhaa kar inhein de deejiye*'[21] the gentleman said, pointing to the officer.

I handed the form to Rajnath Singh. He glanced at it cursorily, smiled at me, '*Su-swaagatam, su-swagatam,*'[22] he said, and handed the form back to me for being given to the electoral officer.

Kalyan Singh intercepted my hand, and took the form. '*Bhai,* schoolmaster *to main hoon.* Form check *karnaa to mujhey aataa hai.*'[23]

And in a moment he spotted a fatal omission. My nomination had to be seconded by ten MLAs. There were ten names, but only nine signatures. Panic. Everyone in the room ordering everyone to locate the missing MLA . . .

After a while, some MLA was located. His name replaced the earlier one, and he signed the form.

An ingenious device

That was a little heart attack, but it was just the beginning. For a candidate to get elected, he had to secure 32.24 votes in the first round. I had been assigned thirty-three MLAs. On the day of voting, one of the MLAs could not be traced. He was coming from Nainital, I was told, and he had missed his train. Exactly the sort of thing I had feared.

But then why wait? Why not ask one of the surplus fourteen to come and vote?

They have already voted.

What? I was in full panic by now, and quite upset: exactly what I had feared was happening, and the simple precaution had not been taken. How could they have voted? And who among us needed fourteen extra votes?

No, no. The fourteen have voted for D.P. Yadav.

---

[21] 'Show this to Rajnathji, and give it to him.'
[22] 'Welcome, most welcome.'
[23] 'Friend, I am the schoolmaster, after all. I am the one who knows how to check a form.'

I couldn't believe my ears. Yadav had a colourful reputation. He had been an MLA several times over. He had even been a minister in Mulayam Singh's government in UP. But he was best known for the nine murder charges that he had hanging over his head, for the dread that he evoked as he was said to be the most fearsome member of liquor and sand mafias of UP, and, therefore, one who'd better not be crossed. How could the Party have assigned fourteen precious votes to such a person?

Someone took mercy. An MLA not among the original thirty-three was fetched and he voted for me.

Like other BJP candidates, I got thirty-three and was declared elected.

D.P. Yadav got forty-two.[24]

'Sir, vote *uskey liye kyon naa padtey? Aur turrant kyon naa padtey?* Vote *daaliye aur apnee* Safari Taj Hotel *sey ley leejiye,*'[25] a local politician explained.

'But how could Yadav be sure that the person to whom he was handing the Safari had indeed voted for him?'

'Sir, *hum aapkey lekh to kab se padhtey aayein hain, par yeh to spasht hai ki aap ko electionon kaa koi ilm hai he naheen.*'[26]

The gentleman explained the modus operandi.

MLAs stand in a queue. Your turn to vote comes. You are handed a slip on which you have to mark a cross against the name of the candidate for whom you are casting your vote.

You enter the screened cubicle and mark the cross against 'D.P. Yadav'.

But you don't put the slip in the box. You bring it out, hidden. And you hand it quietly to one of the two/three coordinators.

The coordinator checks that you have marked the slip correctly for Yadav. He hands it to the next voter. The latter collects his

---

[24] The authorities in the BJP who transferred the votes to him also inducted him into the Party. But such was the uproar that he was shown the door within four days.

[25] 'Sir, why would the votes not get cast for him? And why not before everything else? Cast the vote, and collect your Safari from Taj Hotel.'

[26] 'We have been reading your writings for long. But one thing is clear: you don't know anything about elections.'

own slip, marks it for Yadav, but does not insert it into the box. Instead, he puts in the slip that *you* had marked.

He hands the slip that was assigned to *him* and which *he* has marked to one of those coordinators, who in turn hands it over to the next MLA.

This has to be done only for the MLAs who have been 'persuaded'. Those who belong to your own party or group, they will vote for you in any case . . .

I was as dumbfounded as I was impressed by the simplicity of the device.

In any event, I had scraped through and got into the Rajya Sabha.

No one mentioned what by then almost everyone knew—D.P. Yadav's ingenious device.

I got to meet Yadav several times in the Rajya Sabha. Always the silent presence, he was invariably polite, almost deferential. His battles against the law and perilous rivals continued in subsequent years. Much later, his son was jailed for having fired at and killed a model . . .

An innocent question from Atalji settles the matter

The second time round, five years later, in 2004, the election was a calmer affair. I was better known within the Party, that I had Atalji's backing was also common knowledge, and so the election managers had taken requisite care.

But there had been an uncertainty before the selection as a candidate, one that I was to learn only later from my friend, Yashwant Sinha.

In the Lok Sabha elections of 2004, Murli Manohar Joshi had lost, as had Yashwant Sinha. Their names had been proposed for being taken into the Rajya Sabha. Advaniji and some others had been long opposed to Joshi. So, when the names were being considered, a participant at the meeting said that it had been the Party's principle that those who had lost in the Lok Sabha election would *not* be accommodated in the Rajya Sabha, and so Joshi and Sinha should be excluded.

Atalji knew that no one had anything against the inclusion of Sinha. The target was Murli Manohar Joshi. Sinha was just collateral damage.

He asked innocently, as was his wont, 'Advaniji, *yeh siddhanta to bahut achhaa hai. Par yeh Party ne apnaayaa kab? Kyonki, aap to jaantey he hain ki election haarney ke baad aap bhi aur main bhi Rajya Sabha mein gaye the.*'[27]

That killed the argument of principle.

But then Joshi's opponents turned their fire. Caste sentiments are running high in UP, they said. Joshiji is a Brahmin. We cannot have two Brahmins in a list of five or six.

'*Doosraa Brahmin kaun hai?*'[28] Atalji asked.

'Shourie.'

'*Shourie? Yeh to pehli baar mainey sunaa hai ki* Arun Shourie *ki pehchaan kisi ki aankhon mein Brahmin ki hai. Naheen, naheen,* Joshiji, Sinha, Shourie *sab hamaarey ummeedwaar hongey. Aagey chaliye.*'[29]

Yet another principle

By the time my second term in the Rajya Sabha ended, Atalji had more or less receded from the scene.

A new principle was invoked. It is the Party's principle that no one shall be given a third term in the Rajya Sabha, the most shameless of justifiers decreed. Having got two terms, the person must fight elections for the Lok Sabha.

So, I was out of the reckoning.

As you can imagine, the principle was soon discarded. The very ones who had pressed it continued into their third, and then their fourth terms.

---

[27] 'Advaniji, this rule is a very good one. But when did the Party adopt it? Because, you know that after losing elections both you and I went to the Rajya Sabha.'

[28] 'Who is the second Brahmin?'

[29] 'Shourie? This is the first time I have heard that someone knows Arun Shourie by his caste. No, no, Joshiji, Sinha, Shourie, all of them will be our candidates. Let us proceed.'

But by then, I had lost interest completely in both—the Rajya Sabha as well as the BJP. And for good reason. By then, as Dr Dang once put it, all that mattered in the Party, in fact, in all parties were *paisaa* and *parikramaa*![30]

That was some years away. In the interim, Atalji inducted me into his Cabinet. He was among the most sagacious and gracious of leaders, a wonderful person to work for. His trust and large heart left me free to do many things, to be witness to and even to participate in issues of considerable consequence.

But that is another story, and would require another volume.

---

[30] Currency and circumambulation!

Tu samajhtaa hai havaadis hain sataane ke liye
Yeh huaa kartey hain zaahir aazmaane ke liye
Tundee-e-baad-e-mukaalif se naa ghabraa ai uqaab
Yeh to chaltee hai tujhey oonchaa udaaney ke liye[31]

—Sayyad Sadiq Hussain

---

[31] You think that traumas are meant to trouble you?
They manifest to test your mettle
Do not be afraid of the strong and contrary wind, O eagle
It blows only to make you fly higher

Acknowledgements

I am grateful most of all to Ramnath Goenka who let us do things that no one else would, and to all my colleagues at the *Indian Express* who did them. Some of them were so kind as to remind me of the incidents that should be covered in this book. In particular, I am grateful to Pushp Saraf, Surya Prakash, Coomi Kapoor, Arun Sinha, Ashwini Sarin and N.K. Singh, who recalled several details. They will pardon me for not including the many other skirmishes they listed—by the standards of editors, the book has already exceeded the length they bargained for.

Raj Kumar Srivastava who looks after the *Indian Express* archives and P. Nataraj, research editor of the *New Indian Express,* were most helpful in enabling me to access articles and news reports of those days.

And so did the Nehru Library at Teen Murti House, New Delhi, and the National Library of India in Kolkata.

Rahul Gupta from Prashant Bhushan's chamber, Rahul Unnikrishnan from that of Arvind Datar, and K.S. Roshan Menon from Shardul Shroff's Amarchand Mangaldas helped track down the judgments that I needed to study again after all these years.

My sincere thanks to all of them.

And to Aroon Purie for allowing me to use images from the *India Today* archives.

I am once again grateful to Meru Gokhale and Aparna Kumar, first for deciding that Penguin India would publish this book, and then for seeing it through all the way to printing. Clare Stewart and Binita Roy went through the manuscript and edited it.

I remain in debt to all of them.

Index